The Admiral I knew

A True Story of
Admiral Ronald Lynsdale Pereira

The Admiral I knew

A True Story of

Admiral Ronald Lynsdale Pereira

Mike Bhalla

Vij Books India Pvt Ltd

New Delhi (India)

Copyright © 2018, *Mike Bhalla*

First Published in 2018

ISBN : 978-93-86457-16-5

ISBN : 978-93-86457-17-2 (ebook)

Designed and Setting by

Vij Books India Pvt Ltd
2/19, Ansari Road, Darya Ganj,
New Delhi - 110002 (India)
www.vijbooks.com

All rights reserved.

No part of this book may be reproduced, stored in a retrieval system, transmitted or utilized in any form or by any means, electronic, mechanical, photocopying, recording or otherwise, without the prior permission of the copyright owner. Application for such permission should be addressed to the author.

Contents

Foreword   vii

Preface   xi

PART – I

1.	Background	1
2.	My Journey	10
3.	Matters Military	79
4.	Home	269
5.	Cavalry Generals	307
6.	Visionary	322
7.	Great Orator	325
8.	Post Retirement	335
9.	Golf	346
10.	Accidents	369
11.	Love For Dogs	376
12.	Battle With Cancer	381

PART – II

13.	Encounters at NDA	431
14.	Encounters with Naval Officers	522

15.	Encounters with the Staff	540
16.	Conclusion	563

Foreword

I am delighted to write this Foreword to the biography of Admiral RL Pereira, a widely admired and respected former Chief of the Naval Staff, by one of his former NDA cadets, and for all practical purposes, adopted son, "Mike" Bhalla.

It is a most unusual true story of human relationships and emotions, with complex psychological undertones and can only be described as an unabashed labour of love on the part of the author, who because of his chance association as a cadet at the National Defence Academy with the then Deputy Commandant, Commodore RL "Ronnie" Pereira, and his wife Phyllis, came to be treated as the de-facto son they did not have. It could only have been some deep emotional connect which made Admiral Pereira, despite his onerous preoccupations, eventually as Chief, to find time to write numerous hand written letters, advisory, admonitory, affectionate as appropriate, to a young "Mike" Bhalla as he grew in his army career from cadet to regimental command under the watchful gaze of a caring father-figure.

The chance association would have remained just that but for a curious coincidence; the uncanny facial resemblance that cadet Sant Pratap Singh Bhalla had to the only next-generation male member of the Pereira clan, an upcoming young Indian Air Force fighter pilot with a bright future ahead, Michael "Mike" Pereira, who tragically died in a freak accident while executing an emergency landing at Hashimara. The resemblance also explains how a Punjabi Sikh cadet, came to be called "Mike" Bhalla, first by the Pereiras and then more generally by his colleagues, family and friends in the Indian Army Armoured corps.

"Mike" Bhalla has taken great pains to find out and authenticate information about his chosen idol, "Ronnie" Pereira, and Mrs. Phyllis Pereira, from both sides of their respective families, tracing their origins from Portuguese and Armenian settlers respectively, through generations to the present times. In doing so he travelled far and wide across India, including to the neglected grave of Michael Pereira in a cemetery some distance from Hashimara where he had breathed his last. He interacted with numerous persons, relatives and others, who knew the Pereiras or had knowledge of the extended clan, not least a large number of his former fellow cadets who shared his experiences of their time together in the NDA. His affection and regard was more than reciprocated by the Pereiras who gave of their love of humanity in abundant measure to the young Sikh boy, whom fate in some inexplicable way had brought into the lives of a deeply religious, caring, childless Christian couple. The reproduction of letters exchanged and inclusion of a large number of personal photographs enhance the readability of the account.

I did not have the opportunity to serve directly under Admiral Pereira, but when I first went to sea as a cadet in 1955, the Indian Navy was a small service with barely 400 officers, the majority in sea-going ships based in Bombay (Mumbai). One therefore knew most officers by name and sight, especially if they were prominent in some way, as then Lt. Cdr. Pereira certainly was as Fleet Gunnery Officer.

I met him several times of course over the years. Coincidentally, I also studied for a year in St. Joseph's College, North Point, Darjeeling his old school, in 1951 and was familiar with Mrs. Pereira's school, Mount Hermon, down the hill, where we used to be invited to witness the Girls' Annual Sports Day, which we enthusiastically did because of our great interest in athletics!

I was doing reasonably well in service and was considered a decent sportsman and rider (Army Horse Show, Delhi, 1954) from my own cadet's days, and as a mountaineer subsequently (Basic and Advanced courses at HMI, Darjeeling, Annapurna III in Nepal, 1961). Later, I came to his notice as a submarine captain with a Vir Chakra in the 1971 war with Pakistan, when he was the Deputy Commandant at the NDA, and partly because of our common link to Darjeeling, the Pereiras were always very warm to me and my wife whenever we met.

When he became the Chief of the Naval Staff, he persuaded the Chiefs' of Staff Committee to appoint me Deputy Commandant of the National Defence Academy in 1979, to a position he had loved and for which he had set the benchmark for excellence. Before assuming charge I called on him for guidance, and for over an hour, despite being a busy Chief, he briefed me on the finer points of running the NDA, from the broader aspects of leadership, training and discipline, down to seemingly trivial details such as the number of stitches per-inch in the cadets' uniforms (to ensure that the tailoring firm delivered as per contract)! Though not equal to his prodigious reputation, in my own way I believe I met his expected standards in a job which I too loved doing.

"Mike" Bhalla's being a highly personal account also includes his interactions with distinguished Cavalry generals with whom he has worked or otherwise known. This in no way diminishes his main narrative about the Pereiras, rather it enhances it, as he weaves in episodes in which Admiral Pereira was involved with them. His book will surely be appreciated by the thousands of officers who have passed over the Quarterdeck of the National Defence Academy, many of whom directly experienced Admiral Pereira's inspiring and self-less leadership and today accord him almost a mythical status. **Equally, it should interest all young boys and girls who may wish to pursue a military career, for insights into qualities that go to make a true leader.**

The author's tale of the Pereiras is an adulatory one and makes no claim to objectivity. It is nevertheless completely frank, especially in pointing out his own failings and lapses. I understand an official biography is under preparation, which will also include the views of those who had reason to see Admiral Pereira as a person with human flaws. These will surely be only the first of many books that will bring out the full dimensions of the personality of a dedicated, upright, professional naval officer who devoted his life to duty and the good of the service and the men and women who serve in it, and together with his devoted wife, Phyllis, showered an abundance of love and care on them, while enforcing the highest standards of conduct and discipline. "Mike" Bhalla was fortunate to be particularly favoured and his sentiments to their memory, expressed through his book, are a continuing tribute to a most remarkable couple and a unique relationship.

– Vijai Shekhawat, PVSM, AVSM, VrC
Admiral, Indian Navy, (Retired)

Preface

In early February 1997, I received a letter dated 29th Jan 97 from Mr. Ashok Mahadevan, Editor-in-Chief of Reader's Digest, **quote** "I am writing an article on late Admiral RL Pereira for Reader's Digest and am talking to large number of people who knew him. I plan to meet Mrs. Pereira in Coonoor next month. I understand you were very close to Admiral and Mrs. Pereira and I would very much like to talk to you" **unquote**

January 29, 1997

Colonel Mike Bhalla
C/O 56 APO

Dear Colonel Bhalla,

I am writing an article on Admiral Ronnie Pereira for Reader's Digest and am talking to a large number of people who knew him. I plan to visit Mrs Pereira in Coonoor next month. I understand that you were very close to both Admiral and Mrs Pereira and I would very much like to talk to you. Is there a phone number at which you can be reached or could we meet in Delhi or some other place in the North? My address is as above, my telephone numbers are 2611374 (direct), 2614446, 2617272 and my fax numbers are 2614449 and 2613347.

Yours sincerely,

Ashok Mahadevan
Ashok Mahadevan
Editor-in-Chief

In early March, Ashok Mahadevan paid a visit to Akhnoor, 28 kms NW of Jammu and spent couple of days with us. After that he tried to contact Mrs. Pereira, who for some reason refused to meet him. Ashok requested me to put in a word and when I spoke to her, she out rightly rejected the very idea of anyone publishing anything about Ronnie Pereira. Notwithstanding, Ashok went ahead and published an article- "The Unforgettable Ronnie" in March 1998 edition of Reader's Digest. It was barely 6½ pages article not befitting Admiral's stature.

In April 98, Col Pramathesh Raina (38th NDA) walked into my office in AHQs, and told me that his father Mr. Triloki Nath Raina, who was our English Professor at NDA (1952-80), author of "Cradle for Leadership- History of NDA - 1949 -1996", was not too impressed with the article as it had not done adequate justice to Admiral's personality and he expressed his desire to write a book on Admiral, for which he requested for my support in terms of letters, photos and any other information on Admiral. It was indeed a very noble idea and I would have loved to extend all support, but regrettably, I told him - Sir, am sorry, Mrs. Pereira is inimical to the idea and as long as she is alive I cannot go against her wishes and that was the end of proposed project by Mr. Triloki Nath Raina.

Then in July 2015, I received a call from Commander Anup Thomas, stating that he was writing Autobiography of Admiral and spoke to me for about an hour. We were all sitting on the dining table and after I finished talking to him, my elder son Rabden said; "why are you giving all the information to strangers? Instead why don't you sit down and write a book on Bara Papa (Senior Papa). He gave so much space to you in his life, treated you like his own son and shared his inner most thoughts through his letters written over a period of more than 20 years, I think you have a moral obligation to your course mates and all those who loved him to share his views on various aspects of life." My wife and younger son also insisted, that at least give a '**try**'.

I thought about it and then after few days took out all the letters of Admiral and Mrs. Pereira which I had preserved for past 40 years plus and put them in a chronological order. As I went through more than 300 hand written pages, I realized I have "**treasure**" with me and before I turn up my toes, I must share it with all cadets of NDA 40th-49th course and all those who served with Admiral as well as with the future generations of officers at all levels, from Lieutenant to General. **It is more relevant in the context of present day ugly wranglings by the bureaucrats and politicians vis-a-vis Armed Forces.**

Preface

I was aware that since Admiral's sad demise in Oct 1993, many short articles have been written by officers recounting their experiences with Admiral, who had the good fortune to serve with the great man either on his staff (NA, Secretary and Flag) or during his command tenure at various levels starting with INS Kuthar in early 60's.

However, the version of this book is entirely "**different**". It is a tribute from a son to a father and cadets from NDA to share and spread the legacy of one of the **"most inspirational leader"** of men in post independent India. It is purely based on facts and Admiral's **thought process** and personal views expressed in his **OWN** hand over 20 years of correspondence.

The book encompasses his journey in the navy, personal views on nuances of character building, human values, leadership and man management, integrity, honesty and courage of conviction to withstand the political and bureaucratic pressure on the matters military and above all welfare of men in all shades of uniform to sensitive issues of marriage, friendship and role of a wife in the armed forces. Issues of money and his struggles in building a small abode and then selling it, again building another one and selling that too, without ever touching anything black.

The book also includes Admiral's encounters with Cavalry Generals, his love for the game of Golf and dogs, four accidents including scooter accident and finally his battle with cancer in the last two years of his life.

The script has a series of **amazing co-incidents**, Karmic connections and predictions stretching from his early school days in North Point in 1932 to 2017 while compiling this fascinating relationship of a father and son.

In fact, Admiral himself is the author of more than half of Part I of this book!!

With God's name on my lips and prayer in my heart, I sat down to start the project on 25th Aug 2015, exactly 44 years since Admiral first noticed my resemblance to Michael John Pereira, his late nephew on 4th Aug 1971! I spoke to scores of my course mates, ex NDA cadets and naval officers, who had served with him and recounted their experiences with The Greatman, which are covered in Part II.

I must convey my gratitude to Captain Montee Chatterjee, who very kindly shared his letters received from Admiral and for pouring his heart out about his personal and official relationship with Ronnie P. Commander Hugh

Gantzer, Admiral's nephew, for providing vintage photographs, information about the family and early days in Patna, Dumka and Hazaribagh.

Admiral John Pereira (first cousin), Admiral Dick Schunker, a very close friend, late Admiral Ram Tehiliani, who spoke to me couple of weeks before he was hospitalized and leading to his sad demise, Admiral KK Nayyar, close friend and confidant of Ronnie P, Admiral VS Shekhawat, who narrated Lord Tennyson poem on King Arthur, Admiral KK Kohli (NA to CNS), Admiral Premvir Das (NA to CNS), Vice Admiral Anup Singh, Rear Adm Mohan for getting me all information of Pereira's family in Cannanore, Commodore Jena, Bhaskar Sen and Nalin Dewan, Cdr Vijayan (all Flag Lts to Admiral), and Cdr Shambu Biswas, Captain of Navy Cricket team in 1977.

I would like to thank Air Marshal Mike McMahon, who introduced me to Michael John Pereira's course mates - Air Marshal Subash Bhojwani, Air Vice Marshal Harry Ahluwalia, Air Commodore Ganapathy and Mrs. Jennifer De'Figaeiredo, wife of late Gp Captain D.J.A. De'Figaeiredo alias David and roommate of Michael in Hashimara in 1966/67.

Col RK Roy, Commandant MH Wellington in 90-93, Colonel Surgeon Ashok Chacko, who operated upon the Admiral after the nearly fatal scooter accident in April 1983 and Captain Surgeon Arun Behl who treated him for Cancer in 1991-93 in INHS Aswani at Bombay.

Admiral B Guha, Rear Admiral Ravi Vohra, Commodore P Franklin, Cdr AJB Singh, who served with him in INS Delhi. Admiral Britto who served with him in INS Kuthar in 1962-64.

Captain Biswajit, Director Veteran Cell, Naval HQs, who gave unstinting support in giving the contact numbers of all retired naval officers, who served with Admiral in any capacity. Brigadier Bency P Jacob, (Brig Training) NDA, for providing information and photos of Admiral as Deputy Commandant as well as the Reviewing Officer for POP of 56th and 59th courses. Pradeep Sinha (43/A), who got me all info about Admiral's schooling in Patna and David Taylor for St. Joseph Convent, North Point, Darjeeling.

Special thanks to Sankar Narayan (43/D) for photographs of Admiral's visit to Madras in Mar 79 and Michael and Zarine Pereira (Admiral John's son) for photos of both brothers together in 1948 with Ronnie Pereira, as Best man for John Pereira and as Admirals in 1976.

I would like to express my gratitude to Pratap Muthanna (40/J) Anil Kaul (41/J, Anil Mago (42/J), Sam More(41/F), Himmat Singh(42/H), Kirat

Vaze, George, Anoop, Bedi, Kataria, Grewal, Dharam Ahlawat, CP Sharma, Murlidharan, AK Singh, SP Singh, Joy Nath (all 43), TS Gill (45/A)and host of other cadets who very kindly have shared their experiences with Admiral, which are covered in Part II under the chapter on "Close Encounters". More often than not the contents leave a lump in one's throat and few tears in the eyes.

I must convey my deep gratitude to Brigadier PK Vij, my course mate (43/F) and friend for his unstinted support for publication of the book. He was indeed God sent. I was very apprehensive about the publication of the book and had no idea whatsoever and one fine day spoke to Brig Rahul Bhonsle, my course mate and author of number of books on Security Related Issues. He said; Mike, just contact Pradip Vij, he will do the needful. PK and self were together in Manipur in 1994, where, I was posted as GSO 1 Ops, Hqs 57 Mountain Division and PK was commanding 4 ASSAM. He commanded the battalion with distinction in one of the most difficult counter insurgency area. I spoke to him after 22 years and he was so happy to get a call from me. I informed him that I am writing a book on Admiral Pereira and I need your help. All he said; Mike, you are more than welcome, come to me after you have finished writing with all the material including Admiral's letters and photographs etc. Indeed those were the most soothing words. Thanks my friend!

Finally, I would like to express my deep gratitude for the emotional and moral support extended by my wife Annie, my brother-in-law Yap Rinchen Sonam Gyatso, and sons Rabden and Tashi.

Background

More than 250 years ago Admiral's ancestors migrated from Portugal to a small town – Cannanore in North Kerela in 1759. Initially, they worked in munition factories of Hyder Ali (father of Tipu Sultan).

It is believed that Francis Xavier Pereira, born in 1786 and probably one of the earliest members of his family, who had a written record of the marriage of his son, John Emmanuel (b.1825) at the Holy Trinity Church, Cannanore on 19 January, 1848.

A Mangalorean genealogist Dr Michael Lobo states that " According to one account , a member of his family, an interpreter translated an important document for the Zomorin ruler of Calicut and was provided with land there as recognition for his services- he goes on to say that this person may have been 'Francis Xavier'. Francis was married to Natalia and their only son Emmanuel settled down in Cannanore.

John Emmanuel was married to Eugenia Coelho, daughter of Basilio Coelho and Hyacitha Rosario and had a large family of 6 children. The eldest son John Pereira was born in 1851.

John Pereira ,who went on to become a Sub Engineer in PWD department in Mangalore and later moved to Cannanore in late 1880's He donated a Cast Iron bell, a large Cross and Painting of the Lady while undertaking to build the Oratory- a small chapel for private devotions- in the Holy Trinity Church, Cannanore.

John Pereira

The Pereira family evidently flourished and prospered under JOHN PEREIRA (third generation) patronage. He was a philanthropist, who adopted and paid for the education of at least 7 children, many of whom were Hindus. In gratitude- one of them, a Nair by birth took the name of Peter

Lima and was baptized as a Catholic. The fruits and Jackfruit from the trees in the compound of the Sea View Bungalow were given to the poor.

John Pereira married Anna Clara Fernandes daughter of Miguel Clejus Fernandes and Matilda Teresa D'CRUZ in 1879 in Rosario Cathedral, Mangalore. This is known from the Rosario marriage index, unfortunately, the register of that period is missing and so the precise date of the marriage is not known. Their four sons were baptized at Rosario Church. John was then posted in Mangalore as PWD Inspector. Later shifted to Cannanore, where three youngest children were born.

Anna was born on July 27, 1861 and was baptized on 31st Aug, 1861 in Holy Rosary Church, Tellicherry, India, and died on July 18, 1935 in Cannanore at the age of 74. John Pereira '**will**' was written in March 1920 and he died the next year in 1921, aged 70, and both he and his wife are buried in Holy Trinity Cathedral Cemetery, Doicese of Kannur.

John Pereira had a large family of 4 sons and 3 daughters.

Dr John Michael Pereira	: born 29th May 1880
Francis Pereira	: born 22nd Aug 1882
Robert Arthur Pereira	: born 27th Mar 1884
Sr Mercedes Clare	: born 7th May 1886
Cecil Fredrick Pereira	: born 13th Aug 1889
Hilda Mary Pereira	: born 3rd Aug 1894
Prascilla Mabel Pereira	: born 20th July 1898

John Pereira educated his three sons in England. **His eldest son John Michael (fourth generation) studied Medicines in Dublin, Ireland** and other two sons Robert and Cecil (father of Admiral John Pereira) went to the Crystal Palace Engineering College in London, UK. However, there is no mention of his second son Francis.

John Michael Pereira

Admiral's father, John Michael Pereira was born on 29th May 1880. He did his Medicines from Dublin, Ireland and in 1906 joined Indian British Medical Service and two years later he married Charlotte Louise O' Keefe Lynsdale, (b.29th October 1886, Bellary) daughter of Herbert Lewis Swayne Lynsdale and Charlotte Louise O'Keefe on 21st November 1908 at Cannanore. They had four children.

Arthur Pereira

The eldest son Arthur Pereira was born in 1909 and did his engineering from Electrical Engineering College, London from 1931 to 1935. He then joined Bombay Sappers as volunteer in WW 2. He was Beach Master for Arkan Landings. After the war he joined GEC Calcutta. In early 70's he took a job of 'Secretary of Green' at Royal Golf Club Calcutta and lived on the premises itself till he passed away due to cancer of right lung (same as Admiral) at the age of 84 in April 1993.

Arthur was tall, fair and very handsome man, who married an English beauty; Pamela Atkinson from the family of famous hat makers of UK, a tall and extremely beautiful woman. They had only one child – **Michael John Pereira** - born in 1945, who inherited the best genes from both the parents and grew up to be a strikingly good looking young strapping lad. Unfortunately in 1946, one fine day Pamela decided to leave India and left the one year small baby in the pram with the maid in Calcutta and told her to take the baby to Hazaribagh, where Maj JM Pereira was posted as Superintendent of Jail and she disappeared from the scene, never to be seen again!! As per Hugh Gantzer, probably she migrated to USA. Arthur never married again. The small baby was brought up by Aunty Masie (May) to whom Michael addressed as Chota Mumma (junior Mumma)!

I met Uncle Arthur in Nov 72 when he came to NDA, Khadakwasla to spend few days with Admiral and Mrs. Pereira and I do have a photo taken with him. I remember he told me about his experiences in WW2 and said at the peak of operation at Arkan landings he did not sleep for 72 hours and added, possibly that is the longest period a human being can stay awake. He was a handsome man in great health and looked much younger than Admiral, though actually 14 years his senior!!

Patricia Masie Pereira

Maise (May) Pereira was born on 12th April 1912, she did her schooling in St. Helens, Kurseong, Darjeeling and being the favourite daughter of her father, he wanted her to become a Dentist. However, she decided to marry Mr. Joseph Francis Gantzer, 26 years her senior, Resettlement Officer of

Santhal Parganas, located at Dumka in Bihar at relatively young age of three months short of 18th birthday on 22nd Jan 1930 and that put paid to her ambition of becoming a doctor. Their only child, Hugh Gantzer, was born on 31st Jan 1931. Hugh Gantzer joined Indian Navy in 1953 and left it in late 70's to become a world famous writer on tourism along with his gracious and beautiful wife; Colleen. They live in Mussoorie in their pretty cottage-Ockbrook, bought in 1940. Both of them visited Gangtok in spring of 1981 and spent an evening with us in our small ADC's cottage.

Mr. Joseph Gantzer, a contemporary of Maj JM Pereira was an extremely generous and kind human being and a highly respected Indian official in Bihar. During 1914/15, the farmers of Bihar had revolted against the indigo cultivation. Mahatma Gandhi was requested by local leaders like Dr Rajindra Prasad (later first President of independent India) to visit Champaran to support the farmers. The British moved out the English District Magistrate and replaced him with a native DM Mr. Joe Gantzer with specific instructions to arrest Mahatma Gandhi if he went ahead with the Satyagraha. However, Mr. Joe Gantzer refused to arrest the Mahatma as it was peaceful agitation, much to the annoyance of the British authorities. This was the first time on Indian soil that Satyagraha (Non Violent Civil Disobedience) was successfully put to test.

However, later in mid 30's Mr. Gantzer was awarded the MBE prior to his retirement in 1940 for his outstanding services to the crown.

Aunty May brought up Michael and was very close to him. After I met her in June 1972, she took great liking to me and I spent next 7 summers with her in Ockbrook and she used to tell me stories of good old days of 20's and 30's in Patna, Hazaribagh, Dumka as well as of Mussoorie in pre-independence days.

Joe Gantzer passed away in 1968 after prolonged illness. Aunty May was one of most respected lady in Mussoorie who was deeply involved in many social activities and lived up to ripe old age of 84 years. She passed away in 1996 peacefully while reading the Newspaper. Both Mr. Joe Gantzer and Aunty May are buried in Mussoorie Cemetery on Camel's Back road.

Inez Clara Pereira

Inez Clara (Bobby) was born in 1916 and followed her sister to same school. A very talented and fashionable person, she left India in 1938 to undergo training in London School of Music and eventually became a professional

Concert Pianist and Opera Soprano singer. She married a handsome Polish Air Force engineer- Stefan Watslav Malinowski and after WW2 migrated to Buenos Aires, Argentina. She came back to India in 1982 and died in an Old Age Home in Trinity Church, Bangalore, at the ripe age of 90 in 2006 and is buried in Roman Catholic Cemetery on Hasur Road, Bangalore. She is survived by a daughter Maria, who lives in Argentina.

I met Aunty Bobby in Feb 82, soon after her arrival in India, when we had gone to Delhi to spend few days with Admiral and Aunty Phyllis along with our 3 months old son. I took lots of photographs of Aunty Bobby with my wife and the baby in the lovely and colourful garden of the Navy House, 12 Rajaji Marg. I used to visit her in the old age home Trinity Church, during my yearly visit to Bangalore to see Aunty Phyll.

Throughout the WW 1, Maj JM Pereira was serving in Mesopotamia and came back in early 1920's. They were blessed with their fourth and youngest child, a son, on 25th May 1923, and named him Ronald Dadley Gregory Lynsdale Pereira alias Ron or Ronnie. At that juncture Maj Pereira was posted at Dumka as Senior Civil Surgeon.

Ronald Dadley Gregory Lynsdale Pereira

Admiral was born on 25th May 1923 , just two years after his grandfather, John Pereira passed away, who, thus missed out on his youngest grandson, however, his wife Charlotte lived for another 14 years and had the privilege to see her grandson- Ronnie P grow into teens . Being the baby of the family obviously the Grandmother simply dotted on him as so did everyone else in the family.

Ronnie P spent his childhood in Dumka, where Maj JM Pereira was posted as Senior Civil Surgeon in late 20's and early 30's, later in Patna where his father was posted as the first Superintendent of Patna Medical Hospital as shown on the Name Board (photo) from 1935 to 1938 and thereafter in Hazaribagh, where his father was posted as Superintendent of Hazaribagh Jail in late 30's and later from 1946 to August 1948, as shown on the name board in Hazaribagh Jail. Maj JM Pereira was also Superintendent of Gaya Jail in 1943-45. At all these locations the family lived in big Bungalows with large compound. Ron, as he was addressed by immediate members of the family learnt how to ride a cycle and a horse from his eldest sister Masie (May), 11 years his senior. He learnt shooting from the eldest brother, Arthur. Admiral mother was from Irish stock from her mother's side and Aunty May used to speak a lot about her, **quote** "Mike, my mother was an **'ANGEL'**, very soft hearted person and extremely fond of Ron. **She always told him to do the right thing no matter what is the personal sacrifice.** She instilled in him a very strong sense of religion and brought him up as '**GOOD CHRISTIAN**'. Apparently the early upbringing had very deep **INFLUENCE** on Ron's personality in later years". **Unquote**

Hugh Gantzer

Hugh Gantzer was born in 1931, reminiscences his maternal grandmother very fondly as a small child he always snuggled to her; **quote** "Mike, yes, my granny was indeed a wonderful lady, I still remember the fragrance of her perfume she used during summer months; 'Eau-d-clone' which was imported from Paris in crystal bottles and it was different fragrance for winters. My grandparents always believed in the best quality".

Hugh Gantzer added, **quote** "Ron was greatly taken in by my maternal grandfather's personality. Major JM Pereira, who was recipient of MBE (Member of the Most Excellent Order of the British Empire), was a man of rigid and uncompromising **integrity** and **honesty**. He was a man of great form and style and always immaculately dressed, very proper in his conduct with his superiors, contemporaries as well as his subordinates. He was multi-linguist and could speak number of languages. During his long stint in Mesopotamia he picked up the local dialect and developed deep interest in the Egyptian and Iranian carpets and rugs and over a period of time became a connoisseur. I vividly remember as a child that sometime in early 40's the carpets dealers would come home to obtain my grandfather's expert opinion. Maj Pereira also picked up taste for Egyptian's cigarette as well –Marcopolis, a flat cigarette of one's palm length with golden tip. My grandfather was a heavy smoker and had his quota of cigarettes shipped regularly to India from Egypt exquisitely packed in cedar wooden boxes and duly printed with his initials JMP on each cigarette". **Unquote.**

No wonder Admiral picked up smoking at an early age; 14 years!

Initial Schooling

At the young age of 8 ½ years in Dec 1931 Admiral was taken to Darjeeling, North Bengal, and was admitted in a famous boarding school – St. Joseph Convent, **North Point.**

North Point

The British Government acquired Darjeeling as a health resort in 1835. By 1846 the town had an excellent girl's school run by the Loreto Sisters. In 1887, when jurisdiction over the Catholic community in Darjeeling was transferred to Archbishop of Calcutta, the Jesuits there were able to satisfy a long standing request of Calcutta Catholics to establish a school for the boys.

On the slope above the presbytery was a long low building locally known as Sunny bank? As a provisional measure, this would now house the new school. Accordingly the alterations were immediately decided on and carried into effect.

February 13th 1888 heralded the birth of the new school – St. Joseph Convent, **North Point**. The next day the classes formally opened with 18 boarders and 7 day scholars present.

Boarding School

The information given by the Rector Father Shanjuman, North Point is as follows:-

Admiral was the 2802nd student enrolled in the school. The name given in the register; Pereira, Ronald Dadley Gregory Lynsdale s/o Major JM Pereira, Civil Surgeon, Dumka.

He was a boarder. Date of admission; 5.12.1931 and date of birth; 23.5.1923. He was admitted in Standard 1.

Ronnie P studied in North Point till Standard 6th in 1937. From the very beginning he took active part in sports; in 1932-Std 1, won E Merit; in 1933-Std 2, was Captain of Relay Team; in 1934-Std 3, he won Kangroo Race and in 1937-Std 6 he was one of the Finalists in Tennis Championship.

In 1935 he also took part in a play "Mother of Apostles" and acted as "Thaddeus"- Greek form of Aramic name meaning 'courageous heart' who likes to take role of leader. **Very hard exterior but soft from inside!** Incidentally, these were two major human traits which he imbibed and displayed throughout his life. **Coincidence!**

In 1990 Admiral sent me a photograph with his schoolmate Erach Avary, who came calling at BROADSIDES, Coonoor, incidentally also took part in the same play as one of four 'Beggers', (shown in the school photo of 1935). **Coincidence?**

Apparently with the war clouds looming large he came back to Patna in 1938, where Maj. JM Pereira was posted Superintendent Medical College Patna.

As per the information given by Father Armstrong Edison, SJ, Principal, St. Michael's High School, Digha Ghat, Kurji, a suburb of Patna. Admiral was admitted in class 7th on 17th February 1938 and his admission serial number was 432. He left the school in year 1941.

Thereafter, he joined St. Edmund's College, Shillong, and within a year or so, he went on to join Royal Indian Navy and was commissioned on 25TH May 1943.

Phyllis Beatrice Bedell

Mr. Bedell (photo) was an Armenian of Indian stock settled in Calcutta. They were a trading community with very high sense of integrity and good will. Over a period of time they had made very strong bond with East India Company. Phyllis was born on 7th Nov 1925 in large family of five sisters and a brother. As far as I remember her eldest sister was Mary settled in Sweden, others were in UK, Denmark and Canada. Mary along with her sister from Denmark had visited India in early 1980. Her only brother Benjamin was mysteriously lost at sea sometime in 1958.

At the age of 5 Phyllis was admitted in Mount Hermon School, Darjeeling in 1931 and spent her next 10 years in the hostel. This school is located just next to North Point, but they never met each other in schooldays. Thereafter, she went back to Calcutta and after doing Secretarial course joined Bombay Burma Company in mid 40's. I remember she told me that the first time she saw Ronnie was sometime in late 1940's during the Agha Khan Hockey Championship and Ronnie was representing Navy team as **Right-Out**. Navy lost the match and next day in the local papers, one of the sports critics wrote; that Navy could have produced much better performance, had there been some contribution from the Right-Out! Who was more of **Out-Right** as he could not collect a single ball through the match!

Phyllis was playing for Anglo Indians woman team in the local tournaments and she played as an electric Centre Forward! She was a national sprinter and with her speed and skill she was always a great threat to her opponents. In addition she was great athlete and Bengal state champion of

Tennis and Badminton Ladies Doubles and very knowledgeable about most of the sports but found Cricket rather boring- a game played by 22 jokers and watched by thousands jokers!- It was during these days that they had their first meeting and gradually the relation blossomed.

As per Aunty May Gantzer; **quote** "Mike, I must tell you that it was not all honky dory for Ron. In the spring of 1952, Ron went to Darjeeling to meet Phyllis father, who was Manager of hotel 'Everest'. All other sisters married and settled abroad and naturally her father wanted Phyllis to settle in London.

It was a disastrous trip and Mr. Bedell out rightly rejected the proposal and old man's words were; **I will never let my daughter marry a penniless naval officer** and to add insult he also presented him with the bill for two days stay at the hotel! Poor Ron had to come back empty handed and rather distressed" **Unquote**

Later she moved to Calcutta working for same company and it was here in summers of 1952, when Hugh Gantzer, who was studying in St. Xavier College, met her at the behest of the family and found her very charming and elegant.

Marriage

As per Aunty May; **quote** "however, she left for London for some inexplicable reason and took the engagement ring along with her! In spite of opposition from my parents as Phyllis was Protestant and we being Roman Catholic. Ron still went ahead and again got in touch with Phyllis and she agreed to come out, if he arranged a ticket for her. I believe Commander (later Rear Admiral) Kurvilla, who was in London at that time arranged a ticket for Phyllis to sail back to India and on 25th Sep 1952 they were married in Bombay". **Unquote**

My Journey

Born in a family with total civilian background, in my formative years I had no idea whatsoever about the uniform or rank structure in the armed forces. My parents were educationist in the Government service and served in non-military stations like Bhiwani, Hissar and Karnal in undivided Punjab in 50's and early 60's.

My first exposure to uniform was in 1963 when I joined Sainik School, Kunjpura, Karnal. The founder Principal was Lt Col Eric John Simeon, Registrar; Major EF Edulgee, and Headmaster; Captain MMR Menon. We as children were hardly aware of rank structure in the Army and even less in Navy and Air Force.

However, in the ensuing years we had number of senior dignitaries from Services visit our school for Founder's Day Functions and Annual Athletic Meets. I remember in 1964, Gen JN Chaudhuri, COAS, visited our school, followed by Air Marshal Arjan Singh, Chief of Air Staff and Lt Gen Harbhaksh Singh GOC-in-C Western Command in 1965. Next year in 1966 General Carriapa, the first Chief of the Army visited the school. In 1967, Gen Kumaramanglam COAS was Chief Guest for Annual Athletics Meet. In 1968, Gen Katoch, Maj Gen Jang Shamsher Singh and Maj Gen Ayyapa visited our school. In my final year, in **Oct 1969, Admiral Adhar Kumar Chatterji, Chief of Naval Staff visited as Chief Guest for Annual Athletics Meet.** Indeed he was the first senior Naval Officer I ever saw and yes, **I had the privilege to receive the Inter House Champion's Trophy from him and 47 years hence I still have and cherish the photograph of receiving the trophy!**

At that moment I could have **never imagined in my wildest dreams** that 20 months later, I will be meeting yet another senior Naval Officer, who will follow the footsteps of Admiral Chatterji and one day himself become

Chief of Naval Staff?!! I must mention ,that here I was shaking hands with Admiral AK Chatterji, who had great influence on Ronnie Pereira and to a great extent was responsible in shaping his career for higher ranks. It was a known fact in the Navy in those days of late 60's that Admiral AK Chatterji was very fond of Ronnie Pereira, and recognized his unique leadership qualities which he displayed as Captain of cruiser INS Delhi in 66-68.

My journey to meet Ronnie P started on a cold morning of 15th Jan 1963, when I joined Sainik School, Kunjpura and there on to NDA on 7th Jan 1970.

Sainik Schools were conceived in July 1961 by Mr. VK Krishna Menon, Defence Minister of India, to rectify the regional and class imbalances amongst officer cadre of the Indian Military, and to prepare students for entry into **National Defence Academy**. Initially five schools were established in 1961, including Kunjpura and another six were added next year and today we have 28 schools all over the country including Imphal in Manipur and Punglwa in Nagaland in North East India.

Sainik School, Kunjpura, is spread over 275 acres, and was established on erstwhile fiefdom of Nawab Najabat Khan, which dates back to 1739. The main building of the school is housed in the Nawab's Palace built in 1900.

The first batch for NDA from our school was selected in June 1963 - Deepak Kapoor (later Chief of Army Staff), DDS Sandhu (later Lt Gen, DG Ordinance), BK Berry (later Brig) and TS Hassanwalia (later Col). All of them came for our Old Boy's Meet in Dec 63, attired in NDA blazer looking dapper and handsome (particularly Deepak Kapoor), yes, we as children were totally mesmerized and inspired by them to join NDA. Sure enough six years later 13 students from our class qualified for 43rd course and we reported to NDA on 7th Jan 1970.

A year later in Jan 71, Commodore RL Pereira was posted as Deputy Commandant and rest as they say is history.

National Defence Academy - January 1971

On our return from winter break in January 71, there was buzz in the air that the newly posted Deputy Commandant is one Commodore RL Pereira from the Indian Navy. I would like to highlight that he was the 15th Deputy Commandant and 3rd from the Navy. Incidentally out of the previous 10

Deputy Commandants 9 were from the Army and one from Air Force and the last Deputy from Navy was Captain JS Mehra (7th Nov 55 -27th Sep 58)?! Was it a **coincidence** that NDA got a Deputy from the Navy after more than 12 years! It could have been another one from Army or Air Force, and why Navy now?? As per Buddhist mythology it was in his **karma** to come to NDA at that very juncture. What "**TIMING**"!

Speaking to Admiral Adolph Britto, who served with Admiral in INS Kuthar in early 60's said; **quote** "Mike, Navy was very small in those days with only Western Naval Command and Indian Fleet, and senior naval officers from Captain onwards were known to everyone. By 1969, Ronnie P had put in 26 years of service and already commanded INS Delhi, one of two Capital ships (other one INS Mysore), with great aplomb and success (including winning the 'COCK' in the famous 1967 Regatta in Cochin) and his reputation of a fire brand officer and **inspirational leader** was known to the entire Navy, naturally he would have been the ideal choice for NDA. He just happened to be in the right '**Time Zone**'". **Unquote.**

We were just stepping into our third term and relatively junior to comprehend any earth shaking consequences. The previous Deputy Commandant Colonel HKK Shukla wasn't seen around much, so for us it was no big deal with the new incumbent and we thought that he too won't be visible – **how wrong we were?** - And what was to unfold was way beyond our wildest imagination!!

However, our Squadron Commander Lt Cdr Daljit Singh Brar seems rather excited and proud that the new Deputy is from his service- Navy. He informed all the cadets of Delta squadron that there are two Pereira's in the navy, first cousins, the elder one John is from Engineer branch and the younger Ronnie is from Executive branch. It is the younger one who is posted to NDA. Lt Cdr Brar explicitly forewarned us that Ronnie Pereira is a fastidious officer, a strict disciplinarian and stickler for rules, so better stay out of his sight as even minor offence or violation of rules will promptly invite severe action, so '**BEWARE**'!!

Soon after taking over as Deputy Commandant, the whole academy was ordered to assemble in the Auditorium for Deputy's first address to the cadets. We all were looking forward to hear his exceptional oratory skills, as informed by naval instructors.

At the stroke of 5pm the Deputy entered the hall and Academy Cadet Adjutant Mir Ahmed Shah, roared – **gentlemen, the Deputy Commandant-**

and all of us jumped to attention. Even now after nearly 46 years I vividly remember as Deputy headed for the stage through aisle I could see from the corner of my eyes, **a tall and ramrod officer in immaculate whites with peak cap walking briskly and climbed up the steps to the stage and first action was to kick the stool placed behind the lectern for relatively short speakers!!** Ronnie P was 6.2 feet in his socks and certainly didn't need it.

He stood there and gave a deep stair and thundered in his baritone voice- Gentlemen, - **Duty, Honor and Country**, - comes first always and every time. Let me make one thing very clear that am not here to molly coddle you, am here to make men out of you and mould you as the finest human beings in the world and I will not hesitate to **kick your bloody back sides** if so required. The Government spends helluva lot of money on training and feeding you and it will be my sincere endeavor to make each one of you a mentally and physically strong leader of men, so that when you are called upon by your country to safe guard its sovereignty and integrity you are not found wanting. I want you all to rigidly follow the rules and regulations of this great Academy, and any infringement, however, minor will be dealt with severely. I shall be chasing you all and chasing hard, day in and day out, so be on your toes and I will not spare you.

He spoke for about 20 minutes in very emphatic and articulate manner with American accent and I have tried to give the gist of his address. By the time he finished we were all spell bound, shaking our heads in disbelief. To be honest many words flew over our heads but it was clear **that we are in for tough times ahead.** What he said, he meant every word of it.

14 years later in his letter dated 29 July 85, he wrote, **quote** "*The Commandant of NDA is Rear Admiral Ravi Sawhney, who is a fine officer. However, I don't know who the Dep Com is. It could possibly be an Army officer, but I have no idea who is in the chair at the moment. I will always have a place very close to my heart for the Academy. It was one of my happiest tenure ashore and as a result of that assignment, I really learnt a great deal about human nature and had the pleasure and the privilege to mould the finest devils in the world that I could have ever wished for*".

"*Admiral Sawhney wrote to me two or three times to ask me to preside at the Convocation Ceremony, but it was just after my accident and I couldn't make it. However, I did have the joy and privilege of passing out two courses, and that was something I always wanted to do and will always remember*". **Unquote**

> ADMIRAL R L PEREIRA, PVSM AVSM(Retd.)
>
> "AT LAST"
> 188, MAIN ROAD
> WHITEFIELD P. O.
> BANGALORE-560 066
>
> -3-
>
> The Commandant of NDA is Rear-Admiral Ravi Khuhney who is a fine Officer. However, I don't know who the Dep. Com is. It could possibly be an Army Officer, but I have no idea who is in the chair at the moment. I will always have a place very close to my heart for the Academy. It was one of my happiest tenures ashore, and as a result of that assignment, I really learned a great deal about human nature and had the pleasure & the privilege to mould the finest cadets in the world that I could have ever worked for.
>
> Admiral Khuhney wrote to me two or three times to ask me to preside at the Convocation Ceremony, but it was just after my accident & I couldn't make it. However, I did have the joy & privilege of passing out two courses, & that was something I always wanted to do, and will always remember.

Lieutenant Commander Daljit Singh Brar **was spot** on and within couple of weeks, all 1500 cadets were on their toes and running helter-skelter to avoid getting caught or hauled up by the Deputy Commandant as even minor infringement invited- son, 21 Days Restrictions and 4 Singarh Hikes?? That took care of entire month. No movies, no liberties to Poona and lots and lots of physical pain!

One of my course mate Major AK Singh, author of *Beyond Horizons* has very aptly captured Ronnie P personality, **quote** "Ronnie, none of the cadets really took much note when Commodore RL Pereira of the Indian Navy took over the reins of Deputy Commandant or Dep Com! It was not common for cadets to even see Dep Com unless one was marched up to him either for consistently for poor performance in physical or academics or for committing an act of grave offence and indiscipline or ' moral turpitude'- whatever that meant . In general we were made to see him for not possessing OLQ or Officer Like Qualities. And once marched up to him, one seldom came out without being relegated to the next term. Thereby being put back by six months, or- and this was the really the last rung-being withdrawn from the Academy and losing future career in the Armed Forces as a commissioned officer. So, unless someone has performed a serious act of commission or omission , one could normally rest easy. **One would seldom set eye on the Dep Com, except at functions where he would address all the cadets from the podium, and even more feeble was chances that Dep Com would ever set his eyes on you.**

Not so with Ronnie Pereira. Ronnie soon made it clear that he was the part of academy curricula- through day and night, as all of us, and that he was going to live the academy life with same ferocity he was determined to make us live it. Ronnie the enigma, Ronnie the hero, we worshipped, Ronnie the devil we feared, who would catch our every wrong doing- day in and day out, who was high on do's and don'ts routine and above all we loved what he was, and that he was committed to do- his dedication was as unmatched then as it is even now, over 45 years later, Ronnie was afflicted with human passion for everything he ever set out to do. And above all he was determined to be God and Godfather to each one of 1500 cadets, and turn them into the fittest and finest human beings on earth. It was his obsessive dedication that actually managed to make both work. Ronnie was everywhere at the same time. If that sounds impossible, just ask anyone of us who were there. He certainly was at most unlikely places at most unpredictable times. He could be in the tea queue at 5 am or appear behind you to catch your smart Lecky moves to cut corners! Suddenly who do we see but Ronnie! In fact he saw us before we saw him! We were on punishments like hikes or subjected to restrictions". **Unquote**

No doubt there could not have been better description of Ronnie Pereira and am sure any other cadet with pen as good as AK's would have given more or less same narrative. However, as I go along the journey with the great man I have dozens of **close encounters** narrated by ex NDA cadets to give their own experiences with beloved Ronnie.

Within days Dep Com became Omni present and was everywhere, squadron lines, morning muster, Drill Square, PT grounds, Swimming pool, Equitation lines, Sudan Block, Science Block, Military Hospital, Library, Cadet's Mess, Assembly Hall on picture days, sports fields, training areas and any other most unlikely places, be it on horseback or in his famous White Ambassador car, yes, on bicycle or on foot. With car parked outside Foxtrot Squadron and himself in Delta Squadron! The only time we got forewarned was when his Labrador dog named Ceaser went on his own way and we knew that Dep Com is somewhere around on the prowl, so be on the look out!!

The first causality was the 40th course, the sixth termers, when he caught few of 6th termers were late for PT parade and to teach a lesson, Dep Com sent the entire course for long route marches throughout their mid-term break.

Nearly 40 years later Mir Ahmed Shah, Academy Cadet Adjutant, 40th Juliet squadron wrote about Ronnie P, **quote "Ronnie Pereira-** Yes , I am talking about one and only one Admiral Ronnie Pereira, our Deputy Commandant in NDA during our 6th term, who later became Chief of Naval Staff! May God bless his soul? A man who can never be forgotten by us or for that matter by anyone who ever came in contact with him? Ronnie galvanized the Academy the moment he joined. The NDA revolved around this man, all else was forgotten. He was always looking to improve the working conditions and the morale of the cadets, whether by getting after the Catering Officer to improve our food or by seeing to it that the squadron lines had everything to make our lives comfortable. He was the one who got fans put in every cabin. We could expect to see a tall man in the Navy Whites with the roaring voice at any time, any place- whether it was Muster, PT, Drill, classes or at various sports disciplines. If Deputy Commandant was omnipresent, well you can imagine that the poor Div Commanders and Squadron Commanders were with us 24 hours; And Ronnie could be tough. During our 6th term, he felt that the discipline of 40th course was not up to mark, so instead of letting us go home in our mid-term break, he sent us for long route marches, which really had us!

I must narrate that in early March 1982, I went to New Delhi Railway Station to see off my relative and as we reached the platform I saw a huge crowd and there was no place to stand . I inquired why there was such a rush, somebody told me that they have come to bid farewell to Admiral Pereira! I immediately struggled through the crowd and manage to reach Admiral and shake hands with him. Yes, he remembered me. **What a great man! My eyes still fill up thinking of that moment". Unquote**

Pip squeaks like us in junior term were always on our toes. Throughout my third term from Jan-June 71, I stayed as far away as possible from Dep Com's sights. Though he was all over the Academy almost all hours to catch an earring cadet, and if you were unfortunate one, you simply ended with 21 days plus 4 Singarh Hikes thrown in for additional affects!! Therefore, I never broke any rules, never stepped out of line, always moved in a squad on foot or cycle, and ensured I was before schedule time for all indoor and outdoor activities. Simple rule was not to attract Dep Com's attention for breaking any code of conduct .The closest I came to Dep Com was during practice sessions for Academy Hockey team for which I was playing as a Left Half under the eagle eye of our coach Mr. Bhatnager, who in 1943 played along with great Major Dhyan Chand at National level. Often Dep Com would come and sit on the sidelines to witness our practice sessions and certainly for our matches with local teams from Poona and encouraged us from the side lines. Later we were informed by Mr. Bhatnagar that Dep Com in his younger days represented Navy Hockey team as Right Out. Dep Com would often talk to us and give some tips etc but I still managed to stay out of his close sights. At times he would enter the ground and borrow a stick from one of us to hit few balls into the goalpost. He had great regards for Mr. Bhatnagar.

Singarh Fort

This is an ancient fort (Lion's Fort) with more than 2000 years of history and is perched at the highest point of Sahyadri Mountains at the height of 4000 ft. It is located 14 kms South of NDA. Many famous battles have taken place starting from 1328 when Mohammad bin Tughlak captured it from a Koli tribal chieftain. In 1656 Shivaji captured it and remained with Marathas till 1689. Later it exchanged hands with Mughals and Britishers. It was clearly visible on the skyline from NDA. It was tremendous physical exertion in climbing up the fort, collect the token and rush back to Academy; all within stipulated time frame i.e. about 6 hours .The hike was unfortunately scheduled for Sundays!! Enough to take care of one's Sundays and Mondays with after effects!! I climbed it 13 times!! The minimum Dep Com gave was 4 hikes at a time!!

Nun-Kun Expedition June-July 1971

In all probability I would have remained a **faceless cadet** amongst 1500, had it not been for our 5th term Sergeant Joginder Singh Mann, 41st, Delta squadron, (my schoolmate) who out of the blue forwarded my name for NUN- KUN Mountaineering Expedition in May 71.

Nun (23,409 ft) and Kun (23,218 ft) are twin peaks located in North Western Himalayas, in the Sura valley in Zanskar range. After 5 attempts it was scaled for the first time in 1953 by Swiss- French team led by Bernard Perrie, which also included Claud Kugan- a pioneering female mountaineer.

Even today after 45 years, I still wonder as to why Sergeant JS Mann asked me if **I was keen to go for this expedition.** To get the answer, in April 2016 after many years I managed to locate JS Mann, and informed him - Sir, I am writing a book on Admiral and **if you remember, it was you who triggered this unique relationship.** To be honest, but for you I would have never come anywhere near the 'Dep Com' to give him an opportunity to focus on my face which reminded him of his late nephew- Michael Pereira; otherwise I would have gone through life as one Sant Pratap Singh Bhalla in the crowd.

So I requested JS Mann Sir, please take back your mind by 45 years and try to recollect your thoughts and events leading to this episode of recommending my name for the Expedition? Brigadier JS Mann said, you have to give me some time to recollect my thoughts and call me up in the evening. As per his directions I called up again at 7pm and he went on to narrate the whole episode.

Quote "Ok Mike let me try and narrate you the sequence of events. The previous year in summer of 1970, I was the member of the expedition led by Flt Lt Venugopal, which had successfully scaled MULKILA Peak (21,638 ft) in Lahul Spiti, Himachal Pradesh. However, in 1971, Flt Lt Venugopal decided to include four members of last year expedition to be part of Nun Kun expedition also. Apart from me other three were- Manoj Kumar (40th course) JS Dalal (41st) and MS Gill (43rd), primarily to have some experienced climbers in the team. For the selection of fresh members a formal selection procedure was carried out by the NDA Mountaineering Club. Sometime in the month of April 1971, a circular was sent to all squadrons for selection of Nun Kun Expedition team and asking for volunteers to forward their names with complete credentials to the Mountaineering Club. After perusal of their profiles about 30 cadets were shortlisted and interviewed by Flt Lt Venugopal. Majority of selected cadets were either outstanding sportsmen or attended course in Mountaineering Institutes at Darjeeling, Manali, Uttarkashi or been part of any expedition during school days. The fresh members were also put through endurance test before final selection to comprise a team of 14 cadets. However, after few days of training, I went and informed Flt Lt Venugopal that I will not able to continue due to dislocation of my shoulder during the recently held Inter Squadron Boxing Championship as it will only hamper me to carry any weight (rucksack) and requested if my name could be withdrawn from the expedition on medical grounds. Venugopal initially did not entertain my request but later on my repeated insistence, he reluctantly agreed but on one condition- **to look for a suitable replacement.** I said I will do that, Sir."

I again asked Brigadier Mann, Sir, **why me?**

He replied –"look Mike, because, firstly you were from my school, secondly my squadron (Delta) and thirdly I thought you were smart enough to make the grade, as you were already representing NDA Hockey team and played most of the games for the squadron so I thought you were a suitable candidate". At that time I informed JS Mann that Sir, **I have not attended any Mountaineering course or been part of any mountaineering expedition**, to which Mann replied "don't worry, you leave that to me and all I want is your answer"- **I said, ' Yes Sir'.**

He could have easily recommended any other cadet's name in the whole Academy, **why mine??** That's still **is a mystery**! Even now after 45 years, I often wonder, was it just a **coincidence** or was it in my Karma! There had to be some method in this madness and surely **some super power was at work** through Sergeant JS Mann and trying to create a situation which will eventually get me into **close proximity** of the "Dep Com" and thereby be **noticed** by the great man.

45 years on I still have no answers but am 'MOST' grateful to JS Mann, who was solely responsible for initiating this unique relationship with Admiral and Mrs. Pereira, and gave them the joy of a son they never had. However, my wife, who is a Buddhist, tells me that it was part of my **"Karmic journey"**!

My name was duly forwarded to the team leader Flt Lt Venugopal. Few days later, after we had finished trekking for 4 hours, the whole team gathered at Flt Lt Krishnamurthy's residence to have cup of tea and meet his new bride. After a while Flt Lt Venugopal turned around and asked me; **Cadet Bhalla, what extra qualifications, if any, do you have?** I don't know why, I promptly replied - **Sir, I can sing**! Venugopal Sir was sort of taken aback by my answer but then said, Ok, go ahead and sing. I very seriously sang the song from reigning super star Rajesh Khanna's movie 'Safar' – **Zindagi ka safar hai yeh kaisa safar koi samaja nahin koi jana nahin; hai yeh kaisi dagar chalte hai sab magar koi samaja nahin koi jana nahin**; (What is the journey of life all about? Neither we can understand nor know anything, but we all have to go through it without knowing what future holds for us??). Flt Lt Venugopal liked the song and said **'ok you are in'** and keep us entertained during the tough and challenging times ahead but not with such serious songs!! In fact,

I got to know later that it was Venugopal's, favourite song!! May be the song lyrics changed my life or Kishor Kumar, who sang this immortal song?? I don't really know?? But this much I know that, **JS Mann changed my life and I will be indebted to him till my last breath on this earth.**

The list of all members is given below.

Nun Kun Expedition June/July 1971

Leader

Flight Lieutenant KP Venugopal

Deputy Leader

Captain SS Singh

Photographers

Lt Commander DS Brar and Flt Lieutenant AS Krishnamurthy

Doctor

Captain S Sen

Team

SCC	KMP Singh
ACC	JS Dalal
BCC	Ajit Singh
BCC	SV Kulkarni
SCC	SB Chavan
Cadet	R Kochar
Cadet	PT Joshi
Cadet	BK Sinha
Cadet	SP Singh
Cadet	SPS Bhalla
Cadet	MS Gill
Cadet	RS Chaudhary
Cadet	KS Rawal
Cadet	NS Powar

Prior to our departure the entire team was introduced to General Manekshaw, COAS, who had come to Review the 40th course POP on 5

June 71. We also had photo session with Gen SD Gupta, Commandant and Dep Com. In fact it can be noticed from the photographs that Dep Com was standing barely 3 feet away from me when we were interacting with the Commandant, Gen Gupta and in the group photograph I am, in fact, sitting in front at his feet, but naturally Dep Com paid no attention whatsoever towards me and I passed off as an inconsequential cadet. Not only that, as per Air Marshal SP Singh, who is shaking hands with General Manekshaw in the photo, told me; if you remember one day after our routine training, both of us were very tired and sitting on the steps of Sudan Block to catch our breath and suddenly Dep Com appeared from nowhere and all he said was son, you both seem very tired! We kept our mouths shut, out of fear, and he drove off!! Much to our relief! Even at that time being so close to him, my face did not evoke any memories whatsoever of Michael Pereira!

On 6 June 71, Sunday, our team consisting of 5 officers and 14 cadets left NDA for Poona, where we boarded an Indian Air Force service aircraft to Agra. Next morning we boarded a Packet aircraft and had miserable and uncomfortable journey to Srinagar, where we were welcomed by our ex Dep Com, Col HKK Shukla, who was posted at HQs 19 Infantry Division, Baramulla.

After spending few days in Kargil, on 12 June we headed for base camp and after tiring and long trek of 9 hours through Sura valley we reached the base camp located at the altitude of 15000 feet. The high altitude effect was beginning to take its toll and we were feeling very tired and out of breath due to lack of oxygen and sub zero temperature. The first night was indeed uncomfortable and it took us about 7 days to get acclimatized and steadily got our strength back.

On 2nd July, Joshi, Chaudhary, Chavan and self with 4 Sherpas climbed Tanak Peak 21000 ft, and we just managed to get back to Camp 1 before the billizard hit us. Next four days we were holed up in Camp 1 with heavy snowfall, winds speed over 100 kmp, and temperature minus 20^0 or more. There was no water to drink and we were eating snow and getting dehydrated, the kerosene oil had frozen and tents were completely buried under snow and we had to often come out to clear the snow or lest we get buried under the very weight of the snow. How we survived those four terrible days and nights only God above knows? How we went through the horrifying experience make my hair stand even today after 45 years. At that time I thought as the cli'che goes - this is the end and why did I get into this situation and how I wished I should not have sung that song or sang another one, may be from *Mera Naam Joker*! This would have annoyed Venugopal and rejected me and wouldn't have brought myself **so close to death** and that too buried under snow, what a terrible death and blaming everybody and everything!!?? But with the grace of God, the weather opened up on 6th July and we came out unscathed and alive. We immediately re-establish radio contact with Base Camp and everyone was relieved that we were alive.

On 16th July the Capt SS Singh with senior Sherpa Phinzo, two other sherpas and 4 cadets i.e. JS Dalal, SP Singh MS Gill and KS Rawal commenced their ascent from Camp 2 and established Camp 3 at 22000 ft. The final assault to Nun peak started at 4am on 19th July but it had to be abandoned half way due to bad weather. However, the team made the second assault on 20th and by 2.45pm Capt SS. Singh and Phinzo reached the summit, followed by a Sherpa and Cadets MS Gill and KS Rawal. After hoisting Indian Flag as well as NDA Flag and spending about 20 minutes on the summit, they commenced their descent and safely reached Camp 3 by evening! A great feat in itself and all the credit goes to Venugopal Sir, and his Deputy SS Singh.

It took us about a week to wind up all the camps and reached Srinagar by 28th July and had a nice break of four days visiting Baramulla and Uri and took off for Delhi on 2nd Aug. Next day on 3rd Aug, we boarded Indian Air Force - Super Constellation- a VIP aircraft, as we boarded we noticed in the middle seats a tall Sikh officer seating by himself. We were later told by one of the crew that the officer in question was Air Commodore Dilbagh Singh, AOC Poona, and future Chief of Air Staff!! Sure enough he became CAS ten years later in 1981!!

The Day of Reckoning- "Encounter with Dep Com"

We reached NDA by late evening of 3rd August 71. Next day, **Wednesday 4th August**, early morning we were informed that all members of Nun Kun expedition were required to report to the Conference Hall, Sudan Block at 10 am to meet the Commandant.

I vividly remember it was an overcast day and there was a light drizzle outside. The first thing came to my mind was to find a Barber to have hair cut as I had a long crop of two months and there was no way I could go like this in front of Dep Com, who we knew will be present and he would simply chew me up. There were no sign of Barber and I was beginning to get panicky, however, I was able to locate one and had just enough time for him to go through the process and I told him 'just give me Zero cut' and after he had finished I rushed to Sudan Block and managed to reach minutes before the arrival of Dep Com.

We all had just settled down when Dep Com walked in, he congratulated each one of us and then stood in the middle of the hall and started to give us a talk regarding the experiences and lessons we would have learnt from this dangerous and challenging expedition. He basically spoke about the team spirit and camaraderie to help each other in death threatening situations. At that very moment for some unknown reason I interrupted and said; "Sir, I came very close to death not once but twice"; Dep Com turned towards my direction to see; who is this idiot who spoke out of turn and looked at me. Being a chain smoker he was holding the lighter in his left hand with slight bend at the elbow and cigarette in his right hand near his lips and was about to light it when he suddenly stopped and froze in the same position and stared hard at me , I thought to myself that I have I dropped a brick by opening my mouth and now I will walk out from the room with minimum 21 days Restrictions and what a terrible way to start my 4th term ? After about 10 seconds I looked up and Dep Com was still staring at me and there was pin drop silence in the hall and am sure everybody was looking at me with pity and expecting the worst, after another 10 seconds or so SP Singh (my classmate and course mate, later Air Marshal) who was sitting next to me slowly whispered in Punjabi (hali vi dekh raya hai!), he is still looking at you ; by now I was shivering in my legs and my throat was dry, anyhow after 30 odd seconds which to me felt like a life time, Deputy softly said, son, you know, your face reminds me of my late nephew 'Michael', who tragically died in a plane crash some years ago; I was relieved beyond words that he did not utter 21 days!! He then went on to narrate the entire details of the accident, but believe me I heard nothing as my mind was blank out of fear. I don't know, how he was reminded of Michael, because we had more than a dozen interactions with him prior to our departure in June and he fortunately never gave me second look, thank God or else asking for trouble! May be the angle from which he saw me or my zero haircut or some striking feature which reactivated the memory chip of Michael in his mind, or could be 'Karmic' connection of previous life or whatever it was, it left me totally confused and after the conference I thought that's the end of story and I should now merge with rest of 1500 cadets. I could never imagine that those few seconds would be the beginning of unimaginable and incredible journey; no, not at all, resembling some unknown person is not going to change my life, I thought. In fact I promised to myself never to open my mouth again in Dep Com's presence and shut my mind to this incident and try to stay as far away as possible from Dep Com's sights.

How wrong I was in my perception?

The next day i.e. Thursday, the entire Nun Kun expedition team was invited to Commandant's Residence for high tea. There, Mrs. Pereira, a tall elegant and extremely graceful lady walked in with Dep Com and was being introduced to all cadets, as they came in front of me, before introducing me, **Dep Com asked Mrs. Pereira 'Darling who does he remind you of ?' She gave me one look and in two seconds said 'Mike'**!! I was beginning to get more confused, nervous and intrigued. However, for rest of the evening both Dep Com and Mrs. Pereira stood close to me, I did not speak a word and couldn't even enjoy the eats!!

Lunch

Two days later on Saturday i.e. 7th Aug 71, Cadet Sergeant Major JS Mann called and informed me that I have been invited for lunch at Dep Com residence on Sunday i.e. 8th Aug, I thought that he would have invited the entire Nun Kun team, but I was taken aback when JS Mann said, no, you are the only one invited for lunch. Now that made me more frightened and worried and how I will face Dep Com alone. I could not sleep most of the night out of sheer mixed up feelings. Never been to such a senior officer's residence in my entire life and I kept wondering why me alone, believe me it was no joy to be alone in Dep Com's company. What will I talk to him about? What questions he will ask, whether I will have the correct answer or not? To be honest I was not looking forward to it out of sheer fear and nervousness.

How wrong I was? He had '**other side**' exposed to few; so warm, courteous, self-effacing and large of heart and I dare say, nearest to the God.

Anyhow come Sunday, by noon, I cut my nails, polished my shoes till I could see my face in its shine, shaved twice, washed my cycle and after bath dressed into my best Mufti, checked all buttons in place and got the correct tie knot in 4th attempt. By 12.40 pm with mixed feelings I commenced **my journey** from Delta squadron lines, I turned left on to the main road and went past No 2 Battalion, Ashoka Pillar, along the Drill Square with Science Block on my right, crossed Swimming Pool with Gymnasium on my left and slowly cycled up the slope to D2 and E3 Area, which had Staff Quarters on either side of the road with beautiful front gardens and hedges. I was now within 500 yards from my destination which was little ahead of the road turning right towards Peacock Bay. The total distance of about 3 kms from the squadron lines and all the while I was thinking and trying to figure out what questions they will ask me or what to talk or will I have the right answer ; just tell the truth, don't pull fast one etc. At the end of the road was double storey building –Deputy Commandant Residence (photo); I quietly approached the gate and parked my cycle outside the gate. Yes, I was perspiring, partially due to cycling and more so because I was scared of the impending unknown situation and unfamiliar territory ahead! I checked my dress, took a deep breath and entered the gate, there was drive in to the front porch, a well manicured and lovely lawn and well laid out garden blooming with pink and white bougainvillea flowers and many other flowers whose names I did not know and I still could not believe where I was? There in the front verandah I saw Mrs. Pereira sitting on a Wicker chair deeply engrossed in the Newspaper (later I got to know, she was busy solving crossword puzzle!), I cleared my throat and whispered Good Morning Madam; actually it should have been Good Afternoon - it was past 1pm. Anyway she looked up and replied very warmly Oh! Hello, Good Afternoon, my son, come on in and sit down. I sat down on the tip of the chair almost falling. Mrs. Pereira called; Ronnie, come down our guest has arrived. My legs were shivering, my heart was beating at a rapid rate and my throat was absolutely dry and on the sight of Dep Com I shot up from the chair and stood as stiff as I could and wished him rather loudly; Good Afternoon, Sir. He had a warm and broad smile on his face and gave me a deep look with his big eyes and strong hand shake and said, relax and sit down, son. I dare not, he was such an imposing personality and in last six months had already become a veritable terror catching erring cadets at odd hours of day and night, everywhere and anywhere in the Academy and here he is asking me to sit down next to him!? I couldn't believe my ears and almost stopped breathing!

Mrs. Pereira sensed my terrible plight and discomfort and to make me feel at ease she promptly asked me to sit next to her and shot her first question; son, which part of the country do you belong to? I replied in a hushed tone; Punjab Maam, she said, oh! We in the Navy have lots of Sikh officers and sailors from your Punjab and how smart they look with their beard and turbans. She spoke to me about a handsome senior Sikh Naval officer who tied his turban beautifully. Later I got to know, it was Commodore Kirpal Singh, she was referring to. She asked about my schooling and games I played, I told her am already playing for NDA Hockey team and she was thrilled to know as she herself represented Bombay Women Anglo Indians team as centre forward way back in 1949-50 and participated in Women Hockey Championship at Bombay. She asked me about my school days and where did I study? I told her that I studied in Sainik School, Kunjpura for 7 years and then joined NDA. Then she went on to regale stories about her school days. She told me that she went to Mount Hermon School, Darjeeling in 1931 as a 5 year old girl and studied for the next ten years there only and later went to a college in Calcutta. She remembered her train journey from Calcutta and how they had to cross river Padma on ferry and then cover rest of the journey by train to Siliguri on meter gauge. Thereafter take the Toy train to Darjeeling through most scenic and beautiful landscape. The train would halt at Kurseong for lunch break and get to Ghoom by late afternoon and then walk to school which was located close to the railway station. I kept cracking my knuckles and listened to her quietly. She inquired if I have been to East, I said no Maam, she said son, **one day you must visit East**, and it's the most beautiful part of India. Meanwhile a glass of juice arrived and was offered to me which I sipped slowly like a gentleman instead of gulping down my parched throat. Dep Com too asked me which other games do I play, I replied almost all team games like Football, Basketball and Athletics etc, and he asked me if I played Golf. I told him I have never heard of this game before coming to NDA as we did not have this facility at Karnal an ancient historical place where I lived in my childhood. Then he asked, would you like to learn this game, I replied, yes Sir, and thought to myself that it could not be more difficult than Hockey!

I could not have been farther from truth!!

After a while we moved in for lunch to the Dining Room. They made me sit on the head of the table with Admiral on my left and Mrs. Pereira on my right. I could see the most sumptuous spread out in front of me; there was chicken, fish curry, dal, two vegetables and salad with rice and chappatis. I really enjoyed the lunch and polished off almost every dish on the table as it is **cadets are always hungry**. Then the pudding- ice cream came, after that I was offered fruits and then chocolate and I kept eating! **Now we come to an embarrassing part, after I had my fill, as I got up , my trousers could not sustain the pressure of overstuffed stomach and to my horror I found that my hook and two buttons snapped and I was left totally red faced holding my trousers from slipping down!!** What a situation and that too in presence of Dep Com and Mrs. Pereira! Anyhow, I took deep breath and with doleful eyes picked up courage to ask Dep Com if he could get me couple of safety pins!! He looked at my face, took pity and went up to his Dressing Room and after a while he came down and handed me two pins and I temporarily salvaged the situation and managed to repair the damage, it was indeed most awkward and horrifying situation to say the least. I thanked them and sheepishly asked their permission to leave before I create more nuisance of myself, they walked me to the gate, and I thanked them again, stood to attention and wished them and slowly cycled down the slope much to my relief. As I was out of their sight, I started to smile and laughed to myself all the way to squadron lines and raised my hands and thanked God. My close friends Anoop, Prabhjit Bedi and Arun Chand were eagerly waiting for me and I recounted the whole visit to them verbatim. We all laughed and were generally very happy.

I still had no idea whatsoever, **how the future will unfold – not the faintest idea!!!**

By asking Dep Com for safety pins I inadvertently gave away the short cut procedure of the missing buttons. And thereafter he used to ask cadets to remove their belt to check if they were using safety pins to hold their shorts and managed to catch **few unfortunate ones!!**

After a few days one early morning at about 6 am, Dep Com was walking in the squadron corridor. I approached him and wished him Good Morning Sir, his eyes lit up when he saw me and replied very warmly and said; son, remember today is Wednesday, club day and you must be at the Golf Club at 3pm sharp , OK . I said, yes Sir.

Mike

I was very excited the whole day and looking forward to going to the Golf Course **first time** in my life. I had no idea what the game was all about, but more than game it was meeting the Dep Com again, imagine three days before I was mortally scared of him , but after that Sunday lunch when I experienced his other side, somehow the fear of his presence began to diminish a wee bit. So immediately after lunch I got ready and was the first one to reach the course at 2.40 pm. At sharp 3pm we saw the White Ambassador speeding down towards Club House. Dep Com came out in T-shirt and his white naval shorts and called me out and said, son, go and pick up a golf set and 20 practice golf balls. I repeat, I was totally ignorant about this game. With eager to learn feelings I followed the Dep Com to the practice range and he literally started from scratch about the game. First he told me, son, in this bag you can carry maximum 14 clubs. 4 wood clubs i.e. No 1, No 2, No 3, and No 4. No1 is also called Driver. Nine irons i.e. No 3, 4, 5, 6, 7, 8, 9, plus Pitching Wedge and Sand Wedge and finally a Putter. In addition Golf balls and some practice balls, Tees, markers, left hand glove and cap and also a book on rules.

I was in ordinary Bata PT shoes! He said, son you need to buy a pair of new Golf shoes.

Next he gave me demonstration of a basic stance. Align towards the target with imaginary line, legs slightly apart to shoulder's width, stand erect with slight bend at waist, overlap grip, arms straight, knee slightly bend, ball placed in the line of instep of left heel, body relaxed, don't hold the club too tight and focus on the ball. Now the backward swing, keep left arm straight, lift it slowly, turn your hips, turn your shoulders and cock your wrist, club parallel to the ground over your head at top of the swing, now start down swing, turn in your shoulders and hips, keep left foot grounded, left knee steady and go through the ball and remember one thing that through the **entire swing the head MUST remain steady, that's the key to true swing**. He repeated the whole procedure and then gave me a demonstration by hitting few ball towards the target area, the swing looked so simple, smooth and easy. I was very confident that I will be able to replicate his swing. I thought to myself here you have stationary ball and no one to worry you like in hockey and am also in stationary position, so no big deal, then why such long list of do's and don'ts. So, very confidently I took a stance as per his directions, had couple of practice swings, held the club bit tightly with my hands, held my breath and took a rather wild swing at the static golf ball- lo' behold-I missed the ball completely and was off balance by the time I finished my follow through- I looked towards Boss and felt rather sheepish and embarrassed. Dep Com said, son, slow down your swing, try to have rhythm in your swing and try again and this time I hit the turf behind the ball- agricultural shot- the ball remained unmoved!! I tried couple of times more but failed miserably and finally when I contacted the ball it sliced and flew to the right, by now he was getting impatient, he slowly but emphatically said, son, listen to me carefully, do not hurry your swing, particularly down swing- just let the club come down naturally by its own weight, don't force, the angle of the club will carry the ball to designated distance i.e. 100 yards for no 9 iron and I was trying to get 200!! For additional distance you have other clubs in the bag, so don't use force. Do you understand, son? I shook my head and said- yes Sir; we went through the entire process once again, I tried and failed. At this moment Dep Com realized that I was lifting my head before striking the ball. He repeated keep your head still, my son, keep your eyes on top of the ball till you have gone through the swing and don't hurry up to see where the ball has landed but it wasn't working and I could make out that he was getting exasperated and losing patience and in all probability may soon give it up as a bad joke!! But he was tough coach and determined to teach me the correct swing. In spite of his instruction I was lifting my head too soon, next thing I noticed, he pulled out no 3 iron club from the bag and said, am going to place the shaft end of the club over your head and if you move your head , I will hit you with it, OK, remember your head has to be still and feet rooted to ground till you complete your swing, only then you can maintain balance. To be honest I was getting confused with plethora of instructions and so many parts of your anatomy coming into play, the resultant swing was worse than before and I duly received couple of taps on my head and he kept repeating, Son, don't lift your head, and suddenly next thing I hear; he shouted "MIKE don't lift your head, keep it steady". When he said 'Mike' I was wondering who is he calling and I looked around and realized there was nobody else nearby, it was from that moment at about 3.20pm on 11th Aug 71 when I became 'Mike' and eventually 'Mike Bhalla' and the name stuck through next three terms in NDA and 36 years in the Army and thereafter and shall remain so till Lord says 'time up'. Only my classmates and course mates knew my actual name Sant Pratap Singh Bhalla, but henceforth everybody knew me as Mike Bhalla from Armoured Corps or Mike Bhalla of Ronnie Pereira's connection!

Yes, Mike was genuine name and not nick name like Gary for Grewal or Hardy for Hardeep or Randy for Randhawa or Jessie for Jaswinder or Hunty for Hanut,or Suri for Surinder or Mandy for Mandeep or Kat for Kataria or Ahli for Ahlawat or Viroo for Varinder!! etc, etc. In fact, traditionally in Armoured Corps every officer has a nick name.

Later after few weeks when I was bit comfortable, I asked Mrs. Pereira what was it that reminded her of Mike when she first saw me ?-she said son, apart from your strong resemblance, **it was your zero hair cut**, as she vividly remembered last time she saw Michael many years ago, he supported similar hair cut . It was only in June 1972 in Ockbrook, Admiral's eldest sister - Mrs. Masie Gantzer's (Aunty May) house in Mussoorie, I saw Michael's photograph of 1965 in his flying suit with helmet in his right hand in front of fighter aircraft that I realized what Mrs. Pereira said was correct. Michael had crew cut hair and indeed there was striking resemblance, except that he was big build and much taller than me. Yes, I remember while going through an old album Aunty May showed me a picture of Michael aged about 10 and at that age his features were very similar to mine , almost identical. At that time Aunty May **told me, son, it is believed that in the entire human race, there are seven identical faces across the world!! She was right, I suppose!**

In fact on 4th Aug 71 I did not comprehend anything about the accident as my mind was totally blank! Months later I requested the Admiral to once again narrate the details of accident to me. He went on to narrate, **quote**

"Sometime in 1967, Michael Pereira, only son of my elder brother Arthur Pereira was posted in a Fighter Squadron located at Hashimara Airbase in North East India. During one of his routine training sortie while flying he noticed that his fuel gauge was (incorrectly) indicating very low level of fuel in the tank, so he panicked and immediately requested for priority landing from the ATC. His plane overshot the runway and crashed into the cement post of the fencing, cracked his skull and died on the spot. **He was barely 22 years.** My brother Arthur flew from Calcutta and buried him there only. He was devastated and actually never got over loss of his only son."**Unquote.**

Michael John Pereira

However, I was keen to get more information on Michael and probably his photograph as the one in Mussoorie was not traceable. Sometime in Oct 16, I called up my course mate Air Marshal SP Singh and requested him to try and find out any pilot from 1965/66 batch, from whom I can get some information about Michael John Pereira, He mentioned about Air Marshal McMahon and two days later called up to say, you have hit the jackpot, Air Marshal Mike McMahon and Michael's father were schoolmates at St. Edmund's Shillong!! What a **co-incidence?**

Soon I was on the phone with the Air Marshal Mike McMahon, I introduced myself and also told him that my eldest brother served in the Air Force; Wing Cdr BGPS Bhalla. He said; Oh My God he is my course mate, 84th Pilot Course! **Co-incidence?**

Air Marshal McMahon had this to share with me, **quote** "As a child in mid 50's Michael used to spend most of his time with our family. His father would bring Michael home and asked my mother if he can leave him with us to spend the day. My mother said I have 4 sons and Michael will be the 5th son, no problems. Yes, we grew up together and in late 50's Michael moved to St. Joseph, Nainital and after that we never met. However, Mike, don't worry I will introduce you to the right person who will be able to give you more information on Michael; Air Marshal Subhash Bhojwani, a course mate of Michael". **Unquote**

The above conversation resulted in; Air Marshal **Mike** McMahon sent a mail to Subhash Bhojwani introducing **Mike** Bhalla and requested Bhojwani to share whatever information or photographs he has of late **Mike** Pereira. 3x Mikes- What a **co-incidence?**

Air Marshal Subhash Bhojwani was kind enough to send me a mail the very next day with pictures of Michael and notification of his course mates on commissioning in Oct 1965. Going through the Notification I saw name of Pilot Officer Ganapathy, a Coorg and immediately called up Pratap Muthanna, who of course knew Ganapathy and sent me his contact number. I spoke to Air Commodore Ganapathy, and gave him the background of my reason to approach him. He immediately recalled and said, **quote** "well, Mike I do remember about the sad accident as Michael was the **first causality** from our course. At that time I was posted in "Battle Axe" 7th Squadron (Hawk Hunters) at Hindan Air Force Station and in early 1968 David Figaeiredo was posted from Hashimara. He was not only Michael's best friend but his roommate too. He mentioned about the unfortunate accident. I wish you had contacted me bit earlier as David passed away on 9th Sep 16. However, I will speak to his wife- Jennifer and request her to share whatever she remembers about her husband best friend." **Unquote**. After few weeks Ganapathy was kind enough to send Mrs. Jennifer Figaeiredo contact number.

I spoke to Mrs. Jennifer Figaeiredo, and she was quite moved and had this to share with me **quote** "Yes, my husband was particularly close to Michael Pereira and he used to say that Michael was a wonderful human being, very handsome and like a film star and whenever they went to the Kharagpur Club, the moment they entered all eyes were on Michael and of course they were very popular with young girls, it was indeed very tragic that Michael went away at such young age, my husband could never get over his death. Michael had great sense of humour and one day he was walking down a street in Kharagpur when one young girl approached and inquired about David. With a poker face Michael told her that I am sorry to inform you that David had died in a crash. The poor girl was heartbroken and wrote a condolence letter to David's mother. Who naturally got worried as no one had informed her and she frantically contacted David's squadron to check up and was told nothing like this has happened and David is fine. Later on when the mother got to know that it was Michael prank, she let him have it and shouted at him when she met Michael next!! I wish you had contacted us earlier and am sure David would have lot to share with you". **unquote**

Jennifer then mentioned about another course mate; Harry Ahluwalia who went to same school as Michael (**co-incidence**). As per Air Vice Marshal Harry Ahluwalia, **quote** "Michael and self joined Convent of Jesus and Mary Hempton Court, Mussoorie, for our pre-primary in 1948 and thereafter in 1954 went on to join St. George's College Barlowganj, Mussoorie. Michael spent 2 years in St. George's(estd 1853) and left for Calcutta in 1955 where he joined La Martiniere College (estd 1836). After that I met Michael in Sep 1963 when we both joined as Flight Cadets at Coimbatore" **Unquote.**

I am also informed by Air Marshal McMahon that Michael studied at St. Joseph College, Nainital from where he did his Senior Cambridge in 1962. After completion of his schooling Michael went on to join a college in Bangalore. Hugh Gantzer mentioned that Michael also tried his hand on bit of modeling.

As per Air Commodore Ganapati, **quote**" Michael and self joined as flight cadets in Sep 1963. After initial training of 6 months we were sent to Elementary Flying Training Unit to do 30 hours flying on Pushpak. I went to Nagpur and I remember Michael went to Delhi. In June 64 we all reported to Allahabad and in Dec 64 we went to Air Force Flying College Jodhpur for another 3 months. The Commandant was Air Commodore (later Air Marshal) Shree Hari who was related to Michael through his wife-Beryl Mary Pereira, daughter of his grand Uncle Robert Pereira. Thereafter, all fighter cadets proceeded to Hakimpet in April 65 " **Unquote.**

Air Marshal Subash Bhojwani kindly sent me a mail given in the succeeding paras:-

Quote "I passed out of NDA with 26th course in June 1964 and reported to Elementary Flying Training Unit at Allahabad in July 64, where we flew HT 2 Trainer aircraft for our basic training. We were 45 cadets from NDA and were later joined by 200 Direct Entry flight cadets. Michael John Pereira was one of them. He was a lovable character, a tall, fair and handsome strapping young man (photos). He was one of the most popular cadets of our course and we used to call him a gentle giant as he would sportingly take our needling. After 6 months we all moved to Air Force College Jodhpur and in April 65 all fighter cadets moved for advance training at Fighter Training Wing at Hakimpet, 30 kms north of Secundrabad. Our course was schedule to pass out in June 1965, however, it was delayed due to pulling out all our flying instructors first in May 65 for Bhuj operations and then in September for the Indo-Pak war. Those few extra months meant that we fought the war from the trenches in Hakimpet. Mike was most vocal about missing the action, even though we all knew that even if we had been commissioned as schedule, we couldn't have completed our basic operational training and hence excluded from flying in ops.

We were commissioned on 16th Oct 1965 and Air Marshal Arjan Singh, Chief of Air Staff was the Reviewing Officer. Mike's service no was 9054 as shown in the Gazette Notification. After commissioning Mike and self were posted to 221 Squadron and 24 Squadron respectively, both located at airbase Kalaikunda. For Mike this was great opportunity to go off practically every weekend to Calcutta to see his sweetheart-sorry don't remember her name- we often discussed the possibility on one day beating up at her home. I was posted out of Kalaikunda in January 1966 and next month i.e. February 1966 Mike was posted to 47TH Squadron located at Hashimara, North East India. After that we never met again.

Accident

Unfortunately, Mike was the first casualty of our course of 42 fighter pilots. It happened on 13th April 1967. His "TOOFANI" accident was really tragic, unfortunate and avoidable. The story of accident goes something like this; Mike was in a formation of 4 aircrafts and at some point noticed his fuel content gauge reading way below the normal and suspected it to be fuel leak. He detached himself and headed back to Hashimara airbase for a priority landing. TOOFANI aircrafts were notoriously difficult to land and pilots often got into situation called Pilot Induced Oscillation (PIO) and when this occurs the pilot is well advised to go around and make another circuit. But since Mike was facing an emergency of possible fuel leak, he decided not to go around but to press on with straight-in-approach. In the process he overshot half the runway resulting in Baulk Landing and the aircraft plowed into over shoot area and went straight into the Arrester Barrier and lost it canopy. The barbed wire snagged the exposed ejection handle and caused him to lift clear of the aircraft but not high enough for the parachute to deploy and he hit the ground and died a little while later. Really sad" **Unquote**

I must add that Air Marshal Bhojwani was the only officer who had a camera in his course and sent me all the photos featuring Michael.

Michael Grave

However, I got to know from Hugh Gantzer that Micheal Pereira was buried in a place called Hamilton Ganj near Hashimara. I eventually located the graveyard in Hamilton Ganj, Kalichini, about 30km South East of Hashimara. It is referred to as "EUROPIAN BARRIUL GROUND" (photo). I went there and personally met one Mr. Dalip Chackraborty, (photo) who resided close to the graveyard and as a 12 years school boy had attended Michael's funeral in April 1967 and even remembered Michael's name. The funeral was carried out with full "Military Honors". He showed me the grave, in rather dilapidated condition with no Tomb Stone which had apparently been vandalized and the graveyard is in total neglect and encroached by the locals as shown in the photographs. Michael had Royal n Field motorbike which as per Aunty Masie his father gave it to Michael's roommate and buddy Flying Officer David De' Figaeiredo.

It took me 45 years to finally visit Michael's grave!

Admiral and Mrs. Pereira had no children. Hugh Gantzer and Michael were only children of their generation. Hugh Gantzer was about 14 years his senior. Therefore, Mike was the apple of the eye and **it was indeed a great loss to the whole family.**

On my return from Hamilton Ganj, I sent the pictures of my visit to Captain Montee Chatterjee, who was very close friend and Secretary to Admiral when he was Chief in 1980/81 and this is what he had to say, **quote** "Mike thanks for the pictures. I can see that you have paid your respect at Michael's grave and it is very touching and thoughtful of you and I have no doubts that Ronnie Pereira must be looking down at you with a smile on his lips and a prayer in his heart. As you would have observed from my letters, that Admiral and I had very warm and close personal relationship. This was shared between two of us only and never made known to others, except when he appointed me as his Secretary. In furtherance of this relationship if there is anything that I can do to put some type of Tomb stone on Michael's grave as token of remembrance to Ronnie P, please do let me know. If it means making a contribution to the same, it will be my way of saying "Thank you Sir for the love and affection you gave me and my family over the years". Mike I hope you don't mind my sharing this thought with you" **Unquote**

I wrote back; Sir, I really appreciate your sentiments for the Admiral. However, the locals are so poor that they will vandalize anything and as of now only two graves are left in dilapidated condition, which I am sure subsequently will be soon encroached by the locals. Nobody has visited the grave for last 48 years!

Montee C replied; **quote** "*So sad Mike, with you will die the memory of a young man that Ronnie P tried to keep alive. I know that the Admiral loved you a lot as a son, he and Phyll never had. RIP-RLP and Michael.*" **Unquote**.

In a reply to my letter many years later, Admiral wrote in his letter dated 18 May 1985, **quote** "*When you write to say my son that we have given you a lot and you have given nothing in return. I find that you tend to make two mistakes. We have given you nothing my son. You have given us, what we lost in not having a son, and being very much like Uncle Arthur's son. You became 'Mike' to us and it will always be so. Also, you have your dear parents to whom* *you must always give your attention and affection and they must always be first in your life"*. Unquote.

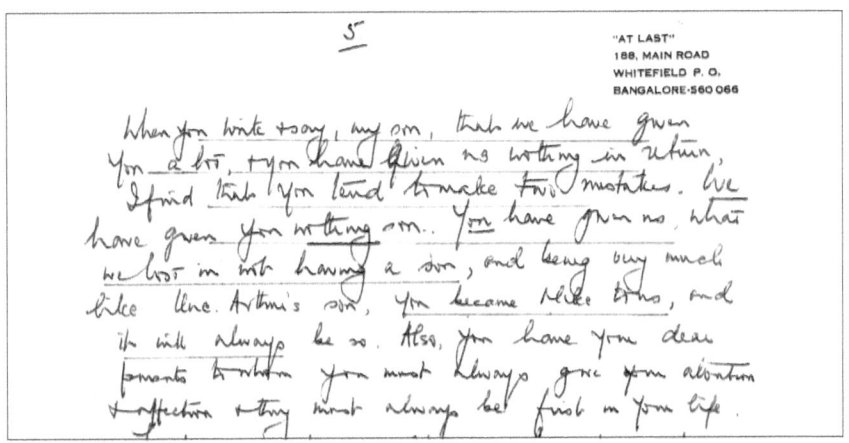

Admiral had earlier expressed similar sentiments, when I wrote to him about Aunty Masie (eldest sister) getting upset with me and felt that I was being spoilt by Ronnie 's over indulgent and some issue of drinking Beer and she told me that – she will write to her brother to keep me on a tight leash! In reply to one of my letters, Admiral wrote dated 24 March 1978, **quote** *"My son, you seem very worried about what Aunty May feels towards you, it seems to upset you a great deal. I really don't understand why you should be so distressed. Aunty May is my sister, but even between us there are not only differences in opinion but I think we are also different in character, and it is so with every human being. I personally know that Aunty May has no animosity towards you whatsoever. However, she may be disappointed in you, but that is her personal opinion. In fact, I think she worries about you, and feel that unless you mature faster; you may not do as well as professionally, as you could have. Again this is her view. However, I can assure you that she does not, and would never, try to alter our feelings for you. So, my son, you have nothing to worry about and as long as you wish to be part of our family, we shall always be delighted to welcome you into it. You don't have to be distressed about anything, as you go through life doing as well as you can, as I am sure you will, and all of us and May will be equally pleased. So quit worrying, son"*. Unquote .

I clearly recall the winters of 78, I was in Delhi when one night after dinner we had taken the dogs out for walk and after about 20 minutes Admiral turned and said, son, don't you ever have any wrong notions in your mind about our relations with you, **and said "my son, remember one thing that even if I live for 1000 years, you will be my only son for those 1000 years,** so quit worrying and do well in your life, that's all I ask for". There was a lump in his throat, I could feel, yes, he was indeed a wonderful human being.

The above two letters and what he told me on that cold night amply give a deep insight to his feelings towards me and believe me he was **the greatest gift of God to me**, but never hesitated to shout at me if he thought I was in wrong and on couple of occasions I came pretty close to be slapped by him. Once I escaped by running around the dining table in 5 Moti Lal Nehru Marg some time in Aug 78! I remember he called me "imbecile"? I did not know the meaning and when I checked up in the dictionary and realized that he was referring to me as donkey or mentally defective! Later, when I caught him in good mood, I told him I did not know the meaning of "imbecile", he said really son! I said yes, and in future when you shout at me, at least use simple words which I can understand? He had a good laugh and said wait till I catch you next time!!

NDA 1971

Initially I used to visit them once in two or three weeks. Then I realized they were really enjoying my company and I started to go more often and eventually went every Sunday or holiday. To be honest, I was still very circumspect in my conduct in Dep Com's presence and gradually started to open up with him and the fear steadily faded away. He used to crack jokes, laugh a lot with me, back thumping, shaking hands just to make me feel at ease and after few months I became comfortable in his presence and if he saw me anywhere in the Academy he would wave at me or walk up to me and say, how are you, my son? One Sunday he challenged me to have 'Panja' competition with him. He was 48 and I was 18 but I couldn't beat him, he was really strong, I tried again but failed!!

NDA 1972

In the spring term 1972 we were preparing for Hockey season and he would come and witness our practice sessions almost every day. One day while playing a practice match with Air Force team from Poona, as usual Dep Com was there to cheer us, I was playing left-half, one of the most difficult position in Hockey as you are always on the wrong side of the opponent Right-Out and more often than not, the Right-out are the best players in the team, this Sikh player was really fast and great dribbler and I was giving him tough time and after some time he lost his cool and swung his stick rather wildly at me and caught the lower part of my chin resulting in deep cut and soon my shirt was full of blood, Dep Com who was sitting on the side lines rushed to the ground and slowly picked me up and drove me to Military Hospital in his White Ambassador along with Major Divine Jones our PTO, where I was administered anesthesia and given four stitches . While the doctor was putting the stitches, Dep Com with twinkle in his eyes and tongue in cheeks said; don't worry son, your good looks are intact!! Yes I do have the scar, but not very visible.

At the request of Mr. Bhatnagar, the Hockey team was permitted to participate in Agha Khan Hockey Gold Cup Championship at Bombay in April 72 and I remember playing at Bombay Hockey Association ground with all leading teams such as BSF, Indian Airlines, Punjab, Railways and Services, with best players of the country --, Ashok Kumar,Balbir Singh sr and jr, Govinda, Ajit Pal Singh,Harcharan Singh, Kulwant Singh, Harmik Singh, Ganesh , Krishnamurthy, Aslam Sher Khan,Vinod, Michael Kindo, Chimni and many more. **It was indeed a great experience for young players like us and thanks to Dep Com.**

After our trip to Bombay Mr. Bhatnagar recommended two names for Hockey Blazer –Anil Bali and self, Dep Com agreed for Bali and only Blue for me!! However Anil Bali missed it too and got Blue as he was marched up to Dep Com for relegation but escaped!! Later he justified to me why he turned down my recommendation as he did not want anyone to point a finger at me and says you got it because of Dep Com!! I lost out but he won't compromise in what he thought was right!

For the Inter Squadron Boxing, I was selected to fight in Light Welter weight category but as we did not have any suitable boxer for Welterweight, my Squadron Cdr Brar asked me to fight in one weight higher and I knew I was not good enough for it but had no choice but to fight. On the day of my bout as expected Dep Com was there cheering me like mad and I managed to win the first round match as well the second round match and Dep Com was almost acting as my second and bucking me up vociferously but my third round opponent was very strong and I just managed to survive being knocked out and he beat the hell out of me!! Dep Com felt sad for me but he was happy that I fought and tried my best. I was black and blue for few days. Thanks to my course mate Satish Singh.

I was not too good at swimming and in our 6th term it was mandatory to jump from 10 Meter board and complete one full length of the pool. Jumping was no big deal, though we had some cadets who wouldn't jump, but I used to climb up and just close my eyes and jump straight down. Now for Breast Stroke , I had to put in great effort, then again Dep Com came to my rescue and walked the entire length of the pool, shouting, come on , son, keep going and I along with Anoop Singh we just managed to pass the test !

I remember Mrs. Pereira asking me in early days, who is your best buddy and I had told her Anoop Singh. One day in our 5th term Dep Com caught 4 cadets cycling down the Sudan Block slope, when the orders were that there has to be minimum 8 cadets to make squad or else must run on foot or with cycle, suddenly Dep Com appeared from nowhere and confiscated their Identity Cards and asked them to report to his office at 9 am the following day. When he reached home for lunch, he casually put the Identity cards on the Dining table and out sheer of curiosity Mrs. Pereira picked up to see who were the unfortunate cadets? The first one she picked was of Cadet Anoop Singh and she told Dep Com this name sounds familiar and after a while she recollected and said oh! **Yes, its Mike's best buddy and said- come on Ron you can't possibly punish him?** Next day Anoop was outside the Dep Com office before 9am. After a while Boss came and went inside without noticing Anoop, after sometime he came out and asked Anoop where are the rest, Anoop repied; Sir, they are coming and Boss said "X-Mas is also coming" The pun flew over Anoop's head! Anyway when they were marched up to him, he let them off!! Sure enough next Sunday when I went home Aunty Phyllis told me how she saved my best buddy. I thanked her profusely and had a treat from Anoop in the café.

We had our Inter Squadron Hockey Championship in spring of 72. Anoop was one of the best players in our squadron and as usual he was on 21days restrictions and was not permitted to take part in the championship and I knew that without him we will end up at the bottom of the ladder. I then explained the case to Mrs. Pereira and she knew that Anoop was my best buddy and I got around her and requested her to plead my case to Boss. All those cadets who were on restrictions and were part of their respective squadron teams should be permitted to participate and complete their restrictions post championship. After lots of pleading and coaxing Dep Com relented and passed an order across the board that all players on restrictions during the competition were allowed to participate in case they are good enough to represent their respective squadrons and complete their restrictions after the competition and that's how we got Anoop to participate. Of course Dep Com would come and witness all our matches and cheer loudly for our team and yes, our squadron ended up in 4th position!!

Ockbrook, Mussoorie

Admiral and Mrs. Pereira were pleasantly surprised when I informed them that I will be proceeding to Mussoorie for the summer break, June 72, to see my parents who had moved there just recently. Dep Com told me that his elder sister Maise Gantzer has been living in Mussoorie since 1940 and I must go and look her up, though the last time he met her was in June 1957 when the family got together at Calcutta for their parents funeral. However, Auntie Phyll who had photographic memory knew the exact location of the cottage 'Ockbrook' and wrote the address on a piece of paper which even now after 44 years still have with me. Last time she visited Mussoorie was in 1953!! After reaching Mussoorie on 8th June, the very next day, as per Aunty Phyll directions I went

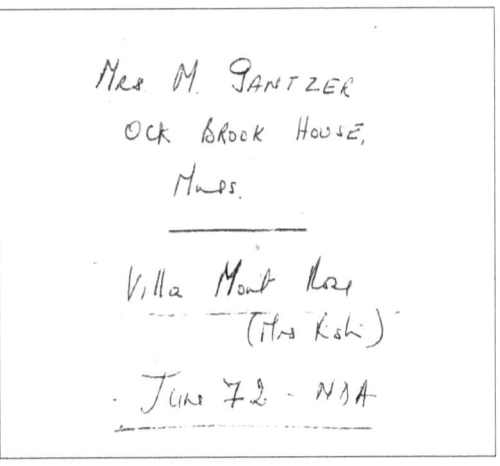

to see Mrs. Gantzer and didn't have much problems finding the arrow – Ockbrook- on the tree leading to the beautiful cottage, only error I made that I entered the cottage from Postman's gate! When she saw me coming down the Postman's gate, she came behind the house to open the kitchen door and asked me who are you looking for? I said Mrs. Masie Gantzer Maa'm, and I have come from NDA, Poona , she asked , did my brother Ron send you , I said yes Maa'm, she was apparently happy and said, come in, son. Mrs. Masie Gantzer had very strong resemblance with Ronnie P, particularly the Pereira's nose, big expressive eyes and same commanding voice as her brother! I told her how I met Dep Com and the whole story about reminding him of Michael and then she looked hard at my face and said, yes, son, you do look like our Mike, who left us at very young age in a tragic manner and I could see her eyes swelling with tears and slowly flowing down her cheeks and softly continued; Mike was brought to Ockbrook by my dear mother when he was a baby in 1947 and he stayed with us till 1956 and used to address me as Chota Mumma (junior) and grandmother as Bara Mumma (senior). He spent his childhood and initial schooling with us" **Unquote**

I was in Mussoorie for a month and spent lots of time with Aunty May listening to her stories about the life in Hazaribagh in 20's and 30's and later in Mussoorie where they have been living for over 30 years since 1940. She also showed me pictures of Michael when he was about 10 years and yes, there was indeed striking resemblance!

NDA- Final Term

On my return in July 72, I straightaway went home and there I saw Mrs. Pereira waiting at the gate and I still remember vividly how she saluted me and said welcome home, son. Apparently they missed my company and more importantly "Scrabble" sessions! I told them about my visit to Ockbrook and how Aunty May looked after me and we often went out for movies and to her friends houses. All in all it was very happy experience.

Being autumn term we had our Inter Squadron Football Championship and I requested Mrs. Pereira to come and witness one of our matches and thankfully Anoop Singh was not on restrictions! One day they landed unannounced on the ground to witness our match against Lima Squadron, who had a very strong team with Ashok Pathak playing centre forward. We kept them at bay but were goal down at half time. As the match was coming to closing stages we managed to win a penalty shot, which I like a fool took it and kicked the ball flying over the cross bar and landed up losing the match, needless to say I was bit embarrassed . Later on Dep Com with a tongue in cheeks said, son, you play at full back position and someone in the forward line should have taken the kick from penalty spot, or were you trying to impress Aunty!! I was speechless.

In Sep 1972, Mrs. Pereira's father (Poppy) moved in to stay with them. He was 72 years old but quite fit for his age. I must mention here that Mr. Beddel was the same gentleman who in 1952 out rightly rejected Admiral's proposal to marry his daughter. It is to the Admiral's great credit that not only old man was made to feel welcome and comfortable and went on to stay with them over next 8 years. In his last weeks before he passed away in Dec 1980 in Navy House, Admiral used to sleep on the floor next to old man's bed to help him to go to toilet at night and also clean and change the soiled linen! That was the **greatness** of Admiral. **So humble, kind and considerate. Amazing!**

Best Buddy

As I mentioned earlier that Mrs. Pereira inquired about my best buddy. I told her that we are a group of 4 in Delta Squadron; Anoop, Prabhjit Bedi, Arun Chand and self, but it is Anoop, who is closest to me. Anoop was an introvert, more of a listener and very fond of reading. Next question was; how did he become your best buddy? Well Anoop and self reported together to Delta squadron on 7th Jan 1970 as cadets of 43rd course. The same evening all first termers (19 of us, 3 joined at later date) assembled in front of Cadet Sergeant Major's cabin in the ground floor centre lobby. As Cadet  Seargent Major Tyagi emerged from his cabin, he barked; turn right and start front rolling and this continued for next one hour plus up and down the corridor, Anoop was next to me and I clearly remember the look of helplessness on his face, it was terrible feeling , but we both stuck together and continued, cursing under our breath , where the hell we have landed and from that moment we were always together through our waking hours at all events; may it be Drill Square, PT grounds, games fields, swimming pool, equitation lines, cadets mess and any other outdoor activities such as movies, liberty to Poona and sort of giving **moral support** to each other. Only place I was not with him was; Restrictions! I just felt comfortable in his presence and was almost inseparable throughout our 3 years in NDA and 1 year in IMA, Dehradun. Indeed he was my best buddy and 47 years hence still remains so.

After that whenever Mrs. Pereira saw me in any function, she observed that Anoop was invariably next to me and over a period of time she began to refer Anoop as my "**shadow**"! Whenever I went home she would always enquire, son, how is your 'shadow'? Anoop used to smoke in spite of the ban; he loved his brand of Bristol cigarettes. Deputy and Mrs. Pereira were almost chain smokers and every time they lighted a cigarette, they would offer me as per the unwritten ethics of the smokers! But I never smoked basically being a Sikh, my religion did not allow me and in fact I never liked to smoke. Then one Sunday Deputy took out a fancy packet of imported cigarettes-Dunhill- and as usual offered me. This time I thought of Anoop and that he may enjoy this expensive brand and asked him if I can take few for my buddy? He stared hard at me and said, you can, but if I catch him then I will have no hesitation in relegating him, choice is yours? I still took few and late in the evening, after taking a deep puff, Anoop remarked, Doggie (our pet name), nice but very light! **He was never caught by Dep Com! Or he did not want to catch him!**

I don't remember the exact date but it was sometime in late Sep 72, Mrs. Pereira asked me to get Anoop home for lunch on the coming Sunday. I told her it may not be possible as he is on Restrictions and he can't possibly miss the afternoon parade at Sudan Block. She said, Oh! and who gave him the Restrictions? I said, who else but the Boss! She checked up with Ronnie P, who said, doesn't matter, he can come home for lunch and all he has to do is to get his kit i.e. FSMO, Dangree, cap FS, shoes and anklets along with him and after lunch he can change and go for his reporting time.

On my return to the squadron in the evening, I informed Anoop to get ready, next Sunday you are coming along with me for lunch to Dep Com's residence. He would not believe me and thought I was pulling his leg. Hitherto fore, no cadet was ever invited for private lunch to Dep Com residence except on one occasion in Sep 71, when he invited his second cousins; Robin Pereira and Charlie Wier along with me and none after that. Naturally Anoop was skeptical, I told him that he has been invited as my best buddy, but he wasn't convinced and wanted to stay as far away as possible from Boss! Then later in the week I met Dep Com on the Golf course, he reminded me about Anoop and I told him Anoop thinks that I am pulling his leg!! Dep Com said really my son, and didn't say anything more.

Back to present 2016. Few months back I requested Anoop to go down the memory lane, some 44 years back and send me a mail of that fateful Sunday of Oct 72! After lots of coaxing and pushing Anoop eventually reproduced the incident as follows;

Quote "On a Sunday morning the last thing the cadet would be looking forward is running Cross-Country race. In Academy every term one Sunday morning was reserved for this activity. On the designated Sunday the whole Academy had assembled at the Glider's Dome waiting for the run to begin. The only saving grace for one's mood was that the damn thing would be over for the term. Suddenly somebody came to me and said; "Anoop, Deputy is looking for you"- since the reader knows who the Deputy was, **I was really at loss and wondered what mistake I have committed?** I saw him seating on the horse, checked my dress in detail, anything wrong will invite trouble, if you are going to meet Deputy. I walked up to him and wished him, Sir, Cadet Anoop Singh. He said what are you doing this afternoon, I said – nothing Sir, and **I was crisply told to join them for lunch that afternoon.** I went straight to Mike and told him, yes, now I believe you, but to be honest **I am**

not looking forward to sitting next to Deputy on the dining table. Mike told me, don't worry, it will be fine.

Immediately after the Cross Country I rushed to the squadron, had a haircut, and took out my best Dangree, gave fresh coat of Blanco to my FSMO kit, polished the metals with brasso, polished my drill boots and counted the 13 nails as I did not want to take any chance with Deputy and end up with more restrictions! Of course I was nervous. I adjusted my kit and boots on the handle and Dangree on the carrier of the cycle.

We started at about 12.45 pm and it took us 20 minutes to reach Deputy's residence near the Peacock Bay. This was the first time in 2 ½ years that I ventured beyond Swimming Pool and needless to say I was bit nervous. As per Mike's instructions we parked the cycles next to the garage and slowly walked to the front verandah and there we saw Mrs. Pereira coming out followed by Deputy. **My heart stopped for a second but then I regained my composure and wished them rather loudly!** After we sat down Mrs. Pereira asked me, son, what will you have? I like a fool said 'nothing' Maam. Anyway little later a soft drink was offered and Mrs. Pereira asked me; where are you from? I said from Rohtak, Haryana, she never heard this name before for obvious reasons! **She made polite conversation about my school days and hobbies and when I told her about reading, she was visibly impressed and said you seem to be more intelligent than Mike!!** I wanted to laugh but couldn't as Deputy was sitting there immerse in the Newspaper. This continued for some time and then Mrs. Pereira went inside to check about the lunch and Mike also disappeared for a while and I was left alone sitting with Deputy, not knowing what to do or say?? Deputy who was reading the Newspaper, looked up and said, son, do you smoke? I did not know whether it was a question or statement of fact. However, before I could answer, Deputy picked up the packet of Bristol cigarette and threw towards me- thankfully I could catch it. Boss went back to his Newspaper. Now, there I was a piddle cadet, me sitting and holding a packet of cigarettes in Dep Com's House, the match box still lying next to Boss. My dilemma was how to ask for the match box. How dare I, and even if I get the match box, how dare I light a cigarette in front of him? In fact I was looking more silly sitting there fiddling with the cigarette packet in my hands. Luckily Boss again looked up, and saw me, and said sorry son, and gave me the match box. Finally I managed to light the cigarette with trembling hands, what a relief!

Little later we all moved in for delicious lunch. The pleasure of having lunch started to reduce with every passing minute when I realized that the time for Restriction Parade was drawing closer. Now how to suggest such charming hosts to hurry up as one of them was the cause of my having to go for that report! I was silently praying to finish off fast and give me sufficient time to change and cycle down to Sudan Block. The lunch mercifully ended for me and I realized that I have no time to waste now.

I looked up at Mike and Deputy said I can go up and change in his dressing room. With the help of Mike I picked up my kit and rushed to the Boss dressing room. Soon I changed and tip toed down the steps to avoid my 13 nails creating a racket on the floor. As I came down Mrs. Pereira said, Oh! Son, you look smart in that outfit. Boss asked me what time I have to report, I said 3pm, Sir. He looked at his watch and said, I don't think you can make it on your cycle. **He asked me to wait outside the gate, and he will get the car out.** I couldn't believe my ears, what I was hearing- here is the man who gave me this punishment, and now he is taking me in his own car, so that I reach there on time or else will end up with some more restrictions!! What a man? But he was human enough to help me when I was stuck. It occurred to me - what GREAT human being he is. **He got the car and said, son, get inside.** I immediately opened the back door and entered and realized that once again I am in trouble. The covers of the seat were sparkling white and self was wrapped in FSMO (Field Service Marching Order) which include two small pouches, water bottle, straps and belt. Now the Olive Green Blanco on all these items loves to transfer itself on to anything it comes in contact with and its worst enemy is white colour! Add to this the fact the Boss was known for his fast driving (he likes to see the flag on the car fluttering, as he put it) and there were curves too many on the road from his house to Sudan Block. I wonder if anyone could at that moment understand my plight. Well all the training I had received in last 2 ½ years or so in the Academy came into play as I tried to device a method of sitting on the car seat without touching it. My total weight was on my hands and legs. Add to this the fact that the weight had to be delicately transferred in jerks to left or right depending on which side the car was turning. Those 5 to 7 minutes or so was one of the longest drives I ever had in my life. As we reached Sudan Block, the Duty Ustad on seeing Deputy's car shouted on top of his voice- parade savdhan! –and there he saw me coming out of the rear seat? Boss said, son, I will wait for you in my office and went away. The perplexed Ustad asked me, how do I know Deputy Sahib? I humbly informed him- old friends! - Ten minutes later I went to Deputy Office and saluted, he said, son it is over, and drive back home was equally testing but the end of it, I ensured that one could make out the original colour of the seat covers was white!!

On our return I saw Mrs. Pereira and Mike deeply involved in the game of "**Scrabble**". I changed back into Mufti. For the last time looked myself in the mirror in the Deputy dressing room and came down and Mrs. Pereira said, son now you look normal and laughed. We had cup of tea with cakes and biscuits and little later started the journey back to the squadron.

What lovely memories and even today after more than 44 years I remember the lunch, the cigarette and drive in the car to Sudan Block and of course Deputy's dressing room!! It was like a dream and I had to pinch myself to ensure that I was indeed standing in front of the mirror in Deputy's dressing room!

The story doesn't end here after few weeks I was informed that there is a visitor waiting for me outside the squadron lines in the parade ground. I came down and there in the staff car, who do I see, **none else but Mrs. Pereira with a big smile. I wished her warmly and she handed me a small packet and said, son, a gift for finishing your punishment, happy reading and drove off with me standing there astonished and dumbfounded!** It was the book titled "The ANTAGONIST" from the author of Fate in the Hunter-Earnest K Gann- with a short note **"to commemorate the end of the 21 days!! What a wonderful gesture and it brought few tears in my eyes. I still have the book with her note as shown in the photograph."** Unquote

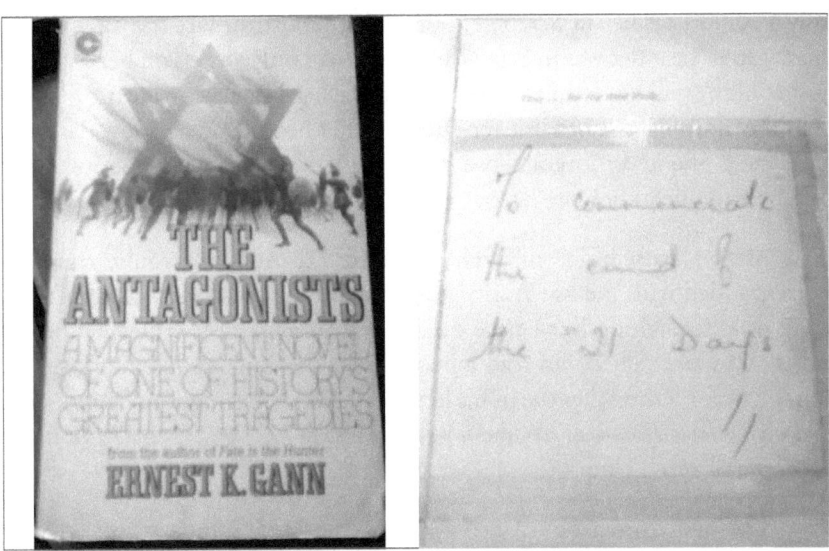

Next week when I went home, the first thing Aunty Phyll asked-I hope your "**shadow**" enjoyed his lunch? I said yes, but to be honest, not as much he

wanted to as he was worried that he might get late for his reporting time. He certainly enjoyed the ride with BOSS in the car! For him it was dream come true and he tried his best not to transfer the OG colour on to the seat covers. **Oh! You are telling me; in fact Anoop left lots of traces of olive green on the rear seat covers!!** And Uncle did not say anything except- poor chap, he could not help it- had it been me or someone from the staff he would have brought the roof down!!

The point I would like to highlight is that Admiral did not compromise on principles. He could have easily given one call to the Adjutant and excused Anoop from reporting on Sunday afternoon parade as he had invited him for lunch to his residence. But he did not do so, because it would have been improper and on the contrary he took Anoop in his car to ensure that he reaches on time for reporting and doesn't invite more trouble for him.

That was the greatness of Admiral and that's why, even today 44 years on, very mention of his name evokes so much emotion, passion and pride for being in NDA at that juncture.

In my final term, I was going home every weekend and after lunch invariably Mrs. Pereira and self would sit down and play game of '**Scrabble**' for two to three hours till sunset; no doubt she had great vocabulary as she was voracious reader and was never without a book to read. So there was no way I could beat her in Scrabble, but play we must. In fact the only time I managed to beat her was in Sep 77 when she had only vowels on her wall and just couldn't pull out any consonants from the bag!! But she made me play till 2 in the morning and beat me repeatedly to her heart content. How dare you beat me?!! She never forgot those days and 3 ½ years later she wrote about Scrabble in one of her rare letters!

After I passed out of NDA in Dec 72, Admiral would regularly corresponded with me but Aunty Phyllis **wrote rarely** as she just wasn't too fond of letter writing but I have over half a dozen letters written by her in nearly 40 years!! She could read a book whole day but was just not keen on letter writing. Admiral wrote in his letter dated 02 Feb 84, **quote** "*Aunty sends you all her love. However, she doesn't even write to her family, and I just don't understand this*". Unquote.

The one written on 12 Feb 81 from the Navy House is indeed very interesting and am sure it must be one of rare occasions for Aunty Phyll to get into such a mood for letter writing, it's quite hilarious too, **quote** "*Mike Dear, - Thank you very much for your letter dated 30/1/81 and as Unc is away in*

Mhow for the night. I am writing this- my 11th letter in one day!! The mail just seems to pile up and I never seem to clear up my pending file!!

Unc has been playing foul golf (not two legged) of late, but has done some shooting- birds- along with Gen Gupta and some others. They claim that Unc is shooting extremely well! He gets back tomorrow from Mhow and leaves immediately for a long weekend shoot. He's also acquired a fishing rod- in anticipation of retirement!! I just can't see Unc sitting on a river bank and waiting for some obstinate fish to bite- can you?!! He'll curse within 5 minutes!

The Naval Band won the Inter- Services band competition again and Unc was naturally dee-lighted (no, you cannot use that spelling in Scrabble!!)

We have had very hectic Jan and Feb, and so many meals out I don't want to see food for a month. Eating vast quantities of food is not my idea of heaven. We saw a super Russian Ballet performance and some good concert- as I say culture comes to North India for 2 months in a year!!- **No offence meant!!**

Did any of those photographs come out (X-Mas 80)? If so what are they like? How about the X- Mas tree ones?

Met Anoop and Mrs. and Chand Major and Mrs. at the Army Day reception. They really look like they did at NDA. I must have them over to the house one day. Apparently they live 50 yards apart in the Cantt.

Am reading "The Second Lady" by Irvin Wallace. Far fetched but OK.

Went to Mahli's brother's wedding- Mahli Sr married Kirpal Singh's daughter. Mahli's junior daughter is an absolute poppet. His father and Aunts have all flown out from States for the occasion- I am sure the guests were wondering who this old lady is involved with two Sikh brothers! That should give them food for thought! Love from Unc and self - Me.

It is indeed rather long letter with subtle sense of humour and she could have you in splits of laughter in her normal conversation and most of the time, butt of the jokes was none else than dear Ronnie P! She would always ask me, son, am I right, and I had to be very diplomatic and wouldn't like to rub the boss on the wrong side!! But it was fun alright.

In her another letter dated 5 June 90 she wrote **quote** *"Hi Mike, A Very Happy Birthday- God Bless and keep you safe and happy.* **This is to prove to you that I am not completely illiterate!!** *Have a wonderful day. I hope your Thambi told you that I did my best to look after him so that you have no opportunity to say that I favor sailors!!! We are still working on the house and garden-* **the work** never ends- in fact the only thing that comes to an end rather soon is- cash!!! Unc has become a first class Mason, any work for him in the regiment. I hope by now you have met Major Bhullar who will tell you that we are in fine fettle, our love to them when you meet. A big hugs for the boys and Annie and of course you. All our love" - Aunty P. **Unquote**

Final Weeks- NDA-1972

It was sometime in Oct 72, Brigadier SK Sinha (later Lt Gen and Vice Chief) visited NDA to meet his childhood friend from Patna days in 30's and he was invited for lunch. It happened to be a Sunday and I too was at home. How, Mrs. Pereira spoke so fondly about Gen Sinha's Gorkha hat when they were together in Staff Collage in 1952/53 as students of DSSC 6. In fact I almost opted to join Gorkha Regiment till Col Mike Skinner, who was very close to Aunty May and lived in Barlowganj , Mossoorie, asked me to opt for Skinners Horse, and ultimately I landed up in 16 Cavalry!

In Aug 2016, I wrote a mail to Gen Sinha and took him down the memory lane 44 years back and he immediately replied that he remembered that trip to NDA. He very kindly had consented to write the 'Foreword' for the book. Unfortunately he passed away on 17th Nov 2016 at the ripe age of 90.

In my final term Dep Com was really getting close to me and he knew that by Dec 72 I would pass out and then there may be long break till they see me again. The frequency of meeting increased, and I visited them on every Sunday and holiday to spend maximum time with Aunty.

However, Dep Com will find me somewhere in the Academy on daily basis now, starting from morning PT ground, where one day he came armed with scissors to trim, anybody who he thought had long hair even by a centimeter, he came to our squadron and put his hands in Nauriyal's hair and whatever hair came above the fingers were trimmed, next was Atul Khanna, 5.3 ft and one of the shortest in the Academy, as Dep Com caught his hair locks and about to put the scissors through when he inadvertently bruised Atul's nose and there was bit of blood, immediately Dep Com apologized and walked him to his car and took him to MH for medical treatment for the unintended injury. After being attended by the Medical Officer, Atul Khanna was taken by Dep Com to his residence and given a sumptuous breakfast! Atul said later that he didn't mind getting injured by Deputy!! At least he can again enjoy the breakfast!!

After few days, Dep Com landed up in my class. It was third period of Chemistry, after double outdoor i.e. PT and Drill, and naturally half the class was sleeping with eyes open!! I was sitting in the last row and on my right in the corner seat was Cadet Sidhu, A sqn, who was fast asleep hiding behind the cadet in front. Out of the blue Dep Com entered the class and instantly everybody straightened up and all were wide awake and I nudged Sidhu hard to wake up, Dep Com is here and expectedly he came and sat next to me on my left side. Sidhu was without notebook and pen, he whispered to me to give him some paper, I quietly took out center page of the notebook and slid towards Sidhu, next he asked me for a pen, I had only one so he said pass me the cap. For rest of the period Sidhu turned his shoulders and pretending to make notes very seriously with the cap of the pen and by turning over the page repeatedly. **All this while Dep Com kept smoking and looking ahead as though he had not noticed Sidhu's cleverness. The class got over and Dep Com stood up and started to move out and suddenly he turned back and asked Sidhu, son, let me see what have you written, Sidhu almost had a major heart attack when he showed him blank page and the cap of the pen in his hand !!** Dep Com barked 21 days and 4 Singarh Hikes and walked off, poor Sidhu slid into his seat and started boxing and abusing me - it's because of you he came here and what I have landed into!! I profusely apologized to him and promised to speak to Dep Com when I meet him next. The coming Sunday I went home and pleaded Sidhu's case and told him that Sidhu was indeed down with fever, he took pity and said tell Sidhu to see me in my office on Monday. Sidhu met him next day at 9am and Dep Com told him, son, this is the last chance and don't let me catch you again, **now bugger off**, Sidhu never ran so fast in his life!! He was let off, and when he met me next, he just gave me a bear hug!!

As the time was passing by and Mrs. Pereira was feeling sad by the day. I remember sometime in early Oct 72 during the mid-term-break Dep Com, Mrs. Pereira and self went to spend a day in Poona. They bought couple of golf T- shirts for me, we then had lunch at Latif Restaurant near West End picture hall after that visited Manney Book Shop where Aunty bought herself some books, she normally read best sellers, and along with Dep Com, they both initiated me to serious reading habit and over the years I have over 250 books in my small library, thanks to them and same bug has bitten both my sons. As per Mrs. Pereira, there can't be better companion than a book, so true.

Last few weeks were rather sad. In the final term my cabin was opposite the Tea Room as I was Cadet Quarter Master Sergeant, later de-tabbed by none else but Dep Com for skipping classes. I remember one early morning at about 5.30 am, I was woken up by familiar voice, son, wake up, and there through half opened sleepy eyes, who do I see? Dep Com with mug of tea in his hand!! That was the father's soft side in him!! As the days were passing by, he would often meet me somewhere or the other in the Academy. Then one day I asked him how do you know about my whereabouts, he said, son, am the Dep Com ok. Yes, he had my classification 5 weekly programme in his pocket and whenever he had time, he would find me.

Passing out Parade of 43rd course was on the 16 Dec 72. After the parade during the tea with parents of the passing out cadets on the lawns in front of Sudan Block, Dep Com walked up to me, congratulated and quietly took out his Rolex watch and put it on my wrist as a parting gift, it was indeed very touching gesture which brought tears in my eyes. I spent rest of the day with them and of course had one final round of Scrabble with Mrs. Pereira!!

Next morning after tearful parting with Aunty Phyllis and Dep Com I was dropped at Kirkee Railway Station in the white Ambassador car.

That was the end of NDA episode, but I have over two dozen stories to share which have been sent to me by all those Cadets who had a slice of good fortune to have interaction the great man, which will be covered separately in chapter on 'Close Encounters'.

Family Photographs

Grand Parents - Mr. and Mrs. John Pereira (1880)

Father – Major (Doctor) JM Pereira

Mother- Mrs. Charlotte Lynsdale Pereira

Brother- Arthur Pereira with Admiral (1992)

Sister- Mrs. Clara Malinowski (1945)

Phyllis and Ronnie Pereira (1952)

Mrs. Masie Gantzer (1930)

Nephew- Colleen and Hugh Gantzer (1960)

Nephew- Michael John Pereira receiving Wings from Air Marshal Arjan Singh, CAS (1965)

Phyllis Beatrice Bedell (1975)

Mr. Bedell (Phyllis's father)

Patna/ Hazaribagh

Name Board - First Name, Major (Doctor) JM Pereira,
Superintendent –Medical College Patna, (1935- 1938)

क्र0सं0	नाम	कब से	कब तक
	अधीक्षक, लोकनायक जयप्रकाश नारायण केन्द्रीय कारागार हजारीबाग।		
1	मेजर जे0एम0 परेरा	सन् 1946	अगस्त 1948
2	श्री ए0 फतह	सितम्बर 1948	जून 1952
3	श्री गंगेश्वर पाठक	जुलाई 1952	अगस्त 1956
4	श्री रमेश चन्द्र सिन्हा	सितम्बर 1956	अप्रिल 1960
5	श्री प्रसादी सिंह	मई 1960	अप्रिल 1963
6	श्री नुरूल हक	मई 1963	मई 1966
7	श्री रमेश चन्द्र सिन्हा	जून 1966	जनवरी 1970
8	श्री नुरूल हक	जनवरी 1970	अप्रिल 1975
9	श्री मथुरा लाल	01/05/1975	17/06/1975
10	श्री प्रदीप कुमार गांगुली	18/06/1975	11/04/1977
11	श्री गुन्जन चौधरी	12/04/1977	31/05/1979
12	श्री नवल किशोर प्रसाद	13/06/1979	31/01/1981
13	श्री कपिलदेव राय प्रकाश (बि0प्र0से0)	01/02/1981	05/02/1981

Name Board - First Name, Major (Doctor) JM Pereira,
Superintendent Hazaribagh Jail (1946- Aug 1948)

Hazaribagh Jail

Jailor House – Balmoral House

Schooling

St. Joseph School

Primary Department 1933
3rd Row Standing - 2nd from left

Mother of Apostles
1st Row Standing - 4th from left

Tennis - seated first from right (1936)

Garnet House - Middle row - 2nd from right

With E. Avari (1990)

St. Michael Patna, Main Building

Admission - 17th Feb 1938, serial 432

Sainik School, Kunjpura

Sainik School, Kunjpura – Main Building

Principal with First NDA Cadets – 1964.
Deepak Kapoor (later COAS) seated third from left

Gen JN Chaudhuri, COAS-1964

Air Marshal Arjan Singh, CAS-1965

Admiral AK Chatterji, CNS-1969
(Author Receiving Trophy)

Tug o war

NDA – 1971-72

Sudan Block

Ronnie – Dep Com 1971-1973

NUN KUN – 1971

NUN KUN -peaks

*Team being introduced to Gen Manekshaw
First from left*

Group Photograph
3rd from left, sitting in front of Dep Com

Author 3rd from left, 3 feet away from Dep Com

Michael John Pereira

Michael at 10 years

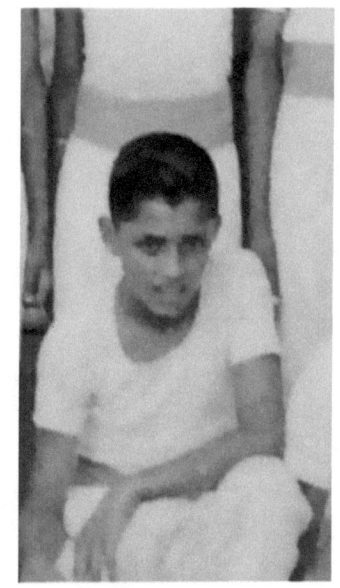

Author at 10 years

Michael in 1965

Author in 1976

Michael standing in the middle - 1965

Michael's grave – 2016

European Burial Ground

With Dalip Chakravarti, who attended Michael's funeral in Apr 1967

NDA – 1971-72

Dep Com's Residence

First photo with Mrs. Pereira –Oct 71

With Foreign dignatory

with Prince of Tonga

with YS Chauhan-Sword of Honour at IMA, June 71

With Gen E. Habibullah Nov 72

Receiving Hockey Blue from Mrs. P, Apr 72

Author with Arthur Pereira – 1972

Training Ship-Ronnie Pereira

Mrs P. with Bedi, Beniwal and self - 1972

Meeting Gen Manekshaw, June 71

POP Dec 72

last photo with Mrs.P, 17th Dec 1972

Vicky Mehta receiving Best Rifle Shooting prize

1973

Academy Under Officer 73

Lt Col Morris Ravinderan (1st Commandant, 1974)

Matters Military

Introduction

Admiral Ronald Lynsdale Pereira PVSM, AVSM, ADC, and ex Chief of Naval Staff, retired from Navy on 28th February 1982 and passed away on 14th Oct 1993, but his memory and any form of association with him lingers on, particularly with the cadets from NDA 40th - 49th courses (15 Jan 71 to 15 Feb 73) for whom he left an indelible impressions on their young minds and even to this day in 2017, still their heart swell with great sense of pride, and helps stiffen their spine, though most of them are on the other side of 60. Nearly half a century later (46 years to be exact) the very mention of the great man's name evokes intense emotions- inspiration, pride, awe, admiration, adulation and respect for his unflinching concern and well being for the cadets. He went around the Academy 24X7 chasing the cadets with single minded aim- to make each one of them into finest human beings and leaders of men.

What a MAN and each one of 2500 cadets still owe him complete allegiance bordering to worshipping the ground he walked.

As late in Dec 2016 I received few photos of the great man from Navkesh Singh 42nd NDA-Golf squadron, with this caption, **quote** "What a great soldier? A truly inspiring man. A few moments I enjoyed in his presence, I cherish all memories of this great man and his wonderful wife. May God bless them, always ." **Unquote**.

He was a man of principles with great sense of integrity, honesty and compassion. He symbolized these human traits which were the very foundation of his character. They were his 'Bible' and he pursued them fearlessly till his very last breathe, without ever compromising, whatever be the consequences or personal sacrifices.

In Aug 1971 I was barely 18 years old when for the first time he took cognizance of my existence and believe me we were all mortally scared of his presence but he had other side like all other human being, to which I was extremely fortunate to have experienced. The following 22 years Admiral had great influence on my life both as a human being as well as a man in uniform. His sole "AIM" was to make me a good officer and more importantly a better human being. As I go through my journey with him, every advice (sometimes in anger) and every word and every action was directed only towards character building and more importantly to be a good leader of men. I tried, but to be honest, I could not match his expectations; he was thus disappointed on some occasions but never discouraged me, in fact encouraged, to get up and try harder next time.

NDA-Dec 71

The only regret Admiral ever had in his heart was that he had to sit out of 1971 Indo-Pak Conflict due to his tenure at NDA at that juncture. One day in rather subdued mood he told me, **quote** "son, it is not often in life that you get an opportunity to lead your men in battle and look at me, am sitting here on the sidelines and twiddling my thumbs" **unquote**

He certainly wasn't twiddling his thumbs!! May be at that time he did not realize that he was ordained for larger responsibility of moulding and shaping future leaders of all three services. I would like to quote what Wing Cdr(retired) Unni Kartha had written about the great man without ever serving under him for a single day :-

Quote "Amongst the many who still love and worship him are cadets of NDA, where he was Deputy Commandant in early 70's, where he kicked butts and turned a whole generation of juvenile delinquents to socially useful and upright gentlemen. The very generation who form the top echelon of Army, Navy and Air Force? This is therefore, an eulogy not from Naval history , wardroom tales, or chewing the cud by old Naval crabs, but an eulogy by the old goats who went to wear drab Olive Greens, Khakis, and Blues, even from the ones who never wore a uniform because of him, all of them illustrious men in their own right. **This is the eulogy from the ones who were fortunate to have been within an arm distance of Ronnie even for few seconds;** this is what one of the cadets remarked "he touched all our lives, kicked our butts, breathed wit and wisdom into our ears and gave us a steady course to steer during the turbulent weather and heavy seas of our youth" **unquote.**

Unni Kartha could not have put his thoughts in better perspective. He is right when he speaks about a generation of officers who had been under Ronnie P wings rose to the highest rank in all three Services, General Bikram Singh COAS, 40TH course, Air Chief Arup Raha 44th, General Dalbir Singh Suhag 44th and Admiral Robin Dowan 45th, apart from them scores of C-in C's in all three services. These were the officers who were commanding over hundred thousands of troops, carried Ronnie P legacy to the last 'T'.

Yes, approximately 2500 cadets from 40th to 49th were impacted by the great man personality. 49th saw him for a short while as he relinquished his appointment on 15 Feb 73.

When I mentioned to my course mates about the book, they were indeed very happy and said this is the noblest act you can do in your life time. Air Marshal SP Singh, who happened to be sitting next to me on that fateful day of 4th Aug 71 when Admiral eyes froze on my face to remind him of his late nephew Michael (Mike) Pereira said "Mike, we all were blessed to be influenced by the Admiral, and yes, you were the most blessed".

Military History

On my return from winter break of 1971/72, I went home on the first Sunday for spending the day with them and Admiral spoke to me at length about 1971 Indo-Pak war and the great leadership qualities displayed by Field Marshal Manekshaw as well as the outstanding performances of officers like Hoshiar Singh PVC, Khaterpal PVC, Sikhon PVC and Captain Mulla MVC, who went down with his frigate INS Khukhri and attack by Sea Hawks on Cox Bazar and Chittagong in East Pakistan and the bravery of our men in general. After a while he gave me a searching look and asked - "son, are you reading any military history books??" I sheepishly said- no Sir, he then said you better start reading. I suggest you go to the library and pick up some books on great military leaders down the centuries. After a while he went inside his study and brought a book and gave it to me- *'Other Side of the Hill'* by Captain B.H. Liddell Hart, to be honest at that age it was a bit heavy for me but I went through it and again many years later when I was mature enough to comprehend the nuances of leadership. But the next book on Alexander the Great by Herald Lamb was fascinating and this eventually led me to read autobiographies of great military commander's i.e. Hannibal, Changez Khan, Napoleon Bonaparte, Shivaji, Maharana Partap, Ranjit Singh and Generals of WW2. After a couple of months Mrs. Pereira asked me if I was reading any book , I told her about the book on Alexander the Great, she then went inside and brought a book ; *Exodus* by Leon Uris and added this book is about creation of state of "Israel" and very interesting reading, which in fact it was. Next book was again given by Admiral; **Last Battle** by Cornelius Ryan about the battle of Berlin and from there on the bug had bitten me and started to enjoy reading.

He also recommended that I should read 'Untold Story' by Gen BM Kaul and later 'The Himalyan Blunder' by Brig John Dalvi and I wondered why? Much later I realized that, our officers and men were not found wanting in spite of critical shortcomings in weapons and equipment. **The main cause of our set back in 1962 was due to unwarranted interference by politicians and bureaucrats in 'Matters Military'**.

Years later he gave me another book, '**Defeat into Victory**' by Field Marshal Viscount Slim, one of the best books of military history. I still have the book duly signed by him, which was bought in 1962 for princely sum of Rs 25/- !! I am grateful to him for initiating me into this wonderful hobby, particularly Military History. Mrs. Pereira always told me, **son, there can't be a better friend than a 'book'**. How right she was and this habit helped me to clear all my exams including Staff College in the 1st attempt!

He often used to tell me-son, I learnt a lot from reading autobiography of great military leaders-their human traits, leadership qualities, to take quick decisions in the battle field under stress and hostile conditions, and remember; human **life is non- negotiable. Why do you think I drive all you devils so hard?' So that you don't buckle under pressure and that's the key to victory in battle.** That was **his vision of leadership** and wanted to inculcate these very qualities in each and every cadet. **A leader must breed his men tough so that they have pride in their abilities, pride in the unit and more importantly pride in their leader.**

Indian Military Academy

On 7th Jan 73, I reported to Indian Military Academy and joined 'Singarh Company'. Our Company Commander was none other than Major Hoshiar Singh PVC, 3rd Grenadiers. A fearless and inspirational leader of men, who drove us hard, and within one year he lifted 'Singarh Company' from last position i.e. **12th to Champion Company** in our final term in Dec 73. I happened to be the Senior Under Officer of Singarh company!

I used to correspond regularly with Admiral, who by then had taken over as Fleet Commander, Eastern Fleet, Vishakhapatnam. His basic advice; "was to work hard and remember there may be host of Leadership Qualities required as per the pamphlet on 'Leadership' but what really matters is two critical qualities i.e. **Professional Competence'** and **'Personal Example'**, the second one encompasses all other qualities", so true. He conveyed so much in those two qualities! Also he kept reminding me to work hard and pass out as high as possible in the merit- "You may not realize at this juncture but later in your career IC No, will matter a lot, in your promotions . I tried very hard and passed out 25th as Battalion Under Officer, in course of over 250 cadets, not bad but Admiral wasn't very satisfied and wanted me to do better. I told him I tried my best, perhaps the others were better academically and more importantly in science subjects!!

I was commissioned into 16 Light Cavalry on 23 Dec 73.

16th LIGHT CAVALRY

I reported to 16th Light Cavalry on cold and overcast Sunday, 13th Jan 74 at Pathankot. I was actually supposed to report the previous day but decided to spend a night with my elder brother 2/Lt KP Singh, 6th Grenadiers at Jullunder. Lt PJS Mamik who was detailed to receive me, came back after waiting for two hours at the Railway Station the previous day and as soon as he saw me, he hurled choicest abuses and barked - check guards every hour from 11pm to 5am in the morning till further orders! **What a welcome??**

16 Cavalry is the oldest Cavalry Regiment in the Indian Army. The Regiment was raised prior to 1776, as the 3rd Regiment of Native Cavalry in the service of Nawab of Arcot, under the command of Captain JD Stevenson. In 1923, 16th Light Cavalry was amongst the first three Indian Cavalry Regiments nominated for the induction of Indian origin officers for replacement of British Officers. Faiz Mohammad Khan and Sheodatt Singh (later Maj Gen) were the first two 'Indian' officers to be commissioned on 19 Oct 1923. The regiment produced 2 COAS, Gen JN Chaudhuri and Gen VN Sharma plus over two dozen General cadre officers. The regiment took active part in Burma during World War 2 and won 6 Battle Honors. It is the only Cavalry Regiment in the Army with 100% Thambi's troops from Southern states.

My first Commandant of 16 Cavalry was Lt Col Morris Ravinderan, a bachelor, introvert and decorated officer of 1965 Indo-Pak War. A great personality with handle bar moustaches and cavalry swagger. Orders from Lt Mamik, Senior Subaltern, were very clear for young officer like me; not to cross Commandant's path and never to open my mouth in his presence. I was sharing room with 2/Lt KP Ramesh and 2/Lt Bajpai and Commandant's room was bang next to ours. We couldn't even play the transistor loudly to hear cricket commentary, if the Commandant was in his room; we spoke in whispers so that he was not disturbed. In the Dining Room we were not permitted to speak in his presence, it was pin drop silence. During Dinner Nights on every Thursday being the junior most I hardly ate anything and after dinner I used to quietly sneak to cook house where cook Raju would provide some left over and few cutlets! All in all he was considered as one of the best Commandant in the long history of 16th Light Cavalry. He tragically passed away in March 78 under mysterious circumstances.

Add to this we had a fiery 'Adjutant' Captain Rajender Mehta, who would not allow me to breathe during day and at night and made me check guards by the hour. By the time I realized couple of months had passed and there was no time to write letters to Admiral and Mrs. Pereira, and telephone was out of question.

Apparently not hearing from me for nearly 3 months, Admiral and Mrs. Pereira got very worried about my well being. In his letter 14th April 74, Admiral wrote, **quote** "*My dear Mike, between Aunty and myself must have written to you at least five or six letters but have not got a single line in reply. We only hope you are well, it's really hard work which is keeping you from replying. In fact I have written to Aunty May 3 letters since your POP and also not had a line in reply.*

My son at least let us know what is your personal number, as there must be hundreds of 'BHALLAS' in the Army , though you have the distinction of being 'Mike', you haven't quite reached the rank or the fame, for the whole of Indian Army to know you such !!

I am writing this letter to the 16 Cavalry, though Aunty got the idea that you were in 18 Cavalry, is such a regiment in fact exists!! **How do you like the regiment and are there a good set of officers with you that can teach you your job as an officer.** *I expect you must have T-55 tanks or is it some other, and must therefore, be busy getting to know it. I like the cavalry black beret, and is it the crossed lances you wear as your crest?*

Well son, I hope you are keeping up your games and playing a lot with your troops as that is the finest way to get to know them. In any case it will keep you fit. You will also have lot of courses to do at the beginning of your service and it is important that you do well in all of them. Write to us when you have time and tell us all about your regiment. Send your letter Registered AD, as lot of mail coming to Vizakh is being tempered with. Aunty sends you her love and best wishes. Yours; Uncle Ron". **Unquote.**

No doubt, my first few months in the regiment were very eventful. I was in trouble most of the time, particularly with the Adjutant, who happened to invariably catch me on the wrong foot resulting in more guards checks throughout the night. After few weeks I started to enjoy the punishment as it kept me far away from the officer's mess and gave more time and opportunity to mix with the troops. Thambi's as the South Indian troops affectionately called are very simple and intelligent lot and I got along well with them. I remember Admiral telling me, son try to remember the names of each and every jawan in your sub-unit, not only I remembered their names but also their numbers (1030334, one had to remember 30 series) and trade i.e. Driver/ Operator/ Gunner.

One night at about 2 am as the Duty Officer I ordered 'Fire Fighting' practice for HQ squadron, and having barely one month of service , the JCO's thought it is not necessary to come out, as it was pretty cold night in the month of February with fresh snow on Dhauladhar Ranges. I refused to take no for an answer and went inside their rooms and got them out. My over enthusiastic action was not appreciated by Risaldar Major, who next morning brought the matter to the notice of Adjutant, who in any case was looking for an opportunity to twist my arm. He went ahead and reported the matter to Commanding Officer. I was informed that I will be marched up to the Commandant in 'Sam Brown' and Peak Cap, at noon. Everybody was mortally scared of Lt Col Morris Ravinderan and the worst was expected for a peddle pipsqueak of 2/Lt and I thought I bit more than I could chew and resigned myself to serious tongue lashing and may be some more punishments.

At 12 'o' clock I was marched up to the Commandant by the Adjutant. The Commandant told the Adjutant to leave and close the door. I kept standing motionless and looking straight into his eyes, in fact between the eyes and expecting the worst!! Next I heard 'sit down'; I could not fathom and thought I heard wrong; again the Commandant said; "sit down". I was taken aback, here I was thinking after being marched up, Commandant will shout the hell out of me and bring the roof down, and now, am being asked to sit down?? I slowly sat down, next he asked me to remove my cap, which I did. Commandant spoke softly; Mister Bhalla, you know, you remind me of my young officer days. He went to narrate the story- **quote** "In 1955/56 as a young 2/Lt with less than 2 years of service, I was posted in Nagaland with the Recce Squadron. One fine day all officers were asked to gather in the officer's mess to welcome a Brigadier. We were enjoying a glass of beer when I overheard the Brigadier passing some offensive and derogatory remarks about the fighting prowess of South Indians troops. Being a South Indian myself and on top of that belonging to South Indian Regiment, I thought it was too insulting and humiliating to digest. I did not react but when he continued with the tirade, I could not digest anymore and walked up to him and said, Sir, your perception of South Indians is totally off the mark, and this is not a fair remark. I would therefore, request you to withdraw your statement and apologize. The Brigadier looked down on me and growled; youngster! How dare you speak to me like this? I repeated myself and he shouted back; shut up. I once again requested him to apologize, which he of course refused and shouted few explicits at me, which was most unbecoming of a senior officer. Being in Counter Insurgency area all of us used to carry our personal weapon- Revolver- my blood raced to my head and I took out the Revolver and pointed at the Brigadier and said; will you take back your words and apologize or I'll shoot you. He couldn't believe my reaction! He panicked and apologized but I got into big trouble with the higher HQs but survived. It's a Court Marshal offence, do you know? He then said, Mister Bhalla, am proud of you and appreciate your enthusiasm and aggression, but be little careful and don't go over the top. Thambis are wonderful soldiers, look after them; they will never let you down, OK. All the best and now you can leave". **Unquote**

I got up totally stunned and saluted him as smartly as I could and walked out of his office shaking my head in disbelief. And three months later he was posted out to Staff College as an Instructor. (He was from 5th NDA course, 4th Dec 1954).

The Adjutant was of course very intrigued at the reaction of Commandant and was wondering what he spoke to me?? I said; he was very happy with me!!

In September 1974, Admiral had a chance meeting with Col Morris Ravinderan at Madras, when as Directing Staff; Colonel Morris had accompanied the Staff College Army students for a visit to Naval Establishments during Bharat Darshan. A Cocktail Party was organized for the visiting students on INS Brahmaputra, anchored at Madras harbour. Captain Subimal Mukerjee, the CO put up the list of Instructors to Admiral for his information and he noticed the name of Col Morris Ravinderan, 16 Cavalry, and immediately recalled that I had mentioned about him in my initial letters from Pathankot!

However, I would like to recount their meeting in the version given by none else than Col Morris Ravinderan himself. In Sep 76, Col Morris Ravinderan made a short trip to the Regiment in Pathankot. I was informed that Colonel would like to meet me. I was therefore, instructed to report to Regimental Head Quarters at 4pm. I was bit nervous but still looking forward to meet my first Commandant.

At few minutes past 4pm, I saw Col Ravinderan in his old Willeys jeep, which he used as CO, approaching RHQ; I immediately came to attention and saluted him. He came out of jeep and met me very warmly; How are you, Mike? I said, I am fine, thank you Sir. Next thing I hear, let's go for a drive towards the hills and asked me to drive, I proudly sat behind the wheels (as youngsters one can't go anywhere near the CO's jeep, leave alone driving it) and drove North towards Nurpur Hills, Himachal Pradesh. After a while he turned around and with pride in his voice said, **quote** "you know Mike, about two years ago in Sep74, I met Admiral Pereira in Madras, we were all invited for drinks on board INS Brahamaputra and as we all were waiting for the Fleet Commander to arrive, we saw a tall and handsome officer in his White Dinner Jacket 6A, entered the hall and he clapped couple of times and in his baritone voice said, Good Evening Gentleman, you are all welcome aboard and am looking for one Col Morris Ravinderan from 16 Cavalry ? Is he here? I was standing near the bar and was bit surprised to hear my name and then I raised my arm and said loudly, yes Sir, am here. Admiral looked in my direction and walked towards me and before I could take few steps, he stretched his hand and looking straight into my eyes and gave me strong hand shake and said; nice to meet you Colonel, there is a young officer in 16 Cavalry, Mike Bhalla, who is like a son to us, wrote a lot about you and am glad that you kept him on a tight leash'!! I was indeed touched by his gesture and said, yes Sir, that's the way we bring up our youngsters in the Regiment , he said 'Good' and Admiral put his arm on my shoulders and said Colonel, now tell me what is your poison ? And have a drink on me. You know Mike; he spent most of the evening with me only."

It was a great experience and indeed surprised to be singled out by the Admiral and of course I was touched by his humility. I think Admiral is very fond of you, Mike" **Unquote.**

I kept driving quietly and imagining the scene in my mind; warm and deep looks in Admiral big eyes and laughing with Col Morris!!

The best part is that, then Admiral's Flag Lt (later Cdr) Vijayan kindly sent me some photos of Admiral just recently in Jan 2016, and yes, in one of the photos, there is Col Morris Ravinderan, laughing and standing next to the Admiral!! What **coincidence**, unbelievable but true.

First Pay Cheque

Where was the time to write letters? Rightly so Admiral and Mrs. Pereira had reason to get worried. However, thereafter, I tried to be regular in my letter writing. In early April 74, we got our FIRST pay deposited in the bank; it was princely amount of Rs 696/- of course I was keen to share a small amount with my parents, Admiral and Mrs. Pereira, it was just a token amount of Rs 101/- I very proudly sent them a cheque of Rs 101/- dated 18 April 74.

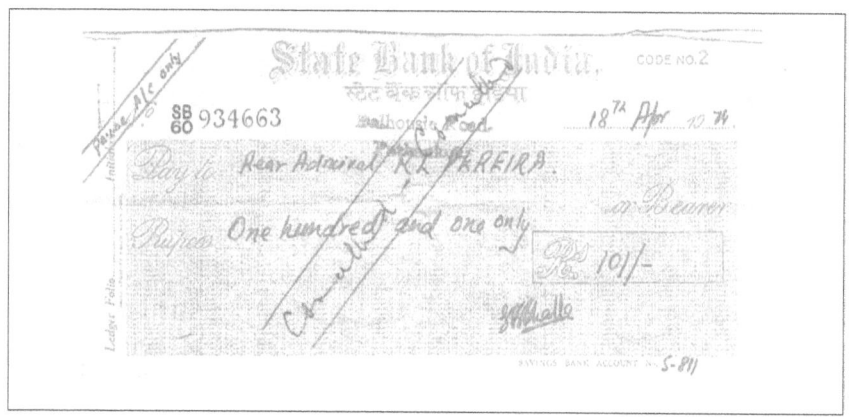

This was promptly replied by Mrs. P, dated 25 April 74 quote *"Dear Mike, thank you for your letter dated 17/4 and we were so pleased to hear from you after ages, 'Sir' wrote to you the other day to enquire how you are? I only hope you got that letter. I fear that 90% of our letters go astray from Vizag. Postal service is terrible here. Everyone complains. You ought by now to have received at least 4 letters from us. I have also not heard from Anoop and Barfi in reply to my last letters and can only presume that they too have gone astray. We find these forms (2x Inland Letters) sometimes get through and though I hate using them, they appear to be more reliable. Thank you so much my son for the wonderful gesture in sending us extremely generous cheque. The thought behind the action is so very sweet and so very typical of you. However, my son, Sir will be returning it to you, as we would like you to save it. You must try to save a little each month. You are by nature is very generous but I fear that in this age and era you must try to curb your generous tendencies! Thank you again son, for your lovely thought of wanting to share your first pay packet with us. As for your leave in June/July- or at any time for that matter-you know that you are always welcome for as long as you like. We are planning to go on leave 18 May- 18 June, so plan your leave accordingly. We will be in Bangalore trying to fix up things in connection with our property. This is so far and since we last went on leave in 1969. I am keeping my fingers crossed. Sir is at sea again today . I will be leaving for Delhi on Friday*

i.e. tomorrow. He will be gone for a week-10 days and thereafter he might be going overseas for a short while, therefore I say we still cannot say for sure about our leave. Sir was away for whole of January, came back early Feb; was in and out throughout Feb end of March I went to Madras as Sir had to go anyway to meet Singapore ships who were visiting India. We both like Madras a lot-very clean. I stayed on in Madras for an extra week and then came back. Sir is as usual very busy but I think he is looking tired and I hope our leave comes through. Tomorrow our new dog arrives from Bombay-a highly pedigreed Sydney Silkie- also very expensive. He's cost us Rs 500/- We are also expecting our new car. I was coming back from welfare center in Jan in our old car when the brakes failed, and only way I could stop was by driving into a gate! The damage to the car was quite heavy but I got out un-ruffled!!

It's hot as hell and I was green with envy when I read in the papers Poona has had her first shower of rain. We don't get very much rain here and we get it very late. We will be sending you a photograph of Sir- I think a very nice one but we had better make sure that it gets to you and not destroyed by some lazy Andhra postman who cannot be bothered ensuring that letters get thru. My garden came up very well and despite the heat I still have flowers in the garden-I think I am the only one in Vizag with flowers!! That's all for now my son, Work hard and don't slacken off and keep up your games- very important. Lots of love from both of us. God Bless-love-Mrs.P". **Unquote.**

As I had mentioned earlier that Mrs. P could finish a book in one sitting, but just didn't like to cook or write letters. So for her to write such a long letter indeed is special. This must be one of her longest letter and that's the reason to share each word of it.

Couple of weeks later I received a letter from Admiral, dated 5 May 74 , **quote**" *My dear Mike,- Thank you a million for both your registered letters, the first with the cheque and second from the camp in reply to mine .*

Son, both Aunty and I are deeply touched for your wonderful thoughtfulness in sending us a cheque of Rs 101/- from your first pay and we certainly appreciate this gesture of yours. We have talked about this a lot and we have decided that we would like you to keep it and open a saving bank account to which we want you to put little money every month, so that in an emergency you have something to fall back on. I must thank you a million, son, for your fine gesture, but we surely feel we would like you to start the saving bank account with it, so that at least when you go home on leave, you have enough money to take with you.

I see that you are having it rather tough, but am sure in the long run you will appreciate this for it makes you work and learn your job far sooner and being a professional officer, this is your whole task in life. It also bring you closer to men whom you will always have to lead, and therefore must know very well, so all said and done it is good for you to begin life in the Army in this way, for it makes far better soldier of you.

Son, we will be delighted to have you with us whenever you come on leave. Just let us know when you are arriving in June or July and we shall meet you at the station. I was myself due to go on leave towards the middle of this month, but I had to cancel this, due to my going to Egypt as part of defense delegation for about 10 days from 15th of May. Thereafter on my return we have lots of exercises scheduled with the Western Fleet, so I don't believe that I will be able to get away before July or August. However, I will have to decide the dates much later after I have worked out the programme of my Fleet.

Mike, I want you son, a little careful in what you write in your letters to Aunty or me. You must always remember that there are lots of people wanting to know about our state of preparedness in the Services, the equipment we use and many other issues and they don't hesitate to open Service's officers letter, to try and get this information. Though you may think there is no harm in writing about these issues to us and one never know who may see these letters and pass on the information to the people who should not have it. The other point is that had the censor seen this letter, you might have been pulled up for it, son. Though I am very interested in what you are doing, Mike, it's better to tell me all about it when we meet.

Had a long letter from Auntie May after ages, and she had not received any of my previous letters other than the last one which I registered. There seem to be something very wrong with our P&T department in this place, and I would not at all surprise if the stamps are stolen off the letters and the letter itself is destroyed. I am sending this one to you 'registered', Mike, as that seems to be the only way that my mail gets through, Aunty Phyll wrote you an Air letter about four or five days ago, while I was away in New Delhi, and I do hope you have received it. Quite a few of her previous letters & indeed mine don't seem to have reached you.

Son you mentioned in your letters that you had sent us some photographs taken at IMA. I am sorry to say that we never received them, and they must have gone astray. This is indeed sad.

I am enclosing your cheque son, which I have deliberately cancelled, to prevent someone getting hold of it and opening an account in my name which will permit him to cash it. Don't forget to open the saving bank account with it.

Aunty May writes to say that she spent a very nice holiday with your parents at Chandigarh, and enjoyed every minute of it. She was particularly happy with Zakir Hussain Rose Garden which was absolutely beautiful.

Well, Mike I will close. Look after yourself and work hard. Be careful with your money as the world is full of sharks who will be delighted to take it off you, one way or the other. Looking forward to seeing you on leave, yours Uncle Ron". **Unquote**

Unit Life

Those were the early days in the regiment; there was no question of asking for leave, firstly with pre-course training for Young Officer's course and operational deployment along the International border in May 74. Inter Regiment Football Tournament in July, followed by Inter Regiment Hockey Tournament in Sep/Oct, and add to this various inspections viz; Administration Inspection of Brigade Commander, tanks technical inspection by CEME (Cdr Electrical Mechanical Engineering) There was just no time for yourself and at the end of the day you just hit the bed and off to deep sleep to wake up early next morning. So I defaulted in my letter writing and in fact got no leave at all for initial 18 months of my service till mid 75 and therefore could not visit Vizag in 1974.

As for the cheque I felt wee bit disappointed as I was keen that Aunty Phyll bought herself a small gift- though very small amount but I wanted to convey my gratitude for their love and affection. I still have the cancelled cheque with me 42 years hence!

Being young with hardly few months service I was trying to impress with the knowledge of the equipment we were holding etc, but it was certainly incorrect and against the security regulations. Admiral aim from day one was to guide me to do the right thing and follow Army norms.

The months passed away rather fast and by the time I received next letter in August and realized I had not written to them for a long time.

In his letter dated 20 Aug 74, **quote** *"Hi Mike- we haven't heard from you for a very long time and I wonder whether you away on course or spot of leave. The last time I heard from you, you wanted to come and spend some time with* us at Vizag and I had written back that we will be delighted to have you with us. When does your leave commence or can you not get leave till after your YO's course which I believe is sometime in October.

Aunty Phyll had a letter from Mahli the other day-he is in 7th Cav and he wrote that he will be going for his YO's in October which seems to be the same time as you. This course will be your very first after being commissioned or at least first course outside the regiment and your position and grading will be an important factor, am quite sure you will do well in it, but remember son that it all counts towards future promotions.

I will probably be moving in December from this job, as my relief who is an officer who will be coming back from deputation in UK and is also an Admiral. I have no idea where I will be going, but I should think that Naval Headquarters will be working this out now and I should know sometime in October and early November. It will mean packing up and moving again, but that is part of the game, and I haven't got many more moves left before we finally retire from the service. The two possible stations could be COCHIN and New Delhi, and I would naturally prefer Cochin as it is an independent command and a very nice one too. Naval Headquarters New Delhi will be desk job and a great deal of paper work and you know how much I would like that! At one time there was also the possibility that I would return to the Academy as the Commandant, but this now seem to be out as AVM Naik, as far as I know will not be moving until late 75 or early 76 which will be too late for me.

I had a letter from Aunty May from Mussoorie and I understand that she is heading a campaign to stop lime quarry trucks from using the main road past the library, as that has damaged these roads with their vehicles. There, in fact a quarry road which keeps them out of town, but it makes the trip longer, and they do not use it. She and some other ladies and gents ran a 'bandh' and blocked the roads for 48 hours and she has got the administration thinking about taking some action against the trucking company. I must say I admire her, as it takes lots of guts to do these things.

We are facing a very serious water shortage in this place, as the rains have failed for third successive year, and it looks as the crops will be very seriously affected again. What is even worse is that the only lake that really supplies us water has now reached the danger level, as its only source is the monsoons. I don't quite know what they are going to do. We have really had hardly any rains this year; the only real shower that fell about 3 weeks ago was so heavy, that it completely flooded the place!! Our own house in the Naval Park was under 2 ½ feet of water.

Has your Regiment been visited by Lt Gen KK Singh as yet? I spoke to him about you, when we were together in Egypt in May this year he said he would see you the next time when he visited 16 Cavalry. By the way Aunty May tells me that your CO is away or under transfer or you have now got a new CO with the unit- I hope you find that he is strict and rigid and chasing about just as much!!

Well my son, I will close, Aunty sends you all her love and good wishes and always remember you. She says she hopes that you are looking after yourself. All my good wishes to you and write whenever you can ; yours Uncle Ron". **Unquote.**

Lt Gen KK Singh MVC, Padma Bhushan was commissioned in 16 Cavalry in 1939, and Commanded the Regiment from 1951-54. However, after 1965, he never visited the regiment and retired in 1975 as Army Commander, Central Command. He passed away on 26th July 2016 at the ripe age of 97 years in Mahindergarh District, Haryana.

In Oct 74 I proceeded for my Young Officer's course to Ahmednagar and by end 74 Admiral moved to Cochin to take over as FOC Southern Naval Areas .So I could not make a trip to Vizag.

Cochin 75

After completion of YO's I went back to the Regiment and finally got leave in mid July 75. I immediately wrote to Admiral that I would like to visit and by second week of Aug I was in Cochin and just missed the famous Snake Boat Race at Alleppy by few days.

I had informed Admiral about my flight details and as I came out of Cochin airport and looking outside for Staff Car to arrive, suddenly from inside the airport terminal I heard someone shout; Mike- and I immediately knew it was Admiral calling and as I looked back there I saw him walking towards me in his Whites and looking very impressive. He came and hugged me, and held my face and said, son, you are looking fine, it was after gap of 32 months that we met and no doubt I was bit emotional and my eyes swelled! He picked up my suitcase and said, come on son the car is on the runway! The airport was within the naval establishment INS Garuda and there I saw brand new Black Padmini Premier Fiat. We drove across the runway to his office. How happy he was to show the new car to me. Later from office he asked me to drive home- but be careful, my son!! Aunty was thrilled to see me.

The Navy House was located at the Southern tip of the Wellington Island along the backwaters of Cochin, with a jetty in front. I spent four wonderful weeks with them. Admiral drove me around Cochin in his car and we visited historical places such as Dutch Palace, Chinese Fishing Nets, Bolgatty Islands, Synagogue and ride in local boats in the backwaters. It was peak of monsoon with lovely weather. We also visited couple of local homes of distinguished people of Cochin. I remember meeting one of the richest couple, but dressed in simple traditional dresses and no jewelry at all! No external show of wealth unlike people in North India?

Of course Admiral was enjoying his Command and as usual he had a story to tell about the sentry who was sleeping while on duty. One night at about 2 am Admiral woke up and decided to check his own guard.

Quote "Son, I went out to see whether the guard was alert or not and quietly walked past him, I found no reaction from the sentry, obviously he was asleep, I walked past second time, still no movement, then I stepped forward and picked up his rifle and after a while threw some stones on the sentry box and couldn't wake up the sentry, obviously he was in deep slumber. Next morning at 5.30am I came out with Smokey for my morning walk and as I went past the sentry he saluted me, without weapon, and I asked him son, where is your rifle and he immediately broke down and said, in the middle of the night a boat came from the channel with few persons and they overpowered me and took away the weapon and left me unconscious , Admiral called Capt Bouncy Malhotra CO, INS Venduruthy, he immediately came and after inquiring came out with the similar story of boat coming etc, Admiral heard him patiently and then went inside and brought the rifle to everyone amazement !! The sentry was awarded NO 11 punishment and was confined to barracks for a month. Admiral wanted to court marshal him for dereliction of duty, but he let him off with lighter punishment as he was the only earning member of the family. He said, son, I had to think of his old mother!" **Unquote**

Egypt Visit

We would sit in the verandah opposite the Cochin channel and discuss about life in the unit, the Regimental history, about my troops, whether I had memorized all names etc and the games I played with them. I requested the Admiral to narrate me about his trip to Egypt the previous year In May 1974. I had few sittings with him and kept taking down notes about the first hand briefing they got on **Yom Kippur War**, Oct 73 from the Egyptian point of view, thinking that it might help me whenever I appear for Staff College Entrance Exams. And sure enough 9 years later in 1984 I was eligible for my first mandatory chance and **Military Campaign for Military History** was indeed 'Arab- Israel War' 1973 (co-incidence). I had kept the notes all these years and yes, they were very useful for my preparations as Admiral gave me the insight to planning and execution from Egyptian point of view, particularly their 'anti- tank' approach and with God's grace cleared the exams in my first attempt itself.

In fact in his letter dated 25th April 84 he wrote, **quote** "*Really Mike, I am not at all sure whether the future wars on land or at sea, cannot be dominated by one Arm or the other. It is really the judicious combination of all arms used to their very best advantage that will produce the ultimate answer of victory. I will never forget our visit to Egypt after the 'YOM KIPPUR' war when we spent a whole day, on one occasion, with the only COPTIC Christian Div Commander that the Egyptians had. He took us on the battle area, and in amazement related an incident when the Israeli's had the impertinence and temerity to put in a counter- attack with a brigade of armour, without any supporting infantry, believing stupidly enough that the Egyptians would run, on the site of armour, particularly at that moment, they (Egyptians) had no armour available to meet the this thrust. In fact the Egyptian infantry, with only a limited number of shoulders operated Russian anti-tank missiles, ultimately accounted for 91 Israeli tanks and the attack was in fact a total failure. The point I make is that no single arm can claim over- riding advantages by use of their equipment; it is always the better team that wins.*" **Unquote.**

I vividly remember how Admiral spoke about the Div Commander, who as per his description; was a huge man much above six foot with very broad shoulders and big smile coupled with loud laughter! As luck would have it in our Military History paper for DSSC entrance exam in Nov 19-24, 1984, there was a question about this very operation!! **Co-incidence!!**

Colour Presentation

By mid 1975, the regiment was officially informed that Colour Presentation to 16 Cavalry and Hodson's Horse is scheduled for 4th March 1976. It was also the Bi-centenary year of 16 Cavalry having been raised in 1776. Being one of the first three regiments earmarked for induction of Indian origin officers (7th Cavalry and 3rd Cavalry were other two regiments), we had over dozen officers in General cadre serving and retired. Accordingly list was drawn to invite each one of them starting from Mr MAR Baig 1925 (later Ambassador to Philipines), Hira Atal 1926 Gen JN Chaudhuri 1928. MS Wadalia 1929, SD Verma 1929, Habibullah 1930. Gynshyam Singh 1933, Bhagwati Singh 1936, Varindra Singh 1937, KC Khanna 1937, Har Prasad 1939, KK Singh 1939, Jang Shamsher Singh 1940 and Zorawar Singh 1940 and few others.

Maj Gen Sheodutt 1923, first Indian officer to be commissioned had already passed away.

Our 2IC Major Opu Sengupta was organizing the whole proceedings for the celebrations. One day I walked up to him and asked his permission to invite Rear Admiral RL Pereira, Flag-Officer-Commanding Southern Naval Areas for the above function. He knew about my relations with the Admiral and was indeed very happy and said "Mike, go ahead and I shall also write and formally invite him on behalf of the regiment". I wrote to Admiral, and so did Oppu Sengupta and Admiral very kindly accepted the invitation to attend the celebrations. But there was some hitch as he was expecting his move sometime in end Feb 76.

In his letter dated **19th Feb 76, quote** "*My Dear Mike-I am sorry I have not replied to all your letters regarding the bi-centenary celebrations of the regiment, but I have been waiting, as Aunty May must have told you, for my next appointment before finally deciding whether I would be in a position to attend or not.*

As it stands at the moment I have yet not heard anything about my next appointment and I have now decided to take few days leave and come up to Pathankot for the celebrations irrespective of where I may be next going .I have therefore, sent you a wire and also written to Maj Gen Virendra Singh to try and get a seat in the air-conditioned bus to Pathankot on the 3rd Mar, and I will also come back by this transport on the 6th March.

Thank you, Mike for all details regarding the ceremonies that will be taking place. You must however have got my wire for clarification as to whether winter or summer uniform will be used and the reason I have sent this is because details of Colour Presentation on 4th refer to spectators being in dress No.1 (this will be full dress winter uniform) while I also notice that for the personnel who will be participating in the ceremony and the JCO's, the dress has been stated as No.2, which is full dress summer uniform. I have therefore, some doubts as to how the spectators will be in one uniform while the participants on the Parade will be in another. I therefore hope you will be able to clarify this issue before I leave and this is the reason of my wire to you.

I am also filling up the Performa, so that you have all the details that you required. I do hope I am not too late.

I have wanted very much to come to Pathankot for these celebrations, but I was regrettably not sure whether I will be able to make it and I did not want to find myself in a position where I would have had to cancel my attendance.

Incidentally, my son, they may want to know my substantive seniority as Rear Admiral. This is the 2nd April 1973. They may require this in regard to the seating plans for the various ceremonies.

Aunty Phyll will not unfortunately be able to attend, but sends you her love and good wishes.

This letter was penned in the office, hence the type written screed. *Thinking it over son, I will only be wearing plain clothes, as I am your private guest. And therefore should not wear uniform.*

All the best and look after yourself- Sincerely-Uncle

Lieutenant Mike Bhalla
16 Cavalry
c/o 56 APO

All arrangements were made for Admiral's reception and I was indeed very excited to welcome him. He had put in application for casual leave for first week of March 76. The CNS Admiral SN Kohli inquired as to why Ronnie wants spot of leave, to which Admiral replied that he wishes to go to Pathankot to attend Colour Presentation and Bi-centenary celebrations of 16 Light Cavalry. The CNS expectedly was rather surprised why on earth to a place like Pathankot!! The Admiral apparently explained the background and his relation with one piddle Lieutenant from 16 Cavalry; the CNS turned down his request and said wait for further instructions from Naval HQ's. Admiral still had no clue what so ever about his impending move. In fact, he was quite certain that he will be proceeding on retirement soon and as per his Flag Lt Jena; during his farewell function at Bangalore **Admiral said in so many words that soon he will be going home.**

FOC-in-C Western Naval Command

However, within one week, there was a big surprise in store for him

Lt Cdr Dinbandhu Jena, Flag Lt to FOC, narrated the sequence of events in his own words, **quote** "On 26 Feb 76, at about 11 am Mr. Chandra Hasen, PA to FOC got a call and as he picked up the phone, to his utter surprise he found Admiral Kohli, CNS on the other end asking to speak to FOC and he immediately put the call through to FOC; Sir, CNS on the line!! Admiral was indeed taken aback, by now PA informed me and I rushed to see through the peep window and saw that FOC who was on his feet and looking very excited, and could hear him saying; Sir, please say again, is it C-in- C Western Naval Command, Bombay? And the CNS confirmed and told him to catch the first flight to Bombay and take over as C-in-C within 24 hours. After putting the phone down Admiral called me and PA and said book two seats for Bombay immediately, by then Lt Cdr KK Nair, Secretary to FOC also came in and told the PA to rush to the airport which was located within the premises of INS Garuda itself, The Naval Air Station, on the other side of runway. I asked him Sir, are you taking over Western Naval Command? He replied yes, I think so!! Admiral informed Mrs. Pereira that he is off to Bombay for some important work. By afternoon flight both Admiral and self in uniform only took the Indian Airlines flight to Bombay. It was 'Top Secret' move and no one but immediate staff was in know of it. We reached Bombay in the evening and stayed in Command Mess and next day Admiral took over as C-in-C, Western Naval Command, still 3 months short of 53 years."**Unquote**

Flag Lt further shared with me his own perception of this sudden move of Admiral to Bombay, **quote** "Sometime in November 75, Admiral Kohli CNS, paid an official visit to Cochin , the station where he had number of tenures earlier and what he saw during his visit really impressed him. The whole station was vibrant and full of energy and all training activities and sports were in top gear. The Ceremonial Parade given in honor of CNS was outstanding. CNS was indeed very, very impressed of what he saw and it could have been the turning point in FOC's career". **Unquote**

I tried to find out the reason why CNS took this step, and I was informed by Ronnie P colleague and very close friend that it was done as 'preventive move' as the Government of the day was indeed keen on someone else to take over but Admiral Kohli, CNS did not approve of it and wanted to ensure that Ronnie P took over while he was still in chair, he retired on 29th Feb 76!! There were manipulations at work and underhand games being played by some individuals with vested interest. Whatever, it may be Ronnie P took over but come April 77, he was controversially shifted to Naval HQ's as VCNS??

Mrs. Pereira packed the house and with help of Lt Cdr KK Nair and shifted the baggage to Bombay.

This move put paid Admiral's visit to Pathankot and he cancelled his trip, In any case I was very happy for him. But he promised me; son, one day I will visit 16 Cavalry, yes, he kept his promise and 4 years later as CNS visited the Regiment in Mar 80 in Jodhpur.

Lonavala

In April 76 I was detailed to attend 'Intelligence Course for Junior Officers' at Poona. I was passing through Bombay and had the opportunity to meet Admiral and Mrs. Pereira. When I landed in Bombay, both of them had already left for a visit to INS Shivaji, Lonavala (Engineering Training Establishment). On my arrival at the Navy House on Shaheed Bhagat Singh Road I immediately got a call from Admiral, who told me to catch a train to Lonavala next morning and I will be picked up at the Railway Station .The journey through Western Ghats was beautiful and reminded me of my journey to Poona while going to NDA. After reaching Lonavala as I got down from the train, there I saw a naval officer in uniform and I walked towards him and realized he was Lt Commander and wished him respectfully and introduced myself. We walked to a station wagon parked outside. He asked ex NDA, I said yes Sir, 43rd course and I apologized to him for the trouble as he was from 36th course. He said I have not come here to receive you, but C-in-C's guest, so you don't have to feel sorry. We drove through beautiful and lush green rolling hills of the Sahyadri ranges to Lonavala, which is located at the altitude of 2000 feet. As the vehicle approached INS Shivaji, we were stopped by the Naval Policeman and asked to park the vehicle beside the Quarter Guard as the cavalcade of C-in-C was passing by. As the Admiral car approached Quarter Guard, he must have noticed me sitting in the Station Wagon and told his driver to stop the car and asked Flag Lt Jena - I see Mike in that vehicle, call him. Jena hurried towards us and shouted- Mike, Admiral is calling you, I jumped out, and as Admiral got out of his car right in front of the Quarter Guard with Admiral's walking stick in hand and looking Regal and impressive in his Whites, the bugler sounded the bugle and at that very moment Admiral gave me a bear hug and said; how are you my son?! Even today 40 years later I remember that scene vividly with Jena standing next to us and sound of the bulge in my ears. He said son, freshen up and we will wait for you. After 20 minutes I was ushered in a hall where all officers and ladies had gathered, Aunty Phyll saw me and just gave me a warm hug. I was quite embarrassed with so much attention. After that we witnessed Command Swimming Championship. I met my course mates, NN Kumar (later Vice Admiral) Thomas Zakarias, Rakesh Tagnet and Samual(45th Delta).

Later in the evening Captain Raju, Commanding Officer, had organized Club function in the Officers Institute. I was seeing Admiral and Mrs. Pereira after 8 months. Admiral was very fussy about long hair and will not stand even a small strand of hair out of place. I being from Cavalry traditionally we have long hair. Now that was something not acceptable to Admiral and he said you can't possibly attend the official function in the evening with such long locks of hair. As soon as we reached Inspection Bungalow, Hazam (barber) was summoned and was specifically told by Admiral to get rid of all my long locks. The barber was bit slow and nervous as Admiral was personally supervising the proceedings. After a while Admiral who did not seem to be very impressed with the barber's effort ultimately snatched the scissors from barber's hand and proceeded to cut my hair himself. All he did was put the fingers through my hair and in one fell stroke he cut them all and told the barber to give me a crew cut!! Aunty Phyll tried to dissuade Admiral and said; come on Ron don't be so harsh on the boy, but no go, and by the time the Hazam finished, he had ruined whatever simple looks I had and waited for next three months for the crop to grow again!! But Admiral had his way! He thought I looked smart in short hair, I resigned to my fate!

I was told later that during his first visit to Goa as C-in-C, the Station Commander called the staff to check up, is Admiral really very fussy about long hair, well he was advised if you don't want to forsake your job you better ensure everyone has proper hair cut. All the barbers who had no job hither to fore were summoned to do the needful and as the time was running out, then all civilian barbers in Vasco too were summoned to meet the dead line next morning. I believe one of my course mates had a curl coming out of his cap on the parade ground and next thing he found, his cap was flying!! Not only that, while attending Command Basket Ball Championship, Admiral noticed few players with rather long hair wearing a net to keep them in place, were immediately asked to leave the court and have proper haircut!!

MCO, Bombay

Next day I was off to Poona. Six weeks later after completion of the course I had another opportunity to spend couple of days with them. Admiral and Mrs. Pereira were invited to NDA by Rear Admiral Manohar Awati, Commandant to attend Passing out Parade on 5th June 76. Incidentally my course also got over on 5th June itself. Admiral in his letter dated 3rd June wrote, **quote** "*My dear Mike, A quick line from office to answer your letter dated 1st June. We leave for NDA on the 4th, Friday and will be there about lunch time and will return on Saturday after lunch, which we are having with Commandant. You could, therefore, come back in the car with us- there will only be two of us and Sharda —and if you wait at RSI, Poona, from 2.30, Saturday, 5th, we shall pick you up as soon as we can. We may be a little late but I will try and make it by 1430 h.*

I am glad that you are working hard, and I am sure you will do well, if you make the effort throughout the course and work steadily

I will not be staying at IB as we had originally intended as Rear Admiral Awati has kindly asked us to stay with him at the NDA .Must end now-our love and good wishes- Uncle Ron".**Unquote.**

On 5th June the Admiral Staff car drove into the main porch of RSI Club at 3 pm. It was a Plymouth car with no pilot or back-up vehicle or escorts, unlike the Army!! FOC-in-C is equivalent to the Army Commander and moving in a single vehicle!! Army Commander even in those days moved with not less than 10 vehicles in his cavalcade. Few years back my course mate; an Army Commander came to look me up at Bagdogra and had 14 vehicles in his entourage!! The times have changed, may be the security factor, I suppose.

By the time we reached Powai about 50 kms short of Bombay it started to rain very heavily and we were moving in 1st gear and managed to reach Navy house late in the evening. Otherwise it was beautiful drive through the Ghats.

Next day Admiral inquired whether I had reserved berth for my return journey to Pathankot, which was over two nights, I told him I haven't but will manage. As a Lieutenant, in those days we didn't bother about reservations and a bottle of Rum would do the job. Admiral was not impressed and asked me to give him my Soldier Ticket No, he then rang up MCO (Movement Control Organization), Bombay and passed instruction to the NCO on duty and told him to release one berth in the Frontier Mail from VIP quota for Lt SPS Bhalla from Bombay to Pathankot, 7th June 76.

On the day of my departure Admiral insisted that he will drop me at the Railway Station and to check about my reservation. I told him there is no need for him to bother and I will manage. He wouldn't listen and took out his Fiat car and drove me to the Railway Station. After reaching there I again tried to impress upon him that I will manage, but he wanted to see me off till my compartment. Then he proceeded to stand in rather long queue, I asked him what's he trying, he turned around and said, son, I must buy a Platform Ticket!! I told him that nobody will check you, but he won't listen and he waited in the queue for 10 minutes and paid 50 paisa to buy the ticket!! When we reached the platform, my name was not on the reservation chart of the compartment to Pathankot, I told him not to worry and he can go back but no way; he hissed- am the bloody C-in-C and they can't manage one seat for you and now he was losing his famous temper and straightaway went to the MCO office and at 4pm in the afternoon there was one poor NCO, who got the wrath of Admiral's ire and gave his card to him and shouted, I am Admiral Pereira and tell your CO to report to my office at 9 am tomorrow morning. With great difficulty I managed to convince him to go and hugged him and said bye, bye. I knew somebody is going to buy it. After 10 minutes a JCO and two NCO's charged in our compartment looking for one piddle Lt Bhalla, and said Sir, lower berth is booked for you and the JCO ordered for cold drink and samosa for me. He requested that I inform the Admiral that all is well. Those were the days of no mobile phone! However, I called up Navy House on the Military line and informed Aunty Phyll that am fine and got myself a berth, and that too lower one, she said ; son don't worry I will inform Ron.

Bombay Aug 76

I came back to Bombay on long leave in Aug 76 and on the day of my arrival there was a tea party in the Navy House which got over just as I reached and there I met Commander DS Brar, my squadron commander in NDA in 1971/72.

The first thing Aunty Phyll told me that your departure in June created lot of crises. The very next morning MCO, one Colonel Sahib was summoned to the Western Naval Command HQs and got a dressing down of his lifetime. Admiral growled, how dare your staff does not take cognizance of C-in-C call? He was told in no uncertain terms that next time the whole MCO staff will be posted out within 24 hours. The Colonel profusely apologized and escaped by the skin of his teeth and after that day MCO staff was on their toes and always on the lookout for any call from C-in-C!!

Admiral by then had spent 5 months in Bombay and had everyone on the run. He used to work for long hours and couple of times in a week would pay surprise visits to ashore establishments. At 9am in the morning before getting into the Staff Car, he would tell the Flag to drive to some Establishment in Bombay, so actually nobody knew where and which establishment will the C-in-C visit?? Everyone, therefore, were on their toes! In the evenings we would sit in the verandah overlooking the Arabian Sea and he would discuss with me what all he has been doing to improve the facilities in Navy Nagar and the Bombay Dock Yard.

Family Accomodation

Admiral was particularly keen to see the progress of work on the High Rise Towers for family accommodation in Colaba and was aware before taking over as C-in-C that this is one project which has been dragging on its feet for many years and he wanted to expedite it. In his own words, **quote** "Son, you know I was keeping a close eye on the construction of towers and I would visit them every 4th Tuesday to see the progress, and in my first two visits I found nothing was happening and the work on foundations was moving rather slowly due to non availability of adequate rigs. I asked the Chief Engineer – what's happening and why there is no progress, he replied; Sir, I have tried to tell these Contractors, who have connection in high places and they don't bother and always come out with some excuse or the other and we are much behind schedule. I told Chief Engineer to arrange a meeting with the top man of the construction company. After a week the CE got an appointment with them. Admiral then said, son now I will enact the whole scene with them and he actually went through with it!! Kept both Aunty and self in splits of laughter but Admiral imitated them really well!!

Quote "These two gentlemen walked into my office; Hello, Admiral- how are you? I am Mr. Paulos, stretching his hand to supposedly get a warm handshake from me. I did not move from the chair and gave them a cold stare and said I have not called you here to exchange pleasantries but to talk about serious business, sit down. Now this frosty welcome deflated their big egos. I looked straight into their eyes and asked why there is no progress in the work. I am told that no rigs are available on the site to work on the foundations; Mr Paulos replied confidently; you know Admiral we have our problems in providing them and due to shortage of equipment etc etc. I butted in and told him- I have not called you to listen to your lame excuses, I want progress of work on ground and yes, what about the rigs operating on your sites in the Middle East, you don't have any problem there because you are making fast buck and you have no concern for families of the Indian Navy, I have to face them, am answerable to each one of them. They tried to justify again. I cut them short and said, I will give you two weeks to get the work going or I will scrap your contract and have you black listed . By now both of them were perspiring, I knew the iron was hot to strike and told them; Mr. Paulos and Mr. Pinto (showing them my open palms) you see these two hands they are absolutely clean and in 33 years in the Navy I have not taken a single kauri (paisa) and I can tell you that I will kick your bloody backsides till you bleed through your noses and you better get going or else I will come down heavily on you, is that clear? And now you can leave. They walked out slowly shaking their heads in disbelief. I don't think they ever experienced anything like this in their lives! I had no choice; they do not understand any decent language. Yes, my son, next time when I visited the sites there were 9 rigs!!" **Unquote**

When I recounted this incident to Admiral VS Shekhawat ex CNS, he said, **quote** "Mike, it reminds me of a famous poem written by a great poet, Lord Tennyson about King Arthur.

"MORTE de ARTHUR"
MY GOOD SWORD CARVES CAST OF MEN
MY TOUGH LANCE THIRSTED SURE
MY STRENGTH LIKE STRENGTH OF TEN
BECAUSE MY HEART IS PURE

When your hands are clean and your heart is pure, you get strength of ten in you and that's what Admiral Pereira was- a man with impeccable INTEGRITY and HONESTY". **Unquote**

Mrs. Pereira told me that we have also incorporated ladies to advice us where all they would like to have switches/plug points in the kitchen and other rooms of the flat so that their convenience is addressed, and ultimately the product was very good. Even today all old timers say without any hesitation that it was primarily due to Admiral Pereira efforts that these towers came up and to great extent mitigated the problem of shortage of family accommodation in Bombay.

Brig Gobindar Singh

It happened in 1976 i.e. 40 years ago and I was very keen to find out who was the Chief Engineer at that juncture? With the help of Brig Rakesh Rana, the present CE, I managed to get the name, Brig Gobindar Singh Jan 75- Oct 76. Next I called up my very old friend, guide and philosopher- Lt Gen (retd) Promod Kumar Grover, Bombay Sappers (we both served together in Sikkim in 1980) who in fact gave me Brig Gobindar Singh's contact number and address. I got through to him and even now at 93 years he remembered everything during his tenure with the Admiral. I have his signed photographs of 1976 and 2015 plus that of Memento presented to him by C-in-C. I personally called on him on 18 Mar 2016 in his residence In Sector 27, Chandigarh. He was looking fit and healthy. He also gave me a write up on important project for modernizing the dockyards, which is produced below:

Engine Test House At Naval Dockyard, Bombay

Many ships had to be sent to distant Russian Ports for testing and overhauling of Engines resulting in heavy expenditure of crores of Rupees. A Detailed Project Report (DPR) had been prepared by the Russians after an inter-government agreement for establishing an Engine Test House at the Naval Dockyard. Unfortunately all the Specifications/Dimensions/Drawings were in their language and according to their standards. A huge effort was required to interpret and re-design these to conform to our Indian standards and conditions. In addition it was necessary to co-relate the revised item to our manufacturing capacities and resource availability. For instance, voltages had to be readjusted to 440 as against the Russian 380 volts. The sizes, thickness and material specifications also had to be changed.

I approached the C-in-C and explained the whole case to him as well as the difficulties to go ahead with it. After listening patiently to my presentation the C-in-C asked me how he can help to kick start this very critical and important project and he will provide whatever assistance is required in terms of specialist and officers.

The project was taken over by the Chief Engineer (West Zone) as a challenge. A Russian team was to be made available for only three months.

It was probably for the first time a consulting Firm (Tata Consultants) was brought in for MES Works. A high powered working group was formed for the task and included the representatives from Navy, the Consultants and the Chief Engineer. They were asked to work round the clock and immediately approach the Chief Engineer in case of any diversions/ disagreements. On the few occasions the top trio of the CE, the Consultant and technical head of local Naval Command had to sort out problems. The Consultant was required to not only re-do the design and specifications but also research and locate available indigenous manufacturers and suppliers of all the items involved and the time frame needed for the same.

The project included about nine different systems as civil, electrification, water and sea water circulation, cooling and heating systems, oil and lubricants and their effluent disposal. It was decided to have only one main contractor so as to avoid inter-coordination problems between different sets of contractors. The main contractor was given the responsibility to sub allotting different works to his selected parties while retaining overall responsibility. Prior permission of Chief Engineer was however needed for sub allotted contractors.

The work started in the right earnest and the joint groups found themselves in the closed room with the instructions to come out only after the day's work is completed and that too without any disagreements. Over thousand odd drawing all in Russian language were redone in a record period of three months. The Consultants (Tata Consultancy Company) for whom this was their first such assignment with the Defense Service did an excellent job finalizing equivalent sizes of various items, designing the equivalent thickness/ diameters of various pipes and channels, their availability in the market, and source of manufacture including the time frame.

Appropriate contracts were completed and such a complicated and unique work was completed on schedule saving the Navy recurring expenditure of a few crores every year. The task was completed on time and appropriate contracts concluded successfully.

I would like to put it on record that without the dynamic guidance and support of the C-in-C, this project would not have gone beyond drawing table let alone executed to its completion. Admiral Pereira was very much involved in its progress right from beginning and today after 40 years I feel proud that I was the part of the project.

Also blessing and approval was taken of the C-in-C on the other major design. The land availability for heavy multistory buildings was restricted in the dock yard area, so was in the residential areas. Almost all buildings were thus designed, particularly the foundations-for subsequent addition of two extra stories in the Dockyard Buildings and four extra stories in residential buildings.

So much so that Air Force had no accommodations and Air Marshal Latif, C-in-C Maintenance Command requested Admiral for some quarters, and on CE advice 8 additional quarters were added to the towers and allotted for Air Force families.

When in early 77 orders for his move were received, the Admiral approached the CNS Admiral Jal Cursetji and requested that he should be permitted to complete his tenure to push these two particular projects to their final stages, but CNS and the government of the day had other plans!! They could not be bothered and moved him out prematurely??

Helmets

Admiral told me that he was coming down rather heavily on those riding the two wheelers without helmet and had passed strict instructions to confiscate the bike /scooter for a period of 3 to 6 months depending on the rank!

He had issued similar instructions while he was at Vizag and Cochin as he strongly believed that it's not worth losing one's life in a road accident. There was an incident in Vizag when one young officer barged into Fleet Commander's office and saluted him and said Sir, I have come to thank you for saving my life. Admiral asked him how? The officer showed a big hole in the helmet and said my bike skidded and without helmet this hole would have been in my skull and that would have been good bye. Admiral smiled and told him, son go and have a glass of beer on me!!

Second incident was in Cochin where a couple was going on a scooter through the bridge on the channel. The scooter went over the puddle of oil on the road and it skidded. The wife who was sitting on the pillion seat with the small baby in her lap lost her balance and to avoid any harm to the baby fell backward with her head hitting the deck and she died on the spot. I believe Admiral got all officers and wives assembled in Sagarika Hall and spoke to them, that I can order the officer to wear helmet but request ladies to wear it. I would not like to see my son lose his life on the road (soft side). Hereafter, if any of you is caught without the helmet, I shall confiscate and jack up the transport for 90 days (hard side).

Initially these instructions were not taken seriously, and then one Sunday Admiral himself decided to go to Navy Nagar with few Naval Police personnel from INS Kunjali and managed to catch dozens of erring officers and jacked up their transport for 6 months. After that Colaba ran short of helmets, every one scurrying around for it. But his aim was to avoid accidents. It worked and in fact, appreciated by all, particularly the families.

Classics

During my stay at Bombay Aunty Phyll and self used to move around in Admiral's Padmini Premier, Fiat. Together we saw couple of old English classic movies. The first one was "Roman Holiday" (1953) starring Audrey Hepburn and Gregory Peck, what a beautiful movie and excellent portrayal of the character by both of them. Few days later again Aunty Phyll and self went to see another classic-"Waterloo Bridge" (1940) starring most handsome actor of his generation; Robert Taylor and gorgeous Vivien Leigh. I am not a connoisseur of English movies but must admit Mrs. Pereira's taste was par excellence!

The only Hindi movie she ever saw was 'Pakeeza'!! However, she was very intrigued that how the heroine can change six dresses in a song sequence and mix summer flowers with winter flowers in the background!!

I spent lovely six weeks in Bombay. However, this time for my return journey to Pathankot I took lift in an Air Force aircraft to Delhi; I did not want to take chances with train journey!! Poor MCO!!

Vice Chief of Naval Staff 77-79

Next I heard in Mar 77 that soon he will be moving to Delhi as Vice Chief. At that time with barely three years of service I could not comprehend the undercurrents and consequences of this sudden move, but was indeed surprised that it was bit too early, as in the Army even in those days Army Commanders had tenure of at least 2/3 years, it seemed odd. When I met Admiral in July 77, at 5 Moti Lal Nehru Marg and asked him why he was moved within one year plus (13 months), he turned around with tongue in cheek and said, son, "my Chief, Admiral Jal Cursetji told me that am a strong contender for next CNS and the Government of the day would like to interact with me from close quarters!! I really don't know whether he was serious or pulling my leg? I remember telling him in Army the Vice Chief (except Gen Kumaramanglam) normally go home and doesn't take over as Chief, and majority were Southern Army Commanders who took over as COAS, and similarly in Navy it is invariably C-in-C Western Naval Command who takes over as CNS, he looked at me bit surprised and intrigued by my analogy said, son, the trend can change, who knows??

Incidentally, it did, the next three Chiefs of all three services were promoted from Vice Chief to Chief!! Malhotra, Latif and Pereira, known as Amar, Akbar and Anthony of armed forces!!

> MARCH 1979 opened a new chapter for India's defence forces with their three service chiefs drawn from three religions. General O. P. Malhotra, Air Chief-Marshal I. H. Lateef and Admiral R. L. Pereira are the Indian military's Amar, Akbar and Anthony—and in the same order. We would challenge any other country's defence forces to cite even a near parallel. —*Imprint*
>
> –*Reader's Digest Jan 1980*

Notwithstanding, he enjoyed his tenure as Vice Chief. However after coming to Delhi, there was a moment when he was toying with the idea of putting in his papers, but better sense prevailed due to sane advice from his well wishers. As far as I remember he had a close knit group of friends, mostly Anglo-Indians and he often spoke about them very warmly. Except John Pereira 94, Dick Schunker 93, KK Nayyar 88 others Denis Pereira, Jack Shea, Eric Barboza, Fraser, Lunel, Guppy Gupta and Ram Tehiliani have left for heavenly abode. Of course he was very close to Montee Chatterjee, who was not only his Staff officer and Golf partner but close buddy though many years his junior .They all loved Ronnie Pereira for what he was.

Inter Services Cricket-77

I was in Delhi for a short break with Admiral and Mrs. Pereira in the autumn of 1977, when Admiral as Vice Chief was residing in 5 Moti Lal Nehru Marg, in Lutyens Complex, New Delhi. One of my regimental officers Captain KP Ramesh, was representing Northern Command Cricket Team in the Inter Services Championship being played at Air Force ground at Palam. Though it happened nearly 40 years ago, but I vividly remember KP Ramesh mentioning about some crises in the Navy team and ultimately Admiral came to their rescue. And one of their key players was flown in from IIT, Poona overnight but I was not privy to rest of the details.

I contacted Bhaskar Ranjan Sen and asked him if he could recall, who was the Captain of Navy Cricket Team in 1977/78? He said, yes, and promptly gave me the contact number of Commander Shambu Biswas, who was Captain at that time and now resides in Kolkata.

I called up Cdr Shambu and informed him that I am in the process of writing a book on Admiral Pereira and expectedly he was really delighted and said with so much of pride in his voice; **"what a great man"**. I reminded of the incident and how Admiral came to their rescue- he had a big laugh and asked me how do you remember? I said Sir, I happened to be in Delhi at that point in time. I requested him to please take your mind back 40 years and kindly relate the whole incident. Few weeks later he sent me mail and I also had the privilege to call him over for a meal in end March 2016, during his visit to Bagdogra.

Quote "Mike, what actually happened, I was the Captain of the Navy Cricket team and unfortunately I could muster only 10 players. I sent number of signals to Indian Navy Sports Control Board, Bombay, and FOC-in-C Western Naval Command but of no avail. I was in great dilemma with regards to the composition of the team. I mentioned about my predicament to Lt Vishram Naphade, 33rd NDA. He was chopper pilot and used to fly Admiral when he was FOC Southern Naval Areas in 1975 and he suggested that we should go and speak to the Admiral. I was very apprehensive, going to such a senior officer's residence and that too Vice Chief, at that time I had barely 4 years of service but Lt Naphade was very confident and said not to worry, let's give a try.

Same evening on his motor bike we drove to 5 Moti Lal Nehru Marg. Admiral himself came out to receive us and I was introduced by Naphade as the Captain of Navy Cricket team. Admiral asked me, son, what's the problem and before I could speak, he asked us about our drink, we both said Rum, he offered us and helped himself with Peter Scot whisky (I observed quite curiously that there was no Scotch in the chest, an extreme rarity at that level).

I told Admiral that despite my best efforts, I have been unable to compile a team and we require at least one player to complete the protocol, otherwise team participation is not possible in the tournament. He asked me the player's names and their ships. I gave him the names of 4 players' i.e.Lt Ved Prakash from Petya Class, Lt Pusalkar (surface ship?), Lt Venket Kumar (a submariner), Lt Cdr Chandershekhar attending Long Course at IIT, Poona. He immediately picked up the phone and spoke to Vice Admiral Rusi Gandhi, FOC-in-C Western Naval Command, Bombay. The conversation goes something like this; "Good Evening Rusi, I say, you can't spare Lts for my cricket team? Admiral Gandhi replied "says who" VCNS said- your Commanding Officers, they are not sparing officers to represent our team in the Inter Services Cricket Championship, I am told, the ships and submarine are at sea, I don't know how you do it , but I want these officers by 1100hrs in the morning and I authorize them their airfare. "Admiral Gandhi replied don't worry Ronnie, will be done". Those days only Captain and above were authorized to travel by air on temporary duty!

What followed was unprecedented in the history of the Indian Navy. The ships were ordered to close in the Bombay coast line and submarine which was snorting were asked to surface and do likewise. Choppers were sent from INS Kunjali and officers were airlifted from the ships and submarine and directly flown to Santa Cruz Airport. They were made to board the first flight to Delhi. Lt Chandershekhar was asked to proceed directly to Delhi and his air travel was also authorized. To my pleasant surprise all the 4 officers checked in at Central Vista Air Force Mess at Janpath around 2300 hrs the same evening, where the Navy team was staying. It was all ecstasy for the team, me in particular. Next day morning at 1100 hrs they were all in Vice Chief's office.

It is pertinent to mention that the team performed brilliantly and reached the finals after 20 years since 1957!!

Admiral told me that he will personally come to witness the matches and accordingly issued orders that at least 4 officers from each directorate to be present to cheer the team. One day while team was having lunch, he dropped into see what we were having; we quickly invited him to share the lunch with us. He was appalled to see the quality of the food (our good old packed lunch consisting of parathas, aloo gobi and pickle). He immediately summoned the Director of Training of Naval Headquarters and gave him a mouthful and instructed him to order Chicken Sandwiches, burger and soup from Wengers, Connaught Place for rest of the tournament.

"I don't think I will ever meet a person like Admiral Pereira, as for me he was Knight in Shining Armor".

Admiral came to witness the finals and also brought CNS Admiral Cursetji along to cheer the team!! **Unquote**

That was Ronnie P at his vintage best and always encouraged sportsmen to perform to the best of their abilities, never mind the outcome. When he saw KP Ramesh on the field, he would cheer him up too, knowing that he was from my Regiment.

China Town

I had come to Delhi to spend few days with Admiral in July 78; Admiral was alone as Mrs. Pereira had gone to Whitefield, Bangalore to start the construction of their 'Home'. One evening Admiral decided to watch a movie. In those days only few picture halls used to screen English movies; Chanakya, Revoli and Alankar. The programme was to go for late night show to see "China Town" starring Jack Nickilson and Fay Dunaway, which was running at Alankar cinema hall. As we were about to leave 5 MLN Marg, senior Topaas Madan Lal came and informed Admiral that Topaas Sham Singh's small daughter is running very high fever. Immediately Admiral asked him to get the child and Sham Singh and we drove straight to Central MI Room near Rashtrapati Bhavan. On reaching the MI Room Admiral introduced himself to the Duty NCO at the reception and asked for Duty Medical Officer. We waited 10 minutes and there were no sign of Duty MO! Now Admiral was slowly getting agitated and asked the NCO as to where the doctor was? And then barged into Duty MO office, doc was not in his chair, next he banged at toilet door, no response and then he kicked it open! In fact the doc was missing and the NCO was trying to cover his absence. After a while the doc appeared and Admiral gave him a mouthful; if you treat Vice Chief in this manner, I can well imagine how you must be dealing with my sailors?? The doc tried to mumble something; Admiral gave him dressing down and just cut him short and told him to attend to the child. Naturally we missed the beginning of the movie!

However, the matter did not end there as the over pampered doctor on duty went and complained to his superior and the matter was reported to the DGAFMS, that the Duty Officer has been humiliated in public. The DG went ahead and informed Gen Malhotra, COAS. When Admiral got to know about it, he went straight to DGAFMS office and gave him his piece of mind; that instead of apologizing and taking stern action against the erring doctor, you are trying to molly coddle him! What kind of message are you trying to send to the organization? Tell your officers to do their jobs with more responsibility. Admiral did not mince his words, but after that day no doctor ever misbehaved (particularly with the sailors) or left his place of duty!!

Visit to Mussoorie

The last time Admiral visited Mussoorie was in summers of 1953 after Staff College, and the last time he met his sister Masie was in June 1957, when the family got together after sad demise of their parents. So, in November 77 he made a trip to visit Hydrographic Institute located at Rajpur, Dehradun, which was headed by Admiral Fraser. From there Mussoorie is just 22 miles, after the visit he drove up the hill to meet Masie Gantzer. While he was there, he also had the opportunity to meet my parents at "Ockbrook", Masie Gantzer's beautiful cottage. My father told me that they were really taken in by Admiral's humility and moved to tears when Admiral holding my parents hands said; "Bouji and Biji, I have taken away your son!" My parents who were standing in front of him with folded hands cried when Admiral embraced them. It was indeed very touching moment. In fact my simple mother was in tears most of the time. I must thank Aunty May for this nice and touching gesture. That's the only time he met my mother, but my father did have another opportunity to meet him at 5 Moti Lal Nehru Marg in Nov 78, when the Govt announced his appointment as next CNS.

House Building Advance

By late 60's and early 70's, the bygone era of colonial bungalows with large compounds was rapidly on the decline. As it was financially not viable for the bourgeoning middle class, who by now preferred a newly introduced concept of residential complexes offering 2/3/4 BHK flats at comparatively reasonable cost and within the reach of middle class including officer's cadre in the services.

Commander Montee Chatterjee who was posted to Naval HQs in mid 70's decided to book a flat in a place called Saket, a suburb of New Delhi and paid Rs 10,000/- as Registration fee. After few years in 1978 when the construction of the flat was in final stages and almost ready for occupation, the builders asked the client to pay the balance amount prior to taking over. The total cost was Rs 87,000/- a huge amount in those days and to meet the requirement Montee Chatterjee had no option but to put in application for House Building Advance for Rs 70,000/-. The application duly signed by his Director Captain Madan Chopra was forwarded to Chief of Personnel (COP) branch. However, the application was rejected as there was no provision in the existing Regulations of the Government to sanction HBA for purchase of flats; the Regulations stated that the HBA could only be sanctioned for building / renovation of the house.

As the time was running out Montee Chatterjee was under great stress and he did not want to lose the flat. The builders wouldn't extend the dead line. During their next round of Golf, Montee game was out of sorts and Admiral noticed that his partner seems pre-occupied and his mind was not in the game which resulted in losing the round! Next day Admiral called up Montee and inquired if anything was bothering him. So Montee went to the Vice Chief's office and informed the Admiral about his predicament about the payment for the flat. His application for the loan has been turned down by the COP branch as there is no provision to sanction loan for purchase of flats, but only for building the house. Admiral was taken aback and said that's rather ridiculous and at that very moment he rang up Rear Admiral Ramesh Atre, Deputy Chief of Personnel, and asked him to come to his office to explain the issue . Rear Admiral Ramesh Atre informed the Admiral that he can't go against the existing rules on the subject as there will be audit objection later on. Admiral told Atre that it's absolutely unfair. In the present day environment majority of the officers at best can afford a flat only, particularly in metros! He directed Atre to immediately take up case with Ministry of Housing and Works as well as MOD and have the necessary amendment issued at the earliest.

In Montee Chatterjee words, **quote** "You know Mike, at the behest of Admiral within two weeks, all the paper work including Statement of Case and file pushing through two ministries was completed and a fresh Notification was issued by the Government of India with appropriate Amendment to extend HBA for purchase of the flat also and thus Admiral ensured, thereafter all officers desirous of purchasing flats will not face similar difficulty as I faced." **Montee Chatterjee looked up towards heaven and said, Ronnie P** thank you so much, wherever you are! Yes, he had tears in his eyes and so did I." **unquote**. Today, the market value of the flat is worth 3 crore!!

Kavita Chatterjee

In 78 Montee Chatterjee was serving in Directorate Management Services, Naval Headquarters. He narrated an incident involving his young daughter. **Quote** "I was the only Commander who was authorized a residential phone as I was heading the EDP Cell and was responsible for introducing computers in the Navy, otherwise only Captains and above were entitled for an official phone at their residences. One night at about 10pm I got a call and the unknown person spoke to me in a very rude manner and threatened to kidnap or harm my daughter Kavita, who was studying in 9th standard in Jesus and Mary Convent, and warned me of serious consequences. Naturally I got very worried as she used to travel in the school bus. Next day while playing Golf I informed Admiral about the call and was indeed worried about the safety of my daughter. After the round of Golf, Admiral, who was very fond of Kavita, immediately rang up the police commissioner and informed him about the incidence and the young girl, is being stalked and her life is in danger. You know Mike, more importantly, from next morning Sharmaji would bring Vice Chief's staff car to 78, Dhaula Kuan and drop my daughter to the school and then again pick her up after school at 2.30pm and this routine continued for three months!! Till Ronnie P was convinced that threat had disappeared. The point I want to highlight is that Ronnie P will not use staff car for Golf or personal activity but in this case he did not hesitate as he perceived it as a part of his Naval duties to safe guard life of his subordinate's daughter !!". Unquote

Unfortunately few months later the next incident was not only threat but ended up into **most heinous** crime committed by two notorious convicts.

Geeta And Sanjay Chopra

This horrific incident which occurred on 26 Aug 1978, was extremely tragic, traumatic and disturbing. It involved two young children of Captain Madan Chopra. Montee Chatterjee, who was involved in this incident, enumerated the sad contents of the episode as follows:-

Quote "Captain Madan Chopra, Director Management Services was two terms senior to me in the Academy and my boss. I used to 'Sir' him during office hours but were on first name basis off duty. Both of us were staying with our families in Dhaula Kuan Part 1, my house No was 78 facing the Golf Course and Captain Chopra was in 95, back to back houses and our children grew up together. I had a car, where as Madan Chopra didn't. One late evening there was knock on the door. Madan Chopra walked in looking very worried and asked for my car, I said no problems, but what happened? Then he told me that his daughter Geeta had an appointment with AIR for a programme and I sent Sanjay along with her, they left the house at 5pm and now it is 9pm and there is neither any news about them nor any call, the moment I heard that I said I will accompany you. As we came out of Dhaula Kuan, we took the Ridge Road, for some unknown reason he asked me to head for Budha Jayanti Park, after about 1km there was total darkness and nobody on the narrow road, and he asked me to turn back, as I reversed my car the rear wheel got off the road and was running free, somehow we pulled up the car to the road and then we went to Lok Nayak Hospital in Karol Bagh to check if they had any accident case in the Emergency Ward. We were told no such case has been reported. I clearly remember seeing a tall and thin chap having his head bandaged, and after that we came back home and there was still no news of children.

I had already called up Admiral before we left the house, and he immediately called up Commissioner Delhi Police Dr KC Paul. Not only that he deputed me officially to investigate the case and liaison with the police. We were worried and didn't know whether they were kidnapped or murdered.

Next morning Madan Chopra informed me that there is a famous Baba on the way to Faridabad, who can tell us exactly where the kids are, so we drove to a dirty looking small village and as we entered I was surprised to see a long queue of posh cars of rich businessmen and all waiting to meet the Baba, who would tell them about auspicious time to start their business ventures etc. Anyway I walked up to the person who was co-ordinating the meetings with Baba. We informed him that we are from Indian Navy and gave him the background of our visit, and it is urgent to meet the Baba at the earliest. He let us jump the queue and were in front of the Baba, the first question he asked the children's names, then he asked to spell the daughter's name, I said 'Gita' but Madan Chopra immediately corrected me and said; 'Geeta'. Baba did some jiggry pockery and made some noises and said, they are between line joining Agra and Hissar and look North of the road and not South and added that they are alive. After giving some 'Dakshana'(money) to him we came out more confused and didn't know where to go?

Next evening i.e. 28th Aug we got information from Commissioner that police has found two dead bodies near the road in Budha Jayanti Park, one girl and one boy. We immediately rushed to the spot. I got out of the car and saw the mutilated bodies of the children, the boy had stab wounds all over the body and the girl body too was disfigured beyond words and they must have raped her before killing her as her clothes were thrown all over- it was terrible scene, and I went back to the car and told Madan, you cannot see the bodies. He insisted but I didn't let him and asked the police to take the bodies for postmortem and they took the bodies to the mortuary; so the Baba told us lies, he was a fraud. The children were murdered the previous evening.

The funeral was arranged next day. At the funeral site Madan ran and saw his son's face on the pyre and broke down and sat on the ground sobbing; Mike, it was most heart rendering site.

Now the sequence of events - both Geeta and Sanjay were standing at Dhaula Kuan and thumped a lift to All India Radio, Parliament Street. What these two guys had done- they had removed both door and window handles from inside, they took them to Ridge Road towards Lok Nayak Hospital- after realizing that they have been trapped inside the car, a scuffle ensued and Geeta was shouting and hitting at the rear glass- a Sardar, Inderjit Singh from Delhi Cantt on a scooter saw something abnormal and followed the car, but lost it near Lok Nayak Hospital, but he had noted the car No and informed the police, that something is not right.

Now look at the **co-incidences**, firstly Madan asked me to go towards Ridge Road, secondly where I reversed the car, the bodies were barely 20 yards from that spot, next we went to Lok Nayak Hospital to check Emergency ward and there Billa was standing getting his head dressed. After the car was recovered by the police, they traced the name of owner Mr. Jain of Hissar! Baba mentioned Hissar, but Mr. Jain informed the police that his car was in his house and he never went to Delhi in last few days. Anyhow the police went to Chandni Chowk area, where 2 or 3 shops paint car number plates. The police showed them the plate and asked if anybody came to get this number painted. One of the young guys said; Sahib, wait, I normally write No's on the wall and sure enough he saw the same No on the wall and described that two chaps had come, one of them tall and thin. When police recovered the car, they noticed the handles inside the car were missing, it was peculiar modus-oprandi and then Bombay police was contacted, where it was reported that some time back, few Arab tourists were picked up, later looted and killed and same modus-oprandi was used, they knew it was Ranga and Billa. However, they kept evading the police.

It was only after few days in early September, when Lance Naik AV Shetty of 237 Field Artillery Regiment (which was later commanded by

Col Robin Chatterjee, son of Captain Montee Chatterjee) while returning from leave and was travelling in a Military Compartment. When the train reached Agra, two guys got into the compartment and when asked for their identity, a scuffle ensued and Shetty recognized them from their picture in the Newspaper. When the train reached New Delhi both Billa and Ranga were handed over to the police. On interrogation it was revealed that both of them were involved in the murder of Geeta and Sanjay Chopra and eventually in Jan 82 they were hanged to death.

Paris

It was terrible experience for Madan and his wife. Next year on 1st March 79 Admiral took over as CNS, and I joined CNS office as his Secretary in mid 1980. One day Madan came to my house and said, Montee, I want to meet the Admiral and request for posting abroad, for change of scene; can you help me? I said of course and arranged a meeting with CNS. Next day Madan walked into CNS office and after hearing Madan, Admiral in my presence called up Vice Admiral Manohar Awati, Chief of Personnel and told him **I want Madan out of the country- is there any vacancy?** Awati said- yes, Sir, Naval Attaché, Paris , so Ronnie P told him send Madan to Paris- Awati replied Sir, it's an Executive Officer job and Madan Chopra is from Supply Branch. **Ronnie P said doesn't matter, you change the criteria and send him and that's how Madan Chopra was posted to Paris**. That was the greatness of Ronnie P and he could not be hindered by Rules and Regulations where he thought it is his bounden duty to look after the welfare of his subordinates. Considering the ordeal they faced there could not have been more deserving case.

Finally Mike' let me tell you that even now, for every meal food is cooked for four and table laid for four people- though only two eat. It has been one of the most horrific and traumatic experience for any parents! Really sad, it was Mrs. Chopra who was the stronger of the two. Even after 38 years my hair stands thinking of that episode".**Unquote.**

I remember in Dec 80 Admiral speaking to me about their move to Paris. He said son, "it was one of the most horrific incidents and my heart goes to the grieved parents. You are the closest to a son we have and we shudder to think if something happens to you and I can well imagine **their grief and sadness on losing both children in such a tragic manner** and yes, when Montee brought Madan to me, I had no choice but to **help him to mitigate their pain to whatever extent I possibly could.** There was opposition for his posting as we were in the final stages of major deals like Submarine and French aircraft but **I said ,doesn't matter he must leave the country at earliest and Paris was the best location for change of scene.**

My Posting

I had already put in more than 4 ½ years of service and within 6 months I would be due for a posting on staff. I was extremely keen to go to Indian Military Academy as a Platoon Commander. In Aug 78, on my specific request to the Commandant, Opu Sengupta, I was detailed to attend 'Platoon Weapons' course at Mhow. It's an eight weeks course and conducted for officers of other arms (less Infantry). For Armoured Corps officers it is a mandatory course in case you wish to be considered for posting as Platoon Commander at Indian Military Academy, Dehradun. At that juncture in my short career I was very keen to be posted to IMA as Instructor as I thought it could provide me an opportunity to train and motivate in two years tenure, may be 80-100 cadets into becoming good officers, albeit a small dream! The course is conducted under the aegis of Infantry School, Mhow. August and September are best months in Mhow, which is located 23kms South of Indore, Madhya Pardesh at an altitude of 2000 feet. I attended the course primarily with the singular aim of getting myself posted as Platoon Commander at IMA, Dehradun. On my way to Mhow I stopped for couple of days at 5 MLN Marg with Admiral and Mrs. Pereira and I informed Admiral that I will need his help to get me posted to IMA at a later date. He said it shouldn't be a problem and he will have word with 'OP'- Gen OP Malhotra, Chief of Army Staff.

In his letter 23 Aug 78- **quote** *"My dear Mike- just had your letter from Mhow this afternoon and before I get bogged down in work, I thought I will quickly answer. I am glad that you have settled in quickly and got down to the course. It is also nice to know that it isn't too difficult, which makes your 'AXI' grading somewhat easier to pick up- good for you. Please give Dalal my good wishes. I remember him well from the Academy and I also met him when I went to the IMA on one occasion to witness the passing out parade- well son, I will close. Work hard and do your best. If you get your 'AX' we will all be very proud of you, and I have strong feeling that you will make it this time. Glad to know that you are off hooch!! affly Unc Ron"*. **Unquote** .

The course got over in the 2nd week of Oct and on my way back to Pathankot again I spent couple of days with Admiral and Mrs. P. Needless to say, they were really happy that at last I was able to secure 'AXI' grading for the first time in any professional course and also informed him that it will certainly help me for posting to IMA after a year or so.

On 3rd Feb 1979 I took over as 'Adjutant' of my Regiment, I proudly wrote to Admiral that for me it was a great honor and am really going to work hard and look after my Thambies (South Indian Troops). He replied in his first letter after taking over as CNS, 16 Mar 79, **quote** *"I am glad that you are enjoying your job as Adjutant. It is interesting assignment as you are virtually equivalent of 'Executive' Officer of a ship who runs the whole thing. It therefore, calls for lot of thought and initiative and it is certainly excellent experience for you. Do it well son, I am sure you can".* **Unquote.**

As I have mentioned earlier that Admiral always used to tell me to remember names of all your subordinates, particularly important appointments at JCO's/NCO's level in the unit with whom you will be interacting for day to day functioning- both officially and unofficially. So the first action was to get the list of names of all Regimental appointments, drivers of all important vehicles, and office runners, the list ran into 60 odd names but managed to memorize all names within two weeks. It worked wonders and the response was quick and effective. I mentioned this to Admiral in one of my letters and in reply he wrote in his letter 6th July 79 **quote** *"I am glad you are enjoying your new job. Its great experience being Adjutant and you will learn a great deal of organization and staff works in this assignment.* ***As you say it is hard work but that is something which has to be accepted, as you slowly climb the ladder of promotion".*** **Unquote.**

Letter to Commandant

In end March 79 Col AK Sengupta, our Commandant called me in his office and showed me a letter which he had just received from the Admiral after taking over as CNS. He asked me to sit down and go through the contents of the letter. I clearly remember; **quote** "My dear Colonel, I am sure you are aware of my relationship with Captain Mike Bhalla, he is the son to us we never had, and both my wife and self consider him as a part of our family. My earnest request to you is that Mike should be treated like any other officer in the Regiment and he should never be given any preferential treatment because of his closeness to us. He should be kept on a tight leash and kicked if so required. Also he should not to be given any casual leave till I personally request you to do so.

Please do drop in whenever you visit Delhi next, with our warm regards- RL Pereira". **Unquote.**

I gave the letter back to my Commandant and he said, Mike what a great man, here everybody is doing backseat driving for their kith and kin and you have a man like Admiral who writes to the CO and asks him, if required, to kick your backside !! He had a good laugh.

In fact it had exactly opposite affect and I was never refused leave and Col Opu Sengupta was indeed very kind to me throughout his tenure till he got posted to Staff College as Instructor in Dec 79.

Years later I mentioned about it to Admiral and asked what made him write that letter. He said, son ,you were young and immature and I did not want my position to go to your head and start misbehaving, so to keep you grounded and for your own good, I thought that I must write to your Commandant and I honestly did not think that he will show this letter to you. I told him, I was his Adjutant and very close to CO and maybe he showed this letter in good faith. Secondly, he never expected to receive a letter from a Chief and that too of other Services? It was a high point in his career!! Any way I thanked Admiral for that letter as it had diametrically opposite effect, and he just laughed off!

CNS – ADMIRAL IN THE MAKING

Early Years in Navy

On 25th May 1943, during World War -2, Ronnie Pereira was commissioned in the Royal Indian Navy (Executive Branch) and saw active service in a Gun Boat in Burma and Malaya in 1943-45. Thereafter, he continued at sea with an amphibious task group based in Iraq till 1946. Next year in 1947 he was nominated to attend Long Gunnery Course at UK. In 1951/52 he served as an instructor in the make shift Gunnery School in Cochin. Then he was nominated to attend Defense Services Staff College Course 6 at Wellington. In mid 50s, he was Fleet Gunnery Officer and thereafter in 1956 he took over as OC Gunnery School. He commanded INS KUTHAR in 1962-64. He also held very important appointments of COMRAX Barracks in Bombay, Director of Weapon and Equipment, Director Combat Policy and Tactics (DCPT) at Naval Hqs and later as NOIC Bombay in late 60's.

Promotion Board -1965

However, Ronnie Pereira journey on the ladder of promotion was not a smooth sailing! He was passed over for the rank of Captain in his first look. His very close friend Admiral KK Nayyar narrated, **quote** "In 1965 I was posted at

Naval Hqs as Deputy Director Naval Signal in the rank of newly promoted Commander and Ronnie P, who was senior most Commander was Director of Weapon and Equipment. Our offices were in 'A' Block and we shared a very close relationship. One day Ronnie P walked into my office looking rather perturbed and said; Krish here is my bloody resignation letter and I am going to leave the Navy, as he had not cleared the promotion board from Commander to Captain. I told him to relax and have coffee. I categorically told him; you will not do any such thing. Firstly you have already lost part of your left lung and on top of that you are penniless and what will you do outside? Phyllis who was working at Bombay can't possibly look after you too on her pay, so you just cool down and have patience and I am sure you will make it in the next board. He reluctantly agreed to my advice and sure enough after six months he was cleared and subsequently given the command of INS Delhi and thereafter was no stopping him from going up the ladder and lo and behold he eventually reached the pinnacle of his career. We remained very close friends right till the end". **Unquote**

At NDA in 1972 he once told me; son, Commodore is a very senior rank, equivalent to Brigadier in the Army and I am quite sure in my mind this is my last rank and from here I will move to Whitefield, Bangalore!! I just kept quiet as I was too young to understand his logic and thought in my mind, that he certainly had the personality and professional competence to go up the ladder. However, 44 years later speaking to one of my course mates Murlidharan who retired as Vice Admiral, **quote** "that Dep Com was partially right when he said this is my last posting because if you remember Colonel HKK Shukla, the previous Deputy went on retirement and took up re-employment in Hqs 19 Infantry Division at Baramulla. With that analogy Ronnie P could have gone home, but Ronnie did so well during his tenure at NDA, that Admiral Charlie Nanda, CNS, had no hesitation in promoting him to Rear Admiral and sending him as Fleet Commander, Eastern Fleet and from there it was no looking back".**Unquote.**

Here I must mention that Captain Montee Chatterjee, though many years junior in Service was indeed very close to the Admiral. He was his permanent golfing buddy and also served as his Secretary when Admiral was CNS in 1980/81. He had something very amusing to share about "**Ronnie's promotion curve**", when I met him in Guwahati in Dec 2015.

Quote "Mike, I must tell you that Ronnie P was very close to me and like my "Godfather". At every promotion over the years Ronnie P would call me up and say; Monts, I have been promoted to Captain and going to take over INS Delhi and with this I have achieved my lifelong ambition to command a "Capital ship", am sure this is the last rank. Next when he got his posting to NDA in late 1970, he called up and said; Monts I have been promoted to Commodore and going to NDA as Deputy Commandant and after that I am sure I will head for Bangalore. Come Feb 1973; Monts, I have been promoted to RA and going to take over Eastern Fleet and this is definitely end of the line. In Feb 76 he was promoted to VA; Monts, I have been promoted to Vice Admiral and going to take over as FOC-in-C Western Naval Command and **this is pinnacle of my career!". Unquote**

Naval Headquarters - 77

Actually it seemed prophetic, when within a year or so Admiral was moved to Naval Headquarters as Vice Chief in April 1977. In those times traditionally Vice Chief meant, going home – bye, bye to the services!!

No doubt Admiral was taken aback as the move was like a bolt from the blue as the normal tenure was 3 years and needless to say he was disappointed by this unexpected turn of events at this late stage in his career. He requested to the CNS, Admiral Cursetji that he should be permitted to complete his tenure of 3 years. Prior to him Cursetji, Kohli, Nanda and Chatterji had 2 to 3 years tenure and even before that in late 50's and early 60's as FOC of Indian Fleet and Bombay Area Admirals Soman and Katari had full tenure and later Tony Jain held the appointment for 5 years!! Then why this change now?? Admiral had initiated large number of major projects i.e. Modernization of Bombay Dockyards and construction of high rise towers for family accommodation at Navy Nagar, and was keen to push them to their final stages. However, Admiral's request was turned down by Defence Minister, Mr. Bansi Lal, who in any case was bending backwards to please Sanjay Gandhi. It is a fact that during "**Emergency**", Sanjay Gandhi virtually ran the government and exercised unconstitutional authority including meddling with "**MATTERS MILITARY**". It was evident that Sanjay Gandhi had a role to play in this unfair and manipulative move. The previous year during the "Review of the Fleet" in Jan 76, there were serious crises due to Sanjay Gandhi presence and it is believed that his official status and credentials were questioned and voiced by many including Ronnie P. However, Bansi Lal insisted that Sanjay Gandhi be accommodated to attend the official lunch on board INS Vikrant, which as per Vice Admiral Dick Schunker, who as Chief of Staff, Western Naval Command and Chief organizer said, **quote** "it entailed changing the seating plan! Many eye brows were raised" **unquote**. It was not taken kindly by Bansi Lal and Sanjay Gandhi, and to make matters worse later in 1976 when Ronnie P was the C-in-C Western Naval Command, did not permit

Sanjay Gandhi to board Navy helicopter from Colaba to Santa Cruz airport!! Apparently Sanjay Gandhi took umbrage; how dare anybody question his authority?? Those were the **"dark days of Emergency"** and Sanjay Gandhi was ruling the roost. Indeed there were no valid, cogent and legitimate reasons to move out Admiral to Naval Headquarters. The question remains unanswered to date!!

A similar incident happened during Army Commanders conference when Bansi Lal brought Sanjay Gandhi along, at that juncture it was Lt Gen Inder Gill who questioned his presence and walked out!

Therefore in early 1977 Admiral who had barely completed a year as C-in-C received orders to move to Delhi and take over as Vice Chief of Naval Staff. He was succeeded by none other than the establishment's **"blue eyed boy"** Vice Admiral Rusi Gandhi to take over as C-in-C Western Naval Command , which in any case the Government and Admiral Cursetji were very keen to move Rusi Gandhi to Bombay in Feb 76. But at that juncture Admiral Kohli, CNS put paid to their unworthy intentions by posting Ronnie P to Bombay, just couple of days before he retired.

No doubt, move of Rustom Khushuro Shapoorjee Gandhi popularly known as "Rusi" Gandhi to Bombay was shrouded with mystery? Who was behind this unfair and manipulative move? Firoze Gandhi connection (both Rajiv and Sanjay Gandhi used to address Rusi Gandhi as **"Rusi Uncle"**!!). Or could it be Lord Mountbatten's intervention for his erstwhile Aide? Lord Mountbatten had very close relations with Nehru family. Whatever may be the reason, the move was against the norms of Services and **politically motivated.** It was an open secret in those days, that the Navy had two prominent lobbies- RC (Roman Catholics) vs Parsi. It is evident that Parsi lobby had upper hand at that point in time. **But just yet!**

Therefore, the move at this juncture had very clear intentions; push Ronnie P out of the way and make Rusi Gandhi the next Chief of Naval Staff. Traditionally the gateway to CNS office was invariably via Bombay- **foregone conclusion!**

It is pertinent to mention here that the only other likely candidate for next CNS, Rear Admiral Kirpal Singh was passed over for the rank of Vice Admiral and proceeded on retirement on 31st March 1977. With Ronnie P and Kirpal Singh out of the way , the "coast was clear" for Rusi Gandhi's elevation to CNS !!.

Famous axiom "**man proposes, God disposes**"- yes, however, a different narrative emerged on 24th March 1977!

Destiny

But destiny had something else in store for Ronnie P. Probably there was a "Guardian angel" protecting him; it had to be as he had been such a righteous human being throughout his life and always treaded narrow and straight path as per the will of the LORD. Admittedly "Divine Intervention".

Come 18th January 1977, Mrs Indira Gandhi released all political prisoners and announced fresh General Elections for March 77.

In the ensuing Lok Sabha election held in March 77, the Congress Party was routed and Janata Party came to power with Morarji Desai as the Prime Minister and Emergency was officially revoked on 23rd March. Babu Jagjivan Ram was given two portfolios of Deputy Prime Minister and Defense Minister. **The whole scenario changed diametrically!**

When I visited Delhi in July 77, the senior Topaas Madan Lal told me; Sir, as per the galley rumours in the Navy (langar gup in Army) - as soon as Congress went out of power, it is believed that Admiral Rusi Gandhi remarked; "that his chances of becoming Chief have vanished in the thin air" and words to that effect. He probably saw the writing on the wall and come Nov 1978, Ronnie P name was announced as "Chief Designate" to succeed Admiral Cursetji. The Janata Government was in power from 24 March 77 to 29 July 79 (two years and 126 days) - adequate time to appoint Ronnie P as CNS.

Nobody can fight "DESTINY".

Hazaribagh 1930's

In late 30's Babu Jagjivan Ram was arrested and held as political prisoner in Hazaribagh jail. Admiral's father Major JM Pereira was the Jail Superintendent. An upright man, he was very considerate towards the prisoners. Babuji a man of great intellect never forgot this good gesture of Maj Pereira.

In 1930's political prisoners were imprisoned in what was known as "political camp" established in Hazaribagh. In those days the Britishers would invariably appoint a senior Indian officer from the Medical Services as Jail Superintendent to look after the political prisoners. The Britishers were very cruel towards senior Congress leaders such as Babuji, Dr Rajindra Prasad (first President of India) and Jaya Prakash Narayan by denying them to indulge in any form of mental activities, thus keeping their mind totally blank with the aim of weakening their "will" to fight the Britishers politically. However, they were never harmed physically. In fact on arrival in the jail, they were weighed and proper medical record was maintained. By the time they were released from the prison, most of them would have gained weight considerably!

Major Pereira being a true Indian found loop holes to bend the law by smuggling in Spinning Wheels and allowing the prisoners to make yarn out of silk worms and also made arrangements for local newspaper and other literature to keep them abreast with the political situation and thus helped to remain mentally active and strong. All in all he was genuinely good to the prisoners in those difficult days.

Babu Jagjivan Ram -1969

An amazing but true incident took place in Mussoorie in 1969 with Mrs Masie Gantzer, eldest sister of Admiral, who had settled there since 1940. Being one of the senior citizen of Mussoorie, she was always invited to attend important civil functions. The incident was narrated to me by Masie Gantzer herself in 1972.

Quote "some time in summer of 1969, Babuji, who was a minister in Indira Gandhi cabinet, paid an official visit to Mussoorie. A civic reception was organized in honour of Babuji, where all senior government officials and distinguished citizens were also invited. When I was introduced to Babuji as Mrs Masie Gantzer, Babuji stopped for a moment and then asked; were you married to Mr Joe Gantzer, Resettlement Officer of Parganas Santana at Dumka? I said yes, Babuji next question was; are you daughter of Major JM Pereira? I said yes, he then instantaneously held both my hands and took me to the sofa in the centre of the hall, where he sat down with me for rest of the evening regaling stories of his struggle and days in Hazaribagh jail about 30 years ago and how good my father was to all of them and particularly to the political prisoners for which he was always grateful. To be honest my eyes filled up with pride to hear about my father. Mike it was at this juncture Babuji got to know that Major Pereira's youngest son, Ronnie, was a Captain in the Indian Navy". **Unquote.**

Nine years later in November 1978, when the new Chief of Naval Staff was to be selected, Babuji as Defence Minister had no hesitation whatsoever to nominate Ronnie Pereira as "Chief Designate"- **What a poetic justice?** - There were pulls and pushes as also external pressure, so much so Lord Mountbatten wrote to Prime Minister Morarji Desai recommending his ex-Flag Lt Rusi Gandhi to be considered as next Chief! The letter was forwarded to Babuji, who remarked, that he may be Mountbatten's good man but for me Major Pereira was a true Indian, in any case Ronnie P was the senior most.

It was indeed an act of gratitude toward Major JM Pereira.

In December 78, Mrs. Masie Gantzer went to see Babuji at his official residence at 6 Krishna Menon Road to convey her thanks. All Babuji said; Masie, firstly Ronnie deserved it, secondly he was the senior most Vice Admiral as per the date of commission and thirdly and more importantly, holding her hands he said; Masie, it is all because of Almighty, he controls the strings. Masie was overwhelmed with emotion and it brought tears to her eyes, the tears of joy to see her kid brother reach the top of his profession.

Somewhere up there Major Pereira must be smiling. The wheel of fortune had turned fully.

Chief Designate

On 27th November Admiral was informed by the Defence Secretary Mr. Bannerji sometime before noon that his name has been cleared for "Chief Designate" by the Cabinet Committee of the Appointments, but requested Admiral not to divulge this information to anybody before it is officially announced on All India Radio at 2 pm News. Expectedly the first person he wanted to share the News was with Mrs. Pereira, who was away at Whitefield, Bangalore for construction of their house. Apparently she was on the site and he could only speak to her when she came to Aunty Dorothy Shea's house for lunch break at about 1.30 pm. Meanwhile Admiral called up his golf buddy and good friend Montee Chatterjee, with whom he had in fact played a round of golf the same morning and said; Montee, believe it or not I have made it to the top of the tree!! Exactly at 2.10 pm that afternoon I received a trunk call from Army Hqs in 16 Cavalry officer's mess at Pathankot. Mess waiter Srinivasan came running to my room to inform that there is trunk call for me from Army Hqs, I immediately sensed that it must be from Admiral and I ran as fast as I could to the phone and heard Commander Krishnan

Secretary to Vice Chief on the other end and he said Mike speak to the Boss. In few seconds Admiral was on the line and said, son, I have made it - I shouted **Chiiieeeef!**- yes, my son, and it took me 35 years to reach here. I was delirious with excitement and happiness and told him I will be on the first train to Delhi. I was on cloud nine!!

Incidently Mr. GM Kapur, General Manager, Northern Railways had come to our regiment to meet his young brother Major BM Kapur and was leaving the same evening by his Saloon to Delhi. I got myself a lift by buying a second class ticket. Armed with few Rum bottles I reached next morning at 5 Moti Lal Nehru Marg. As Mrs. Pereira wasn't there and Admiral had left for office, so I decided to celebrate with the staff - Senior Topaas Madan Lal and Sham Singh, Stewarts Shardha and James and Cook Negi. We all drank to glory and last thing I remember before I passed out that I was being carried by the staff to my room. It was about 6.30 pm when Admiral came to the room with a glass of strong coffee and woke me up and said get ready son, lots of guest are expected soon. I got up and hugged him as hard as I could and was so happy for him. Because at one time in my presence, Aunty Phyll almost convinced him to leave the Navy after he was unceremoniously moved out of Bombay, but Admiral said now that I have come so close after putting in 34 years of service, so let me stay on and try my luck, though he had actually given up deep in his heart but then few months down the line the whole scenario changed!

I believe the previous day more than 100 people came to congratulate Admiral and there was no space for car parking inside 5 MLN Marg and cars had to be parked outside on the road. All ex Chiefs including AK Chatterji, SK Kohli, Nanda and Admiral Cursetji had come to congratulate him.

At about 7pm people started to troop in, those scenes were very touching. I vividly remember Commander Shyam Rattan Verma, Sport anchor on DD walked in and physically lifted Admiral and with tears flowing down his cheeks said; "Sir, I told you in 1954 that one day you will become CNS and that day has dawned and my wish fulfilled. God is great and Navy is simply fortunate to have a man of your stature at the helm". How happy he was? It is seen to be believed. Even today after 38 years those words ring in my ears and my eyes swell up!

There was his long time golf partner and cousin Denis Pereira with his beautiful and famous daughter Valleri Pereira and her husband actor Jalal

Agha. Captain Reggi Sahwney who was married to Admiral's cousin Phyllis and was the first Deputy Commandant of NDA in 1950-52. Ex Chief of Air Staff ACM Malgoankar, crickter Abbas Ali Baig, many senior officers from all services, Ambassadors and their reps from number of embassies.

The reason for so much happiness was that Ronnie P was one of the few officers with strong sense of conviction and integrity to have reached the top. It is people like Manakshaw and him who were fortunate to have beaten the system, otherwise officers of their reputation and honest approach couldn't have gone beyond the dizzy heights of Major or Lt Commander!! They both continue to be ICONS for the future generations.

So much so in 1989, the Navy had conducted the survey from the present generation of officers- Who do you think in your opinion was the best CNS the Navy ever had? Yes, it was none other than Admiral Ronnie Pereira with overwhelming votes of over 80%. Ronnie was CNS from 1st March 1979 to 28th Feb 1982.

In his letter dated 19th Mar 1987 Admiral wrote, quote "*Son, as I look back at my career, there were numerous occasions when I was sure, it was the end of the line. As Commander in 'G' school, when I argued incessantly with my Commodore-in-Charge. As a Captain, at sea , on one occasion , when I had Delhi in problem in confined waters, thinking that I could do something which was not at all possible. As a RA when my C-in-C couldn't see eye to eye even for 5 minutes and this lasted for almost two years while I was with the Eastern Fleet. As C-in-C Western Naval Command, when I was sure that, that was the end of the line, though I was sure that I was going to thoroughly enjoy the assignment. However, I survived, and ultimately got to the top of the tree and for that I have great deal to thank God for. So my son, just take on what comes to you, and provided you do it with good professionalism , zeal and enthusiasm , it will always pay dividends.*" **Unquote**

With all humility, apart from Mrs. Pereira and Montee Chatterjee perhaps I was the closest to Admiral, who poured his heart out to me in his letters and I saw him from very close quarters for over 22 years. He was a hardnosed Deputy Commandant to a terrified cadet; an adoring and considerate father to a son; an **ICONIC** Chief to a young Cavalry officer, in addition friend, philosopher and guide to me. At times I used to wonder that how a human being can be so driven by righteousness, probity, honesty and integrity. He NEVER wavered from his chosen path, whatever be the consequences till his last breath.

> As I look back on my career, there were numerous occasions when I was sure, I was at the end of the line. As a commander at B's School, when I argued heavily with the Commander-in-Charge. As a Captain at sea, on one occasion, when I had delvi in problems in confined waters trying to do something that was not at all possible. As an R.A, when my CNS & I were not see eye to eye for over 5 months, that lasted for almost 2 years while I was with Eastern Fleet. As CinC Western Naval Command, when I was sure that that was the end of the line, though I was sure I was going to the end of the assignment. However, I survived, & thoroughly enjoyed the assignment, & ultimately got to the top of the tree, & for that I have a great deal to thank God for. So, my son, just take on what comes to you, & provided you do it with good professionalism, zeal & enthusiasm, it will always pay dividends.

Parents Influence

His eldest sister Masie Gantzer told me, **quote** "you know son, I see so much of my father in Ron and he has inherited his complete personality as Ron grew under the long shadow of my father. When Ron went to North Point in Jan 1932, he was hardly 8 ½ years old and by then my father had an "aura" around him. My father was a man of rigid and uncompromising integrity. My husband Joe (26 years older) was contemporary of my father, though 7 years younger to my father; he was also a man of very high integrity and held my father in great esteem and respect. In fact both of them were awarded MBE (Member of the Most Excellent Order of the British Empire) by the British Government for their outstanding service to the Crown.

My parents were very religious and devout Christians. Ron grew up in clean environment bereft of any malicious or manipulative tendencies. My mother who was of Irish descent had great influence on Ron in his childhood and being the youngest in the family of four and 14 years junior to my eldest brother, Arthur. Naturally Ron was very intimately attached to my mother;

he was in fact "Apple of her Eye". My dear mother was an "Angel" and taught Ron the difference between right and wrong, good and bad and always told him to do the right thing whatever be the consequences or personal sacrifice. That was the beginning of his character building which was as prominent in his personality as he went along in his life. I vividly remember an incident in 1930, when once late in the night there was a knock on the door and as my father opened the door, he saw an old man standing with his folded hands and said in shivering voice that his wife has been taken ill and requested my father to come and attend to her. My father took out the car as the old man's hut was some distance away. When he returned late into the night, my mother inquired about the woman and said I hope you did not take any fee, my father replied; no, darling, they were too poor to pay. Ron was 7 years old and this incident had deep influence on him and that's why he grew up to be such a kind human being. "**Unquote**

However, the fundamental difference was that Admiral's father lived in an environment of 20's, 30's, 40's when society at large respected "human values". The greed and desires were minimal, whereas by the time Admiral reached the higher echelons of service in mid 70's, the environment sadly was totally hostile to "human values". There was rampant corruption at all levels of society. He had to deal with corrupt politicians, wily and manipulative bureaucrats and still worse increasing personal ambitions and jealousies within the services itself, where everyone was bending backwards to keep the powers that be on their right side just to garner some favours post retirement, such as gubernatorial jobs etc.

Notwithstanding Admiral never compromised on his principles and stood his ground what he perceived was fair and just and in the interest of his beloved Navy. He was symbol of probity and integrity for the generations to come.

Chief of Naval Staff

After taking over as Chief of Naval Staff on 1st March 1979, I still remember his initials words in his interview with Doordarshan, **quote** "Human being is most vital factor both in peace and war. His welfare and well being will be uppermost in my mind". **Unquote**

In words of Admiral KK Nayyar, **quote** "Ronnie P was the greatest leader the Navy ever had and the men simply loved him. He never compromised on the interest of the Navy with Government or bureaucrats. His concern for men was unmatched and he had very close relations with the officers and above all "**integrity**" was something to learn from him". **Unquote**

Similar sentiments were echoed when I spoke to Admiral Ram Tehiliani, Admiral VS Shekhawat, Admiral Sushil Kumar and Admiral Madhvendra Singh – **a man of great integrity-**

1st March 79

Commander Montee Chatterjee, who was posted at Naval Hqs in 1979, narrated a very touching incident, **quote** "Mike, on the evening of 1st Mar 79, at about 7.30 pm there was a knock at the door of my residence at Officers Colony, Dhaulakuan. I went out to check and there I saw Sharmaji, driver of CNS Staff Car and I inquired what brought him to my house? He softly said; Chief Sahib is sitting in the car! I immediately went out to meet the Admiral and wished him Good Evening Sir. Admiral asked; Montee can I come inside? I said, of course Sir, the honor is all mine, please Sir. Admiral came inside and sat on the sofa and asked me to fix a drink for him - Old Monk rum with water. He then asked me to switch on the TV and tune in Doordarshan No 2 channel. In those times DD had only two channels! Same morning after Handing/Taking over ceremony, Admiral was interviewed by Doordarshan and the crew had informed him that the interview will be telecasted on No 2 channel at 8pm. We were joined by my wife and Sharmaji, who sat on the cane stool to watch the interview. After about an hour Admiral profusely thanked my wife and self and departed.

The point I want to highlight here is, that **Ronnie P did not own a TV at home**. Mike, what an amazing human being- no pretence whatsoever, down to earth and humble" **Unquote**

Staff Car

Admiral was very particular and unrelenting about using staff car for personal activities. Admiral KK Nayyar remembers, **quote** "I was posted as ACNS Lands in Naval Hqs and Ronnie was Vice Chief. Sometime in Sep 1978 we were invited to German Embassy for dinner. I was driving with my wife in our car. At the traffic lights, my wife remarked; I think I saw Ronnie on a scooter, to which I answered what nonsense you must be mistaken. Sure enough some time later as we were having a drink, a scooter entered the embassy premises and who do we see but our Ronnie Pereira!! Needless to say we were all taken aback- Vice Chief on a scooter? Never heard or seen anything like this before. Anyway next morning I barged into Vice Chief's office and told him; Sir, are you out of your mind? Coming to an embassy on a scooter? He softly replied; Krish, what else I could do? I have already disposed off my car to raise money for the construction of the house and I don't want to use staff car for private activities. I told him in no uncertain terms that you were not invited by your Uncle, you were the official guest of the German Ambassador's but he won't relent" **Unquote.**

In Nov 78 when I had gone to Delhi after the announcement of "Chief Designate", two days later we decided to play Golf at Army Golf Course, Dhaulakuan. We both took a taxi and went to the course. After playing nine holes we came out and were looking for a cab but couldn't get any, and then we started to walk towards Dhaulakuan roundel. I remember carrying the golf bag and Admiral walking in his Golf shoes with hand towel hanging from his back pocket. Those days the traffic wasn't much and as we approached the main gate of Dhualakuan officers club, we hailed an auto rickshaw and got inside. When we reached 5MLN Marg, one of the staff stopped the auto and asked the driver as to where does he think he is going and when he looked inside and found Admiral and self sitting, he almost fell down while saluting the Admiral!! He was of course shocked and we had good laugh. I remember telling Admiral – who will believe the "Chief Designate" of the Navy sitting in an auto rickshaw? He just laughed off. What a man? But he won't use the staff car!

Admiral's first round of Golf after taking over as CNS was rather interesting in Montee's words. **Quote** "Mike on the first weekend after becoming Chief, Admiral asked me to fix a four ball for a round at Delhi Golf Course. The foursome was Gen OP Malhotra, COAS, Lt Gen Heera, Admiral and self. Admiral true to himself came to the course in a taxi! As he perceived that Golfing was a private activity thus inappropriate to use the staff car. I would argue with Admiral that it is very embarrassing to see a Chief coming in a cab and being received by the President and Secretary of the course. I told him in no uncertain terms that you can't do this and as a Chief you are on duty 24 hours and there is no private moment for you, but he won't budge!!" **Unquote**

Colonel Divine Jones who was our Physical Training instructor at NDA would often leave his Standard Herald car at the Navy House whenever he went out of town. Admiral would happily use it for Golf, going to church and market. Also his Flag Lt Bhaskar Ranjan Sen would leave his old Fiat car at Navy House when he went on leave, primarily for security reason as lots of thefts were taking place in the officer's mess and few officers had lost their music system. When Bhaskar returned from leave after one month, he found rattles in doors had disappeared, few indicators, brake lights which were non functional were functional and above all petrol tank was full to the brim. When Bhaskar quietly inquired from the staff, he was informed that Admiral had taken the car to Prem Nath Motors, Connaught Place for servicing and repairing. When offered to pay the expenditure, Admiral admittedly gave him his peace of mind and Bhaskar never uttered a word about it again.

Similarly Captain Premvir Das left his Fiat car at Navy House when in June 1980 he proceeded to USA to attend a long course; details are covered in "Admiral Remembered".

In 1981 Reader's Digest edition had published a short snippet about Admiral- "The following was overheard while Admiral recounted; It was a winter Sunday morning, which saw Admiral, the Chief of Naval Staff in lounge suit along with Mrs. Pereira, the first lady of the Indian Navy walking briskly down the Rajaji Marg in New Delhi. A passing civilian bureaucrat who knew the CNS stopped his car to enquire where they were going. To the church, came the crisp reply. Is your car off road Admiral? The tone laced with sarcasm, lost on uncompromising uprightness for which Admiral was well known. No! I don't have personal car and my official car will not be used for my private purposes. And if you will excuse me, I must hurry or I will be late for Mass. The Admiral rushed to join his wife.

The bureaucrat shook his head in disbelief and walked slowly to his waiting car".

Amenity

In spring 1980, Captain Krishnan was posted to Moscow as Naval Attaché and was relieved by none else but Montee Chatterjee, who was posted as Secretary to CNS. Montee was determined to ensure come what may, CNS will not come to Delhi Golf Course in a taxi and somehow he must find way to cease this practice. So one fine day he managed to dig out a 1958 Government Notification on use of Staff car by Service's Chief for their personal management. This Notification was issued when Gen K S Thimmaya, DSO was the Army Chief. It entitled the Chiefs of Services to use their official cars for personal management by paying Amenity of Rs 128/month. This Notification was put to Admiral, who then instructed Montee Chatterjee to deposit the said amount at INS India and thereafter Admiral had no qualms of using the staff car for going for Golf or church.

When Gen Malhotra and ACM Latif got to know about this, they were livid and threw a fit and admonished Ronnie P- how on earth you could do anything like this and was setting a wrong precedence; After all who can question Chiefs regarding use of official car? But Admiral stuck to his stand much to dismay and annoyance of the other two Chiefs.

I never dare asked him for the use of staff car, as I knew the answer but at times he used to relent. There were three occasions when I used the Staff Car; The first one was in Sep 77, when I received a call from my Senior JCO Risaldar Janadharan, B Sqn, late at night of a Tuesday to inform me that Inter Squadron Hockey Championship will commence from Thursday and I must try and reach latest by Wednesday night. I had no choice but to catch a bus from Old Delhi Inter State Bus Terminal to Pathankot, a journey of over 12 hours. I informed Admiral that I have to leave early next morning. Sure enough at about 5am, Admiral woke me up with a cup of coffee and told me to get ready for the long journey. Yes, he himself drove me to Old Delhi, a distance of more than 10 kms from Moti Lal Nehru Marg; so that I could catch the first bus to Jullunder and from there to Pathankot to play the first match next morning against 'A' sqn; it was a draw against the best team! Second time it was in Aug 78 when he drove me to Tuglakabad Railway Station where our Military Special was stationed to go to Babina. Third time was in autumn of 1979 I was coming to Delhi from Jodhpur for a short break. The Murdhar Express train from Jodhpur used to arrive at Old Delhi Railway Station at about 6am in the morning. When the train arrived Delhi Junction, as I got down from the train and there on the platform I saw Admiral standing. I walked up to him and embraced him and asked; what on earth he was doing on the platform so early in the morning? He said; son, I have come to receive you. I was taken aback and told him that he could have sent Sharmaji with the car. He turned around and said; you are a peddle Captain in the Cavalry and not entitled to a staff car! I kept quiet and we walked out to the car park and got into the black Ambassador, the No. 2 staff car with no star plate or car flag and Chief himself behind the wheels- we drove to Rajaji Marg! That was the 'father' in him.

The only time he sent the car to pick me up with the driver was at the Palam airport in Feb 1982 when I visited them with my wife and small son- Rabden, barely 2 ½ months old. In fact Admiral told me that he was sending the car for Annie and the baby, so don't be under any wrong impression!

However, he never hesitated to help a jawan. It happened twice with Thambis from 16 Cavalry. First time when in May 1979 I had sent a parcel of Basmati rice and Rajma from Pathankot through Dafadar Mohinderan and Sowar Radhdkrishnan. Both reached Navy House early morning and after having breakfast Admiral inquired about their train and realized they might miss their train to Madras, so he immediately took out Col Jone's Standard Herald car and in full Chief's uniform drove them to the railway station to ensure that they do not miss the train. That was vintage Ronnie P; rank and position did not matter where the welfare of the men was concerned.

Next time I had sent a parcel from Jodhpur in Aug 79 with Dafadar Palangappa, Lance Dafadar Machayya and Sowar Ponnappa and this time Sharmaji was asked to drop them to the railway station in his No 1 staff car to catch a train to Bangalore.

Tosha Khana

Tosha Khana is a word of Persian or Sanskrit origin that literally translates in "Treasure House". Under British rule, the official of East India Company were not allowed to accept gifts or presents, often weapon and jewels known as "Khilat" from Indian rulers and their subjects. When the procedure required that the official, who received such a "Khilat" will deposit it in East India Company Treasury.

As per the Notification of Ministry of Home Affairs dated 22 June 1978. No one can retain a gift which is valued at Rs 1000/- or more. The assessment and valuation of the gift to be made within 30 days, if it exceeds Rs 1000/- at market value then it must be deposited in Tosha Khana.

In 1980, Defence Minister of Oman from Middle East during his visit presented a gold watch each to all three Services Chiefs. Next day Admiral gave the watch to Montee Chatterjee and told him to have it valued. The Flag Lt Nalin Dewan was dispatched to Omega show room, Connaught Place, to verify the value. When the watch was presented to the person concerned, he was taken aback and said such watches are made to order and therefore cannot be valued, in fact it is invaluable! When Montee Chatterjee informed Admiral, he was immediately instructed to go and deposit the watch in the Tosha Khana and get the receipt for the same! No Chief had done anything like this before and this action was not at all appreciated by other two Chiefs!! Who of course retained their watches with themselves? Admiral was in fact getting under their skin and they just could not figure out how to deal with a man of such fierce integrity!

Same year in July 80, I had lost the watch Admiral had presented to me on my POP at NDA on 16th Dec 1972, it was a ROLEX watch. I had mentioned about it to Mrs. Pereira and she had replied in her letter of 5th Aug 80, quote *"sorry to hear about your watch- Unc is on tour at present but leave him to choose when he returns"* unquote. I remember telling Admiral instead of depositing such a beautiful and expensive watch in the Tosha Khana, he could have given it to me, he said; son, he couldn't, as it was question of probity and integrity and yes, that is the reason, when I put my head on the pillow, am fast asleep in no time because I have nothing to fear or hide anything in the world. Perhaps he was right and maybe that's why right till end he hardly had any grey hair!

Staying with the subject of watch, eventually when I had gone to see Aunty Phyllis in June 99 in Bangalore, she was staying in the Annex of Mathai's family at 32 Museum Road. After a while she went inside and came out with a old and withered leather box (photograph at page 419) and said; son, this was the only luxury Ronnie ever had and nobody else deserve more than you and wherever Unc is, I am sure he will be very happy to see it on your wrist - it was LONGINES watch with gold dial which was presented to Admiral by his elder brother Arthur in Dec 78 when the government announced his name as the "Chief Designate". I stood there speechless with tears flowing down my cheeks and embraced Aunty who too had few tears in her eyes. It is indeed very expensive watch and I have kept it as a souvenir and never wear it and leave it for my elder son Rabden!

Photograph

Admiral was never fond of being photographed and generally avoided coming anywhere near the camera. No doubt he had very good looks and even in NDA in 71/72 he would always tell me that I should stand in front of the camera and not him, well he had his way, I had no options. Aunty Phyll would make fun of him and say, son, whenever you ask Uncle to pose for photograph, he will invariably come out with some funny expression on his face and become very conscious of his good looks and laugh under her breath. Ronnie P would give her a hard look but won't utter a word. Over the years I managed to capture lovely photographs and the best of course the one he sent me in July 78 as Vice Chief with his remarks: *"Mike, With my very good wishes"*, Unc. Jul 78

After taking over as CNS, Admiral had to sit for photo session, as Chief's official photograph is required to be displayed in all Naval establishments. Apparently he was struggling to get some good results and he had to sit through more than one session!

In his letter dated 16th Mar 79 **quote** *"I have had perforce to do some photo posing for official photograph and I have just seen the results which I don't find very good .I say this advisedly, as a face like mine does not lend itself on anything bordering on "glamour" nevertheless, my otherwise poor appearance comes out* even worse in the official photographs and I shall have to try again in the next week or two!! As soon as I can make it to reasonable standard, I shall send you one of them, if you want it." **Unquote**

Within two weeks Admiral sent me a photograph and wrote in his letter dated 27th Mar 79, **quote** "*Hi Mike- I am enclosing long promised photograph with a face like mine, there is little to inspire, but you asked for it! Sincerely Uncle Ron*" **unquote**.

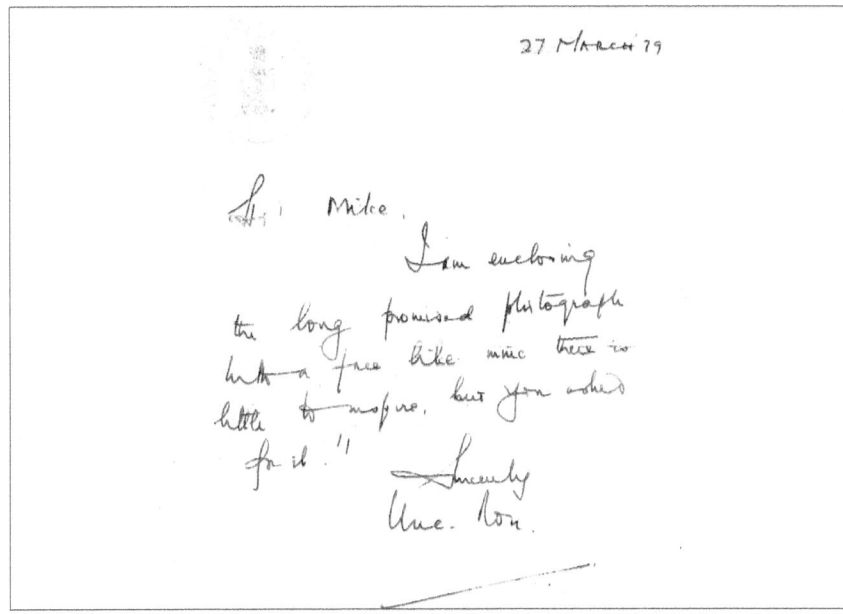

However, I have scores of photographs in which he looks very handsome and dapper. Some have been sent to me by his staff, Montee Chatterjee, Vijayan, Jena, Bhaskar and my course mates Bedi, Sankar Narayan and Muralidharan and ex cadets from NDA.

The first letter after becoming Chief was dated 16th Mar 79, **quote** *"Hi Mike- I am penning this from the office as I have slight lull in work and your letter with lovely pictures came in today which made me realize that I have not written to you for quite some time- so here I am.*

Thank you, a million, my son, for the photographs which have come out very well. You will generally find that the colour film calls for little more exposure than normal film, on that automatic super duper camera of yours, there should be some way of indicating this to the automatic exposure meter, either by insertion of ASA no or some other way. A little more exposure would have brought the colour even better, though they are nice as they are.

I go on my first tour from the 19th to 24th of this month and will be visiting Visakh and Madras. I will also be stopping over for few hours at Bangalore and Hydrabad on my way out and in to call on the Governor and CMs of the states. I will also be picking up Aunty Phyll at B'lore and she then return from Hydrabad on my way back.

Delhi is beginning to get warm up and the days are certainly hot, though the nights are still very pleasant. We finally went to "Whites" on Thursday; it was not a day soon. Our garden is looking lovely and is at the moment in full bloom. In fact we won the garden competition this year, for best govt house with 1 Mali, while the Chief of Air Staff won for govt house with 2 Malis. The staff and the Mali (gardner) in particular very happy, and so of course was Aunty Phyll. She had worked very hard on it and it was really her effort that paid off.

Aunty May is still here with me. She was leaving on the 15th but in view of the fact that I will be away from 19th to 24th Mar, she is staying on until I return. In fact we have just heard that Hugh and Colleen Gantzer will be coming in from Cochin, on their way to Kathmandu, so Aunty May will be able to meet them. They go off to Kathmandu on the 24th and will be returning on 2nd or 3rd April.

You will see that we are still at 5 MLN Marg and will not be moving to no 12 for at least 3 months, as the house needs lots of repairs and we must have it done before we move in. It is particularly subject to seepage and calls for extensive work on the base of all the walls, which they are working now.

Well, I will close. Our love to you and look after yourself. God bless and thank you for the photographs- sincerely Uncle Ron" unquote

Chief has very tight schedule but still Admiral found time to write whenever he could.

Chief of Staff Committee

General OP Malhotra took over as COAS on 1st May 1978, Air Chief Marshal Idris Latif was promoted on 1st Sep 1978 and Admiral on 1st Mar 1979. Gen Malhotra being the senior most was the Chairman of Chief Of Staff Committee. The Chiefs used to meet every 4th Tuesday to discuss the matters about the Services followed by meeting with Defence Minister. In Montee Chatterjee words, quote "Mike, from day one Ronnie P had major disagreements on "Matters Military" with Malhotra and Latif, who were apparently toeing the Government line and they continued till their retirement.

Gubernatorial Appointments

The policy of offering gubernatorial appointments to Services Chief after retirement has been in vogue since the days of Pandit Nehru in 50's. Gen KM Carriappa, first Commander-in- Chief, after retirement in 1953 was appointed as High Commissioner to Australia and New Zealand till 1956. In 1959, Gen Nagesh was appointed Governor of Assam and later Andhra Pardesh. In 60's Gen JN Chaudhuri as High Commissioner to Canada, later followed by Gen Raina in 70's, Air Marshal Arjan Singh to Switzerland and Keneya, and Gen Bawoor to Denmark .

However, Admiral's view was contrary to the existing practice and was of firm belief that it was detrimental to the Services interest.

Admiral was the junior most Chief and the first agenda he took up with other two Chiefs that a joint proposal is forwarded to the Government that the Services Chiefs should NOT be offered any gubernatorial appointment after retirement. It was exactly what the other two Chiefs did not want to hear. How could Admiral possibly recommend such a preposterous proposal? They out rightly rejected the very idea. Admiral pushed his case and said; fine if the government wants to utilize the experience of the retiring Chief, then we can go in for a "Cooling Period" of 5 years or at least 3 years, but no go. Admiral tried to put across his point of view, that there is a perception in the Services, that the Chiefs DO NOT fight for the cause and betterment of the Services and instead toe the government/ bureaucrat's line with the hope of being rewarded suitably after retirement. Therefore to remove this ugly perception, we should collectively send message to our men, sailors and airmen that we are working for the Services and not the government. However, his proposal was shot down and he was told in no uncertain terms by Gen Malhotra that he was senior and the Chairman of Chief of Staff Committee and Admiral should not speak out of turn. In Montee Chetterjee word, quote "Mike, Admiral had TAKKAR (head on collision) relations with other Chiefs! So much so Latif remarked that he will never support such a ridiculous suggestion. Evidently both had their personal interest to vehemently oppose the very idea. Sure enough after retirement Latif went to Bombay as Governor of Maharashtra (1982-1985), after he pushed out his ex Chief Air Chief Marshal Om Prakash Mehra to Rajasthan. Later he went as Ambassador to Paris (1985-88). Malhotra after retirement stayed on in Lutyens Complex till he was sent as Ambassador to Indonesia (1981-1984) and later as Governor Punjab (1990-91).

Notwithstanding the resistance from other Chiefs, Admiral waited to become Chairman of Chief of Staff Committee on 1st Sep 1981. By then Congress was back in power and Prime Minister Mrs. Indira Gandhi was also holding the portfolio of Defence Minister. Admiral discussed the matter with Mrs. Gandhi and put up a draft to the Government recommending minimum "cooling period" of 3 years. Expectedly the recommendation was not accepted by the Government and the file was literally thrown out of the window!

There were many detectors in the Government and more so in bureaucratic circles those were sure that Admiral won't be able to sustain his high moral ground on the issue and sooner or later will come around. How wrong they were? Admiral did not change even an iota from his stand in spite of external pressures.

Prior to his retirement Admiral went for farewell call on the President, Mr. Sanjeeva Reddy, who suggested to Admiral that he should stay on in Delhi till the Government finds a suitable job for him. Admiral with all humility turned down the suggestion and left Delhi on 6th Mar 82, within a week after he retired.

Yes, Admiral stuck to his word, what he told me in Nov 1978, son I am here to serve my men and the Navy and under no circumstances will compromise on this aspect. After 39 years of outstanding service he just walked into the sunset and comfort of his humble abode AT LAST at Whitefield on the outskirts of Bangalore.

High Commissioner

In early May 1985, I wrote to Admiral to convey my best wishes for his birthday; 25th May. In this letter I also mentioned to him that his successor Admiral Stan Dawson has been appointed as High Commissioner New Zealand. I felt sad for Admiral and wrote, I wonder at times what did you gain by sticking to your convictions and rubbing everyone on the wrong side in position of power in the Government as well as the bureaucracy. **As you see the system has not changed a wee bit**. Most of your contemporaries have been placed all over the world in most exotic locations. Idris Latif in Bombay as Governor of Maharashtra and later in Paris, Gen Malhotra in Indonesia, Air Chief Dilbagh Singh in Brazil, Gen KV Krishna Rao .Governor of Nagaland and Manipur, Air Chief Om Prakash Mehra in Rajasthan, Rusi Gandhi, Chairman of Shipping Corporation of India and now Dawson to New Zealand. Look at you, holed up in Whitefield with Vespa Scooter and Black and White TV!! Was it worth it?? You know better than me that we Indians do not appreciate people with high morals and integrity. They are misfit in our corrupt society! After being slave to Muslims invaders for over 800 years and later British Colonial rule for 200 years, everybody is downright selfish."Everyone for himself and devil takes the care of hind most".

The contents of my letter were indeed unworthy to say the least, but I was stating the truth and prepared to receive serious tongue lashing. Well, he replied and wrote in his letter dated 18th May 85, **quote** *"Yes, I see that Admiral Dawson is going to New Zealand as High Commissioner. I understand he is leaving in June. I think I have told you the background of my discussion with late Prime Minister on the issue of Ambassador and High Commissioner so I will not repeat.*

Amongst us Indians there is hankering to be in the limelight and any assignment that might do this for an individual is always sort after. If a Chief of a Service after about 40 years of service can accept an assignment after retirement, held by equivalent of Deputy Secretary to the Government, as did Bewoor and now Admiral Dawson, it is the decision of the individual. However, that factor alone will prevent me from taking anything like this, particularly as Dawson's predecessor would have about 12 years of service- somewhat less than a Major and Lt Commander, and the Foreign Service itself would look upon retired serviceman as a bit of nit wit to say the least in accepting such an appointment. I am equally sure Chief's own service would not be too impressed either! Latif is different to anyone. He will always in my mind remain, as the most slippery, slimy Chief that I had the displeasure to serve with. He will possibly land up ultimately as a Chief

Minister of a state and do better politically than any Chief Minister before him. He had all qualification of a politician and a diplomat, ably assisted by his wife"

- 2 -

Yes, I see that Admiral Dawson is going to New Zealand as the High Commissioner. I understand he is leaving in June. I think I have told you the background of my discussions with the late P.M. and the some of Ambassadors & High Commissioners, so I will not repeat it. Amongst us Indians there is a hankering to be in the limelight and any assignment that might do this for an individual is always ought after. If a chief of a service after about 40 years of service can accept an assignment after retirement, hired by the equivalents of a Deputy Secretary to the Government, as did General Bewoor and now Admiral Dawson, it is a decision of the individual. However, that factor alone would prevent me from taking on anything like this, particularly as Dawson's predecessor would have about 12 years of service — somewhat less than a major or a Lt Commander, and the foreign service itself, would look upon the retired servicemen as a bits of a nit-wit, to say the least, in accepting such an assignment. I am equally sure that the chief's own service would not be too impressed either! Each of us is different to anyone. He will always in my

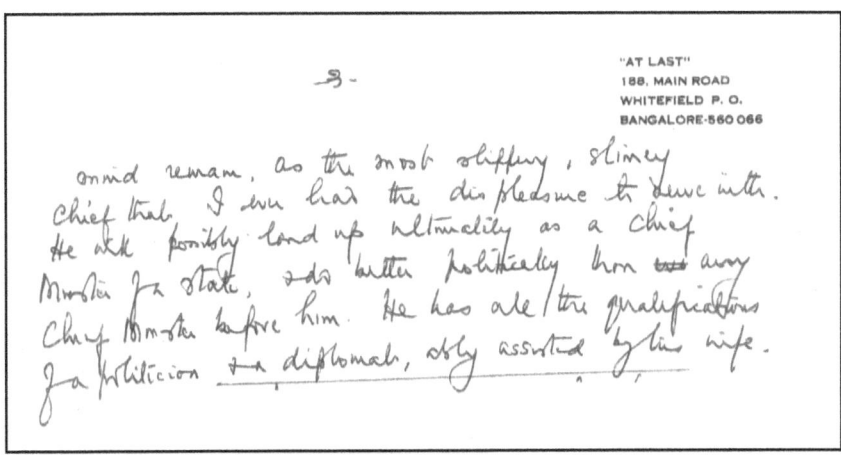

I don't have to elaborate further on this issue as Admiral's strong views on the subject are all too evident and self explanatory. I was simply stunned by his forthright reply. That's why Admiral is held in such a high esteem, I suppose!

About his discussion with Mrs. Gandhi on the subject as Chairman of Chief of Staff Committee, Admiral tried his best to somehow convince Mrs. G, but she will have none of it. Probably due to pressure from bureaucrats lobby.'

I vividly remember in Nov 78, he told me he will not accept any Government appointment and work for betterment of the Navy. The Government always plays the game of carrot and the stick!! Admiral never wavered from his aim. In fact Admiral Dick Schunker mentioned to me that Ronnie had given in writing that he will not accept any government job after retirement.

However, sadly for Services, apart from a few Chiefs (Carriapa, Thimmaya, Manekshaw and Ronnie P) rest have been servile and subservient to say the least, to the Government of the day.

July 1979

Well Admiral was very busy to write for next three months. It was only in July when I received his letter dated 6th July 79, **quote** "*My dear Mike-I have just got your letter dated 30th June and if I don't reply to this, it will be third one that will go unanswered, so here goes!*

To begin with, son, please do come and spend a day or two with us when you are passing thru Delhi on 19th or 20th. You are more than welcome. The house unfortunately is still in total chaos. As there are lots of works to be completed, but we have to move in, as the new Chief of Material arrived in Delhi on 30th June. I had asked him to take over 5MLN Marg, so that we didn't lose this marked house which is Vice Chief's. The present VCNS has only 8 months to go before retirement and it would have been unfair to ask him to move from his present residence. The COM will, therefore stay at 5 MLN Marg till the new VCNS in Mar next year.

We have done extensive repairs at 12 Rajaji Marg and when it is finally finished, it will be a good house, but at the moment we have yet to do the polishing and upholstery and get new curtains. However, it had to be done as we had a house at 5 MLN Marg; it was worth doing these essential jobs.

Delhi is very warm and the rains are yet to break. This year it has been far warmer than the last year and the humidity has been extremely high, it is not much different to the weather at Bombay! Coolers are also little use in this weather, so Aunty is really going through very trying time at the moment. The Met expert tells me that the rains will be with us in next few days and we are certainly waiting for them-God Bless-Unc" **unquote**

Lord Mountbatten's Funeral

Lord Louis Mountbatten, Ist Earl Mountbatten of Burma, KG, GCB, OM, GCIE, GCVO, DSO, PC, FRS was tragically assassinated on 27th August 1979, when his luxury boat was blown up by suspected IRA in Mullaghmore, County Sigo, Ireland. Other causalities were his twin grandson Nicholos 14, his local friend Paul Maxwell 15, and Baroness Brabourne 82.

The funeral of the Royal family is planned well in advance. However, in Lord Mountbatten's case, it is believed that he had written the whole proceedings himself, which involved 507 personnel from Royal Navy and Royal Marine. The list of Pall Bearers included representatives from Burma, India, France, USA and Canada. All reps were Chiefs of their respective services and from India it was the incumbent Chief of Naval Staff.

The Pall Bearers were placed on either side of the Gun Carrier in the following sequence:-

Left Side	Right Side
*Rear Admiral Chit Hilang	* Admiral RL Pereira

*Gen de Boissieu	* Admiral Heyward
*Sir Williams Dickens	* Gen Sir Robert Ford
Marshal of the Royal Air Force	Admiral of the Fleet
*Lt Gen John Richards	* Sir Edwards Ashmore

(Senior Pall Bearers on the Right)

On 5th Sep 79, Lord Mountbatten received a Ceremonial funeral at Westminster Abbey which was attended by the Queen, the Royal family and members of European royal houses. Watched by thousands of people, the funeral procession which started at Wellington Barracks, included representatives of all three British Armed Forces and Military contingents from Burma, India, France, United States and Canada. After public service which he had planned himself, Lord Mountbatten was buried in Romsey Abbey.

Admiral being the incumbent CNS was detailed by the Government to attend the funeral ceremony and I remember meeting him after his return from UK and he showed me the album of complete ceremony which was sent to him by the British Embassy. Admiral said that he has never before seen Royal family from such a close quarters and almost touching distance (photo). The entire Royal families of Europe were in attendance including 4 Kings and 2 Queens. It was solemn occasion with silent tears and no wailing, conducted in a very traditional and professional manner. Lord Mountbatten was related to numerous Royalties of Europe through his great-grandmother **Queen Victoria.**

Visit To Western Fleet

In between Admiral was busy with tours and obviously had no time for letter writing and the next letter was dated 22nd Nov 79, quote *"My dear Mike, I have just got your letter and if I don't start to reply immediately (I have no idea when I will end) I will not get down to this; so here goes. We have just returned from three days visit to Bombay, where I had gone to spend this time with the* **Fleet at sea***, and get a feel of their operational preparedness. Aunty Phyll stayed on in Bombay and didn't come with me.*

It was wonderful to be back at the business end of the Navy and to be with boys at sea. They fared very well and I was delighted with the standard they achieved in missilery which was very high. For lack of actual missile targets we de-activate a missile (neutralize its homing head) and then fire it and use it as a missile target, the results were 100%.

I transferred to three ships, starting with HIMGIRI, then transferring to HERSDURG, a new acquisition, and finally spending a night on a tanker DEEPAK to observe an anti-submarine exercise while she replenish the Fleet.

We have certainly advanced a great deal, and technology has brought tremendous benefits in weaponry and sensors. I am now totally convinced that the advantage of **human experience**, at least in military or professional sense, pay very small dividends towards the decision –making at sea in a tactical situation. Let me explain.

The days of large fleet at sea are now dead. The necessity to manoeuvre large naval forces, to get into position of tactical advantage before battle is joined is totally out- as dead as dodo- The environment of the missile as a threat, with tremendous range and great accuracy, coupled to great destructive power is what we will face in future. Technology has made the problem even greater; by making available large punch on a very small or comparatively small ship and its loss against the advantage of its punch is now well within the calculated risk. The hub of the problem therefore is one of the two factors- either destroy the ship or neutralize her capacity to use the weapon, or if that fail, destroy the weapon before it destroys you. In final analysis one must destroy the weapon because that will always guarantee survival, so work towards this aim.

But basic problem is that the threat can develop and destroy in matter of seconds- not even minutes or hours. The human being therefore plays no part at all in this final battle scene, and to rely on the sensors, his ECM, his ECCM and his computer that will analyze and give you the best answer, and it will be the computer that will find the initial data to the gun or the missile system to lock on and engage. The human being is reduced to an observer- an anxious one at that too!!

Maintenance, availability and constant training therefore, become imperative because it is these that will ensure 100% availability for those few seconds when you fire in anger!! The human being is certainly important at the preparatory stage but when battle is joined his contribution is small to the actual success.

That is why I have set my heart on the issue of maintenance and support. It is these factors- unglamorous, routine and mundane- that makes for actual success and unless they are always remembered, we will certainly miss out when the crunch comes.

Son, when you arrive on the 30th morning, we will not be there, as we only return from Visakh on evening of the 30th. But please come, as the staff will be there, and the room is always ready.

Uncle Arthur was with us for few days. He has now gone up to Mussoorie to see Aunty May, but will be back on Sunday, the 25th, then leaves for Calcutta on the 27th. He is looking very well and certainly keeps very fit.

It's still not anywhere near cold as it should be. The nights and mornings are chilly and one wants a sweater, but the days are quite warm. However, it has been much cooler for last 48 hours with cloudy sky and chill wind blowing. I don't know how long it will last. Love to you and work hard-affectionately Uncle Ron" **unquote.**

Navy Day 1979

I was in Delhi for a week in end November and had the privilege to attend the Navy Day on 4th Dec 79 on the lawns of 12 Rajaji Marg. The garden was looking splendid and beautiful on which Aunty Phyll had worked wonders, she indeed had "Green fingers". There was President Sanjeeva Reddy, Prime Minister Chaudhry Charan Singh, Deputy Prime Minister Babu Jagjivan Ram, Army and Air Chiefs plus host of senior officers from three Services. I remember looking at Babuji, who was smiling to himself and must be happy for Admiral's father. There was Admiral Manohar Awati, who walked up to me and said, Oh! You are the one that Ronnie and Phyll are very fond of? I was speechless and just said, yes Sir.

Next day before leaving I again requested Admiral to visit 16 Cavalry before I am posted out within 6 months or so. He promised to come.

Visit to 16th Light Cavalry

In July 79, my Regiment, 16th Light Cavalry moved from Pathankot to Jodhpur, Rajasthan, a historic city known as 'The Sun City' which was founded in 1459 by Rao Jodha, a Chief of Rathore clan. It is the 2nd largest city in Rajasthan. On my way to Jodhpur in July 79, I spent few days at Navy House and once again reminded Admiral about his much promised visit to 16 Cavalry before I proceed on posting next year. He promised he will come and in his letter dated 22 Nov 79, **quote** "*I will certainly make to the Regiment before you pull out. I must visit 16 Cavalry, and I must say that I am disappointed not to have made it in the past. None the less I will-our love to you and work hard- affly Unc Ron*".**Unquote.**

Admiral kept his word and started the process to visit Jodhpur in Dec 79. His Naval Assistant Captain Premvir Das was the one who was coordinating the visit of CNS with AHQ.

Recently when I spoke to Vice Admiral Das after a gap of 36 years, he told me at that time we were wondering why would a Navy Chief visit an Army unit as it has never happened before, then we got to know that Admiral's adopted son is posted in that unit and Admiral ensured that he kept his promise with Mike Bhalla.

I promptly requested our new Commandant Col JP Singh to write and send an official invitation to the Admiral to visit our Regiment sometime in March 80. Accordingly Commandant wrote to the Admiral who replied in his letter dated 8 Jan 1980, **quote** *"My dear JP, -Thank you very much indeed for your letter 9001/AS dated 18 Dec 79 inviting my wife and I to spend a day with the Regiment on the celebration of Meiktila Day in the first week of March 80.*

Both of us will be delighted to come. But I understand from Mike that the first week of March may have certain problems and you may, therefore, like to change the dates a little later. My own forecast of tours at present scheduled me to be out of Delhi from 13th to 16th March and after that, I will have the Chief of Naval Staff of Sri Lanka Navy. In fact he will be with me at Delhi from 24th to 27th March.

If you would like to change the dates, I would be happy to be with you on 9th and 10th of March, and any date between 16th and 24th will be little tricky as it will be the end of financial year and the last two weeks, therefore, are fairly hectic in getting our budget in line with the our estimates for the year. It results in series of meetings and consultations which will keep me tied up at Delhi.

I propose to arrive on the afternoon of the 9th, if this would suit you. And leave after lunch on the 10th March. I will, therefore, have an opportunity to spend an evening with the Regiment and also have some time to see the unit and perhaps talk to the men.

Formality and ceremonial are not my strong points so the more informal you keep the visit the greater would both of us enjoy it! However, I leave the programme entirely in your good hands and would be delighted to speak to the men in my own elementary Hindustani or in English, which ever may suit them. I believe your boys understand English far better than other Regiments in the

Army and I would prefer to talk to them in English, though I can certainly do it in Hindustani.

May I bring along two of my staff officers which will include my Flag Lieutenant? With my good wishes; RL Pereira" **unquote.**

Lt Col JP Singh
Commandant
16th Light Cavalry
C/O 56 APO

Accordingly the programme for the Admiral visit to the Regiment was finalized and forwarded to Naval HQs for approval.

9TH March 80

1.	1600h	Arrival- Jodhpur Airport	Received by GOC and Comdt
2.	1615h	MES IB	Received by Adjutant
3.	1700h-1800h	Baseball Match Admiral's team vs GOC's team	Sports Ground
4.	1800h-1830h	Tea with Ex-servicemen	Sports Ground
5.	1930h	Call on GOC 12 Inf Division	Flag Staff House
6.	2015h	Dinner	Officer's Mess 16 Cavalry

10th Mar 80

7.	0700h-0900h	Golf	Sardar Golf Club
8.	1000h	Inspect Lancer's Guard	Regiment Quarter Guard
9.	1030h-1130h	Visit Mehrangarh Fort	Tourism Department
10.	1130h-1200h	Tank Ride	Training Area
11.	1200h- 1245h	Durbar Parade	Garage Area
12.	1245h-1345h	Lunch	Officer Mess
13.	1350h	Depart for Airport	
14.	1400h	Departure for New Delhi	Seen off by Commandant

The detailed programme and all Invitation Cards for various events were neatly put into a file and duly sent by hand to Naval HQ's through Dafadar Karup, recipient of Sena Medal in 71 Indo- Pak Conflict . A smart NCO, and instructed him that he must meet the Chief personally and hand over the file. When he came back to unit, I asked him 'did he personally meet Chief Sahib', he replied - Yes Sahib, and the Chief asked him 'Kaisa hai'? aur hamara beta app ka dekhbhal karta hai ? (how are you? hope my son looks after you all) so Karup gave some answer which made the Chief feel very happy and proud!

On 9th March 80, at 4pm the door opened and Admiral disembarked. He was received by Maj Gen PM Menon, GOC, 12 Infantry Division, Air Commodore ML Trehan, VrC, AOC Air Force Station Jodhpur and Lt Col JP Singh, Commandant 16 Cavalry. Admiral was driven to MES Inspection Bungalow, where I received him and the Ceremonial Guard Commander Dafadar KK Bhaskaran, shouted- General Salute, Salami Shashtra and bugler sounded the fanfare, but as Admiral got out of the car and he walked straight towards me and hugged me and said, son how are you? I have made it and I replied 'THANKS' – the scene was reminiscence to the one enacted in front of Quarter Guard, INS Shivaji, Lonavala in Apr 76. So much of warmth and even today after nearly 37 years I get a lump in my throat.

The first event was the Baseball Match between Admiral's Team vs General's Team. The whole regiment and ex-servicemen were there to witness the match. I was of course playing for Admiral's Team. Admiral won the toss and decided to field. We placed Admiral on Base no 1, so that he wouldn't have to run much and be rooted to the base to catch the ball to run out the opponent's batsmen. One of the officer, who was fielding at silly mid-on position collected the ball and slowly looped it towards Admiral thinking he may not able to catch a fast throw! How wrong he was? Admiral, after catching the ball, threw it back to that officer like a bullet and shouted **'don't throw it like a woman, throw it like a man' that was Ronnie P of old times in NDA!!** The poor Major was of course embarrassed.

When our turn came to bat, I was batting at no 3. The first two batsmen had managed to fill base no's 1 and 2, and then I came in to bat and bunted the ball and ran to no 1 base, now all three bases were full and next Admiral came into bat. I remember how the whole crowd clapped and cheered for the **Chief.** I reckon, in the annals of our history, it must be the **only occasion for a Chief to play baseball match along with the officers, JCO and jawans and that too Naval Chief with Army personnel!** With all four bases full, all we needed from Admiral was to connect the ball and our team will certainly pick up couple of runs. Admiral had never played baseball in his life but had represented Navy in Hockey in late 40's and of course was an excellent Golfer and naturally had good eye-hand co-ordination. Expectedly, he missed the first two strikes and was now left to face the last strike, so I walked up to him and told him "look Unc, you are swinging your bat a bit too soon, so wait for the ball to come on to your bat and then swing and hit it hard"- sure enough **he connected the next ball** from the sweet spot and as it sailed over BP Singh who was positioned at long off, I shouted for him to run to the first base- he ran , I again shouted to follow me to 2nd base and then to 3rd and he was getting bit tired but I coaxed him and kept shouting 'run, run, run' and finally he ran as fast as he could to the home base and whole Regiment cheering and clapping and **ran straight into my arms on the home base huffing and puffing heavily, he just held on to my shoulders till he got his breath back to normal beat, remember he was 57 years and never ran like this for last 20 years or more but he didn't give up and completed a 'Homer' and we won the match. What a sport he was?** Later on I realized that I should not have pushed him so hard to run all four bases, he had lost part of his left lung in 1956 and was still smoking heavily! Anyway he made it and enjoyed the game thoroughly.

After the match there was high tea with officers and ex-servicemen and he then along with Major Arun Kaishta, his Liaison Officer, left for MES IB. After reaching the IB Admiral instructed Arun Kaishta to break off the Staff Car, escorts and the Pilot vehicles. Then after a while he asked Arun Kaishta - son, do you have a vehicle and he said yes Sir, I have a jeep. Admiral said OK let's go to the Mess and meet Mike. Arun Kaistha was aghast at the very idea, **how can a Chief travel in a squadron commander ordinary jeep, not even modified, no star plate, no car flag, no pilot or escort vehicles,** Arun protested and asked for few minutes to get the fleet of vehicles back but Admiral insisted and said '**I want to surprise Mike** ! We had lots of ex-NDA cadets who had come from outstation units to meet their beloved Dep Com and due to shortage of accommodation they were all sharing rooms with us and I had 4 officers sleeping on the floor in my room, and it was in total chaos to say the least. We were all in high spirits and making lots of noise when I heard someone calling '**MIKE**'. It sounded like Admiral's voice but then he had left just a while ago for IB, and how could he come back and that too without any pilot hooter, and before we realized he called again and I looked out from my first floor balcony and saw Admiral with Arun Kaishta walking towards our rooms. Most of the officers were in towel or state of undress. I ran and tried to stop the Admiral as he was walking up the steps and with my arms open I stood there blocking his way and told him surely you can't catch me off guard and my room is in a mess. **He said doesn't matter son, I** wanted to catch you with your pants down and he came to my room, before I realized 4 officers hid themselves in the bathroom ! He looked around and saw his photograph as Navy Chief on my table and said, son, who is that? He looks very familiar!! And we all had a big laugh. He was keen to see the condition of the bathroom, I told him someone inside is having a bath and he could hear the sound of flowing water!! He knew they were hiding inside, and with great difficulty he departed! Those were flashes of his NDA days!

The same evening we had a gala dinner party in our Officer Mess. Apart from guests from the Army we had also invited His Highness Raja Subegh Singhji of Jodhpur Royal family and Major Mohindar Singh, 17 Horse, who attended Staff College with Admiral in 1952-53. Lt Colonel JP Singh, our Commandant, was a great connoisseur of Scotch whisky and had huge personal collection of finest whisky brands in the world. Also being the oldest Regiment the mess bar was well stocked. Col JP wanted to offer the best brands to the Admiral. After a while as Admiral walked into the bar, Dafadar Srinivasan, senior Abdar (barman) in his new attire with smartly tied 'Pugree' (turban) approached Admiral with variety of Scotch Whisky displayed on antique Silver Tray and **Col JP very proudly asked Admiral, Sir, which brand do you prefer, we have the best ones available in the world? Admiral had a good look, put his hand on JP's shoulders and said, son, I will be happy with a glass of Beer!! (Photo).** That floored JP Singh and he then offered Beer in the old Silver Beer jug, no doubt JP had form of old colonial days. That's what Admiral drank for rest of the evening, he interacted with all young officers and danced and had a great evening.

Early next morning a game of Golf was fixed at Sardar Golf Club which was established in 1901 by HH Maharaja Sardar Singh Bahadur GCSI, KCSI of Jodhpur and thus named after him. Admiral was joined by HH Raja Subegh Singh, who played to a handicap of 2 in his hey days in the 50's apart from being National Squash Champion for number of years. In those days the course had nine browns and being arid area one had to play off the mat and it was first experience for the Admiral. Major Arvind overslept and had to rush in Commandant personal jeep which he could not start!! Anyway by the time he reached Admiral was already on no 1 tee, as he saw Arvind Kumar rushing towards them, he shouted , you are late , my son! Anyhow for Admiral it was a novel experience to play off the mat and still had a good round.

At sharp 10 am Admiral reached the Regimental Quarter Guard for turning out the Lancers Guard – **it was first time in the history of more than 200 years that an Admiral of the Navy was taking salute in a Cavalry**

Regiment- he looked regal in his Whites as one can see in the photographs. He signed in the Visitor's Book, went around the Quarter Guard including Armory.

After paying brief visit to the Mehrangarh Fort Admiral came back to the unit to have a Tank Ride, so he got inside the tank and stood erect on the Commander cupola and enjoyed himself a dusty ride for about 20 minutes. Major (later Lt Gen) BM Kapur reminiscent the famous tank ride, **quote** "Came from AHQs (MO Dte) for my farewell too, for I was to go to the new regiment; 43 as it's first Commandant; and yet JP, the CO of 16th, made me take out my old C Squadron Cdr's tank no 74Y 204 N and take the CNS for a ride of his life. Admiral Pereira would not even wash or dust up before taking the "Regimental Durbar"; for he looked like nothing on earth with his spanking white uniform totally covered with dust and grime from the horrific tank ride, as was his face and balding head.... and he addressed the Regiment beautifully.... Great man". **unquote**

In his letter dated 8th Jan 80 Admiral had expressed his desire to address the men. Accordingly a Durbar was organized for Admiral's address at noon of 10th Mar in Alpha Squadron tank garages. The Durbar commenced by traditional procedure of reporting by the Squadron Dafadar Majors, Transport NCO, Signal NCO, Intelligence NCO, Regimental Police NCO, Quarter Master NCO, followed by Senior JCOs and finally Woordie Major. Admiral started his address;

Quote "Commandant Sahib, Officers, Sardar Sahiban and my dear bahadur (brave) jawans of 16 Light Cavalry- at the outset I would like to thank Commandant Sahib, Col JP Singh for giving me an opportunity to visit the unit and speak to you all fine troops of 16 Cavalry. You all must be wondering what the Chief of Indian Navy doing in a Cavalry Regiment? Well, as you know, your Adjutant Sahib Captain Mike Bhalla, who is like a son to me, is part of your Regiment and I am here on his long standing request to visit the Regiment and of course with kind permission of Commandant Sahib. I was in fact, scheduled to visit your Regiment in March 1976, for Bicentenary Celebrations at Pathankot. However, I had to cancel the visit at the very last moment as my 'Chief' Admiral Kohli ordered me to report to Bombay forthwith to take over as Flag-Officer-Commanding-in-Chief, Western Naval Command. **Notwithstanding, I have kept my promise and I am very happy to be amongst you all.**

I have been in your Regiment for the past 24 hours and I must admit that I am indeed impressed with what I witnessed , particularly the turning out of the Lancers Guard at the Regimental Quarter Guard . What impressed me most were the cavalry dress and the drill movements with the lances! It took me back to good old Cavalry days of the bygone era. Yes, I enjoyed the tank ride and it was bit rough and dusty but it was indeed a unique experience and so was the Baseball match, in which I was made to run around all the 4 bases by your Adjutant Sahib!! (Loud laughter)

I am privileged to have great friends from the Army who are holding very high positions in the hierarchy and the closest is Gen SK Sinha, Corps Commander 2 Corps, with whom my association goes back to pre World War 2 days in Patna where his father was Superintendent Police and my father was Senior Civil Surgeon. We also attended the same Staff College course at Wellington in 52/53 and Gen Sinha was expectedly declared as the best student. I must admit that I joined Indian Navy in 1943 and which very kindly elevated me to the rank of an Admiral, am sure had I joined the Army, in all probability I would have retired as a Major!! I also have great friends in the Cavalry, Gen Habibullah and Gen Varindra Singh, Gen KK Singh with whom I visited Egypt few years back, all from your Regiment and do have soft corner for them. I like their black beret with crossed lances on the badge, the dash, the élan, the swagger, the riding crop, the flamboyance and of course cavalier attitude.

Armoured Corps is the main punch of the Army and it calls for brashness, courage, fearlessness and ability to take quick decisions in the changing situations of mobile warfare. It is therefore, very important to learn to take independent initiative early in your career. Always keep your powder dry, and remember that more you train in peace time the less you will bleed in war. **Being from the Gunnery Branch of the Navy I fully understand the importance of quick and precision firing. It calls for very high standard of training and you must ensure that you destroy the enemy's tank before he can fire at you- it's a split second decision, which will make the difference between life and death.**

Your regiment is the oldest Cavalry unit with outstanding history of valour and bravery for over 200 years and as I have been told also has the distinction of producing maximum number of General rank officers in the Army. I am sure you all will continue to work hard and uphold the traditions and name of your fine Regiment.

I finally I would like reiterate that I immensely enjoyed my stay and would like to thank Commandant Sahib once again and each one of you for your warm hospitality and making my visit really memorable one . I wish you and your families all the very best and I am sure you will give a bloody nose to Pakis, in case it dares to do any mischief- Jai Hind" **Unquote**

Admiral was a great orator and he kept everyone spellbound and attentive to catch every word he spoke. Post Durbar a group photograph was taken with Champion Squadron -'A' squadron and all officers. Admiral was also presented a 'Portrait' (photo) by Dafadar Appuni, Regiment Intelligence NCO, made from single HB pencil. It was a great effort by Appuni which was duly appreciated by Admiral.

We then proceeded to Officer Mess for lunch. Gen Menon and Mrs. Menon joined us for lunch. Admiral was taken around the mess by Col JP who showed him all the trophies dating back to 1877-Pardoe Cup-, the oldest trophy, also Admiral was shown the- Pigeon Hole Board- presented by Maj Gen Bhagwati Singh: IC 00001. Col JP also requested Admiral to sign his autograph in the Mess Visitor's Book across two full pages, which Admiral obliged. Lots of group photographs were taken and I must admit that **Admiral was indeed looking splendid in his Whites, particularly the one with the ladies. This must go down as the best ever photograph. He himself couldn't believe when I sent them to him!!**

Mrs. Pereira for once agreed that Admiral was indeed looking handsome!!

At sharp 2pm the door of the Avro aircraft closed and took off for Palam Airport. I remember Admiral saying bye to me through his window by pointing his finger in my direction. **It was indeed most memorable 24 hours and all who came in contact with Admiral were taken in by his conduct and humility. Unbelievable but true.**

I wrote to the Admiral firstly to **THANK** him and secondly to tell him how everyone in the Regiment enjoyed his visit. Everyone was simply in awe of him, particularly the troops to witness such a senior officer of the rank of a **'Chief'** from other Services, to mingle with them, play with them, take photographs; they never experienced anything like this before. The last occasion a serving Chief visited 16 Cavalry was Gen Raina in 1976, just for lunch at Officer Mess and no contact with the men!!. Gen JN Chaudhuri made short visit to the unit in the 60's but unlike Admiral - **who spent full 24 hours with the Regiment!!**

Admiral in his letter of 27th March, **quote** "*My dear Mike- **Well my son, I certainly enjoyed every minute of the stay with the unit. It was nice to be with them, and of course, I was really overwhelmed with kindness and hospitality. The Army besides being fine professionals is also great gentlemen and your unit is*** undoubtedly at the head of that category. I am indeed most grateful for all they did for me. Somehow I am prejudice towards cavalry and armour, I don't really know the reason, but I have certainly had very good friends amongst them. They also form the main punch of a service and one has to be tough, resilient and at the same time professionally competent to use this arm to its full advantage. It calls for brashness, risk and a certain requirement to stick your neck out. Putting all this together I believe make the cavalry a different breed!"* unquote.

Visit to Andaman Islands

Admiral was not particularly fond of desk job or file pushing as by nature he was more of an outdoor man, who loved to be at sea with his sailors and the next letter reveals his discomfort.

In his letter of 27th Mar 80, quote *"My dear Mike- it is just around 5.30pm and I seemed to be tired of going through of whole pile of files- they have certainly left me mentally tired today, so I have decided to stop work and catch up with some letter writing. As I had your letter today, I have decided to reply immediately and lest months go by and I continue to be defaulter!!*

Before he could proceed much further with his effort, somebody walked in to meet Admiral! Next I see on the left side of the page written -3rd April! He started again with the letter, **quote** *"What I suspected has in fact happened. Someone walked into my office as I was penning you the letter, and now I see that I am 7 days adrift already, so here I am try and finish it on Thursday morning from my office.*

We will be off to Port Blair on the 7th. I will be going via Calcutta. Where I will stop over for the evening and then go on the next day. We will spend three days in the islands which I have not visited since I took over this chair and we shall be returning via Vishakhapatnam, doing the whole haul- Port Blair- Visakh and New Delhi, in one day which will mean 7 hours of flying. The "748" though comfortable, is a very slow aircraft and the cruising speed is about 185 miles an hour, it really comes within the category of "Jatka"!! Aunty Phyll will be coming with me and so do Chauhan, the Master- at-Arms, who has just been promoted to Chief Petty Officer! He has never seen PB, and therefore, very anxious to come with me.

Delhi is still surprisingly cool and there continue to be a distinct nip in the air in the mornings and evenings. The days get quite warm, but it is certainly nowhere near as hot as it should be at this time of the year. In fact we still use couple of blankets at night and when I take the dogs out for a walk in the morning; one could always do with the sweater! I am sure this is not going to last much longer, but we certainly cannot complain for this pleasant diversion.

Hugh and Colleen were here with us, in between their visit to Maharashtra. They finally left for Cochin and have taken a train back home. This will get them to Cochin in 48 hours, which means that they will be there on Saturday morning. Aunty May will be leaving on the 6th for Mussoorie, as she has to get back to her many activities now that the weather is somewhat better in the hills. In fact she leaves a day before we go on tour to Port Blair.

Well son, I will close, thank you again for everything and I am sorry that I have taken so long to write. My good wishes to everyone-sincerely-Unc Ron" **unquote**

It is indeed a fairly long letter and I have excluded the paragraph about his visit to the regiment, which I have included in chapter on his visit to 16 Cavalry. Imagine he came early to the office to finish off the letter? Speaking to Admiral Shekhawat, he remarked; Mike I wonder how did Admiral Pereira find so much time to write such long letters while he was Chief? He narrated an incident, **quote** "I was posted in Naval Hqs as ACNS in 1984 and used to interact with then CNS Admiral Stan Dawson and one day he told me - Vijai I just can't find enough time to reply to my friends letters and they must be wondering that I have become too big to respond to them !! It is only nine years later when I took over as CNS and I realized that busy schedule indeed gave you no time for yourself to indulge in letter writing. Therefore, there has to be some deep or Karmic connect between Admiral and you which made him share so often his inner most thoughts through his letters". **unquote**

Foreign Tours

In his letter of 3rd April he mentioned in detail about his tours abroad, quote *"I have been invited by Sir Henry Leach, 1st Sea Lord and CNS at UK, to visit England in September this year and he has asked me to bring Aunty Phyll and my aide. I have gone to the Govt for their approval and as soon as this is given, I shall get into dialogue with him about our programme. It is also likely that I will be visiting Australia in February, next year and probably Japan in April. Thereafter, I propose to call a halt to these visits. As I do feel that my last year in the office should be inviting my counterparts to visit India, so that my successor can start his tours as soon as he gets into chair.*

I had invitation to Iraq in March this year, but the invitation came to us in February and there was no time to process. I, therefore, declined the invitation due to other engagements, but I did mention that I would like to take advantage of the invitation early next year." **unquote**

I would like to mention here that once Admiral discussed about his foreign tours. If I remember correctly, CNS is entitled to nine visits abroad during his tenure of 3 years i.e. 3 visits per year and may be few more to neighbouring countries. He said I would not like to make any trips abroad in my last year. He also mentioned that the previous Chief made a trip to USA in early 1979, that is couple of months before he demitted office, and Ronnie P could not visit USA in his tenure! Admiral visited only 5 countries in his tenure viz UK, Russia, Australia, Sri Lanka and Kenya. He was personally invited by Admiral Sergey Georgyevich Gorshkov, Chief of Russian Navy (1956-1985), to visit Russia in Sep 1980, which included 4 days at Moscow and a two days visit to the Black Sea Fleet at Sevastopol, where Admiral was accommodated in famous Datcha of the Fleet Commander!!

Internal Tours

Admiral was travelling a lot in those days and in his letter of 30th April, **quote** *"we will be going to Calcutta from 6th to 8th to do my inspection of one of my units there and I shall also be visiting Garden-Reach Ship builders who are doing lots of work for us, and not doing very well or in the set time frame. Thereafter I will be in Bombay on 15th and 16th May to be present for launching of a frigate- the 7th which is the first of the new class and will be done by Mrs. G. The next day is commissioning of TARAGARI- the 6th and last of original Leanders which I will be doing. I will be staying in Delhi for most of monsoons and will be only start touring in September.*

We are certainly in midst of summers with the temperatures in the 43* and 44* C- dry and hot'. However, we had the first of the dust storms about 2 days ago, and it certainly gives us a bit of relief for a day or two thereafter. Well Mike I will close, our good wishes and all the best sincerely- Unc" **unquote.**

Visit to UK - Sep 80

After a long break I received a letter dated 18th Nov, **quote** *"My dear Mike- I haven't written to you for ages and I must apologize. But I seemed to be really snowed in with work and just as I have caught up with it, I go on tours and I am* faced with another lot of files to get rid off!! It really is not the paper work that bothers me a lot but that fact that I seem to perpetually have people coming in to see me, or else I have meetings to attend and the result is that you don't really get a couple of hours to yourself to do the work that comes each day.

My tour to Britain was both interesting and fascinating, and both Aunty Phyllis and I got around seeing and meeting people that we wanted to. But the pace was really in top gear the whole time and we were kept going from seven or eight in the morning to 11 or 12 at night, with the result, I was really tired at the end of the eight days that the official visit lasted. The trip included rather intense programme in London itself, which included lots of calls and just as much discussions with the Admiralty with whom I had lots of issues to go through. We then visited Plymouth, Portsmouth and Edinburgh, Coventry for the visit to the Rolls-Royce's Engine factory where I had considerable interest; Yeovilton which is the HQ's of Naval Air Command and Dunsfold where the Harrier is being manufactured by the British Aerospace.

We stayed in London at a lovely hotel in Sloan Square called the Carlton Towers and moved either by car- a super Daimler, or helicopter for short haul, or by the VIP Service Aircraft for long hauls.

On the completion of the official visit, I took five days leave and spent with my sisters-in-law. It gave me two days at Bristol and three days in Denmark, I then flew back with Aunty following me a week later. England was very expensive to say the least, but Denmark was just prohibitive and one almost paid for the air one breathed!!

21st Nov - This always happens, with my letters to you. I never seem to finish them in one sitting but I must get this away today.

Am off to tour to spend four days with the fleet at sea- the Western Fleet and I am certainly looking forward to this as it gives me the opportunity to see how the sharp end of the Navy is doing, to meet and speak to all my Commanding Officers. We leave on the 26th and will be returning to Delhi on the 30th. I then get a week in this chair to catch up with the backlog before I go to NDA for the POP on the 6th December. This will be my last POP but I have been fortunate to take two POPs in my tenure and cannot ask for more. The entire old staff- academic- have more or less left and whole lot of new ones have come in is nowhere as good as the old guard. It is really sad for the Academy as it will certainly have adverse effect upon the quality of the cadet and this set back will be very difficult to make up. We have been fighting a case at least step their pay up to the scales set by the University Grant Commission(UGC) but the government keep talking of the necessity of the academic staff being given certain research project if the pays are to be increased, the whole issue has been unnecessarily bogged down. Unless pay can be increased, we will get all the wrong people and that would be disastrous.

Aunty is well, but working as usual on the garden with great fervor and enthusiasm. She is trying to have the whole place looking as lovely as possible for the Navy Day on the 4th December so everything is aimed at this. All the best and look after yourself-affly-Unc Ron". unquote

My Posting to IMA

I had already completed over six years in the Regiment and was due for staff posting. As I had mentioned earlier that my main aim of attending 'Platoon Weapon' course in Aug-Oct 78 was primarily to meet the QR (Qualitative Requirement) for posting to Indian Military Academy, Dehradun. Minimum grading required was BY and I had secured AXI, highest grading. So when I visited Delhi in April 80, **I again requested Admiral to put in a word to Army Chief for my posting to IMA,** and with my excellent grading, there should not be any problem or hitch. My aim was to groom cadets the way we were groomed by our first Div Officer at NDA, Captain Manmohan Bhardwaj, a handsome officer from Para Arty Regiment. In IMA our Platoon Commander was Captain VK Buchhar, 3 JAT Regiment. A firebrand who kept us on the run and of course what we learnt from Admiral in NDA. Somehow my idea of an Instructor convinced the Admiral and said he will do the needful.

In his letter dated 30th April 80, quote "*I had spoken to Gen OP about your ERE assignment to IMA and he said that he couldn't really see any difficulty in getting it done, particularly you had AXI in your Weapon Course. I have given him the particulars and I should think your assignment will be through as soon as there is a vacancy. However, DON'T MENTION THIS TO ANYBODY including your buddies."*

> *[Handwritten note:]* Kamal, ... I had spoken to Gen OP, about your ERE assignment to the IMA, he said that he doesn't really see any difficulty in getting it done, particularly as you had an "axi" in your weapons course. I have given him the particulars & I should think that your assignment will be through as soon as there is a vacancy. However, DON'T MENTION THIS TO ANYBODY, including your buddies. Please remember this. We shall be going to Calcutta...

After a couple of weeks I went to Delhi to check up about my posting and I was pretty sure in my mind that I will be off to IMA soon when the new session commences in July. But I was in for a rude shock when Admiral turned around and said, sorry son, I don't think your posting to IMA will materialize as there seem to be some problem in your ACR (Annual Confidential Report), one of your CO had graded you pretty low, particularly in asterisk qualities such as integrity, loyalty etc and you can't make it, but if you are still keen I can speak to OP again, I felt my stomach turning upside down and said; Unc, no need, I don't want you to be embarrassed and that was the end of my dream of going to IMA. Admiral noticed the pain and disappointment on my face and offered to check again, I said leave it, and am sure some good will come out of it, **if two Chiefs out of three can't manage a posting of a piddle Captain to IMA, Dehradun, then there has to be some hidden agenda, I suppose.** Admiral looked at me rather surprised by my reaction and didn't say anything. Yes, indeed there was, as I was soon destined to meet two human beings who will have great influence in my life; **a young 'Buddhist girl' and a Saint-Soldier 'General' as the story unfolds!!**

What amazes me to this day, how the Army Chief could not post a piddle Captain to IMA and that too on the request from a Chief from other services?? Nobody can fight destiny, I suppose!

Posting to Sikkim

Yes, my destiny took a new turn. One month later on 17th June 1980, I got my posting as ADC to GOC 17 Mountain Division, Gangtok. There also was a twist to the story as Major Gen VN Sharma (Tich), though commissioned in 16 Cavalry on 4th June 1950, but in 1966 was posted to a new raising- 66 Armoured Regiment as 2IC and later took over as 2nd Commandant after Narinder Singh in late 60's. Naturally, his first choice was to have an ADC from 66 AR and not 16 Cavalry. However, when I got to know that Gen Tich Sharma is going to Sikkim, I spoke to my ex squadron commander Major PK Chakravarti who was posted as MS-6 in MS Branch, at AHQ's, that I am keen to go as ADC to GOC, Sikkim. He expressed his inability to do so as ADC was a personal appointment and the General has to concur and recommend your name. Tich was not at all keen to have an officer from 16 Cavalry. I requested Maj BM Kapur to put in a word to Gen Tich Sharma, he said, he will give it a try and just to placate 16 Cavalry, General forwarded my name to MS-6 as 2nd choice, though Gen Sharma made it amply clear that he wants an officer from 66 Armoured Regiment. But as luck would have it, the officer's name from 66 AR was included in the panel for a new raising, 41st Armoured Regiment and Col HS Sandhu, Commandant 66 AR expressed inability to spare another officer for ADC to General Sharma. Major PK Chakravarti, then offered my name which was already on the panel and very reluctantly Gen Sharma accepted my name as a last resort. That is how I got posted to Sikkim, much against Gen Sharma's wishes.

Sikkim

On my way to Sikkim I stopped in Delhi for couple of days, yes, I was there when Sanjay Gandhi was killed in an air crash near Safdarjung airport on 23rd June 80. It devastated Mrs. Indira Gandhi as he was being groomed to be next Prime Minister and all her hopes collapsed in one fell stroke. Sanjay Gandhi was just 33! Destiny!

Admiral was quite surprised by my posting and asked me if I was happy about it, I said yes, at least it will give me an opportunity to see North Eastern part of our country. Admiral told me that he has never visited Sikkim but remembered that it was a tiny Himalayan Kingdom and indeed there was a Prince from Sikkim, who was in fact his class mate in early 30's in St. Joseph's Convent, North Point, Darjeeling!

Admiral spoke to me at length about the duties of an Aide and how I have to be careful not to lose my balance. **Quote** "You will experience that, many senior officers will be extra nice to you so that you can put in a good word for them as you as an Aide will always have ears of GOC, **so better be on the lookout and don't cross the line and keep your distance from your boss, don't try to get familiar with him**, however, it is his prerogative to be free with you. **It is a glamorous appointment and you can also pick up lots of invisible enemies who will try to settle score with you at a later date, so keep your feet on the ground."** Unquote.

What a sane advice and I kept my nose clean!

I boarded North East Express from New Delhi on 26th June 80 with my small pup; German Spitz; Sumitra Devi and headed for Barauni, from where I boarded the connecting meter gauge train to Siliguri. I spent couple of days with my friend Captain (later Lt Gen) Velu Nair and his wife Kiran both from Medical Corps at a nearby Sukhna Military Cantonment and before I left on 30th June 80, I really don't know the reason but **Velu Nair specifically told me, Mike, mark my words and I promise you that within 6 months you will get married to a local girl**, I turned around and said, Velu, I have never been to Sikkim in my life and how can you make such an assumption?? **8 months later he came for my Wedding Reception to Gangtok!! His prediction came true!**

Sikkim was out of this world and I was mesmerized by its natural beauty. It is nestled in the lap of Himalayas and bounded by some of the highest mountain peaks including majestic Khangchenzonga amidst spectacular terrain, pristine lakes, luxuriant forests, roaring rivers and gentle streams. Sikkim is veritable paradise and destination for all seasons.

Gen and Mrs. Sharma was very affectionate, warm and outgoing couple and soon they were the toast of local Kazi clan. Their son Vikram and elder daughter Nandita, who were staying with them soon found local friends through Chief Justice Gujral's children, Anand and Biki. **I remember on 5th July 80 we all went to witness an Inter Departmental Football match and enroute Nandita asked me that we have to pick up two of her local friends, two pretty Sikkimese girls- Annie and Babeila.** In fact they were sisters belonging to one of the oldest Kazi family- 'Libing' and it was their elder brother Tashi popularly called "Speedy" who was participating in the match. I vividly remember when I saw them for the first time; they were in early 20's and really pretty with peach and cream complexion!! On arrival at the ground we were also introduced to their younger brother Richen, who subsequently became a very close friend and was major contributory factor for my marriage to his elder sister Annie!

Expectedly the first couple of months the GOC and self were on the move by heptr, Jonga, mule and on foot all over North and East Sikkim for operational familiarization.

In July GOC and Mrs. Sharma along with Vikram and Nandita visited Kalimpong and Darjeeling, and being Aide I also accompanied them. It was my first visit to Darjeeling and how I remember the first time when I had lunch with Admiral and Mrs. Pereira on 8th Aug 71 and Mrs. Pereira regaled me with the stories about her school days in Mount Hermon from 1931 to 1941, and the train journey from Siliguri to Kurseong and Ghoom, so the first thing I did after reaching Darjeeling I went to see Mount Hermon (estd 1895) as well Admiral's school North Point (estd 1888) and was indeed fascinated to see those iconic buildings and standing there taking my mind back to 30's and how pretty Darjeeling must have been in those wonderful times. How Admiral and Mrs. Pereira spent their childhood years!! However, due to inclement weather could not see Khangchenzonga Range.

I had managed to collect Swiss cheese from Swiss Dairy, Kalimpong , run by a Swiss National, also Sikkimese Cardamom, Sikkim Liqueur, and some ethnic Dragon paintings and sent them to Navy House, 12 Rajaji Marg .

Aunty Phyll was indeed not very fond of letter writing, but this time she got into that rare mood and wrote a very nice letter dated 5th Aug 1980 in reply to my letter of my visit to Darjeeling.

Quote *"Dear Mike- many thanks for your two letters- one to me and one to Unc and for the lovely gifts. How lucky you are to be where the Sun doesn't shine with a vengeance and one isn't in the state of outright exhaustion! I have never known anything like this year summer- ghastly.*

We have had a house full of guests for almost a month and 2 huge Cocktail parties and 2 big dinners to be organized- **in addition to the work on this sadly neglected house (Navy House) and garden.** *Work on latter has been slow owing to non-stop rain. Needless to say my bone idle malis are delighted!*

Both the tinned and the fresh cheese were really excellent- by far the best of all over local cheese and with all the parties of late you can imagine how handy it came!! In fact yours boss's brother (Lt Gen Tindi Sharma, Engineer- in- Chief) was at one of our dinner:

The painting on silk is really exquisite and I had them framed straight away! They match my Dining Room perfectly and have been very much admired. **Your taste has really improved considerably!!** *The elachi (Cardamom) arrived today. What huge ones. I never realized that they grew your side of the country – one lives and learns! The Pan liqueur is also very popular and also came as God sent for the parties.*

So glad that you visited Darj . It really is I feel our most beautiful hill station. You must confess **it knocks blocks off Mussoorie**. The Mountaineering Institute is just next to Unc's and my schools! It used to be **Birch Hill Park where both Unc and I had innumerable childhood picnics.** Sorry you missed seeing Khangchenzonga- its beautiful sight.

You will never believe Unc and I (with flag) saw two movies in one week. 'Tiawan Rainbow' and 'Alice doesn't live here anymore 'The former light and delightful. Unc and Flag didn't like the latter- my choice!

Unc went to Mussoorie about one month ago- I declined the invitation.

Sorry to hear about watch. Unc is on tour at present but will leave him to choose one when he returns.

Captain Das and his family left for USA for one year so Unc has a new NA now, (Captain KK Kohli).

Heaps of letters to write, but it is too hot to write more than one a day! We might be going to UK in September. I hope in that case divert on the way back and see my sister in Denmark. Let's see . That's all for now Mike. Again many thanks for all the gifts. But do try and save.

Dad had another toss- and cut his head right down the back, had 2 stitches and now back to normal- but getting very feeble. But I thank God that he is not sick.

All the best, son and God Bless- Love – Aunty P. **Unquote**

The Helicopter Accident

On the night of 20th Aug 80, I was reading one of Ayan Rand's book late into the night and I heard my small dog making noises, as I opened the back door, there I saw a big black dog trying to eat leftover of my pet, I just shooed him and went to sleep. After a while I had a nightmarish dream, the same big black dog entered my room and attacked me and I vividly remember that he was trying to bite my forearm through the quilt and I suddenly woke up to see a huge man standing in front of me, I instinctively shouted 'Kaun Hai' (who's there) and kicked him with all my might only to bang my legs into the cupboard, as I put on the bed side lamp there was this cupboard with box and sleeping bag on top of it making a figure of human being. I was totally wet with sweat, scared and disturbed .Next evening on 21st Aug, when Rinchen (Annie's brother) came to the mess to meet me, I told him about this weird dream and Rinchen softly remarked that as per their superstition **seeing** a black dog in one's dream is inauspicious and harbinger of bad tidings. He repeatedly asked if I saw any blood in my dream, I said no, may be the thickness of the quilt saved me from his canine tooth to puncture my skin but I was shaken up alright. He went home and told his mother, who also repeatedly asked him the same question, did Mike see blood or not? Rinchen said NO. **Amla, his mother said, some horrible thing or accident will take place in next 24 hours but he will survive.**

Next morning on 22nd August GOC and Col GS Col Yogi Bali were scheduled for air recce of North Sikkim and I had gone to Libing Helipad to see off the GOC. Just before takeoff Col Bali got a call from higher HQs and his presence was required in office, so he informed the GOC accordingly and said; Sir, - I have some important work to attend to so let Mike accompany you, I was more than happy to jump in the chopper as North Sikkim is really beautiful and no better opportunity than to see it from air. It was an Air Force chopper (Chetak) flown by Squadron Leader Mann and Flt Lt Subramanian. We took off from the helipad and headed North, over the Kabi Ridge, flew along Teesta River, Chungthang and through the Lachen valley and on to the Giagong plateau in North Sikkim. As we approached the Donkayala pass (18000 feet), it was blocked by the clouds and the pilot turned back but GOC was rather keen to go across the pass to Lachung valley, and he saw a window in the clouds and told Mann to turn back again and make another attempt, as he took U turn for the 2nd attempt he made a **figure of 8** and chopper suddenly lost power and started to descend. I was sitting at the back seat and wondering what was happening and why we were going down rather fast or is Boss trying to do close ground recce ?!! The **rocks started to get bigger and bigger and before I knew the chopper crashed into huge rocks** and I lost my senses and blacked out and little while later hazily saw the GOC who was sitting in front on the left side, unbuckled his belt and jumped out and next thing I hear someone shouting Mike, Mike, Mike, and I regained my senses and made some noises and GOC shouted again Mike- are you alive? I said, Sir. He shouted; Mike get out before chopper goes up in flames I was hanging upside down but the belt saved me I immediately opened the belt and stood up and again GOC shouted: come out. I said Sir, what about the pilots, he asked; are they alive? I saw the two pilots totally crouched against the instrument panels and tried to move them, Sir, Sir' are you ok? Mann made some movement and couldn't believe that he was alive, so I pulled both of them out, picked up maps, and came out. A while later I was asked to go inside the chopper by Maan who instructed me to put off three switches to turn off the fuel tap. **What really saved our lives was that the chopper crashed into relatively soft area surrounded by big rocks and** fortunately did not burst into flames and indeed it must have been due to 'Divine' intervention. Luckily, nobody was seriously injured, Gen Sharma bruised his coccyx and experienced discomfort while sitting for a couple of months, I sprained my right thumb trying to save my head and both pilots were relatively unharmed. After a while I wanted to pick up a piece, and GOC asked me what the hell are you looking for? I said Sir, am trying to find a souvenir to remember this accident, after all how many times one comes out alive from chopper crash!! GOC rebuked me what bloody nonsense! The time of crash was 9.11 am. Yes, I picked up a tail light!

In those days only one platoon of 17 Assam Rifles was deployed on the plateau at Kerang (17000). The Platoon Cdr Naib Subedar Jawahar Singh saw the chopper going towards Tso Lhamo (17000) lake and did not see it going over the Donkayala pass (18000), so he knew something was not right and immediately took out a Patrol Party of ten men with stretchers, hot coffee and First Aid Box and headed towards the pass. After walking for about 2 hours we saw the Patrol coming in our direction and Jawahar Singh later told me- Sahib, I was really surprised to see all of you walking towards us. He thought that all of us were probably killed in the crash!! It was a great initiative by the JCO because at that altitude we were breathless and finding it difficult to walk leave alone carrying anyone, and if anyone of us had been seriously injured the situation could have been life threatening and that's why Jawahar Singh initiative was critical and praiseworthy.

The crash took place next to Tso Lhamo Lake near Kerang post from where river Teesta starts at altitude of approximately 17000 feet. The floor of cabin crashed into the rocks and possibly absorbed the initial impact, the chopper toppled over on its right side with front and side glass smashed into smithereens and main rotors were totally damaged and rear half of tail with small rotors blown away. We came down from over 1000 feet at more than 50 knots and survived. Few days ago in early Dec 2016 a Cheeta helicopter lost its rear rotor and crashed and rolled over from just 20 feet killing two pilots and another officer!! Life is strange.

After reaching Kerang Post GOC asked me to inform Col Bali, Col GS, and just tell them that we had an emergency landing and not to mention about the crash or else it will unnecessarily create panic. By 2pm two helicopters appeared on the horizon. Group Captain Maithani OC 112 Helicopter Unit, Bagdogra and Flt Lt Attri landed first in Chetak and followed by Lt Col Chatterjee, OC Air OP Flt (later Lt Gen and DG Aviation Corps) and Capt Parminder Singh in Cheeta. **They hovered over the accident site for a while** and could not believe how on earth any human being could come out alive from this crash, and said it is simply miracle. (as shown in the photograph!)

By the time rescue choppers arrived, the Lachen valley was rapidly getting blocked. Gen Sharma and Mann were evacuated by Maithani and Attri where as Subramanian and self by Chatterjee and Parminder Singh. As the choppers approached Thangu, the valley was totally blocked. Maithani went straight into the clouds and with the help of the compass he kept going up and up till he broke the cloud line and saw Khangchenzonga on his right – West- and headed South East to Gangtok. Gen Sharma said that it was blind flying for five to ten minutes and he thought he survived the crash earlier in the day but may not survive this one!! In our case Chatterjee tried to go under the clouds hovering few feet above turbulent Teesta but could not make any headway and came back and landed at Thangu helipad. After about an hour Chatterjee saw an opening in the clouds and could see blue sky. We immediately took off and managed to reach Gangtok safely by 4pm in the afternoon.

After reaching my room I changed, went to the mess and armed myself with couple of bottles of Scotch whisky and rushed to Rinchen's place. There nobody believed me that I have just survived a chopper crash, but when they noticed my swollen thumb and few scratches on my back then they believed me. After a while we were joined by Amla, and then Rinchen told me that Amla, his mother, had already **predicted** the previous evening that something terrible will happen to Mike but he will survive. God saved us and **Gen Tich Sharma went on to become 15th Chief of Army Staff (1 May 88- 30 June 90) and I went on to marry Rinchen's elder sister Annie on 18th Feb 1981!!**

My eldest brother Wing Commander BGPS Bhalla was Staff Officer to Air Marshal Wollen, AOC-in-C Eastern Air Command, Shillong, and within minutes the report of accident reached Command HQs and immediately my brother rang me up to check about my well being, however he could only contact me late in the evening when I returned to my room and I requested him to inform Admiral and Mrs. Pereira and tell them all is fine. Sure enough next day there was a call from Naval HQs and Admiral was on line and I told him God saved us, both he and Aunty Phyll were relieved.

15 Sep to 15 Nov 80 the Divisional Head Quarters was deployed in forward area for 'OP ALERT'. Most of the days GOC and self were on the move visiting each and every post down to Company level. Admiral in his letter dated 21st Nov 80 wrote, **quote** *"How are you? Son, I am sure you are enjoying your assignment in the North. It is an opportunity for you to learn a*

great deal professionally, and you must not lose out on it. To have such an excellent General to 'flag' for is indeed a privilege and **you must serve him with great loyalty and devotion** *. What is more, you will hear and see things, that you not normally have access to, as a young Captain, so it is vitally important never to discuss them with your buddies. Always remember that"* **Unquote.**

Disillusioned

By the time Admiral finished 18 months in autumn of 1980 one fine day he walked up to his close friend and confidant Admiral KK Nayyar and shared rather disturbing thought with him. In Admiral Nayyar words, **quote** "I must tell you that after about half the tenure as Chief, Ronnie told me; Krish I think I made the biggest mistake of my life by becoming "Chief". I was very happy as Vice Chief, because **I was like a Tiger**, and everyone listened to me and I could have anything done I wanted, but as a Chief nobody listen to me and I can't get anything done because of unwarranted external pressure from politicians and more so from the bureaucrats and look at me; **I really and honestly feel like a "HIZIRA" (Eunuch)-totally ineffective**- He must have felt downright helpless and frustrated as there was NOBODY to support him within or without the system. Yes I did understand the feelings of a man whose shoulders had stooped with sheer helplessness, when he wanted to do so much for his beloved Navy and he couldn't." **unquote**

There were many issues which Admiral realized were deliberately obstructed by the bureaucrats and to make matters worse he had no support from other two Chiefs, it seemed they were all in cahoots with the Babu clan to grind their own axes.

Politicians and Bureaucrats

These were two words which Admiral was **anemic** to! He was of the firm belief that the root cause of all ills afflicting the Services since independence was unnecessary and unwarranted interference by politicians and worse by bureaucrats in **"Matters Military"**. It was Babus clan which has been biased towards the Services.

In Nov 78 when I visited Delhi after the announcement of "Chief Designate", the very next morning when we went for customary walk with the dogs he told me, **quote** "son, since independence we had very few outspoken Chiefs who stood up to the politicians/bureaucrats lobby. I can think of Gen Thimmaya and Manekshaw only. They have systematically sidelined officers who showed any sign of courage of conviction or speak up for the betterment of services. Sadly, Gen Bhagat was superseded by Mrs. G by giving extension to Bewoor, who not only got Padam Bhushan but was also sent to Denmark as Ambassador!!

I have my resignation letter in my pocket and I will not allow them to brow beat me" **unquote**. But soon he realized it is impossible to fight deep rooted moth eaten system - still he tried but...

In April 83 Mrs. Gandhi again superseded Gen SK Sinha, it was done at the behest of bureaucrats who were rather uncomfortable with his forthrightness and were aware of his reputation and strong views. Admiral was dismayed by the Government decision to sideline Gen Sinha and wrote in his letter dated1st July 1983, **quote** *"Yes, I was indeed very sorry to see Gen Sinha stepped over for Chief, though I am sure Vaidhya will be equally good. However, I knew Manney well and he certainly had excellent pen and firm belief in his concepts which bureaucrats would have found disconcerting to say the least. What I have never understood is this esoteric manner the govt employs in choosing the Chief, leaving it, more often than not to the last moment when speculation runs rife; and ultimate choice is subject of unnecessary conjecture".* **Unquote**

With this background Admiral ventured into rather hostile environment and eventually had repeated clashes with influential bureaucrats and at times with political hierarchy. He did mention that he will extend all respect to the Prime Minister and Defence Minister, but certainly not entertain any interference from other quarters, particularly bureaucrats that he was very certain about in his mind.

Deep Sea Rescue Vessel

Soon Admiral's fears were proved right and he encountered hurdles at every step but he went ahead full steam! The maintenance of sub-marines has been huge task for the Navy. The operational life of a submarine is 25 years in active service and the Navy had to refit its sub-marines fleet to keep them in running condition much beyond its operational life. However, the Government has been rather sluggish on issues of purchasing critical items and clearing new projects. Still worse Navy did not have a full fledged Deep Sea Submarine Rescue Vessel which was hanging fire for quite some time.

After taking over as CNS, the Admiral immediately took up this issue with Ministry of Defence. Expectedly the Finance Department in MOD was dragging the case due to supposedly lack of funds. I vividly remember one evening when Admiral came back from the office, he looked withdrawn and preoccupied, so I just kept quiet. He then said, son, I will join a little later. After changing and refreshing himself, he asked me to come to the side lawn facing Rajaji Marg to have a drink. After a while he spoke to me about Deep Sea Submarine Rescue Vessel and said, son, you know it is very critical to rescue a submarine in distress and sadly we do not have such facility. The crew in submarine in distress can survive up to about 48 hours and it must be recovered in that timeframe to save the crew. We have put up a project worth Rs 300 crores and the MOD finance is trying to cut down the budget which Admiral remarked is "Chiseling Syndrome" whereby slice down the budget by 25% to 30% and if you accept then the evaluation of the project has to be prepared from scratch resulting in loss of time and by then inflation catches up and you are back to square one. It's a vicious cycle and Admiral was not ready to accept. Same day in a meeting in MOD staff, one of the bureaucrats commented; Admiral by the time the Rescue Vessel reaches the submarine in distress, you may end up in saving few or no sailors at all. Admiral caught on the sarcasm and his blood rushed to his head. He got up and looked straight in that official's eyes and replied in his baritone voice; that even if it saves one human being, I will go ahead with the project. **Life of human being cannot be measured in money, it's invaluable.** Let me tell you I will not accept 5 paisa less in the proposed project. The bureaucrat tried to justify and mumbled something as Admiral walked out. Admiral said; how these people can be so insensitive? He was sad but could not make any headway during his tenure. Anyhow the project made no progress for the next 30 years or so.

The government woke up to the reality after series of accidents in 2014/15. INS SINDURATNA resulting in killing of 2 officers and injuring 7 sailors. INS SINDHURAKSHAK killing 18 sailors and collision of fishing boat with INS SINDHUGOSH.

Above accidents led to unfortunate resignation of CNS, Admiral DK Joshi, PVSM, AVSM, YSM, NM, VSM and ADC- the most decorated Chief ever. The government and Mr. Anthony, Defence Minister just washed their hands off.

However, it is believed that the present government has seen the light of the day and taken action on the issue.

Admiral must be smiling up there!

Maritime Role

The aircrafts employed for maritime coastal patrolling were under the direct command of the Indian Air Force and were flown by the air force pilots. The Admiral was keen that the Maritime role should be handed over to the Navy independent of the Air Force, where as Air Chief Latif thought that anything that flies in the air should be controlled by the Air Force. He in fact went ahead and said that Navy was not competent to fly Sea Harriers and opposed their induction to the Navy. Basically it was turf battle between Admiral and Air Chief, who was strongly supported by his ACAS (Ops) Air Vice Marshal Wollen.

Unfortunately the bureaucrats were playing their own dirty games and were siding with the Air Force and not putting across Navy point of view to the Defence Ministry. In fact the Army was on board with the Navy as the Army too was in the process of establishing Aviation Corps independent of Air Force.

This struggle was going on for some time and not making any head way. Obviously Admiral was losing patience resulting in bitter arguments with Air Chief Latif. One day Admiral decided to meet the Minister for State Defence and complain against the Defence Secretary for not putting across the Navy case in correct perspective. Admiral called his NA Kailash Kohli to discuss the issue. Captain (later Vice Admiral) Kohli in his own words narrated the incident, **quote** "Mike, we were facing stiff opposition from the Air Force, who just would not entertain anything on the subject and we were up against the wall and Admiral was literally at his tether end, so one day CNS called me and said Kailash I am going to meet the Minister and complain against the Defence Secretary that he is playing ball with the Air Force and not putting up correct picture of the case to the MOD. I was not in favour in this line of action and politely told the CNS that it will be counter-productive. I tried to dissuade him that by complaining directly to the Minister may not be taken kindly by the Defence Secretary and he may construe as back stabbing and ultimately lead to problems for our officers who on daily basis deal with MOD officials at lower level and in the long run Navy will suffer. But nothing will convince the Admiral and he was adamant and as the argument got hot, I just lost my patience and banged my fist on the table; Sir, you cannot do this and immediately realized that it was not proper, after all he was Chief. Before I could apologise, Admiral hissed "you are right, you bastard" and now tell me what should I do? I told him the best option is to take the Defence Secretary along with him to the Minister and put across your point in his presence. He immediately picked up the phone and called the Defence

Secretary, Mr. Kaul and told him that I have some important issues to discuss with the Minister and would like you to come along, he said fine and asked what time? So at about 2pm we walked to Mr. Kaul's office, corner room, which was on the way to the RRM's office and Admiral knocked at the door and said; Mr. Kaul am here and we went and had a long discussion together and we were able to put across our point of view. And that's how we managed to tide over potential crisis!! Otherwise Ronnie P was not the one to mince his words where the interest of the Navy was concerned.

The greatness of the man is, that Admiral accepted his mistake and went along with the advice of his NA in the larger interest of the Navy, he so loved" unquote

Eventually all the maritime assets and command and control were transferred to the Navy.

Naval Academy

The Admiral was very keen to go for a new site for the Naval Academy which was established at Cochin in 1969. With expansion and modernization of the Navy there was indeed requirement of new Academy with adequate land and all latest training facilities. A number of locations were proposed but somehow the Defence Secretay-Mr. KPA Menon was keen for setting it up in his home state of Kerala which the Navy did not agree to.

In Nov 1983 I had written to Admiral to help my ex Head Clerk (Honorary) Lt MBK Menon to get a job in the proposed Naval Academy in Kerala. Admiral replied in his letter dated 23rd Nov 83, quote *"The Naval Academy in Kerala is still in very nebulous state. I, personally never wanted it there, as the site to my way of thinking is not suitable. However, the decision, in spite of all my remonstrations was delayed while I was in the chair, as the Def Secy KPA Menon wanted it in Kerala, so he decided to prolong the issue as much as possible. The problem now faced by the Navy is the fact that the locals do not wish to give up their land and there have been number of demonstrations and representations to move it out!! I do not know the present situation, but I am sure that it will not come up in near future. The question, therefore, to get your head clerk appointment to this establishment is a very dicey issue."* unquote

It is a clear case of bureaucratic wrangling and I am sure Admiral faced many more. However, 20 years later state of Kerala did manage to allot an area spread over 2452 acres, located at Ezhimala, near Payyanur, Kannur district, North Kerala. It has 7 kms of beach front on the Arabian Sea and was inaugurated by Prime Minister Dr Manmohan Singh in 2009.

Finally Mr. KPA Menon had his way.

Free Rations For Officers

Sometime in mid 70's the government put up the proposal for issue of free rations to officer cadre till the rank of Colonel/Captain/Group Captain in all three services and MOD accordingly asked for comments from the Service Hqs.

Admiral Kohli. CNS deputed Rear Admiral Ronnie P, FOC Southern Naval Areas to study the proposal and give his recommendations during the Senior Naval Commanders Conference in Oct 75. The amount earmarked was Rs 183.84 paisa per month, paltry amount to say the least. However Ronnie P was of the firm opinion that services should not go for "cash payment" and recommended that we accept "in kind" and set a committee to work out the details of rations and ingredients required for officer per month. The recommendation was accepted by Admiral Kohli and accordingly forwarded to the Chief of Staff Committee. The bureaucrats as usual dragged their feet and 4 years later it was again pushed by Admiral when he took over as CNS in Mar 79.

The bureaucrat lobby along with two other Chiefs; Malhotra and Latif were not on board and insisted that it will be demeaning for the officer's cadre to accept free ration "in kind" and should go for "ration allowance". Admiral refused to be brow beaten by this lobby and stated that over the years the purchase value of the Rupee will steadily reduce and we will end up in a situation where the officers won't be able to buy ingredients or bread with so called "ration allowance" in times to come. So prophetic!

Captain Premvir Das, NA to CNS, **quote** "Admiral was CNS when free rations for military officers up to the rank of Colonel and equivalent were approved. They were priced at Rs 215/- per month and Services proposal was to compensate in cash as it will avoid logistic issues. Admiral was in minority when he said that this approach was short sighted and would be counterproductive. In the event the Cabinet accepted his advice and opted for issue "in kind" and that is why and how the system has functioned so successfully. In 1983 it was extended to cover all ranks" **unquote**.

The point Vice Admiral Das has brought out is that the bureaucrats could NEVER think well for the Services and our Chiefs invariably fell into their trap for own selfish interest. In Ronni P words- they never saw beyond their noses".

Mrs. Indira Gandhi

Mrs. Indira Gandhi was a very authoritative, strong and tough Prime Minister. Before I proceed further I would like to put it on record that Mrs Gandhi was indeed very fond of Admiral. He had very respectful and cordial relations with her, except he would not be pushed by her if he thought she was not right. Admiral always had very high regards for Mrs. G, and told her once; "Madame, in line of duty, I will lay my life for the country but I will not let anyone trample over my self respect, dignity and authority and therefore, will not entertain any political interference in the functioning of the Navy"

Over heard from one of the senior Secretary in the PMO, quote "Whenever any Minister or Governor of the state was summoned by PMO to meet the Prime Minister, the person in question would be literally perspiring in the waiting room wondering what act of commission or omission he/she has committed to get a call from PMO! Once they entered her office, there was only one voice heard i.e. Prime Minister's. When the Services Chief came to see her, you could hear both sides talking but when Admiral Pereira went inside you could not only hear them talking but laughing, yes Admiral's laughter could be heard by all and it would reverberate through the PMO like a breath of fresh air!!

Admiral KK Nayyar reminiscences about Admiral's relation with Mrs. Gandhi, **quote** "I must tell you about the most famous incident during Senior Commanders Conference in Oct 1980, traditionally held in Room No 129 D of the MOD. Mrs. Gandhi while addressing the Senior Naval Commanders said "Gentlemen, I want to tell you, that you must not ever think that your Chief doesn't tell me about your problems and what should be done. **He probably is the only person, who comes and thumps my table.** I may or may not agree with him, but I want to tell you, that your point of view he has brought at the highest political level i.e. Prime Minister. There are so many things which I can't do due to political compulsions but your point of view is well and strongly represented" **unquote**

She was a powerful personality and nobody dare opened his mouth in her presence and more importantly she never spoke like this of any other Services Chief.

Sadly this equation changed diametrically in "one fell stroke" consequent to disagreement over a promotion issue from Captain to Rear Admiral in autumn of 1981??

Promotion Board 1981

Navy is the smallest of the three services. In 80's the Promotion Board from Captain to Rear Admiral was traditionally held once a year during the Senior Commanders Conference in the month of October. The board is chaired by the CNS with Vice Chief Dick Schunker, three FOCs-IN-C i.e. Vice Admiral Barboza, Western, NK Roy, Eastern, Stan Dawson, Southern Naval Command, and Manohar Awati, Chief of Personnel.

In those times there were barely 15 Rear Admirals in the Navy and may be 2 or 3 vacancies were up for grab out of 20 odd candidates! However, even before the board was convened, the Naval Headquarters got a message from Mr. T Singh, Secretary to the Home Minister, Giani Zail Singh stating that the Honorable Minister desires that one Captain IJS Khurana must make it to RA. Probably it was done to pre-empt any adverse reaction against Khurana, who it is believed as Naval Attaché to Moscow had come under some cloud over an inappropriate interaction with Arms dealers lobby. Navy in that era was reputed for having senior officers of very high integrity. Imperative that Admiral will not accept any officer with questionable integrity, whatever be the political pressure. When Gianiji realized that Admiral is not the one to entertain his request, then he put pressure through the bureaucrats from MOD. When that also did not work, then the PMO came into the picture and conveyed that Prime Minister desires, that the officer in question must clear. Admiral said, he will do it if it is given in writing to him and that was of course not forthcoming.

After the board results were compiled, Admiral called his NA and showed him the list and Khurana's name was way down, apparently there were few officers above him who did not make the grade. There was no way that he be permitted to jump the queue and Admiral refused to comply with the PMO and said "over my dead body". When the list was put up for Prime Minister approval, who was holding the portfolio of Defence Minister also, without Khurana's name, Mrs. Gandhi approved it but with a remark- "**I don't know what this Admiral's coterie is up to?**

Resignation

When the file came back to Naval Headquarters and Admiral saw the remark, he sat down to give three pages reply on his official letter pad stating " All promotions are strictly as per merit and no pressure whatsoever from any quarters is entertained to interfere with functioning of the Navy and least of all in promotions and postings. We work with honesty and never compromise on integrity- and words to that effect. When the file went back to PMO, the Prime Minister was livid and very annoyed with the Admiral, as the written remarks stay on the file forever and ever! Yes, she contemplated to sack the Admiral and told the Defence Secretary in so many words, who walked out without saying anything at that juncture. Words were sent to Admiral Barboza to be prepared to take over as the "Chief" - Admiral Barboza said ; that I will not accept it in the circumstances"- Prime Minister was informed by the Defence Secretary; incase she went ahead with sacking of the Admiral, she will have serious problems on her hand and there may be mutiny in the Navy as well as other two services as more than 2500 officers have been impacted by Admiral inspirational leadership while he was Deputy Commandant National Defence Academy in early 70's. She stands to lose more than to gain. Better sense prevailed and she quietly withdrew. Imagine George Fernandez sacked Admiral Bhagwat when his government was in minority and **Indira Gandhi could not sack him when she was not only in majority but a very powerful PM, she dare not, that was the standing of Admiral Pereira.**

But meanwhile Admiral was drafting his **"Resignation Letter"**. As per Montee Chatterjee, Secretary to CNS, **quote** "Mike, I was informed by the Flag Lt Nalin Dewan that Admiral is drafting his "Resignation Letter", I immediately went to CNS office and told him; Sir, you can't do this, you are playing into bureaucrats hands- it's a trap and that's what they are waiting for- but he wouldn't listen and told me to "bugger off". I immediately went to the office of Deputy Chief, Admiral Ram Tehiliani and informed him what the CNS was up to? He called up Admiral Barboza and requested him to come to Delhi at the earliest and control the situation. By late evening Admiral Barboza landed in Delhi and went straight from the airport to the Navy House and told CNS; Ronnie you can't do this, don't be foolish and take any action in haste, just hold your horses and we will resolve the problem. Admiral won't relent and in fact tried to be aggressive, at that point Barboza told him in no uncertain terms; that if you go ahead and resign, in that case I too will resign- Ronnie was taken aback but that put an end to the discussion." **unquote**

The government hereafter tried to act awkwardly with Admiral but couldn't lift a small finger to implicate him, as Admiral was too honest for them to handle him. He was a fearless man, who could walk alone in a dark alley.

Here, I would like to add that this was not the first time when he threatened to resign, there was another occasion when after heated argument on some issue concerning the Navy with PM. Admiral told her; Madam, I am going home and you can find another Chief! This has been corroborated by one of my course mates- Vice Admiral Muralidharan, who was Flag Lt to Admiral Barboza at Bombay, **quote** "sometime in mid 1987 I had gone to call on my ex boss at Bangalore, years after he had retired. Admiral Barboza shared an incident about Ronnie P and PM; one day I received a call from Ronnie and he told me; Bamby, you better get ready to take over as CNS, because I have informed Mrs. G that I am going home. I told Ronnie that you will not do any such foolish thing and just hang on and put some sense in his head. At times Ronnie was very rigid on his principles and won't compromise, well that was his nature and Indian Navy loved him". **unquote**

Irony

But the irony of the whole episode is, the moment Admiral relinquished his chair on 28th Feb 1982, within few weeks Khurana was promoted to Rear Admiral with ante-date seniority and appointed as Fleet Commander, Eastern Fleet.

That is the way of functioning of the politicians and bureaucrats, I suppose!

Later Khurana was promoted to Vice Admiral and took over as DG Coast Guard and two years later had the temerity to put up his case to come back to the main stream of the Navy and stake his claim over Podgy Nadkarni for the post of Chief of Naval Staff after Ram Tehiliani.

Admiral Ram Tehiliani himself told me when he invited me along my wife and in-laws for lunch at Raj Bhavan, Gangtok, when he was the Governor of Sikkim in 1991- **quote** "I just shut the case, enough is enough" **unquote.**

Christmas 1980

In December 80 I proceeded on annual leave to Chandigarh. I spent **X-MAS week with Admiral and Mrs. Pereira** and had the opportunity to take lots of photographs on the 'X-MAS' eve and both of them were looking very elegant and splendid. At that time I mentioned to Aunty Phyll that I was seriously contemplating marrying a local Buddhist girl from Gangtok but I am facing stiff resistance from the mother as she does not have faith in me. **She doesn't approve of her eldest daughter to leave her roots and go and settle down in an alien land of Sardars with different culture and language,** maybe she had a point but then that's why they say '**love is blind**'. Needless to say Aunty was worried and said what about your parent's views; I said they have no problems whatsoever. Aunty Phyll advised me to try and get the parents around somehow. That will be good for both of you.

On my return to Gangtok in early January 81, I managed to get Pala, Annie's father convinced and I wrote to Aunty Phyll about the latest development. In her letter dated 12 Feb 8I, **quote**" *Mike, your letter certainly led me to believe you have battled all elements-**including the turbulent seas**-to get to the engagement stage of your life. Something in life my son, have to be won the hard way and am glad that you and Annie has realized that you would not have been happy had you married without the consent of both sets of parents.* ***This way you will start your life with blessings from both sides and no 'recrimination' later; 14 letters if you can do that in scrabble!!*** *But jokes aside Mike, am glad you have been patient and won Annie's parents over. Now you can plan ahead*". **Unquote.**

My Marriage

On 18th February 1981 our marriage was solemnized at my brother's residence at Shillong. On 11th March my parents, brothers and relations from Punjab came to Gangtok for the Wedding Reception. It was during the wedding reception that General Sharma told my parents that he tried his best to get an ADC from 66 Armoured Regiment but he couldn't! Mike had to come to Gangtok to marry Annie, it was in his destiny and no human can do anything to change it.

Admiral and Mrs. Pereira could not attend and grace the occasion due to previous engagements but **Admiral promised that as soon as he finds time he will certainly visit Sikkim and check up with Annie if she really made the right decision to marry you!!**

Marriage and Friends

I must mention here that sometime in April 1980 I visited Delhi for one day basically to see a prospective bride for myself, who my parents were very keen that I meet her before they finalize the relationship. After arriving Delhi early morning I went straight to the Navy House to spend some time with Admiral and Mrs. Pereira. At the breakfast table I informed them the purpose of the visit and I will be returning the same evening to Jodhpur.

Admiral apart from 'matters military, gave me advice on my personal matters too and I wrote to Admiral that I have seen the girl and I have no objections whatsoever.

Admiral immediately replied in his letter dated 30th April 80, **quote** *"Well son, both Aunty Phyll and I are delighted to hear the news that you are engaged. I am sure this girl must be a very sweet and kindred soul, and she will really be to you, the most important human being in life.* **She will become your companion for life**, *in addition to being your wife. I say so, because the Hindu relationship to a wife is strange, and I don't completely understand it. She is not merely there to bear your children; she is certainly not there to do all the chores of the house; and she is definitely not there to meet your every whim and fancy. Beside you agreeing, or wanting to marry you, so has she; and that is important factor. Both of you, therefore, become equally important and it is only by realizing this, that you will have happy and complete relationship.* **There has to be mutual respect, love and affection.** *What your wife wants or desires is more important than what you want, but it has limits, remembering that you serve a unit and an Army, whose demands upon you, don't always, and often cannot always consider our wives and families. So their lives become tough and difficult and our understanding of their problems at least makes it easier for them to bear these problems.*

Your bachelor friends, like my bachelor friends may also be friends of your wife, but we are human being and there can be differences on this score. You must therefore always remember this, and not necessarily inflict all your friends on your wife. I am always quite sure that women are far more discerning than men, and you will sometimes find that your wife advices you against many of your so-called friends. It is well worth considering her judgment. In life, I am sure you will find, on a careful analysis, that there are few friends, but a large number of good acquaintances, and quite a few parasites, which hide under the guise of "friends". I have often tried to analyze what is the **deep meaning of friend**, *and I believe you will find that it is a kindred soul, with your outlook and interests, you will always, when you are in difficulty or distress, be right by your side. There are few of these. When you ride the crest of a wave, you will find lots of souls around you all ready to share your glory, and certainly share your money. But when you have problems, very few of these will be at your side, and it is only those few- and there are very few- who can be considered your friends- the friends of your wife and yourself.*

And finally son, marriage is far more give than take, and that applies to both of you. You must give, before you can take, so when it's a question of "I or You", it must always be "you", and very often our lovely kind wives always give it back to you". **Unquote**

What meaningful words for the most enduring human relationships: **Marriage and Friendship.**

However, due to unfavorable stars, there were some reservations and proposal was amicably closed. Two months later I got posted to Gangtok, and 36 years hence I am still in Gangtok! **That's destiny!** I followed Admiral's advice and sage words for past 36 years of our marriage. Fortunately my wife is a **"Buddhist"**. **Undoubtedly one of the most compassionate and forgiving religion!!**

Admiral Visit To Sikkim

Expectedly in early April 81 the Army Head Quarters informed HQ's Eastern Command, Calcutta that Chief of Naval Staff, Admiral RL Pereira will be visiting 33 Corps Sector from 6th to 8th May including visit to Gangtok on 7th and 8th May. I had mentioned in one of my earlier letters to Admiral that as and when he visits Gangtok, my father-in-law, Kazi Sonam Gyatso would like to host a traditional Sikkimese dinner with Chang (local brew) and local cuisine at his home which Admiral happily accepted and was looking forward to interact with senior locals from old Sikkimese families.

HQs 17 Mountain Division was directed by HQ's 33 Corps to forward a draft programme for approval. GOC, Maj Gen VN Sharma was well aware that the prime reason for Admiral's visit to Gangtok was to meet my wife and in-laws. After the draft programme was finalized the GOC called me to the office and said, Mike, we have included a meeting with your father-in-law between 1540h-1600h on 7th May, and Admiral can have cup of tea with them. I was totally aghast and tried to explain to GOC that the very aim of Admiral visit was to meet Annie and her family, otherwise why would a Naval Chief visit a Mountain Division and requested to schedule a dinner for Admiral and Mrs. Pereira with Pala (my father-in-law), he said, no way, the state is hosting a State Banquet with Governor and Chief Minister in attendance and in any case protocol wise Pala can't invite a Service's Chief to his residence. That's the maximum time we can spare for your in-laws. I came out of the office very upset and rather low and how will I inform Pala, it would be very humiliating.

I sat down and shot off a long letter to Admiral giving him the details of the programme and how the GOC has out rightly rejected the very idea of his having dinner with Pala in preference to State Banquet. Only option left is that either you turn down the invitation for State Banquet or extend your stay by another 24 hours to accommodate Pala's dinner invitation. **If you can't spare time for Pala, then forget about meeting Annie or myself.** I had to get under Admiral's skin and I knew he will find a solution to ensure that I am not embarrassed in front of Pala. Mean while the final programme was forwarded to 33 Corps HQs – Eastern Command – AHQs and finally to Naval HQs.

After a week I got a call from Captain Montee Chatterjee, Secretary to CNS- '**Mike you can go ahead for Admiral's dinner with your father-in-law'**. I put the phone down and went and informed Gen Sharma about the call from Naval HQ's that **Admiral will have dinner with Pala**. GOC couldn't believe what he heard and said that's not possible as we had already confirmed to the Governor and Chief Minister and the rest of the VIP guests, I said; Sir, I am just conveying the message of Naval HQ's. GOC said he will have it officially checked up from AHQ's. So the 33 Corps was informed, and matter was taken up with Chief of Staff, Maj Gen Himmat Singh, HQs Eastern Command, on to AHQ's and finally to NHQ's. Montee Chatterjee told the AHQ's; **yes Admiral is available till 2000 hour and after that at the disposal of Captain Mike Bhalla!!**

The message was conveyed to HQ's 17 Mountain Division; **Gen Sharma was in a quandary and did not know how to get back to His Excellency for cancellation of State Banquet!!** He called me and said, it will be awkward for him to cancel State Banquet and why don't you **invite Admiral for lunch**, I said sorry Sir, I can't do that because it is Admiral who has expressed his desire to have Sikkimese dinner and there is no way I can speak to him. He will clobber me! Gen Sharma tried once again and the AHQ's got the same answer from NHQ's and he had to reschedule the whole programme. The original copy of the programme is given on succeeding pages.

The GOC had to get back to the Governor His Excellency Mr. HJH Taleyarkhan and it was a bit of embarrassment for the GOC to say the least. **The Governor was upset and took umbrage as to how a Service's Chief could turn down the State Banquet**. However, may be to placate the Governor, the GOC extended him an invitation for Cocktails on 7th May at Black Cat Institute!

1512/INS/12/GS(SD)

Mukhyalaya
17 Parvatiya Khand
HQ 17 Mtn Div
C/O 99 APO

05 May 81

HQ 63 Mtn Bde
HQ 64 Mtn Bde
222 Sig Regt
534 ASC Bn
490 Pro Unit

VISIT ADM RL PEREIRA, PVSM, AVSM, CNS
07 & 08 MAY 81

1. Adm RL Pereira, PVSM, AVSM, CNS will visit this Sector on 07 & 08 May 81 as per programme given at Appx 'A' att. CNS will be accompanied by Mrs Pereira. Programme for Mrs Pereira is geven at Appx 'B' to this letter.

2. **Adm Arrangements**. The security arrangements, provision of gds & all other arrangements will be made in a similar way as done for COAS. A & Q Branches this HQ will issue necessary adm instrs for the visit of CNS.

3. **LO**. HQ 64 Mtn Bde will detail LOs as under. LOs detailed will report to GSO1 this HQ on 05 May 81 at 1100 h for briefing.

   (a) One Offr (Lt Col) for CNS.

   (b) One Offr (Maj/Capt) for Mrs Pereira.

4. **Comn**. 222 Sig Regt will make comn arrangements, where necessary, during the course of visit.

5. **Helipads**. All helipads in the div sector will be activated on 07 & 08 May 81.

6. Programme of visit will be destroyed on termination of tour.

(MC Bali)
Lt Col
GSO1

Copy to :-

HQ 46 Mtn Arty Bde
HQ 112 Mtn Bde
103 Engr Regt

Internal

GS(Int)
'A'
'Q'
Med
17 Mtn Div Camp

2

Appx 'A'
(Refers to HQ 17 Mtn Div
letter No 1512/CNS/12/
GS(SD) dt 5 May 81)

VISIT PROGRAMME OF CNS

Serl No	Date & time (h)	Events	Remarks
	07 May 81		
1.	0745	Arr Gangtok from Kalimpong	Received by GOC 17 Mtn Div.
2.	0800	Dep Gangtok & overfly East Sikkim	By heptr, accompanied by GOC 17 Mtn Div.
3.	0830	Arr Chhanggu	
4.	0835	Dep Chhanggu	By rd.
5.	0930- 1000	Visit Natu La Post	
6.	1050	Arr Chhanggu	
7.	1055	Dep Chhanggu	By heptr.
8.	1105	Arr Gangtok	
9.	1110	Dep Gangtok	By rd.
10.	1200- 1230	Visit Rumtek Monastery.	
11.	1235	Dep Rumtek.	
12.	1330	Arr Gangtok	Lunch at 'A' Mess 17 Mtn Div.
13.	1430	Dep for Raj Bhavan	
14.	1600-1630	Call on Governor of Sikkim	Raj Bhavan.
15.	1830- 1900	Call on Chief Minister of Sikkim	State Guest House.
16.	1905 -2010	Cocktails	Black Cat Institute.
17.	2015	Dinner	Capt SPS Bhalla's residence. Ni halt at Raj Bhavan.
	08 May 81		
18.	0745	Dep Raj Bhavan	
19.	0800	Dep Gangtok for Bagdogra	By heptr.

Matters Military

SECRET

Appx 'B'
(Refers to HQ 17 Mtn Div letter No 1512/GNS/12/GS(SD) dt 5 May 81)

VISIT PROGRAMME OF MRS PEREIRA

Serl No	Date & time (h)	Events	Remarks
	07 May 81		
1.	0745	Arr Gangtok from Kalimpong	Received by Mrs Surinder Khera & Mrs Guna Chopra.
2.	0930-1000	Visit Cottage Industries.	
3.	1015-1100	Visit Institute of Tibetology.	
4.	1110	Dep Gangtok	By rd with CNS.
5.	1200-1230	Visit Rumtek Monastery.	
6.	1235	Dep Rumtek.	
7.	1330	Arr Gangtok	Lunch at A Mess 17 Mtn Div.
8.	1430	Dep for Raj Bhavan.	
9.	1600-1630	Call on Governor of Sikkim	Raj Bhavan.
10.	1830-1900	Call on Chief Minister of Sikkim	State Guest House.
11.	1905-2010	Cocktails	Black Cat Institute.
12.	2015	Dinner	Capt SPS Bhalla's residence. Nt halt at Raj Bhavan
	08 May 81		
13.	0800	Dep Gangtok for Bagdogra	By heptr.

I immediately informed Pala that he can go ahead with dinner and organize something very, very special.

On 6th May Admiral and Mrs. Pereira visited their old schools at Darjeeling, in fact at North Point Admiral was presented a copy of 'certificate' by the Principal; winner of 50 yards Kangroo race- E Division, 1934!! They halted for the night at HQs 27 Mountain Division, Kalimpong

On 7th May 1981 at 7.45 am Admiral and Mrs. Pereira landed at Libing Helipad, Gangtok , Sikkim.

Karmic Journey

It was indeed an **amazing coincidence**; when I got Admiral's Primary Department photograph of 1932, Standard 1 from North Point, the small boy in spectacles standing next to the Admiral was none other than the **Prince Paljor Namgyal of Sikkim**!! There were about 78 children in the photograph and imagine Ronnie P had to stand next to the future King of Sikkim!! At that juncture Admiral could have never imagined in his wildest dreams that **nearly 50 years later he will visit Sikkim to meet a Sikkimese girl who happened to marry his adopted son, Mike Bhalla**; was there any **Karmic connection** between Ronnie Pereira and Prince Paljor!! Yes.

Unfortunately the Prince who was the Heir Apparent to Chogyal, King of Sikkim, was tragically killed at the young age of 20 when his plane; Westland Lysanders crashed while coming into land and bursting into flames on impact on the runway at Peshawar airport, NWFP, on 20th Dec 1941, while serving in Number 1 Squadron with Royal Indian Air Force. Exactly in the same manner 26 years and four months later Michael Pereira crashed on the runway while coming into land at Hashimara airport on 13th April 1967. Aged 22! Is it **Karmic connection or coincidence?**!! Both died young, both met their end in identical and tragic circumstances at two diametrically opposite directions of British India: Prince Paljor from North East (Sikkim) died in Peshawar in North West and Michael from South Western Coast (Cannanore) died in Hashimara in North East!! And some where both of them left their legacies to be fulfilled 50 years later.

The photo was taken in 1932. Michael was born in 1945, self in 1953 and my wife in 1958!? There has to be some connection somewhere.

Admiral and Mrs. Pereira were received by Corps Commander, Gen and Mrs. Balaram, who had driven all the way from Sukhna and Maj Gen Tich Sharma.

I was there standing at the edge of the helipad and as Mrs. Pereira noticed she remarked' Ronnie, there I can spot Mike and walked towards me and gave me a bear hug followed by Admiral; **so warm and affectionate display of their emotions, cannot be described in words. It has to be experienced!**

After a while Gen Sharma while discussing the visit programme mentioned to Admiral that he will be staying at Raj Bhavan, thinking Admiral will be happy! But Admiral who had antipathy towards political class, turned around and said **General, I don't want to stay at Raj Bhavan,** put me up in MES IB. Now this was bit too much for Gen Sharma to digest, who had already borne the brunt of cancellation of State Banquet and now Admiral reluctance to stay at Raj Bhavan will be the proverbial 'last straw on the Camel's back'! The GOC looked at me and conveying with his eyes to bail him out of this potential predicament. I told Admiral; Unc, it is very difficult to make arrangement for Chief in MES IB at such a short notice, maybe he understood and said OK son- its fine by me.

The Admiral flew to Nathula to visit forward posts and meet troops deployed in High Altitude Area. I escorted Mrs. Pereira along with Mrs. Khera, w/o Brig NS Khera, Deputy GOC and Mrs. Chopra w/o Brig AS Chopra, Cdr 64 Mountain Brigade for breakfast at the Raj Bhavan.

Meeting With His Holiness

After about 90 minutes we came back to helipad and along with Admiral we headed for Rumtek Monastery, which is located about 23kms from Gangtok, for an audience with His Holiness Gyalwa Karmapa, the 16thKarmapa and a charismatic leader of Karma Kagyu order of Tibet Buddhism (Yellow Sect). Pala was at the helipad and I introduced him to Admiral and Mrs. Pereira. Admiral met him very warmly and said I hope you won't mind if we also address you as Pala, and thank you very much for inviting us to your residence for dinner, Pala just smiled. Being steep climb to Rumtek Monastery we travelled in GOC No 1 Jonga. Admiral and Mrs. Pereira got into the rear seat and Pala, as he was climbing into front seat with me, Admiral said Pala please come and sit with us. They really enjoyed the journey through small hamlets and beautiful flora and fauna. **On the way Admiral asked Pala questions about the history of Rumtek Monastery. In fact way back in 1959 when Karmapa fled Tibet, at that time Pala was ADC to the Chogyal, the King of Sikkim and assisted Karmapa to settle down in Rumtek.** Enroute I told Admiral that cancellation of the State Banquet, has not been taken kindly by His Excellency the Governor and he was apparently miffed! May be to placate him the GOC has invited the Governor for Cocktails at Black Cat Institute in the evening. It was little odd as the Cocktails were in the honor of the Naval Chief and the Governor who is much higher in order of precedence than Services Chief was also invited!? **I told Admiral that the Governor has a habit of coming pretty late for functions,** but Admiral won't believe me and said, son, how can he have ladies waiting for him? I said you will see for yourself in the evening.

After 45 minutes of drive we reached the Monastery and as we were being ushered into the Durbar Hall for the audience with His Holiness, I started to take out my shoes, so Admiral looked at me and **he also started to take out his shoes, I told him you need not do it as all VVIP are permitted to go inside with shoes on**, and I, myself have escorted GOC and many guests in last one year. He gave me a stern look and said "what do you mean, son, he is a Holy man and must be given due respect and took out his shoes. Not only that unlike other VVIP's he refused to sit on the sofa and yes, Admiral and Mrs. Pereira sat on the carpet , it was OK for Admiral to sit crossed legs but imagine Mrs. Pereira, who in her entire life never sat crossed legs on the ground but she managed very well that morning out of sheer respect for His Holiness, Karmapa; that's the kind of HUMILITY they possessed, unbelievable but true.** His Holiness offered them Khadha (holy scarf), spent some time and took lots of photos with Admiral and Mrs. Pereira and Pala and staff. Mrs. Pereira was fascinated by the flowers and orchids around the Monastery as well as a white Peacock, who in fact displayed its beautiful feathers and danced to welcome them!!

From Rumtek we drove straight to Officer Mess for lunch. It was here that for the **first time they met Annie**, who, with her peach and cream complexion in pink brocade Baku (Sikkim's traditional dress) literally looked like a doll. **Admiral and Mrs. Pereira as usual were very warm and Admiral holding Annie's small hands addressing her 'doll' and asked; my sweet little doll, what did you see in this silly fellow??** In case he doesn't look after you let me know, I will twist his ears. Annie became more red and smiled, rest of the time Annie kept following Admiral as he wouldn't leave her hand and it was some sight to see Admiral six plus and Annie just five feet!!

Next appointment was calling on the Governor at 4pm. Just about 10 minutes before the schedule time ADC to Governor informed Maj Khanna, 2/4 GR, Liaison Officer to CNS , that his Excellency is preoccupied and will see the Admiral at 4.15 pm, it was clear ploy to convey his displeasure. **Admiral lost his famous temper and said; in that case cancel the bloody meeting, Mrs. Pereira sternly told him 'come on Ronnie behave yourself and subsequent meeting was expectedly cold.**

At 6pm Admiral had appointment with the Chief Minister Mr. Nar Bahadur Bhandari, who knew Pala very well and **told Admiral that Annie belongs to one of the oldest and most respected families of Sikkim, so quit worrying, Captain Sahib could not have asked for better choice, good luck to him** . That made them feels really happy.

Cocktails at Black Cat Institute – 7th May 81

The Cocktail at BCI was schedule from 7.05 pm to 8.10 pm, and all officers and wives of the formation were invited, it was fairly large gathering (more than 100). Admiral and Mrs. Pereira walked in at 7.05 pm and were introduced to all senior officers and wives, and soon all ex-NDA officers surrounded them, some they recognized and some they didn't but none the less were happy to meet them. After about 15 minutes when **there was no sign of Governor**, the GOC asked me to check up with Raj Bhavan and I called up the ADC Capt Anil Thapa and inquired about the Governor and he said that His Excellency is preoccupied and will be delayed a bit. **At 7.35 pm still no sign** and now GOC was beginning to get worried and asked me to check again and I got the same answer from Anil Thapa. I bluntly told the ADC; Anil, you do not know Ronnie Pereira, if His Excellency comes late, the Chief will not hesitate to leave for next engagement at the appointed time, so to avoid any embarrassment you better get him over soon. **At 7.55 pm the band played the National Anthem announcing the arrival of His Excellency**. I looked at Admiral across the hall and gestured the time with my watch. **After a while Admiral came over and put his arm around my shoulders and said, son, but I will leave in next 5 minutes as I can't keep Pala waiting for us.** I said you can't be serious the Governor has just walked in, he said; doesn't matter son, but I can't be late for my next appointment!! The cocktails were in honour of Chief of Naval Staff and by tradition Admiral was supposed to deliver a 'thank you' address to all officers and ladies and present a Memento from the Navy to the Division, which he couldn't in the presence of the Governor. He called his NA Captain Kailash Kohli and asked for memento which he handed over to GOC, thanked him and **walked past the Governor and said Good Night Governor**, followed by Mrs. Pereira, KK Kohli, Flag Lt, Brig Khera, Mrs Khera, and Maj Khanna (LO). The GOC's head kept moving sideways as so many were trooping out in presence of Governor which is against the protocol as no one can leave before him but **I don't think the Governor had the faintest idea about Ronnie Pereira reputation, who never entertained any such nonsense from politicians.** Finally GOC told me, Mike, you carry on with Admiral and I will come after the Governor leaves. When I reached down the Admiral asked me where is Annie? I ran up the steps and saw Annie standing between Governor and Gen Sharma. I whispered in General's ears, Sir, Admiral and Mrs. Pereira are waiting for Annie in the car. I slowly pulled her out and hurried down the steps.

I was later told by one of the officers who overheard the Governor telling GOC that **I will have to break the protocol and stay for a while**. After that day Governor never came late for any Army engagements!!

By now it was raining very hard and by the time we reached Sonam House (Pala's residence) at about 8.30pm, on arrival the first thing Admiral told Pala, I must apologize that we are bit late!! Pala had invited close family members, Kazi Sonam Gyatso married to Chogyal youngest sister, Kazi Barfungpa of Khenzong, Kazi Tashi Topden , Kazi Sonam Dadul of Libing family and Dr Gyatso . It was here Admiral mentioned about late Prince Paljor to his brother-in-law Kazi Sonam Gyatso that they were together at North Point in 1932. Pala served traditional Sikkimese cuisine for a sit down dinner in traditional Sikkimese 'Thalis'. Admiral and Mrs. Pereira tasted 'Chang' for the first time in their lives and seemed to enjoy the flavor. It is local brew made of fermented millet and tastes like light beer. The container is called Thungba made of mature bamboo which is filled with millet and then you keep adding hot water and you sip with bamboo straw. After 5/6 topping up you change the Thungba with fresh millet. They all enjoyed the dinner and Mrs. Pereira kept telling me Mike, I did not let you down and had two Thungbas!! **She really enjoyed herself and Admiral admitted this is the first time he is seeing her bit tipsy!!**

Departure

Next morning i.e. 8th May Admiral reached Libing helipad 5 minutes before departure. However, there was delay as the baggage 1 Ton had not fetched up and Admiral was getting bit impatient and hot under the collar and shouted at the Flag Lt Nalin Dewan, who rushed in a Military Police Jonga to look for the vehicle. After 10 minutes Maj Arvind Sharma, commander of the baggage vehicle, (1Ton) reached and apologized for delay due to some snag in the vehicle but Admiral will have none of it and gave his piece of mind and said- **son, you can't possibly have the Chief waiting at the bloody helipad and gave him some tongue lashing** and everyone present was stunned and ultimately the chopper took off for Bagdogra after 20 minutes delay. In 2004, Lt Gen Arvind Sharma visited HQ's 57 Mountain Division, Imphal, Manipur, as Army Commander, Eastern Command and I happen to sit on the same dinner table, and said 'Mike do you remember Admiral Pereira's visit to Gangtok in May 1981?' He recounted that incident to everyone present and said that it was for the first time he experienced a Chief losing his cool!! Ronnie Pereira was famous for his short fuse but he would soon cool down too and in spite of this he was loved in the Navy and who ever came in contact with him. In fact when I met Admiral later that year he asked me **to apologize to Major Sharma on his behalf** and I conveyed to Gen Arvind after 23 years and he had a big laugh and added **what a great man Admiral was?**

Captain Montee Chatterjee told me that after their return Mrs. P mentioned,- you know Montee; Ronnie created a scene in Sikkim; and he wondered what was it all about, till I narrated the whole incident to him when I met him 34 years later in Dec 2015 at Guwahati. He said it is expected of Ronnie and nobody else got the guts to put these people in their place!

Nalin Dewan, Flag Lt to CNS, (later retd as Commodore) who accompanied Admiral to Gangtok reminiscences the trip; **quote** "Ronnie P, as he was commonly called was people's man. He liked to keep in touch with the people at the ground level. Apart from several visits to Naval Establishments, as Chairman, Chief of Staff Committee, he also visited Army and Air Commands. One visit that stands out was to 17 Mountain Division in May 1981, particularly to Nathu La Pass in East Sikkim. This was truly amazing experience for a Naval Officer. After landing at Libing helipad, lower Gangtok, we took off for a short flight to a place called Chhanggu at the base of Nathu La and from there we were driven in a Jonga by the GOC himself to the post located above 14000 ft. From the vantage point we could see the Chinese troops just few yards away, eye to eye contact! The interaction with the jawans was informative, highlighting that the camaraderie prevalent in the Armed Forces is the backbone of discipline, valour and honor.

On return to Gangtok we visited the Rumtek Monastery and had an audience with his Holiness Karmapa – another memorable experience. The Monastery is on top a mountain. The view was spectacular. The gardens were beautiful with orchids of all hues. There was even a white Peacock that spread the feathers in its glory as if to welcome us. Ronnie was keen to meet Capt Mike Bhalla. Mike was a cadet with him during his tenure as Deputy Commandant NDA. Mike bore resemblance to his late nephew Michael. Ronnie P had taken a great liking for him and considered him as son. Mike had married a local Sikkimese girl and Admiral and Mrs. Pereira were keen to meet them. Admiral and Mrs P, Captain KK Kohli (NA to CNS) and self were invited that evening for Sikkimese dinner to Kazi Sonam Gyatso (Mike's father-in-law) house. This was one of the oldest families of Sikkim and we were regaled / educated with their history during the sumptuous meal of local cuisine and brew-Chang.

One must admit that this particular visit to Sikkim will be remembered with great fondness for years to come". **Unquote**

Captain KK Kohli too was fascinated by Sikkim that after a month Mrs. Kohli along with her two lovely daughters, Rachna and Arti, paid a visit to Gangtok!

Rinchen's Sickness

In months of July/August 81, Bangladesh was afflicted by conjunctivitis called 'Joy-Bangla' and thousands of people were affected by it and within weeks this epidemic spread to North Bengal and ultimately Sikkim. By end August every member of Annie's family had contacted it, only Annie and self somehow escaped from it. Annie was in family way and carrying our elder son and it was very important for her to stay free of it. In fact she was cooking food for her entire family at home, but ensured that she did not touch her eyes with fingers nor touched anybody's towel. The worst affected was my middle brother-in-law, Rinchen, who was very close to me. He eventually suffered initial attack of paralysis and couldn't get up from his bed and walk to the toilet. I used to sleep on the floor next to his bed in case he needed any help. He was in real bad condition and had to be carried up the steps. In fact, that year, there were many conjunctivitis related deaths in Delhi. We were really getting worried.

I called up Admiral and told him about Rinchen's condition and he asked me to get him over to Delhi at the earliest. In mid September we took the Indian Airlines flight from Bagdogra, the return ticket cost me Rs 440/-(with 50% concession) and I could afford it!! Today it is over Rs 10,000 one way! Admiral was kind enough to fix an appointment with Brigadier Varinder Kumar, Senior Neuro Surgeon, one of the best in India at Army Base Hospital, Delhi Cantonment.

Rinchen and self reached Navy House in the evening. At the dinner table Auntie Phyll asked Rinchen; son, where did you do your schooling from? **Rinchen replied 'Mount Hermon, Darjeeling, maam '- Auntie Phyll couldn't believe her ears and said, my God, really, that was my school too (1931-1941)** It was enough to establish the bond, next question – which house?-'Stahl' - she said, my first Principal in 1931!!, what a **coincidence** and rest of the evening they spoke about the school with Admiral and self as mute spectators!

Next day we had an appointment with Brig Varinder Kumar, and lo' behold **Auntie Phyll volunteered to accompany us and take care of her schoolmate-Hermonite.** By then Admiral being the senior most Chief, was the Chairman of Chief of Staff Committee and sure enough Maj Gen Sharma ,Commandant, Base Hospital was there to receive us and accompanied us for quite a while , till Auntie Phyll told the General we can take care of ourselves and requested him to attend to his official work. We were in the hospital for over three hours carrying out various tests and she walked along with us in the hot Sun just to give moral support to Rinchen. Gen Sharma was there to see her off at about 2pm.

Next two days again we went to the hospital and eventually Rinchen was admitted for further tests and treatment. I remember Aunty Phyll patting herself own her shoulder and said, **Mike, my son, I did not let down a 'Hermonite' and gave him moral support right till the time he was admitted.** Soon I had to get back to Gangtok. Aunty Phyll assured me not to worry son, and I shall take care of Rinchen.

Rinchen was sharing room with another officer in the Officer Ward, and a week later one morning at about 9am, suddenly two Senior Nursing officers with couple of attendants and sweeper hurried into the room and first they asked the Rinchen's room mate-a Major- to shift to another room, and then asked Rinchen to move out and sit in the verandah. They moved out the second bed, cleaned up and swab the room and toilets, changed the linen, curtains, put new soap and oil in the bathroom and did some flower arrangement in the room to make it look presentable. **They asked Rinchen to get dressed in decent clothes as Chief of Naval Staff, Admiral Pereira will be coming to see him and were rather intrigued why would a Navy Chief come and see a civilian,** initially they thought that he may be from Bhutan Royal family and then could not resist asking Rinchen; How does he know the Admiral? He told them that he was related to his brother-in-law and gave them some story!! Rinchen dressed up in traditional Sikkimese shirt with Chinese collar called-'Kyesha'.

At 1100h Admiral arrived at the Officer Ward and was received by Maj Gen Sharma, Commandant, Base Hospital and ushered into Rinchen's room and where he spent about half an hour with Rinchen and told him that he and Aunty Phyll are leaving for an official tour to Kenya, but James, the senior Stewart in the Navy House is there to look after him once he gets discharged. **It was indeed very kind of Admiral to find time and meet Rinchen.** In fact in NDA also as Dep Com he used to frequently visit the Military Hospital to see sick cadets and I have lots of stories to share mailed to me by ex-NDA cadets who had interaction with Admiral while they were admitted to the MH , which I shall cover in a separate chapter.

James, the senior Stewart in the Navy House visited Rinchen everyday in the hospital and spent time with him. James was indeed very smart and could speak fluent English. After a week or so Rinchen got discharged and spent couple of days in the Navy House. Rinchen took James out for a movie in Chanakya picture hall followed by dinner in nearby restaurant. On the day of departure James came to the airport to see off Rinchen. Presently Rinchen is Secretary level official in Sikkim Government.

To express his gratitude, Pala sent a box of apples for Admiral and Mrs. Pereira in appreciation of their kindness and concern for Rinchen during his stay in Navy House.

Admiral in his letter dated 24 Oct 1981, **quote** *"Dear Mr. Gyatso, Thank you a million for your kind thoughts and the lovely apples which you sent us. They are excellent and we are enjoying them. Both Phyllis and self were very pleased to hear that Rinchen is improving .He is really a very fine son as indeed Tashi is- and you and your wife can be very proud of both of them. They are a great credit to a very fine family. Our visit to Kenya was a very memorable one and country as a whole is a paradise with game reserve that has seen to be believed- such a profusion of animals.*

Our thanks again for lovely apples and our love and good wishes to Annie, Mike and their son! **Should Rinchen want any further medical attention please do not hesitate to let us know?** *With our good wishes, sincerely Ronnie Pereira .* **Unquote.** My son was not yet born, but Admiral intuition was correct.

Yet another **coincidence**; Tashi is Rinchen elder brother and from same school as Admiral – **North Point, Darjeeling** and he had couple of meals at Navy House with Admiral and Aunty Phyll and the conversation on the table would invariably lead to which of the two schools was better? - **Mount Hermon** (Aunty and Rinchen) vs **North Point** (Admiral and Tashi) and poor me from Sainik School, Kunjpura, had nothing to contribute in their discussion. They used to have heated argument about education and sports standard and who had better Soccer team?? Mrs. Pereira invariably won the argument! I was silent spectator but enjoyed listening to them!!

I must mention here that; a Roman Catholic Admiral (25th May 23) and Buddhist, Pala(25th June 23) born within one month of each other in two different countries and more than half century later; **both were attached** to a Sardar from Punjab!! Indeed both had similar human traits also!! Unbelievable!

Rabden

We were blessed with our first son on 1st Dec 81 and I called up Admiral and Mrs. Pereira and they were indeed very happy and sure enough, first question from Aunty was –does he have chinky or big eyes? Fortunately he had pretty big eyes for his small face. Later I was asked about his name; Sikh or Buddhist? I said it doesn't matter and no issue at all. Few weeks later we took the baby for naming ceremony to a revered Rompochi of the oldest Monastery in Gangtok, after chanting prayers from Tibetan scripture, he took out a letter and wrote a name on a small piece of paper and gave it to my mother-in-law who passed on to my wife and I asked- what's the name? She replied; **Rabden**- I said oh! My God this is a **Punjabi name** meaning; **gift of God**!! In Punjabi language, **Rab means God and Den means gift**!! What a **coincidence** and **surely the Rompochi could not have been conversant with Punjabi from time immemorial!**

Final Days

In his last few months Admiral was looking rather weary and forlorn and tired of fighting with the corrupt system and as per his staff he was beginning to feel sad that soon he will be leaving his beloved Navy after nearly 40 years of glorious service. One of his last letters as CNS written after their trip to Kenya, he wrote in his letter dated 26th Oct 81, quote *"My dear Mike, Thank you very much of your letter of the 19th Oct. I also received Pala's letter with lovely apples and immediately wrote back to him and thanked him for his thoughtfulness. He has also given a parcel for Tashi, which Gen Rao's ADC has delivered directly*

Our trip to Kenya was wonderful experience and we enjoyed every minute of it. The country is beautiful one and undoubtedly the most progressive in whole of Africa. The people are very kind and hospitable and the whole place runs with considerable organization and method. It surprised both of us a great deal.

We were overwhelmed with kindness and hospitality and our visits to 4 of the game sanctuaries were out of this world. The whole tour of game reserve has been meticulously and precisely planned for the tourists and there is no doubt that they have done extremely good job. The animals are in the "hundreds" and it is absolutely amazing sight to see them as you drive along the game track in the sanctuaries. We moved largely by service aircraft and service helicopters so there was little or any delay and the whole tour was a refreshing experience'.

I am glad Rinchen is doing well. His visit to Delhi was the best thing for him and I am quite sure that he will steadily improve. Our love and good wishes to Annie and the family, please also convey our good wishes to Pala - affly Uncle Ron" unquote

Next couple of months were spent on his farewell visits and Admiral had passed specific instructions that he should not be given any expensive gift excess of Rs 200/-. The best gift was given during his visit to Bombay. After taking off from INS VIKRANT, the C-in-C asked the helicopter pilot to turn around and he said; Ronnie look down and what he saw was indeed touching-all sailors on the ship doffing their caps and made a formation of "BYE RONNIE", yes it brought tears to Admiral's eyes! The photo of the same was the center piece of their Drawing room.

Last Visit to Navy House

In Dec 1981, Admiral had only three months left before his retirement on 28 Feb 82, and I was very keen that they must meet our baby and bless him. I wrote to him in end Jan 1982 that we would like to come and spend few days with them at Navy House before he retires.

Admiral replied in his letter dated 3rd Feb 82, **quote** *"My dear Mike, thank you very much for your letter dated 29th Jan 82, which I have just received.*

You, Annie and the baby will be welcome to visit us this month, but I would suggest a change in your dates. I am on tour up to evening of 14th February and I would, therefore, suggest that you come to Delhi on Monday, the 15th or Tuesday the 16th February. Unfortunately for most our evenings would be out as this farewell programme. That apart, we will be very delighted to see you.

Regarding the pram for the baby, I am afraid I do not go anywhere near the embassies or their sales except for official parties. However, I am sure you will be able to get a pram in the town and I think it is best that you and Annie have a look around and select something that you want.

*Please let me know the details of your arrival and **I will have the transport available at the airport to meet you.***

***Forgive the typewritten note.** It is the quickest way to reply - affly Unc Ron"*. **Unquote** .

In his correspondence of nearly 20 years with me, Admiral always wrote in his own hand, except couple of occasions and invariably apologized for the same!! An "ART" long forgotten and lost!

In fact letter writing is an "ART" and Admiral letters were like someone is speaking to you. I was told by Hugh Gantzer, the only son of Aunty May and a writer of international repute, **quote** "My maternal grandfather, Major Pereira had excellent command over the English language and could write fluently in beautiful hand. Both my dear mother and Ron inherited these skills from their father. He was an eloquent speaker, so naturally Ron picked up all these qualities from his dear father". **unquote**

Grand Parents

We arrived in Delhi on 16th Feb by the evening flight: 6.30 pm, Sharmaji was at the airport to receive us. While driving he mentioned, Sahib, this is the first time I have come to pick you up in 3 years. I told him that the car has been sent for Madam and Baby, I just happened to accompany them!!

They were thrilled to see the baby and he was indeed a bundle of joy for them as they were playing part of **Grandparents** for the first time in their lives and would take turns to carry him around- probably they never handled such a small baby in their lives. Admiral would finish his meals quickly, just to get an opportunity to carry Rabden and speak to him in baby language and make him smile. Aunty would be worried and keep reminding the Admiral to be careful and say – Ronnie, mind his head, put your hand under his head. By then Admiral had developed small beer paunch and the baby would soon sleep on his belly!! **How they enjoyed carrying the baby for four days and at times the baby did trick on him but Admiral did not mind but himself cleaned up the baby and changed diapers too, as also feeding bottles!**

The Navy House garden was in full bloom and I had the opportunity to take lots of photos of the baby with Aunty Phyll and Admiral elder sister Aunty Bobby who had just come back to India from Argentina after 44 years.

The next time when they met Rabden in Dec 86, he was 5 and younger son- Tashi- whom they saw for first time was already three years old.

Back To Gangtok

By April I was back in Gangtok and next month Gen Sharma was posted to AHQ's and was succeeded by another Cavalry officer- **Maj Gen Hanut Singh,**

MVC, from Poona Horse (17 Horse).A saint-soldier, who I will be covering separately in another chapter 'Admiral Encounter with Cavalry Generals'.

As my posting was due, Admiral gave me a long sermon, on how I should conduct myself on my return to the regiment and he wrote in his letter dated 12 Oct 82, **quote**" *I hope this letter gets you before you are transferred; in any case the HQ's will know where you are; if you have gone on leave or posting, so it should catch up with you. I am glad that you are getting back to the regiment and my congratulations and good wishes, my son, at picking up your majority as soon as you report. I see that Col Arvind Kumar is your Commandant. I believe I met him when I visited you in 1980, so please give him my very best wishes.*

This will now be very crucial time for you in the regiment . You will have your own company, responsible for its professional standards and the moral of the men . You will have young officers to mould and train in the right traditions of the Army and the regiment. **You will be under the microscopic scrutiny of your men who will analyze every word and every action of yours and that analysis will be deep and searching one, with the whole company comparing notes to find out exactly what you are like.** *You will finally have a fine CO deciding during this tenure in the regiment, whether you are suitable for promotion and the capacity in which you should be promoted.* **Finally, son, the answers that ultimately come out, may NOT be the one you hope for and you will be disappointed. At that stage never give up or never turn sour or disgruntled.** *Provided you have done your best and if you have, then you would have surely got a great deal of satisfaction from your work- there is nothing else you can desire or want. So to become sour or disappointed and critical is just not worth it."* **unquote**

It's amazing being a Naval officer with over 40 years of service and experience in handling human beings- his analysis and assessment of life in the Army and particularly at the unit level were '**spot on**'. Naturally he understands human behavior better than most. **That is why Navy still consider him as the "BEST CHIEF" they ever had!**

More importantly Admiral reading of the officer class was very accurate; "**men never let you down, if you look after them, breed them well and breed them tough they will be 100 % loyal to you;** The problem is in the officers cadre or colleague who may be envious or jealous, who may misbehave or try to create unnecessary awkward situations for you."

I went through the contents a number of times before I reported back to the unit in Nov 82. Needless to say Admiral's words were '**pearls of wisdom**' for me. It was quite smooth for me to get back to the grind of the unit life. Nothing like being amongst your own men with whom one has grown up and learnt the basics of Centurian / Vijayanta tank from them – Dafadar Janadharan- Radio , Satharaman- Gunnery, and Ulagnan-Driving and not to forget Risaldar Kutty Krishanan who taught me basic troop level drills ,so I just melted into them without any difficulty whatsoever.

Amritsar

In April 83 the regiment moved to Amritsar, Punjab, and on the day of arrival of our Military Special Train on 24th April 1983, the headlines in "Tribune" Newspaper read- DIG AS Atwal assassinated within the premises of Golden Temple! In fact Atwal had gone to pay his obeisance and like any other Sikh he went around the Parikrama, the marble pavement which surrounds the sacred pool. He went inside the Har Mandir Sahib, and prostrated himself before the Guru Granth Sahib, the Sikh scriptures and after a while holding Prasad in a leaf he came out and then walked towards the main gate. As he was climbing up the marble steps, he was fired upon and he died on the spot. He was 39.

Punjab was on fire with Khalistani Movement and **Amritsar** was in the **'eye of the storm'**.

Admiral and Mrs. Pereira and my parents were very concerned about safety of our lives. Soon we settled down and kept them posted about the situation. No doubt it was indeed very stressful.

In June we went out for 'Operational Familiarization' followed by exercise with tanks and troops. In his letter dated 1st July 83 **quote**" *My dear Mike- Both Aunty and myself were delighted to hear of the excellent performance of your squadron in the last exercise. It is always gratifying and professionally satisfying to see your unit not only perform well but to have that performance recognized by your 'Boss'. It more than makes up for all the sweat and toil that one has to put in and it makes all the difference to the men to know that they have not only be well led but their endeavours have been appreciated*". **Unquote**

In early June 83, my squadron was out on exercise with 86 Infantry Brigade near the International Border in a historic village called Kalanaur (Dist Gurdaspur, Punjab) where on 14th Feb 1556, Akbar was crowned as 3rd Mughal King and the structure of Thakht-i-Akbari still lies there in ruins. At the end of the exercise the Brigade Commander Brigadier RN Bhalla, VSM wrote a DO (Demi Official) letter dated 22 June 83, **quote**- "I write this letter to convey my grateful thanks to you and your men for being with us during "Ex HIMMAT". I wish to further say that the spirit of cooperation, sense of urgency and vigor shown during execution of all tasks given to your Sqn, and the accuracy with which the given tasks were executed is praiseworthy. **With the dedication and sense of coop shown by you and your men I will have no hesitation in choosing you to be with me any time the real need comes.** Please convey my appreciations to all ranks of your Sqn. Well done and keep it up- Ravi".**Unquote.**

I sent the photocopy of the DO to Admiral, who was indeed happy to read the contents of the letter and thus his reply in the above letter. Admiral always encouraged me to work hard and **"look after your men"**.

Dafadar (Safaiwala) Mohinder Singh

Dafadar Mohinder Singh was a senior Safaiwala (sweeper) in my unit; 16 Cavalry. In those times by tradition the vacancy of the father on retirement went to one of the male members of the family. Just a couple of years back on the retirement of Dafadar (Safaiwala) Babu, his son Ramesh was enrolled in our unit in early 80's.

However, Mohinder Singh decided to break away from this tradition and wanted better future for his son, Manoj Kumar, than following in the footsteps of his father. In mid 70's a Central School was established near Sujanpur Colony, Pathankot. In early 1977 Mohinder Singh approached me to get Manoj Kumar admission to the Central School. Being from schedule caste there were no problems at all getting admission and in June 1979 the regiment moved to Jodhpur. Armed with Transfer Certificate we faced no problem at all for admission to Central School, Jodhpur.

Four years later in April 83, the Regiment moved to Amritsar and by now Manoj had passed 7th Standard.

By then the nomenclature of the Central School had changed to Kendriya Vidhyalaya. The KV School in Amritsar was located within the cantonment itself. One day in the month of July, Mohinder Singh came to my office and told me that he was facing problems for admission of Manoj Kumar in 8th Standard. I immediately went to the school and met the Principal; Mr. Kaul whom I found rather rude and disrespectful. Still I ate a humble pie and requested him to please admit the boy, he did not sound very positive and expressed his inability to help and remarked that it is too late for admission in the 8th Standard. When I insisted, he asked me to come after one week and see what can be done about him. After one week I met him again, and the answer was the same, come back after one week. I was getting bit impatient and mentioned that the boy is from Schedule Caste and surely you can help him, but no go. Third time when I met him, he asked me in a rather sarcastic tone; Major Sahib yeh apka beta to nahin hai (he is not your son?), then why are you taking so much interest. I still held my cool and explained that his father is serving in my unit and I will be grateful if you could admit the boy- almost pleading! He said sorry there is no vacancy whatsoever.

I very politely asked him in case you can't help then there must be someone above you whom I can approach for help and release of additional vacancy. Mr. Kaul thought for a while and gave me hard look and sarcastically said; Bhalla Sahib, in case you want to approach higher up, then why don't you speak to the Commissioner of KV Sangathan in New Delhi. I asked for the name and he said – he is too powerful a person and controls over 400 KV Schools and won't have time to meet you. I again asked for the name and he said; Commodore Satbir Singh- the moment I heard the rank, I straightaway thought of Admiral and then told Mr. Kaul in no uncertain terms –Yeh bachha apke school mein hi dakhil hoga (mark my words, this boy will get admission in your school only). He was taken aback by my reply and said let me inform you Bhalla Sahib, Commodore Satbir Singh does not entertain any such unnecessary requests, there is no hope whatsoever.

I said we will see and walked off!

Commodore Satbir Singh was reputed to be unbending, strict and unapproachable person and maybe that's why Kaul gave me no chance. But then, he was not aware that I had the most potent weapon with me in form of the "Admiral" and nobody, I repeat nobody in Naval Whites, including Satbir Singh could possibly say "NO" to Admiral. I was 100% sure that Admiral will do the needful, more so because Manoj was from Schedule Caste.

I sat down and penned down a long letter to Admiral explaining him the situation and why it was important to educate this boy to give him better life than his own father. Without your help the father won't be able to fulfill his dream for his son. I knew Admiral will never say no when it comes to helping a sailor or soldier's cause. He was too kind a man and very sensitive to such issues.

I was in Delhi on my way to Gangtok for a long leave for arrival of our second child and stopped over to spend a day with my course mate and close friend Prabhjit Bedi, Adjutant President's Body Guard and I happened to mention about Manoj Kumar's case and also about the letter to Admiral to approach Satbir Singh for help. Prabhjit turned around and said, **quote** "Mike, forget it, Satbir is known for NOT entertaining any such requests and to be honest I am skeptical that he will heed to even Admiral's request. In fact I tried to approach Satbir through his son, to whom I had given the membership of the Polo and Riding Club, for admission of one of my jawan's child. Commodore Satbir did not oblige his own son's request. So Admiral stands no chance, just forget it" **Unquote.**

I did not agree with Parabhjit Bedi and told him whatever you may say about Satbir Singh, I don't think he will have the heart to turn down Admiral's request, and that too for a son of Sweeper, whom he does not even know from Adam!

Yes, I would have agreed with Prabhjit Bedi, had it been any other retired Chief, but NOT Admiral Ronnie Pereira, who had a reputation of impeccable integrity of 40 years in the Navy and surely Satbir Singh too would have been impacted by it while serving in the Navy.

On receipt of my letter, which I sent him by Registered Post AD, so that it does not get misplaced enroute, Admiral immediately shot off a letter to Commodore Satbir Singh requesting him to help the child and later wrote to me in his letter dated 20th Aug 1983, **quote** *"My dear Mike- this is very short and quick letter, just to say that I have written to Cmde Satbir regarding the admission of Dfr' Mohinder's son. Satbir will certainly help if he can, but with academic year already two months past, it will be difficult for the young lad to catch up. Secondly, you have not given me anywhere, the full address of the Sangathan and merely to put it 'New Delhi' which may not-indeed will not-get the letter to him as it's not quite as well known as Rashtrapati Bhavan!! I have, therefore, sent the letter to Naval Headquarters, to be delivered to the Sangathan. I hope something comes of it.*

Thank you very much for your long and juicy letter which you sent registered. Our love and good wishes to Annie. I am sure all will go well with the new baby, but I am glad that you are going up for spot of leave. The weather will be lovely and the baby will arrive before real cold sets in.

I will end now, so that I can get this off to you by today "Oakrunner"!! Will write again at length. God bless you and all the best. My warm regards to your in-laws – affly-Unc Ron". **Unquote.**

Admiral's letter was personally delivered to Cmde Satbir Singh by CNS office. I am certain in my mind that Cmde Satbir must have got surprised to receive a letter from Admiral, it could well have been the **first** letter ever received from Admiral in his life! After going through the contents, an urgent message was sent from Sangathan office to Mr. Kaul to admit Manoj Kumar forthwith and forward completion report within 48 hours for the information of the Commissioner!? I can well imagine how Kaul's stomach must have turned inside. He immediately called my regiment and feverishly tried to contact me. He was informed that Major Bhalla is away on leave to Sikkim. He now panicked and requested the Adjutant that one Dfr Mohinder Singh from your unit must contact him at the earliest!

Next day Manoj was admitted in the school.

When I returned from leave, Squadron Senior JCO Risaldar Uthaman was at Amritsar railway station to receive me, and as I disembarked from the train, I inquired about Manoj's admission; Uthaman told me; Sahib a few days after your departure Principal KV School was frantically looking for you and later we sent Mohinder to the school and Manoj was immediately admitted. As I reached Officer's Mess, there I saw Mohinder Singh standing outside my room on the first floor with a box of sweets in his hands and he walked towards me, saluted and bent down to touch my feet with tears flowing down his cheeks, I held him and embraced him and he cried to his heart content and kept **repeating** –thank you Sahib. I too had tears in my eyes to share the happiness of a father for his son and told him he can only thank God, we are mere mortal tools of the God.

God bless Admiral's soul and yes, next time when I met him in person in Dec 86 in Whitefield, I narrated the whole incident to Admiral and he too was moved and all he said ; really my son!

That was the **GREATNESS** of Ronnie P, **"GOOD Human Being"**. He never met Mohinder Singh in his life but felt for his son's future.

It has been over 33 years but it feels as though it happened just yesterday and I vividly remember the sarcasm in Kaul's voice and tears of happiness and joy of Mohinder Singh!

Staff College Exam

In his letter dated 28th July 83, he suggested that I should start preparing myself for **Staff College Entrance Examination**. By then I had 9 ½ years of service and as per regulations my first mandatory chance was due in Nov 84, which was some 16 months away but he insisted that I must concentrate and start preparing and wrote , **quote** " *Well, my son, you must get down seriously to your Staff College Examination. This is very necessary for you to get over this hurdle and it is certainly worth while course, professionally. Not only is it necessary for you future professional career , but an opportunity to know and study with a fine bunch of your contemporaries and have a absolutely magnificent library to do your professional reading is the opportunity that does not come very often in your career. It will certainly mean studying, in addition to running your company **but the sooner you put the examination behind you, the better it would be**". **Unquote**

1983 was a bad year for Punjab as the militancy was at its peak and Sikh militants were carrying out systematic killings of the Hindu Intelligentsia leading to their exodus to other states and here our regiment was located right in the heart of their struggle. It was very stressful and dangerous situation for us; however, after receiving Admiral's letter, I started to collect material for all six subjects, particularly Military History. It seemed insurmountable task, **but try I must.**

Notwithstanding, our commitments in Internal Security duties in Amritsar, Admiral kept pressurizing me not to lose anytime and start preparations for the exams in the right earnest. In August I had gone to Gangtok for birth of second son, born on 30th Sep 83. In response to my telegram Admiral wrote in his letter dated 10th Oct 83, **quote** "*My dear Annie and Mike- our love and good wishes and God's blessings on arrival of second son and heir, which we were very pleased to hear about, on the receipt of Mike's telegram. I hope you have since received our telegram which I sent to you on your father's address at Sikkim. I am glad you were at home, Annie, for your confinement, as it really is best place to be when expecting a baby.*

*Now that there are two sons to ensure the Bhalla line of succession!! Mike must now begin to get ready for Staff College, which will mean him, qualifying in an entrance exam. This is very important hurdle to cross, and a very necessary one, as it is the key to all future avenues of employment and promotions. Indeed for you, Annie, Staff College is lovely 11 months, for though it will be a plenty of work for Mike, it is a lovely change for the wives. **What is even more important is the fact that you will meet a lot of officers and their ladies from other arms and services that you would not have normally met in your own service environment and these friends will stand you and Mike in good stead,** in the years ahead- well Annie and Mike our love and good wishes to you, to the 'heirs apparent'! Look after yourself- our very good wishes to your parents, Annie – affly Unc Ron'.* **Unquote**

Well I **heeded to his advice** in the right earnest and started to prepare myself for the upcoming Junior Command Course at Mhow in November 83, which is in fact a precursor to preparation for Staff College Exam. However, Admiral next letter did not bring good tidings for me. Somehow he got the wind that I have been damaged in my Annual Confidential Report and it was my first Command Report as Squadron Commander and would certainly damage the prospects of my promotion to next rank i.e. Lt Colonel, whenever the promotion board is held.

Annual Confidential Report

In his letter dated 25th Nov 83, **quote** " *My son, I hear that your last ACR was not a very good one and I tried to personally analyze the reasons as I know you must not only be good with the men, but you should be equally good professionally, having done well for most of the courses since commissioning .*

*I feel that you must remember primarily that you are in a very competitive environment and it takes very little to be superseded to Lt Col, as the competition at this stage is really tremendous. The Army, if you wish to make it a career-is literally your mother, father, wife, child and this is not an unreasonable assumption as it is only by giving everything to your service that you have, can you move up in the ladder of success and promotion. You can get outdated very fast; you will be observed for this out datedness; any shortcoming in lethargy or delay in execution of orders, must be observed in close society like regiment , so it is only by going flat out, can you keep up with the rest. Finally, you have just finished a spell as an ADC and I have always found that those young officers, who come back from such an assignment, take time to settle into mundane and regular activity of a unit. As a **Company Commander** you must forget your time as an aide and remember you are back in the run of the mill. Lastly, your family, at this stage of one's career cannot have priority, it must be your men and your unit and it is always advisable to keep the family with your in-laws, particularly at this crucial stage, this is important.*

Don't above all get discouraged. Get stuck into your profession and work and you will certainly do well. Besides it is only one ACR and there will be many good ones to balance out. However, you cannot afford another mediocre report.

*I have not seen or been told the contents of your ACR. It was matter of luck that I heard of this report, so don't worry how I came to know. However, I felt I should write to you about it, and have, therefore, done so. **The point is to correct the error and make up for the lost ground**".* **Unquote**

Admiral was right about my rather below average report as a Squadron Commander initiated by my CO. It was indeed damaging and detrimental to my future prospects in the Army. It is just not possible to balance out a poor ACR with 2 or 3 outstanding ACR (which is pretty tough). The below average ACR stays in your Master Data Sheet and pulls you down and enough to damage your career progression and **for all practical purposes I was fixed for good with little hope to go up the ladder. But Admiral kept encouraging me not to ever give up and keep working hard.**

Admiral as everybody knew was workaholic and he had great energy and mental strength to work for 10 to 12 hours whether as CO INS Delhi, Dep Com in NDA, or Fleet Commander or C-in-C Western Naval Command. He was simply unbelievable and amazing and actually loved what he was doing.

Honestly nobody could match up with him and I tried to suggest that I may not be able to meet his expectations in spite of my best efforts. In his letter dated 2 Feb 84, he made an effort to explain and elaborate the contents of his previous letter about work ethics, **quote** "*Son, the only reason I mentioned that your profession must come before your family, was to try and point out to you,* **the intense competition that arises once you get into the selection grade of promotion** *and to compete in that environment one has to sweat professionally to make the grade.* **Perhaps 1 officer in 100 makes it to Brigadier and one in thousand to General rank.** *This gives you an idea of steep pyramid one has to climb, it cannot, I am sure be done by giving equal time between your profession and your family. And it's* **not** *a question of neglecting your family,* **but it is certainly a question of putting a great deal time in your profession.**

However, son, this is the decision that only you can make, it is up to you to make anyway you like. **However, if and when you ever miss the boat don't ever blame your seniors, a little objective analysis will always find the shortcoming within yourself.** *All the best to you son, and work hard. You must come out with an AX. Look after yourself – affly Unc Ron".***Unquote**

Admiral was pushing me to work, work and work hard and I was fully aware that whatever he was suggesting was ultimately for my own good.

Operation Blue Star

By the time I came back from course the situation in Punjab, particularly in Amritsar got very grave and soon we were deployed for IS Duties in and around Amritsar. It was indeed getting worse by the day leading to 'OP BLUE STAR' on the night of 5th/6th June 84, when Army stormed sanctum sanatorium, Har Mandir Sahib, "The Golden Temple".

In his letter dated 9th June 84, **quote** "*Your dear mother and Father, you and the family and all the fine young Sikh cadets who were with us at the Academy, have been in our minds over the last few days with the events in the Golden Temple, distressing us a great deal. The whole episode has been one of great sorrow to us, and after seeing the tremendous coverage given to the beautiful shrine in Amritsar, it seems unbelievable that it could have been the focus and centre of a movement that sort the wonton destruction and death of mankind, so indiscriminate and unnecessary that it can only fill the hearts and souls of men with grief.*

We have been watching every T/V programme and following the whole episode very closely. Both Aunty and I felt very proud of the excellent task the Army had done and one cannot speak too highly of the way the operation was conducted. It was sad that the Army had to go in, but there appeared no answer but this, to the problem; however, **the truly magnificent way the Army officers and men conducted himself,** *made both of us realize the excellence of our soldiers . 55 men dead and 355 casualties are heavy to say the least, but this can confirm the sincerity and maturity of the troops who acted with such great restrain. I only hope that this is the end of activities of the extremists, and Punjab will now return to normalcy".* **Unquote**

Admiral couldn't have been farther from the truth as the militancy in Punjab continued for another 6 years, before DG Police Mr. KPS Gill brought an end to it in early 90's.

Staff College Nomination

Time was running out for me as **only 5 months were left for preparations of Staff College Exams scheduled from 19th-24th Nov 84, at Jullundur.** I went ahead and sat for the exam and with the **grace of God was happy to see my name in the nomination list on 31st Jan 85!!** I immediately sent wire to Admiral, my parents and Gen Hanut Singh. Admiral who was at the back of me to get this hurdle behind was indeed very happy and in his letter dated 5th Feb 85, **quote'** *My dear Mike- Thank you very much for your telegram with the news that you will be going to the DSSC for the next course.* **Both Aunty and I were delighted** *and send you our love and good wishes.*

I presume this means you will be going for the next course which commences in Jun 86 and not the current one on which Benny is and which must have started early Jan. However, the main thing is to get P.S.C. and in doing so, meet a lot of fine officers from other two services and indeed many of your own course mates from the 43rd. You will certainly enjoy and get an opportunity to do lots of professional reading from one of the best Services library in the country

Our love and good wishes to Annie and the children who must be with you . I am sure Annie must be looking forward to Staff College, as the weather will be lovely she will be away, poor girl, from the grueling heat of Punjab, which she has yet to face. "**Unquote**

I received scores of congratulatory letters from my well wishers and of course the best was from one of the most revered officer from Cavalry- **Maj Gen Hanut Singh, MVC (later Lt Gen)** dated 22nd Feb 85, **quote** "*My dear Mike- I was away at Ahemadnagar, attending a Seminar. It was there I learnt of your success in the DSSC Entrance Exam. **I was delighted to hear this news** and wanted to drop you a line to convey my felicitations, but they kept us infernally busy: quite against the ethos and established traditions of 'Nagar', they made us attend long afternoon sessions, ending as late as 1830 hrs. Of course, they did this at their own risk because, usually, the only person awake was poor bozo who was presenting his paper.*

On return, I received your letter also. In that you sound rather apologetic and go to the extent of "confessing" to having committed the unpardonable crime of having passed the DSSC Exam. I guess that is in the best traditions of the Cavalry. It was considered rather improper in old, horsy days to even sit for the Staff College Exam, let alone passing it, because if you did some such thing, you would be labeled " intelligent and clever officer"; which in effect meant that you had been damned by your brother officers , as the cleverness of any sort was always suspect in the eyes of the old " Koi Hais". Officers from Cavalry Regiments were usually nominated to the DSSC, and the Commandant usually nominated those whom they did not like, or those who were proving to be an embarrassment and had to be got rid off !Times change.

I was happy to learn that Annie and the kids were doing fine. You can look forward to a very pleasant one year at Wellington. The officers are kept reasonably busy, but the wives have a real jolly time. So you must take Annie along; she will enjoy her stay there; it is a lovely place.

The important thing is not simply to get into Staff College; in fact, I had no doubt in my mind that you would make it. The important thing is to do well there. I am equally confident that you will do very well, and I expect you to get posted as a BM to an Armd Bde. This will be the best way of thumbing your nose at those who tried to belittle your professional worth. **The fate of individuals is not controlled by petty human beings; however, much such people may like to believe otherwise.**

Fond regards and best wishes to you, Annie and the kids–affly Hanut."**Unquote**

Gen Hanut too was hinting at that damaging ACR, which Admiral had mentioned in his letter of 25th Nov 83.

Traditionally, Staff College courses since its inception in Oct 1947 commence in the month of September, later in early 70's from January and from DSSC-42, our course, with effect from last Monday of June. Our course commenced on 30th June 86. The aim was to coincide with school calendar of the children and the reporting period of officers.

Television

Colour TV was the flavour of the season and as usual didn't have sufficient finances to purchase one. I wrote to Admiral if **he could loan me Rs 5000/- to enable me to buy one, expectedly he out rightly turned down my request** and maybe he had his reasons that was the first time I ever asked in 15 years. In his letter dated 21 Feb 85, **quote** *'My dear Mike- Two days ago one of your boys brought me a letter from you and I was surprised to read that you had not received two of my earlier letters, the last of which was in reply to your telegram telling us about the Staff College examination, which delighted both Phyll and I.*

I just don't understand this as all my letters have gone to you care of 56 A.P.O and they should certainly get to the regiment, where ever you may be, I therefore taking the precaution of sending this one Registered AD to confirm whether you have received it.

Of the last two letter. The first one was written quite some time ago, in reply to your request for Rs 5000/-. I wrote you a very long letter, to explain why we could not give you this, as well as to say that even if I could, I would not give it and then went on to explain why.

I don't understand why this should not have got to you, though I did not have a reply. Again, when we received your wire about Staff College, I immediately wrote to you again and this letter as I note from your letter sent thru one of your lads has also not got to you. However, this will go Regd AD.

Our love and good wishes to Annie and the children . I am sure you will all like Staff College, it will get Annie and the kids out of summer heat of Punjab. The Army unfortunately works hard at the college, but you will certainly find the course very interesting and you will not only meet your old course, but a bunch of fine officers- look after yourself and drop me a line if you receive this letter- affly Unc Ron". **Unquote**

After that I never mentioned about the money to him ever. May be he was from the old school, where parents never spoil their children- go and earn yourself. Worse my father too refused to help! In hindsight I think he was right, make you learn to look after your needs yourself. **Admiral was a straight man and never minced his words - yes, I was on the receiving end a number of times. He had no shades of Grey, just Black or White!**

All officers who qualify for Staff College are put through a short 'Scientific Orientation' course at IIT , Girinagar, Pune, located at the base of famous 'Singarh Fort'- which as a cadet I climbed 13 times - it was a popular punishment doled out by none other than Admiral himself !!

It's a six week course and I mentioned to Admiral about this course and in reply in his letter dated 29 July 85, **quote** '*I see that you are going for a course to Pune,* **but your writing being what it is, I haven't have the faintest idea, what course this may be as it looks like ATOC and I haven't any idea what that could stand for!!.** *Armament Technology covers a pretty wide field, so it could not be an 'acquaintance' with the subject, which could be just as successful as trying to make a doctor out of a dispensary assistant by short medical acquaintance course!!".* **Unquote**

In his very next letter dated 30 Sep 85, he was once again reiterating on professional front and life in the Army, **quote** "*You are in a very competitive Army; you MUST command your battalion. If you do that I would be immensely proud of you, as I know how good you would be as a CO both professionally and indeed to your men. When you are there, I will, without a shadow of doubt come and visit Annie, children and you. So, my son don't neglect your profession, though the sport has its place in the unit and certainly in your life. Finally, my own pride and joy to see you in command would be nothing in comparison to the joy in Annie's heart and that is what really matters. All the best, son, and work hard . You are always in our thoughts-affly Unc Ron".***Unquote** .

Apparently he was trying to tell me not to waste too much time playing Golf!!

From day I got commissioned in Dec 73, Admiral has been always encouraging me to do well in all courses, clear the Staff College Exams and ultimately make a sincere endeavour towards **one single goal- that is to command a unit** and thereafter it is all bonus. In fact, in by gone era, **command of the unit, was considered as a pinnacle of one's career.**

Commanding Officer appointment is the last in the chain of command where one has direct contact with the men you command and thereafter it is always from standoff distance. To encourage me he would always say- "**son, I will be there to congratulate you personally, even if I have to come in a wheel chair!** Unfortunately he never lived to see that day as he passed away in Oct 93 and I got command in April 95.

In his next letter dated 26th Nov 85, **quote** "*When will you be leaving for DSSC? I think the course starts sometime in Jan, so you will have to be there just before this. Hold it- I think you mentioned in one of your earlier letter that the course had been rescheduled for July, so you may be leaving later. Anyway, my son, I am sure you will do well, **but what will burst my heart with pride, will the fact of your possible posting after the course as Brigade Major.** That is really where I would like to see you go, **for that is a top slot for a Major from the DSSC**. I know you can do it and my prayers are always with you on this issue*"

Role of Serviceman Wife

*Dear Annie must be with you and so do the children. It is always wonderful to be together and **a wife to a serviceman is really like rock of Gibraltar**. Just two days ago, I was writing "middle" for our local paper called the 'DECCAN HERALD' and in it I spoke of the part played by serviceman's wife.*

I said "he is really married to someone who compares with the status, for she is really the economist, financier, interior decorator, professional packer and peace maker; in fact a great magician and last but not least, a very devoted wife. She cooks his food and runs his household on a shoe string; she clothes and feeds his children and caters to all their whims and fancies; she entertains his guests and never lets him down even if it means raiding the oldest child piggy bank. She buys his uniform, polishes his shoes and provides his civvies. She always keeps her man proud of himself, his unit, the country that he serves. Finally she sets him off to work every day never to be discredited to himself or his fine associates. She is a star; she is "poppet"-

It's a 500 words article and if it is published, I will send you a copy. I have asked that it should be published under the **pseudonym of A.D. MIRAL!!** I have called it "The Serviceman". **Unquote**

What a beautiful and meaningful article by someone whose wife was a working woman. Much before she was married, Mrs. Pereira was working for Bombay Burma Company in Calcutta in late 40's early 50's, staying at YWCA hostel and later moved to Bombay and it was only in early 1971 she gave up her job as her presence was mandatory at NDA as Dep Com's wife. **She was indeed rock of Gibraltar for Admiral. Very elegant and superbly dignified in her conduct and was admired by all the ladies in NDA and Navy.** She had serious problem in conversing in Hindi and one day instructed the staff car driver Bahadur - "memsahib ko raste mein girakar ghar aana"!! What she meant was- after dropping Mrs. Rikhi at her residence, come back home!! I used to give her Hindi lessons and we laughed like mad! **It was she who single handedly constructed 'AT LAST' at Whitefield, Bangalore at the peak of summers in 1978. Hats off to her!**

I remember sending him a letter through two of my jawans; Parmeshwaran and Sajan Babu, who were proceeding on leave to Bangalore. Parmeshwaran's wife was in advance stage of pregnancy and Admiral very kindly took her to the Command Hospital himself and had her admitted there. He wrote in his letter of 23 May 86, **quote** "*Thank you Mike for both your letters thru your two boys. I took Parmeshwaran down to the hospital to have his wife checked up, and she since had a baby girl. Parmeshwaran left yesterday for Kerela.*

Regarding the job for Sajan Babu's wife, this will be a problem. The reason is simple. With about 5000 officers and sailors, there are many who graduates with an additional B.E.D ! These are also looking for job in the naval school. However, I will try but the competition is very stiff." **Unquote**.

Many of my unit JCO's and Jawans used to approach him. Though he couldn't succeed every time but he **always tried**. It is because of his concern for my men; I had very good standing with all of them. Throughout my stay of 18 years in 16 Cavalry, I hardly raised my voice leave alone punish any Thambi, they were simply wonderful.

Admiral and Mrs. Pereira were very keen to meet the children and toying with the idea if we could spend few days with them on our way to Coonoor. In his letter dated 23 May 86, **quote** "*Son, what are your plans?* **Phyll and I were discussing the possibility of you, Annie and the children, spending a few days with us, we would be delighted to have all of you , thou you will only** *have a single bedroom to live in. However, coming down from the North, to Bangalore will require a number of changes, and the problem of reservation. This will also inconvenience the kids a lot. On the other hand, it may be better to get up to Staff College, quickly, settle into your house, draw your rations and do all the initial chores as quickly as possible. And when you do your Bharat Darshan which includes B'lore, you could bring Annie and the kids with you. I reckon we will still be here at 'AT LAST ' If by chance, it is sold, then Coonoor will be our destination and Aunty intends to come up, as soon as any future sale is finalized and spend some time at Dunmore , the office of the Naval Hydrographic where Southern Command have a nice VIP, Suite. Nonetheless, this depends at the sale of AT LAST. However, whatever you decide to do I will leave it to you, but let us know your plans.*

Thank you for the photo of the children. They are really looking wonderful and very cute, Our love to both of them. When are their birthdays and Annie's as well our love to all of you and God bless you, affly -Uncle Ron". **Unquote**

Due to very long journey of more than three days which would have entailed changing at least two trains, coupled with hot weather and two small kids it would have been very inconvenient and uncomfortable journey to say the least, particularly for the kids, who were still not fully acclimatized to the heat and dust of the plains of North India. **Thus, we very reluctantly decided to skip the Bangalore trip and hopefully make it during mid-term break in Dec 86.** We travelled to Mattupalayam by Staff College special train from New Delhi, which is in fact, has only ambulance coaches and children have great fun running up and down the coach. It went via Eastern coast route, rather dry and few stations to provide food and milk for children and got us to our destination after grueling four days of very tiring and pathetic journey.

Defence Services Staff College 42

As young GC (Gentleman Cadet) at Indian Military Academy in spring of 1973, I vividly remember when the Staff College exams results were declassified and published in the leading Newspapers, there was lots of excitement. Three officers from IMA had cleared the exam; Major Binny Shergill from 7 Cavalry, Major Gandhi from Artillery and Major MP Singh from Education Corps (originally Artillery) and they all seemed very happy and top of the world. **We thought that they were all great officers to make the grade for Staff College.**

In Jan 74 I joined 16 Cavalry, part of 16 Armoured Brigade which had three of the oldest and best Regiments plus top Mechanised Battalion;

Hodson's Horse, Commanded by Lt Col Gurinder Singh, 17 Horse by Lt Col Ajai Singh , 20 MLI by Lt Col Satish Nambiar, and 16 Cav by Lt Col Morris Ravideran. All outstanding officers and Satish Nambiar had attended Staff College in Australia. In addition there were nearly dozen Majors who were PSC (Passed Staff College) in the brigade. Perhaps it was best collection of highly professional officers in a single formation. I as youngster like many others in the brigade looked up to them with great awe and admiration and wondered, if one day I too could make it to Staff College? Academically being just above average, at that juncture it seemed almost **impossible** to cross this massive hurdle?!

That magic moment arrived 12 years later in the last week of June 86 as we were driving up the road from Mattupalayam to Wellington in the Staff College bus - **a dream come true** ;

Within a week we went straight into the whirl wind of work, work and work. My God, with Staff Duties and Appreciations, home work and preparations for next day tutorials, we did not know whether we were coming or going!! And to make matters worse our DS for first tutorials was a fire brand Col RR Palsokar from the Regiment of GUARDS who had attended Staff College, Camberley, Surray in UK, a very serious and hard task master, we were beginning to wonder was it worth the effort to come here??

This hectic schedule gathered pace and it was becoming difficult to cope with it! Admiral must have realized my plight and tried to motivate me to face the grind, in his letter dated 08th Aug 86, **quote** *"I am sure you will thoroughly enjoy Staff College, from every aspect of work and play, **though I well know that the Army tends you to work, just a little too much and to my mind that doesn't really make sense**. Any student will never have the opportunity to read from such a fabulous library; to discuss and understand from the members of other two services, their positions, their necessity and their slot in the jig saw of war; **to establish that very important human relationship with the other services, that makes for the most important aspect of co-operation that wins battles**; and finally to let the officers off the hook, to do what they want in building up their professionalism.*

*However, son, my views don't really matter a great deal and what Aunty Phyll and **I want from you is a posting as a Brigade Major when you leave next year!! I know that is well within your ability** , so I leave it you to work on.*

I hope Annie likes Coonoor. It will certainly give her and children a better climate than she had to put up with at Amritsar!! In fact winter is really enjoyable and pleasant and will possibly bring back memories of Sikkim, though there will not be any snow. Our love and good wishes to all of you. Look after yourself-affly Uncle Ron". **Unquote.**

Admiral letter did make some difference to lift my sagging spirits and knowing well that the pressure of work is a continuous process, soon another letter followed dated 14 Sep 86, **quote** *"The first tutorial is indeed a bit of sweat, what with minor SD and appreciations and a campaign study or two thrown in for good measure! I am quite sure we didn't have the same pressure as you do now and our afternoons were always P.S. time!*

I am sure you must have fair deal of tutorials or some form of instructions, and sand models or **whatever the devil the Army do**, *but I personally feel that P.S. was a great advantage, for it gave one time to go into that 'Super' library- which must be even better now- and catch up on your professional reading, whether it was part of study you were working on, and indeed just browsing thru professional literature. In fact one never ever gets this sort of opportunity again, in the whole one's professional career. Other than possibly when you come back for NDC or Higher Command course- and lot of water will flow under the bridge before that! Look after yourself son, all the best. You are all in my prayers every day- affly- Uncle Ron".* **Unquote**

Undoubtedly there was great deal of pressure of written work and hardly any time to do anything else. Notwithstanding, the ambience, the weather, the working environment in the college were excellent to say the least. The Directing Staff were all top class and possibly the best lot as instructors. I remember in one of the central classes for Management taken by a team of officers from College of Defence Management, Secundrabad, led by Brig Agarwal of Rajput Regiment. Brig Agarwal asked a question from the class- What are the major advantages of doing Staff College? Most of the students spoke about learning staff duties, syllabus, sand models and lectures etc. Brig Agarwal, who I knew from before, turned towards me and asked -Mike what do you have to add? I got up and said- Sir , the biggest advantage is that you meet your own course mates, not from the Army but Navy and Air Force, plus officers from foreign countries and creating a bond with them. Secondly more importantly, there are 52 Colonels in the DS body, each one of them will become Brigadier, 90% will become Maj Gen, 80% Lt Gen and you may have future Chiefs sitting amongst themselves- everyone had big laugh- and later in my service apart from all the students of DSSC 42nd course, am sure I can walk up to anyone from the DS body, irrespective of their rank and appointment for any assistance whatsoever, the answer will be always 'YES'. Brig Agarwal was left speechless and he nodded in agreement and said I think what Mike had stated has deep meaning to it, learning professional subjects is one thing but creating human rapport with each other is something more important as this particular aspect will play very important role towards the outcome of future wars !! To be honest I was echoing Admirals thoughts!! But it worked and got lot of back thumping after the class!!

There was no let up in the pace of work but I kept in touch with Admiral and Mrs. Pereira. In his letter dated 27 Oct, **quote** *"My dear Mike and Annie- you must now be in the middle of another tutorial and sweating on OP ORDERS and snap appreciations and country studies and plenty of sand models thrown in for good measure! This tutorial will possibly be sweat and then things will begin to ease up though you possibly never think so, as my recollection of the Army go back to them sweating on PS of some manual of 400 pages which they were required to complete in 4 hours of PS !*

Read as much as you can, son, as you will never get this opportunity again which gives you a fantastic library to go through". **Unquote**

There is no doubt that Staff College library was one of the best we have in all three Services and it had books on every possible subject, military campaigns, military leaders and famous battles down the centuries. Our problem was of finding adequate time to spend in the library, leave alone reading at home as it was difficult to cope with the syllabus!! Admiral was a voracious reader and so was Mrs. P who had great collection of books on almost every subject **except cooking!!**

Somehow going through my letters Admiral must have sensed that I was having a tough time with my written work and I must confess that **I wasn't brilliant** and was just average student in school and as cadet in NDA and IMA. No great shake with academics. Just to pep me up he wrote a very nice letter dated 26 Nov 86, **quote** *"My son, you sound a little 'choker' 'with the course and all the written work you have to do. I see your point that written work of the type you do at DSSC will never figure in the field, but the point is, that if you learn to be logical in the written work, the rest will follow in the years later. You are being schooled, all over again, but this is professional schooling. Someone is trying to teach you logical thought, be it an OP ORDER, APPRECIATION, or anything else. Once you get that in your head, everything follows, whether it is snap appreciation, or an OP ORDER under stress, or a written report for an operation. It is absolutely essential, and you MUST and WILL benefit from it. I still remember AMOSS Could Eat Five Custard Apples- Aim, MORAL, Offensive Action, SECURITY, Surprise, cooperation, Economy of Effort, Flexibility, Coordination and*

Administration. I don't even know if these principles of war still exist, but I have never forgotten them. Don't let all the work let you down. It's not like you, as I always believed you to be someone who can take a great deal, however, adverse and come right back. Just keep batting with your head down and your eye on the ball and you will come through with flying colours. As I have studied you, watched you, with fair degree of objectivity and no bias. I believe you have a great degree of common sense and ability to establish a rapport with human beings. This is all that matters, as these are the qualities that make good leaders. Look after yourself and work hard- affly Unc Ron". **Unquote**

Even today when I go through the contents of Admiral letters nearly 30 years later, make my eyes swell with memories of those struggling days and how Admiral tried to **motivate and encourage** me to get over the hump. **He was so concerned and expressive in his letters as though he was speaking to you and telling you don't worry, son, you will make it.**

After very hectic five months and tutorials we were looking forward to our mid- term break in December, a very welcome respite from précis, study table and syndicate rooms, sand models and outdoor exercises. It's a short break of one week but long enough to enjoy it!!

Visit to Whitefield

Bangalore is overnight journey by train from Mattupalayam. Admiral and Mrs. Pereira were very keen to see the children. In between I had gone to Bangalore after Admiral's scooter accident in April 83. Last time they met Annie and Rabden was in Feb 82 in Navy House, and the younger son was not born as yet! I wrote to Admiral that we would like to come and spend few days with them. They were really excited and Admiral in his letter dated 26 Nov 86, **quote** "*We will be **delighted** to have all of you with us, for the break in December, but please let us know your firm programme. I think it will be better to come down by train, as you then can get off at Whitefield- at an unearthly hour of 0600 h in the morning- but I **shall get someone's car** and meet all of you. The station is about 4 kms from the house, but the bus terminal will be 24 or 25 kms.*

I am afraid that you will have to rough it out a bit, as the bedroom has two beds and I will be able to squeeze in a camp cot. It'll not however, take 4 beds!! None the less it will be nice change and I am sure you will enjoy it.

The weather in Whitefield is certainly not cold. One needs a sweater in early morning and again in the evening, but beyond this you can be in a shirt during the day.

*I did have a car of a buddy of mine, who was away in UK. It was an Ambassador, old, but ran reasonably well. However, he comes back on 28th November we shall **be car-less after that**. My intention is to buy Maruti 800- if and when 'AT LAST' goes, but that is now somewhat nebulous. Anyhow, buddies of ours go into town quite frequently, **it is not difficult to take lift with them".*
Unquote

Leave alone car Admiral did not have a scooter, all he had was- 'MOPED'??

It was cold December morning when the train slowly trudged into Whitefield Railway Station, it halted for few minutes only and we were able to disembark and there in the darkness at a distance on the platform I saw Admiral standing with a torch in his hand, as we walked towards him, he was so delighted to see the small boys and he lifted both of them in his arms, hugged them, kissed them and simply loved as they were his own blood grandchildren!

Yes, he borrowed a car from very close friend and colleague Commodore Jack Shea (retd), who joined Navy one year after Admiral in 1944. Commodore Jack Shea and Aunty Dorothy were very close to Admiral and Aunty Phyll. After a while we reached AT LAST and Aunty Phyll was indeed very happy to see Annie and two little fellows!!

After breakfast we got both the kids ready to go for a joy ride with "Bara Papa "on his famous 'MOPED'. Rabden would sit behind with his arms tightly around Admiral's waist and he could not fully put them around him as Admiral had developed beer pounch! Tashi would stand in front holding the handle! It was beautiful sight and I had taken photos and not been able to trace them, though I have many more of that visit. Admiral used to carry both of them on his shoulders and he would take them for long walk across the main road to "St. Theresa Novitiate" church and beyond. On their return Admiral would ask them to take out their shoes which were full of mud and dust and would sweetly hold them in the palm of his hands and clean and polish them, brushing them till the children could see their face in the shine! Then at lunch time he would keep the Riding Crop with him on the dining table and bang it on the table and shout –come on **EAT**- both of them would quickly clean up their plates. It was some sight and Aunty Phyll would say- come on Ron don't frighten the poor children but he won't listen and would say they must have full meal and only then they can grow strong and big!!

Admiral spent every minute with the kids and whole day he was playing with them. He borrowed Jack Shea's car and took the children to Cubbon Park, Vidhan Saudha in Bangalore and other places of interest including Toy Train journey and the famous Lal Bagh.

Every time Admiral went to market, he would take the kids with him on his Moped. It was indeed a wonderful break for the children and both Admiral and Aunty Phyll thoroughly enjoyed the kids company.

On our return journey we came back by road and Admiral insisted that he will drop us at the bus terminal which was 25 km away. I noticed that Admiral was having difficulty in driving at night and I felt very guilty but he wouldn't let us go in a taxi .I really felt sad for him when he bid good bye to the kids, kissed them many times over and we had tears in our eyes and he never saw the kids again, though Aunty met them a number of times as both of them did their graduation from Al-Ameen college, Bangalore, from 2002-2006.

Staff Posting

Since the time I passed Staff College Entrance Exam in Jan 85- Admiral always had one small dream, that on completion of Staff College I must get a posting of **'Brigade Major', which indeed is the top appointment for Major in the Army**. In almost in all his correspondence during Staff College every time emphasized on this particular issue. I tried my best but eventually could not make the grade and my posting came as **grade 2 in Mechanised Division**, Hissar. I wrote to Admiral and apologized that I could not meet his aspirations in spite of my best efforts. He must have realized my disappointment and replied by return post, dated 19 March 86.

Quote *"My dear Son, your letter of 12th just came in, and as I read thru it, I decided that I must reply to you immediately.*

To begin with, I am not disappointed in the least, about your posting, and I certainly don't think that you should be. If you have not been posted as a BM, it's nothing to mourn about and possibly the staff job that you will go to, will be equally interesting. No son, never worry what is behind you; that is only useful for the lessons you learn, for the experience that you gain and that is important. What you must think about is what is ahead, and I have no doubts that you have a fine future in the next few years. A BM is possibly an independent staff job; it may get one in or out of the lime light quickly, but that is only one course, so to speak. All staff jobs are equally important as they contribute to giving a Commander a good and clear picture of what is ahead, so you play your part equally well in any staff assignments. My advice therefore is forget about BMs and do your best what lies ahead.

Secondly, son, don't worry about one report, having set you on not quite the course that you expected. **There are many ways of getting where you want to, without compromising your principles.** *So don't change those: you have excellent ones which you must stick to, and those will always be respected.* **Life if you look back runs like a Sinnsvidal curve - it has ups and downs. But provided the general trend of that curve, moves in an upward direction,** ⌒ **- you don't have anything to get discouraged about!** *Nonetheless, Mike,   the system always caters for straightforwardness and the courage of one's convictions- certainly- but at times it may cause a bit of ruffle!!*

What Staff College has certainly done to you, is that **it has really improved your written expression of thought, a thousand times, and that is particularly important in a Staff job. You now write with great fluency and very clearly and it does my heart good to see that.**

I am glad that Annie and children are going home. It will certainly be too much for them to take the heat of Hisar in any case you had you had mentioned that Annie was thinking of taking up teaching assignment for a year or so, in Sikkim. Possibly too, with you taking on your first staff assignment, I think Annie and the kids safely settled in Sikkim without anything to worry about would give you more time to settle in. Give Annie all our love and good wishes and Rabden and Tashi too, our love and hug from Aunty Phyll and myself.

I am sorry Hissar has not got a golf course. Obviously the Mech, Div have never had a keen golfing Commander!! However, son as you say, you can keep your hand in, with a bit of practice. I see that Hissar (spelt in Atlas as Hisar) is in Haryana, and quite close to Rewari, where there is a petrochemical complex- HARYANA Petrochemical-run by a great Naval officer, now retired-Commander Radhe Shyam Aggarwal. Indeed, he is, in fact, the owner!

Well son, our love and good wishes to you. Finish the Staff College well, and put your heart in the last semester. Doing the course has been a great benefit to you and I am sure you will realize this, as soon as you are in your first staff chair! Our love again to the kids and Annie and DON'T WORRY -affly Uncle Ron". **Unquote**

It was indeed very encouraging letter written with so much of **concern** and right from the bottom of his heart and it indeed helped lifting my sagging feelings. To be honest I was sad that I let Admiral down and denied him a little sense of satisfaction. **But I had my limitations, I suppose.**

After a month I received another letter dated 28th April 87, **quote** " *My dear Mike and Annie,- I have not written for a long time, and I apologize for this lapse, as there is no valid reason, other than the fact that each day came and went without me getting down to penning you this line!*

Well son, you must be at the fag end of the course, and everyone must be busy packing up for their next move. ***Dear Annie must be very busy for I confess that my intuition tells me that one Mike Bhalla must be busy in other directions trying to improve his golf handicap!!*** *I am glad that Annie is taking the children and going home, for there is always the problem of housing, and until you are allocated of your own, there is no point for her being with you, as it will add to both your problems. It will also give you a chance to settle into your new job, and get to know it well before Annie joins you.*

I see from the papers son, that the pay rise for service officers- and indeed the revised pensions as well- are through, so you should be picking up a reasonable amount of back pay, possibly the 1st week of May or June at the very latest. The pensioners- Harijans of the Service- are reliant on the CDA(P) sending details of revised pensions to all the Pension Paymasters , before the latter can do anything and the possibility of all of us be given the revised rates, will not to my mind materialize in the current financial year!! There seems to be no limit to total inefficiency and indeed apathy of the CDA (P) and yet the Government cannot find a better answer to this vexed problem. ***The organization should be exterminated, and if only Pakis could do this with a bomb, it could be the greatest service that they can think of!!***

There is car at the gate and if I don't wind this up, this letter will not go! Our love to Annie and the children . Look after yourself and all the best-affly- Uncle Ron". **Unquote**

Within a fortnight my posting was shifted to HQs 7 Infantry Division, Ferozepur as GSO-2. Relatively better, but very hot and dusty place. However, my connection with Ferozepur goes back more than 70 years. Both my parents were born there, father in Ferozepur City in 1916 and mother in Sadar Bazar, Ferozepur Cantonment in 1914!! Married in 1938 and left for Lahore in 1942.

On 8th May 87 we left Staff College for long journey of three days to Sikkim.

I wrote to Admiral and informed him of my new posting to HQs 7 Infantry Division. In his letter 02nd June, **quote** *"My dear Mike – We were glad to hear that you are now going as G-2 to HQs 7 Inf Div at Ferozepur. I haven't the faintest idea what a G-2 does in an Inf Div, as the only G-2 I have ever come across, was someone at NDA, who was associated with training! But as far as I was concerned, everyone at NDA had finger in training so the G-2 contribution was not spectacular enough for me to remember his precise functions.*

Our love and good wishes to Annie and children. Annie must be enjoying herself being at home, the kids must be getting thoroughly spoiled by their grand-parents! As Phyll often says what else are grand- parents for?!! Please give Annie's mother and father our warmest good wishes. Look after yourself and please give me your new address at Ferozepur.-affly-Uncle Ron". **Unquote**

After spending nearly six weeks in Sikkim, I left for Chandigarh to meet my parents, and thereafter reported to my new appointment at Ferozepur on 18 July 87. Ferozepur is located close to river Satluj which flows towards South into Pakistan. It was founded by Sultan Feroze Shah Tughlaq (1351-88), a Muslim ruler of Tughlaq dynasty. It is the oldest British district established in 1833 even before Ludhiana and Amritsar, as also one of the earliest British Cantonment established in mid 19th century during Anglo-Sikh wars in 1840's.

The Ordinance Depot was established in 1880, which catered for entire North Western Region in pre-partition days. It was well laid out cantonment with huge bungalows known as Old British Grant Bungalows with sprawling area of 3 to 5 acres. Incidentally I was the occupant of one of these bungalows as Infantry Brigade Commander in 2003-04- "Khemkaran House" built in mid 19th century!

This was my first exposure to staff appointment and I was determined to work hard. In reply to my letter Admiral wrote in his letter dated 7th Oct 87 **quote** *"Well son, I am glad that you are enjoying the job. It's really what you make of it and am sure you will fulfill the assignment with credit.* **Don't play too much Golf at the expense of the job, but play is essential to keep the cobwebs away.** *Nonetheless, as this is your first real staff job,* **it is crucial and the first report will be important one, on the way up the ladder"**. **Unquote**

In May 87 a book on Staff College- **DSSC, Wellington 1947-1987**- authored by Colonel RD Palsokar MC (retd) was released by the Commandant, Lt Gen Billimoria. It had photographs of all ex Chiefs - "Eminent Alumni"- which somehow missed out the photograph of Admiral, and I mentioned to

Admiral as also to Col RR Palsokar, our DS at Staff College and son of Col RD Palsokar. In his letter dated 27th Oct 87, **quote** *"Talking of Palsokar's book, the Commandant gave me a copy of it when I came up to Coonoor just about a month before leaving Whitefield. I observed that I was not amongst the list of the 'Eminent Alumni', but that was possibly DSSC's mistake in not providing the author with the correct details. However it matters little, if at all and I find my golf handicap of far more importance than a reference in a publication!*

We had the CNS and 1st Sea Lord U.K – Admiral Staveley- and his wife visit DSSC last week and there was a lunch and dinner for him to which Aunty and I were invited. He was Vice Chief when I made my official visit to Britain in 1980 and then went as Fleet Commander, from where he was appointed as 1st S.L. His great grandfather- General Staveley was C-in-C Madras Army- and is buried in the Ooty cemetery, while the General's son, ultimately fetched up as C-in-C Bombay Army!! The Admiral visited his g,g,f's grave and very impressed on how it had been maintained. A spot of org by the DSSC transformed an otherwise uncared for grave, into what Staveley saw." **Unquote.**

Annie and children joined me in Dec 87 and we had to stay in the Mess till we were allotted a house. In his letter of 28th Feb 88, **quote**" *Son, I hope you have got your own house by now and Annie and children have managed to settle in. What I don't understand is why you brought Annie and the kids down before getting your home. It just put the family to unnecessary inconvenience.*

The morning paper brought the news of General Sharma, succeeding Gen Sundarji. Is this not the 2nd Chief that 16th CAV have produced? As I recall, General Chaudhuri was also from 16th, but I may be wrong.

You were Gen Sharma Aide when we came to Sikkim, and I remember him well. His brother, E-in-C, was also an excellent hand. Unfortunately the papers said that he will not get his full tenure of 3 years in. well I'll close. Our love to Annie and the kids- affly Uncle Ron. **Unquote**

By mid June 88 Admiral was able to finalize the land deal at Coonoor. Thereafter, he got bogged down in working on the design and construction of the new house. It naturally took him a while before he could find time to write the next letter dated 26th Aug 88, **quote** *"My dear Mike and Annie,- Thank you Mike for your last letter, and the delay in replying to you has been the fact that I have been out from Coonoor from late last month till the 18th of*

August, except for two days in between, when I paid a virtual doctor's visit to EVERGREEN.

Son, in my travel around I some time stay in a mess, as I did the other day at B'lore, and I must say, I begin to get a little distress at what I cannot but help to observe on these occasions. As the Army jumps into 21st Century so to speak-and I am sure this is necessary and imperative- and the advances in the technology in the field, give you better equipment, better sensors, better kill potential and therefore much better technical and material Army, ***you are forgetting the man, the man who will continue to be the vital link in binding together these technological advances into a vital, and the ultimate answer. The man MUST continue to play an important part, be he an operator, maintainer, intelligent user of technology, or just an occupier of ground in denial to an enemy- indeed he is indispensable, and therefore he must be bred as a serviceman and never forgotten or permitted to soften.*** *It is this I see occurring and it certainly distresses me- sentries who have chairs to sit on, jawans who seem to be getting pot-bellied, men who don't necessarily salute officers, and officers who don't seem to worry about these 'trivialities', uniform worn casually without pride, jawans and officers sheltering in uniform, under umbrellas and worse still ladies umbrellas'.* ***It is this host of small irregularities that will undermine discipline, weaken men, with the result when the crunch comes, they will not be able to take it- softened and spoiled by bad leadership, bad officers- and all the technology in the world will not at that time help you win. Watch it, my son, carefully. Look after your men always, but breed them tough with pride in themselves and their unit.***

Command of Unit

Yes son, it will be for me certainly the greatest day of my life when you command 16th Cav, and really for you, that is the ULTIMATE. After that everything is bonus. But as you aspire to that assignment, don't be depressed, cynical, or upset with what you believe is around you. You must remember we are Indians, regrettably after 150 years of Brit rule we are still to develop a personality of our own. So you will have the hypocrites, the sycophant, the boy who lacks character and in a few cases, the outspoken Indian. The latter normally gets killed, before he can really be of use and that is sad. So it is better to bide your time, be little diplomatic and then when you are in a position of authority, **to mould men and officers,** *and do so with determination and zeal. It is then you will be appreciated.* **Don't worry son. You WILL command 16th, and will be there to congratulate you.** *Look after yourself. Our love to Annie and the children- God bless you – affly-Unc Ron".* **Unquote**

"In my travels around, I sometimes stay in a mess, as I did the other day at B'lore, and I must say, I begin to get just a little distressed at what I cannot but help to observe, on these occasions." As the Army jumps into the 21st Century so to speak - and from time this is necessary + imperative - and the advances in technology in the field, give you better equipment, better sensors, better kill potential + therefore a much better technical + material army, you are forgetting the man, the man who will continue to be a vital link in linking together these technological advances into a vital system, and the ultimate owner. The man must continue to play an important part, be he an operator, maintainer, intelligent user of technology, or just an occupier of ground in denial to an enemy. — Indeed he is indispensable, + therefore he must be bred as a serviceman + never forgotten nor permitted to suffer."

It is this that I see occurring + it certainly distresses me. — "Sentries who have chairs to sit on, jawans who seem to be getting fat-bellied, men who don't necessarily salute officers + officers who don't seem to worry about these "trivialities", uniforms worn crookedly without pride; jawans + officers sheltering in uniform, under umbrellas + worse still, ladies umbrellas." It is this host of small irregularities that will undermine discipline + weaken men, with

The Admiral I Knew – A True Story of Admiral Ronald Lynsdale Pereira

the navy that when the crunch comes, they will not be able to take it – offered & spoiled by bad leadership, bad officers – & all the technology in the world will not at that time keep you to win. Watch it, my son, carefully. Look after your men always, & treat them tough, with pride in themselves & their Unit."

Yes son, it will be for me certainly the greatest day of my life when you command 16 CAV, & really for you, that is the ULTIMATE. After that, everything is a bonus. But as you aspire to that important, don't be depressed, cynical, or upset with what you believe is around you. You must remember we are humans, & expectantly after 150 years, but will be are still to develop a personality of our own. So you will have the hypocrite, the sycophant, the boy who lacks character, and, in a few cases, the outstanding human. The latter normally gets killed, before he can really be true, that is sad. So it is better to bide your time, be a little diplomatic, & then when you are in a position of authority, to mould men & officers, do so with determination & zeal. It is then that you will be appreciated.

Don't worry son. You WILL command 16 th. I will be there to congratulate you.

Look after yourself. Our love to Annie & the children. God bless you –

Love Mac. Ron.

In September 88 Punjab was hit by severe floods with Beas and Satluj in full spate much above the danger mark. Both these rivers merge at Harike barrage, about 55 kms North East of Ferozepur. To save Harike Barrage from bursting, the sluice gates of Harike Barrage were opened to release water downstream into Satluj River which resulted in submerging the entire distirct of Ferozepur more than 6 feet of water and the cantonment area was totally inundated that we had to shift with kids and all our belongings on to the roof of our house. It took about a week plus for the water to recede after the sluice gates were opened at Hussainiwala Barrage, 10kms West of Ferozepur!

Admiral and Mrs. Pereira were indeed very concerned about the situation in Punjab and wrote in his letter dated 8th Nov 88, **quote** *"Sorry to hear of the floods inundating your house, son. However, I am glad that you had time to clear the house before water got in. Both Phyll and I were also distressed to hear that the kids had a bout of illness. We hope they are both well again. Dear Annie must have had her hands full. What with moving house in a rush and looking after the kids in their illness. Give her all our love.*

In the same letter he mentioned about the crises in Maldives *"The para-commandos and Navy have been in the news and the Services seem to have done a fine job in Male.* ***I am glad that we decided to help the Maldives, as I am sure British or Pak would have otherwise moved.*** *Some of the reports spoke of Naval Commandos being used in the actual operation of boarding the Merchant ship which had the mercenaries.* ***But I am not sure if such a Naval Commando unit exists.*** *Look after yourself. You all are always in our prayers, affly- Unc Ron"*. **Unquote**

From Sep 88 onwards Admiral was completely busy with the construction of his new house in Coonoor and the contents of majority of letters written in next one year were relating to the construction work, which have been covered in the chapter on "**HOME**".

The normal staff tenure is of 2 years and by Aug 89 I had already completed more than two years and Admiral was very keen that I should move back to the regiment amongst my Thambi troops as it's always better to be with your men than to pushing files as a staff officer.

Admiral emphasized this point in his letter dated 30th Aug 89, **Quote** *"Well son, you will be going back to your unit and that is certainly an important assignment, if as I hope,* ***you eventually make it to command of the 16 Cavalry.*** *There is no point on worrying about past reports. Get stuck in your work in the Regiment, as quickly as you can, I am quite sure it will pay off. You must* *also remember, you are in a peace time environment and it can have its disadvantages, because it is difficult in this atmosphere to sort out the sheep from the goats. However, one must accept it, and work hard for Command. I am sure that two good or above average reports from the Regiment and you will be thru. So hold your horses, son, don't unnecessarily blow off your steam and remember it's Command that you want ,I am sure will get; look after yourself – affly- Uncle Ron"* **Unquote**

PS, My apologies for 'official' paper. After instructing the printer to put my name on only half the quire, he did the whole lot!! Unc Ron.

Somehow he always refrained from writing on official papers, and preferred to write on normal pad, even the correspondence as Chief, only few times he used his official letter pad, and that too for short and quick note. It's amazing, may be **this is the way of showing his personal touch and closeness**; people of his generation were definitely a different breed. Yes, even Gen Hanut Singh would mostly correspond in his own hand!

I continued in my staff job till end 89 and Admiral was getting anxious that I should be moving back to the regiment. In his letter dated 29 Dec 89, **quote** "*When do you think, son that you will be definitely moving back to the unit? I am not quite sure how your relief could be appointed and not appear at the date and time, so set, but things seem to have changed quite a bit in all the Services- sadly I feel, and certainly not for better. However, as long as you can get back to the 16th sometime at the beginning of the New Year, it will be good for you and you will surely enjoy being with your own men again. Who is commanding the unit, at the moment?*" **Unquote**

On 3rd March 90, sadly my dear mother passed away due to old age and multi organ failure, she was 76. Admiral in his letter dated 18th March, **quote**" *My dear Mike- your letter regarding the sad demise of your Mother arrived on Saturday afternoon, and so I am writing this letter on Monday hoping to send it by an officer on his way to Delhi who will post it there.*

Both Aunty Phyll and I were deeply distressed with the news of Mother's passing away, and we offer you my son, a very deepest condolences, and love and blessing of God to carry this cross.

The loss of one's parents always hits you hard, and the hole it leaves in your heart, never really heals, for dear and good parents are irreplaceable in life. However, son, one must remember it would have been far worse for dear Mother to be in a state of suffering and pain, so her passing away is really a happy release, and am sure the blessing of God will be showered upon her for all she did in life, and for the many sacrifices I am sure she made for all you children. It is good for Bouji to be with Rupu or one of you, for it would otherwise be very lonely for him, on his own. Love, Unc Ron". **Unquote**

Unit

Ultimately, I was back in my unit by end April 90. The regiment was located at a picturesque town called - Akhnoor, 28 kms North West of Jammu on the banks of river Chenab with breathtaking view of famous shrine of Mata Vaishno Devi, which incidentally I visited 22 times!

Akhnoor is an ancient town established over thousands of years ago and is considered the place where Pandavas hid themselves from Kauravas during the period of exile. However, it came to known as Akhnoor, when the Mughal Emperor Jahangir died on his way back from Kashmir at Sarai Sadabad in 1627, and to overcome the revolt by his sons, it was necessary to keep his death a secret. The body was preserved and entrails were removed and buried in Chingus Fort near Rajouri, at place now called Narian means 'intestines'. While crossing river Chenab Jahangir corpse fell in the boat and the Empress Noor Jehan believed to have shed tears- 'Ankh' means eye and 'noor' means tear- and thus named Akhnoor.

However, the unit did not stay long and in September 90 moved to Babina, near Jhansi in Central India for conversion to new equipment, T-90 tanks. Notwithstanding, those 4 months in Akhnoor were most enjoyable and it was so nice coming back to your roots. Prior to my departure from Akhnoor, **on 5ᵗʰSep 1990** I went to pay my obeisance to Mata Vaishno Devi Shrine and prayed that I should get another opportunity to serve at Akhnoor. **Yes, my prayers were answered in Jan 95!!**

However, the sudden move of our Regiment to Babina, which came under Central Command, in fact was GOD sent and indeed game changer in my career!!

In his letter of 5ᵗʰJune 90, **quote** *"It is good to know that you are enjoying yourself in the regiment and running a tank squadron. Men like it, because it helps to build up their ego, and as they do better and better, in every field of activity. They feel good and the 'Izzat' of the Squadron grows. It is indeed, so important that you are with them, for, as you rightly say that they all want to measure your ability, and when that out strips them, their respect for you grow. It is this growth, this respect, this admiration that builds leadership, and leadership is after all, the hub of success in peace and war".* **Unquote**

I was given the Command of 'A' squadron, though my original was 'B' squadron. Therefore, the first task was to memorize the names of all the 120 Thambis as well as their trades (Driver, Gunner and Operator). Within days I knew everyone by name and trade and it was a joy to attend every parade with them starting from early morning PT to evening Roll Call.

Selection Board

My batch i.e.; 1973 commissioned, was coming up for selection to the rank of Lieutenant Colonel in early 91. Since my days in Indian Military Academy in 1973 Admiral has been motivating me to do well in my chosen profession. Starting from my Young Officers course, as also in other courses and then from 1983 he started to emphasize the importance of passing Staff College and later to work, with single minded 'AIM' of making to rank of Colonel and **ultimately Command of 16TH Light Cavalry. It was nonstop and continuous motivation for 17 years.**

I was working sincerely and honestly to fructify Admiral's **'dream'** to see me as **Commandant of 16th Light Cavalry.** But deep down in my heart I knew that I have been damaged in couple of ACR's and in spite of PSC (Passed Staff College), I still may not make the grade to Lt Col leave alone full Colonel !? I had rubbed couple of my bosses on the wrong side by trying to be argumentative and too straight laced and shot myself in the foot. **You may work hard for 364 days and one disagreement on the 365th day can harm your career- it is as simple as that.** Due to a Pyramidical structure of hierarchy in the Army it takes **one Average report** by Initiating Officer, (which as a thumb rule is endorsed by Reviewing Officers) to **write off your career.** Just "no go" and **I had couple of them!!**

I, therefore, decided to write and apprise Admiral of the true picture. Admiral was already aware of the ACR of 83, which he mentioned in his letter date 25th Nov 83. Without mincing my words I wrote to him "**there is no way I can make it to the rank of Lt Col, leave alone full Colonel, until unless my damaging reports are expunged. However, you can help me by putting in a word to the present Chief of Army Staff, General Rodrigues**". General was a Brigadier when Admiral was the Chief in 79 and like all others, he too held Admiral in very high esteem and I was certain that General would have taken cognizance of Admiral's **minor** request. In fact, I remember Admiral was very fond of Rodrigues when he was Chief and interacted with him being from the same faith and would say; son, mark my word, one day Rodrigues will become your Chief!!

I mentioned to him about 'backseat' driving in the Army. It is a known fact that most of General's sons and sons-in-law, prodigies and personal staff officers are normally placed in protected appointments (including posting on their own staff; ADC, AMS, MA, MS, Deputy MS, Col MS) for upward progression as well as foreign posting/UN Missions. So much so that they even interfere at the Academy level to get their ward an appointment (additional OLQ points), prior to their Passing Out to accrue higher position in the merit, and so and so forth. **I thought I was trying to convince the Admiral, but I was really far from my intended aim. Deep down I did feel that it was not correct on my part to ask but out of sheer frustration and helplessness, just took a blind chance with Admiral.**

Alas! I failed miserably!!

The reply he gave in his letter 27th Oct 90 **quote** " *I was delighted to get your last letter, see that you have really got stuck in your job and am sure doing it very well indeed. There is really, son, no better job than Regimental tenure. It is same as commanding or serving on a ship.* **Men are wonderful people to work with, and once you have their confidence and trust, you have the greatest team in the world.**

Son, I certainly did get your letter about dropping Gen Roddy a line on you, but I have not done this, as I do not believe that it'll work. To me, it would not be correct or helpful to you and I do feel that if you do well in the Regiment in this tenure, then your promotion will come, without any doubts. I pray that you will command the 16th and I know you will make a spot Commanding Officer, and that would be my life ambition achieved, to see you in command. Thereafter, it's in God's hand for anything further.

Who is commanding 16th Cavalry at the moment? **In many ways, I see in you, myself, as young officer with the troops. I loved my men too, and they gave me everything, and to them I owe whatever I have achieved. But as I went up the ladder, I missed my men,** *if I had any qualities at all, it was the ability to motivate men and look after them too. I therefore always missed them, as I went up the ladder.*

Our love and good wishes to Annie and the children. I know it must be rather lonely without the family, but possibly this is blessing in disguise, for without them, **you obviously can spend a great deal of time with the men, knowing them, and knowing your equipment, and this is so important at this crucial**

Ken, I certainly did get your letter about dropping Ronald Roddy a line re you, but I have not done this, as I do not believe that it will work. To me, it would not be correct or helpful to you, & I do feel that if you do well in the regiment in the future, then your promotion will come, without any doubt. I pray that you will command the 16th, & I know you will make a super commanding officer, which would be my life's ambition achieved, to see you in command. Thereafter, it's in God's hands for anything further.

Who is commanding the 16th at this moment? In many ways, I see in you, myself, as a young officer with troops. I loved my men too!, & they gave me everything, & to them I owe whatever I have achieved. But as I went up the ladder, I missed my men, & I had my greatest work, it was the ability to motivate men, & look after them too. I therefore always missed them, as I went up the ladder. Our love & good wishes to Anne & the children. I know it must be rather lonely without the family but possibly it's a blessing in disguise, for without them, you obviously can spend a great deal of time with the men, knowing them, & knowing your equipment, which is so important at this unusual juncture. However when Anne joins you next month, you must have already been a fair time with the regiment, & tested out any problems, if they are there.

*juncture. However, when Annie joins you next month, you would have already been a fair time **with the squadron** and sort out any problems, if they were there.*

*Our love and good wishes to your family. Keep your cool although things may upset you. By flying off the handle, nothing will be achieved, only way to put them right is to remember them, and then **when you are in command**, set them on the lines you consider just and correct. Look after yourself and God bless you, affily Uncle Ron."* **Unquote**

Admiral's reply **did not surprise me** at all as instinctively I knew it was against his **convictions** and **principles** but I thought may be out of his emotional attachment and his strong desire to see me in Command may turn the tide, **but he was not the one to compromise on his rigid principles and he stood by them.** At that moment I thought what kind of a man is he? All these years he was at the back of me and pushing me hard to work, work and work with single minded "aim" for command of the regiment and it was **also his dream**, and when I am so close to achieving it, he will **not help and compromise** on his principles. Without any doubt he loved and cared for me much more than a son, **but when it is question of his Integrity, he won't bend even if it hurts him!!** In fact he told me, "son, you can go home as a Major, it'll saddened me but I will not do what is not correct!" It just showed his character, to do the right thing whatever be the consequences. Unbelievable human being! But he added, "I will pray for you".

The promotion board was held from 11 Mar-22 Mar 91 and within a month the results were de-classified and expectedly I was **rejected**. I took some time to reconcile to inform the Admiral. By then I received a letter from Admiral dt 1st May 91, **quote** *"Your board, if what you mentioned in an earlier letter is correct, must have been held. However, Mike, whatever the results don't get worried over them. If you are through, I will be delighted, but if you are not, it makes no difference at all, in any case you still have two more looks, so the loyalty and devotion and training of your men should never suffer. Some of the 43rd, now on the course (DSSC) were quite sure that your board would not be held till 92, but I did mention to them that you had said that it was due in March 91"*. **Unquote**

Annie and self were devastated, but then destiny took unexpected turn??

In Sep 1990 the regiment moved to Babina (Acronym for British Army base in North Asia), near Jhansi. The regiment was orbatted to 27 Armoured Brigade; Brigadier RS Randhawa was the Brigade Commander, popularly known as Dhiru Randhawa, a war casualty of 71 Indo-Pak Conflict, a handsome and vintage cavalry officer of the yore and above all proud father of Ace Golfer Jyoti Randhawa.

In 1987 both of us had participated in Western Command Golf Championship at Amritsar and here at Babina, we regularly played on an uncared and dilapidated Golf Course with 9 Browns near the Field Firing Ranges. One day in Nov 90, he called me to his office and said –"Mike, Babina is one of the oldest Armoured Corps Military Station from the British Raj days and it is shame that we in the Cavalry cannot boast of proper Golf Course in the station. It is my dream to lay out a new Golf Course with 9 greens and I need someone dedicated to help me and then asked me "Mike can I bank on you," I said **certainly Sir**, but you will have to take my CO into confidence. He said, don't worry on that score and I will speak to your CO.

I worked day in and day out at the new Golf Course site and in next 4 month cleared about 60 acres of area between Gurari Nala and the Officers Colony of all undergrowth and leveled it with grader. Brig Randhawa was very happy with the progress. (Photo)

Redressal of Adverse ACRs

Lt Gen FN Bilimoria, The Army Commander, Central Command, was scheduled for an official visit to HQs 31 Armoured Division, Jhansi, in the last week of April 91. He was Commandant Staff College in 1986/87 and I played lots of golf with him at Staff College.

Dhiru Randhawa suggested that I should approach the Army Commander and request him to visit Babina and show him our efforts for laying the new course. The main aim was to ask the Army Commander to release some funds for infrastructure and equipment for the new Golf Course.

Accordingly, I wrote to the Army Commander about our project and requested him to **please** spare sometime for Babina during his visit to Jhansi. Fortunately, he agreed for a short visit to the new Golf Course location.

On the appointed day Army Commander came accompanied by the GOC, 31 Armoured Division, Maj Gen AK Gulati. Army Commander greeted me very warmly and was very pleased to see me after 4 years. He was also accompanied by his Dy MS (Deputy Military Secretary) Brigadier Arjun Singh Narula, who was posted as AQ in Div HQs, Gangtok in 1980 when I was Aide to Gen Sharma. The moment he saw me he shouted 'Mike' and embraced me much to the amusement of Army Commander and GOC and told them, Sir, he is my 'Baccha' (boy) and meeting him after 10 years!! They all had good laugh.

After the visit and seeing the reaction of Army Commander and Brig Narula, Dhiru Randhawa literally ordered me; "Mike, catch the first train to Lucknow and put up a 'Non Statutory Complaint' to expunge the adverse ACR's and I am sure Army Commander and Brig Narula will do the needful". Army Commander had the power to write off adverse ACR up to the rank of Major. Dhiru Sir, was 100% right! This visit by Army Commander indeed changed my destiny!

Next morning Annie and self were in Lucknow. I met the Army Commander and Brig Narula, who were indeed sad to hear about the board results and said not to worry and put up the complaint through proper channels. Yes, within 6 weeks, I got a letter dated 19th June 91 from Brig Narula; a gift before I hand over the charge-! The affected reports were set aside. Had the regiment not moved to Babina, which came under Central Command, I would not have got the adverse ACRs expunged and gone home at best as Time Scale Lt Col! The Regiment was destined to come to Central Command under Gen Billimoria who retired on 30th June 1991, just enough time to help me! What a **coincidence?**

Yes, Admirals prayers were answered!

After I received my redressal, I immediately wrote to give the good news to the Admiral; however, **he was not convinced and refused to believe me.** In his letter dated 27th July 91, **quote** "*Thank you Mike, for both your letters of the 4th and 25th June and I am sorry I am just replying to them.*

Well son, I am glad that two of your adverse ACR's have been set aside and you will be coming up for a fresh look in the next few months. It is not often, as my memory serves me that this sort of thing was done in the past, obviously there has to be very valid and cogent reasons, to accept your representation. However, son, how do you know that the two adverse reports have been set aside? Have you received an official reply to your representation stating in clear terms, that this has been done, or is this galley rumour which you have heard from your buddies.

I do not, by any means, want to be pessimistic, but it is very seldom that ACR's are really set aside and unless this is done officially, it could still be a problem to your promotion. Whatever anyone may say to the contrary. People do have the tendency of glossing over the problems and telling you something or the other to boost your morale. It is for this reason that I am asking you these questions.

WELLINGTON BARRACKS P.O.
WELLINGTON - 643 231
NILGIRI'S, TAMILNADU.

27 July 91

My dear Mike & Annie,

Thank you Mike, for both your letters of the 4th and 25th June & sorry I am just replying to them.

Wilson, I am glad your Fit: Adverse Ack's have been set aside & that you will be coming up for a fresh look in the next few months. It is not often – as my memory serves me that this sort of thing was done in the past. Obviously there must have been very valid & cogent reasons, to accept your representation. However Son, how do you know that the two Adverse reports have been set aside? Have you received an Official reply to your representation stating in clear terms, that this has been done, or is this a godly rumour which you have heard from your buddies. I do not, by any means, want to be pessimistic, but it is very seldom that Acks are really set aside, & unless this is done officially, it would still be a problem to your promotion, whatever anyone may say to the contrary. People do have a tendency of glossing over problems, & telling you something or the other just to boost your morale. It is for this reason that I am asking you these questions. As I have always said, it does not matter whether you are promoted or not. What matters is that all your decisions must be based on the true & factual factors, & if then, your views do not meet with your SO's views, it matters nought. Anyway son, I hope you are right, & in any case, you will always remain in our prayers.

Now comes a very vital question not posting & do what even attempt to get something that may be what you want. You must take whatever comes, be it good, bad, or indifferent. What really matters is what you make of the job, what you now think of you. These are the only two factors that really count

As I have always said, it does not matter whether you are promoted or not. What matters is that all your decisions must be based on the true and factual factors, and then your views do not meet with yours SO's (senior officers), it matters naught. Anyway, son, I hope you are right, and in any case you will always be in our prayers.

Now don't worry about the next posting and do not even attempt to get something that may be what you want. You must take whatever comes, be it good, bad or indifferent. What really matters is what you make of your job, what your men think of you. These are the only two factors that really count.

Well, my son, I'll close our love and good wishes to Annie and the boys and yourself. I do hope all goes well for you. You are certainly in our prayers. **Work hard son, worry about your men and everything else will fall in line.** *Aunty Phyll sends her love to all of you- affly –Uncle Ron".* **Unquote**

My name was considered as fresh case in No 4 Selection Board held from 3rd Sep to 5th Sep 91 and before the results were declassified Admiral wrote in his letter dated 28th Sep, **quote** "*Well son, I hope you have been cleared and will indeed make staff and then Command. I know how much you want this and how important it is for any soldier to command his own regiment. I always pray that you may get this. However, son, should it not happen, DON'T be disappointed or get sour. That would be far worse than not getting command. Your best confidential reports come from your men, if they think you are a great guy then you surely are, no matter what the boss may think or record. As long as you serve in the Army, you serve men; provided their professional enlightenment and molding gives you satisfaction in your work, then everything else is secondary and peripheral. If your squadron ended up being Champ; then you have certainly done well by them;*".**Unquote**

Apparently the next letter did not reach me as he mentioned in his letter of 2nd Dec 91, **quote** "*I thought, son, I had written back after your letter regarding promotion, about which Phyll and I were delighted. I am sure I sent that letter to C/O 56 APO, though you may not have been there at the time.*

Dear Hanut's (Gen Hanut Singh) advice to you is solid and pragmatic in your next assignment as a half Colonel you will have to play it cool, as your reports in that assignment will have direct bearing on your subsequent promotion to full Colonel and **chance to command the regiment.** *So watch it as soon as you take up the assignment; work really hard, but don't have too many arguments with anybody. The service today is totally different to what I knew as a young officer. However, you want to command 16th Cav, and I think nothing could* *be better and satisfying than this. You must therefore, work for it, by doing your very best and playing it cool!"*. **Unquote**

General Hanut Singh also wrote very expressive letters in his own hand like Admiral. After I cleared the board to Lt Col, he wrote in his letter dt 11 Oct 91, **quote** *"My Dear Mike,-Just received your letter of 30th Sep. I was very happy to learn that you have been cleared for the next rank. Though I have started enforcing my self- imposed isolation, I had to break it to convey my felicitations and share in your happiness.*

I look forward to the day when you take over command of 16 Cav. It is fine regiment, but it has never been able to develop its full potential because of poor officer leadership and indifferent to poor CO's. **With your total dedication to the men and to the regiment, 16 Cav will at last get an opportunity to come into its own, when you take over as Comdt.**

I would also like to put in a **word of caution**. *Though you have crossed the main hurdle, you can only be assured of command if you get approved for Col. I have known many fine officers who failed to make to Col from Lt Col, because of the subjective reporting of some distasteful superiors. Therefore, it is important for your future prospects as to where you serve and under whom you serve for the next 2-3 years. Also it is important that you avoid confrontations as there are few officers in our Army who can appreciate a subordinate being frank and forthright in his views.*

But God has brought you so far, and I am sure he will take you to **your cherished goal of commanding 16 Cav**. *Fond regards to you and Annie- yours Hanut"*. **Unquote**

Assam and Manipur

My aim was to get out of the regiment before initiation of another damaging report and I had my well wishers to help me, and I was ready to be posted to most difficult areas. Sure enough in Jan 92 received my posting as GSO -1(ops), HQ's 57 Mountain Division located at Guwahati, Assam. In Sep 92, the div was inducted into Manipur for counter–insurgency operations. We walked straight into an internecine and very volatile situation, where Nagas and Kukis were involved in systematic cleansing of each other's tribes. The entire villages were being burnt and everyone killed mercilessly including women and children. The Security Forces were frequently targeted by the insurgents resulting in large numbers of casualties to both Army and Para

Military Forces. It was the worst period in the history of insurgency in North East. I served there for 3 years and survived!

Unfortunately, Admiral started to have severe health related problems from early September 91 and by Dec, he was advised by the doctors at Kuppuswamy Naidu Hospital, Coimbatore to proceed to INHS ASVINI, Bombay for further tests and check up at Tata Memorial Cancer Hospital. The details are covered separately in the chapter on "Battle with Cancer".

Command

In his first letter from INHS ASVINI dt 30th Dec 91, Admiral explained to me in detail about the sickness, which I will cover separately in chapter on cancer but the last paragraph is relevant to my promotion, and I **quote** "*Now the reason I wrote this, is to have no panic whatsoever from you. I don't want you to come down under any circumstances. It is wholly unnecessary. I have told May and Arthur precisely this Phyll is with me and that more than meets my requirement. So son, get on with your job. What you can do is to sweat and sweat hard on your job, for what I want of you, is to see you in command of 16th. That would give me more joy than anything else. That will still call for very hard work, for you will not be the only one wanting that command, and the best must slot into the job".* **Unquote**

By now Admiral was well aware of his sickness but what amazed me was that he still had my concerns in his heart and displayed so much positive energy in his thoughts and words. Prior to my departure for Assam in first week of Feb 92 I wrote to Admiral and he immediately replied.

In his letter dt 20th Feb 92, **quote** "*My dear Mike,- Thank you very much for your letter of the 10th February, which came in on the 18th. I had also written to you, C/O 56 APO also on the 10th, but I don't know when that will catch up with you, as it will now has to be re-addressed to HQ's 57 Mountain Division.*

To begin with, this gives you a big break, but the assignment must meet the standard expected of a G-1 and that will mean that you must sweat. Nothing comes on a platter and G-1 (ops) job is a key one, and you must be up to it. It certainly will require logical thought, maturity, foresight and planning and the ability to express yourself clearly and lucidly on paper. The latter is very important. I am sure you can do it all, if you put your mind to it, but I am equally sure that it will require all out effort from you, for that is the only thing that makes certain that you go thru this hurdle successfully.

*Having said, forget leave, forget family and forget everything but work. Anything other than work is a mere distraction, so forget the peripherals and keep the aim in view. **Don't get yourself in debt, don't misuse your office, and don't misuse transport or men. Remember men serve you only. They are not servants to cut costs and don't do menial duties in a house, whatever may be views of other officers.***

*There is lot to think about your job. Give it all your time. **Finally success is always due to putting together a good team and failure is always attributed to you alone; don't blame others for it.*** Unquote

Admiral's letters were indeed very inspiring and motivating and needless to say I went ahead with single minded aim of working as hard as I possibly could do. To be honest I was not too great at pushing files, writing drafts, but I made up my mind to do my best and also gave up playing golf! I had no margin whatsoever to pick up another mediocre report as that will put paid to my aspirations and **Admiral's dream to see me in command of 16th Cavalry.**

In his very next letter dt 16 Mar 92, **quote** *"I don't know what documents you take over as GSO-1, but am sure the secret and top secret publications must be there, and you should have **done a page by page muster** (which is certainly required in the Navy) before you signed, as having taken them over. If you have not done so, do it now, to ensure that all is well and correct. What, son, is the organizational set up of a Div Hqs? I presume that the 'ops' Div is headed by a Brigadier and you come under him as GSO-1(Ops). Do you also have a COS (Chief of Staff) for the Div and who is your Div Commander? I will surely not know him; as all my contemporaries have long since retired. Well, son, look after yourself, and work hard. **Get everyone involved under you, as a team and look after them. Remember that your attitude towards work, men, life in general, will be what is critically analyzed and dissected by those below you. Your example in everything is therefore important**- all my love-Uncle Ron".* Unquote

By third week of March I proceeded to College of Combat, Mhow, to attend Senior Commanders Course, serial 63. A very important course and nomination is purely on merit. Armoured Corps had only 7 vacancies so I considered myself to be lucky to be nominated after the debacle in the first Selection Board in March 91!

The course indeed was very interesting and it was nice to meet one's course mates and as luck would have it my instructor was none other **Brig RR Palsokar** who was my DS in Staff College in 86/87. **Coincidence!**

In his letter dt 24th April 92 written from the hospital bed, when he was undergoing second course of radiation, which is very painful and discomforting to say the least but Admiral still sounded very positive in his thought process and **quote** "*You are now running, son, in a highly competitive field, and everything that you do, will have a bearing on the next rank- full Colonel- which is necessary to be achieved, if you are to command those fine Thambies of yours. I say this because you may not realize it-the result of current course SC-63; you're dealing with your boss in the Division, your daily work and discussion with the boss; yours views as expressed or written down which may find their way to GOC's table, all this and more have a bearing on your future and therefore, calls for determined endeavour and thought; the very best you can give, as you are now certainly part of very harsh rat race which begins from now, to separate the sheep from the goats. Some of this is done wholly unethically, some very professionally, some illogically. However, those that are responsible for separating the breeds, are mature enough to realize that the rising stars are future leaders of the services and therefore, they must be able to discern genuine from fake and many of them do so. The answer, therefore, seems to be to keep your nose to the grindstone, and your mental faculties on fine-tune and just keep going, hoping for the best. Work hard and sweat blood. Well my son, I will close. Look after yourself and remember survival at this stage is in sweating blood and not being distracted by anything, other than work- affly- Uncle Ron*". **Unquote**

What beautiful expressions, written under great pain and after effects of radiation, still so clear and emphatic in his thoughts. Even at this moment, 24 years later my hair stand on my back as I type these words, so much love and care for my progression in my career. Nobody could have expressed it better and he continued to do so right till the end!! At times I wonder how many fathers must be writing in this manner to their sons- I suppose, very few!! I consider myself singularly fortunate to have a **MENTOR** in Admiral, and that too Ronnie P- amazing, to say the least.

In his letter dt 4th May 92, **quote** "*Son, what is the general content of your course-minor SD, higher direction of war, certain aspects of administration, aspects of tactical command or what?? I find the Army is very good in giving its officers periodical refreshers in aspect of professionalism and this is certainly imperative in the light the constantly changing factors of the prosecution of war. We, in the Navy did not do so previously, but it is certainly now being brought in at all levels of command. In fact, as you may know, we have now set up our Naval War College at Bombay- Uran to be precise- and it is proving of great value for Captains cleared for command, who do this course, before they* take over their ships. *Well son, work hard on the course and do well and when you get back to the Div really **sweat blood** and give it all you can. All the best to you – affly Uncle Ron* . **Unquote**

By third week of June the course got over and I went back to Assam and of course there was lots of paper work to do. In his letter dated 7th July written from INS AGRANI, Red Fields, Coimbatore-641018, **quote** *"Well son, your course at Mhow must be behind you and I hope you have gained something from it. At this stage of your career, not all the courses give you everything new, however ,if they have a certain contents of professional information that you were previously unaware of, there is always that , to gain from them .*

You will be serving a host of new bosses. All of them will be interested to see what contribution you can make it to the formation. You will, therefore, have to work hard and will really keep your nose to the grindstone. You must also remember, that this job will be one of the stepping stone to the next rank, and so sweat and toil that you put into it, will be measure of your success Forget leave, forget family forget everything that might or could affect your ultimate professional result in the chair. Just slog as hard as you can- I am sure this will be good step to command". **Unquote**

In early July 1992, 57 Mountain Division got a new GOC- **Maj Gen AK Sengupta** - my regiment!!He was Commandant 16th Cavalry from July 77 to Nov 79 and I was his Adjutant, therefore for me **he was God sent**. Gen Sengupta came on promotion from Washington DC, USA, after a long tenure of 4 years as Military Attaché. Somehow I had premonition and wrote to him on my arrival in Guwahati in Feb 92 that he might land up as GOC 57 Mtn Div or 3 Inf Div, Leh. Come July 92, he was posted as GOC 57!! What a come down from Washington to Assam to Manipur, the worst affected Counter Insurgency area in North East!! **He cursed me and my black tongue! I didn't mind, for me this was the best situation, both morally and professionally.** Yet another **co-incidence!**

Admiral had met Gen Sengupta in Aug 78 when along with two other officers of 16 Cavalry (Maj and Mrs. JP Singh and Maj and Mrs. PK Chakravarti) had called on Admiral at 5 Moti Lal Nehru Marg. As the CO of 16 Cavalry, he also received a letter from Admiral after he took over as CNS in Mar 79, in which he had mentioned that; "Mike should not given any preferential treatment due to my close proximity to him and if need be do not hesitate to kick his backside!"

In his letter dated 11 Aug, Admiral wrote, **quote** *"It is good to know that your new GOC is from 16th Cav.* ***Indeed that would be one more reason to really sweat for him.*** *As you know him, it should be far easier to work for him, and we both hope all goes well".* **Unquote**

In Aug 92 I was diagnosed with 'Falcipram' Malaria or serious cerebral malaria with very low chances of survival and I must admit that I reached the gates of heaven and was saved by proverbial '**gong**'. I was running temperature of 106 * F and slipped into coma with just no chances of survival to come out alive but after 14 hours I miraculously came back to my senses, hospitalized for a month and followed by 4 weeks sick leave. By the time I reported back to the Div, it had already moved to Liemakhong, 28 kms North West of Imphal, Manipur. Initially I did not inform the Admiral and wrote only after I was discharged from the hospital.

In his letter dated 2nd Oct 92, **quote** *"My dear Mike- just received your registered letter dated 14th Sep and both Phyll and I were distressed to hear of your illness. However, it is good to know that you are over the worst and it's a matter of getting back your strength. This will take a little time. I see you are in Gangtok so I am addressing this letter there. With Malaria you must be very careful for at least 3 to 4 months and you must lay off all liquors.*

Phyll sends all of you her love. Look after yourself and take it easy on leave. ***You must be absolutely fit, by the time you get back to duty, so that there is no question of you not pulling your weight*** *- affly-Uncle Ron."* **Unquote**

It is really tragic that after 10th Feb 93 Admiral's condition deteriorated rapidly and for next few months he was in and out of Military Hospital at Coonoor and on 20th Aug 93 was evacuated by heptr to Bangalore.

My board for Colonel was held in July 94 and yes, I picked my rank, but could not get Command of 16th as Lt Col AK Kaistha, got priority over me being senior.

Admiral passed away on 14th Oct 93 and 18 months later I got the command of 6 Armoured Regiment.

On 25th Jan 1995, I reported to a relatively new regiment raised on 1st Feb 1984 - 6 Armoured Regiment as 2IC and took over as 5TH Commandant on 18th April 95. Yes, it was located **at Akhnoor**, my prayers of 5th Sep 1990 were answered by **Mata Vaishno Devi** and I had most wonderful and happiest tenure of my entire service and relinquished Command on 5th June 1997, and **I owe it to rank and file of 6 Armoured Regiment.**

Gen Hanut Singh in his letter of 30th May 95; **quote** *"My dear Mike. I was delighted to learn that you have taken over the command of 6 Armoured Regiment; At least you have an independent command of your own, where you can implement all the many ideas on Training and Man management that you have patiently nurtured all these years.* **These were being stored up by you for your first love, 16 Cav, but that unfortunate Regiment is jinxed. Firstly, it seems to attract only self seeking officers; then, the few devoted officers that land up there by accident, get weeded out for one reason or the other. Without being able to give the regiment the benefit of their professionalism and dedication.**

We in Poona Horse have a paternal interest in 6 Armd Regt- the first Commandant and the first RM (Risaldar Major) were both from Poona Horse. Notwithstanding, the unfortunate manner in which Ravi Deol's command was terminated, I would like to think that some at least of the PH spirit and traditions permeated into the Regiment.

I cannot now place RPS Brar, but from your description of his character (or lack of it), I am guessing that he is a progeny of Surjit Brar (GOC 33Corps). KD had also written about his foul character. He appears to have been a pain in the neck to the entire Regiment. There has been audible sigh of relief at his departure. Equally, there has been a palpable exhilaration at your taking over. Expectedly you have endeared yourself to all ranks during the brief time you have been with them. I am sure they all look forward to 2-3 years of happy and professionally rewarding time. I am certain with God's grace; you will have an enjoyable and deeply satisfying tenure of command. With my best wishes, as ever-Hanut". **Unquote**

Admiral was always in my mind and I had kept his famous photograph as Chief on my office table and every morning would pay my homage and take his blessings before starting my day. I am sure he must be looking down and smiling to himself!

"God bless his soul"

Admiral

Chief of Naval Staff 1st March 1979

Admiral

As Lt 1948

Best Man at John Pereira wedding- 1948

Captain 1968

Captain 1969

Dep Com –NDA- 71

Fleet Commander 1973

With Rear Admiral K K Nayyar, FOC Eastern Fleet, 1979

With Col Morris Ravinderan, Madras, Sep 74

FOC Southern Area, Cochin 1975

With Admiral AK Chatterji and Dick Schunker, Bombay 76

With Mrs. Schunker, Bombay 77

With Captain Perera, Sri Lanka Navy

Address to sailors, INS Angre 76

Taking over as CNS, 1st March 79

POP - 56th NDA Course - June 1979

POP - 59th NDA Course - Dec 1980

With Montee Chatterjee, Sydney, 81

Lord Mountbatten's Funeral – Aug 1979 (Admiral standing extreme right)

With Prime Minister Mrs. Indira Gandhi 1980

With Prime Minister Mrs. Indira Gandhi 1981

16th LIGHT CAVALRY

Toss; Base Ball Match

Arrival ; Officer's Mess

With Lt Col JP Singh

Turning out the Lancer Guard

Inspecting the Guard

Tank Ride

Addressing the Men

With officers and ladies

Admiral with ladies 16 Cavalry – 1980

Admiral with Mike – Mar 1980

Sikkim – May 1981

Annie July 1980

Helicopter Accident, 22nd Aug 80

Primary Department Photograph 1932 (1st Row standing 9th from left)

Prince Paljor Namgyal of Sikkim (specks) with R. Pereira on his right.(standing behind Mr. Gerald & Mr. Cowan)

Prince Paljor as pilot in 1940

With His Holiness Karmapa

with my father-in law Kazi Sonam Gyatso

Rumtek Monastry

Dinner at Home

Dinner at Home

Home

Sea View Bungalow, 1880s Cannanore

Ockbrook, Mussoorie 1975

Rabden and Tashi at – AT LAST, 1986

BROADSIDES, Cannoor, 1988

BROADSIDES - 1990

ATLAST-2016 (Ruins)

HOME

Introduction

The very first mention of ancestral property in Pereira family dates back to 1880's, when Admiral's grandfather Mr. John Pereira (third generation), who was a Sub Inspector in PWD in Mangalore, bought a **Sea View Bungalow** from a Muslim family in Cannanore (now Kannur) in North Kerala. Presently it is located opposite Mascot Seaside Hotel and just outside the (DSC) Defence Security Services Headquarters. Regrettably, the sea view is totally blocked from the property due to urbanization over the last 100 years. The bungalow remained with the family till 1972 and Cecil Pereira (b. 1889) and his two younger sisters - Hilda Mary (b.1894) and Perscilla Mabel (b. 1898 and youngest in the family) were the last occupants.

Thereafter, the bungalow was sold to Mr Janardanan Nair, relative of Leela Krishanan Nair (owners of Leela Hotels chain) and was renamed as '**Harisree**'. Cecil apparently moved to the four room property behind the house and lived there till his demise in 1985. Both sisters moved to Ahmedabad.

The original building is intact except the kitchen which was outside and at rear of the house has been dismantled. It is a single story bungalow with a drive in to the porch, drawing room, three medium size rooms, two large bedrooms and a hall as family room in the center of the house. Pantry and stores were in the rear covered verandah. Layout of the house is as shown in the sketch.

Admiral's father, Major JM Pereira, retired as Jail Superintendent, Hazaribagh, in August1948. He had no property and lived in a rented accommodation in Hazaribagh till summer of 1957 when their health began to deteriorate and both were admitted to Woodland Nursing Home Calcutta, where Admiral's parents passed away in June, 1957 within 9 days of each

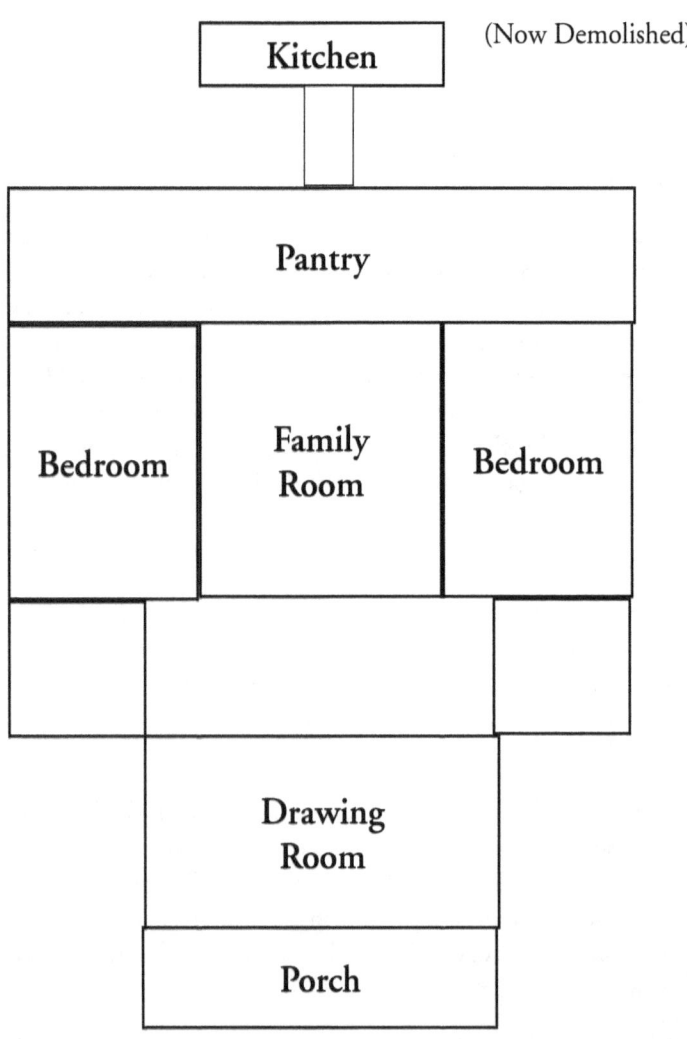

other (9th and 18th June). Incidentally both of them were not aware about the death of the other!

Will

The properties owned by Mr John Pereira, Sub Inspector PWD, were bequeathed to his three sons in his famous "WILL" written on 31st March 1920. The same is given below:-

(a) 'Sea view' should go to Jack.

(b) 'Rose Cottage' at Calicut, should go to Roberts.

(c) '4 rooms' at Cannanore should go to Cecil.

However, names of John Michael Pereira and Francis Pereira have not been mentioned. Jack remains a mystery!! As per Commander Hugh Gantzer, his grandfather, **Major JM Pereira did not own any property whatsoever, and lived in a rented house in Hazaribagh.** However, as per Michael Pereira son of Admiral John Thomas Pereira, Jack could be Major John Pereira nick name, but none the less he never stayed in Cannanore and apparently left the property to his brother Cecil and two younger sisters.

Property

Admiral elder brother, Arthur Pereira, after his retirement from Calcutta Electricals picked up a job with Royal Calcutta Golf Club as 'Secretary Greens'. He resided within the premises of the club itself till he passed away in April 93, aged 84 years, and he too did not own any property.

The eldest sister Masie Gantzer and her husband Mr. Joseph Francis Gantzer bought a beautiful cottage - '**OCKBROOK**', just below the Library Stand in Mussoorie in 1940 for a princely sum of Rs 10,000/- ! Presently their son Commander (retd) Hugh Gantzer, 86, and his elegant wife, Colleen is residing there. The second sister Bobby migrated to UK in 1938 and then in early 50's to Buenos Aires, Argentina.

Fortunately for Admiral sometime in late 60's, he was given a plot of land by one of his very generous cousin **Dr Dorothy Sommers**, who had property in Whitefield, Bangalore. I remember, in Autumn of 1972 Admiral once mentioned about it, and said, **my son, do you know we were very fortunate to get a small piece of land from a very kind cousin of ours in Whitefield near Bangalore and with a twinkle in his eyes and tongue in** cheek added, son, I paid her next to nothing!! I do hope that one day Auntie Phyll and self will make a small cottage for our old age! Indeed Dorothy Sommers whose children were settled abroad in Australia, gifted the land to Admiral as also to another cousin, named Dr Peter. All Admiral paid was for Registration fee!!

There is brief mention of the property in Aunty Phyllis letter dated 25th April 74, **quote** *" We are planning to go on leave from 18 May to 18 June and will be in Bangalore to fix things in connection of our property"* **Unquote** . However, the leave never materialized as Admiral was nominated to be part of a Defence delegation for study tour to Egypt in the month of May 74.

Cuffe Parade Bombay

In June 1976 when Admiral was FOC-in-C, Western Naval Command, Bombay, a gentleman by the name of Mr. SFS Engineer, who was involved in the construction of high rise residential buildings in Cuffe Parade, Colaba approached Admiral and offered him a flat. The deal was - initially make a down payment of Rs 17000/- with the undertaking that after completion of the flat, it will remain in the custody of the builders for a period of five years, in which they will accrue and recover the cost of construction and thereafter the flat will be handed over to the buyer for possession. **A very fair deal but Admiral will have nothing of it and out rightly rejected the offer as he perceived it to be inappropriate and may undermine his status and position - he wouldn't budge to the temptation and politely showed Mr. SFS Engineer which way the exit door was??** Surely he missed an opportunity to own a flat in Colaba. Today in 2016 it is between 10-15 crores!! Yes, one of my course mates Guddu Sharma bought a flat in one of the high rise building in Cuffe Parade in 2015, and he **paid only 10 crores** !! Along with Admiral, Captain Montee Chatterjee was also offered but he too had to turn it down!!- What a missed opportunity?

Whitefield

The very thought of a house dawned on them in early 1978, when Admiral and Mrs. Pereira realized that it was high time that they start thinking about a 'Home' as Admiral was very close to superannuation.

In his letter dated 24th March 78, **quote** *"My dear Mike- let me begin by giving you some of our news and the best one is that I have decided to get down and **build this house of ours**, which has always in my mind, but has not got beyond the stage of some nebulous planning and a great deal of discussion!! What finally led me to get down to the project in the right earnest was the fact* that I was on temporary duty at Bangalore, about 10 days ago , and everyone I met , spoke of the rising cost of the building. To add to this, **I suddenly realized that I was inside a year of my possible retirement, and unless I got down to building immediately, we could find ourselves in a position of having to leave the service without a house to go to.** Lastly I visited a friend of mine at Bangalore who is just completing a lovely house- simple but very elegant and the design was just what we wanted.

I therefore got down to planning immediately on my return, and the final drawings will be going to Bangalore for the approval of the Panchayat on the 29th. As the DG (Works) - General Nanda – has been kind enough to offer to take them down himself, and get them passed. I should have them approved by end of the month, when I will get down to **getting a loan** from Ministry of Works and Housing as well as **my provident fund**, and soon thereafter I will begin the project.

I hope to go on some leave- perhaps 30 days- in mid May, when I will possibly motor to Bangalore and get down to obtaining licenses for cement and steel, fixing a good contractor and getting them cracking on the foundations.

You know that we have two small plots of land in that area. I have a small agricultural plot of -3 ¾ acres- South of Bangalore, about 14 miles from the centre of town and another ½ acre of urban land in **Whitefield** where we intend to build- East of B'lore.

We were, at one time to develop and build on the agricultural land, but without any neighbours and as far from the town as 14 miles, it is really not practical. We have decided to build in Whitefield, **where a cousin of mine gave me ½ acre which we now own.** Whitefield itself is about 12 kms from Bangalore. But it is a little township of its own, and is a very nice area, though scarce of water. However, the Cauvery water scheme is through, Bangalore itself has got sufficient water and the supply now is being extending to Whitefield, where it will be available in a year's time.

I do want to try and finish the house by January next year. If I can achieve this, I shall certainly feel very pleased with myself". **Unquote.** The friend in question is Commodore Jack Shea, who had built a small cottage in Whitefield.

Whitefield is a neighbourhood of Bangalore in state of Karnataka, established in late 1800's as a settlement of Eurasian- Anglo Indians. On 27th April 1882, His Highness Chamaraja Wodiyar IX, the Maharaja of Mysore granted 3900 acres of land to the Eurasian and Anglo Indians Association, Mysore and Coorg for establishment of agriculture settlements in Whitefield.

Named after David Emmanuel Starkenburgh **White**, the President of E & AI Association was pioneer for development of the village. Today in 2016 it has become IT hub and boasts of most expensive prime properties in B'lore!

After getting the loans sanctioned and withdrawing money from provident fund, Mrs. Pereira arrived in Whitefield in the summers of 1978. She put up with Cluff family, who lived close to the main market of Whitefield and it was quite a walk to the site-about 20 minutes.

It is to her great credit and courage that Mrs. Pereira, went ahead with the construction work on her own, as Admiral couldn't get any leave and get away from Delhi. She used to be at the site dot at 9 am every morning without fail. For lunch break she would walk (10 minutes) to Dorothy and Jack Shea's residence, relax couple of hours and be back on the site at 4 pm till sunset. On most of the occasions, Dorothy Shea's lovely daughter Debbie, (who was christened by Mrs. Pereira on 22nd April 1959 at Cochin and was her God daughter) would take Aunty Phyll up and down the site on her Vespa scooter and sing Rajesh Khanna's movie songs (*vada tera vada* from film 'Dushman'!) for her dear Aunty Phyll, though Mrs. P could not understand a word of song but she appreciated the tune and rhythm, alright! This fact was narrated to me by none other than Mrs. P herself, as also by Debbie Shea.

The cost of construction was going through the roof as all construction materials and the skilled labours, like mason, plumber and electrician were coming from Bangalore and Mrs. Pereira was finding it difficult to cope with excessive expenditure. Soon she ran out of finances and sent a SOS to Admiral, who in any case had already scratched the bottom of the barrel.

New Car

It was way back in early 1974, while in Vizag Admiral decided to purchase a new car. In his letter 05th May 74, **quote** *"We have at last got to the top of senior officer roster for a new car; I expect my allocation for new Fiat, sometime this month.* ***It will be our first new car in 32 years of service.*** *Though it is costing us a fortune- 26,600/-, we have just got to take it, as our present one is certainly getting old being a 56 Land Master! As soon as I get my allotment, I shall take delivery of it in Kakinada- about 100 miles from us and drive it down to Vishakapatnam. Before the petrol hike, Aunty and I had decided to wait for the car and then spend our 30 days leave driving around the South. However, with prohibitive price of petrol that is now impossible"*. **Unquote**

As per Flag Lt (later Commander) Vijayan, **quote** "Admiral did not go to Kakinada to collect the car. In fact it was delivered by the local dealer at Vizag itself. Admiral and self drove to the showroom in a Staff Car and after collecting the new car Admiral himself drove it back home along with me and he was indeed very excited and told me with lots of pride- **son , this is my first new car in 32 years of service !!** Unquote

The car was very close to his heart and he would religiously clean and wash it every Sunday and nobody was allowed to drive it including Aunty Phyll. However, during my stay at Bombay in Aug-Sep 76, every morning he would leave the car keys next to my bed and would say, **my son, the tank is full, enjoy yourself!** At Delhi also in 77/78, I would drive Aunty Phyll to Khan Market for shopping. But he made it very clear that if the car gets even a minor scratch, then he will not hesitate to shoot me!! Indeed I was very careful but enjoyed driving around Delhi Lutyens complex.

Disposal of Car

Therefore, when Mrs. Pereira sent 'SOS' for financial help to Admiral, **he had no option but to put the car on sale** and I really felt sad for him when I got to know about it. In his letter dated 23rd Aug 78, **quote** *"I wonder if you know that I have sold my car. It went within two hours of an advertisement in 'Times' and was taken by a civilian engineer with Engineer Project (India), who gave me exactly what I asked, which was 28000/- In fact there were three people who wanted at this price, and one even offered 29000/-, but I had asked for 28000/- and refused to budge a paisa on it, when I was, therefore, offered it. I gave it to the first individual, who though I say so, myself, he got an excellent vehicle. **I needed the cash for the house; its sale was really inevitable. I don't really regret it, as it was an excellent price, as the house was far more important. I had no hesitation in disposing it off".*** Unquote

Golf Set

In fact Admiral had also put his second Golf Set for sale to raise some money for the house! This story was narrated to me by Lt Gen Thomas Mathew, GOC, 33 Corps. In June 2006 I was posted as Sub Area Commander, 111 Sub Area, Bengdubi, near Siliguri, North Bengal. As per the norm on taking over the Command, I went for the customary interview with the Corps Commander, Gen Thomas Mathew.

I entered the GOC office and saluted - Good morning Sir, - Gen Mathews nodded and said, come sit down. After exchanging pleasantries,

General said, **quote** "Mike, let me narrate you an incident which happened nearly 30 years ago way back in 1978. In fact, it was at that juncture when I heard about you first time in my life from none else but late Admiral Pereira himself! And since then I always had a desire to meet you!!

It was month of September 1978, then as a Major I was staying with one of my course mates in Delhi preparing for Staff College Entrance Examinations, which were schedule in the third week of November. One day I read an advertisement in Times of India Newspaper for a **sale of golf set**, only contact number was given. At that point in time I was quite keen to buy a set for myself and so called up the number and inquired about the golf set, the voice on the other end of the line replied, son, you better have a look and then make a decision. I then asked if I could come next Sunday after the Church service. He said, ok and gave me the address 5 Moti Lal Nehru Marg. I could sense that it was voice of a senior officer. On Sunday on my way back from Church at about 1100 h I decided to go to 5 MLN Marg. As I reached the house and read the name plate –Vice Admiral RL Pereira, I was bit hesitant and almost changed my mind, but then I thought, now that I have come thus far, let me try at least. So I went inside and rang the bell in the front verandah, and after a while Admiral opened the door himself and I introduced myself and told him, Sir, I spoke to you about the golf set. He introduced himself - Admiral Pereira and firmly shook hands and said come on in, son, I will show you the set. We went to his study and he showed me the set. After a while I noticed a black and white photograph of young Captain in uniform on his Dressing Table and out of sheer curiosity asked him- Sir, is your son in the Army? It was your photo Mike and he said, yes, he is like a son to us as we do not have any children and presently serving in 16th Light Cavalry and for next 15 minutes or so he went on to narrate the entire story- how he met you in NDA in 1971 and you reminded him of his late nephew Michael Pereira, who died in an air crash in Hashimara and subsequently gave you the name- '**Mike**'. I stood there awestruck and motionless listening to the Admiral and the description of his first meeting with you. Indeed it was very unique and touching story and I could make out how much he loved you as a son. 28 years on, here you are sitting in front of me. Amazing story isn't it. Admiral was a great man and we were indeed proud of him" **Unquote.**

The General eventually did not buy the set, as the set had customized clubs and made to order for Admiral who was good ½ feet taller than him and the Admiral in fact advised the General not to buy it! Admiral could have made 4000/- bucks but he won't make an unfair deal!! This set was ultimately sold to a Naval officer in Staff College in 1989.

Garden

Mrs. Pereira was very avid and keen gardener and put in lot of effort in maintaining a well laid out and beautiful garden, where ever they were posted. Indeed, she had "green fingers". She won Best Garden competitions in all the stations i.e. Dep Com residence at Khadakwasla, Navy House Vizag, Navy House Bombay, both 5 Motial Lal Nehru Marg and Navy House, 12 Rajaji Marg , New Delhi.

Mrs. Pereira was very passionate about gardening and naturally, she planned the layout of her possibly final garden very meticulously. She worked out where all she will plant flowering trees like Bougainvillea with different colours, the seasonal flowers, perennial flowers and fruit trees and started the work on the garden along with the construction of the house with her favourite gardener Rammanah. I was lucky to capture the glowing garden with my two small sons posing at different corners of the compound amongst bevy of colours and beautiful flowers, when we visited Whitefield in Dec 86.

House Plan

The house plan was rather simple. The building was constructed at the back end of the property about 30 yards inside from the main gate. The total plinth area was 70 x 30 feet. It was like a long barrack with two bedrooms (15x15) with attached bathroom (10x8) back to back, pantry and kitchen. The front portion of the house was a long covered verandah. With drawing room ,coffee table, dining table, bar and library from left to right as you face the house On the left side near the fence was a garage cum workshop, where Admiral stored extra baggage, and every possible tool required for the maintenance of the house concerning electrician , carpenter or plumber, and even for mason work .

Interior Decorations

Mrs. P was also an excellent interior decorator, and she kept a lovely home with different colour combinations for each room plus attached bathroom. "Orange Room" meant orange paint, orange linen, orange bed cover, orange curtains, orange towels including hand towel, orange bucket and mug, orange door mat, orange bath mat , orange bath curtains, orange soap dish with orange soap, orange picture on the walls, orange carpet, orange table cloth and orange cushions covers and orange shades of lights etc, etc !! Similar get up for Rose Room, Mediterranean Blue Room or Green Jade Room. She was very fastidious about cleanliness in the house. The floor must be spotlessly clean, brass knobs, door handles and bolts to be polished every day. Ash trays strategically placed at every nook and corner of the house to ensure no ash drops on the floor-if you did, then it was at your own peril and hell to pay!! (Thank God I never smoked) but Admiral used to err at times!!

Once during monsoon in Aug 76, Bombay, Admiral came back presumably after a bad round of Golf and he walked in with his soiled and muddy Golf shoes on the spick and span floor, expectedly Aunty Phyll threw a fit and shouted ' look Ronnie what have you done to the floor? He shouted back 'To hell with your bloody floor and to make matters worse dropped ash on the floor!!- which was proverbial last straw on the camel's back- immediately Topaas Madan Lal was summoned to clear up the mess created by 'Sahib'!!

A similar incident took place in winter of 80 in Navy House, 12 Rajaji Marg. Admiral walked in, of course with a cigarette in his hand to the side verandah facing the Rajaji Marg, Aunty Phyll noticed the ash at the end of the cigarette and as it was about to drop on the floor, she rushed towards Admiral with an ash tray in her hand to catch the ash before it dropped on the floor and sure enough she missed it and said; there you go again Ronnie? Admiral snapped back and said damn your bloody floor and shouted for Topaas Sham Singh who was in the staff quarters and took a while to arrive at the scene and by then Admiral famous temper was rising and as Sham Singh appeared Admiral snatched the broom from his hand and shouted – Kitna waqt lagta hai pahuchne ke liye ? (How much time do you require to reach here?) and started to sweep the floor himself in anger. I said Unc, give it to me and I will do it- he hissed –**shut up** and muttered some explicit under his breath and continued to sweep till he finished with whole verandah. Aunty Phyll walked out to the rear lawn! I went after her to pacify and **she retorted- Unc is unnecessarily getting hot under the collar- typical Pereira's genes!!**

With the announcement of Chief Designate in Nov 78, fortunately they got another three years to complete the house. It was indeed God sent and it was not additional time but also additional financial support. Thus a great deal of pressure was taken off the shoulders of Mrs. Pereira. But thereafter, unfortunately could not devote much time and a lot of work was still pending to be completed on their arrival in Bangalore on 7th March 82, after Admiral's retirement!

They named the house 'AT LAST'. The final place!!

Why Admiral chose this name? Though, it was self explanatory. One day Admiral sat down and wrote a poem on AT LAST and gave it to Montee Chatterjee, who very kindly sent me the copy;

AT LAST

AT LAST- it's taken quite some time,
The sweat of MA, much toil and grime,
But now we have AT LAST a house,
To call our own and no more grouse,

AT LAST- we have got ourselves a roof,
To MA it should be solid proof,
We have AT LAST a house, our own,
To rest our heads, and weary bone,
AT LAST was built without a bean,
For MA and I never seen,
A bank account AT LAST in black!!
How did we build a house a shack?

AT LAST- we scraped the pot, a car was sold,
MA had no goodies, nor no gold,
To the "boss" AT LAST was put in pawn,
That's how it managed to be born!!

AT LAST-a question of a name,
But MA was having no such game,
To give AT LAST a naval tang,
AT LAST! AT LAST! She merely sang,
AT LAST- we are ready to go home,
Dear Ma will reap what I have sawn,

And when AT LAST we stepped inside,
T'will help us in our even tide,

And LAST DEAR GOD we YOU do thank,
In earnest prayer both loud and frank,
We are LAST to so deserve,
Your kindness, mercy and reserve,

AT LAST our time will, but draw nigh,
We've done, our best; we will not sigh,
And when we leave AT LAST for home,
The Lord will tell us how we've sown.

- *23 May 80- RLP*

During his tenure as CNS, 79-82, Admiral and Mrs. Pereira (MA) were busy with their official and social engagements and therefore, could not pay much attention to the house. However, most of the construction work had been completed by the time Admiral retired in end Feb 82. They moved to Bangalore on 7th Mar 82 and initially put up at MES IB, located on Rest House Road, Bangalore. It was about 14 kms from Whitefield and increasingly becoming difficult for Admiral to commute daily to and fro on a scooter and therefore, decided to move to AT LAST.

Final Touches

In his letter dated 12thApril 82, **quote** *"My dear Mike; thank you for both your letters and my apologies for the delay in replying.*

We arrived in Bangalore on 7th March and all of us stayed at the MES Inspection Bungalow until the 11thand then we moved over to AT LAST, at Whitefield. This was essential, as there was lot to be done in the house to get it the way as we wanted and nothing was possible unless we moved in. We have now been here exactly a month and we are still living in the boxes as the house is nowhere finished.

When we built ATLAST, **we just didn't have the resources available** *to finish the two built in cupboards, each of which is 7 x 12 feet. A large show case in the drawing required completion and this was 12X6 ½ feet and finally I had to* build a side-board in the dining room which will be 2 ½ X 8 ½ feet . In addition there is a requirement for a front wall and a shutter to the garage which is now open and has about 40 crates in it.

The cupboards were completed soon after we arrived. Aunty Phyll has her dressing table incorporated in hers and mine has closet of drawers, the top of which is my dressing table. Both were done very well, but the carpenters could not stay on, as they had great deal of work to complete in B'lore, and promised to be back to do the rest of the work in the second week of April. The result is that until all this is completed, I just cannot unpack.

Any way, they were in today to take the final measurements and will be back with the material and men on the 14th, promising to complete everything in week. If this can be achieved we shall be very lucky and I will certainly be pleased. Our little house is not really too bad and will certainly serve the three (including Aunty Bobby) of us very well. Once we unpack, we shall certainly feel more settled and life will be normal again.

It is fortunate we can get men from B'lore as Whitefield has great shortage of artisans- carpenters, masons, plumbers and the like. The whole lot has been drawn away by the industry and it is therefore difficult to get anyone. It is equally difficult to get any domestic help, other than a young girl, who we have employed to do washing, sweeping, scrubbing and cleaning; we are still without a cook. However, I am enjoying myself though there is great deal to be done. I find it is satisfying to do it for one's own house.

My transport is a **scooter- a Bajaj Super** and it certainly gets me around. To give you an idea of running that I do, **I have now clocked 1200 kms since I got it on 8th March".** Unquote .

There was indeed problem of the cook and Aunty Phyll did not like to enter the kitchen as she was not very good at cooking, so perforce they had to get Tiffin for their lunch and dinner from one of the restaurant in the village market.

In May and June 82, I did not hear from the Admiral and apparently they were very busy settling down and giving finishing touches to the interiors. Then in July I was surprised to receive a long letter written from Margao, Goa! In his letter dated 16th July giving me the details of events of preceding two months, **quote** *"My dear Mike- I have not written for ages, and I must apologize for this lapse. I must also thank you very much indeed for your thoughtful gesture for my birthday. This certainly warranted a reply a long while ago, but I have been really busy, and I will tell you why.*

After leaving Delhi on the 7th of March, we came straight down to Bangalore, and moved into AT LAST on the 12th. The house was by no means ready for occupation, but we appreciated that nothing would be done unless we were on site. The three of us therefore- Bobby, Aunty and myself- decided ATLAST was where we should be.

The house was not ready for occupation, as the large built-in cupboards- 12X7 feet in each bedroom had to be manufactured. We needed a large show case-12X7 feet in the drawing room, a side board 7X4 feet- in the dining room, the built-in office furniture for my little office, and a great deal of work outside including the compound wall. Finally our roof was leaking. And the entire surface 70X30 feet- had to be water proofed.

However, we got stuck into the problem, and were fortunate to get the most excellent carpenters, masons and other skilled labour, all from Bangalore as nothing is available in Whitefield, and after three months of constant effort and endeavour, and 3500 kms on my scooter, we have finally finished it! AT LAST is finally in the shape that we want and we all are very pleased. I have one last job to do, and that is to build a servant's quarter, and I hope this will be completed by the end of the year.

It has cost us much more than we anticipated, but it has all gone into our very home, so I am not really concerned.

It's wonderful having a home of your own, but in Whitefield it is impossible to get any staff. After being there for 4 ½ months, we have only managed to get a young girl to scrub, clean and wash. I have not been able to get a cook or even a watchman at the rates we can afford is not possible. The reason for this position is that the Industrial Estate in Whitfield- and this is a big one- has taken every human- being, man woman and child- who can walk on two feet, and the wages they pay have no bearing on what we can offer. It is for this reason that I must build a servant's quarter, as the added attraction of free accommodation will help us to get a cook". **Unquote**

Admiral stayed on in Goa till end 1982 and came back to Whitefield. However, 1983 was a bad year for Admiral as he met with a serious scooter accident in April and thereafter he was hospitalized and confined to AT LAST for most of the year.

One time there was talk of taking up job with an international shipping company and I wrote to inquire if he was indeed contemplating to settle down abroad? In his letter dated 02nd Feb 84, **quote** *"As far as Aunty Phyll and myself are concerned, we could never settle down at this age in a foreign* *environment, not that either of us, have a desire to do so.* **In any case having put in a large amount of our limited savings into AT LAST, it's here that we must remain, until the Lord say 'Time'.** *I personally enjoy this little village of ours; Phyll sometime finds it trifle lonely. However, it would be almost impossible to find an ideal environment anywhere, and to settle down in a city within the confines of a flat, would just about put paid, to both of us. As I always say, we are lucky to have what we now possess, so let's count our blessings and thank God for his generosity and kindness".* **Unquote**

Shifting Out of Whitefield

In 1984 Admiral was 61 years and the scooter accident the previous year somehow restricted his movement between Whitefield and Bangalore and to be honest he was bit chary of driving, particularly after dark in the crowded and unruly traffic on the road. At the same time Aunty's patience were running thin with Whitefield local residents, as she felt they were only interested in silly gossips, add to this she just couldn't take the heat. Notwithstanding, Admiral was quite happy as he had his old friends such as Vice Admiral Fraser, Commodore Jack Shea and Commander Lunel all residing close by in Whitefield itself. But Aunty Phyllis had made up her mind to shift out of Whitefield sooner or later. Aunty Bobby had already moved out and was staying as Paying Guest at 25 Magarath Road. Gradually the seed of selling AT LAST was sown in by end 1984.

Sadly Admiral admitted in early 1985 that- yes, they are thinking of shifting out of Whitefield. In his letter dated 05th Feb 85, **quote** *"I am obviously getting old, as I cannot remember if I had earlier mentioned to you, that we are now toying with the idea-indeed decided in fact-* **to sell 'AT LAST'** *and move into Bangalore. The reasons are that any activity in town entails a haul in, often after dark and return also in the dark hours and with steadily increasing traffic- impolite and inconsiderate-it's a journey I am beginning to detest!! Also the hospital is 14 kms from us and finally though there is no problems just now, running the bungalow between the two of us, in our old age will raise security problem later in life. All said and done therefore we have decided to move. However, it will take a fair time and* **we can only think of a flat after selling 'AT LAST'.** *We are not in hurry and will await a buyer who will agree to our price, before we think of anything else-Aunty Phyll is well, but* **rather bored with Whitefield.** *In fact, when we do actually move into town, she will be rather pleased to say the least!!"* **Unquote**

Sale of At Last

Two weeks later I received another letter dated 21st Feb 85, **quote** " *My dear Mike- I don't know if I have told you that we have decided to* **move into town** *and this will necessitate in selling 'AT LAST' and reinvesting our money in a flat. It is a decision which we have very carefully made and our basic reason for this move centre around three factors of distance into town, difficult to motor after dark with a heavy traffic, secondly the distance to IAF Hospital is 14 kms and when and if we need it, it will be an awful fag for the other half of the family and lastly the security in a bungalow may become a problem in the years ahead and would* **much better in a flat**. *We have no intention of hurrying our move and until we sell 'AT LAST' for the price that we want, we shall not move. Fortunately the properties have escalated a great deal, particularly, independent bungalows, on the other hand there has been not only a slight drop in the price of flats, but they are not moving and this suits us a great deal as the two flats we like a great deal are part of a complex that is moving very slowly, this gives us time to sell AT LAST and yet pick up one of those flats".* **Unquote**

It was indeed sad that Admiral and Mrs. Pereira had made up their mind to put AT LAST on sale - apart from money it was 'emotional' investment- so much time had been put into planning and construction and herculean effort by Aunty Phyll walking up and down the Main Road from one end of the village to another in such inhospitable summers and monsoons- and kept at it all by herself without making complaints about Admiral absence at the site. Last time Admiral availed leave was in 1969!! Not only that Admiral had to sell his new car to raise funds, in fact he, eventually spent all his savings on AT LAST. Apart from that they had put in so much effort in doing the interior after retirement and above all Aunty beloved garden, every tree and plant was planted under her personal guidance and supervision. It was indeed hard decision but I would say pragmatic. Admiral had a point about **distance** to the hospital and, yes- **security**. Finally, Aunty Phyll antipathy towards the local residents and above all, she just could not take the heat and dust of Whitefield anymore. Her patients were running out fast!!

The fundamental problem of sale was that Admiral wanted a buyer who would give him 100% white money, either in cheque or demand draft and not a penny under the table. Now that was a big ask and almost impossible proposition in Indian environments but he still went ahead with the sale and hoped some NRI may appear on the scene?? The moment the perspective buyers mentioned number 2 (black money), Admiral would simply show him the gate!!

Admiral told me, son, it is indeed very difficult to build a roof over your head while you are in Service, leave alone after retirement. Apart from sharing a house in Staff College in 1952/53 they never lived in a flat and always lived in sprawling bungalows. Therefore, the very idea of shifting into a flat did not appeal to them, notwithstanding its advantages at this stage of life. But at the same time to go in for another construction of the house was also **not advisable** as Admiral was 62 years and Aunty Phyll pushing 60. It was a difficult decision to make. Not only that they will have to find suitable piece of land, which by itself was not an easy proposition to say the least.

About a year back, I was allotted a flat in AWHO, Noida, and almost surrendered it due to paucity of funds. The advice given by Admiral in his letter dt 2nd Feb 84, **quote** *"Regarding your house, Mike DON'T, if you want my advice, ever take your name off AWHO. Its, by far, the cheapest and best way to get a house, which is what everyone wants as time goes by. It doesn't matter whether you stay in Delhi or not. Property today is the finest investment and if ultimately you want to settle somewhere else other than Delhi, the escalation in the price of your flat, will permit you to obtain another anywhere you choose. You certainly never be able to lay out the money for another, so DON'T be shortsighted and swing this wonderful asset of the future for silly fridge or TV set. You will really make the biggest mistake of your life if you did this"*. **Unquote**

As per Admiral's advice I did not surrender the flat, however, when in 1990 AWHO asked for payment of first installment of 2 lakhs, we hit the wall and could not raise the money and regrettably surrendered the flat!!

Unfortunately sometime in late 85 and early 86, there were security concerns in Whitfield and local residents were subjected to a series of dacoities and burglaries, which had never happened before. Admiral in his letter of 21st Feb 86 **quote** *"We have had a spate of dacoities around Whitefield, and in fact the gang which has now been operating for about three to four months, have raided nine houses, and unfortunately shot 5 people in their raids, so there is fair amount of anxiety. We are actually very well situated and in a safe locality and the gang have been concentrating on the isolated farms and houses. The police reckon that there are six people in the gang with 4 guns.*

The police have been very active, but unfortunately unsuccessful to pick up the gang, as none of the unfortunate inmates of the houses that have been raided, were able to give them any description of the gang. They usually shoot anyone resisting and then lock up the rest. However, I am sure they will be eventually picked up as everyone is now alive to the problem and even in Whitefield the locals have special vigilance parties patrolling at night. I have two weapons in the house, and would not hesitate to use them if it was necessary. Whitefield at this moment therefore, is very dacoit conscious and it's the talk of the village! **Unquote**

Though AT LAST was located bang on the main road with lots of houses in close vicinity, but still the incidents of dacoities made their resolve stronger to move out of Whitefield sooner or later and purchase a flat in Bangalore.

However, the sale of AT LAST did not materialize throughout 1986. Admiral was still looking for a buyer who would pay him in cheque. Meanwhile, Admiral and more importantly Aunty changed their mind about shifting to Bangalore and instead decided to move to Coonoor and buy or build another house as and when AT LAST is sold. **Indeed a wrong decision!**

Move to Coonoor

In his letter dated 27th Oct 86, **quote** *"We have now decided to make another house when AT LAST is sold.* ***This will be at Coonoor****, possibly I have already told you this in one of my earlier letters and it is obvious that I am getting old, as my memory keeps fading. Anyway let me repeat the thesis! The point is that the houses in Coonoor are very expensive, going for 6 to 7 lakhs. Over which we, as buyers will be required to pay 14 % in stamp duty for the transfer and another 1% approx in lawyer's fees. This is certainly a lot of money and as I am not regrettably- Paul Getty or Onassis, I have decided that building will be far cheaper proposition. It happens that a very good friend of ours- Dev Mukerji of Consolidated Coffee, has acquired, with buddy of his, 2 acres of land in Coonoor, which they intend to develop with roads, electricity and services and then sell them in ½ acre plots. I happened to run into Dev in Cochin in September, and we have booked a plot from him. Even if it costs around 70,000/- it will be worth it.*

Our home will be built around three bedrooms with a plinth area of about 1700 sq feet. Estimates from architect working in Coonoor put the current rate of construction to Rs 200 /- per sq ft and it will therefore cost us about 3,50,000/-. The total will then be well under 4 ½ lakhs, which would be far cheaper than a readymade house, which I am sure will never suit Aunty Phyll. Even if our furniture goes to another 50,000/- we shall certainly be much better off.

Aunty Phyll reckons that I will have a hell of a sweat, but that doesn't bother me in the least. In any case we shall get a good architect who is at Bangalore to design and supervise the house and with a bit of rank to throw around, I don't see any problem of getting steel and cement at control rates. This then is the plan. Also having built a house already, we know the snags and we will be able to get fairly good result in our second attempt! I shall work on PERT charts and critical paths and will have great fun, getting myself into a really good SNAFU!!

AT LAST is not sold as yet- at least the deal is not finalized in payment, as the buyer- a very nice couple- is now trying to sell their house in Bangalore, also in white, and that is always a problem. However, as he has agreed to our price, and is very keen to move in, we are happy to wait till his property is sold.

I have already worked out the list of priorities, once AT LAST is sold!! They are:

(a) *A car –a Fiat or Dolphin*

(b) *A set of MACGREGOR MUIREFIELD, golf clubs (I am already in correspondence with my buddies on this one!!)*

(c) *A holiday for Aunty P in Europe with her sisters.*

(d) *The house in Coonoor.*

The deal for sale continued for another ten months as Admiral refused to touch anything but white, and in doing so he was prepared to lose over Rs 10 lakhs and ultimately I believe he sold for just 9 lakhs!! The amount was not at all commensurate to the value of property (approximately 22 lakhs as per the market value). Admiral would tell me, my son, even I accept black money, where will I hide it?? I won't be able to sleep. Without it at least I can sleep peacefully. The moment I put my head on the pillow, within minutes I am fast asleep!! He had a point there, no doubt!

Admiral in his letter mentioned that he will prepare PERT chart. It is 'Program Evaluation Review Technique'; a methodology developed by US Navy in 1950's to manage the Polaris submarine missile program. It helps you to schedule and manage complex projects.

When I visited AT LAST during mid-term break from Staff College in Dec 86 with my wife and two small sons, I inquired from Admiral regarding the sale of the house and tried my best to dissuade them from selling AT LAST. He admitted that it is indeed very difficult to find a buyer who would give him a cheque and most of them spoke of No 2 and invariably shown the gate !! Anyhow, we have a buyer on our terms, but he is finding it difficult to dispose off his property, hopefully it will materialize.

In fact Aunty Phyll's BEST friend Aunty Dorothy Shea lived few blocks down the road from AT LAST and she had known her since late 40,s. Then what happened? I told her in case you move out, you will have to make new friends and it is not easy as everybody is busy with their own lives. Here at least you and Unc have many old friends from the navy, think of the advantages of Whitefield, please, I fervently tried to change her mind but no go and Aunty Phyll was adamant and just would not entertain the very suggestion. Her words were "I am fed up with this place; it's like a hell hole". I told her you have put in so much of effort and resources to build such a beautiful home for yourself, and where on earth will you get a perfect environment? Don't sell it please, but she will have none of it and walked off in a huff much to the dismay of Admiral, but he kept quiet. After that for next 4 days I did not broach the subject. But to be honest given a choice Admiral wanted to stay on in Whitefield or at best move into a flat in B'lore. However, come hell or high water Aunty Phyll had made up her mind to move to a hill station to escape the heat!! Not realizing the inherent problems in doing so!

In his letter dated 02nd June 87, **quote** *"Aunty Phyll is well, but not at all pleased with present weather. She really cannot take the summer at all, this is the main reason that we must move to a hill station, when we sell AT LAST".* **Unquote**

AT LAST Sold

Finally the deal was through by August 87 and in his letter of 7th Oct 87, **quote** *"My dear Mike and Annie- Thank you very much for your letter of the 17th Sep which I received yesterday, but I think that the delay has been in the Staff College as the Coonoor post mark is 21st. However we are in our own rented house, my earlier address will not hold good anymore.*

We left AT LAST on 30th August and motored up to Coonoor with Cindy very comfortably. It was lovely weather, and as it was a holiday, there was precious little traffic on the roads, the car ran like a bird, so all in all, it was just as the doctor ordered.

The Navy had put the Guest House- DUNMORE- which is just above the Coonoor club at our disposal, there we stayed for about 10 days, till we found something to rent. We were fortunate in hiring the present accommodation, which is nice two bedrooms house on Quail Hill, fully furnished, we moved in and intend to stay here, till we find our own.

Properties are very expensive and have escalated 5 to 10 times in the last 5 years, so we are in no particular hurry to grab the first one that we see, and we now toying with the idea of possibly getting a small piece of land on which we might even build a '*jopra*' (hut) of our own. However, its question of cost effectiveness- a piece of land or a house-cum-land which may or may not require remodeling- we will look around, therefore, for a month or so before committing ourselves.*

I bought a FIAT in excellent condition, totally refurbished, and she is running like a bird. I had looked at both the DOLPHIN and the MARUTI van, but did not feel comfortable in the former and could not fit in the latter, and we therefore, went for the FIAT.

Aunty is well and loves Coonoor. She delights in the weather, and the change has done her lot of good. If we can find something suitable for our own abode soon, that will be final answer. She sends Annie and you all her love and hopes that you are now willing to do a little more work around the house and help Annie! Our love to children as well.

It's been raining almost every day since we arrived and the planters around are very happy indeed. We seem to have brought the rain, as there was precious little before our arrival.

Well Mike I'll close.I am off for lunch to DSSC Mess, as the college is being visited by Admiral Sir William Staveley .The First Sea Lord and CNS from Britain. He was the Vice Chief when I visited Britain. God bless you and family. Lovingly-Uncle Ron" **Unquote**

This was the first letter I received after they left AT LAST and apparently Aunty seems to be happy with the weather and social engagements and the Coonoor itself. However, I must mention here that initially she was very excited when they moved to Whitefield in March 82 and for first two years enjoyed their stay in AT LAST. The idea of shifting out of Whitefield came up sometime in summers of 1984, and that too when both of them were keen to shift to Bangalore and buy a flat, which would have been far more easier to maintain, better security arrangements and availability of domestic help. Also hospital would have been in close proximity. Admiral was 62 and Aunty was pushing 60 so the idea was indeed worthwhile, particularly for later years.

However, over the next two summers Aunty was determined to shift to a hill station to avoid the horrible heat and dust of the plains! This decision was taken by Admiral and Aunty, much against the sane advice of their very close friend Air Marshal Doughlas Kinglee, who had a flat in Bangalore. **He tried very hard to explain to Admiral that it will NOT be wise to shift to Coonoor and build an independent cottage.** Firstly it will cost lots of money, secondly it will be a herculean effort for Admiral to go through the construction process, particularly at this late stage of life, thirdly and most importantly there will be security concerns later in life (that was one of the main reasons to shift out of Whitefield) and no way Mrs. P could stay alone by herself, God forbid something happens to Admiral. Lastly, the Military Hospital at Wellington does not have equipment or specialist to provide necessary medical support and one will have to travel down to Bangalore / Coimbatore for any major/ critical surgery or operation. **All in all it was just NOT advisable to move to the hills.** However, the **'SAGE'** advice of Air Marshal was not heeded to, and come June 93, regrettably they had to put BROADSIDES on sale also due to Admiral's sickness, and doctor's advice that he must shift to lower altitude at the earliest?? . **I remember vividly, how sad Admiral was in his last days and he confided in me" Mike, I think it was the worst decision of my life to sell AT LAST, I wish I had listened to you and my dear friend Doughlas Kinglee's advice not to move to Coonoor !! And now I am leaving Phyllis without a roof over her head?! There was so much pain and regret in his voice and sadness in his eyes**

Coonoor

Indeed, Coonoor is a beautiful hill station and the second largest town on the Nilgiris Hills. It is situated at approximately 6000 feet and 19 kms from the town of Ooty, and famous for its verdant environs and variety of wild life, flowers and birds. In mid 19th century the Britishers came here and started tea plantations. In 1880 Madras Regimental Centre was established in Wellington. Post independence, Brigadier Shiv Dev Verma 16th Cavalry (my regiment) Senior Instructor at Staff College, Quetta (now in Pakistan) was given the task to find a suitable location to establish Staff College in India. When I visited him and his lovely wife Thelma Verma at their beautiful cottage - 'Longwood' at Kasauli in May 1986, a month prior to my departure for Staff College, the General narrated in his words, **quote** "Mike, I nearly did not visit Wellington and eventually it was only after second thought that I decided to take the Blue Mountain Express Train and arriving at Mettupalayam next morning took a little train to Wellington and as it entered Nilgiris, I just fell in love with the Blue Mountains and that's how Staff College was ultimately established there in autumn of 1947".**Unquote.**

I understand that Admiral and Aunty had special attachment with Coonoor as immediately after their marriage on 25th Sep 52, then, a young and dashing Lt Commander RL Pereira along with his beautiful bride proceeded to Wellington to attend DSSC- 6. They shared a house with another couple in upper Coonoor, and spent memorable 6 months.

Secondly, I believe that Admiral thought, that he will be in good company of Field Marshal Manekshaw and General Sundarji. I think it was a misplaced perception as Gen Sundarji was confined to his fortress like accommodation and Manekshaw had a nice cottage for himself since early 70's. The Army provides them with complete staff and security to look after them, unlike in the Navy. **Admiral had no help at all from the Navy**?? Nor he would accept it. In fact he barely had one civilian bearer in the house, that's all! He interacted with General Sundarji a couple of times. In his letter of 26th Aug 88, **quote** *"Yes Gen Sundarji is here and has now moved into his house. Sadly within 8 feet wall around the whole house and very tight security throughout the day, life becomes not only grim but I am sure it can get overpowering. I sometime drop in to see him. And we have had him and his wife over for a quiet evening as his life now, is certainly not his own".* **Unquote**

Anyhow, now that, they were in Coonoor and they had to work out their future plans. In his second letter dated 27th Oct 87 from Coonoor, **quote** *"My dear Mike –Thank you very much for your letter of the 17th Oct, which came in last week. Here I am to reply as the bloody electricity has broken down in the middle of the match between Australia and New Zealand!!*

Indeed any continuity, so to speak, in the electrical supply to consumers in T.N, is a total myth!! We have a break-down at least once every 48 hours, and it really occur at the crucial stage of a sporting event- recently during the Reliance matches. I was under the misconception that the Karnataka was the worst in India, as far as power was concerned, but T.N, I now realize is at the very bottom of the hill!

We have a new SOLIDAIRE CT/V and stay glued to the box for the feast of cricket that RELIANCE now affords. *Our reception on Quail Hill is not bad, compared to rest of Coonoor, but it is not as good as B'lore. However, it gives us reasonable picture and I can't grumble. I do so hope that we win for Kapil's sake. I reckon it will rub the noses of all these so called sports critics in the deck- Patuadi and Puri in particular.*

Our love and good wishes to Annie and the kids . They are often in our thoughts. Smack 'Goonda Gowdah' (my younger son) *on the bottom from me!! affly Uncle Ron.* '**Unquote**. This was the first colour TV they ever had!

By early 1988 Admiral and Aunty had more or less settled down in their rented house – Evergreen - Quail Hill, Coonoor and were quite busy with social activities at the Staff College.

In his letter dated 17th Feb 88, **quote** *"The search for suitable piece of land seems elusive as Scarlet Pimpernel!! We have, as I might have mentioned in one of my earlier letters found a lovely piece of land in Wellington, just after Black Bridge overlooking the MRC (Madras Regimental Centre) Training Centre. However, the property is jointly owned by 4 brothers and sisters, three of whom has been overseas for last 45 years! I have therefore, seen my lawyers at Coonoor and Bangalore , and I have managed to convince the owner that he has to get a Power of Attorney from his relations overseas, giving him the authority to sell. He also has to go to RBI to seek their approval, not only to sell on behalf of his relations overseas, who are now all foreigners but to ask the RBI for permission to permit his brothers and sisters to hold that land since 1976, when they should have made a declaration to the effect that they had held land in India, since 1976 as foreigners. I will possibly have to go down to Madras in regard to RBI permission, but this may not be too difficult, as none of the relations overseas desire to have anything from the sale proceeds, which they are quite happy to let the brother in India, hold in Toto. All this should take about 2 to 3 months, but the land is excellent and worth waiting for".* **Unquote**

As per Admiral assessment the deal did materialize by June but from another party, in his letter dated 14th June 88, **quote** *" Well the best news is that we have at last bought a piece of land in Wellington, about 1 ½ km from the MRC. We got this from a very lovely couple called Mehta's. Balbir and Sujata- who settled here about 8 years ago and have about 3 acres , which they had no intention of selling but were kind enough to offer us a lovely little portion, about half an acre, out of goodness of their heart . The transfer was registered on the 9th, and we have now got our young architect planning our house. I hope we shall turn the first sod in an about a month's time, and have the house completed and ready for occupancy by March next year. It is really a relief, as we were both worried, but now that land is ours, things will start moving quite fast".* **Unquote**

Broadsides

Yes the work started pretty soon and In his very next letter of 26th Aug 88, **quote** *" My dear Mike; Well let me begin by saying that we have started the work on the house and are at the moment clearing the land of tea bushes- and then leveling it to the extent that we desire for the house , this should be completed in next 15 days, when we shall then peg out the foundation and start digging, simultaneously I intend to build a garage, which I hope, will be completed in 30* *days time. As I will need a place to store all the materials, as we purchase them, be it timber, cement etc as well as having a place for the carpenter to work on the joinery.*

I am trying to get everyone on CPM chart in regard to the house, but it's not easy as everyone- contractor, architect, supervisor agrees, but does nothing about it. I am therefore, intending to get them all together next week and see if I can't knock something out on which we can monitor progress. As I see it, it should take about 9 months, and this will bring us to **May 89, when I hope we shall be under our own roof**". **Unquote**

The full form of CPM chart is 'Critical Path Method, it provides reduced project duration due to better understanding of dependencies leading to improved overlapping of activities and tasks where feasible.

Evidently Admiral got stuck in the construction from morning to evening and in coming 2 months just had no time to sit down and write. It was only in early November when I heard from him, letter dated 8th Nov 88, **quote** "*BROADSIDES- a good gunnery term- is the new name and I hope we'll at least be able to move in by May 89, though I don't think all the work will be completed by then. At the moment we have cut and leveled an area 52X 72 feet on the upper terrace- 20,000 cu feet of earth has been a problem to dispose, but we are gradually getting rid of it, by dumping it in a stream by the side of the property. By leveling we hit a large outcrop of granite stone on the left and right rear of the cut and this required to be blasted and cut. However, it has now given us 7500 granite stones, about ¾ x ¾ x ½ feet which will be more than sufficient for the foundation and plinth, which will be 2 feet above the foundation.*

We have dug and cleared the foundations and everything was ready to start the 6 feet of concrete on the base of foundations before starting the actual stone and masonry work. In fact, Monday was the D-day, but a low pressure formation in the bay has brought the rains which have given us a wet Diwali, and I will therefore; wait till there is a **break in the weather**, *before we go. It is rather like the* **Normandy landings** *though not quite as dramatic!!*

My intention is to try and get the foundation completed, and if we are lucky even 2 feet of plinth by the end of the month, and then wait till NE blows itself out by the end of December, before starting the brick walls and the roof. The garage is ready and completed on the lower terrace and this will be our work centre and store while we build the house". **Unquote**

By the beginning of 89, Admiral and Aunty Phyll shifted from Quail Hill to Naval guest house DUNMORE, Club Road, Wellington, which was much closer to the construction site and fully staffed to look after them.

The time flew past for next 6 months and I did not hear from Admiral in spite of writing regularly at least once a fortnight; I realized that he must be busy with the construction and to meet the deadline of May 89. Knowing him so well I could imagine that he must be the first one to reach the site and probably the last one to leave, but one important factor he was overlooking was, his **advancing years,** as he was nearly 66 years and he must be working like 46 years !! Apparently he must be dead tired by the time he got back. Aunty Phyll was the last person to write and as per Hugh Gantzer, **quote** "in fact she never communicated with our family throughout her life".**Unquote**. Ultimately I sent them a telegram to check about their well being.

At last I received a short letter written on inland letter dated 1st May 89. **Quote** *"My dear Mike- thank you for your telegram which arrived two days ago. I must apologize for not having written for a very very long while, but the house, now in its final stages has kept me very busy, and by the time I get back home by 6.30 pm, I am really tired. However, I am otherwise very fit and so is Aunty, but both of us are anxious to move into the new house as soon as we can, if we are a just trifle lucky, we should be in occupation by June.*

At this final stage, there is not only a lot of running around, but the small jobs that require completion seem to take too long and are never ending!! We make check off list and 'aides memoire' but in spite of our entire attempt to cover all the nit wits, something always seems to get out of the net!!

Cost of construction today is phenomenal, and in spite of all our attempts to keep a tight budget, we have far over spent. However, it is now almost finished and both of us are looking forward, to finally having our own roof, over our heads." **Unquote**

This letter gave us a great sense of relief, and I repeatedly wrote to Admiral that in case he needs my presence, I will take long leave and come, but he wouldn't listen and say your responsibility is to your family and the men you command. I am fit and in case I need you I will not hesitate to call you. Exactly the same argument when he was admitted in ASVINI, Bombay in Jan 92. To be honest even today after 27 years I do feel guilty and regret not being of any use to him at that juncture! He wouldn't listen and it was impossible to make him change his rigid ideas!

In his letter 6th June 89, **quote** *"BROADSIDES is almost ready but we are stuck on our electrical connection which has not been given as yet. However, I have been informed that it will be provided by next two weeks, as soon as that is done shall move in. Both Aunty and I believe that it will be better to move in, as soon as possible and then continue the completion of the small jobs while we are in occupation.*

I don't quite know what will be the **condition of our luggage***, which has been in* **storage for last two years***. However, we could not have in a better place – THE MRC Centre- so we hope it will not be too bad".* **Unquote**

The construction of BROADSIDES kept Admiral totally immersed and busy for **nearly 9 months at a stretch**, so much so he got mixed up with my postal address!! He addressed the letter to HQs 107 Infantry Brigade instead of 7 Infantry Division. Fortunately, a smart Havildar Duty Clerk sent the letter back to Admiral with a note (which I still have) attached, "not present in 107 Inf Bde." It reached back Coonoor on 15th Sep and Admiral then posted it with correct address with a remark "PS. My mistake, instead of 07 I sent it to 107!! sorry and I received it in the end of Sep 89."

Above letter dated 30th Aug 89, **quote** *"My dear Annie and Mike- It's been ages since I last wrote to anybody, but the trials of building a house and trying to get it completed in a schedule I had worked out and was determined to stick to,* **had me wholly tied up from 9 in the morning to about 6pm in the evening when I was on site, six, if not seven days a week***. By the time I get back home, I was so burnt out that there was time for a bath, dinner and bed. Anyway it is just memory, for you will see that we have since moved in, at this moment are in the process of unpacking- unpacking after almost two years- and settling in. This is always satisfying and delightful part of life, particularly you are settling in your own house, as every picture that goes up, or plug that is put into the wall, is there for keeps and exactly as you want it.*

Sadly one never has enough space for all the little things, some totally innocuous but sentimental- that one wants to display or keep, and finally they have to be discarded or given away. This is inevitable but sad and if one has to keep and display everything that one had gathered over the years the house has to be enormous and otherwise purposeless. Unlike AT LAST, - 'BROADSIDES' has separate dressing room-cum-office, with its own bathroom which I wanted. In addition we have two bedrooms and two bathrooms, a sit out with main entrance a drawing room, a dining room. Kitchen with its own store room leads from the dining room. This gives us 1700 sq feet of plinth area. I also have separate garage which is 18x12 feet internally.

I actually started the house on the 7th Nov 88 and wanted it to be complete by first week of June 89. However, the electrical connections from TN Electrical Dept, took us a while to get, till I blew up, and as a result we moved in on the 4th of July- American Independence Day- **and of course like everything American there was chaos and disaster.**

Our plans to save some money from the sale of AT LAST, did not work out at all. We had hoped to keep the construction within 200/- a sq feet, but it ultimately went over 250/-, and we had to dip into our **savings** *to finish the work. There wasn't a great deal saved into which we dipped, so* **most of it has gone** *we have to start again.* **However, with my pension just over 3000/- a month, we manage to keep going and run a strict budget, which is the only way, we can manage".** Unquote

I wrote three letters to Admiral in the month of Sep 89 and finally got a reply in the first week of October, in his letter dated 2nd Oct 89, **quote** *"My dear Mike-Thank you for all three of your letters -12th, 20th and 26th September – and let me try and reply today, as I am not quite as busy, as I somehow find myself in the house, on most days.*

Aunty has two occupations now, her garden and the kitchen?? Peter, our dear old cook, found that 'BROADSIDES' was too far from his house and therefore, decided that he would pack up working for good, as he is really getting rather old and even the walk from the bus stop to the house, about 1 ½ km used to leave him rather tired and weary. We certainly miss him, but Aunty has taken over the galley responsibility and is really doing rather well, **though she does not like cooking at all.** *We have lass who sweeps and clean and generally does all the jobs around the house and she now helps Phyll, but I can see that we shall need a cook on permanent basis. Today in Coonoor a cook can ask 500/- a month with pay, rations, his lunch here and his bus fare to and from his house. However, it is difficult to get a good one and we don't really want a woman in the kitchen. However, we have sounded all our buddies and see what turns up".* **Unquote**

However, by December they had settled down well and celebrated their first X- Mas in 'BROADSIDES' with their friends, in letter dated 29th Dec 89, **quote** *"My dear Mike and Annie-Thank you a million for your letters and greeting cards for X-Mas and the New Year and I do hope you got ours, as we were not sure where you would be, till we got Mike's last letter.*

We have had a quiet but very enjoyable X-Mas with our friends. The weather was beautiful and Phyll had put up a lovely X-Mas tree in the house with

all the wee decorations that we have gathered. It looked lovely and was really very unique.

Sadly, amidst all this joy and happiness, we lost a friend of ours who lived in her own small house on Quail Hill, very close to EVERGREEN, where we lived for about 18 months after our arrival in Coonoor. She was either murdered or inadvertently asphyxiated by the culprits who entered the house sometime in the evening of 27th. Her servant, next morning, could not get a reply from her, to open the door, when she came at about 7.30 am, and the door had to be ultimately broken open by the police, who found her bound, hands and feet in the bathroom, with a cloth covering her head and her mouth, and in putting the latter, they evidently restricted her air- intake which I think, led to her death.

The old girl was 72 and often visited us at EVERGREEN. It was therefore, quite a shock when we got the news. Indeed, this sort of offence is unheard of in Coonoor and it has shaken lots of old residents a great deal. Ironically, she had very little money, jewellery or anything worth stealing and the whole thing therefore, seems very sad and purposeless. In fact we are not sure how these people got onto the house, as she would never open the door to anyone she could not identify. Her funeral will be at 5.30 pm this evening and we shall be going.

The NE monsoon is now behind us, we shall be starting some of peripheral work that is yet to be completed around BROADSIDES. Our first priority is outside drains- they are now kachha ones- and then the painting of the stone work of the plinth. At the moment plinth which is granite stone is plastered but not painted. The later will make it look better and this is necessary that this is done. We have also put the guttering along the eves at the back of the house, to save a bad splash coming into wall and discoloring it. These three small jobs are about the maximum we can do at the moment. **We shall wait for another year and to do the other work as this helps us to build up some resources!!**

One of the problems of moving into a new house, too soon, is that fact that having not dried out completely- it takes all of 12 months for this- spaces like cupboards, store rooms and areas that are not vented get mildew and this effect clothes and anything in storage. It has certainly affected my camera lens and my binoculars which I am rather sad about. But nonetheless, I have taken some photos of the house- rather poor indeed- which I am enclosing. It will give you some idea of what we have built. Auntie's garden is yet to take shape. As she will only be planting her annuals- limited to a few beds- in January, to have them in flower in March, when it is little warmer.

Well Annie and Mike, I'll close. Our love and good wishes to both of you, and may 90 be a good year, full of happiness, joy and grace of God. Our love to the children, whom we shall have in our prayers; indeed, so will both of you will be there. Affly Uncle Ron". **Unquote**

This was the beginning of the best 24 months (Aug 89- Aug 91) in BROADSIDES and in fact post retirement, they truly deserve every minute of it. Both of them were enjoying good health and had no complaints whatsoever.

Aunty Phyll was working on her garden and Admiral in his letter 18th Mar 90, **quote** *"I sent you some photos- at least one photo of BROADSIDES in one of my last letters and I hope you have received it .It was taken soon after we moved in, on July 89. Aunty Phyll has now started on the garden and I am sure she will have it looking lovely in a few months. Our love to Annie and kids, affly Unc Ron".* **Unquote**

By end May 90, apart from odd jobs like second coat of painting and some carpenter work, BROADSIDES was more or less completed , however ,to get to this stage, it made rather **very deep whole in Admiral's pocket** and he came face to face with the hard realities of his financial situation .

Admiral seems to be living in world of his own and he thought that everyone else will be as good as a human being as himself. His very close friend Admiral Raja Menon remarked, **quote** "that Ronnie P lacked acumen in money matters, he trusted others to be like him and invariably got trapped in wrong situations as far as financial deals were concerned". **unquote**

Firstly, the sale of AT LAST did not accrue its full market value as Admiral would not touch anything but **white**, which had its own disadvantages. It is not easy to find a buyer who would make payment in cheque –very few, if at all. Secondly, the value of the property will be much lower than the market price. Having gone through the sale, his decision to buy land and to build a house was based on apparently incorrect estimates leading to a situation, where he could not leave construction half way and literally had to scratch the bottom of the barrel and ultimately spending the proverbial last penny to complete BROADSIDES. **Finally, he was back to square one - his pension of Rs 3000/- (three thousands only) ! What a situation to be in!??**

Life Interest

This is what precisely Admiral had to say in his letter dated 5th June 90 **quote** "I wish, my son, I could help you with your NOIDA flat, but we *are really* *flat on our coffers after building BROADSIDES and indeed had to dip into our very meager savings to finally complete this little home.* **It is for this reason that we have decided to ultimately sell BROADSIDES;** *three years after its completion-July 89- but will retain what is known 'as a life interest'. In other words we continue to live here till Phyll and I pass on, and only then it will go to the new owner. This has many advantages. Firstly you get back your investment plus: and then you have enough liquid assets to live in a degree of comfort at this stage of your life. Lastly, when we do turn up our toes, there is no real estate to cause any problems.*

Both Phyll and I would during our life time like to bequeath our assets once and for all. There will be Tashi, Rabden, Annie and yourself, and the Little Sisters of the Poor. The question of division of the real estate is both a hassle and indeed impossible. It is only if one has the liquid assets available, can one provide for those for whom one cares and loves.

I say all this merely to point out that till we convert BROADSIDES into liquid assets, life will be difficult, then I have been permitted to build myself a lovely house in beautiful environment, and that itself is a great deal to thank Almighty for .

We have already had a fair amount of rain in May and my rain gauge clocked up over 200mm for the month which was more than average. The planters are very happy, the tea prospers and everything seems rosy in the garden.

Talking of the garden, we –actually Aunty has just laid down the lawn in the front of the house , and she did it in about February plant a lot of flowers that are now in full bloom. The result is a feast of colour and BROADSIDES certainly looks rather nice"

The new Commandant- Lt General Wadera-from 9 Inf Div at Meerut has now taken over the college from General Brar, who has gone, as you know to Eastern Command. Wadera and his wife were kind to call on us, just after he took over, and they seem to be a very nice couple.

Well, let me get this letter away to you. Look after yourself, affily Uncle Ron". **Unquote**

In the next 4 months the lawn had really come up and in his letter of 27th Oct 90, **quote** *"Aunty is well and enjoying herself looking after the garden . The lawn in the front of the house has come up beautifully and there has been quite a change since we have moved in, in July 89. We are at the moment getting* *a little work done in the guest room , as it was rather neglected, while we got rest of the house in order"* **Unquote**

Next 6 months I did not hear from Admiral, in spite of my writing to him regularly, though I did get news of their well being from my friends doing the Staff Course, particularly who sometime saw him on the Golf course .It was only in early May 91 that I received his long letter dated 1st May 91 , **quote** " *My dear Annie and Mike-I haven't written for ages and there has not been any particular reason, other than the fact that there are always seems something to do in the house , which certainly keeps me busy. Indeed, one realizes it, its dinner time and soon after that I am fast asleep!!*

It was only today that I realized that I had not got a letter away to you for ages, so here I am to try and give you all the news.

It's been lovely weather over the last month or so, with short sharp showers of rain, usually in the evening or every other evening, giving us something between 5 to 10 mm. of rain and then beautifully bright clear mornings with the warm sun bearing down on us, to warm our old bones up. The nights are not cold, but they are certainly pleasant enough to pull up a light cover, just to remind one that we are still in the hills. Our lawn has now come up as well as it should, and I am really very pleased with it. We prepared the ground very well, having dug up the whole area; we removed every stone, and then mixed it with good forest soil. Having done so we left it fallow for about a month, so that we could remove any weeds, and then, did we plant the new grass which is now really super.

The current course is almost on its way out, as all the students will be leaving between the 3rd and 5th May. The area is now full of large trucks, all trying to get a full load to the 4 corners of the sub- continent, every now and then, one of them pulls away, often with the car perched amongst the boxes, which always surprises me.

Aunty Phyll spent a fortnight at Bangalore last month, and she certainly needed a break, as she had not been away for about 4 months. B'lore was really warm, nay hot, and lot of people said that they have never before experienced as much heat. I have no doubt with the tremendous building activity, destruction of all our greenery, and general increase in traffic and humanity. Every city of ours is heading for serious trouble, with population out stripping every other facility, the ultimate degradation of our cities and metropolises into large and unhealthy slums. Well I will close with our love and good wishes affly Unc Ron". **Unquote**

It is quite evident from the contents of the above letter that both of them were in pink of their health and generally enjoying the salubrious climes of the Nilgiris. Indeed, these were the best months and in his very next letter dated 27th July 91, **quote** " *Both June and July have been really quite wet and humid, as I am penning you this letter, it is, in fact, raining at the moment. If one totaled up all rainfall over these 2 months , it would just about 10 inches (250mm), which is not bad for Coonoor, as we really get our rains during the North-East, but it is certainly not excessive. However, except for 7 or 10 day dry spell over the last two weeks, we have had it generally wet throughout, with very little sunshine, and a strong westerly wind most of the day.*

Aunty is well, thank God, and is at last off cigarettes. Indeed, she has been off it, for about 2 months, and it has really done her a great deal of good". **Unquote**

However, Aunty went back to 'Charms' within couple of months, when Admiral was admitted in the hospital!! Apparently due to stress, I suppose.

Admiral's health started to deteriorate from Sep 91 and thereafter it was down hill, never to recover again! For next year and a half he was moving to and fro Coonoor, Coimbatore and Bombay and ultimately Command Hospital, Bangalore.

In end Dec 91 Admiral was advised by the doctors to move to INHS ASVINI for further tests and subsequent treatment, Aunty Phyll followed him and stayed for over two months in Bombay and went back to Coonoor in early March 92.

In his letter dated 16 March 92, **quote** "*Aunty Phyll left for BROADSIDES on the 5th and got home on the 7th afternoon. She went by train, as she had quite bit of shopping to take with her. I spoke to her a day later, and other than the hot journey thru Andhra Pradesh, it was uneventful, and she was up the hill and at BROADSIDES by lunch time. I have just had her first letter, and she writes to say that our young bearer- Shankar- had kept the whole house immaculate and she was very pleased with his work. I have therefore, written to Aunty to increase his pay by 50/- as this is the really only 'Thank you' that means something. I was glad that Aunty decided to go back as we have been away for over 3 months, and that is really long time by any standard."* **unquote**

On 5th May 92, Admiral was discharged from ASVINI and was asked to go home for two months break before his next round of check up in July 92. Admiral was indeed very happy to be back at BROADSIDES after more than 5 months.

When he left for Bombay in Dec 91, there was still some pending work in BROADSIDES, so as soon as he reached back, he got busy completing the pending jobs in the house. In his letter of 2nd July 92 written from INS Agrani, Coimbatore, **quote** *"My Dear Mike-This letter should have gone off a long long time ago, but with a long list of jobs to be completed at BROADSIDES and just 60 days to do them all, I kept going- and indeed enjoying myself- in an endeavour to put them all behind me, only to find that there was still quite a few to be completed when I get back.*

For 4 weeks from late May we were in total chaos in the house, with painters, carpenters and plumbers and their entourage of labourers, all working on BROADSIDES to give it a face lift. When we moved-in, in 1989, the contractors had just given the house a base coat of white colour wash, as it is not advisable to distemper or snowcem a new house, for at least one year after it is constructed. We tried to get it done in 1990 and early 1991, but it was either raining or else the contractor was busy on the other project. Finally Phyll and I decided that something must be done, so she got onto the contractor as soon as she got back from Bombay in March, and I got on his tail from the time of my arrival in early May. The invasion ultimately hit us in late May, and continued till end of June, when we were almost going around the bend, with the house in total disarray as each room was taken in hand.

We just managed to settle down and I must say that BROADSIDES looks very very lovely. We have repaired all the plaster cracks, a few large cracks in the walls. We have given the whole of the outside surface two coats of SNOWCEM. The plinth has been done in grey and the ledge between the plinth and the upper walls in terracotta. The inside has been done in oil bound distemper and all the wood work, windows, barge boards etc have had white enamel paint. Sadly, my camera is giving trouble, but a buddy of ours has done some photos for us as soon as I get them, I will send you the copies. I also intend to make a video of the property as I think the College has 5 or 6 cameras available '

Aunty is well and the garden is really looking beautiful. *Much of the afternoon is spent by Aunty with the bearer in the garden as both of them work on it very hard".* **Unquote**

In his letter of 10th July 92, **quote** *"A friend of ours came home just before I left and took some photographs of BROADSIDES. Unfortunately after the three shots taken of the family, he ran out of film, and had to load another roll, with* *which he took shots of BROADSIDES which should be good if they came out. The 3 that he initially took are enclosed, and as soon as the others come out, I'll send you the copies".* **Unquote**

The friend was Erach Awary, who was with Admiral in North Point in 1935! Yes both acted in a play "Mother of Apostles". **coincidence!**

I wonder if it was advisable to work nonstop for two months, when he was still under serious medication for cancer, with whole house turned upside down for painting work!! Not fair at all and how I wish if they had only shifted to a flat in Bangalore, Admiral could have lived much longer! His first cousin Admiral John Pereira is one year senior and still up and about at 94 and Admiral Dick Schunker is 93 and of course close friend Gen Manny Sinha passed away on 17th Nov 16 at the ripe age of 90!!

Sale Of Broadsides

By beginning of 1993, Admiral's health was steadily failing, and as he was suffering from lung cancer the doctors advised him to move from Coonoor (which was at 6000 feet) to lower altitude as his lungs were struggling to produce adequate oxygen resulting in breathlessness. In his letter of 14th March 93, **quote** *"I don't know if I have mentioned it,* **but now we have decided to sell BROADSIDES and move to B'lore, as the doctors reckon that the altitude is too much for me and I would be better at a much lower height. It is certainly sad, after we built it to exactly what we wanted,** *but it is unavoidable. We intend, God willingly,* **to buy a flat at Bangalore, as neither of us would be able to live alone in a place like BROADSIDES.** *(Advice which was sadly rejected by Aunty prior to sale of AT LAST!! What an irony of fate?)*

Sale will take some considerable time. Money is fairly tight, and I will not accept anything under the table. However, we hope on NRI will pop up and buy it, as there will then be no bother about payment- well son, I'll close. Our love to Annie and kids-affly Uncle Ron". **Unquote**

> I don't know if I have mentioned it, but we have now decided to sell 'BROADSIDES' & move back to Bangalore, as the doctors reckon that the altitude is too much for me, & I would be better at a much lower height. It is certainly sad, after we built it to exactly what we wanted, but its unavoidable. We intend, God willing, to buy a flat at Bangalore, as neither of us would be able to live alone in a place like Broadsides.
>
> Sale will take some considerable time. Money is fairly tight & I will not accept anything under the table. However, we hope an NRI will pop up to buy it, as there will then be no bother about payment. Will sign, I'll close. Our love to Aunne & the kids.
>
> Affy 'Uncle Ron'.

Unfortunately this was the **LAST** handwritten letter from Admiral; his hand was still as steady as ever, very legible and expressive.

The next letter dated 16th June 1993 was typed and it indeed was the **"FINAL"** letter, which brought down curtains to the "JOURNEY "of our correspondence – really, really sad!! Even at this moment in 2016 more than 23 years later, my eyes just fill up with sad tears!!!

In his last letter of 16th June 93, **quote** *"The doctors feel that it would be prudent for me to move down to a lower altitude, and this has meant that B'SIDES would have to be sold. We think that the sale is almost through, and we should be signing the agreement to sell. Sometime next week, as soon as that is done, we have asked for 90 days to move down to Bangalore, where we think we are able to find ourselves a small two bedroom apartment to move into. It has saddened us to move. Phyll will certainly miss the garden and Bangalore being as* *warm as it is, I believe we will have to air-condition one bedroom for Phyll, who will certainly feel the heat of the plains.*

Our wee garden is looking rather nice. Phyll had got some open mouthed antirrinum seeds from overseas and they have now come up in a flash of colours that is almost unnatural, with a variety in colour that I would not believe, but for the fact that I see it in our garden. The pansies are also very large and in spite of lot of rain, survive weather like a punch drunk pugilist.

My dear brother Arthur passed away at Calcutta on the 26th April 93. However, he did not have to suffer at all, and went in couple of hours. It has left the whole family very sad and depressed, as he had so much of my dear father in him, and we were all very fond of him- with our love-Phyll and Ron"-**Unquote**

During his stay in Bombay Admiral had put up an advertisement for sale of B'SIDES in Times of India. There were few buyers who contacted Admiral to strike a deal, but again the big hurdle was -no money under the table and only WHITE!! He could not find any buyer who will meet his requirement and ended up showing the exit to most of the buyers!!

Commander Anup Singh, (later Vice Admiral) who was posted at Staff College as Instructor was the one who was looking after Admiral and Mrs. Pereira - told me "Mike there was no way you could make him change his views as far as the colour of money was concerned and made it very clear that —only above the table and nothing under the table and only 'white', he just would not budge on this issue."

Eventually Commodore (retd) SS Sodhi, who had settled down in Coonoor sometime in mid 70's, after his tenure as Chief Instructor Navy was approached by Anup Singh, and requested him to use his good offices to find a suitable buyer who will make payment in 'white'!

One fine day SS Sodhi informed Anup that he has found a buyer, it was none other than the youngest of famous 'Hinduja' brother, who had settled in B'lore and had chain of up-market show rooms' WEAR HOUSE" dealing with sale of readymade garments. Mr. Hinduja was shown photographs of BROADSIDES and he was very impressed by the property and agreed to sign the sale deed without personally visiting the site and finally a deal was stuck for fairly big amount. Broadsides is still in very good condition and well maintained as shown in the photographs very kindly sent by Air Marshal Harry Ahluwalia. Where as AT LAST is regrettably in total ruins!

Final Days

I have no idea what happened to that money except that Mrs. Pereira did purchase a small flat C-309, Inner Circle, Whitefield and few years later was disposed off to some local party in Whitefield ! She then went on to stay at an annex at 27 Rest House Road, owned by Commander Thomas Mathais and later moved to 32 Museum Road and from there she was shifted to old age home - Holy Ghost-much against Debbie's and my advice. Debbie in fact offered Aunty to stay with her in their home in Whitefield. So much so, in early 2009, she made arrangements for a trained Nurse and maid to look after Aunty, and brought her home. But for some reason Aunty did not feel comfortable and wanted to go back to Bangalore. By then Aunty was suffering from dementia and it was not advisable for her to stay alone but still she turned down the offer. Then Debbie called me up and asked me to speak to Aunty and convince her to stay on with her, but Aunty refused to listen and told me- nobody can tell me where I want to stay and insisted to move back to Bangalore. She was adamant and added that if Debbie can't have her dropped, she will then start walking to Bangalore! No amount of pleading could make her change her mind. She went back to Bangalore. Soon thereafter she was shifted to old age home by Admiral's second cousin to whom she bequeathed whatever little she had. She ultimately passed away in the old age home on 18th November 2013. It was sad end. She was buried in the Protestant Cemetery on Hasur Road, Bangalore (photo).

CAVALRY GENERALS

Brigadier Hanut Singh

I vividly remember it was 22nd June 1980, when I stopped in Delhi to spend couple of days with Admiral and Mrs. Pereira. I had just reached 12 Rajaji Marg and sitting on the dining table with Aunty Phyll, and after a while Admiral walked in briskly to join us for breakfast. He was looking very imposing in his white uniform and sat down on my left side. He seemed rather preoccupied and looked at me with wide open eyes and finger pointing towards me, and asked with a tinge of anger in his voice, "son, who is Hanut Singh from the Indian Army?" Do you know him? I said; no, I have never met him personally, but yes, this much I know that he is known as "Saint-Soldier" and is treated like an "Icon" in the Cavalry. He was awarded MVC in 1971 Indo-Pak conflict. Poona Horse (17 Horse) under his Command literally destroyed two Armoured Regiments of Paki's 8 Armoured Brigade in the famous "Battle of Basantar" in Shakargarh Bulge.

Admiral was not too impressed and seemed annoyed. He said; "well son, whatever you may think of him in your damn Cavalry, he is fortunate that he is not in the Navy and I can assure you, had he been in the Navy this would have been his last rank!!" I was taken aback and I asked Admiral- what happened?

A bitter tussle was going on between Navy and Air Force for command and control of Maritime Long Range Patrolling Aircraft Squadron. At that point in time Army was in the process of establishing independent Aviation Corps and was also facing stiff opposition from the Air Force.

Therefore, Admiral was keen to get the Army perspective on the subject and asked his NA Captain KK Kohli to check up from the Army HQs who is the officer who can brief him on this issue. Accordingly Kailash Kohli contacted DGMO and was informed that Brig Hanut Singh DDMO was dealing with the subject.

Same evening Admiral after reaching home, called up Hanut Singh's residence to speak to him and personally request to give a presentation on the subject at his convenience. Lance Dafadar Harbans Singh,(from Sikh squadron of Poona Horse) General's man Friday answered the phone and said 'Sat Sri Akal', Admiral asked for Brigadier Hanut and he was politely informed that "Sahib is in Pooja" (meditation). After about 30 minutes, thinking that Pooja would have got over, Admiral called up again, Harbans Singh gave the same reply- "Sahib Pooja mein hai"(still doing meditation). Admiral was getting bit impatient and was wondering what kind of Pooja is Brigadier involved in?? When Admiral called for the third time after a while and got same reply, he lost his shirt and shouted down into the phone –I **am Admiral Pereira speaking, Chief of Naval Staff and I want to speak to Brigadier Hanut Singh!** Poor Harbans could not comprehend a word of Admiral's English and murmured 'Sat Sri Akal' couple of times and Admiral banged the phone down in anger, wondering why he can't speak to Hanut Singh!

Admiral said, son, am the **Chief of the Navy** and I can't bloody well get through to a Brigadier of the Army. What did he mean by Pooja, how many hours?? What nonsense!! I tried to explain that he does meditation but at that juncture I was not fully informed about Hanut's schedule.

Anyway I proceeded to Sikkim as ADC to Gen Sharma and when I came back for winter break in Dec 80 and met Admiral, first thing he told me with a broad smile, **quote "Son, you were correct about your views on Hanut"**. I had an excellent interaction with your Brigadier from the 'Cavalry' and what an incredible presentation he gave on the creation of Aviation Corps for the Army and must say without an iota of doubt, that it was **by far the best presentation I have witnessed in 37 years of my service**. He was absolutely clear and lucid in his delivery and answered all my queries with complete clarity and to my entire satisfaction". **Unquote.** I said-didn't I tell you, that he is one of the finest officer ever produced by Armoured Corps. Yes, he indulges in meditation for long hours and that's why he is known as **Saint - Soldier**. In fact, he is the author of all précis written on mobile warfare as well as on Technique of Shooting of Centurion tanks in Armoured Corps. Being a Gunnery expert himself, Admiral said "really son! Yes, he appeared very proficient and knowledgeable". I also narrated couple of famous stories to Admiral which had become folklore in the Army and he heard very patiently and was indeed intrigued, that Hanut is still serving??

Navy and Army eventually got their Aviation Arm! Much against the stiff opposition from Air Chief Latif !

Background

Before I proceed ahead, I would like to shed some light on Gen Hanut's background.

Hanut Singh was born on 6th July 33 in 'Rawal' clan, (established in the 14th century) in a small village –Jasol, Dist Barmer, Rajasthan. After his schooling in Colonel Brown School, Dehradun, he joined 10th JSW (Joint Services Wing), Dehradun (1st NDA course) and passed out in Dec 1952 and was commissioned in 'The Poona Horse'. He was a tall, lean and smart officer with handle bar moustaches and piercing eyes. He was considered one of India's finest Military leaders in the mould of great Cavalry generals of WW 2 i.e. Guderian, Rommel and Meinstien. Master gunner, a tactician extraordinaire and a man of sterling character, who had no time for fools- which was soon apparent to those in this category!!

Hanut commanded Poona Horse and relinquished his command in Sep 73, just few months before I joined 16th Light Cavalry in Jan 74. Both Regiments were part of 16 (Independent) Armoured Brigade; I missed seeing him by 4 months. But as youngsters we heard lots of stories of Hanut's act of bravery in 1971 Indo-Pak conflict, as also his run in with awkward senior officers and thus my initial answer to Admiral's query in summer of 1980!!

GOC 17 Mountain Division

In May 1982, Gen Hanut was posted to succeed Gen VN Sharma (later Chief of the Army Staff) and take over as GOC 17 Mountain Division. I was very excited that I would get an opportunity to meet him in person before I get posted back to my parent unit. As I was sure, some youngster from Poona Horse will soon be posted as his ADC.

Fortunately for me, Gen Sharma detailed me to go and receive Gen Hanut at Bagdogra Airport. On the day of his arrival I reached Bagdogra airport and requested the ground staff, whom I was acquainted with, that I would like to receive the General on the tarmac itself. As Gen Hanut came down the steps, I saluted him as smartly as I could and firmly shook hands with him.

We had 4 hours drive up the hill to Gangtok along river Teesta. Gen inquired about my family and how a Sardar from Punjab got married to a local Buddhist girl. I replied –destiny, Sir- he laughed and I went on to narrate a long story to him; "how I tried to get my posting as Platoon Commander to IMA, Dehradun, and in spite of Admiral speaking to Gen Malhotra, it did not work out. I added Sir, imagine two Chiefs out of three tried and failed to post a piddle Captain to IMA, so I was destined to come here to find myself a wife!! I told him about our small son, Rabden etc. I also told him what Admiral thought about him when he could not speak to him that fateful evening and poor Harbans Singh was totally confused and terrified! But later he was very appreciative about the presentation given by you, Sir. Gen laughed and said -"he was well within his rights to think like that, as who will dare not attend Chief's call. Anyhow next morning Harbans informed me about the call and as soon as I reached my office, I called up Naval HQs and spoke to Admiral and duly apologized. I asked him when can I brief him and on appointed date he came to DGMO ops room".

I categorically told Gen Hanut, that I have a hunch that he will not stay long in Sikkim and within a year he will move out and take over as 1st Armoured Division, he replied; "no way, having always served in Armoured formations except one tenure as BM in 66 Mountain Brigade the MS Branch has, finally consigned me to the mountains for good and he laughed!"

After Gen Sharma departure I was packing my luggage to move back to my unit. However, a couple of days later Gen Hanut called and asked me to see him at MES IB. When I reached there, General turned around and asked; Mike would you like to stay on as my ADC? I was nonplussed and couldn't believe what I heard; I replied 'my honor Sir'. But you will have to handle 16 Cavalry, Poona Horse and the MS Branch at AHQs. Gen replied; you leave all that to me, I want your answer first; I said 'Yes Sir'.

I was very excited and immediately wrote to Admiral and informed him that Gen Hanut has taken over as GOC 17 Mountain Div and I will be staying on as his ADC. Admiral replied in his letter of 16th July 82, **quote** *"I am also glad to know that you have a fine Gen to work with. These opportunity don't come often, and the more you learn from him, better will be your professional standing"* **unquote**

Schedule

It was simply a pleasure to work with Gen Hanut. He was a bachelor and had no interest in socializing, instead he was happy with a book to read and of course he was voracious reader of Military History. General's schedule of work was out of the ordinary. Gangtok had wonderful climate in summers and at the hour of 10am both of us would walk to the office (10 mins) and at sharp 1pm he will leave office for lunch. The staff was instructed not to make any telephone calls after office hours at his residence until unless there is an emergency and it can't wait till tomorrow. The General used to retire to his Pooja room at 6pm for 'DHYAN' (Meditation) till midnight. The instructions were very clear, that no calls to be put through to him after 6pm from anybody including Chief of the Army Staff, and he will only be disturbed in the event of an attack from China!! He did not attend any social functions; at best he will accept official lunch in the Mess. He was a teetotaler and pure vegetarian- no meat or egg, no onions or garlic, and never had dinner.

Throughout his stay in Sikkim of one year, the only local family he ever visited was when my father-in-law, Kazi Sonam Gyatso invited General for lunch and yes; General drank the local brew 'Chang' in traditional 'Thungba' (bamboo container)?? That was the nearest he came to tasting alcohol in his entire life!! He enjoyed it as well as the traditional lunch (vegetarian).

Call from the Corps Cdr

In those days we had field exchange and all calls to GOC after office hours were put through the ADC. One evening at about 8pm I got a call from Corps HQs exchange and Col MS came on the line and said; put Gen Hanut on the line for Corps Cdr, knowing full well that Gen Hanut doesn't entertain calls after 6 pm, so I politely informed Colonel Mani, Col MS to Corps Commander, Lt Gen Surjit Singh Brar, that General is in his Pooja and I can not disturb him. After a while there was another call from Corps HQs and this time the Corps Cdr himself was on the line and said in very authoritative voice –"this is big big Tiger speaking and I want to speak to your Tiger"- I said, Good Evening Sir, but I can not disturb the GOC as he is in his Pooja, he growled again, but got the same reply and he banged the phone down !! Early next morning, we got a call from Corps and this time I put it through to Gen Hanut, apparently the Corps Cdr was very upset and told GOC, how dare your ADC refuse to put the call through? Gen Hanut politely replied; General, he was simply following my instructions and please tell me what was the emergency for a Corps Cdr to speak to GOC at 8pm at night, which could not wait till next morning and in any case my staff is available to answer any queries. The Corps Cdr had no answer and that was the end of conversation. Thereafter, Hanut Singh had rather rough innings as GOC 17 Mountain Division, till Gen Krishna Rao, COAS, intervened at the behest of his ex boss in MO Dte Lt Gen KK Singh (retd) and posted Gen Hanut to Ambala to take over 1st Armoured Division in May 83. **My prediction was proved right!**

I spent most wonderful 6 ½ months with the General, and he gradually became very fond of me. He used to narrate famous Rajput's stories of valour and sacrifice and also the reasons why they lost out to the Mughals etc.

I used to write to Admiral about my experiences with Gen Hanut. Admiral in his letter of 12th Oct 82, **quote** *"I am glad that you have had the privilege to serve under **such a splendid man as General Hanut**. You have learnt a lot from him, it is now for you to put it in practice, but remember one important point. You are now coming back to the unit after being ADC to a Divisional Commander. There will be some waiting to get even with you, just for the hell of it. So take it easy, until everybody realizes that you are still a nice guy and being the General's Aide has not spoiled you!!* **Unquote**

By now, i.e. October 82, Gen Hanut was pretty free with me, particularly when we were alone travelling to visit formations and units. Otherwise a very introvert person who did not speak much, but with me, I really don't know the reason, he used to talk nonstop and narrate all his experiences and run in with distasteful senior officers and laugh freely and had a great sense of humour. One day I asked him why he offered me to stay on, he said "Mike I have done Dhyan (meditation) for over 20 years and it takes me few minutes to see through a human being and with you there has to be some kind of connection of previous life because I feel very comfortable in your company" Many years later he admitted that; "Mike, you are the only person with whom I feel emotionally attached". I really don't know how he felt like that? Otherwise he was totally detached from what he called; the materialistic world! Yes, like Admiral he also wrote most expressive letters over next 20 years and most of them in his own hand.

There were so many incidents in his service which had become folklore in the Cavalry. I would like to share one in Gangtok in 1982 while I was his ADC.

Governor of Sikkim

This particular incident is on Civil Military relations which involved His Excellency Mr. HJH Taleyarkhan, 2nd Governor of Sikkim. A man with huge ego and behaved like a colonial ruler and demanded various privileges which went beyond laid down protocol. He expected the GOC or Brigadier rank officer must receive him wherever he visited in the state. The Governor had taken over in early July 81.

Gen and Mrs. Sharma by nature was very warm, outgoing and social couple and often interacted with the erstwhile aristocratic families and civil dignitaries. Expectedly they got close to the Governor and were often in and out of the Raj Bhavan for various official and private engagements.

On taking over as GOC in May 82, Gen Hanut called on the Governor with Gen VN Sharma as per the protocol. Anyhow, after he took over Gen Hanut put a full stop to all this exaggerated socializing by senior Army officers with Raj Bhavan. Brigadier Ajit Singh Chopra who frequented Raj Bhavan was posted in North Sikkim and had invited the Governor for a visit. However, by the time Raj Bhavan scheduled Governor's visit to North Sikkim, Gen Hanut was in the chair!

Gen Hanut directed me to convey to Brig Ajit Chopra that he should stay away and not to hobnob with the Governor during his visit to North Sikkim and let the civil administration look after him. I accordingly informed Brig Chopra. When the Governor landed at Chungthang helipad, he was received by District Magistrate and other civil dignitaries. The Governor observed that Brig Chopra was conspicuous by his absence. He saw one young Captain of 17th Assam Rifles, who was detailed to look after the administration arrangements at the helipad and asked him the where about of Brig Chopra and he informed His Excellency; Sir, he is out on operational recce. The Governor took umbrage and felt that his position has been undermined and he directed his ADC Captain Anil Thapa, to pass a message to Raj Bhavan that I would like to meet the GOC on my return at 3pm. The message was conveyed to me by Captain Varinder Kumar, No.2 ADC that His Excellency would like to meet the GOC at Raj Bhavan at 3pm. I accordingly informed Gen Hanut and he turned around and asked me why the hell he wants to meet me? I frankly informed him that the Governor is upset that Brig Chopra was not present to receive him when he landed at Chungthang. The GOC said; Oh! In that case please inform Raj Bhavan that GOC is not available due to previous engagements and added that the Governor cannot summon a General Officer Commanding of a Division like a Sergeant Major!

The Governor landed back at 4pm thinking that the GOC must be perspiring waiting for him. But to his great disappointment he was informed that GOC is not available. He then told Captain Anil Thapa to send a message, that His Excellency is in office and GOC should come and meet him. I walked up to General and conveyed the message, he said; tell them I am still not available! After a while Anil Thapa called up and said Sir, please request GOC to speak to Governor on the telephone. When I informed the GOC, he said, tell them that the GOC is not available on the phone also! At this juncture His Excellency lost his cool; how dare GOC refuse to speak to him on telephone?? He directed Anil Thapa to book a trunk call to Gen

Krishna Rao, the Chief of the Army Staff. I must mention in those days all such official calls were booked on Army line. Unfortunately Gen Roa was out of station and not available. Next he booked a call to Lt Gen AS Vaidhya, Army Commander, Eastern Command. He profusely complained against Gen Hanut. Army Commander said he will look into the matter. The Governor was livid and not satisfied and then he booked a call to Lt Gen Surjit Singh Brar, Corps Commander 33 Corps. By now Sub Joginder Singh, Duty Signal JCO came running to the ADC cottage and told me something is not right Sahib and I must come with him to the exchange, I immediately rushed to telephone exchange and there Joginder Singh put the headphone on my ears, before putting the call to Raj Bhavan and I listened to the conversation, the Governor was shouting on top of his voice and complaining against the GOC and saying that GOC was not extending appropriate courtesies etc and the Corps Commander assured that he will sort out Hanut, don't worry Sir. I rushed to Flag Staff House and met the Gen just before he retired to the Pooja room, and informed him about the calls, he was totally calm and at peace with himself and softly told me; don't worry Mike; let it be .We will handle it tomorrow.

Next morning the BGS called up Col YS Bali and informed him that GOC is required at Corps HQs next day at 10am for Op discussion. As the GOC is entitled to fly in chopper, a demand was sent to Corps HQs for the same. Next morning we reached the Libing helipad at 7.30 am. But there was no sign of chopper. Col GS contacted Corps and was informed there is bit of delay. Anyhow, after waiting for nearly 1½ hours we were informed that no chopper is available and GOC to travel by road. Apparently this was all preplanned to harass Gen Hanut. We then started the journey by Staff Car, and on the way I told Gen that there is no Op discussion and Corps Cdr has called you in connection with Governor's complaint. Gen did not agree with me and said I don't think that the Corps Cdr will be so immature to take serious cognizance of such a trivial matter. I said that is my gut feeling and they deliberately made us wait at the helipad just to inconvenience you. Gen would not believe me, and then I just kept quiet for rest of the journey.

We arrived at Corps HQs, Sukhna, near Siliguri at about 1pm. I thought GOC will take some time, so instructed Pandu, the driver to park the car under the tree and started reading my book –'The Fountain Head' by Ayn Rand. After about 20 minutes suddenly I found GOC getting in the car and said Mike, let's go back to Gangtok.

After a while he looked at me and said, **quote** "Mike, you were right it was about the Governor's complaint. After some polite conversation he came back to the topic of Civil-Military relationship and suggested that I should be more interactive with the state government and particularly the Governor. He said, after all how many GOCs in the Army get an opportunity to visit Raj Bhavan, and added whenever I am in Gangtok, I try to amuse the Governor and keep him in good humour. I told him; Sir, you may amuse him but I am neither prepared to amuse him nor I am keen to visit Raj Bhavan other than on purely official engagements and secondly as far as Civil- Military relations are concerned, I officially called on the Governor with Gen Tich Sharma and beyond that I think there is no need for unnecessary socialization. Further on the Governor resentment of not being received by Brig Chopra, Commander 64 Mountain Brigade at Chungthang helipad is not justified, as he was on civil visit to North Sikkim and was duly extended Civic Reception by the District Magistrate and Army had no role to play. Apparently the Corps Cdr was taken aback and said I think I will have to express myself in writing. I replied; that's your prerogative and walked out and that was the end of Op discussion?!" **Unquote**

The Corps Cdr shot off a nasty DO letter to Gen Hanut, which was appropriately replied and shown to me before dispatch! However, Gen Hanut was given rather damaging Annual Confidential Report which resulted in his being overlooked for promotion to Lt Gen rank. But somehow I had intuition that Gen Hanut will not only make to the rank of Lt Gen but I mentioned to him that he will command "The Strike Corps"- 2 Corps and again he did not believe me as he had been overlooked and was seriously contemplating for putting in his papers and retire to his Ashram in Dehradun.

Correspondence With Admiral

It is at this juncture I wrote to Admiral and gave him the whole background and requested him to write to Gen Hanut and dissuade him from resigning or else Indian Army will lose a very fine General. Yes, Admiral wrote a very long letter to Hanut to convince him, that our system need officers of his calibre otherwise it is bound to collapse under the weight of incompetent senior officers , so hang on and don't give up hope. Gen Hanut was indeed touched, that an officer of other service and that also from highly respected and retired 'Chief of Naval Staff', writing to him in such glowing terms. Yes, Gen Hanut acknowledged his wisdom and sage advice and did not put in his papers.

In his letter of 25th Aug 83, Gen Hanut wrote; quote *"My dear Mike- I received a delightful letter from the Admiral today. I remember you telling me that he was proposing to write to me, but I thought he would have forgotten about it. Obviously he is not the type who forgets. And he seems to echo all your thoughts* and phrases. *The day we create a brain washing cell in our MI Dte (Military Intelligence Directorate), I am going to recommend you head it!"* **Unquote**

PS; Could you please let me know the full rank, name and decorations of the Admiral? I do not want to slip on that when writing to him.

In fact just before Admiral wrote to Gen Hanut, he wrote to me in his letter dated 28th July 1983, quote *"I am glad you met Gen Hanut, I am sorry to hear that he may be leaving, I sincerely hope that he does not. Of course people change, and as one grows old, and I believe mature and wiser, you begin to see the ability and professionalism in every individual, however you may feel about him personally. In any case with record like Gen Hanut's, it would be almost impossible to stop him going up the line. I therefore hope all goes well with him and I must write, but has not got his address. Can you give it to me please?"* Unquote

Admiral was undoubtedly **the finest Naval Chief** in independent India and Gen Hanut **the finest Military Commander**. I humbly submit that I was instrumental in small extent to **connect them** and share their views.

Yes, Gen Hanut was promoted to Lt Gen and at the personal intervention of Army Chief; Gen Sundarji and was given the **command of Strike Corps, 2 Corps, in early 86 and my prediction once again proved right**.

In his letter of 28th April 1987, Admiral wrote; **quote** *"Had a long letter from General Hanut, whom I had written sometime ago.* **He has really wonderful, expressive and clear pen, backed by an incisive brain, and his letter was a delight to read.** *He also sent me an article written on Ex "Brass Tacks" which was written by his brother Jaswant for Illustrated Weekly. I think Jaswant must be a non- congress MP and a journalist, as the article find great fault with the stand that Government took vis-a-vis Paki and what I might describe as the over-kill reaction that ensued".* **Unquote**

Mr Jaswant Singh was holding two major portfolio during NDA rule under Prime Minister Atal Behari Vajpaye, ie- Foreign Minister (1998-2004) and Defence Minister (1999/00).

In May 1989 names of Gen Rodriques (IC 6119), Gen RM Vohra (IC 6122), Gen Gurindher Singh (IC 6123) and Gen Hanut(IC 6126), all from 1st NDA Course, came up for consideration for the appointment of Army Commanders. It was quite evident that Gen Hanut, who had Commanded 14 (Indep) Armoured Brigade, 1ST Armoured Division and 2 Corps, (all three at Ambala) was the most competent and experienced to take over **Western**

Interaction with Cavalry Generals

Army. However, due to some dirty political manoeuvering and machinations Gen Hanut was superseded.

In his letter of 16 May 89, **Gen Hanut wrote; quote** *"My dear Mike, Thank you for your letter dated 9th May. What you were referring to as **rumours, were facts**. Tich (Gen Sharma, Army Chief) has been waiting all these years to get his own back, for I don't know for what reasons. The Ministry has also played along for their own sleazy calculations. So **finally your famous intuition has been proved wrong**. I enclose an article, which you may not have read, which gives the whole sordid story".* **Unquote.**

Supercessions rankle army

By KANWAR SANDHU in Delhi

THE belated appointment of Lt Gen S.F. Rodrigues as Central Army Commander and Lt Gen V.K. Sood as Vice-chief has provoked a controversy within the army. The promotions, which indicate unsubtle political interference, also signal the supercession of Lieutenant Generals Hanut Singh, presently Commandant, Armoured Corps Centre and School, Ahmednagar, R.N. Mahajan, Deputy Chief of Army Staff and Y.S. Tomar, Adjutant-General.

Five months ago, Army Headquarters intimated the government of the need to appoint three army commanders and a vice-chief in view of the vacancies arising later this year. While the Central Command post fell vacant on March 31 this year (with the retirement of Lt Gen Sami Khan), those of Northern and Western Commands required new incumbents by May 31 and October 31, respectively.

Still, the government dilly-dallied until a terse announcement of Rodrigues' appointment came last week. Implicit in the action was Hanut's supercession. As on March 31 (when the first command post fell vacant), Rodrigues was senior-most. Others in order of seniority were: Gurinder Singh (Commandant, Defence Services Staff College, Wellington), Hanut, V.N. Bilimoria (Corps Commander, western sector), Mahajan, Tomar and V.K. Sood (Corps Commander, western sector). While Gurinder, Bilimoria and Sood escaped the axe, Hanut, Mahajan and Tomar haven't. And the government has resorted to a complicated maze of appointments both to cover its manipulations and to escape the two-year rule that forbids posting of army commanders with less than two years left for their retirement at 58.

While Gurinder's posting to the Northern Command has not attracted flak, Rodrigues' is tricky. Rodrigues, who has taken over the Central Command, will move to the Western Command when its present occupant, V.K. Nayar, retires on

continued on page 2

LT. GEN. HANUT SINGH.

continued from page 1

Army morale affected

October 31. Bilimoria will take Rodrigues' place on November 1. In normal course, Bilimoria would be ineligible for that posting considering that from November 1 onwards, he would only have 1 year and 4 months to go for superannuation. Hence, his appointment has been predated.

The case with Sood is even more blatant. He has been "paper posted" as vice-chief, passing over Mahajan and Tomar, until he can take a shot at either the Eastern or the Southern Commands, both of which fall vacant on May 31, 1990. Without the supercession and the paper posting, Sood would have faced disqualification for the 1990 appointments under the two-year rule.

The two-year rule, which became operative on January 1, 1988, was first bent for Sami Khan when his appointment to Central Command was backdated to November 1987. Said a recently retired Lieutenant General: "The present exercise will adversely affect the very fibre of the officer cadre... By paper posting Sood as vice-chief, the mistake is being repeated as when Rodrigues was appointed vice-chief without command experience."

Perhaps the most controversial supercession is that of Hanut. He has often discomfitted his superiors with his deep religiosity and strong convictions. But his tactical genius is acknowledged even by his critics. He has had differences with the Army Chief, Gen V.N. Sharma, but it is not clear if the recommended Hanut's supercession. Said a senior Defence Ministry official: "The government feels that selecting an officer who is known for his devoutly Hindu and solitary lifestyle may not send the right signals at a juncture when the country is faced with communal problems which require close civil-army coordination."

THE government is reportedly picking on two or three "negatives" in Hanut's otherwise spotless army career. While commanding a mountain division, his corps commander felt his religious attitude was not in step with soldiering. However, later, he commanded an armoured division with distinction. The late Gen A. Vaidya and Hanut differed in the conduct of the 1971 war, a campaign in which Hanut, commanding an armoured regiment, won the Maha Vir Chakra, and Vaidya, the brigade commander, bar to

The animosity surfaced in the promotion board from major general to lieutenant general. The voting among the members (army chief, vice-chief and five commanders) was 6-1 in Hanut's favour, with Vaidya dissenting. The chief won out but Hanut got his promotion in a review. He later commanded 2 Corps which gained prominence during Operation Brasstacks. Now the fact of his having missed the first board is being held against him.

G OVERNMENT tinkering with army promotions has caused considerable resentment in the forces. It is a topic army commanders discussed with the prime minister during the annual Army Commanders Conference held this past week.

A glaring instance of such meddling: the then Minister of State for Defence, Arun Singh, had three years ago approved Harkirat Singh for the major general's rank (command stream) despite the army selection board having decided otherwise. Harkirat's leadership of the IPKF in Sri Lanka vindicated the doubts of the selection board.

Some board decisions have been overturned by the government this year too. In three cases, the Defence Ministry approved officers only for staff stream, though they had been cleared for command stream by the board. In the case of J.C. Pant, an officer with political connections, the reverse was done, causing much consternation in South Block. He was rejected by the first army board, approved for staff stream after a representation, and is now secure in the command stream.

The Army Chief persisted with the board's recommendations but after a four-month delay, the ministry had its way. "Selections are made after a thorough deliberation of the computerised data by the board and they cannot be tossed around," a senior officer said ruefully. Also, the army has still not been able to convince the government to bring at par the retirement age of officers in command and staff streams. Staff officers retire a year early.

My first two predictions of Commanding 1st Armoured Division and 2 Corps were proved **right** and the third one to Command Western Army was in fact **denied** to the General?

In his last days Admiral often used to inquire about Gen Hanut Singh. I wrote to inform General about sad demise of Admiral, and by the time the letter reached at his Ashram, Dehradun, Gen had already left for Balaji Temple at Jodhpur for winters and hence the delay in reply. The letter is covered under chapter on 'Battle with Cancer'.

Apart from Gen Hanut, Admiral had lots of acquaintances with senior Cavalry Generals. I was aware that he was very fond of Maj Gen E Habibullah, 16 Cavalry, and my regiment, a 1930 vintage officer who was founder father of National Defence Academy at Khadakwasla and was the first Commandant of NDA from 7th Jan 1953 – 26 Dec 58. Gen Habibullah visited NDA in autumn of 1972 was received by Admiral and Mrs. Pereira, as shown in the photograph.

16 Cavalry Tie

One evening in winters of 1979 Admiral was invited by Maj Gen Varindra Singh, 16 Cavalry for dinner, and Admiral decided to wear 16 Cavalry Regimental Tie which I had presented to him before he visited the regiment in Mar 80. As soon as he entered, Gen Habibullah said, Hi Ronnie, how are you? And then noticed the tie and said; Ronnie, that's my Regimental tie and how on earth you got it!? Admiral then had to narrate him the entire story of how he met me in NDA in Aug 1971, which Gen Habibullah found very interesting, after about half an hour another senior Cavalry Gen noticed and asked same question, Ronnie that's 16 Cav tie? Admiral narrated the story again. When I came to Delhi next time Aunty Phyll told me –Son, your Regimental tie created ripples in a party we attended with Army crowd and whole evening was spent by Uncle repeatedly narrating how he got this tie!!

Lt Gen JM Vohra

In early Dec 1979, an Army delegation headed by Lt Gen Sundarji visited Russia to witness a large scale exercise with troops, organized by Russian Cavalry to showcase the fire power of T 72 tanks, which eventually were inducted in the Armoured Corps as Main Battle Tank. **Maj Gen JM Vohra,** GOC 31 Armoured Division was one of the members of the delegation.

JM Vohra was our Brigade Commander; 16 (I) Armoured Brigade at Pathankot from Aug 77 to Feb 79. Both General and Mrs. Janak Vohra were very fond of me and I must have had over one dozen meals in the Flag Staff House during their stay at Pathankot. On his return from Moscow Gen Vohra stopped over in Delhi for couple of days and I thought it will be nice to call him over to Navy House for a drink with Admiral and Mrs. Pereira.

General Vohra, passed out with 5th JSW course on 4th June 1950 as Best Gentleman Cadet and winner of both Gold Medal as well as Sword of Honour. **He belonged to an amazing family of 4 brothers that has no parallel in the annals of Indian Army and in fact all Armies of the world.** Their family migrated from Pakistan during traumatic partition. All four brothers were commissioned in four different Armoured Regiments; Inder Mohan - 8th Light Cavalry, Jagat Mohan - 9 Horse (Deccan Horse), Raj Mohan - 14 Horse (Scinde Horse) and Satish Mohan - 3rd Cavalry. All of them took active part in operations; Gen Inder; Burma and Bangladesh, other three took part in 65 and 71 Indo –Pak conflicts and Satish also took part in OP PAWAN in SriLanka. Jagat and Raj Mohan were decorated with gallantry awards SM and MVC respectively. What really makes them truly unique that all of them went through competitive selection process to end up in '**GENERAL**' rank, **unprecedented achievement by a single family in all the Armies of the world!!** The eldest Inder Vohra was commissioned in 1942 and the youngest Satish retired in 1996 and between them they served the Indian Army for 146 years collectively. **Indeed extraordinary feat!**

Accordingly I spoke to Admiral and requested him to spare an evening for Gen Jagat (Jimmy) Vohra. At the outset he dismissed my request on the pretext; "that it is contrary to the protocol to invite Maj Gen to Chief's residence and that too from other service and secondly I do not know the gentleman, yes, I served along with his elder brother Inder Vohra who was Area Commander Bombay in 1976 when I was C-in-C". I told him that he is coming to the Navy House as **my personal guest**, it is just question of one hour and believe me they were very kind to me when I served under him in Pathankot and I just want to return their hospitality in a small measure. **I got Mrs. Pereira support and he reluctantly agreed but for 60 minutes only.** I said fine and thank you very much. I immediately called up Gen Vohra who was staying with Maj Gen Mohinder Singh Mann (GUARDS) at Dhaula Kuan. I requested Gen Vohra to please join us for drinks at 7pm at 12 Rajaji Marg, and he was delighted to accept the invitation.

Sharp five minutes before 7pm, both Admiral and Mrs. Pereira got ready to receive the guest. We waited till 7.15 pm, no sign of Gen Vohra, I called up Gen Mann and he informed me that Gen Vohra had left at quarter to seven and he should have reached by 7pm as there wasn't much traffic on roads in those days, particularly in the evenings. **7.30 pm and still no sign** and I was beginning to get worried and Mrs. Pereira asked me, son, where is your Gen? I could sense Admiral was getting impatient and said **where is your bloody Cavalry General?** I ran to the gate and stood on the road and after a while I saw a Fiat car speeding past the gate and then suddenly screeched to a halt and reversed and there to my great relief, I saw Gen Vohra. He said, **Mike I lost my way** as I had never been posted to AHQs. We came in, it was 7.40 pm!! As we entered the front varandah and Gen was writing his name in the visitor book, Admiral came out and said- **Hi, General, how come a Cavalry Gen lost his way in Lutyens Complex?** Gen Vohra stood to attention and said Good Evening Sir, I am terribly sorry, I missed one turning and landed in Khan Market as I have never served before in Delhi and not at all familiar with the geography of this area!! Anyway to make him feel at ease Admiral said; General, you look a lot like your brother Inder, except you have no hair! And touched his head, both laughed and the tension was defused a bit, and we went inside and he met Mrs. Pereira and profusely apologized for keeping her waiting.

At that level **nobody comes late even by one minute** to **Chief's Residence** and one can well imagine General's embarrassment! It was close to 7.45 pm!!! Soon Admiral asked the General for a drink and as Admiral had recently hosted a Russian delegation, they got talking about the T - 72 Tank and about the Russian hierarchy etc. It went to 2nd drink, then 3rd and soon 4th and now both of them were laughing and saying 'Khorosho' i.e. how are you? Russian and 'Velmi-Dobji'- am ok-and they were really enjoying each other's company and **it was past 10pm!!**

Now Gen Vohra said; he can't have more drinks and he has to drive back to Dhaula Kuan and this time he did not want to lose his way!! After thanking Admiral and Mrs. Pereira, General got inside the car, and supposedly engaged reverse gear and when he released the clutch the car jumped forward as he had in fact engaged 3rd gear! And lo and behold Mrs. Pereira was standing right in front of the car! General immediately pressed the brake and was most apologetic and sheepishly said; am sorry Maam, I have never driven Indian Fiat car in my life. Mrs. Pereira calmly remarked; **General do you think you are driving T-72 tank?** Gen Vohra was speechless!

That was the end of most eventful evening and I hugged both Admiral and Mrs. Pereira and thanked them for being so considerate and understanding. **They held my hand.** What more can I say?

Speaking to Gen Vohra who is pushing 90 years (17 Nov) still remembers that evening 37 years ago with so much fondness and we had hearty laugh about losing his way to the Navy House. He found both Admiral and Mrs. Pereira very humble and down to earth and added; "**Mike, it was indeed one of my most memorable evenings of my life**".

I have written about Admiral's interactions only with Cavalry Generals. Otherwise he had close friends from Infantry, such as; Lt Gen Manny Sinha, Lt Gen Manezies, Lt Gen RK Jasbir Singh and Maj Gen Rajendra Prasad.

VISIONARY

Visionary is a person who has power of perceiving imaginative mental images or foresight to look far and beyond .Indeed Admiral had the uncanny ability to gauge worth of a human being. He spoke and wrote to me about half a dozen senior naval officers in the Navy and 5 of them went on to become Chief of Naval Staff.

Ram Tehiliani

I was on long leave in Aug-Sep 1976 to Bombay when Admiral was C-in-C Western Naval Command and I used to accompany him for morning walks towards the harbour. One fine day as we went past INS Vikrant, Admiral remarked, son, the Captain of the only aircraft career in the Navy is Captain Ram Tehiliani, an outstanding officer and excellent aviator and I am sure that one day he will reach the top and become "CNS". The only problem is that, **he is too young!** In fact few years later in 1980 Ram Tehiliani became the youngest Vice Admiral at the age of 50! And four years later he took over as 11th Chief of Naval Staff in Nov 1984.

In 1991 I had the privilege of being invited for lunch along with my wife and in-laws, to Raj Bhavan, Gangtok, when Admiral Tehiliani was the Governor of Sikkim.

I mentioned to his Excellency about Admiral's remark 15 years back. He just laughed and said, you know Mike, Ronnie P was a **visionary** and his assessment of human being was par excellence, a rare quality of great military leaders down the centuries and we in the Navy are indeed very proud of him.

VS Shekhawat

In July 79, on my way to Jodhpur, I spent couple of days with Admiral and Mrs. Pereira and I vividly remember Admiral telling me; son, it is Navy turn for Deputy Commandant appointment at NDA and I am going to send the best possible officer. I was back in Delhi in Dec 79, and Admiral said; son, I have posted Vijai Singh Shekhawat in Oct 79 to take over as Deputy Commandant and mark my word one day he too will become CNS. Come Sep 1993, Admiral Shekhawat took over as 14th Chief of Naval Staff.

In summer of 1981, Commodore VS Shekhawat came to Sikkim to spend some time with his brother-in-law, Col Sishodia, Commanding Officer, 17 ASSAM RIFLES at Chungthang, North Sikkim. When I got to know about his visit, I told Col Sishodia, Sir, as per the present CNS Admiral Pereira, your brother-in-law (both were married to two sisters) Cmde Shekhawat will one day become CNS. He laughed, but I told him please convey this to him and sure enough 13 years later he became the "Chief".

Admiral Shekhawat was present at Admiral's funeral on 16th Oct 1993 at Bangalore. I met him in the corridors of South Block later in the month and told him what Admiral Pereira thought about him way back in 1979. He looked deep into my eyes and said Ronnie P was a great man and a **visionary** and we in the Navy are very proud to have an officer of his caliber. He was a man of great integrity and probity.

Next I spoke to Admiral in Sep 2015 and I reminded him of the family photograph which I saw at Col Sisodia's residence in Chungthang in 1981 and where he was standing in the photograph. He of course knew I was stating fact and he laughed.

After the sad demise of Gen Sinha on 17th Nov 16, I called up Admiral Shekhawat and requested him to write the foreword of this book, which he very kindly agreed to.

JG Nadkarni

Admiral wrote in his letter dated 27th Oct 87, **quote** *"As you must have read in the papers our Vice Chief Nadkarni - has now been selected for the "gaddi", after Admiral Tehiliani retires on 1st Dec. Admiral Nadkarni is an excellent professional, with a fine reputation and I am sure that the appointment was welcomed throughout the Service. He will certainly get his 3 years in, in fact, if the tenure is changed to 4, which may be on the cards in spite of bureaucratic opposition, he will even then make the full tenure"* **Unquote**.

KK Kohli and Ramdas

Admiral wrote again in his letter dated 14 June 88, **quote** *"The CI (Navy) - my old Naval Assistant- has now been promoted to Rear Admiral- Kailash Kohli- and he has already finished a year in the college. I expect that he will get another year,* *and then go back into the main stream. Certainly in the Navy having made it to R.A, a lad like Kailash who has a very incisive and clear brain should make to V.A. and thereafter it is in the hands of the Lord. However, I am sure rank and promotion are really incidental. What matters really in life is how you live it, and if one can honestly say that life was an honest attempt to run the gauntlet in accordance with one's conscience, then, not only we are personally satisfied, but the reward from God is immeasurable, for He loves us greatly, when we serve Him, as he wishes us to do so. As an example, the present C-in-C (South) - Vice Admiral Ramdas-is in my view, is very upright and straight officer. It was his good fortune, that he took over C-in-C (South) on the day, Admiral Nadkarni took over as Chief, so both their clocks started together, and unless there is a major SNAFU, Ramu Ramdas, will be the next Chief. Yet, I am quite sure; he certainly did not think so, when he started life as Midshipman."* **Unquote**

Madhvendra Singh

In his letter of 28th Sep 91, **quote** *"The new CI (Navy)- Rear Admiral Madhvendra Singh- has gone to Sikkim and Arunachal Pradesh, on the tour and would be meeting Admiral Tehiliani, who is now the Governor. The Navy had fortunately some excellent CI's over the last few years. I think you had R Adm Kohli, who used to be my NA when I was the Chief. He was followed by RAJA Menon- a submariner and also an excellent officer, who rode, sailed and played golf with same enthusiasm as he put into his work. Menon spoke 5 languages including Russian and French. Now there is Madhu Singh, who is equally good. Have had 3 commands of TALWAR, RANVIR and VIRAT, is a gunner, and one of the few that did a dagger "G" thereafter in UK and his Staff Course in USA. His father who retired as GOC Delhi Area, when I was Lt Commander, was IC 1!!!"* **Unquote**

I later informed Admiral that Maj Gen K Bhagwati Singh IC 1 was indeed from my regiment 16 Light Cavalry. He then turned around and said, son, mark my words, one day Madhevendra will become Chief, which indeed he did in Dec 2001 when he took over as 17th CNS.

Out of these 7 officers, 5 made to CNS, and other two, Kailash Kohli retired as VCNS and Menon as Rear Admiral.

GREAT ORATOR

Introduction

Since time immemorial all great Military leaders had one 'singular characteristic' which was prominent in each one of them, and that was **'oratory skill or public speaking'** – the inherent ability to convince and motivate the men they led into battle field to perform much beyond their known capabilities.

This unique aspect in their personality to great extent had been the deciding factor between the victory and defeat down the centuries from Alexander the Great, Hannibal, Julias Caeser, Napolean Bonaparte, Hitler, Winston Churchill, Patton and our own Manekshaw . Each one of them had the uncanny knack to mesmerize their audiences and that is why they were great **Military Leaders.**

Even before Ronnie P arrived in Jan 71, his reputation of fire brand naval officer and eloquent speaker with exceptional oratory skills had reached NDA.

Expectedly, in the third week of Jan 71, we witnessed this extraordinary skill, when as the Dep Com, he gave his opening address to the Academy and what he expected from the cadets, half of it went over our heads! He spoke with bit of American accent and was indeed, very articulate.

By early 72, I was quite comfortable in his company and told him, to be honest we did not comprehend half of your address to the Academy in Jan 71, he looked at me bit surprised and said , really son ? I said yes, maybe we were all in awe of you!! He just laughed. But I picked up the courage to ask him; Sir, how did you learn to speak so well?

He said; son, I think it is part hereditary and part hard work and sincere effort. Yes, to be honest, I did inherit this skill from my father. He was very articulate and an excellent speaker. He spoke very fluently but more importantly very correctly. He had great command over the English language. My eldest brother, Arthur, too spoke very good English, Aunty May was as you know was very articulate and Bobby was an Opera singer-soprano and of course my dear Mother with Irish background spoke very gently and was as articulate as others in the family. So I grew up in an environment where everyone spoke 'Queen's English'.

As per Commander Hugh Gantzer (retd), Admiral nephew, 86 years old on 31 Jan 2017, told me-"Mike it was in their genes, and Ronnie being the youngest picked up not only good spoken English but also he could express very well on paper, again inherited from his father, who not only wrote well but had a beautiful hand-Ronnie too had very fine hand like his father. It was an inherent advantage, I suppose".

No wonder Admiral would always tell me, son, ensure that you speak to your men off the cuff and not from a written script. Also look straight into their eyes when you speak to them, your words should flow without any pregnant pauses. And it calls for lots of effort and hard work to achieve that.

In spite of the inherent advantage of command over the language being his mother tongue, Admiral admitted that he worked very hard on his speeches. He would prepare a script, and go over it a couple of times, rehearse with a tape recorder. He had great sense of timing and would prepare his speech according to the occasion i.e.; Address to the men, official functions on board ship or ashore or during his visits to Naval establishments, or after a sports events and even during his visits abroad, he always added some witty anecdotes and spur of the moment remarks to lighten up the atmosphere. He once told me that even the greatest orator of 20th Century, Mr. Winston Churchill also worked very hard over his speeches and even went to the extent of rehearsing in front of the mirror to check his facial expressions as well as the movements of his hands.

INS Angre

It is believed in Navy circles that the address given by Admiral as FOC-in-C Western Naval Command to the Petty officers and sailors in Aug 76 in INS Angre was one of the finest delivered in Indian Navy. I was on long leave in Bombay and I clearly remember how he prepared himself and practiced repeatedly in my presence on the tape recorder, and would ask me how it is son? all I could say - excellent - I still remember first few lines - Gentlemen, when I joined the Navy in May 43 during WW 2, it was my Petty Officer who taught me the nuances of operating a Gun boat. I learnt to fire the gun from my fellow sailor, and they were responsible for my initials grooming as a young officer and it helped me as I gradually went up the ladder. I owe to those sailors, who helped me to learn to serve with pride and respect. I learnt a lot from my sailors of INS Delhi, who performed far beyond their capabilities and my imagination. The speech was long and he emphasized on man management and leadership at all level. I wanted to go along with him but then he thought it will be improper to see a young Captain around in civvies, so I missed out, though later he told me if you were so keen you could have come, but when he showed hesitation I kept quiet.

Defence Services Staff College

In his letter of 26th Oct 81, **quote** *"We got back from Wellington on the 23rd. I had gone to deliver my Annual talk on the Maritime Power and I always find it a simulating experience, as you are faced, after the lecture, by barrage of questions-largely from the Air Force- who does not ultimately accept Naval Aviation as integral arm of the Navy! It is good to have an opportunity to answer their thoughts directly and more this comes in the open; the better it is, as it clears the air for everyone else.*

I had prepared this lecture carefully and had series of dummy runs on my tape recorder, which I find extremely beneficial, as the replay helps you to hear yourself and often brings out the shortfalls in a talk which you may not otherwise realize". **Unquote**

I remember Mrs. Pereira narrating about an over eager student who got up and asked long and winding question on 'Pay and Promotions' – after he had finished Admiral with tongue in cheeks said , son that sounds like **'loose motions'**(as he merged pay with promotion!) and whole hall erupted in a loud laughter !!

Sri Lanka

Then during his visit to Sri Lanka in early 1981, he was hosted to a State Banquet where Chiefs of three services of Sri Lanka were in attendance.

Admiral got up to give his thanks giving speech and his opening sentence was –'Lt General Denis Perera, Chief of Army Staff, Sri Lanka Army, Air Marshal Dick Perera, Chief of Air Staff, Sri Lanka Air Force and Rear Admiral Henry Perera, Chief of Naval Staff, Sri Lanka Navy, and finally, myself - Admiral Ronnie Pereira, Chief of Naval Staff, Indian Navy!! So Ladies and Gentlemen all in all it's a 'Pereiras Nite'!! Every one present was in splits of laughter. What a coincidence and never again one is likely to come across this unique occasion, and Admiral must have realized it. One can summarize it simply "Sense of timing" for the occasion, a hallmark for great public speakers. He was mesmerizing, and he could keep the audience enthralled and totally captivated.

NDA - December 72

However, by far his best speech was the one which he delivered at '**Hut of Remembrance**' **to the passing out course of 43rd NDA on 15th Dec 72**. I vividly remember that he started his speech -"Gentleman, look to your right, look to the left and look to the front and this is the last time in your life that all of you will be standing together as a course, here after you will proceed to your respective Services-so '**SAVIOUR**' these moments", he gave a pause for one minute and then started to read:-

(original text of speech is given on opposite page)

Great Orator

TALK BY COMMODORE RL PEREIRA, AVSM, DEPUTY COMMANDANT NATIONAL DEFENCE ACADEMY TO THE PASSING OUT CADETS OF THE 43RD NDA COURSE AT THE HUT OF REMEMBRANCE IN DEC 72

We have today gathered at this Hut of Remembrance on the eve of your passing out from this Academy, to commemorate young men like yourselves who have not only reaffirmed the qualities of determination, guts and loyalty that we endeavour to teach you here, but to pay homage at this permanent monument, to young men who have unstintingly laid down their lives for this wonderful country of ours. They died without hesitation, without thought, and without seeking fame or fortune in doing so.

It is these illustrious and wonderful officers to whom you pay tribute this morning; a very small tribute over a few minutes, during which I would ask you not only to remember them and to thank them, but ask of their spirits that rise from this Hut of Remembrance, to give to you these same qualities that they were fortunate to be gifted with.

This Academy has sent to the three Services well over 10,000 Cadets todate. Amongst them are many living without their limbs, their speech, and their eye sight; many serve no more in the Service of their choice; many indeed have made the supreme sacrifice of their lives. They have done all this in the normal service of their country; in the normal execution of their duties, with no thought for one iota of gain. It is these young men that have laid, brick by brick, stone by stone, with the mortar of blood and torn flesh, the real traditions of this Academy, the traditions enshrined in this Hut of Remembrance that should make you intensely proud of belonging to the same select fraternity, and make you determined to develop the qualities that they had.

....2/-

: 2 :

In the next few minutes, I would, therefore, ask you to remember them, to thank them sincerely from the very depth of your heart. Some indeed, you may well know; dwell on them gentlemen in the next few short minutes for their excellent character and determination and try, if you can, to remember them again when you are called upon to face similar circumstances that they underwent. Think deeply of them gentlemen, in battle, when fear tears at your intestines and tries to stifle your better judgement; think of SALARIA and KHETARPAL, the real gold in the colours of this Academy; think of all those enshrined in this little Hut, and remember that it is from their dust and ashes that rise the glorious traditions of this magnificent Academy, of which you are also a self-same part.

May, I, therefore, ask you, gentlemen, to repeat after me this little prayer:

> Dear God, we pray, that those of us who have yet to be tested on the forge of battle, may whenever that time arises, give of the same devotion, the same courage and tenacity and the self-same leadership and determination, in the service of our country, as those of our compatriots that we have chosen to remember in this Hut of Remembrance.
>
> Let their example inspire us in our endeavours, help us to emulate them in integrity, and may their inspiration help us in tribulation, to overcome our shortcomings and weaknesses. AMEN.

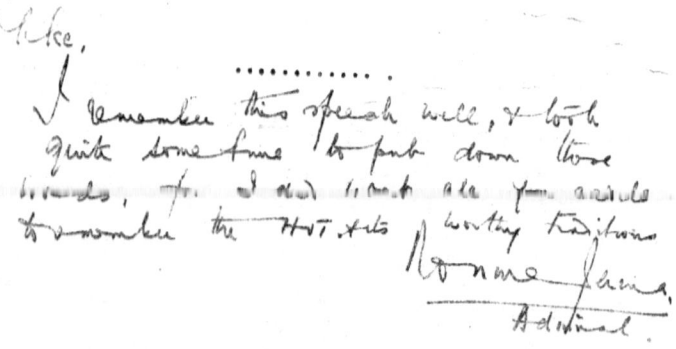

It was in May 1979 when I sent the copy of original speech to Admiral, requesting him to endorse his signature with short note. He replied in his letter dated 3 May 79,

Quote "*Mike, I remember this speech well, and took quite some time to put down these words, for I did want all you cadets to remember the HUT and its worthy tradition- signed Ronnie Pereira, Admiral,* **unquote**

Along with his short note of 03 May 79, **quote** "*My dear Mike, - Just (2 minutes ago!) got your letter. Am returning the speech which you want .*

Am very busy. Look after yourself, afftly Unc Ron" .Unquote .

POP-NDA 56

The address at Passing out Parade of 56th NDA Course on 9th June 79 by Admiral;

Gentlemen of the 56th Course,

Nothing pleases me more than to pass you out today, after 3 years of zealous and hard training at this excellent institution. As I climbed the ladder of success in my Service, I have had but one single regret , and this was my disappointment at not having been able to pass through this Academy when I joined as a young officer some 36 years ago. It was my misfortune that it did not exist. It is equally your great fortune that you have been given an opportunity to be trained, moulded, and schooled for 3 years here, so that you may be able to face, what I believe is, a very heavy task of leading the most magnificent human beings you could wish for, in your respective Services.

In a few minutes, you will be marching over this quarter-deck for a very last time. It will be, in fact, the very last occasion that you will be together as a course. Never, ever, gentlemen, will you so gather again in life. Bur remember this, you now belong to a very select fraternity- the fraternity of this Academy, and believe me when I say that it is very powerful one, and brings together for your future life, not only the members of your own course, but every single officer that has been privileged to be trained at this select institute.

It makes your task in conflict a much simpler one, for co-operation today is the cornerstone of success in the unfortunate event of war.

I do not know what thoughts are running through your minds at this very instant. Indeed, I wonder why the whole lot of you might have considered it fit to join the Services, but I would like to enlighten you on one or two points. If you happen to be under the mistaken impression that you have joined for money, gentlemen, I am afraid you are making a grave mistake. Wealth in that peculiar form of lucre does not come to us in any great share, but I thank God that money is not the sole motivation in life. Equally, I would like to firmly assure you that we do have great wealth in other forms.

I speak firstly of wealth of brotherhood and camaraderie. As you will each eventually join your respective Service, you will find, without doubt, a great wealth of brotherhood. It is not only accidental, for brotherhood and co-operation between human beings is vital to winning wars and that, indeed, is the only purpose of our existence, should our country ever call upon us to defend this great land of ours.

There is great wealth of pride and satisfaction in serving your unit, in professional competence, in knowing your weapons and equipment, and this, indeed, is the crux of your very existence.

There is a deep and lasting wealth on our status. It is perhaps a misleading word, but I speak not of a status of a snob, but status that 640 million of our countrymen have unstintingly accorded us as a good citizens , as dedicated human beings, and as a competent professionals in the service of the country. We are proud of that status, and never must you ever do anything to soil that image.

Finally, gentlemen, we have wealth of tradition- tradition born of hard conflict where our brother officers and men have died valiantly and bravely in the defence of this nation of ours. Very shortly, I believe you will spend a few minutes in reflection at the Hut of Remembrance before you finally leave. Go there today, bow your heads and think deeply not only those who are dead, but for those who still live without their limbs, without their sights, without their hearing- who have given all this, and, indeed, their lives not only for our country, but as an example to you, that you may NEVER fail in this one singular assignment for which we are trained throughout our lives, and for which our government sees it to mould young people like you at great expense, so that in conflict, we will always win, for, as General Omar Bradley once said," There is no prize for runner-up in war".

Go then, gentlemen, to that little Hut, and thank the spirits of all your illustrious predecessors for the tradition they have left to you, and when conflict is upon us, the nation turns to us for its defence, we may rise and give off our very best, and the spirits of our dead will then certainly give us strength and fortitude in that critical moment of trial.

Your parade has been excellent, but that is routine in this Academy, which cannot accept any standard lower than excellent.

I wish all of you great success. May you all have enormous satisfaction in the wonderful assignments that are before you, and whether you rise and fall in the ladder of promotion, which you have not even begun to climb, may you never turn away from the high standards of achievement that are vital to us in peace and war.

May God be with you.

POP NDA-59
Address to Passing out Parade of 59th NDA Course on 6th Dec 80;

I always look forward with considerable pleasure to visiting the Academy, which I regard as one of the finest institution of its kind, and though this will be the last occasion that I will have had the privilege of passing out a course. I consider it as an honor that I would have done so on two separate occasions during my tenure as Naval Chief.

When you finally complete your training and are commissioned to your respective units in the three Services, you will only then begin the arduous of becoming a professional- a professional not merely in the theory of arms and war but, what is far more important, in its practical application- and this will take you a lifetime, which may, at this moment, seem odd to you, but it is indeed true in every sense of the word.

In this profession of arms, life will be complex enough- learning and mastering a diversity of equipment and its practical usage- that will often compound you with its enormity. But this is only part of the problem, because in our way of life, it is not always the genius that makes to the top of ladder, or is the successful commander in peace or war; it is not always the bright boy in a classroom who ultimately climbs the ladder of promotion. To us in Armed Forces, professional acumen is not merely knowledge from book because, without the shadow of doubt, wars are ultimately won by well-led teams, both at unit level as also the level of an army formation or task force of ships. **It is the team of human beings working in total unison and belief in each other that ultimately achieve success.**

What are these qualities that make successful team? Some of them, surely are; respect of one human being of the other; respect for men that understand distress, anxiety, fear and want, and many other emotions that run through this complex animal called man; admiration for professional competence; great regards for integrity, honesty and devotion; the ability to perform a task as a leader better than any of those below you. There are some of the many qualities you must develop and they take time and experience; but without them you will surely be lost, no matter how brilliant you may be academically.

Finally, in your way through life, the strength of your character will often be tested in peace and war- tested by fellow human beings who believe that conscience and conviction can be sacrificed for material benefits. It is here that you will have your greatest battle; for once you sacrifice principle against better judgment, you have not only compromised yourself in the eyes of your fellow human beings, but you have fooled yourself, which is, perhaps, the worst thing you can do in life. This is one aspect that you must watch with great care and, no matter what the price you pay for honest judgment and belief, it matter much more that you can hold your head high with pride and satisfaction, in the knowledge that you have at least served the organization and the nation to the best of your ability.

As you march off this quarter deck for the last time, gentlemen, I wish you great success and that element of good luck which is so essential to all of us. You will never have money in great abundance, but I am positive that you will have far greater satisfaction in camaraderie and good spirit that prevail in Services; you will enjoy every moment of this great calling to Arms, for which the entire nation respect us a great deal. And for which we have the onerous responsibility never to fail in that great trust which we have earned by our performance in war and peace.

So, gentlemen, as you finally pass through the portals of this Academy in the next few hours, I would ask you to remember at least the last part of the NDA prayer which read something like this; **Grant us opportunities of service to Thee, to our country, and to the men we lead and help us place service above self.**

Go, gentlemen, and God be with you.

Admiral was not at all comfortable with Hindi, and had problems getting the right word. In Dec 79, as CNS he had to give an address on the Navy Day in Hindi on All India Radio. He had the written script in Roman English and he rehearsed it a number of times in my presence and he would keep asking me if it was fine. I remember he used to maintain a small dairy in which he would write Hindi words; eg approval –"anumati" in Hindi or doubt-shaque or right –haque so and so forth and he would enjoy writing them.

Admiral also spoke to the men of 16th Light Cavalry during his visit on 10th Mar 1980, which I have covered in the chapter on his visit to 16 Cav.

POST RETIREMENT

Introduction

The day his appointment was announced, he told me; son, **I will not** accept any government job post retirement, beat it. He made this fact very clear in his first meeting of Chief of Staff Committee, which was vehemently opposed by other two Chiefs!

However, come 6th March 82, Admiral left for Bangalore. AT LAST was still not ready and there was lots of work to be done, particularly interiors. In his first letter after retirement dated 12th April 82 Admiral mentioned that he was totally immersed in giving final touches to AT LAST. (Refer chapter - 'HOME')

Goa

The next time I heard from him was through a letter written on 16th July 82, surprisingly with a tongue twisting new address:-

> *244, ANTONIO CAETANO PACHECO ROAD*
> *BORDA*
> *MARGAO*
> *GOA-403602*

Quote *"My dear Mike and Annie – I have not written for ages and must apologize for this lapse. I must also thank you very much indeed for your thoughtful gesture for my birthday. This certainly warranted a reply a long time ago, but I have been really very busy and I will tell you why.*

*I did not intend to do anything for first 3 or 4 months, as my presence was essential with Mrs. P and indeed the physical effort was considerable as there was **no staff or Staff Officer to run around for you**!! However, I enjoyed doing it and* the nicest part is **that I have lost 8 kg**, largely around my middle, which pleases me intensely.

There then came the question of a job, not only to keep me busy, but **to restock the family coffers which as you will appreciate had gone rather low!** I had some nice offers oversees, but did not touch any of them .However , as luck would have it , I was approached to take the job of the Chief Executive of a new company- SIMA HOTELS AND RESORTS PVT LTD- to co-ordinate the building of first leisure project in India , which was to set up at Goa . This is the reason I am now in MARGAO, at this mouthful of an address, which is our office.

The project I am with will ultimately set up a leisure resort in South Goa , at a place called CANACONA, about 33 miles from MARGAO where I am at the moment staying in a hotel called METROPOLE.

The project aims to meet the holiday requirements of the businessman's family and the foreigners. It will set up on 300 acres, right along a very beautiful beach at CANACONA, and will compose of 120 independent, fully air-conditioned villas of 1 and 2 bedrooms respectively. We will even have a super kitchen in each villa, so that if the wife of the family wishes to cook, she can happily do so. Each villa, down to the kitchen will be fully provided, so that one only has to move in with one's suitcases. The centre piece of the resort will be a super club and this will provide the customer with all his activities- outdoor and indoor. There will be a Golf Course of 18 holes to international standards and this will be laid out on 120 acres. There will be squash courts, tennis courts and badminton courts ; three swimming pools, a riding school with 10 horses, billiards , table tennis, cards rooms, health club and yoga; video games for the kids and a marine with every possible water sport including sailing, water skiing , fishing and surfing; there will be usual run of coffee-shops, restaurants and bars and there will also be a hotel with 160 rooms.

The whole project is aimed at the family and attempt is to give that family, anything possible, within our 300 acres. It is a really unique concept and has never been attempted in India before. The brain behind the project is Dr G.S.Dugal, a fine gentleman with a great mind and in fact he is my Chairman.

I have been in this chair for about three weeks and there is a great deal of work ahead of us. Land acquisition, water, power, materials management, contractors, staff and hundred other problems, but I am thoroughly enjoying it. At the moment I am alone, as Aunty Phyll is at Bangalore, as it is impossible for us to close up the house. However, as soon as I can get a house for myself, we will have to decide how we play it.

Goa is much like Bombay, weather wise. With 120 inches of rain in the year! The wettest month is JULY as you might have guessed; it is raining at the moment!! It's sticky and humid, with humidity around 80 to 90, so you can well imagine what it is like. However, 90 % of the rain falls between MAY and AUGUST, so it will be all over in the next month.

Our love and good wishes to Annie and Ron 2. We are glad to know that both are well. God bless you; look after yourself my son, affily Unc Ron". **Unquote** (Ron 2 is my elder son).

I personally felt that he took up the job too early. Just few months into retirement and having served for 40 years in the Navy like a 'Tiger', he will certainly have **difficult time in adjusting** in altogether a different or bordering to alien environment, where the people have the trade union mentality and very casual work ethics- how will he stomach their attitude ?? I wondered and mentioned in one of my letters to him.

Prior to his retirement I remember Admiral mentioned to me one day, that his **pension after retirement will be Rs 1700/-, that was Feb end 1982.** Today in 2016 one can't possibly imagine that a Chief of service would get so meager an amount after putting in 40 years of dedicated service, no wonder every Chief kept the Government of the day on their right side to get some job post retirement, and **Admiral indeed had the courage of conviction to turn down such an offer and it called for tremendous sense of integrity.**

Nevertheless, just to confirm the ridiculous figure (Rs 1700) I sent a mail to Admiral's very close friend and colleague Admiral Dick Schunker, 93 years, who retired as Vice Chief in 81, and his reply was, quote **"Mike, Yes, RP pension would have been in that region (Rs 1700) and mine little less-Peanuts- must have been lot of Monkeys in the armed forces whom nevertheless were the corner stone!".** Unquote . It is from the horse's mouth. Admiral after completing BROADSIDES in Aug 89 wrote that he is now managing on a tight budget from his pension of Rs 3000/-!!(Refer' Home').

When Admiral and Mrs. Pereira along with Aunty Bobby moved to ATLAST on 12th March 82, there were still lots of work to be done and soon Admiral was literally scratching whatever little savings were left at the **bottom of the barrel.**

Therefore, Admiral was right in saying that he took up this job in Goa; "**to restock our depleting coffers".**

A couple of weeks later in his letter dated 2nd August 82, **quote** *"My dear Mike-Just had your letter of the 27th July, which came in with Monday morning mail and here I am to reply as there isn't a lot happening in the office at the moment.*

I was glad to read that all of you are well and that the little fellow thrives. He seems to enjoy the weather in the North, and indeed it's good that he has begun life in that bracing and clean environment. Dear Annie will feel it when you ultimately get your next posting, and as you will have to fetch up, somewhere in the plains, she will find it a little difficult to settle in.

Goa is in the midst of monsoons, and nothing to my mind can be quite as depressing and dreary as the general environment during the rains in Goa. As a matter of preference, I am found of my sunshine and blue skies and the degree of temperature does not really bother me a lot. Since I have been here over the last six weeks, it has been overcast and wet, with the sun hardly making its presence felt and that for the shortest of time. Everything around me is damp and humid and mushy, whether it's the hotel room, the clothes in the cupboard, or the office. When it's not raining- which is not very often- it's warm and sticky- and I am therefore, looking forward to the end of this ghastly wet spell.

Goa has 110 inches in the year, but 90% of it falls in the months of June, July, August and September, with July and August being the worst and accounting for over 50% of the total rainfall. Being right in it, so to speak, I am not at the moment in the best of spirits.

I have had to live in MARGAO, the so called the commercial capital of Goa. The reason I have decided this, is the fact that it's the closest to our site in South Goa-CANACONA- which is 45kms from here. Had I moved to VASCO or Panjim, the capital, both of which are much nicer places, relatively speaking, then it would have added another 30kms of distance to CANACONA!! It's not that I go to the site very often, but ultimately that will be the focus of all our attention, the further our office from it, the more time we would be spending in a car.

At this moment I am trying out my second hotel in MARGAO and I have been for the last 5 days, at the something called the" Silver Sands"!!! The Romanticism of its name, is as remote as one could imagine from its mundane way of life- so casual indeed, that I often wonder how they survive as a hotel, with the temerity to apply for a 3- star license, when they can hardly justify a single star!!!

However, as far as hotels are concerned my options are very limited in MARGAO. I almost spent a month at a hotel called METROPOLE where I was about the only occupant in a 50 rooms venture, **and the only other occupants** *that I ever saw in the residence were some lousy looking Arabs who come in for a few days with some equally miserable women –local of course- who must have been picked up in Bombay.*

The METROPOLE could have been much worse and the hotel generally looked after me with reasonable efficiency. However, I moved out as it was located in the middle of the city and one couldn't even enjoy a walk or bit of exercise, at the end of a day . The Silver Sands on the other hand is on the sea, at a well known beach called KULVA and there are facilities for a walk or a bit of exercise. It also has a video, and this permits me to see either a film, or some of the world cup soccer matches in the evening.

I cannot say that I am greatly enamored with Goa, which I personally find rather disappointing. The Goans are 60 % Hindu, 25% Catholics and 15% other denominations. The place is full of churches , Shrines and bars , and one can literally throw a stone , anywhere in Goa , one would be sure to hit one of the three !! **The Goan is not too interested in work, having had years of Portuguese tradition; the whole state enjoys its siesta from 1 to 4 in the afternoon!!** He drinks a great deal, and bar is therefore a good business!! Finally the Christian Goans has a very narrow, bigoted concept of religion, and a broad outlook of a true religious philosophy does not exist. This is indeed sad, but that is the situation. I have found him a surly suspicious human being, unkempt, and unshaven, living in the belief that God has made him the chosen race and he does not have to do very much in life!!! **I hope I will be able to change these impressions in the months ahead, but at this moment, he is not my idea of fine human being!!** I realize that I am getting old and my concepts of life tend to be more and more rigid. However, in spite of this, I still believe that I am quite liberal but even then the Goan is not my cup of tea.

I have been looking around for a house, so that I can get Aunty Phyll down to Goa or at least have a house which will permit her to come down when she feels like it. Indeed, this is one problem that needs to be settled.

Having moved into ATLAST after doing it up and spending a lot of money, to have it as we want to, we find it impossible at this stage of life, to pack up again and move. On the other hand to keep ATLAST open means that Aunty Phyll will have to stay on there and therefore we cannot have a permanent home in Goa. At one stage we thought we might be able to lock up the house for some time, and let Aunty Phyll move down to Goa, but that will really be impossible as we have everything out and it would really be asking for trouble to leave it like that and go off. Indeed, we have yet to find an answer and until then we will both be rather unsettled. Personally I find it very lonely, living on my own, with no friends at all in Goa, I just don't know how to pass my evenings after work.

The Navy at Vasco, about 20kms from me, but all the officers there are young and very junior to me, so that doesn't really help. Two of my own contemporaries who retired many years ago, are at Panjim and have been working with SESA Goa for many years. However, Panjim is one hour's drive from Margao and there is a ferry to cross which can take anything between 15 minutes to 2 hours depending on the traffic!! So, all said and done Mike, it is not bed of roses!!

Your friend Major Mishra - at this moment we are not taking any additional personnel, and it will remain this way until about the middle of 83, when we should have done a fair degree of building, and will then be requiring an increase in our staff. I shall certainly keep Mishra's, bio-data in my files, if he could write to me around mid 83, I could then see what may be available. Ask him not to waste money and come down at this moment. It would be much better to do so in mid 83.

God bless and all the best – affly Unc; Ron". Unquote

It must have been one of the longest letters, but I do understand he had lots of time on his hands, but still one has to sit down on the table to put his thoughts on paper. There is no doubt that he had an **excellent pen** and wonderful flow of thoughts and it was indeed a great pleasure to read them many times over, and yes, I had my Oxford dictionary next to me !!

Apparently he must have bogged down with the task at hand and after a break of two months Admiral wrote in his letter of 12th October 82, **quote** "My dear Mike-There is lull in the office work, so I am trying to get this letter away to you, as I have not written for ages!

Let me begin by saying that I have received all your letters and the lovely photographs of Annie and the baby. They are both looking very well and our love and good wishes to them.

The rains are at last behind us in Goa, and I find it refreshing to have the blue skies and bright sunshine again, in spite of the fact that it is warm and humid most of the day. However, I much prefer this to the depressing environment of the monsoons, so I will not grumble!!

The project is moving ahead very slowly, and I sometime wonder when we will really get it off the ground. The rules, regulations and administrative machinery all lend themselves to delays and every gentlemen (or otherwise!?!) in the chain wishes to establish his importance by "studying the papers". **Indeed**, *much of this study, as I see it, is to ascertain whether you can be " touched" for some money, when this is not forthcoming, there are further delays. I have always realized that my countrymen are by no means the most honest in the world, but am fast coming around to the view that they could perhaps most dishonest in this universe!! However, let me not depress you on this issue.*

I was back at Cochin at the end of September, as I am also on the board of a firm called" Malayalam Plantations" who have very big interest in tea and rubber, and I had to go to Cochin for the AGM and a board meeting. It was great to be back with the service, **and I stayed with the C-in-C Vice Admiral Tehiliani** *- I saw lots of officers and their ladies. Cochin has always been a favorite spot of mine, having known it from the days when I was a young Lieutenant and I have, therefore, seen it grow and develop in the present shape. It is today, well established and is ideal for bachelors and the young married officers with accommodation being no problem at all, and the base affording the officers, the men and their ladies every possible amenity. The Admiral himself has a huge Doberman-Pincher, except this dog is as friendly to friend as to foe!!I took to him a great deal and had I been little longer, might well have stolen the dog!!!!"*

My love to Annie and the little fellow, God bless you and all the best, afflty –Uncle Ron" **Unquote**

This was the last letter from Goa and apparently he got fed up with the functioning of the civil administration and the babus, and he could not cope with their negative attitude and apathy .By December 82 he left the job and went back to Bangalore. He was succeeded by Air Marshal MB Naik!

In his letter dated 1st March 83 to Montee Chatterjee he wrote, **quote** *"I came home just before X-mas 82 and have stayed on, thou' my Chairman was very keen that I stay with the firm. However, work had really come to standstill, and the Goa government was totally indecisive as to what they really wanted from us. I saw no use merely drawing my pay, from month to month. I have however, told the Chairman, that if the tempo picks up again,I will help them on in any way that they would desire."* **Unquote**

I have no idea, how much the company was paying him? I tried to get the information from Admiral Dick Schunker, who did speak to Air Marshal Naik, but some how could not get any info about the 'emolument'!

Cochin – Madras

Admiral was on board of directors with 'Malayalam Plantations' and had attended the last AGM in end September 82 and he was again on a visit to

Cochin in Sep 83 for the same reason. In his letter of 10th Oct, **quote** *"I was down at Cochin at the end of last month on some work, and as it had nothing to do with the Navy. I had made no mention whatsoever of my programme to any Naval officer. On my arrival, therefore, I was surprised to see the C-in C at the airport and immediately realized that he was possibly meeting a certain V.I.P on the same flight as mine. I was therefore, surprised when the C-in-C came up to me, as soon as I disembarked and insisted that I come home with him. He wouldn't take no for an answer and so I went along with him, to spend three wonderful days with the Navy,* in between various meetings which I had to attend as the director of the company for which I had officially come to Cochin. In fact, I stayed in my old house in Cochin; it was really looking very nice to say the least. I was keen on taking Aunty with me, but she couldn't come, as she did not want to leave our house totally unattended. She, therefore, sadly missed the reunion with the service.*

I will be going in late November to Madras for some work and this time I am determined to take Aunty with me, as she must have some sort of break after the last eight months tremendous tension and anxiety that she has undergone since my accident." **Unquote**

One of my course mates Captain (IN) Sankar Narayan , 43rd Delta squadron, had very kindly sent me few old photographs of Admiral's visit to Eastern Fleet as CNS in March 79 . There were couple of photographs of the Fleet Commander, Rear Admiral KK Nayyar with CNS and from the body language and the way Admiral was looking at KK Nayyar, one could make out that Admiral was very fond of KK Nayyar, so I got his contact no from Vice Admiral Anup Singh and called him up. I humbly gave my introduction and mentioned about the book on Admiral and his photographs with Admiral in Madras during his visit to Eastern Fleet etc. I requested him that I would be grateful if he can share few thoughts about the great man with me. Initially he was hesitant and spoke about couple of incidents and then said that it will be better if I come and meet him personally at his residence F 8/9, Purvi Marg, Vasant Vihar, New Delhi. I took an appointment to meet him in Delhi on 24th Feb 2016 on my way back from Chandigarh, I stopped at Delhi for a day but unfortunately he was preoccupied and I could not meet him. Thereafter, I tried on telephone but still I could not reach him. I then requested Admiral Anup to put in a word, and also asked him , who was the C-in-C in Cochin in Sep 83- lo and behold it was none other than Adm KK Nayyar. I immediately took out Admiral letter of 10th Oct 83 and next time I got Adm Nayyar on the line, I literally pleaded to give me two minutes, Sir, to read the excerpts of Ronnie P letter, he agreed, and when I went through the contents, he was really moved and taken aback and said yes, I was the one who received him at the airport and took him home. Then, he asked me – are you the boy who was like a son to him? - I said, yes Sir.

The letter did the trick, as I was reading it out to the person who himself was there at the airport to receive Ronnie Pereira some 33 years ago!! Admiral Nayyar did share a lot with me which I have mentioned in the chapter on "Admiral in the Making".

Norway

Admiral had mentioned earlier from Goa in July 82 that he had got some nice offers from overseas but he did not touch any of them with the barge pole and was determined to stay in India. However, he once contemplated to take an offer in Norway. In his letter of 25th April 84, **quote** *"I have been asked to take on Chairmanship (non-executive) of a shipping company that is just being formed and as the project looks to be a very interesting one, I have accepted it. This company will be building hard- chemical carriers in Norway. In other words we will carry very highly conserve acids, which will be by-products of petro-chemicals complexes which are now mushrooming in the mid-East and Saudi in particular, as a counter to the slump in oil prices. Hard chemicals are used in variety of industries in Europe and there will be paucity of carrier in the near future. Going in for these carriers at this juncture, would appear to be very wise step. I will be going to Madras sometime next month for further discussion on the new job and may have to go abroad towards the end of the year"*. **Unquote**

However, there was no mention of this job after this letter nor he ever travelled to Norway. Evidently the company never took off?

Other Jobs

In his letter dated 18th May 85, he answered to my query about post retirement jobs, **quote** *"I am not really working for anyone though I serve on the board of Directors of three companies. These are, Harrisons Malayalam Ltd, Marar Shipping and ASDAC. The last two are just getting off their feet, but Harrisons Malayalam Ltd, is the new name of Malayalam Plantations Ltd and Harrison and Crossfield (India) Ltd, which has now been merged to 1 company. I have always on the board of Malayalam Plantation Ltd, and now continue to serve on the board of the merged companies-HARRISONS MALAYALAM LTD."*

In his letter dated 26th April 90, there was a mention of his visit to Cochin, **quote** *"My dear Mike and Annie; Thank you a million for the goodies,* *which your boys very kindly delivered to the house. I was away at Cochin and only got back home yesterday.*

Have not really seen many of the old cadets, but they seem to be very busy and work keeps them fully occupied. However, when I was at Cochin, the Gunnery School very kindly invited me to go around the establishment, and I was delighted to see Ajay Parmar- the PT boy at NDA- as a Commander, and doing a fine job as Training Commander.

Look after yourselves. Our love to Annie and the boys. All of you are always in our prayers. Write when you have the time, afftly Unc Ron" **unquote.**

That was the last time he mentioned about his visit to Cochin.

Mr. Thomas Chacko

Mr. Thomas Chacko, who had worked with Malayalam Plantation for a long time and rose to be the CEO of Harrison and Malayalam Ltd. As a young employ of the company he had interacted with Admiral in 80's, he remembers Admiral very fondly, and sent a short snippet;

Quote "Ronnie P was one of the most upright human being I ever knew. My association with him was from the day he joined Malayalam Plantations Ltd Board in 1982.

In April 83, Admiral blacked out while riding his scooter and seriously injured his stomach which required immediate surgery. When Mr. Peter Weavers, who was Chairman of Malayalam Plantation Ltd and Managing Director of Harrison and Crossfield (India) Ltd heard that Ronnie had met with a very serious accident while riding a scooter, he went to Command Hospital, Bangalore and gave him the keys of a car and told Ronnie that he did not want him to ride a scooter again (Weavers was paranoid about two wheelers) and that he appointed Ronnie as Manager of the Harrison and Crossfield Bangalore office.

Weaver did not expect Ronnie to do anything. The Manager title was given so that he could ensure that Ronnie could have the use of company car.

But Ronnie couldn't accept that. He insisted of going to the office everyday and also going out to meet clients. In those days the board sitting fees was limited by the Government to Rs 250 per meeting. Ronnie, however, would not charge anything by way of expenses for attending board meeting, saying that he received sitting fees and the company bought his flight tickets.

A few years later when someone on the board just mentioned the work he was doing in Bangalore office, Ronnie said that he did not want to continue that. By then Peter Weavers had retired from the company, so there was none to insist on it. Ronnie continued on the board of the company even after it merged with Harrison and Crossfield and became Harrison Malayalam Ltd.

However, in 1983 Malayalam Plantation started giving the non executive directors up to Rs 36000-/ per year. It would be paid in September, after general body had approved the accounts. It could be paid out of the profit of the company .So if there were no profit, nothing could be paid and if the profit were low, the amount could be less than Rs 36000/-. The company made enough profits throughout Ronnie's tenure and he received Rs 36000/- every year. Ronnie P was on Board of Directors from 27th Sep 82 to 10th Dec 91.

Field Marshal Sam Manekshaw was also on the board of the company and after Peter Weavers retired, he became non executive Chairman. At one meeting prior to Weavers departure, there were heated discussions after Manekshaw had said something. Ronnie clasped his hands together and leaned towards Manekshaw and looking him in the eyes told him "Sir you are my senior in service, but you are talking rubbish. You are talking utter rubbish! That was Ronnie true to himself" **Unquote.**

GOLF

Inroduction

Golf is an amazing sport which can trace its roots to Roman Empire- 'pagancia'- a game popular with country folk in ancient Rome. It was played with a bent stick and a ball made from leather which was filled with feathers.

Indeed, Golf was probably played at St. Andrews for well over a century before the passing of the charter in 1552 which gave the citizens of the town rights to use the links for Golf at all times with other manner of pastime.

The first course to be established outside British Isles was Royal Calcutta Golf Club in 1829. Royal Bombay was established in 1842, Wellington Gymkhana Club in Coonoor in 1885 and Ooty in 1891 and now we have hundreds of Golf courses all over India from metros to remote tea gardens in North East to highest golf course in the world -Kapup (13000ft) in East Sikkim.

However, I had never heard of this game before I joined NDA in Jan 1970. Even in the first three terms in NDA, I had no idea at all what this game was all about. We used to pass the Golf Course so many times but never entered. It was only on the second Wednesday of August 71 that for the first time in my life I entered the Golf Course- that too when I was ordered by Dep Com to report to the course on the club day- Wednesday, 11th August 71!!

Admiral was a dedicated, passionate and hard core Golfer, who simply loved this game and never missed an opportunity to play a round of 9/18 holes depending on how much time he could spare, but on weekends/ holidays it was always a round of 18 holes.

Hazaribagh - 48/49

Admiral was initiated to this wonderful game by his father, sometime in 1948/49. At that time his father was posted as Superintendent, Hazaribagh Jail (1946 - Aug 1948) as shown on top of the first board in Jailor's office. There was a rugged Golf Course, 9 holes (browns) in an area known as Elephant Lines- it was located in an open area around three famous lakes (constructed in early 20th century by Hugh Gantzer's grandfather, Mr. Alfred Herbert Gantzer, Chief Engineer) and the course was poorly maintained. So they would pick up some small boys from nearby village as caddies and enjoy their golf. Admiral's elder brother Arthur, used to come home on leave with his Golf set and join his father and his kid brother for a round of Golf. In fact Ronnie P would borrow clubs either from his father or brother. Hugh Gantzer, his nephew, 8 years his junior also learnt his Golf at Hazaribagh, by borrowing clubs from his grandfather. So it was here that Admiral was baptized to this wonderful game and enjoyed for next 44 years till 1992.

Wellington

Admiral attended Defense Services Staff College – 6th course in 1952/53 and he told me how he enjoyed playing at Wellington Gymkhana Club as well at Ooty course, one of the most picturesque course in India. I had the privilege of playing on both the courses when I was at Staff College in 1986/87.

60's

In 60s during his posting at Naval HQs, Admiral used to play regularly at Delhi Golf Club with his first cousin Denis Pereira. At that time he was playing to single figure handicap. One morning both of them reached Golf Course to play and were waiting to tee off from No 1 tee, when the gentleman on the tee asked in case they would like to join them, the offer was accepted. Just moments before the civilian gentleman was about to tee off, he said the stakes are 1: 1: 2, both Pereiras nodded their heads in agreement thinking that these guys play rather low stakes!! They went on to play 18 holes and fortunately for both Denis and Ronnie P had fairly decent round and obviously they won by some margin. So at the end of the round the civilians calculated the score and arrived at the figure of Rs 1400!! Which left both Pereiras astonished and surprised and it was then they were told that actually 1; 1; 2; meant 100; 100; 200! Admirals own words said "son, I had my heart in my mouth and thank God they did not specify the exact figure before the commencement of the game or else I would have been under great pressure and in no way produced similar card"! It was big money in those days. However, in 60's Admiral's game was at its peak.

I was fortunate to contact one of very senior officer of 1957 batch, Commander KS Sood, member of the Navy Golf team from 1966 to 1976 and also the FIRST Naval officer to represent Services team. He narrated an incident about Admiral while playing Golf with him way back in 60's; quote "Mike, **Ronnie Pereira was the most wonderful man, a pure gem, honest, truthful and down to earth.** One day we were playing in a tournament in Delhi Golf Course and he had average score of 7 over in first nine and he told me , KS here's my card and don't bother to fill it anymore. You know in the second 9 holes he played only 1 over and I told him Sir, may I fill your card as I remember the score on each hole and you will be in contention for winning a prize! No way, he turned down my suggestion out rightly and said – it **will not be proper.** That was the level of his integrity, though minor incident but it speaks volume of his character".Unquote .

Commander Sood was the finest golfer ever produced by the Navy with best handicap of 5! In 1968 Admiral AK Chatterji was invited as Chief Guest for Inter Service Golf Tournament, at Delhi Golf Course , and Cdr Sood happened to be recipients of a prize, Admiral, being a non golfer himself was surprised to see a Naval officer winning a prize, asked him where was he posted ? Cdr Sood, said –Bombay Sir, the CNS immediately posted him to Naval HQs Delhi to pursue his talent!! Incidentally, while in Bombay in mid 60's, KS Sood taught Golf and was 'Guru'to three officers –Commanders/Lt Cdr who later on went to become Chief one after another –Admiral Tehiliani (84-87), Admiral Podgy Nadkarni (87-90) and Admiral Ramdas (90-93)!!

Montee Chatterjee remembers that there was only one instance when Ronnie P had an 'Ace' (hole in one) at Delhi Golf Club sometime in 60's. I called my friend Brigadier Sanjeev Mehra, Secretary DGC and asked him if they had record of 'hole in one'. They did, but only from 1988 onwards!!

In 60's Navy had excellent Golf team-Admiral , Denis Pereira, Jawahar Lal Gupta, Henry Menezes, Davar, KS Sood and of course Montee Chatterjee. All of them played to single figure handicap with KS Sood and Montee at 5/6.

Montee Chatterjee, first interaction with Admiral was in early 60's, quote " Mike, the first time I ever met Ronnie P was when he was posted as Commander Barracks or COMBAX in Bombay and I clearly remember he was staying in a colonial bungalow named' Somerset House' opposite Colaba Post Office. I was then posted as Secretary to Captain RN Batra, Commanding officer, INS Angre. Those days I only knew him socially, it was only in 1966 that we started playing golf together and our permanent four ball was Ronnie P, Cdr RN Bhatta, Cdr Bapu Madholkar and self, and almost every afternoon we were on the US Club Golf Course and it continued till Ronnie was posted to NDA in Jan 71. Next we were together when he got posted to Naval HQs as Vice Chief in April 77, as I was already posted in Delhi , and for next 5 years, we really had **best golfing of our lifetime till he retired on 28th Feb 82"** unquote

NDA 71

In Jan 71 as Dep Com, he was playing to single figure handicap and true to himself took immense interest in running of the NDA Golf Club. Invariably, every Wednesday- Club Day-he was at the Course sharp at 3pm to coach all the newcomers and took great interest in improving the playing conditions on the course, we had 9 Browns and later extended to 12 and as of now i.e. June 2016, there are 13 greens!

The membership was restricted to about 25 cadets and there were many officers who played excellent Golf, i.e. Cdr Rishi, Capt Kipgin (Manipuri) and war casualty who had lost one leg in the mine field blast in 1971 Indo-Pak conflict, Capt Rakesh Das, Capt MM Bhardhwaj and, Capt SJB Sharma and few more. Many cadet members had Army background i.e. Navkesh Singh, MS Gill, Mantaj, Gurtaj, Rajinder Lange, Arun and Ranjan Chand, and most of them represented NDA team. There was only one like me who had not heard about this fascinating game – RK Beniwal from Shamli, Dist Muzaffarnagar, Western UP and he had the distinction of picking up this game rapidly and within one year came down to 12 handicap. He represented Air Force team for over 20 years! My best handicap was 17!! My only achievement was ending up as Runners-Up in Single Club Tournament in Nov 72 and received my first Golf Trophy from Mrs. SD Gupta, wife of Gen SD Gupta, Commandant. I still have the photograph and the small trophy with me! In fact same day Mrs. Pereira won the Ladies Putting competition and she too received the trophy from Mrs. SD Gupta as shown in the photograph.

In the spring term of 72, during mid- term break Dep Com took a group of about 15 golfers to Bombay to play at Bombay Presidency Golf Club, Chembur East and United Services golf course just to give all cadets the experience of playing in different courses. I missed out as the NDA Hockey team was participating in Aga Khan Gold Cup Hockey Tournament. In addition Golfers had outing to Poona playing at RSI Golf club and CME Golf Course. Aim was to expose all members to maximum number of courses, though at times it was very frustrating for relatively green horns like me as most of the time we were looking for our ball in the deep rough!!

In my 6th term, on many occasions Dep Com would play a round of golf with me alone primarily to teach me the "**Etiquettes**" of golf. The first thing he told me ; son, never cheat in golf by filling incorrect score or moving your ball to improve its lie unless there is 'preferred lie' as per local rules of the club. Next, always repair divots on the fairway, must rake bunkers after playing a bunker shot. Repair pitch mark on the green and finally do not cross the putting line of the opponent. These were the basic golf etiquettes but very important. He would then teach me on how to plan ones game on the course or get out of hazard or any difficult position. It was a learning curve for me and he was not only excellent golfer but indeed a very good coach. In fact, he could hit anything between 240 – 260 yards with the Driver, straight as an arrow. My problem basically was trying to use strength instead of having natural rhythm in my swing and invariably ended up with blisters on my fingers. **He would say son, don't try to hit the ball, just play your swing!** And would add that **these were the words of my dear father way back in 1948** when I started this beautiful game.

After I passed out from NDA on 16th Dec 72, I did not venture into serious golfing till 1977. As youngster we were so busy playing troop games and had no time at all whatsoever for golf.

Vishakhapatnam

However, Admiral kept me abreast with his golf activities. In his letter of 20th Aug 74, when he was posted as Fleet Commander at Vizag, **quote** *"son, I am still keeping up my Golf and will be going down to Bombay for the Indian Navy Championship, which will run between 26th-28th September next month . I am, however, no more playing at 9, am now on 12, though I seem to play quite well. Last Sunday-yesterday in fact-I took part at the tournament at the **club** (**Vizag**) **which was a Medal Round and managed to win it by playing to a 10!** This was very surprising, as I hardly get in golf more than once a week, as the course is good 20 kms from where we live. It's also a rough course with browns and one has to be very careful not to ruin your clubs"* **unquote**

One weekend Admiral decided to take his Flag Lt Vijayan at Vizag for golf and wanted to introduce him to this wonderful game. This is what Vijayan had to say about that outing;

Quote "Admiral was a very keen and ardent Golfer. One Sunday Admiral asked me to come along with him to the course and he will introduce me to this fascinating game. After reaching the course, he showed me how to hit the ball etc for about half an hour. Then he gave me 20 balls and asked me to practice hitting while he went for quick round. At the end of his game, when he got back to me, I could return only 5 balls as I had lost the others. He remarked jokingly "son, you are a very expensive player as 15 balls cost a lot of money. Any way never mind, son, I hope one day you will learn and then we can play together. That's how **humane** he was" **unquote**

Notwithstanding, consequent to heart attack, Vijayan started to play again Dec 1985 as he could not pursue any other rigorous sport and within 6 months was playing to 18 and ultimately to 11. He is now playing to good 14 and has a fixed four ball i.e.; Admiral Arun Prakash, ex CNS, Vice Admiral Dhamle and Commodore Sanjay Gupta, and they play three times a week (Monday, Wednesday and Friday) at Naval Golf Course, Vasco, Goa !

Cochin

In Dec 74 Admiral moved to Cochin to take over as FOC Southern Naval Areas. Navy did not have a golf course; however there was a nine holes golf course at the famous Balgatty Islands. The course was laid out on the palace grounds of the Balgatty Palace, the oldest Dutch palace constructed in 1722. In 1903 the Britishers took the island on lease and soon they laid out a short nine holes course, initially for the British officers only but later in 1920's it was open to select native public.

The only way to get to the islands was by boat. The Flag Staff House was located at the South-East tip of Wellington Island and it had its own Jetty. Every Sunday/holiday Admiral's Barge would come along the Jetty with full crew. Admiral along with his foursome-Commander Bouncy Malhotra, CO, INS Venduruthy, Cdr SK Sood and one more would take 25 minutes sail along the Cochin channel to Bolgatty Islands. All the ships were anchored along the channel and Admiral with his hawk eyes was always on the look out to catch any erring crew on the Quarter Deck , who showed any signs of lethargy or casualness would immediately invite one month 'Gating' for the entire crew on the ship!

One Sunday Flag Lt's course mate Lt Patnaik, who was commanding a small Patrol boat INS Abhay earned the wrath of the Admiral as the drill movements of the crew were not up to the mark and entire crew was gated for one month. Poor Patnaik went and requested Flag if he could help him to get out of the punishment or have it reduced. Well, Flag promised to do his best but for that he must catch Admiral off guard and in good mood, yes; he managed to have the punishment mitigated to half!

Bombay

In Feb 76 Admiral was ordered to move to Bombay on a very short notice(only two hours) to take over as FOC-in-C Western Naval Command. Bombay had number of golf courses and Admiral had earlier served for fairly long time in Bombay, therefore, from Golfing point of view he was indeed very happy and more often than not he preferred to play at United Services Golf Club. His regular partners were Mr Ravi Tikko, Mr Latif Shah and Cdr Jawahar. Indeed he had hectic schedule but whenever he had the opportunity to play, he never missed it.

Delhi

In April 77 Admiral moved to Naval HQs to take over as Vice Chief and it was here in Delhi that **for next five years he had best golfing years of his life.** Primarily due to his golfing buddy Commander Montee Chatterjee, who was already posted at Naval HQs? They played every Wednesdays, Saturdays and Sundays and **invariably** his partner was Montee Chatterjee!

It was in early 78, after long break of 5 years I started to play golf by borrowing Maj Chahal's dilapidated half golf set! When I came to Delhi in mid 78 Admiral asked me if I was keen to become member of Delhi Golf Club, I declined as I was totally out of touch and my game was rusty. I was aware that one had to play a round with a member of general committee at DGC to earn your membership, to be honest I could not have made it and as such did not want to embarrass the Admiral. I never tried again and now it is almost impossible to get membership with a waiting period of 30 repeat 30 years, yes, confirmed from old friend Brig Sanjeev Mehra, the present Secretary DGC!

That's the time I decided to procure a golf set for myself and wrote to Admiral to help me to get one. In his letter of 23rd Aug 78 , **quote** " *Have recently playing a lot of Golf, both at Delhi Golf Course and Army Golf Course and I find that this regular effort has done my game a lot of good, and I am hitting a reasonably a good ball.* **I am playing to about 12** *and if I can keep this up I will be more than happy. What pleases me a great deal is that I am driving very well and getting anything between 220 to 240 yards off my drives. This is not only a good distance,* **but at 56 more than reasonable!!**

Haven't seen any reasonably good but cheap set for you as yet .Most second hand sets today are frightfully expensive and people are asking between 2500-4000/- for a full set. I wonder Mike, why don't you put down your name for a

Bobby Locke half set, which will cost about 1600/- . These are good and should be available in your canteens, if you do want one of these, I shall also try and get it, but let me know if you are interested". **Unquote**

In Delhi he used to play more often at Army Golf Course at Dhaulakuan. His partners were Gen OP Malhotra, COAS, Lt Gen Hira and Montee Chatterjee. Montee was the marker with handicap of 6! And give strokes all around. It used to be Army vs Navy and most of the times Navy won!

There was an unfortunate incident which prompted Admiral to give up his membership at the Army Golf Course. Narrated by Montee Chatterjee himself, **quote** "It was sometime end December 1978, after the round Admiral would order a cup of tea and soft drink for me. Somehow the quality of the tea was of sub standard and Admiral called the waiter and told him that he needs to improve the quality. However, it had no effect on the waiter and he produced same sub standard tea the next time too. Admiral got annoyed and asked for the complaint book and he wrote that the quality of the tea is horrible and not up to the mark. Next time again no improvement and now Admiral got hot under the collar and asked for the Secretary of the Golf Course-Colonel Malhotra- and Admiral complained to him about poor standard of the tea, which he had put it in writing in the complaint book. Col Malhotra turned around and told Admiral that he is not entitled to write a complaint as he was not a permanent member of the course. Naturally till then Admiral never bothered to check about the status of his membership- so he asked; what do you mean, Colonel? Malhotra replied, Sir, you are an '**Associated**' member of the club!! And only permanent members are permitted to write complaint?? At hearing this Admiral lost his shirt and asked for a piece of paper and wrote 'I hereby resign' and walked off, never to play at Army Course again. I also resigned then and there. The matter was brought to the notice of Gen Malhotra but he apparently took no action"!!**Unquote**

Montee continued- "Mike you know the genesis of the 'membership' goes back to late 60's, sometime in 1967, when Lt Gen Paintal was the Quarter Master General at AHQs and he had come up with a proposal to lay out Inter Services nine hole golf course in the vacant land between DSOI and Rajputana Rifles Centre. For this project the Navy and the Air Force were asked to contribute Rs 25000/- each, with Army putting in much more. However, the CNS, Admiral AK Chatterji, a non golfer himself said that no way, as very few Naval officers play golf and refused and for some reason so did Air Chief Arjan Singh. So at that time as per the club constitution only Army officers were permitted to become permanent member and officers from Navy and Air Force could become only 'Associate' members, and it continued till recently". **Unquote**

However, as per new rules introduced in 2015, there is no permanent membership across the board!!

During his long tenure of 5 years in Delhi as Vice Chief and CNS, Admiral really enjoyed his Golf. Montee Chatterjee, who was posted in Directorate Management Services, Naval HQs since 1976 and had a non golfer for boss -Captain Rao. As per Montee, **quote** "Mike, on every Wednesday Ronnie P as Vice Chief would ring up my boss and tell him – please inform Montee that tee off is at 2.30 pm!! The next boss also happened to be non golfer Madan Chopra and Admiral would send message through him! The ploy was simple, so that I am not held back for some imaginary important task??" **Unquote**

In early 1980, Captain Krishnan, Staff Officer to CNS was posted to Moscow as Naval Attaché. Montee Chatterjee was immediately posted to CNS office as Secretary to CNS!! He took over in May 1980 on his return from USA.

At that point in time the regular four ball was Admiral, Commodore Sanjana, Rear Admiral Bhatta and of course Montee Chatterjee; otherwise with Gen Malhotra and Gen Hira and later Gen Hoon.

In his letter of 30th April 80, **quote** *"It is just after 12.30 in the afternoon. Being a holiday, I was out on the golf course this morning and was playing with your Chief, and I managed to take some money off him, in spite of having come down to a 10".* **Unquote**

The next letter of 19 June 80, **quote** *"My dear Mike, I was on the course about a week ago and came across a young Sardar from the Regiment, who mentioned that he was your room mate. He said that you are playing some very good golf and I remembered that I have few things for you, that you might require. I therefore asked this officer whether it will be possible for him to pick up these items- a golf cap, a left hand glove and three new golf balls- before he returned to the regiment. He promised to do so, by the 19th but has not come either to the house or office, and I fear he might have gone back to the regiment today. If he has, he* **really needs his backside kicked,** *because I even volunteered to deliver the parcel to him, but he promised to come and pick them up himself.*

Son, if you have any one coming this side, ask him to drop in the office or see me at home, I shall pass these few things to him for you. In the meanwhile should anyone be going to Jodhpur, I will send them along". **Unquote**

Captain Manjit Singh from the Ordinance Corps was the culprit, he somehow felt little scared to meet the Admiral. However, 3 days later on 22nd June I was in Delhi on my way to Sikkim and picked up light blue cap, glove and three Top Flight balls.

I met Captain Montee Chatterjee after a gap of 34 long years in Dec 2015 at Guwahati and he said, **quote** "You know Mike, while on the course with Ronnie P, not a single day would pass without mentioning your name, and I used to wonder, there has to be something in this boy than just having a strong resemblance to his late nephew Michael to love somebody like this, you must have been his son in his previous life, I am sure, otherwise such relationships are unheard of, **you were simply lucky to be loved by a man of Ronnie P stature** ! He may have gone but I still carry his feelings for you, Mike" .**Unquote**. I was speechless and my eyes just swelled with tears.

In June 80 Montee Chatterjee took over as Secretary to CNS and they played golf three times a week. Every Wednesday Admiral would come out of his office at dot 1.30 pm and say Montee let's go; tee off at 2.30pm!!

Pushing Files

Montee Chatterjee narrated, **quote** "You know Mike; there is a twist in the story. Ronnie P loved his game of golf, he was not only outstanding golfer, but was very passionate about the game. Then one Wednesday he told me- Monts, I don't think we can play on Wednesdays, as there are too many files to clear and I do not want to leave the back log. I just kept quiet and nodded my head, and I also knew how much Admiral enjoyed his Golf.

Every evening it was my job to clear Admiral's table after he left the office. Admiral seldom took files home, in very rare cases only. So I used to put all the files in the cupboard and lock it. Next morning again take them out and put them on Admiral's table. **So what I did on next Wednesday, I put only three files on the** table and rest remained in the cupboard, **so at dot 1.30 pm, Admiral walked out and said; Monts, no work, all files cleared, let's go for Golf!! And this procedure continued for next year or so!"** **Unquote**

Captain Montee had put in papers for premature retirement in Oct 81 and got a good job as Secretary Delhi Golf Club in Jan 1982, primarily to organize golf championship for the Delhi Asian Games, which was won by Laxman Singh. On Montee's dining out, Admiral in his farewell speech said- **'Gentlemen, Montee thought he was being very clever and had fooled me all this while and on every Wednesday mornings he would put up only three files, when the previous day there were 43 files. I knew he was doing it deliberately, but we went for Golf!!**

In Oct 81 Admiral visited Staff College to deliver talk on Maritime Power, in his letter of 26th Oct, **quote** "*Unfortunately I could do little else but lecture, as I was laid up in bed for most of the three days at DSSC with very bad throat that hit me, soon after I got up the hill and gave me a temperature around 101*or 102*. The weather was also rather bad; with a continuous drizzle most of the time and mist shrouding the entire Nilgiris. **No golf was therefore possible**"*

One week after his retirement Admiral left Delhi on 6th March 82, and headed for Bangalore. After spending 4 days at MES IB, Rest House Road, Admiral with Mrs. Pereira and his sister Aunty Bobby shifted to AT LAST in Whitefield and for the next three months they were still in the process of settling down as there was lot of work to be done inside the house and so, **there was no question of Golf.** Then in June Admiral moved to Goa and picked a job with Sima Hotel and Resorts Pvt Ltd and within six months resigned as he could not cope with the corrupt civil administration. Due to tight schedule and Golf course being long distance away at Vasco, **he could not get any opportunity to play golf in Goa.**

Then in April 83 he met with unfortunate scooter accident .In his letter of 28th July 83, **quote** "*I am now all but 100* fit. The arm or the left shoulder to be precise is much, much better, **though I can still not swing a golf club**, I am sure I will be able to do so, in a little while*".Unquote .

1985

Admiral couldn't play golf for rest of the year. So effectively he was off golf for nearly two years .It was only in early 85 that he mentioned of golf in his letter dated 5th Feb 85, **quote** "*Have recently playing lots of golf, but have been playing very badly!! I cannot find the reason, but I am pressing on, hoping it will gradually improve. I find that I am hitting with my hands and not with my body and this is really bad for golf, as you can neither get the distance nor accuracy, and with right handed person, the right hand tends to take over and you keep hooking every shot. As you know there is now new system of handicapping with the necessity of every golfer have to put in 20 cards, thereafter as many cards as possible each month. It was this that got me back to the course and I am now on a 17 handicap with prospect of going down to*

20!! This does not worry me, as a bogus handicap is about the worst thing that can happen to a golfer". **Unquote**

By beginning of 1985 I was playing to 14, still with a half set! In his letter of 23 June 85, **quote** *"My dear Mike, thanks for your letter of 17th June which came in on Saturday. I am really penning this hurried reply to give you the latest on Driver and No 2 wood.*

Gullu and family were over on the 9th and I then gave him both the clubs to get down to Bedi at President's Body Guard, New Delhi. Gullu is expected to do within a week. The no 2 wood will be with Bedi and I asked Gullu to tell him to either inform you or get it to Amritsar. The driver is being collected by **Captain Montee Chatterjee**, *my last Secretary to whom I have written asking him to get it re-gripped and then give it to Bedi to get it to you at A'sar, so Montee will get this done before the driver is given to Bedi.*

I am arranging for a Golf magazine to be sent to me and when these start arriving, I will send them to you, as soon as I have finished them. **In the meantime I will be sending you two books on golf- one on putting and one on game by a pro called Jassop. In fact, better still, I will send a soft book by Jack Nicklaus and not Jassop".** **Unquote** (Gullu is my eldest brother and Bedi is my course mate 43/D)

Co-incidentally, Montee Chatterjee sent me the copy of above mentioned letter written by Admiral in most humble manner requesting him to get the No 1 Wood re-gripped in his letter of 11 June 85.

Quote *"My dear Montee, - This will indeed surprise you, and I am really writing this with a "Matlabi" intent! Forgive me.*

To begin with how are you? I understand that you have left the Golf Club and it will certainly be their loss. However, I hope you have managed to get something to keep yourself busy. This should not be difficult with all your excellent contacts from golf.

How is Leela? Our love and good wishes to her and Poppet. I haven't heard from her for a long time.

The reason I am writing Montee is to ask for your help. It concern my No 1 Wood-a Wilson K 28 that I have sent through a friend of mine to Captain PS Bedi, the Adjutant of President's Bodyguard, and one of the cadets I had with me at the NDA.

The No 1 requires to be re-gripped and I will be grateful if you could get this done for me at Delhi Golf Club and let me know what it costs. After the refurbishing can you give it back to Bedi, as it will be then collected by Major Mike Bhalla of the 16th Cavalry, who is at Amritsar. The collection will be done by Mike, to whom I have already written. Sorry to bother you Montee, but I will be grateful if this can be done.

All the best to you Montee, and our love and good wishes to the family- your sincerely Ronnie Pereira. "Unquote.

Bedi immediately sent the clubs to me through one of his jawans coming on leave to Amritsar without changing the grip of No 1 Wood and apparently the Admiral got to know about this when he checked up with Montee and, he lost his cool and ordered me to send it back to Delhi in his very next letter, dated 29th July 85, **quote** "*To begin with, you should NOT have both the clubs, as am quite sure that the driver has not been re-gripped, and* **a bad grip on club is no use at all.** *I told your brother explicitly to tell Bedi to hang on to the driver, till it was collected by a Naval officer, who could get it re-gripped, but he does not seem to have done this. So please send the driver back to Bedi and let me know when you have done this. The present red rubber grip is falling apart and is no use to you at all.*

Secondly, **putters,** *there are no such putters as the finest or the worst. It is unquestionably the man behind the putter which counts all the time. There are literally hundreds of well balanced putters and you have to get used to your own and get results. Merely having a PING doesn't really mean anything, as it would be no use to you if doesn't suit you. I have a spare 'Golden Goose' which is a centre shaft- putter, but it works well and many golfers use it. I will try and get this to Bedi, but it will take me sometime. However, don't worry about a PING"* **Unquote**

By now my game was picking up and Amritsar had a beautiful 18 greens course and my house was next to no 16 green! I used to play almost every day and would partner Maj Gen Chikki Dewan, GOC 15 Infantry Division, a good 14, and passionate golfer, Col MMS Sohal at 10, Col Rakesh Das 12, and I was down to 12. Every week I would write the summary of my performance to Admiral and he too was taking keen interest in my progress over the weeks. By now I had also won couple of Monthly Medal Rounds which gave me encouragement to practice hard and particularly short game.

In his next letter of 26th Aug 1985, **quote** "*My dear Mike- on the 12th I sent you the latest rules of Golf, incorporating every change as promulgated by*

R and A. I don't think these rules, would be readily available in Amritsar and it is something you must know on your fingertips. **My own experience has been that the rules of Golf as played or accepted by the Army are based largely on the rank, with senior officer doing what he likes on the golf course to the unanimous acceptance of the juniors?! Certainly the handicapping rules for Army officers are so dictated!!** However, as you see from the Rule Book, the R and A, have NOT as yet accepted this practice!! I am also sending you in the next 24 hours, two magazines on Golf. They are GOLF and GOLF DIGEST, and I am now getting the later on regular basis from Manny's at Pune. You will find them very good as golf compendium of golf instructions that you always be turning to, ever so often.

I am going to Delhi on 8th September for about 3 days and will- if the IA doesn't mix up this club for hijacking instrument – take up a centre-shaft putter for you, which I will leave it with BEDI after it had been re-gripped. **I now realize that you have not re-gripped the driver, as your ominous silence to my query remains unanswered!! Really a bad grip is worse than a bad club".**
Unquote

In spite of playing to 12, I somehow had problem with my 'chipping', sometime hitting the turf behind the ball or topping it. Any error around the green will certainly end up in an extra stroke and on the contrary a good chip can certainly save you a stroke. So I wrote to Admiral about my predicament. In his letter of 30th Sep 85, **quote** "*Now your golf and* **chipping** *which seems to be bugging you. To begin with read the books I sent you and magazine I posted sometime ago, 'Golf World' I think. There are always useful tips in them which you must study. I do hope you have received them, as I sent them by Book Post, a long while ago.* **Chipping and putting are fundamental to low scores. A chip in particular can save you an extra putt and each is unfortunately is a stroke!! In chipping your stance must be open, with the weight on the left foot.** *It is really executed with the hands and very little of any shoulder turn. It doesn't matter what club you use, each to his own choice, but I like a seven or eight, unless it is necessary to go over a bunker, when a chipping wedge become necessary and you want bite on the ball, which means you must hit through the ball. However, with a seven or an eight she will run a bit, after pitching on the green and therefore, the use of same clubs ensure that you get used to the run of the ball to bring it up to the hole. I use this technique when I am within 75-50 ft of the hole.* **However, READ the books which will give you all the gen.**

Now golf is a recreation and not your profession, so don't neglect the later and I hope you also read lots of professional literature which is absolutely essential. When you come into the zone of selective promotion in the next few years, **please** *remember, that your handicap does NOT figure in your confidential report. Indeed, I have seen comments such as "if he spends as much time on his profession as he does on a golf course, he would be an excellent sailor"!! So watch it.*

Lastly, you cannot carry 15 clubs in bag . You would be disqualified in any tournament and that is straight from the Rule Book. You must also know your rules which are an essential part of the game." **Unquote** .

Talking about rules and their interpretation by Senior Army Officers!! Admiral once told me; son, I can write the ACR of an officer after playing one round of Golf with him. This is one game which reveals the true character of human being, as at times one has to perform under pressure particularly 'money holes' and there are so many other occasions when one is tempted to break rules or fill in incorrect score in his card or move the ball from difficult lie or wrong calculation of strokes, and anyone cheating or indulging in these practices immaterial of rank is not a gentleman or an officer of integrity!!

I was still playing with a half set and I kept Admiral abreast about my achievements on the golf course including winning 'Armoured Corps' Championship , both Individual and Team events, held at Army Golf Course at Dhaula Kuan, New Delhi during Cavalry Dinner' in November 1985. By now Admiral managed to get a putting- aid for me. In his letter of 21st Feb 86, **quote** *" I must also apologize for not having sent the putting aid , but the problem was to get it packed sufficiently well, so that it would not get damaged, as it is very light alloy and the handling by the postal authorities could well have wrecked it , if the packing was not good .*

Fortunately, only today Aunty received a X-mas wall plate from Denmark packed beautifully in thermocole, cut to its size and it came very safely. As I saw the packing, I realized that it would do for the putting aid and in fact, it fitted beautifully. I have, therefore, packed and dispatched today, and also sent you separately by book post a golf magazine. Both should arrive soon after or indeed with this letter and your putting should then theoretically improve!! The magazine that I send you, always have an article or two on chipping or on approach shots and if you read them and practice them, I am sure this aspect of your game will certainly improve. The point is that practice is absolutely essential for better golf and playing a round only help to establish whether your practice has been fruitful or otherwise. Personally I cannot get to the first tee without some practice and I normally hit 50-75 balls before I play a round , using at least five clubs from 8 to 3 wood. I have 50 practice balls specifically for this purpose which I get from Delhi at rupee 4-5 a ball, however, it is necessary to keep this stock which lasts a long time and once you have built it up, it is only a matter of replacing 2 or 3 every month. I would therefore, suggest that you do so and in fact keep 3 or 4 days in a week only for practice without playing a round of golf". **Unquote**

Admiral did everything from encouraging and sending golf literature to me but sadly could not afford a set for me , he told me later , son I wanted to buy you a second hand full set but found it bit expensive for my pocket, I felt so sad for him. By April 86 I was really getting desperate to get myself a full set but didn't have the resources to buy a new set. Fortunately for me, one of very senior officer of our Regiment – Lt Gen Shiv Dev Verma (retd) who had joined 16 Cavalry in 1929, later commanded it in 1945 came to my rescue. During my visit to Kasuali, Himachal Pradesh in May 86, I along with my wife and two small sons went to see him and his gracious wife Thelma at their cottage –Longwood- Gen Verma was an outstanding horseman and Polo player with a handicap of 4 goals. Though he told me, **quote**" you know Mike the Goras (whites) never gave me good ponies or else I would have ended up with 7/8 goals handicap"? **Unquote** He later took up golf and played to handicap of 8. He had a full 'Wilson 'golf set of 1970 vintage in pretty good condition with a trolley of 1954 vintage! He offered me the set with one condition that I have it priced at Delhi Golf Club –Pro shop. He asked me to meet Maj Gen KC Khanna, 16 Cav and requested him to personally take the set to Delhi Golf Course and have it priced. I got the set and trolly for Rs 3200/- and was happy that now I have complete set, never mind a second hand one.

The course at Staff College is laid out in tea country with undulating terrain and is very pretty indeed. After my arrival the next day I was on the course!

All senior officers at the college were die hard golfer. Lt Gen Billimoria, Commandant, with whom I played Golf at Kalimpong , where he commanded 27 Mountain Division in 1982/83. Maj Gen Bulbul Brar was the Chief Instructor Army of 'OP BLUE STAR' fame, was my Brigade Commander in Pathankot in 1979. Senior Instructor was Colonel Binny Shergill, a diehard Cavalry officer was one of Company Commander at Indian Military Academy in 1973 and I often played in their four-ball with Gen Brar as my partner!!

Admiral in his letter of 14th Sep 86, **quote** *"I hope you enjoyed your golf with the Planters and you were able to keep up your end with Gen Brar, as your partner. The General has been in my mind a great deal since dear Vaidya's assassination. To think that he can never really lead a life of peace and tranquility, and do what he wants, when he wants just because he was doing his duty is really sad. To think the human beings can really degenerate to the level of animals – nay* *below that- and kill for sake of killing for what they describe a just cause, leaves me with a feeling that we are gradually losing our basic God given sense of reason and understanding and it will surely anger the Good Lord a great deal. There seems no end to such stupidity and inhumanity. If ever I come up to Coonoor, I must meet him, for he must be a very fine and dedicated soldier"*. **Unquote**

Yes, Gen Brar was given Z plus security and was on the hit list of Khalistani militants for leading the attack on Golden Temple on 6th June 1984. In fact, he showed me a letter written in Punjabi on the Khalistan Commando letter pad, in which they had written about his minute to minute schedule of the day including playing golf and had asked him to give a choice of the place and time where he would like to be killed by them ! Therefore, he always had few armed guards around him, including on the Golf Course. One day as I lined up for a fairly tricky putt, from the corner of my eye, I saw a barrel of AK 47 gun pointing at me; I slowly walked up to the huge man with handle bar moustaches- Thambi-and moved the barrel of the rifle towards the sky- Gen Billimoria and Gen Brar had a good laugh !! But I didn't want to die on the Green! More than my life I was worried about the putt?? It sank!!

By Oct 86, Admiral had already made up his mind to put ATLAST on sale .He happily informed me in his letter of 27th Oct 86, **quote** *"I have already worked out the list of priorities once ATLAST is sold and one of them is - a set of MACGREGOR MUIRFIELD golf clubs . I am already in correspondence with my buddies on this one"!!* **Unquote**

In fact the list was long and included golf clubs. Imagine, he had no resources all these years to buy the clubs of his choice and had to wait till he sold his house to raise sufficient funds to buy them!?

In Feb 87, we were out on Bharat Darshan, which included overnight halt at Bangalore. As soon as the train reached Bangalore Railway Station, I headed for the bus stand and barely managed to catch the last bus to Whitefield. It was past 10 pm when the bus reached Whitefield and sure enough Admiral was waiting with a big torch at the bus stop near the village market. We both walked home and talked late into the night, Next morning I requested Admiral that I want to bring my golf buddies home to meet him and Auntry. He not only accepted my request but offered to pick them up from the golf course. So we drove to golf course in Ambassador car and waited for an hour and then picked up Wing Cdr TS Randhawa, Cdr Arvind Bali, Maj RS Kanwar and Mantaj and brought them to AT LAST. They spent three lovely hours with Admiral and Mrs. P, had beer and simple lunch and laughed a lot on jokes about golf. Before leaving Admiral went inside and brought four packets of three new golf balls and gave one each to all of them, but I was left out? I remember he said I must look after your buddies first! After completion of the course Maj Kanwar and his family dropped in to see Admiral and Mrs. P. Admiral in his letter of 2nd June 87 **quote** "*we had a very pleasant surprise when Major Kanwar and his family dropped in on us, on his way out from Staff College. I think his wife is Sai Baba devotee, so they came through Whitefield and spent a night at the Ashram as they were leaving the next morning. They dropped into the house and it was nice to see them.*"**Unquote** .

Admiral in his letter of 19th March 87 Admiral wrote, **quote** "*our warmest good wishes to Randy, Bali, Kanwar and Monty. It was great to have had all of you with us. Even for a few hours. Thank them for their letters*". **Unquote**

The one who enjoyed most was Commander Arvind Bali- to have an opportunity to be free and frank with his **most dreaded ex-"Chief"** – but he loved him, none the less!

After reporting to Ferozepur in July 1987, I wrote to Admiral about my new assignment and he replied in his letter dated 7th Oct 87, **quote** "*Well son, I am glad that you are enjoying the new job. It's really what you make of it and I am sure you will fulfill the assignment with credit.* **Don't play too much golf at the expense of the job,** *but play is essential to keep the cobwebs away-None the less as this is your first real staff job, it is crucial , the first report will be important one, on the way up the ladder.*

I am still without my golf clubs, which arrived in India on 21st August and apparently in oscillation between Bombay and Cochin, having been entrusted for delivery, to an obvious damn fool, with initiative of scared hare! They came down to Cochin, so I understand, by a ship, two days before I got there, and a day after it had sailed back to Bombay. Being sure that the clubs were somewhere in the base, I looked all over, but had no luck at all. Ultimately after much phoning, I discovered that they had gone back to Bombay in the same ship in the custody of a stupid Lieutenant, who had brought them with him!! It's a shame I am not in Service, **as 21 days restrictions would be a minor issue, after I had done with him!!** *They are a set of Rider Mk 3 clubs.*

Incidentally as your bag is falling apart, I will get you one for the safe custody of your clubs! Will somehow order it from Bombay and get it sent to you-NOT by the same ass of a Lieut-via Delhi and Bedi, who is possibly still in the Bodyguard. However, if you have a better idea, please let me know. It will take little time, as the pro in the Wellington club who makes good bags is rather slow. Alternatively, **I will also write to Montee Chatterjee- my old Secy- at Delhi, and ascertain** *availability from Delhi Golf Club. This is an advance birthday present".* **Unquote**

In his next letter of 27th Oct 87, **quote** *"Have started my golf again, with the arrival of my Rider Mk 3 set, which finally got home about a week back. I had asked for 3 woods-a 2, 3, and 4-as I never use a driver, and nine irons- 3 thru 9, a pitching wedge and a sand wedge. They are really a lovely set and suit me well, seeing that I am hitting a not unreasonable ball, after almost 18 months of no golf at all. My first game which was far from good-was with Kaushal, Loomba (both 43rd) and Ashok Kumar (39th) - and in spite of problems, I really enjoyed it. I practice 3 or 4 times a week and play over the weekends. Unfortunately, my golf bag and covers for the woods are still adrift, but I will get them over the next fortnight.*

As soon as I have news of your golf bag .I will try and position it with Bedi at PBG and you can pick it up from there. Is Bedi still there? If not, let me know where you want it positioned". **Unquote .**

Yes I received a lovely bag-white and green combination, plus, 3 Top Flight golf balls , glove and Titlists golf cap from Montee Chatterjee via Major Prabhjit Bedi Adjutant President Body Guards.

I wrote to Admiral and thanked him; All these years if he ever gave me anything it was always related to golf; bag, clubs, putter, caps, golf gloves , balls new and practice, tee, putting aid, 3xTshirts, golf books and magazines and yes, once he paid for my golf shoes-Rs 300/-! Never gave me anything material except a watch on my passing out parade at NDA and few military history books to read. He never wanted to spoil me; in any case he didn't have any spare money to throw around. He was **HONEST** to a fault, unbelievable.

Golf at Wellington

Winter of 87/88 offered good golf for Admiral and he was on the course almost six days a week and mentioned about golf in his letter of 14th June 88, **quote** *"My golf is at last improving and am really delighted to be hitting a very reasonable ball. In fact last Sunday, I had the best game I have ever played with a 12 over par which was extraordinarily good for me at 65! We cleaned up the opposition, took 20/- off them, which did my heart a great deal of good!!I have never used more than 3 woods off the tee, but am now hitting a good 2 wood, and only wish that I had also got myself a driver. However, I am certainly happy with present results.*

The course has not really been looked after, as the Captain was a fellow called Col Gole, who though playing off 12, has not the faintest idea of his duties as a Captain. He was totally useless, but now has been replaced by Col Dube, a 5 handicap and DS In charge, Brig Rajaram, who is equally keen on getting the course back to reasonable state.

I get about 4 days golf in a week- Saturdays, Sundays, Wednesdays and Thursdays- when I play 18 holes, and usually fit in an hour's practice on Mondays and Fridays. Its only way to improve my game and I would like nothing better than to play to reasonable 12 which will be difficult but not impossible" **Unquote**.

By August 88 Admiral started the work on the construction of their new home-'BROADSIDES' and apparently had little or no time for golf, and that too when he was **just beginning to enjoy his game** ! In his letter of 8th November 88, **quote** "*It is rather cold and damp at the moment, with the rains having set in over the last few days but otherwise it has been beautiful weather. I* **have not set a foot on a golf course since the end of August.** *When we started the work on the house, and I am sure,* **I will not be able to play***, till it is all over. I could possibly get a game on Sunday, but playing once a week does my golf no good and I don't really enjoy that sort of game, unless I am hitting a reasonable ball.*

Saw an excellent video of the 88 British Open last Saturday at the WGC. They put it on, with 3 separate T/V sets and close circuit and it was really excellent. Bellesteros won it, by a stroke from a white Zimbabwe-Nick Price- who seems to be doing very well on the European Circuit". **Unquote**

As expected Admiral stayed away from Golf, he mentioned about this in his letter of 1st May 89, **quote** "*The construction has kept me* **completely off golf since August last year** *and the fact that both of us are generally quite weary at the end of the day and has kept us from accepting a lot of invitations to the parties".* **Unquote**

On 4th July 89 they shifted to their new abode-BROADSIDES-. In his letter of 30th Aug 89, **quote** "*I am looking forward to a little golf which I have not played over a year. The golf course is just about 2 kms from the house, so I should be able to get a game in or at least practice three times a week*". Unquote.

Back to Golf

In his very next letter of 2nd Oct 89, **quote** "*Yes, I have got back to golf, but I am at the moment, hitting about 100 balls in practice every 3 or 4 days a week , and will only get on the course when I feel that there is some consistency in my* *play. In any case I don't want to give my knee too much strain, though at the moment it shows no sign whatsoever, of any problems' must be walking 4 to 5 kms in a day and knee takes it very well. However, I do not want to overdo it, just yet".* **Unquote**

Admiral had a nasty accident and had fractured his femur in end July 89 and that's why he did not want to take any chances. I have covered it in detail in the chapter on 'Accidents'.

However, it was only in his letter of 1st May 91 when he mentioned about golf **quote** " *The golf course now got an absolute excellent Captain- Colonel Nicky Bajaj- who has improved it beyond all recognition . The tees have been doubled in size, the greens are much better and a sprinkler system has been installed which makes a great difference. The Commandant has given about 2 lakhs from the club funds for the golf course and I managed to get a lakh from Naval Chief during his visit last month. Fortunately Nicky will be staying on as a Captain of the Golf Course for another one year and I am quite sure he will really have it in A-1 shape by the time he finally hands over.* **I play about twice** *or thrice a week, though my game leaves a lot to be desired, I certainly enjoy it".* **Unquote**

In his letter of 27th July 91, **quote** *"Both June and July have been really quite wet and humid, and as I am penning you this letter, it is, in fact, raining at the moment. If one totaled up all our rainfall over these 2 months, it would just about be 10 inches (250mm),which is not bad for Coonoor, as we really get our rain during the North- East' but it is certainly not excessive. However, except for a 7 or 10 day dry spell over the last two weeks, we have had it generally wet throughout, with little sunshine, and a strong westerly wind most of the day."* **Unquote**

It is evident from the above letter that he did not play much golf in June and July and by late August Admiral suddenly started to have serious bouts of cough and breathlessness and was **admitted in Wellington Military Hospital in first week of September 91.** Thereafter, for over a year he was in and out of ASVINI hospital at Bombay for cancer treatment and checkups.

Final Visit to the Course

After **nearly one year** he did visit the Golf course and he mentioned in his letter of 11 Aug 92 (exactly to the day when I first entered the Golf course at NDA on 11th Aug 71!! **Co-incidence!**), **quote** *"I went down to the club last Saturday, thinking I will see a number of students playing, but was surprised to find hardly three or four of them on the course. There was also a tournament at Ooty, and I was told that a lot has gone up there, to take part.*

In the same letter he continues "We have been watching a lot of Olympics thru the kind courtesy of Doordarshan. Both Aunty and I however, felt that the 'sport' does not exist anymore. It's really a rat race for the gold which then brings a great deal of money by sponsorship. So, in fact, it's become a business and in endeavouring to succeed in this "business" athletes are on steroids, and all sort of drugs to achieve the goal of winning. The whole concept has got totally warped and the original aims of **clean and healthy sport** *just don't exist anymore. I was particularly sorry that the Hockey team of which so much was expected just faded out for no real reason and dear Limbu Ram did not quite achieve the standard of a medal, though I think he did us very well".* **Unquote**

That was his last visit to the Golf course, and brought down curtains to his beloved game 1948-1992, what a sad end!

This chapter on Golf has brought back so many memories with him on the golf course. How can I forget the 2nd Wednesday of Aug 1971 when he taught me, for the first time in my life, how to hold a golf club- overlap grip-my first baby step in the wonderful game of Golf and even today after 45 years whenever I enter a golf course, **I always look up and thank Admiral**, but for him I would have missed out the experience of this most exciting game and the **thrill** to see the ball roll from the fringe of the green towards the pin and hear it dropping in the bottom of the cup!! It can't be explained, it has to be experienced!! **God bless his soul.**

Yes, I still have the Golden Goose putter with me as souvenir and whenever I look at it so many memories just come flooding back to my mind, and few tears!

PS. Admiral always played in the afternoons on Sundays, primarily to attend Church Service, which he never missed. On holidays he would play early mornings and never disturbed Mrs. P and he would quietly tip toed from the bedroom at 5 am !

Pereira Cup

As CNS, at times Admiral played with retired Naval Officers. One day the retired officers came up with the proposal of starting a Golf Tournament in Admiral's name and requested Montee Chatterjee to initiate the proceedings. Admiral was informed of it and he immediately agreed to the proposal. Montee Chatterjee himself designed the trophy with three Dolphins and got it approved from CNS. The first Pereira Cup was played in autumn of 1980, initially only naval officers both serving and retired were permitted to participate and later it was upgraded to Inter Service Tournament. This tournament continued till mid 90's and then for some unknown reasons it was discontinued. However, Pereira Cup was once again revived when Admiral Sushil Kumar took over as Chief on 30th December 1998.

Admiral Sushil Kumar was very close to Admiral and Mrs. Pereira when he was posted to NDA as Lt Commander in the Naval Training Team in 1971/72, when Admiral was the Deputy Commandant. Army was requested to field two four ball teams. Captain Oberoi, Indian Navy (40TH, NDA, Delta), who was organizing the event came to my office and requested to give him some photographs of the great man, and he also informed the AHQ that Mike Bhalla be included in the Army team due to his close relations with the late Admiral Pereira. However, Vice Chief did not accept my name being too junior as he wanted to field team of senior officers only!? Notwithstanding an invitation (photo) for lunch at the Army Golf Course, Dhaula Kuan was extended to me on behalf of Admiral Sushil Kumar.

I asked Captain Montee Chatterjee if he ever took part in Pereira Cup post retirement. He replied; "Mike I was the founder member and designed the cup myself but unfortunately was never invited by the Navy", there was tinge of sadness in his voice!!

Finally, during my last posting before retirement, as Commander 111 Sub Area Bengdubi, suburb of Siliguri, in my tenure of 3 years I was able to make 18 greens golf course with help of two die hard golf stalwarts; Major Pradeep Gurung (retired, 42nd NDA, Delta Sqn) and Col TT Bhutia. The course (photo) is 6 minutes drive from my house!! Whenever I enter the course I always look up and **THANK** Admiral for introducing me to this fascinating game and I feel sorry for those who have missed out this amazing game called **GOLF!**

ACCIDENTS

Ronnie P grew up as a healthy kid who loved nature and outdoor activities. He was the Captain of his house E division relay team in 1934 and took part in all sports during his school days.

After joining the Navy he maintained very good health. Therefore, it was very surprising that, when he was barely 33 years old, suddenly he got an attack of Tuberculosis in 1956 and was immediately admitted in the Aundh Hospital near Poona for lengthy treatment. Unfortunately, the disease resulted in loss of lower part of his left lung. He recuperated but was very apprehensive whether he will be able to get back to SHAPE-1 category or he would be permanently downgraded, which will put paid to all his hopes of going further in his career. God was kind and he pulled through and regained his health without any permanent damage to his lungs and in due course was upgraded.

Cochin 1951

The first accident happened when he was posted at Gunnery School, Cochin in early 50's. Admiral Dick Schunker, very close friend narrated, **quote** "*After partition the make shift G school was established at Cochin and both of us were posted their as Instructors. As the guns had not been installed, a Frigate visited Cochin from time to time to meet the requirements of live firing at sea. RP had taken a class of sailors for close range Anti- Aircraft firing at sea (Bofors) when there was a miss fire and after waiting for stipulated 30 minutes the breach was opened and there was a blow back and RP who had stationed himself at the peep hole had his left arm shattered. I am told that RP slid down against the baulk wall and asked for a cigarette. He was rushed to a civil hospital where the first opinion was Amputation but on second thought Dr Khan the civil Surgeon decided to operate, fortunately the nerve was intact and the arm was saved. His left arm had a permanent bend at the elbow".* **Unquote.**

In fact the bend was quite prominent while lighting the cigarette.

After retirement Admiral had no money to buy a car, not even second hand one and he finally bought a Vespa scooter from the canteen! I spoke to Vice Admiral Kailash Kohli, who was NA to CNS in Feb 82 and he was the one who arranged the purchase of the scooter, **quote** "Mike, Admiral had no transport as you know he had to sell his Padmini Premier Fiat car in July 1978 to raise money for the construction of AT LAST, so he asked me to contact General Manager CSD, Bombay and get a scooter released on priority. When I approached the General Manager, he was taken aback that a retiring Service Chief is asking for a scooter, he apologetically told me that it does not behove of the status of a Chief and it is embarrassing and suggested, instead he should purchase a car, however I told him that Admiral cannot afford a car and you better release the scooter on priority!. **Unquote**

In last 25 years he must have driven scooter just couple of times including the ride to Germany Embassy for dinner in Sep 78, after he sold his car. Within first one month Admiral had clocked 1200 kms on the scooter and he seems to be enjoying it. However, Aunty Phyll used to keep cautioning him to keep a check on his speed, instinctively he used to drive rather fast, particularly in NDA where roads were wide with little or no traffic. It was over a year in Whitefield and Admiral by now had become accustomed to making regular trips to Brigade Road, Commercial Street, Canteen at RSI Club and MG Road on his scooter, which was about 14-16 kms one way. He never forgot to wear a helmet. On return to AT LAST, he would invariably shout "**Am home Phylloo**".

Scooter Accident 83

It was afternoon of 4th April 83, when Admiral was on his second trip to Brigade Road on that fateful day, he had made a trip in the morning and supposedly forgot to get Aunty Phyll's sandals, which he had given for repairs and in spite of Aunty trying to dissuade him from making second trip and telling him not to worry and pick them up on his next trip to town, but Admiral insisted to go and get the job done and told her; I will be back in an hour. At about 3pm after lunch he took off, it was a warm afternoon and as he approached ASMT School, Domlur (about 10kms) he started to feel bit dizzy, may be due to combination of full stomach and hot wind hitting him in the face, he momentarily blacked out and lost control of the scooter but he had the sense to go towards the curbside to avoid the oncoming traffic, which wasn't heavy in those days, he ultimately lost conscientiousness and hit the curbside right in front of the Air Command Hospital main gate, the scooter handle caved in and hit his stomach and he fell on the road. At that very moment a few MES workers were passing by and they immediately picked him up and took him to the MI Room in the hospital. The Nursing Assistant on duty took out the Identity Card to verify Admiral's identity and entered his name in the register as Administration Officer Pereira and took it to Squadron Leader Suri, Duty Medical officer. When Suri verified the ID card and realized it was Admiral Pereira, panicked and called up the Maj Ashok Chacko, Surgeon on call.

Recently I spoke to Ashok Chacko after a gap of 23 years and took him back to that fateful day, and requested him to narrate the sequence of events on that unfortunate day, **quote** "Yes , Mike I remember that day very vividly. I was 'on call' Surgeon on duty and was taking round of the wards, when Suri contacted me and informed that a retired Admiral is admitted in ICU and having dire problems with breathing. I immediately went to ICU Ward .There were no head injury, the helmet saved him , however on inspection I realized that his abdomen was very tense and decided to carry out Quadrant Check and as I poked two needles in two corners of abdomen, blood oozed out of right lower quadrant, evidently it was not head injury and immediately informed Senior Advisor in Surgery, Group Captain Ujjal Singh Pruthi , that a retired Naval Chief is in serious condition, and he rushed down to the ICU immediately and decided to operate and open up the abdomen. The operation started at 6 pm and went late into night. The spleen was totally damaged and removed through splenectomy surgery. Due to excessive bleeding, Admiral was transfused 14 pints of blood starting from pre operation, post operation and over next few days!! There was also some damage to the liver.

Being a retired Service Chief, the Army HQs was informed and immediately Air Force came into action and flew in Gen Ahuja, Senior Consultant in Surgery at AHQs to Bangalore. At the same time another Air Force aircraft was positioned at Poona to fly in Brig Harish Puri, Professor of Surgery at AFMC, Poona. And within 24 hours Admiral had the best doctors the Services could provide by his bedside.

After keeping him under observation for couple of days, Gen Ahuja felt that there may be 'bleed inside' and he carried out 2nd operation, but luckily there was no damage and closed him up. **Unquote.**

I tried to contact Group Captain Ujjal Singh Pruthi but was regrettably informed that he passed away in Feb 2005. However, I spoke to Mrs (Wing Commander) Pruthi and she said, **quote** "I am sorry to inform you that my husband passed away in Feb 2005. Yes, I remember Admiral and Mrs. Pereira very well and they were indeed very humble, lively and down to earth couple.

They were very grateful to my husband and we often visited their home at Whitefield. However, in 1987 my husband got posted out as Senior Advisor in Surgery, Command Hospital, Lucknow and after that we lost contact with them. My husband always spoke very highly of them. We were indeed sad to hear about Admiral's demise in 1993". **Unquote**

On my request Mrs Pruthi was kind enough to send me a picture of her husband.

Air Marshal Wollen , AOC-in-C, Western Air Command paid a visit to Air Command Hospital to meet the Admiral and pay his respects to him. Air Marshal was accompanied by his Staff Officer, Wing Commander BGPS Bhalla, my eldest brother, who contacted my Regiment in Amritsar and was informed that I was away on leave to Gangtok. He then called up 17 Mountain Division HQs and spoke to Gen Hanut Singh, my ex GOC, who immediately sent me the message and next day I was on my way to Bagdogra-Calcutta-Madras-Bangalore flight and reached the hospital late in the evening. On arrival in the hospital, I was told Admiral is asleep, so requested the Nurse on duty to inform Admiral as and when he wakes up that Major Mike Bhalla from Sikkim is waiting outside. The moment I mentioned my name, she told me Sir, every day Admiral used to inquire about you and ask if Mike Bhalla has come or not, I had such a sinking feeling and couldn't stop my tears. Anyhow, after waiting for 20 minutes the Nurse went inside and saw Admiral was awake and informed him, Sir, Major Mike Bhalla is waiting outside. Admiral in spite of being in pain had not lost his sense of humour **and with twinkle in his eyes he asked the Nurse; does he have long hair?** (As per tradition in the Cavalry we normally support long hair and Admiral was a stickler for hair cut!) For a moment she was perplexed and then nodded; yes Sir. OK send him in. She came out and asked me to go inside. It was for the first time since I met him in 1971 that I saw Admiral lying in a bed, his eyes were closed and I was really shocked to see him, totally emaciated, gaunt face with teeth jutting out and half the size of what I saw him a year earlier in Delhi, tears flowing down my cheeks, I held his hand and he opened his eyes and I asked him; what have you done to yourself? He held my hands as firmly as he could and softly said, **how are you my son, you know the Services saved my life, within 24 hours they had the best doctors by my bedside and I owe my life to them, particularly Pruthi.**

He mentioned about Air Chief Dilbagh Singh, Admiral Dawson and Gen Krishna Rao; they all came to visit him in the hospital. I asked him any message from Mrs. G (Prime Minister) **he said no, not even a flower!!** I stayed in Bangalore for 12 days and spent every minute with him. We used to talk and laugh, later; twice a day I would take him for short walk within the hospital compound.

So many people used to visit him. I remember one gentleman from Malayalam Plantation Ltd came and left the car key by the bedside and said; Ronnie , here are my car keys and you will not ride that bloody scooter anymore !

In his letter of 12 May 83, quote *"My dear Mike – I have just got your last letter. I came home on the 22nd April, semi-ambulant, and have since getting back, been worried with a very bad left shoulder that has severely curtailed my activities and keep me in bed for half the day. Aunty Phyll therefore runs around, looking after me, worrying about the house and generally doing far more than she should be. We therefore, both tied up in small way, and until I get back to normal which will take at least a month,* **I have not got a lot of time for letter writing. Indeed, as I pen this letter from the office table, a I am in considerable pain from my left shoulder.**

We are going through a very hot summer, with temperature in April being the hottest in the century. Till date, we have not had a shower of rain and it looks as if May will be as bad as the last month.

Just today, I had a card from Rajan-Hitler-who had heard from you, of my accident. It was thoughtful and kind of him, and I will write to him as soon as I am little better.

Our love and good wishes to Annie, babe, and her family. I have not got down to writing to them, but find it difficult to do so, in my present condition- love to you- Unc Ron". **Unquote**

Rajan was from 42nd NDA course and was relegated by Admiral in June 72 a few days before Passing out Parade for manhandling. A colorful and controversial character and his story is covered in chapter on 'Close Encounter'. Notwithstanding, he held Admiral in very high esteem like thousands of other cadets in NDA!! When Admiral asked Rajan; where do you come from? He answered; Rohtak- "Texas of India"- where everyone draws a gun before asking question? Admiral was taken aback and quite intrigued!!

He steadily and slowly got his strength back and but his movements were restricted within AT LAST. It was one of the worst summers. In his letter of 1st July 83, quote *"Since early June, we have had a fair bit of rain, and it has at least cooled the place down quite a lot.* **Bangalore was otherwise very** *warm and uncomfortable throughout April and May and we could certainly have done with a desert cooler. Which I shall install next year*". **Unquote**

Imagine at this stage, he could not even afford a desert cooler, as he had spent all his resources on AT LAST??- No car, no air conditioner, no desert cooler and no colour TV!! Some price for being honest!!

By end July he was getting better and he wrote in his letter of 28th July 83, quote " *I am all but 100% fit. The arm or left shoulder to be precise is much, much better and though I can still not swing a golf club I am sure I will be able to do so, in a while. It's really great to be able to do all the things that I used to, without asking for someone to help me or being unable to do them, and I therefore, really feel good.*

The weather in Bangalore is now beautiful. We have had a fair share of rain- not excessive, but enough to keep the place pleasant and cool and to call for a blanket in the early hours of the morning. It has been overcast for last week with few showers, and it's just the weather for Aunty who is now busy in the garden, getting it into the shape that she wants. After an unprecedented summer- one of the hottest on record- it's been a great break, and given Aunty the much needed relief that she wanted. **She just cannot take the heat, and it really knocks her out.** *"* **Unquote**

Dog Bite

Admiral, by mid 1984 had completely recovered from the scooter accident when he had another unfortunate mishap; bitten by a stray dog! In his letter of 9th June 84, **quote** "*Once a year, I seem beset to be subject of some mishap, on the 6th May 84, coming back one evening from a visit to some friends, I was bitten quite badly by a dog that came into our compound and attacked Cindy. I was in fact trying to separate them and on lifting up Cindy who was in the middle of brawl, the other dog leapt up and bit me. In fact his canine tooth caught me for about 3 inches, deep and long wound.*

Dr Pruthi as usual treated me, but Cindy and I had to have anti-rabic shots. I however, cannot take our own vaccine made in Kasauli, as this is quite harsh drug and can cause and result in quite a few effects, like paralysis. I therefore, had to get the new French vaccine-MERIEUX- which the Navy immediately flew down from Delhi. It is however, expensive-300- an injection- and one has to take 6 injections over a period of three months. There is no necessity to take in the stomach. It is very small injection which comes with disposable syringe, it's own *needles, the vaccine and is taken in the arm. I have finished 5 and will have the last one on 6th August which is the 90th day"*. **Unquote**

Bus Accident

On 4th July 89 Admiral and Aunty moved to their new abode **BROADSIDES** at Coonoor and as they were in the process of settling down Admiral met with a minor accident with a bus, which kept him immobile for a month or so. In his letter of 30th August 89, **quote** *"Just as we almost finished the move, I had an Argonaut with a bus, which resulted in my fracturing the patella or knee-cap of my right leg this landed me in the hospital for 15 days, with dear Aunty Phyll having to sort things out and settle in on her own. The patella fractured into 5 pieces, but as my leg was also lacerated and required about 20 stitches in various places, they could not put me in the plaster immediately, till the wounds heal and stitches came out. I was therefore, in a splint in hospital and was extremely well looked after. After 10 days the stitches came out and the leg was put into plaster, and on 15th day I hobbled home happily.*

As of today, I am all but normal and just have a crepe bandage, which the doc wants me to retain for another month. It gives the knee added strength, but does not hinder me in anyway, and I am back at driving the car. In fact, there is no pain whatsoever- in fact there never was any real pain and patella has set beautifully without it being removed. I am now looking forward to playing golf". **Unquote**

Apart from these minor to major mishaps, Admiral maintained a very good health for most of his 70 years. In fact while in service for nearly 40 years, except for attack of Tuber-Culosis in 1956, Admiral was **never** hospitalised what so ever.

All three accidents were post retirement and could have been avoided if he had listened to Mrs. Pereira and been more careful!!

LOVE FOR DOGS

Admiral belonged to a family of dog lovers and they always had more than one dog in their house during their stay at Dumka, Patna and Hazaribagh in 20's, 30's and 40's. The best house as per Aunty Maise Gantzer was "Balmoral House" of Superintendent of Hazaribagh Jail.(photo)

Ceaser

In 1971, in NDA , then our beloved and terror in the same breath 'Dep Com' had a lovely golden Labrador- Ceaser, very cute and playful dog but most feared by the cadets as his early morning (between 5am and 6am) appearance in the squadron lines heralded the arrival of Dep Com , and he is somewhere around the corner and most of the occasions Ceaser will be roaming in Delta squadron and Dep Com will be on the prowl in Foxtrot squadron and the staff car in front of Ecko squadron ! Why I say Delta Sqn because Ceaser knew the location of my cabin and he would climb the steps to the first floor and come to my corner cabin which was opposite of Tea Room, looking for me with his tail wagging vigrously. However, Ceaser did not live long as he was diagnosed with cancer and unfortunately was put to sleep sometime in March 74 at Vizag . Both Admiral and Mrs. Pereira were heartbroken.

However , I have been informed by Hugh Gantzer that Ronnie Pereira first dog was a black Cocker Spaniel named '**Okay**' sometime in 60's.

Smokey

Anyhow within a month they got another lovely pup in the house. Aunty Phyll in her letter of 25th April 74, quote "*Tomorrow our new dog arrives from Bombay – a highly pedigreed Sydney Silkie- also very expensive - he cost us Rs 500/-*" unquote

They named him 'Smokey' and both Admiral and Mrs P loved the little fellow. They made a small bed for him in a round cane basket with mattress and small pillows and placed it between them at night. Every morning at dot 5.30 am Smokey would make funny noises in Admiral's ears to wake him up for the morning walk. Smokey was barely 8 inches tall, grey shade and very cute indeed. Admiral would bathe him, then scrub him dry, comb his long hair, put ear drops in his ears and eye drops in the eyes, and tick powder all over his small body while talking to Smokey in dog language, no doubt Smokey enjoyed all the attention and would continuously make all kinds of small noises with his perked up ears moving up and down and giving euphoric looks and Admiral ,would say -Hold it boy, hold it !!

In his letter of 20th August 74, Admiral wrote, **quote** *"We have really had hardly any rains this year, and the only real shower that fell about three weeks ago was so heavy, that it completely flooded the place!! Our own house in Naval Park was under 2 ½ feet water and the whole compound was covered in sheet of water, the only fellow who really enjoyed it was our little 7 months old puppy-Sydney Silkie called Smokey- who kept jumping off the verandah and taking himself for a swim, while Aunty Phyll fretted and fumed thinking that he will get drowned!! Sydney Silkies are very small dogs- hardly 8 inches above the ground and this fellow of ours is really small. However, not only did he prove himself to be a good swimmer, but he was not in the least scared of water. All that happened every time he jumped into water, was that Aunty would shout, and I would take off after Smokey and he would have wonderful time dodging me!!!* **Unquote**

Smokey followed them to Cochin, Bombay, Delhi and finally to AT LAST.

My first encounter with Smokey was in Aug 1975 in Cochin, when I spent about a month with Admiral and Mrs Pereira. Smokey was very cute grey coloured dog with silky coat, whose height was less than the length of the body. I was informed that his breed was named after famous Australian city of Sydney, as most of this breed was found in this particular city.

Every morning Admiral would take Smokey out for a walk and he will run around and if he wondered away, then Admiral would shout 'heel' and immediately Smokey will fall in line and obediently follow at Admiral's heels giving him soulful looks, as though telling him I haven't done anything wrong!! Most of the mornings during my stay with Admiral I would accompany him for morning walks along the channel. In Cochin there was an open ground next to the Navy House, and Smokey would have a field day running around. I believe now a Golf Course has come up there. During my stay in Bombay in July/August 76 every morning without fail we would walk along the breakwater towards the sea with Smokey following Admiral's heels.

The Admiral I Knew – A True Story of Admiral Ronald Lynsdale Pereira

When Admiral moved to Delhi in April 77, he was allotted a bungalow 5, Moti Lal Nehru Marg in Lutyen Delhi and there also every morning the same ritual followed, and Admiral ensured that Smokey did not stray on to the road, though the traffic was minimal at that time of the day.

However, when Admiral moved to Navy House 12 Rajaji Marg in June 1979, the traffic had increased a wee bit and Admiral was very careful with Smokey as he was so tiny that a driver may not notice him on the road.

Few days later exactly that's what happened which Admiral had feared all this while. He would come out of the Navy House and turn left towards the roundel to Race Course Road and being VIP area of Lutyens Delhi there were very few cars on the roads. One fateful morning instead of going towards Race Course Road Admiral turned left towards Akbar Road, on which Air House is located on 23 Akbar Road. Few moments later a Staff Car came speeding down the road and before Admiral realized Smokey was in the middle of the road right in front of the car and being so small the driver apparently did not notice Smokey and reacted at the very last moment and brought the car to screeching halt and Admiral heart came to his mouth thinking the worst for Smokey, he rushed towards the car and there to his great relief Admiral saw Smokey crawling out from under the car!! He immediately picked him up to see that there were no injuries and fortunately he was fine except his small heart was pounding like a drum! By now Admiral had lost his cool and let the driver have it, he shouted the hell out of the driver and said- you don't know how to bloody well drive the car, just because you are driving VIP car, it gives you no right to drive like a maniac etc etc – embarrassed driver was almost trembling and muttered, Sorry Sir. Admiral would have nothing of that apology as he almost ran over his beloved Smokey. Admiral gave his identity to the Sergeant and asked his name and directed him to report the matter to his superior, whoever he is and - I will deal with you later.

Admiral came back fuming with Smokey in his protective arms and Smokey supposedly telling him- "Papa I am sorry, it was my mistake and I did not see the car coming towards me , it was my fault and am grateful to the driver, who did not hurt me so please don't punish him and I promise I will never step on the road again, please I am sorry and words to that effect"- but Admiral told Smokey to shut up and notwithstanding your plea I still hold the driver responsible for rash driving and severe action must be taken against him !! After reaching home still hot under the collar Admiral told Aunty Phyll - how a nincompoop of an Air Force driver just about killed Smokey !! Aunty immediately retorted – Ronnie, I always told you to keep Smokey on leash and don't let him wonder about when you go for walks outside the

Navy House, but you wouldn't listen to me !! And taking Smokey in her arms she said -my poor little baby, you must have got the fright of your life and **Smokey replied** "dear Mommy, what you mean by fright, I almost had a heart attack" !!!

This must have happened at about 6.30 am and by the time Admiral left for office 2 ½ hours later, his famous temper had cooled down and he realized he was bit too harsh with the poor driver and as he drove out of 12 Rajaji Marg , he directed his driver Sharmaji to drive to Air HQs !

Admiral reached Air HQs unannounced and without any prior information resulting in bit of a commotion on seeing a 4 star Staff Car. A senior officer came rushing out to receive the Chief of Naval Staff and saluted smartly and welcomed the Admiral. The frightened driver was standing in the car park fearing the worst! Admiral spoke to the officer about the incident in the morning and requested that no action to be taken against the driver, then he called the driver - Sergeant - and put his arm on his shoulder and said, son, be careful in future and drove off !!

That was Ronnie Pereira at his vintage best - a 'Chief' concerned about an airman, never mind from different service?

Cindy

Smokey was the only dog in the house for over 4 years. Then one morning Admiral came across a beautiful black mixed Apso, who seemed to have lost his way and was looking quite confused, Admiral immediately sensed that it was a domesticated dog and called him, and he responded, and brought him home and gave him water, milk and bread. It was in fact a female dog and was very friendly and affectionate dog and kept following Admiral around the house. Admiral took her photograph and put up an advertisement for lost and found in TOI paper and few days later an Army jawan came to 5 MLN Marg claiming the lost dog. Admiral asked him – where had he come from? - and he said that he is presently working with a General Sahib, so Admiral asked him - what's the dog name? - **Cindy** - Admiral said OK call out her name, as he shouted Cindy the dog inside responded and on release from her chain she ran straight into the arms of the jawan. Admiral knew it is indeed General Sahib's dog because unlike human being dogs never lie! Later in the day, Lt Gen Nanda, DG Works walked to Admiral's office and profusely thanked him .

After 6 months the same jawan came back to 5MLN Marg and this time he was carrying a small pup in a basket with ribbon tied around his neck and handed it over to Admiral, saying General Sahib has sent this pup as an act of gratitude. They named him '**Cindy**' after his mother!!

Cindy was a playful dog but his presence was resented by Smokey ? As he found that Cindy was given undue attention by Admiral and am sure he complained to Aunty Phyll- Mommy, I don't like Cindy as he is getting more attention than me!-. Anyhow after few months they smoked a peace pipe and thereafter, all was well between them. But Aunty always gave preference to Smokey being senior or politics!!!

In summer of 1979 Admiral and Mrs. P visited Srinagar on the personal invitation of Lt Gen Jasbir Singh, GOC, HQs 15 Corps. They also made a trip to Leh, HQs 3 Mountion Division and were felicitated by GOC, Maj Gen CM Somanna, GUARDS, who presented them with a pair of pure Tibetan Apso. But Admiral accepted only one as they had two dogs at home. This pup was eventually given to Aunty May in winter of 79, she named him 'Honey' and lived for over 17 years and died within 2 weeks of Aunty May's sad demise in 1996 ! I do have photograph of Honey with Aunty May, Hugh Gantzer and Colleen taken in June 89.

Smokey lived to 11 years and in 1985 he lost his eyesight and was knocking his head around and sadly was put to sleep.

Cindy lived with them for 10 years and when we went for a short break from Wellington to Whitefield in Dec 86, my children had field day playing with Cindy. He went along with Admiral to Coonoor as mentioned in his letter of 27th Oct 87, quote *"we left AT LAST on 30th August and motored up to Coonoor with Cindy very comfortably"* unquote . That was the last time they mentioned about Cindy.

Cindy didn't live very long thereafter and he was dead before they moved into BROADSIDES in July 1989.

BATTLE WITH CANCER

Admiral kept very good health and he had energy to work for 10 to 12 hours a day even as Chief of Naval Staff. After his retirement in March 82, apart from three accidents, (two very serious and one minor), which I have covered separately in the chapter on 'Accidents', he never complained of any pains or aches nor did he have any serious ailments till Sep 91!

In reply to my letter of birthday greetings to him in May 90, he wrote in his letter dated 5th June 90, **quote** "*Thank you son, for the last letter of the 24th and your good wishes for my birthday. I am now in my 68th year- it sounds really old, but I must thank God for the fact that I am still generally very fit and have nothing to grumble about. An odd ache and pain appear, but passes away, but I give these small ailments, if one can call them that, little thought, as they are not worrying about. Life has certainly been good to me, to say the least and I have lot to thank God for*". **Unquote**

Admiral good health also permitted him to look after old age people, particularly those who were alone and had no member of the immediate family to look after them. While in Whitefield, he was the first person to extend help to such victims. He often used to visit the Little Sisters of the Poor, Old Age Home, Richmond Town, Bangalore. This is one of the traits he inherited from his father.

After a break of nearly three months, in his letter dated 27th Oct 90, **quote** "*My dear Mike- I have not written for ages and I do apologize for this lapse, must thank you for all your letters. The reason for my silence has been the fact that we have been tied up with a dear old lady of 84, who sadly fell and broke her femur and this was indeed a big disaster. The husband a serviceman, since long retired and passed on. I had her in the MH for some time, but though they looked after her very well indeed, there was **no orthopedic surgeon** to do special job on her. She had almost a month in Nursing Home **with Phyll doing 24 hours** nursing on her every other day, and a friend stepping in for Phyllis off-*

days. She is now back home and doing splendidly, though not quite 100%, which may take another month or so.

However, this has kept all of us very busy and little worried, as she has just no one in India, with three daughters married in Britain and all working, one having lost her husband 3 months, one divorced and looking after 3 children and one girl nursing & also supporting a large family, and therefore unable to give up her job and come out.

Fortunately the old lady had resources to meet all the expenses, with 24 days at the MH costing the **large amount of Rs 144/-(!!!)** and about 40 days at Nursing Home, setting her back the lady **a sum of Rs 26000/-!!!**. Whenever I see something like this I thank God that most of us still have a Military Hospital to fix us in our ailments.

Smoking

In 1956 Admiral was diagnosed for Tuberculosis and was hospitalized in Aundh, Poona and ultimately resulted in loss of two lower lobs of his left lung. In spite of this mishap he just could not get rid of what he called 'wretched' habit of smoking 30-40 cigarettes a day and some time more. He tried to give it up many times but couldn't sustain. The last time he seriously tried to give up was as late as in November 90. In his letter dated 27th July 91, **quote** *"I have been off cigarettes since late Nov 90, but until one has gone for at least one year, it is as easy to give it up, as to go back to the 'wretched' thing! I don't miss them at all and never have in earlier attempts, but more often than not, just when I reckon that the habit is behind me, have gone back to them"* **Unquote**

During the 16th Cavalry, Raising Day Celebrations on 8th Sep 91 at Babina I happened to meet Mrs Neelam Dewan w/o Colonel Wandy Dewan (who was my first Squadron Commander in Jan 74 at Pathankot). She was on her way to Coonoor to see her sister Rekha Butalia w/o Col Bob Butalia of Hodson's Horse, who was posted at DS, at Staff College. I requested her to take a small parcel of Basmati rice and Rajmah for Mrs. Pereira and a letter for the Admiral. She called on the Admiral on arrival and handed over my letter with the parcel.

Breathlessness

Soon thereafter, I got a letter from Admiral dated 28th Sep 91 **quote** *"My dear Mike and Annie- Thank you son, a million, for your last two letters, the second of which was brought by Mrs. Dewan with a parcel of lovely goodies for Phyll and I.*

It was really very sweet of you to do this, but you just must not in future. You have a family and they are your main concern. When you have little extra at times, it is them that must be catered for and not us. Thank you son, again very very much, but you must not do this in future.

The reason I have been amiss in writing is that I have not been keeping well, over the last two or three weeks, with a considerable degree of breathlessness which effects me in my activity. I had no such problem at all earlier and really did not tire, no matter how much I did during the day and I certainly enjoyed doing things round the house. However, **this ailment came upon me quite suddenly,** *and as a result I have had our hospital check me out, which has been done very thoroughly.*

The Medical Specialist has given me a very detailed check though with ECG, X-rays and whole host of chemical tests. They seem to attribute it to a problem in my right lung- **it was the left lung which worried me 35 years ago-** *and I am now on course of treatment for 7 days, before going back for further tests. Fortunately for me the hospitals at Coimbatore are really excellent and if any further tests are required outside of the scope of our MH, I can get them done at Coimbatore. My cousin Dr Shiela Pereira- was at Vellore for 40 years and has now retired in Coimbatore. If Coimbatore is indeed necessary, I will contact her and she will certainly put me on to the best institution there.*

However, there is nothing to worry about just now, nor am I in the least concerned or perturbed, except that I am restricted a bit in what I can do, physically till the condition improves. At the end of 7 days, I am sure I will feel better" **Unquote**

Admiral's cousin, Dr Sheila Marie Pereira, MECP, FRCP, born in 1927, was daughter of Mr. Robert Pereira, younger brother of Admiral's father and did her medicine from Edinburgh, Scotland.

Colonel RK Roy

At this juncture in 2015, I was very keen to find out who was the Commandant MH Wellington in Sep 1991. It was not an easy task to look for someone you don't know from Adam, nor his name or where about, but I had no option but to try and locate him. So the first action was to contact the present Commandant at MH Wellington. Brigadier GS Gurunadh, who I found very supportive and within 24 hours he gave me the name-Colonel RK Roy, but no forwarding address or contact number, obviously I was asking for someone who left Wellington more than 22 years ago. The MPRS at Army Hqs gave names of half a dozen Col Roy, I tried the one with address in Kolkata and sure enough I got through to Col RK Roy. As I inquired about Admiral, initially he was speechless and then he spoke with so much love and affection for him that he almost had lump in his throat recalling those sad days.

Quote "Yes, I remember vividly that Admiral came to our hospital sometime in mid Sep 1991 and he was suffering from a severe bout of cough and breathlessness. I immediately put him through all chemical, blood, lipid tests, plus X-ray and ECG. He was personally attended by the Medical Specialist Major Batra. Being a VVIP patient we were very very careful in deciding the course of medication. It appeared he had bronco-pneumonia. As you know he had problem with his left lung way back in 1956, when he lost lower part of his left lobe and over a period of time the outer membrane thickens leading to infection which in medical terms we call PLEURISIO and due to dust and allergy his right lung seems to be suffering from bronco pneumonia. He was immediately admitted to MH and put on 7 days of medication by giving him tablets, pain killers and cough syrup etc. During his stay at MH I would meet him every day, morning and evening to check up his health condition and Admiral would say; don't worry Doc I am in safe hands and hospital is like my home. He was always cheerful and full of optimism and positive in his outlook. However, after a week the Medical Specialist once again subjected Admiral to all tests including X-ray and he found a patch on his right lung which was indeed cause of worry.

Patch on Right Lung

As MH was a small establishment of few specialists e.g. Medical, Surgical and Gyneacologist plus small det of Dental. The hospital did not have the necessary equipment to carry out any further tests on Admiral and we had to refer him to Kuppu Swamy Naidu Hospital at Coimbatore. After due tests it was discovered that there was a "patch" on his right lung which was malignant and requires immediate chemotherapy/radiation. Accordingly in mid Dec 91 Admiral was evacuated to INHS ASVINI, Bombay" **unquote.**

Apparently he was on medication in Oct and Nov 91 and I did not hear from him and was beginning to get worried once again and sent him a long telegram and he Immediately responded.

In his letter dated 02 Dec 91, **quote** "*My dear Mike and Annie-thank you for your last letter, the subsequent wire to which I immediately replied c/o 56 APO, though the telegram came from Allahabad, which had me quite foxed. As I said in the telegram, I am certainly much better with my cough about 99%*

*better and the breathlessness greatly improved to the extent of 80 % or even more. However, the last X-ray indicated that **the patch on the right lung which is the one giving me problem,** is still there and the MH at Wellington has not quite got the equipment and facilities to do further tests to find out the reason for this. I have, therefore got the summary of my case from the Med-Specialist with the results of all the test as well as the X-rays and will be going down to Coimbatore to the Kuppuswamy Naidu Hospital, where the Dean is General Krishnan to get their thoracic specialist to do the necessary tests and continue any treatment that may be necessary. However, it is **nothing to worry about** and I am quite sure that the problem will be resolved in a month or so. I will be in Coimbatore this coming Friday".* **Unquote** (I had gone to Allahabad as instructor Pre Staff College)

Notwithstanding, the grave situation, Admiral still seemed to be very positive and hopeful and did not let the results of tests depress him and feel low or worried. **He always took life as it came and thanked the Almighty for his kindness.** It was his strong and devout religious bent of mind which kept him going ahead fearlessly and I personally experienced this attitude till the very last moments of his life on 14th Oct 93.

INHS ASVINI Bombay

Expectedly by mid December 91 he was advised to move to Bombay for further tests and treatment at Tata Memorial Cancer Hospital. In his letter of 30th Dec 91, **quote** *"As you will see I am at our Naval Hospital I.N.H.S ASVINI, where I had myself admitted at the middle of this month, for all the tests concerning the patch on my right lung. I was advised to do so, by the Kuppuswamy Naidu Hospital at Coimbatore whom I also visited to give me a check, as though I was not feeling any ill- effect whatsoever, **the patch remained on the lung and this was of concern to the doctors.** Indeed the doctors at Kuppuswamy Naidu Hospital then asked me to go down to ASVINI and get a full check up at TATA MEMORIAL to try and find the reason for the patch.*

Malignant Growth

*My tests have all been done, and **the final verdict of the medics is that it is a malignant growth on the right lung,** which has been there for about a year or more. Fortunately, there is very close liaison between the ASVINI the Naval Command Hospital and Tata, the naval doctor who keeps an eye on me- Surg Commander ARUN BEHL had just finished 2 ½ years attachment at the Tata Memorial after his post graduation in Surgery. He is now handling my treatment which will be Chemo-therapy and not radiation at this stage and I am at the moment just going through my first course. **This is a 23 days cycle,** with the* *first injection on day 1, then a break of 20 days, then the last three injections on day 21, 22, and 23. The reason for this that Chemo-therapy can have reactions- falling hair, nausea, ulcer in the throat and mouth etc which may occur, and they watch for these after the first injection. I started on the 28th Dec and yet I have not had a single reaction. My appetite is enormous- I am eating like a horse, there is no nausea at all, this is very usual and certainly I find no sign as yet of ulcer in my mouth or throat.* **I therefore, have lot to thank God for.** *At the end of the course they will re-assess my condition and start the second cycle, and possibly on a different time frame to the first, but it will again be 4 injections.* **In fact depending on progress- and I have no doubt that it will be there-** *I can be given a course of radiation if they consider that my lung can take it . Initially they had avoided radiation, as* **my lung capacity is low-45 %** *and though radiation will expeditiously attack the growth, the peripheral effect of the radiation can also lower the lung capacity further, which they do not desire. So the whole question is matter of watching, re- appreciating and starting another cycle of treatment.*

I could not have been in better hands anywhere in the world. The doctors of Tata Memorial are the finest in the profession and some are world authorities. The Navy has laid on everything for me – car, liaison officer, lovely ward , TV, phone, VCR- and it has got to the stage of almost embarrassing. My room is full of flowers, there are so many callers, friends that they had to cut my visitors, as at this initial stage they don't want me strain my vocal cords or use my lung too much. The Nursing Staff is excellent, and my dear niece, Jennifer- Admiral John Pereira's daughter who is married and lives in Colaba- insist on sending all my food- absolutely super fare which she brings herself. I am therefore, not only in the very best hands and excellent care, but I just don't require anything at this stage.

I came down alone, by train-DSSC laid it all- but as soon as I went to the hospital Aunty Phyll followed and she has lovely suite in the mess which is hardly 1 ¼ kms from the hospital. Personally I feel fine, like I have felt all these years- not a twinge of pain, excellent appetite, steady weight, **but cancer is there** *and must be treated and I am sure our* **Lord** *will have me home in about 3 months and back to normal.*

I think I must do something in return for all that 'He' is doing for me. I am sure He wants something of me and I pray and ask Him to enlighten me .May be it to work for the underprivileged or in some measure. Help Him to get a wee bit of sense in this totally materialistic earthy stupid community of human beings. I would really like to be of some use at this fag end of my life, for God has really been over-kind, generous and infinitely good to me.

I will be writing regularly, I will keep you precisely informed for I will not pull the wool over your eyes, but don't come down. If I need you I will say so". Our love and good wishes to Annie and the family. Look after yourselves and may 1992 be a great year for all of you. affily Uncle Ron. **Unquote**

Bombay

Same evening I was on the first train to Bombay after I received the letter. I knew he will shout and ask me to go back to the unit. I arrived next morning and rushed to ASVINI, of course he was surprised but happy and gave me a big bear hug, yes, and I had tears rolling down my cheeks. How could I not come and give him the moral support. I stayed for three weeks and spent every minute by his bedside. It was seen to be believed how many people of all shades from Admiral to retired sailors and all his well wishers, who came to meet him. There was so much laughter in his presence, particularly the ladies, to whom he always addressed as 'my girl', but the moment they came out of the room, stood next to the pillar in the verandah and quietly cry to themselves as they could not bear to see such a good human being in pain. I vividly remember the famous artist, Mrs Eilla Menon w/o Admiral Menon, she sat with Admiral for while, chatted and laughed talking of good old days in the Navy and how they all lived as a close knit family just to humour the Admiral and he would nod his head and kept repeating, yes, my girl! I escorted her to the car and remember how kneeling against the car, she just broke down and it took some time to compose herself, the question was same –why should nice people suffer? When I came back to the room, Admiral told me, that Mrs. Menon was lady of international fame and repute and her husband Raja Menon was an outstanding human being of great intellect.

In spite of being in pain Admiral never complained. Though he laughed whenever someone came to see him, but it was bit subdued , at times, there was sparkle in his eyes particularly when in Admiral's presence Aunty Phyll narrated the incident of an ex sailor Darshan Singh , who served in INS Delhi, came all the way from Punjab to see his beloved Commanding Officer and so sweetly brought Uncle's favourite Mango pickle, and with tears in his eyes, said - Sahib my wife sent this for you, Admiral gave him a tearful hug, though he knew he could never eat it, but it is the very thought which moved him. **Admiral always loved his men and Darshan Singh made him feel GOOD.**

In spite of Doctor's instructions on the contrary, Admiral specifically told me, son, don't let anyone go without meeting me even briefly, after all they have taken great trouble to come and see me - through the horrible Bombay traffic. The doctors had actually put a curfew between 2.30 pm to 5 pm- No Visitors Allowed- board was displayed on the door. Still people used to come and wait to see him. In case Admiral heard any sound in the verandah, he would immediately say son, go and see who has come? There I saw an elegant lady , very fair with deep navy blue eyes and someone of European origin, was waiting in the verandah and I wished her, she said- I am Mrs. Peck . She came in and said in her lovely voice 'Hi Ronnie' , you are looking good- and she embraced him, so much to talk and share old memories. Later I got to know that her husband was Rear Admiral Surgeon Peck, Admiral's colleague and very close friend. At times Aunty Phyll admonished me for allowing visitors to see him, but Admiral would bail me out and say, I asked him, don't blame the poor lad!!

One day Admiral Barboza came to see him and how they laughed and cracked jokes, later Admiral mentioned to me, son, you know in Navy nobody has better sense of humour than Eric Barboza and great brains !

The Indian Cricket team was playing one day series in Australia and we would watch all the matches and he would really enjoy them and shout along with me cheering the team. He was not particularly happy with Azaruddin's captaincy as he lacked aggression!!

There was no question of any one smoking in his presence, and Aunty Phyll was still smoking on the quiet. On the very first day she asked me to go the Paan shop next to Colaba, Post Office, and get her 4 packets of Charms, and told me not to mention it to Unc?? Admiral would ask me, son, is Aunty smoking? - no, she is not! But deep down within he knew the truth!!

Initially Admiral showed no sign of nausea but after a week he had few bouts of nausea and used to rush to the toilet, but most of the times he could not vomit , it was only the sensation to throw up , but still he never complained, he would lie down and close his eyes with Rosary in his hand. He had great faith in God and would say son, 'Lord will look after me. He never had a frown on his face, still at peace with himself.

He told me how he survived the attack of Tuber-culosis in 56 and lost lower part of left lung. At one time after the TB sickness , he thought that he may have to quit Navy and he was not sure of his future , leave alone promotion but he did not give up and continued to work as sincerely as he could and ultimately reached the top, for which he always thanked the Almighty.

How he almost lost his left arm in the firing incident in early 50's in Gunnery School, Cochin. In fact at first the Doctors decided to amputate his arm but then one civil surgeon Doctor Khan realized that the nerve was intact and carried out a successful operation, however it left permanent bend in his left elbow. Then the scooter accident in April 83, the Lord saved him as it happened right in front of Air Command Hospital, Bangalore. The details are covered separately in chapter on 'Accidents'.

Though he enjoyed my company but one day he did mention, son, honestly I am not happy that you came in spite of my advice, but I told him, I also have a conscience and how can you expect me not to come, after all you have given me so much love and affection in last 21 years and **it will take me many lives to ever repay you or Aunty, he looked deep into my eyes, listened and didn't say anything.** At times he spoke with his eyes and conveyed a lot by his body language -such as holding your hand tight, it meant a lot! I stayed till the end of first cycle of chemo-therapy, in fact I wanted to stay longer but he insisted that I go back and look after the squadron and my men.' I am getting better and Aunty is here to take care of me'. I left Bombay very reluctantly and didn't know when I will see him again?

In reply to my letter, he wrote dt 10th Feb 92, **quote** *"My dear Mike- thank you very much for your letter dt 27th Jan, which came in last week. I am quite sure that **I am now much better and have no doubt that I will be back to normal by the time the hospital finishes with me in 2 months.** There is, therefore, no reason to be worried because I am in the best medical care that is possible in India, as far as cancer is concerned; this is comparable anywhere in the world. Therefore, Mike, DON'T think of coming down again. It really upset me far more to see you waste your money, as there is absolutely no need. Indeed, I have stopped my own family from doing so, for the same reason, though May had decided to come down with Colleen for three days as Colleen is to see her mother, before she and Hugh go to Austria for winter sports and thereafter to Germany and Britain. They leave on the 18th Feb, if I did need you or the family; I would have no hesitation in asking you to come, so don't unnecessary waste your money".* **Unquote.**

By the time I received his next letter dated 20th Feb 92. I had already been transferred to HQs 57 Mountain Division, Guwahati, Assam. **Quote** *" Son, thank you very much for your letter of 10th February which came in on the 18th.I had also written to you C/O 56 APO also on the 10th, but I don't know when that will catch up with you, as it will now has to be readdressed to HQs 57 Mountain Div. I am very well and feeling better every day. DON'T come down to see me at all. That would be waste of money and totally upset me. Any case , I* will be out of the hospital for three weeks at least in the next few days and am still deciding what to do during this break and depending upon its length, as Aunty is going back on the 29th Feb. Your dear father wrote to me a very sweet letter. I am replying immediately. Our love and good wishes to Annie and the family; afftly Unc Ron". **Unquote**

By 21st Feb 92, doctors asked the Admiral to take three weeks break. In his letter dt 16th Mar, **quote** "*My dear Mike- thank you very much for your letter dated 26th Feb which I collected from the hospital early this week, on my return from URAN, where I spent a week of total relaxation with Admiral John Pereira who runs a motel- cum- restaurant on his 10 acre property which he has had for about 25 years on Uran.*

I am at the moment at the mess, have been here **since 21st Feb, when I finished my 2nd course of chemotherapy.** *The reason for break is that the hospital wants about 3 weeks or little more, to let the second course of injections have their effect, before I am given a thorough examination to determine the effect of the treatment and the subsequent line of treatment which the doctors recommend for me. Some of the tests will be done at ASVINI and some at TATA's and this will possibly take about a week. I shall continue to remain at the mess until it is all over and they decide on the actual line of treatment. However, at the moment I am feeling much better and I am sure this will show up in all the tests. Let us see.*

Today, rather this evening, is something called "HUSBAND's NITE" and 500 couples, all Servicemen, are expected. I don't quite know what it is all about but there have been great activities through the day, with stalls being put up by the ladies, and some sort of entertainment being feverishly rehearsed by a crowd of them. C-in-C had asked me to join him and his wife, but I have declined, as I find any sort of a late night tends to tire me out. **In any case tomorrow is a Sunday, and I have early church at 0700, which means getting up at 0530 hrs and that will be little doubtful with late night".** **Unquote**

A devout Christian, who imbibed this sage quality from his dear mother. **It is because of this strong faith in 'Almighty' that kept him going and was still hopeful that he will come out of this illness.**

In early April 92, he was administered radiotherapy. In his letter dated 24th April, **quote** "*My dear Mike-thank you very much of your letter of the 16th April which came in yesterday, and for your letter of 10th March, which found its way to me today !!! The address on the envelope is correct, but it is franked 18.4.92, so I am not quite sure where it has been. Nonetheless, it was nice hearing from you.*

The mess has just had a dish antenna installed and all the cabins are wired up for cable TV. We get Star Plus and BBC and it is reasonably good, particularly for Sports which I always enjoy. There are some reasonable films but I have yet to see a good comedy as most if the films have morbid and grim theme. **As for the music channel, I have never believed that anyone could watch such utter bilge and discordant noise, shouted out at the top of one's voice so that one just can't discern what the devil the singer is singing about!!!!**

Radiation

I am now completing **my second course of radiation** *which finishes on 30th April and I will then be going home for about 2 months before I return for possibly some more treatment.* **The growth has now gone down 40-50 %, which is good,** *though I feel they were expecting even greater regression. However, I feel good and the break at home will certainly do me a lot of good, as I am really getting a* **little tired of Bombay after about 5 months of being here.** *Aunty went back in the 2nd week of March, as we have both been away from 'BROADSIDES' for close on 3 months, and it was necessary one of us got back and opened up the house. However, it was in good shape and had been well looked after by the bearer."*
Unquote

Within ten days Admiral was discharged and left for Wellington. In the letter dt 4 May, **quote** *"My dear Mike- this is going just a day before I leave Bombay, by the time it arrives at Mhow I will be home at* **'BROADSIDES'**.

Had two lovely letters from Mahli and Bedi, both of whom you must have spoken to about my hospitalization, I have written to both of them.

Bombay is certainly is back to high humidity and hot and sweaty days and since about last week of April, it has been uncomfortable. However, I will be out of it soon enough and though Wellington may not be as cool as one would like it, the humidity will certainly not be there- **Bombay is 75 % at the moment and steadily rising and it will, therefore be much nicer than this hell hole** *!*

I am feeling much better after all my treatment and also looking forward to my two months at home, as I have been away since December 91. The rains have fortunately now broken in the Nilgiris, so it is much cooler and the tea which was in terrible condition after months of drought has now picked up and began to recover". **Unquote** (I had gone to Mhow to attend Senior Command Course)

Next six weeks I did not hear from him and was beginning to get worried and it was only in early July, I received a letter dated 2nd July 92, and by then I was back in Assam after my SC course, **quote** "*My dear Mike- this letter should have gone off a long, long time ago, but with a long list of jobs to be completed at 'BROADSIDES' and just 60 days to do them all, I kept going- and indeed enjoying myself- in a endeavour to put them all behind me, only to find that there were still quite a few to be completed when I get back.*

*This letter is being written from INS Agrani, the Naval Establishment at Coimbatore, where I am spending few hours, before catching my train to Bombay today at 2230 hrs. I am on my way back, **after really lovely 60 days at home** and will possibly be in Bombay for about 30-60 days depending on what treatment I am put on.*

*The growth has actually **decreased by about 50 %** and the doctors did tell me that they were very pleased with the progress as they reckon that they have it under control. **However, it is necessary that I have some treatment- either chemotherapy or radiation- before they can really say that the malignancy has been totally killed.***" **Unquote**

Within a week I received another letter dated 10th July, **quote** "*As you will see I am at Bombay and have been here since the 4th.* **Getting all my tests and X-Rays done and indeed bone scans and ultra sound scans of my abdomen, to make certain, that nothing has spread and that the malignancy is confined to the lung.** *Finally, yesterday we took all the results to TATA's and saw their top Surgeon Dr RAO, and head of radiation, Dr Dinshaw. Both of them went very carefully thru the documentation and gave me a thorough check- up. They were very pleased with the progress and said this was much more than they expected. In fact their decision was that I **needed no further treatment at this stage** and I could go home and **come back after three months for the normal review!!** I was delighted to hear this and have already got a reservation back, for the 14th, which will get me home by mid-day on the 16th.*

Bombay is hot and sticky and has an added problem of a very grave shortage of water, as the monsoon has literally disappeared and except for one or two showers initially, there has been nothing further. The result is that the lakes are almost empty and unless it rains in the next fortnight, there could be very serious problem. I hate to think what might happen if 12 million of people have no water to drink." **Unquote**

It is evident from this letter that Admiral was slowly and steadily getting his strength back and indeed he never felt like this in a year, so it was very encouraging sign and I felt really happy for him as he has been through very rough one year.

Check Up

In his letter 02nd Oct 92, **quote** "*I am very well and will be going to Bombay on the 15th for my quarterly check up. I don't really like going, as Bombay is really a dreadful place, but I will have to continue these **3 monthly checks till the end of 93** and then if all goes well, **it will be once in six months**, for the subsequent year*"

25th Sep 92 was their **40th Wedding Anniversary** and Admiral and Mrs. Pereira were very keen to celebrate in style. He also requested his brother Arthur to come and join them for the occasion, which he did.

He added "*Son thank you very much for your good wishes for the 40th Anniversary. We decided to have all our buddies to lunch at the TAJ Hotel- the Garden Retreat- which has now been set up at Hampton Manor which they have bought over. They did us very well indeed and I had saved three bottles of Champaign for the occasion, which they kindly permitted to open without corkage. This was certainly gracious of them.* **My brother is also here from Calcutta, so it was really good get together. He is now 83 but very fit indeed.**

I don't know if you saw the Davis Cup matches between Britain and us, which were played in Delhi. Peas and Krishnan played very well indeed and Brits were badly beaten- indeed they were out- played without any doubt. It always delight me to have us beat them in any sporting activity, as the Brit is sadly always under the impression that the Indian is no competition for them. I am quite sure that in tennis it was a question of over confidence and he was seen off in no uncertain manner. They will surely blame the heat of Delhi, but if they expected us to play it where the weather would suit them, is just too much!!

Our love and good wishes to Annie and the kids. Frankly, I think you are shirking responsibility by leaving them with your in- laws. Remember, you as their father, must be responsible for bringing them up. At least, keep them with you during the holidays, with our love –affly Uncle Ron". **Unquote**

It can be seen from the above letter that Admiral was in a better state of mind and enjoying every moment of life. Deep down he was not sure whether he will be able to celebrate next year so they went full hog ahead this year. **Admiral was particularly HAPPY that his brother Arthur could join him for the occasion.**

However, the re-union with Arthur was cruelly short lived, in his next letter dated 22 Nov 92, **quote** *"I got back from Bombay on 3rd Nov after clean chit from all my doctors. I will not be seeing them again till Feb 93. Sadly my dear brother Arthur, who was with us at Wellington for our 40th Anniversary, has been diagnosed as having cancer of the right lung, exactly as I have it. At 83, fortunately, he is still very fit and has taken the news very well. He is being treated at Calcutta with radiation and am sure this will do him lot of good".* **Unquote**

I think Admiral was very upset to hear about Arthur's sickness. Eldest sister Aunty May, 80 (Mrs. Gantzer) was suffering from acute arthritis, Aunty Bobby,75 was staying alone as Paying Guest at 29, Museum Road, Bangalore- all these put together were taking its toll on him. He was particularly worried about Aunty Bobby, who had come back to India from Argentina after 44 years and she was good to him when he was doing long Gunnery course in UK in 47/48. And for some reason she and Aunty Phyll could not see eye to eye and perforce she had to shift out of ATLAST in early 83 and thereafter had to fend for herself in alien city till she passed away in 2006 at the age of 90!

Relapse

In his letter dated 14 March 1993- **quote** *"I got back from Bombay on the 10th Feb after all my checks and tests and the doctors were very pleased with the progress. That evening while resting at home, Phyll found me having ague and shivering a great deal and I was immediately admitted to the hospital, where they found out that I was feverish. I think it was the long journey- 36 hours from Bombay- and the fact that I had a very bad cough which was not responding to anti-biotic or any treatment. Anyway I am still in the hospital, but the cough is now very much better and I am certainly feeling well again. I expect I may be here for another week and will then be home again"*. **Unquote**

I was amazed why he had to take such a long and dusty journey by train when his health did not permit him to travel for such long hours and it surely aggravated his cough. He could have easily taken a flight to Bangalore instead and he would have been home in 8 hours. But his answer was that he could not afford it. In fact Aunty Phyll also travelled by train .I wonder what did he gain by being so straight and neglecting his own comfort. The system surely didn't appreciate his INTEGRITY but that's the way he lived, one need courage and mental strength to withstand the corrupt system. Unbelievable man, from different era!!

> "BROADSIDES"
> Wellington - 643231
> Nilgiris.
> 14 MAR 93.
>
> My dear Mike,
>
> Thank you for your letter of the 25th February which got to me on the 28th. It's good to hear you have been busy + officiating for GSO (Ops) That would certainly be good experience.
>
> I got back from Bombay on the 10th Feb. after all my checks + tests, + the doctors were very pleased with progress. That evening while resting at home, Phyll found me having ague + shivering a great deal, + I was immediately admitted into hospital, where they also found I was feverish. I think it was the long journey — 36 hours from Bombay — + the fact that I had had a very bad cough which was not responding to anti-biotics or any treatment. Anyway, I am still in hospital, but the cough is now very much better, + I am certainly feeling well again. I expect I may be here for another week, + will then be home again.

I spoke to Colonel RK Roy in Feb 2016, who was Commandant MH Wellington at that time, -quote "Yes Mike, I do remember Admiral being admitted in Feb 93 and he was suffering from DYPNEA or severe breathing problem and bad cough, I immediately put him on oxygen for 48 hours, and positioned a Nursing Officer (Major) to monitor the flow of oxygen as per the instructions given by Medical Specialist and thereafter we were giving him intermittent supply of oxygen depending on the requirement. At night we used to disconnect the supply of oxygen, however, a Sister was detailed, who kept a constant watch over Admiral and in case there was any uneasiness he could be administered supply of oxygen even without disturbing him as we had a tube inserted in his nostril .This continued while he was in the

MH for nearly 1 ½ month and after his discharge, we had also made similar arrangements at BROADSIDES to meet any emergency. BROADSIDES was about 1½ km from MH and ambulance would take 7 minutes to reach. Evidently the weather as well as altitude of Coonoor was not suiting him. In addition our being a small hospital we were not well equipped to look after a VVIP like Admiral and I advised him that it will be better if he moves down to Bangalore at the earliest. **Admiral would smile and say – don't worry Doc, I know I am in very good hands and this hospital is like a home to me, you and your team has taken good care of me and I am happy here, and if I have to die I better die here only**"- still I insisted that it will be more comfortable at lower altitude, Sir. However, after his discharge in late March 93, I ensured that he was kept under constant observation by the hospital staff by making regular visits to his home. Then one night sometime in later half of May Admiral got a serious attack of breathlessness and he was immediately shifted to the hospital and put on oxygen and he stayed on for a week and seeing the seriousness of the condition, I requested that he must go down to Coimbatore for a checkup." **Unquote.**

Commander Anup Singh, who was posted at Staff College as DS Coord Navy was indeed very close to the Admiral and Mrs. Pereira and he and his wife would make it a point to call on them 3 to 4 times a week.

He told me, **quote"** Mike, after Admiral returned from Bombay in Feb 93, his condition started to deteriorate. He spent nearly 6 weeks in the MH Wellington and was put on intermittent supply of oxygen through April and May including spending one week in the hospital in later half of May. I remember it was early June and Admiral was indeed having great difficulty in breathing, and the doctors at MH were getting very worried, so they advised him to go down to Kupuswami Naidu Hospital at Coimbatore for a detailed check up.

Kupuswami Naidu Hospital

Admiral refused to travel in an Ambulance and directed me to arrange a Staff Car. I accompanied Admiral and Mrs. Pereira to Coimbatore and before we started Admiral asked me about the advertisement in the Times of India regarding the sale of B'SIDES, and made it clear he will accept nothing under the table. I told him Sir, I have done it. Secondly, he told me that he would like to be alone when he interacts with the doctor at Coimbatore, as he wanted to discuss serious and sensitive issues with her and under no circumstances Mrs. Pereira to be present.

After reaching the hospital I informed Mrs. Pereira that she should stay out when Admiral meets the doctor, to which she out rightly refused and insisted to be present and listen to the doctor views. However, I managed to convince her on the condition that I will stay along with the Admiral during his interaction with the doctor. The doctor happens to be **Dr Shiela Minakshi, his first cousin**.

Admiral; Doc, please let me know how much time do I have? Weeks or months?

Doctor; Admiral why are you worried, you are fine and on to the road to recovery.

Admiral; That is not the answer to my query, I want you to be specific, how much TIME do I have?

Doctor; Listen you are such a great man, who has served his country so well, don't worry. You will be fine.

Admiral; listen my girl, I have lot of issues to attend to before I go and I must know how much time I have? I need to sell BROADSIDES, then buy a flat for Phyllis in Bangalore and settle her before I turn my toes!

Doctor; I would advise you to please move down to B'lore at the earliest as Coonoor is not suiting you. That's all I can tell you, Ronnie!

As he came out of the doctor's chamber, he turned around and remarked- Anup this is the **damn result of smoking for 56 long years**! And added let us look for Bata showroom; I want to buy a new pair of sandals!!

Anyhow, Admiral did not get the answer he wanted and we drove back to Coonoor and reached B'SIDES by late evening. It was indeed very sad and particularly I was feeling sorry for Mrs. Pereira as in her heart of hearts she knew that the situation was grim and they must move down to B'lore at the earliest."

After his return from Coimbatore, my wife and self used to visit them most of the evenings and have drink or two with them. One evening Admiral was in rather good mood and decided that he himself will pour drink for Commander Anup, to which Aunty objected as Admiral was on oxygen and did not want him to get up from his chair and insisted that she will pour drinks for two of us. After a while Admiral noticed that Mrs. P had poured Indian whisky and in an instant Admiral disconnected the tube from his nostrils and walked over to the kitchen and said, no, **today we will have**

bloody scotch- so he took both the glasses from Mrs. Pereira and threw the drink down the sink and fixed two glasses of large scotch for himself and me and said 'cheers' and gave the drink to me. Even in that late stage of cancer, Admiral never lost hope and always positive and never wanted to attract pity from anyone. Not only that he would come out and see us off and once insisted that he would like to come down the steps, (about 20) to see us off till the car, here I put my foot down and humbly told him Sir, in case you come down to see us off then am afraid we will not come to look you up again. Admiral heeded my advice.

Few days later, one evening during our regular visits Admiral went inside and took out his 'Sword' and said Anup this is yours and when you become Admiral you will need it. I did not accept it and told him, Sir, I suggest that you present the Sword to his ex Flag Lt Bhaskar Sen, he deserves it more than anybody else but Admiral won't have any of this and insisted I accept- I did not budge- then Admiral turned around and said I know why you are not accepting it, because being an ex CNS I will be buried in full uniform and Sword will be kept next to the body- doesn't matter if you don't accept it now, **but it will come to you after I go**- And sure enough one year after his demise during my visit to Bangalore I called up Mrs. Pereira, she said you better come and see me, and I went to see her. Mrs. Pereira went inside and took out the Sword and said- Anup this is yours- it was Admiral last wish and am not going to violate it, so you better accept it, I had no choice and accepted with tears running down my cheeks". **Unquote**

Yes, Anup retired as FOC-in-C Eastern Naval Command!

Admiral final letter was dated 16th June was typed letter, because he wanted to Xerox it and send to all his relations and friends. **Quote** *"My dear dear Mike- with my inability to really catch up on my letter writing, I will try and give you, all our news in this rather rambling epistle, I will then Xerox, and send it around to all of you- friends and relations- to keep you updated.*

I went down to Coimbatore last week, to the Kupuswami Naidu hospital and got my check up done by Dr. Shiela Menakshi, an oncologist at that hospital, who has wealth of experience. The cancer is well under control, and the doctor was pleased what she saw= said I had not a thing to worry about at this juncture. However, as I may have mentioned earlier, **the treatment of lung cancer with radiation , has resulted in some of the live lung tissue being destroyed** *. This result in reduction of lung capacity, with the result that the body does not get enough oxygen, and you are therefore severely restricted in your movements. A* **walk of 20 feet leaves you puffing and blowing like a whale.** *However, one*

has to learn to live within this capacity, which is not easy but very necessary."
Unquote

Rest of the contents of the above letter are covered under chapter on 'HOME'

Command Hospital Bangalore

Admiral condition drastically deteriorated in August 93 and on 20th Aug he was evacuated by IAF helicopter to Air Command Hospital to Bangalore accompanied by Major Batra, the Medical Specialist, who was looking after Admiral at MH Wellington.

At that juncture I was posted at Imphal and our division was deployed to contain the worst ethnic cleansing in the history between Nagas – Kukis in Manipur. On 23rd Sep I received a call from one of my friend Col Anil Bhatt and he informed me that Admiral's condition is very serious and he is admitted in Air Command Hospital Bangalore. I immediately took a flight and left for Bangalore via Imphal-Calcutta-Madras and reached on 25th Sep late in the evening and rushed to the hospital. As it was pretty late and Admiral was already asleep so came back early next morning.

Last Days

He was indeed very happy to see me and I sat next to him holding his hand and tears flowing down my cheeks , he slowly asked me how are you , my son ? I couldn't speak, he said why didn't I come early? I said nobody informed me! He was surprised as he had requested Aunty Phyll to inform me, but she did not as she said she got confused about the address. Anyway, I was with him and used to spend 12 to 14 hours sitting by his bed side. Every morning during my visit to the hospital, the first action was to touch Admiral's feet and put my head on them and same ritual before leaving at night, just to thank him for touching my life and being more than a father for over 22 years. He would hold my hand and take short naps and then open his eyes and smile at me and speak halting and asked about the kids and my job in Manipur, but never complained about any pain. He always had Rosary in his hand and would keep praying. At times I used to go out of the room and if he woke up and did not see me, he will immediately shout '**Mike**' and the Sister would come running out and say Sir, Admiral is calling you.

He used to wait for Aunty Bobby and would repeatedly ask me has Bobby come to see me and don't let her go back without meeting me, doesn't matter even if I am asleep, wake me up. She was his blood sister and he felt guilty that he could not look after her and she was staying as Paying Guest, it used to hurt him a lot.

By now his kidneys were packing up and whenever he felt the pressure, he would say, son - bottle - I would first make him sit up by propping him against 4 or 5 pillows, then get the enamel urine bottle and hold it, Admiral would take long and deep breath and try to release but nothing would come, after holding him for over three minutes I asked him Unc have you come? He turned around and said with a twinkle in his eyes – **son, I am in no hurry!!** Even at that late stage he had not lost his sense of humour!! In fact not once did he complain. I used to change his clothes and clean him up as and when required, though Sister objected, I told her please let me, **you don't know how good this great man has been to me for past 22 years and even if I try for 7 lives I can't pay him back, so please try to understand** and after that she did not say anything. In fact, the only way I could thank 'Almighty' for blessing me with love of such a great 'human being' was that **I never punished a jawan in my entire service of 36 years!** Instead woke up every morning with single minded aim- how can I help somebody? Immaterial whether I knew that person or not.

Admiral used to feel sad and guilty about Aunty Phyll and say "Mike, I feel sorry for Philloo that she has no roof over her head and now I realize that I should have listened to my friend Doughlas Kinglee for not moving to Coonoor, it was a **terrible mistake** and now we have nothing. You look after her and he would say same to Debbie Shea, Aunty's God daughter, whenever she came to see him. And yes, Debbie kept her promise and **indeed looked after Aunty Phyll very well**. I spoke to Aunty every other day and later from 2000 almost every day between 9am and 10am, just to ask her, how is she? I also made regular trips to Bangalore to see her and Aunty Bobby.

Last few days were painful and uncomfortable, and before they put him on ventilator and life support system, he spoke to me alone-he did not want even Aunty Phyll presence, who first tried to dissuade Admiral from speaking to me, as she felt he is not in a position to speak, when Admiral insisted, she wanted to be present in the room **but he was adamant and told her firmly-" leave the lad alone with me".**

Final Advice

I sat next to the bed on my knees with folded hands and tears flowing down my cheeks, in any case, those days at hospital most of the time I was crying-

Admiral spoke to me in halting manner, as it was difficult to speak, he said- "son, listen to me very carefully,-in life, never, never hanker for MONEY, never be greedy- if the Lord wants he will find ways to help you and the wheel of fortune will turn, but if Lord doesn't want, then you can try as hard as you can, the wheel will not move and it will be no win situation, always remember this. Son, always try to be a good human being and look after you men, love them and breed them tough and they will follow you to the end of the earth. There is no better soldier than the Indian soldier in all Armies of the world and I am sure one day you will command 16th Cavalry. I will look down from the heavens (making a gesture toward the ceiling) and feel happy and proud of you, my son- look after your Thambis. Look after Aunty Phyll and Aunty Bobby, and I do feel guilty that I was not able to look after her, she was a good sister, and God bless her. Also be good to Annie, she is simple but a wonderful wife and mother. Imbibe good human values in your sons and make sure that they grow up to be good citizens. Then he slowly bent down held my face in his palms of his hands, looked at me for a while and kissed me on my forehead and said all the best my son; thank you, you were always a son to us which we never had, take care of yourself and God Bless. He kept looking at my face for a while, exactly as he did on 4th Aug 1971, only difference was, the sadness in his eyes, then softly he said, son, I want to lie down now and I slowly put him against the pillows and that was the LAST time he spoke!! I stood there numb and speechless. He opened his eyes couple of time and smiled and held my hand tightly.

Next two days were very difficult and he was put on life support system and he could only speak with his eyes and would gesture to remove the pipes. Group Captain MM Singh senior surgeon came to me and said it is no point keeping him on ventilator and we should remove it. I told him he must ask Mrs. Pereira, he asked her but she didn't reply. Admiral Dawson who was by his bedside would ask me to call Ronnie in his ears and as I used to say Unc, he would react and open his eyes briefly.

14TH October 93

On the morning of 14th Oct 93 he started to sink ,Col Ashok Chacko, who had looked after Admiral after his accident in April 83 had arrived for his mother's birthday also on 14th the previous evening from Kapurthala, Punjab, he came straight to hospital in the morning and at noon he came out and told me, Mike Admiral's pupil are dilating and the end is very near, he took me inside and flashed torch at Admiral's eyes and there was no contraction of the pupil, which indicated Admiral sad demise. I was blank and stunned and after little while Mrs. Pereira came back from town and held Admiral's head in her hands and quietly cried to herself.

In him I lost a father, friend, philosopher, guide, mentor and a GREAT HUMAN BEING.

However, right till the end he never compromised on his principles, no matter what ever be the consequences. He was true 'ICON' to the future generations of the three services and society at large.

State Funeral

Honestly this was the first occasion in my life when I was handling a dead body. Helped by Commander Anup Singh, Commander Bhaskar Sen and Lt Col Ashok Chako we washed the body and dressed him up in Admiral's whites with full medals. The Admiral was given a state funeral on 16th Oct 93 and the burial took place in the Cemetery, Hasur Road, Bangalore. Prior to the funeral the body was placed in ASC Centre South for Wreath Laying. I remember we had to carry the coffin for last KM and there were 8 Pall Bearers, and after 100 meters they were being rotated, but I refused to be replaced though my shoulders were bleeding as the stars were digging into my skin, but that was the least I could do for a man who has been so good to me, **to give him a shoulder in his final journey!**

There were more than dozen Admirals including the serving Chief Admiral VS Shekhawat, two retired CNS-Admiral Dawson and Admiral Ramdas. Air Marshals and senior Army officers plus hundreds of officers and sailors and civilians. It was indeed a heart rending experience to lower down his coffin to the sound of Last Post. A great soul consigned to history.

Tribute By General Hanut Singh

Gen Hanut in his letter of 5th Jan 1994, **quote** *"My dear Mike- I had gone to Jodhpur on my annual visit to the Ashram of Pujya Sati Mata, at Bala, and received your letter on return. It carried sad tidings and the sadness was enhanced because the news of his passing away was so unexpected. I did not know that Admiral was so ill. Cancer in final stages is extremely painful, though with modern medicines much of the pain is ameliorated. I do hope he was free of pain and passed away peacefully. I, for one, have antipathy for the so called life support systems. If there is hope for recovery, then there is some meaning in putting a patient on life support system, but if a person is terminally ill, it is tantamount to* *cruelty to extend his life by few more days, because he is only clinically alive; and for all other purposes, he is virtually a vegetable.*

The news of the passing away of people whom one has known, serves to remind us of our own mortality. And when we look back, we regret all the wasted years, because the main purpose of our having attained human birth, remains unfulfilled. The way is long, and for people like me, the time remaining is very short.

It is indeed a blessing, if God spares you infirmities and indignity of old age, and calls you away while you are still up and about. The greatest blessing, of course, is to die young and in battle, at the head of your men and with your face to the enemy. In England they hold an annual remembrance day for their dead, where they pay homage by very apt and moving prayer:-

" they shall grow not old as we that are left grow old; Age shall not weary them nor the years condemn; At the going down of the sun and in the morning, we will remember them!"

The English do these things rather well! The Admiral may have gone, but I hope I am around to see you attain your lifelong ambition to Command 16th Cavalry. Hope this finds you Annie and the children well. With good wishes- yours as ever Hanut" **Unquote**

Every winter Gen Hanut used to visit Sati Mata ashram 65 kms from Jodhpur on Ajmer-Jaipur road and spend over 3 months there and was totally cut off from the world, hence delay in sending his condolences. Amazing human being and had great following world over.

PURGATORY

Speaking to Cdr Hugh Gantzer regarding the pain and agony suffered by Admiral in his last years of his life , I mentioned to him " Sir, I saw Admiral from very close quarters for over 22 years and believe me I never ever saw him doing anything which was wrong or outside the parameters of "goodness and good human conduct". I don't think he ever harmed a human being or failed in his duties to help a needy person"

Hugh Gantzer replied, **quote** "Mike, you may be gauging him from your own prism and refuse to see any faults in Ronnie, which in my opinion is subjective assessment. There must have been many who hold totally contradictory view. It's very likely that in his long career of 40 years, he would have certainly made some people unhappy or rubbed few on the wrong side!! Let me explain to you;

There is something known as 'PURGATORIUM'. This word is derived through Anglo-Norman and Old French from the Latin word-**purgatorial**- has come to refer to a wide range of historical and modern conception of post mortem suffering short of everlasting damnation and is used, in a non-specific sense to mean any place or condition of suffering or torment especially one that is temporary.

According to Catholic Church doctrine, it is an intermediate state after the physical death in which those destined for heaven "undergo purification, so as to achieve the holiness necessary to enter the joy of heaven"

In simple terms it is a **half way house** between hell and heaven. To get to heaven one has to be cleansed of his misdeeds by a process of 'purgatory' and good men, chosen by God wipe out their misdeeds by suffering from pain and anguish. **That is why Admiral had to undergo so much of pain and discomfort for his entry into heaven.**

RIP, God Bless his soul!

REMEMBERING THE LEGEND

SURGEON CAPT ARUN BEHL, VSM

Admiral mentioned in his first letter dated 30th Dec 91 from INHS ASVINI that Surgeon Commander Arun Behl is keeping an eye on him. Therefore, when I started to write on his battle with cancer, Arun Behl was in my thoughts, however despite my best efforts I could not contact him for over 6 months and finally it was on 26th September, 2016 when I got his contact number from Manoj Asthana.

After nearly 25 years I called up Surgeon Captain Arun Behl and introduced myself "Good morning Sir, I am Brigadier Mike Bhalla speaking", before I could go further he replied, **quote** "Hi, Mike you have a long life, it was only the previous evening, I was at Jennifer Pereira's (daughter of Admiral John Pereira) residence along with her brother Michael and his beautiful wife Zarine and all of us were discussing the chapter on 'Pereira's family' in your book! (I had sent the draft to Michael for the information of his father) and here out of the blue I get a call from you!!" **Unquote**, could it be Karmic connection!?

I immediately came to the reason of my call and requested him to please share his experiences with the Admiral while he was treating him some 24 years back.

After about a month I received a mail from Arun Behl.

Quote "See, Mike, Admiral was a formidable human being and I have never come across anyone like him in my entire life. On the day of Admiral's first consult in the hospital, Rear Admiral Sharma, the Commandant of INHS Asvini along with the team of all specialist HOD's from Surgical, Medical, Pathology, Radiology, Cardiology and a few more were at his bedside taking his history of illness, examining him to arrive at a diagnose and find out what was ailing the Admiral. I was in fact, called there on second thoughts by the

Commandant. So I went and joined the group and they were all of the collective opinion that the Admiral was suffering from Pneumonia/Tuberculosis. I did not get a chance to examine him with the entire medical hierarchy present there but managed to get close enough to have a good look at him and asked the HOD medicine about the lung findings. When all had expressed their opinion, he looked me straight in the eyes called me to his side and asked. "Young man what is your opinion. Why are you quiet?" I looked him in his eyes and described a text book picture of Superior Vena Cava Syndrome, his puffed eyelids and face, engorged, tortuous and bounding Jugular veins in the neck, along with dilated veins around the right shoulder and told him Sir, you have a patch, which in spite of good antibiotics over a period of three months at MH Wellington has increased in size, I suspected that my first diagnosis would be cancer with may be an associated pneumonitis patch.

The Admiral inquired, how this could be proved, so we took him to the Radiology department had his X-rays followed by a CT scan done and by the evening it was an all too obvious diagnosis that he was suffering from a **malignant cancer of the right lung** which had entrapped his superior vena cava. Thereafter, pointing his finger at me he told the Commandant that hereafter, Surgeon Cdr Arun Behl is going to look after me. So I was picked from the crowd of the doctors to deal with his sickness.

We did his CT guided biopsy and I explained to him the stage of his disease and prognosis and generally people with SVC syndrome had a poor prognosis and he has 4 to 6 months to get his house in order. He told me he understood the scenario but requested to keep him going for 18 months. He explained that his only interest was to look after his wife after he was gone. "**I have no money and I have to sell my house in my life time.** I can only do that after a period of 5 years. We bought the land 3 ½ years ago and I don't know what you do but you will have **to keep me alive for next 18 months so that I can do the needful**". I told him, "Sir in such cases you do not survive beyond 6 months, it's a natural course and there are no negotiations on this aspect." Admiral said, doctor "that's your problem not mine -1½ years I want, get it!" So strong was his will power and resilience that he survived for 22 months!

I must tell you why I was apprehensive to meet the target of 18 months. Firstly Admiral had suffered from Tuberculosis in 1956 resulting in loss of two of his lobes of left lung. On top of that he had been a heavy smoker.

He was already surviving on compromised respiratory system i.e. 1 and 1/3 lung. Though, he was upgraded to carry out military duties. The real problem was that the tumor was too close to the heart and the radiation would certainly effect the functioning of the heart and lung.

He tolerated the first two cycles of chemotherapies very well, but after the third he developed low white blood count with fever, what is called febrile neutropenia. This is a life threatening condition, he was administered heavy antibiotics and put in barrier nursing, with no visitors allowed only nursing staff fully gowned with mask permitted. One fine Sunday morning I got a call from the Security personnel that Admiral had walked out of the hospital with a bed sheet wrapped around him in pajamas, the security staff requested him to please go back to the ward but he walked on to the direction of the RC Church. I immediately got dressed and rushed to the church and sure enough Admiral was sitting in the front row. After the service and receiving the Holy Communion as he walked out, I went up to him and asked him how he could walk out of the hospital in his present medical state? ; "Sir, you can't do this, it is not acceptable, you don't realize that you can easily pick up an infection which could precipitate further complications". He said,"Son, I have never missed a single Sunday service to receive Holy Communion and I am not going to start now, If the good Lord has given me a cross to carry he has also given me the strength to carry it, however, I do appreciate your concern". With that he got in my car and we drove silently to the hospital.

I then told him that I could arrange the Holy Communion to be delivered to him at the hospital itself whenever he desired. I then went to RC Church and met Father Matthias and gave him Admiral's name and the background of the sickness and requested if he could come to hospital on Sundays to deliver the Holy Communion, he happily agreed. Hence forth as long as he was in INHS Asvini he got his holy communion every Sunday.

The balance of his chemotherapy and radiotherapy went off well. He was then put on a medical surveillance schedule and every three months he used to come from Wellington to INHS Asvini for a review, His malignancy had been checked, and we were steadily inching towards the eighteen-month target.

On one such visit Admiral was staying at the Western Command Officers Mess; a staff car with LO was detailed to bring him to hospital for a periodic check up. Firstly he dismissed the LO and told him that you don't work for me, you work for the Navy. That was that. He was scheduled for an appointment with me at 1030 hours I waited for him for 30 minutes beyond his scheduled time, checked twice with Western Naval Command Mess,they confirmed that he had left. Those were the days of no cell phones, and so

I left a message at the OPD reception to bring him in to my consultation room as soon as he arrived and got on with the job of attending to the rest of the OPD. At about 12 o' clock I came out to once again check and noticed the Admiral sitting quietly in the corner. I went up to him and asked, 'Sir, why didn't you come inside?' His answer stumped me; he said, 'Doc I was late for my appointment, **I have no right over the other patients who are also waiting to see you, I will come in when my turn comes.**' typical of Ronnie Pereira; I had to tell him that this was not acceptable and attended to him. Actually the reason for delay was.... That enroute, while passing through NOFRA (Naval Officers residential area) to the hospital he noticed an overflowing sewage drain in front of an Officers block and he immediately asked the driver to turn the car and drive to CWE office. There the Chief Engineer was in a conference and Admiral walked in and introduced himself and personally took the CE to the site on the ground, and told him Naval officers don't stay in such conditions, please attend to it immediately. On the way back he checked that pumps were in action to clear the block. What can you say of a man like this?

Another occasion when I was seeing him off after an appointment at 4 pm, he suddenly turned around and asked me to come and sit in the car. I told him that I would just get my cap, he said doesn't matter you come, I want to meet Mrs.Behl and want to have a cup of tea with her, if you don't mind and I hope I am not imposing myself! So we drove to my flat unannounced. I was staying in Archana apartments on the 12th floor. We went up and were sitting in the balcony from where one gets a beautiful view of the US Club, and the sea. Suddenly Admiral said; 'where is the bloody wall? I don't see any wall! Get Johnny on the line'. I didn't know who Johnny was? But soon then realized he is referring to Admiral Johnson, FOC-in-C Western Naval Command, a little while later Admiral Johnson was on the line, I requested him to hold the line while I got Admiral Pereira. 'Johnny where is the bloody wall between the Western Command Officers Mess and US Club, which I had personally sanctioned before I moved out to Naval HQs in April 1977'. Admiral Johnson was taken aback as he had no clue about the wall, but said, 'Sir I will look into this and come back at the earliest.' The CE managed to dig out the file and indeed a sanction was given by the C-in-C. Admiral Johnson called up Admiral Pereira and told him that he was right and didn't know the reason for it not being made, however, he would give a fresh re-sanction and see that the wall was constructed. After a few months when Admiral again visited our home, he was happy to see the wall between the mess and US club!!

After the chemotherapy and radiation Admiral's heart started to weaken. When he came back to ASVINI in Feb 93, I told him 'Sir, your cancer is well under control but I am worried about the condition of your heart and you MUST consult a Cardiologist".... which he did.

Few days later I proceeded to Pune to attend a medical conference. A formal dinner was schedule for all the participants. Knowing that it will be a typical Fauji affair I decided to make a face presentation linked up with good friends and decided to skip dinner and instead go to one of my close friend's house. We were all having a nice time when suddenly at about 12.30 am, there was a call from GOC-in-Chief Southern Command* and my host Col K S Rao, Cardiologist, went to attend the call. The Army Commander asked to speak to Surg Cdr Arun Behl. I was wondering how the Army Commander knew I was here and why would he like to speak to me at this unearthly hour. The Army Cdr told me that Admiral Pereira had been taken ill and he had received a message from Admiral Ramdas, CNS, and you need to speak to the doctor at MH Wellington, the exchange would patch you in a minute. What happened was Admiral had told the doctor at MH Wellington that he would not accept any medication until Surg Cdr Arun Behl vetted it! I spoke to the doctor, who informed me that Admiral's heart was not in good shape, may be due to long journey of 36 hours from Bombay to Coonoor. The doctor asked me to speak to Mrs. Pereira. I told her not to worry the doctor was on the right lines.

In fact the same evening Admiral Ramdas had called up my residence and spoke to my wife and he was informed that I am out of town to attend a conference at Pune and by the time they traced me it was past midnight.

When I got back to Bombay, Rear Admiral Tandon, Chief of Staff, Western Naval Command called up and said that he was sending a staff car to take me to Santa Cruz airport, the Navy Chief has placed an aircraft to fly me to Bangalore and from there by chopper to Coonoor to attend to Admiral Pereira. I told him, 'Sir, this is not a case of cancer; the problem is with his heart and you need a good Cardiologist to be placed there and that I was a cancer Surgeon and that the cancer was well controlled.'

"The point I want to highlight is the CONCERN of Indian Navy to look after Admiral and extend best medical support". Unquote

Lastly, I asked Captain Arun as to why the Admiral did not travel by air instead of taking the 36 hours journey in which in all probability he could have picked some infection. Arun answered, **quote** "I recommended to him to travel by air, but Admiral bluntly told me he has to make 4 trips to Bombay for check ups and he just can't possibly afford the air travel. In fact even Mrs. Pereira always took the long journey by train". **Unquote**

Hereafter Admiral never really recovered and it was a downhill journey till he was shifted to Air Force Command Hospital, Bangalore in Aug 1993, where he breathed his last on 14th Oct 1993.

*Lt Gen Moti Dhar of Poona Horse was the Army Commander.

Cavalry General

Lt Gen KK Singh, Padma Bhushan, MVC

Lt Gen JM Vohra, PVSM, SM

Cavalry General

Lt Gen Hanut Singh, PVSM , MVC

Maj Gen Varindra Singh

Whitefield 1982

With Debbie Shea

Admiral with Dorothy and Jack Shea

At Roger Shea's Wedding

Golf

Lady's Putting, Mrs. Pereira, 9th green, 72

Mrs. Pereira receiving Winners prize from Mrs. SD Gupta, Nov, 72

Runner's up in Single Club Competition Nov, 72

Pereira Cup cap 1999

Bengdubi Golf Course

Admiral off for Golf, 77

Dogs

Honey with Mrs. Gantzer, Colleen&Hugh Gantzer, Mussoorie, 1989

Cindy with Mrs. Pereira, Navy House, 1980

Family Photographs – 1975 to 2002

Cochin 1975

Bangalore-2003

Rolex watch presented by Admiral (1975)

Admiral's Longines watch given by Aunty Phyll in 1999

Navy House – Dec 1980

With Rabden, Feb 1982

X-Mas – 1980

With Tashi in 1986

With Rabden in 2003

With Tashi in 2003

With Annie & kids

Navy House 1982 - Annie with Rabden and Aunty Bobby

Staff

VA Premvir Das, NA to CNS 1979-80

VA KK Kohli, NA to CNS 1980-82

Captain Montee Chatterjee, Secretary to CNS, 1980-81

Cdr Vijyan, Flag Lt, 1973-74   *Cmde Dhinbandu Jena, Flag Lt, 1975-76*

Cmde BR Sen, Flag Lt, 1976-77 & 1979-80

Cmde Nalin Dewan, Flag Lt, 1980-82

Doctors

Lt Col Ashok Chacko, Air Command Hospital, Bangalore, 1983

Gp Captain Paruthi, Air Command Hospital, 1983

Cdr Surgeon Arun Behl , INHS ASVINI, Bombay ,1992-93

Col RK Roy, Commandant, MH, Wellington, 1991-93

Funeral

Flowers on the grave, 16th Oct 1993

Final Service

Mrs Pereira's final resting place

Admiral's Final resting place

Final journey

Cemetry at Kannur

Part - II
Close Encounters
Personal Narrations

At National Defence Academy

PRATAP MUTHANNA

Pratap Muthanna, 40th course, Juliet squadron was **the First cadet who came into close contact with Admiral**. When Admiral joined NDA in Jan 71, 40th course was the 6th termers and within two months they had experienced the wrath of famous 'Dep Com' with the whole course going daily on 'long route marches' during the mid-term break, for not measuring up to 'Dep Com' standards.

There were two incidents involving Pratap Muthanna, one in NDA and another in IMA. At that juncture as a third termer we do remember that Pratap Muthanna was pulled out of some very serious situation by Dep Com. To be honest I was not fully aware of the incident, as it happened more than 45 years ago. I managed to get Pratap Muthanna's contact no; and, yes, spoke to him after more than 30 years and requested him to please go down the memories lane 45 years back !! This is what Pratap Muthanna had to share:-

Quote "Admiral had a **big heart** for me and at times I wonder if my story will be understood in the right perspective by all who read it. My acts were impulsive as far as I can recall, I hardly gave a thought to the consequences of my actions and for reasons I cannot fathom today.

Admiral was such **a revered person, so affectionate, kind, and always helpful**. In the present day, there are few exceptions of his stature, caliber, affable, no–pretentious and **gentleman to the core**. We will always miss his towering and soothing presence.

I remember our new Deputy Commandant, Commodore RL Pereira joined early in January 1971. From day one, we as 6th termers realized that we were dealing with a reputed firebrand from the Indian Navy and our instructors from Navy warned us not to cross his path. One day in March 71, I committed an irresponsible act of consuming something resulting in my immediate evacuation to the Military Hospital in a very grave condition that necessitated stomach wash. Being an emergency case the matter was reported to the Dep Com and that was the last thing I wanted because it will invite serious trouble for me. Admiral came to the hospital to check my condition. I was expecting to be seriously questioned but by God's grace he only politely enquired about my health. I was in the hospital for a week and **Admiral made** it a point to come and see me every day without fail and tried to cheer me up. **And not once did he try to interrogate me.** At that time I was in hazy state, and could not fully comprehend the consequences of my action. At the same time, I was experiencing his **wonderful side** as he was treating me like his son and was genuinely concerned about my well being.

After a week, I was discharged from the hospital and went back to my squadron. A few days later, one early Sunday morning at 6 am, there was a knock at my door and lo and behold, I see Dep Com standing outside my cabin. He said son, come with me, I told him that 'I have not even shaved'. He said, don't worry about being presentable and come out as you are. I hurriedly changed into decent pair of pant and shirt, and left my cabin. He made me sit in his car and drove me to his residence without speaking a word. When we reached his residence I was taken to his guest room and he told me to shave, have a bath and then come down. I was totally perplexed and my mind was blank, imagine getting ready in Dep Com's house. After about half an hour I got ready and came down. I was guided to the dining room where Mrs. Pereira was laying the table for a sumptuous breakfast, with cakes, fruits, eggs, ham and bacon plus toast, jam and peanut butter. I had my fill and never enjoyed such a wholesome breakfast throughout my stay in NDA. After that he asked me to come along for outing to Poona as he wanted to pick up a golf shirt and cap. In the sports shop at Poona, he selected the items while casually engaging me in conversation about the choice of colour etc. I was getting perplexed by the minute. Anyway after wondering on MG Street, we headed for the famous restaurant- Latif's for lunch. There were few cadets already having lunch and **sight of Dep Com put a damper on their laughter and they ate in complete silence as they were mortally scared of the Dep Com. Those who came in later quietly withdrew.** We had delicious lunch, following which he asked me for my choice of ice cream. When I stated chocolate ice cream, he stated 'so is mine' and ordered the same. For the rest of my term, he made frequent visits to Juliet squadron to see me. After our final social where 6th termers are subjected to ragging, and in some cases beating with knotted wet towels, I too was the victim and could hardly walk the next morning. Dep Com pulled me out of the parade and enquired as to why I was sloppy. On hearing my explanation he just said that if you are not fit, you should not be on the parade and left it at that. My parents had come for the POP and Admiral greeted them with warmth and personally supervised their accommodation and seating at the Cultural Show and projected me as a good cadet. When I took leave of him before leaving NDA, **as per my request he gave me a photograph in whites which even today after 45 years, is on my table - my most valuable gift from the great man."** Unquote

Pratap Muthanna was right in being apprehensive of Dep Com reaction and was expecting the worst including withdrawal from Academy, instead Admiral showed him his different side, a soft interior and handled the case as a caring father. This incident had been under wraps for past 45 years, and only his course mates in Juliet Squadron were privy to it ! Pratap's problems did not finish with passing out from NDA, and he once again got himself into more serious trouble in IMA.

Quote "I joined IMA in early July 71, and was posted to Sangro Company. After about two weeks, I again got into my unpredictable mood and thought that enough is enough and decided to abscond. I packed my travel bag and left. I could not find any conveyance at that unearthly hour and walked to Dehradun and caught a taxi for Delhi. On arrival in Delhi I went to New Delhi railway station and boarded Frontier Mail to Bombay. After reaching Bombay I did not know what should be my next action as I was pretty confused and decided to go to Poona. And from there I proceeded to NDA. I reached NDA early morning before muster and I went straight to my classmate from school, Kulkarni, who was Squadron Cadet Captain, Echo Squadron. As he was busy in discharging his responsibilities, he handed me over to a mutual friend, Ranjit Muthanna (later IPKF casualty, God bless his soul). Ranjit informed about my presence to Aditya Gaur from Juliet squadron who then came and took me to Juliet Squadron. Gaur then informed Squadron Cadet Captain Rajindra Singh (later Lt Gen) who immediately reported the matter to the Squadron Commander Major SK Sharma, 2 LANCERS from the Armoured Corps, and excellent human being and outstanding sportsman. Major Sharma soon arrived on a scooter and met me. He knew what I have done is against the rules and can get me into very serious trouble **for an act of grave indiscipline.** He told me, I am going to inform your old friend Dep Com. Sometime later Dep Com reached the squadron. He made me sit in his car and took me for a long drive on the periphery of the Academy including Pashan Gate and Khandwa Gate making polite conversation and for reasons best known to him did not grill/interrogate me and made me feel at ease and finally said will you promise to continue training at IMA and become an officer to which I agreed. He then said you have two options; either I send you back to IMA with an officer escort or you go back on your own to which I replied "Sir, I will go on my own". He also stated that he will be writing to Major General Rajindra Prasad, Commandant IMA. After spending two days at NDA, I left for Dehradun. Apparently Admiral and Commandant, Gen Prasad were very close friends and both had attended DSSC 6 at Wellington in 1952/53. The Commandant called the IMA Deputy Commandant Brig CM Carriappa from Garhwal Rifles and briefed him on handling my case.

I had no knowledge of the contents in Admiral's letter. I was duly marched up to the Deputy Commandant who gave me his piece of mind and told me in no uncertain terms that I had not only let down the institution like NDA but also the community of Coorgs. **After giving me mouthful, he awarded me a token restriction as punishment to regularize my absence and closed the case.** In hindsight I realized it was all due to Admiral's letter to General Rajindra Prasad, **who held Admiral in very high esteem**. I then worked hard, did well in my service subjects, represented IMA in Dehradun district sports where I secured 2nd position in 1500 meters and finally passed out with my course in March 1972."**Unquote**

In both cases Pratap was simply fortunate to be subjected to a '**father figure**' in Admiral who decided to give him second chance to save his career. It were these **sensitive qualities towards the cadets** which made him to be different from others because Admiral's mission was to mould all cadets into strong human beings and leaders of men who could withstand the pressure of the battle field and still take correct decision under stress. He always gave the cadets a chance or two to redeem themselves, if he felt that their act was for reasons beyond their momentary control and not at the cost of willful disobedience of orders. That is why he evokes such **passion and respect** even today in 2016, after all these years.

However, there is another twist to Pratap's story!! In December 1982, he was posted as Platoon Commander, Naushera Company. Incidentally in the same block where he had spent one year as a cadet in 1971/72. After one year as a Platoon Commander, on promotion to Major he took over as Company Commander of the same Company. Pratap had a long tenure of 3 ½ years in IMA and thereafter proceeded to attend Staff College DSSC 42, which incidentally I too attended!

Pratap continued to be in touch with Admiral by correspondence. Sometime in early 1983 Pratap happened to be on leave in Bangalore and went to see Admiral and Mrs. Pereira. Admiral in his letter of 28th July 83, **quote** "*I wonder if I mentioned that Pratap gave us a very pleasant surprise by dropping in on us about a month ago, when he had come down from IMA to Mercara for wedding of his brother. He was looking very well and seems to be enjoying his tenure at IMA. He feels that the caliber of the young men now coming into Army is not the same as was the case few years ago .But I do believe that everyone feels this. The snob school attitude as I call it!!! It is really how one moulds the young men and what example the staff sets. If this is good and honest, then the product will be the same no matter what background will be. Well my son, I will* *close. Our love and good wishes to Annie and Ron 2-Uncle Ron"* **Unquote.** Ron 2 was my elder son, Ron 1 was Admiral himself.

So that is the story of Pratap Muthanna who went on to command 6 GUARDS and retired as Colonel in Feb 2000. I can say, Pratap was very fortunate to have been blessed by Admiral's real concern for his well being.

THE NEW DEPUTY COMMANDANT

DHARM AHALAWAT

I was probably the first cadet of 43rd course to meet the Admiral. It was end of November 1970, I had been recently relegated from 42nd to 43rd course. Commandant Major General SD Gupta, probably for the first and the last time had called all recently relegated souls for High Tea at his official residence. Many DSs felt that the relegated type would boycott the event, so we were herded in a bus at the Mess and taken to NDA Commandant's residence.

It was there that we saw Captain Pereira for the first time. He was then on a recce and said he will soon be joining NDA as Deputy. He was then very different from his later Avtar (personality) and consoled all 'dukhi atmas' (pained souls) and cheered us up. I remember both of us helping ourselves with large portion of Rasgullas. Soon thereafter the Commandant's daughter came to him and invited him to take a walk around the residence. I remember Admiral Pereira telling me 'come along' and we both went around that palatial bungalow with the lady. I must be a rare cadet and that too, relegated type to have gone around the Commandant's residence! Thanks to Admiral.

In 1987/88 while doing Staff College, we remember meeting him many a time in the DSSC bakery in the tea break collecting our respective bread. His mere sight cheered us up so much that it can't be described in words. He had real charisma which pulled you to him, in a system where juniors tend to avoid the senior, if they can do so. Later one saw so many Generals in service but none could command the kind of respect that we personally had for him. He was genuine, had no double standards and that's why '**he was different. We were fortunate to have been his brood!**

SMOKING INCIDENT

ANIL KAUL (40TH/J)

The National Defence Academy (NDA) has its own set of customs and conventions. All cadets who had cleared their Drill Square test were permitted to go to Poona on liberty on Sundays/holidays that meant a day out of the hard daily training schedules. The normal routine would be that one could leave after breakfast and come back by dinner time, possibly after having lunch in a MG street restaurant followed by movie or meeting your friends. These friends either belonged to Pune or were studying in various colleges/AFMC. It was during these outings that unfortunately a few cadets got involved with drug peddlers and ultimately 18 cadets were somehow caught and the matter was brought to the notice of Deputy Commandant (Dep Com) Ronnie Pereira. His first reaction was to relegate the whole lot, however, for some unknown reasons the Commandant Maj Gen SD Gupta over ruled the Dep Com's decision. This may have been due to pressure from high-ups in the Army as a few culprits were from an Army background and all 18 cadets were let off with 28 days restrictions. A kind of punishment with all avenues of relaxation closed for that many number of days.

The Dep Com was not happy with the decision and very next day the whole Academy was summoned in the Assembly Hall and first thing that the Dep Com announced was that smoking which hither-to-fore was permitted for fifth and sixth termers was banned forthwith and he categorically made it very clear that hereafter any cadet caught smoking or in the possession of tobacco/cigarettes would be relegated, he had warned.

Few days later Naval Cadets of the 39th course who had already passed out in Dec 70 and who were on midshipman training off the coast of Bombay had come to NDA for musketeer training, basically training with personal side arms. The ex cadets from Juliet squadron armed with imported cigarettes and whisky decided to visit their old squadron lines to revive memories of the good old days in NDA, an activity for any ex NDA cadets is absolutely very normal. They all gathered in the central lobby and as my cabin being the CSM was located right there was commandeered and converted into a quasi club house. There was a lot of mirth and laughter and everyone was enjoying this sudden change to the normal routine. After sometime 2/Lt Arun Chopra, of 66 Armoured Regiment also an ex Juliet of 37th course along with a few officers also landed up in Squadron lines and joined the party. Apparently Arun Chopra who was doing Young Officer course at Armoured Corps Centre, Ahmednagar had come to Poona on weekend and could not find suitable accommodation in Pune so decided to come to NDA and landed up in their Squadron. It became a kind of re-union with lots of foreign fancy cigarettes and liquor flowing it created chaos in my cabin and after about two hours at 11.30 PM there were loud knocks on the front door of central lobby, I went to open it and found Maj SK Nag, India Squadron Commander and Flt Lt Oberoi standing and they asked me what the noise was about. I told him that some ex cadets of the squadron had gathered in my cabin and he found that most of them were in inebriated condition as were the two officers. Maj Nag had earlier been with Juliet Squadron and Flt Lt Oberoi had been a div 'o'. They asked me to muster all sixth termers immediately as they wanted to meet all their protégés. They also joined in the party with the young officers and midshipmen. By the time everyone wound up it was almost 1 'o' clock, the young officers and midshipmen were adjusted in junior cadet cabins, while the officers went home and my course mates went to sleep.

I then went back to my cabin which was in total mess with cigarette butts thrown all over and liquor bottles scattered around. I cleared all the mess and collected about 30 to 40 butts and as I was in the process of throwing them out of my window facing the battalion quadrangular, there I found Lt (IN) LN Mishra, the duty officer staring back at me.

He asked me that had I been smoking against the explicit orders of Dep Com, I tried to explain to him that I do not smoke and these butts were left by ex cadets of 37th course who happened to be in my cabin the whole evening.

Lt Mishra did not buy my explanation and the next morning reported the matter to the officiating Battalion Commander late Lt Commander TK Das who immediately brought the matter to the notice of Dep Com. Expectedly Dep Com directed Lt Cdr Das to have me marched up to him and added that Anil Kaul should consider himself relegated to the next course. My Squadron Commander, Maj SK Sharma (later Lt Gen) tried his level best to save me but to no avail. The next day I was marched up to Dep Com and I tried to give my side of story but he would have none of it and said this story won't get past my nine years old niece and remanded me to Commandant.

Meanwhile I got in touch with my father Brigadier KK Kaul, then Commander 16 Independent Armoured Brigade and who knew Gen SD Gupta well and requested him to give Anil any punishment except relegation. When I was marched up, the Commandant looked at Dep Com and said that relegation is bit severe and pronounced de-tabbed and 28 days restrictions, which meant that I was to relinquish my rank of CSM and undergo the 28 days of punishment. Subedar Major Kashi Ram barked and marched me out. I saluted and came out and heaved a sigh of relief, my wrist band was taken away by the Subedar Major. As I was going down the steps of Sudan Block I heard a shout "Cadet come back" and lo behold I was marched up again and this time I was relegated to 41st course.

Apparently what transpired in those few moments that Dep Com thought that his authority has been undermined because just few days back he had committed in front of the whole Academy that he would relegate the next offender for smoking. **As I was marched out I believe the Dep Com took out his Stripes and kept them on Commandant table and said Sir, you cannot compromise my prestige and authority in front of the cadets, either you relegate him or accept my resignation.** Gen Gupta was astounded but being a weak man in front of the Dep Com imposing personality and had no option but to have me marched up again and relegated. A total miscarriage of military justice as you cannot be punished twice for the same offence but as a 19 year old one did not understand these intricacies of Military law, surprisingly, between the Adjutant, Squadron commander, officiating Battalion commander neither did they. Or was it just to satisfy one man's ego that justice was thrown to the winds. Something that served me well in the 32 years of service in the Army where I always stood up to the correct dispensation of justice irrespective of the level of intimidation, in one case from no less a person than a COAS.

But the story does not end here. **The Admiral pushed the cadets very hard, did not believe in molly coddling, he was stern and unbending task master with single minded AIM in moulding all cadets into good leaders of men. His punishments were supposedly always corrective and never associated with any malicious intent except I felt in my case.**

I passed out with 41st course from NDA and with 50th IMA Regular course as Senior Under Officer in Dec 1972 and was commissioned into 65 Armoured Regiment which was raised by my father on 01 Sep 1966. I had salvaged my reputation to some extent. I was to add to it by being awarded the VrC in combat in 1987.

One sunny morning in Oct 1975 I along with my mother had gone to Chandni Chowk Market in old Delhi to purchase some jewelry for my impending marriage scheduled for 20th Nov. As my mother was selecting some pearls she asked me to go and look for needle and thread from the adjacent shop. As I was walking to the next shop out of nowhere I heard someone shouting Kaul in a baritone voice and as I turned there I saw Admiral in his Whites uniform in shorts, he had come to Delhi to attend Senior Naval Officers conference at Naval HQs. I just froze and stood to attention and wished him. He shook hands with me very warmly and inquired which regiment have I joined and asked me what I was doing in Chandni Chowk? I told him that I have come here with my mother to buy some jewelry for my marriage. I requested him to please come and attend my marriage scheduled for 20th Nov. He chatted with me for about 15 mins and suddenly his Flag Lt (Lt Jena) produced a box which Admiral handed to me and said all the best and walked away. Yes it was silver salver. I was really touched by his gesture.

The second incident took place in March 1984 during my Staff College course (DSSC 40). During the mid-term break I along with my family decided to spend few days with my cousin Maj Sunil Kaul, who was posted at ASC Centre Bangalore. One day my wife and self borrowed his scooter and drove to Sai Baba Ashram located at Whitefield about 14 kms from Bangalore, on our way back I noticed a name board ATLAST and below it was written Admiral RL PEREIRA, I immediately stopped my scooter and told my wife we must meet them, of course she was hesitant and told me you cannot walk into such a senior officer residence without prior intimation, but I was determined to meet them. **So I parked the scooter outside the gate and walked in and there I saw Mrs. Pereira watering the plants. I wished her and to my amazement she said, 'Kaul 40th Juliet Sqn', I was shocked at her memory and she shouted Ron look who has come to see you.** Admiral came out and met us very warmly and asked us to come inside. I had a cup of tea and lots of snacks as well; we spent two beautiful hours with them. Admiral told me, **quote, 'son, I think you were right, you did not lie that day, I am sorry.' Unquote. Those few words made my day and all demons against the man that I had harboured for over thirteen years in my mind disappeared. Such GREAT human beings are few and far between." Unquote**

That was Col Anil Kaul, VrC's true story. When the Admiral passed away on 14 Oct 93, I received a touching letter from Anil Kaul. **Quote** "My dear Mike, It was terrible to hear of the demise of the "ADMIRAL". Please accept our heartfelt condolence on this tragic occurrence. Please also convey to Mrs Pereira.

May the Almighty give all of you strength to bear this irrepairable loss and we pray to GOD to allow the soul of the departed to rest in peace. your's as ever Anil " Unquote

'RONNIE' AN OFFICER AND GENTLEMAN

SAM MORE (41ST/F)

The world is full of good people but you need divine vision to see them and feel their presence around you. Also, you need to be amongst the blessed few to have touched their Aura.

Admiral R L Pereira [Ronnie] and his charming wife, Phyllis, **was one such Celestial couple to have walked this Earth,** and very fortunately, around the time we were training at the NDA. Roughly around the year of the Lord 1971 to 1973, Ronnie was the Deputy Commandant at one of the World's most prestigious combined Defence training establishments, the National Defence Academy, Khadakwasla, near Pune. **It was sheer destiny and my good fortune to be there at that time.**

Having made it to the Academy Polo team in my very second term, as I was already an accomplished Polo player prior to joining, catapulted me into the elite few upon whom the Sun shone more brightly than the lesser mortals! The instant benefits included being excused the gruelling X-country run and full protection of senior Horsemen from the treacherous ragging, a great necessity in those formative days at the Academy. In the process I instantly caught the Dep Coms' (as the deputy was referred to) eye, and thereafter I could do no wrong. During that period or shall we say "in those days Sportsmen took precedence over 'Specky' (cadets who wore glasses and considered studious type) Torch holders and Polo was always a glamorous sport !

It is rare that two individuals with similar bent of mind, interest and mental makeup are posted together thereby creating a synergy that not only helps in the smooth running of the organisation but creates an atmosphere of tremendous positivity all-round. Major General S D Gupta [Arty] and Admiral [then Commodore] R L Pereira were two such people at the helm of affairs, and it was an instant hit. Both outstanding officers and great soldiers, who understood what it took to be a true leader under adverse conditions. As the saying goes 'The battle of Waterloo was won on the playfields of Eaton', same was true of the NDA. A few anecdotes to highlight the greatness of a man affectionately called **"Ronnie"**! **A man with a hard exterior but all soft inside.**

It was the beginning of the Spring Term and we were in the middle of the Southern Command Polo and Horse show being hosted by the NDA. That particular morning, I happened to be in 'all white' medical category dress slowly trudging up the Sudan Block road near the Assembly hall to be precise. I suddenly heard a thundering voice "MORE", and I looked skywards but there were no clouds to cause the thunder but I soon discovered the origin of the BOOM! - a tall slim figure in immaculate white stood on the parapet of the Sudan Block, the Dep Com. I quickly changed direction and started limping towards him, another BOOM "Stop, stay there", and he walked up to me and asked "What's wrong Son? Are you ok? And where's your cycle? "I stammered, 'Sir I was injured in yesterdays match and as for the cycle, the entire course has been grounded as a punishment. "Oh I see, OK carry on to your class, and well played yesterday!" period. When I went back to my Squadron after lunch I was immediately summoned to the Squadron Office. There I saw my Squadron Commander, my Div Officer and the Squadron Orderly standing with my bicycle with valves and correct tyre pressure et al. I was woken up by a loud bark "you idiot! Here take your bicycle and never be seen without it again, is that understood! "Yes Sir", is all I could manage before saluting and scampering out? Ronnie had called up the Squadron Office and done the needful.

Ronnie was not only a true soldier but a leader amongst men. He took his responsibilities seriously but "Without Losing the Common Touch "as Kipling would have said! He taught us to light the Cigarette with the wind instead of away from it [smoking was strictly prohibit at the Academy]! His one regret -.He was not trained at the NDA!

I can never forget the Exhibition Polo Match I played on the eve of my passing out in which I, surprisingly, played for the Navy team. It was on this occasion that I was given the "BEST RIDER" Trophy! Mrs Phyllis Pereira was so overwhelmed that she made me pose with the Trophy and had Goyal [of Goyal studio] take picture of me. She got my picture from Goyal Studios the very next day, made out a beautiful card with my picture on it and **wrote a few golden words** wishing me luck for my onward journey, a treasure I keep close to my heart even today [photo of card enclosed].

The Admiral, most deservedly, went on to become the Chief of the Naval Staff. And as luck would have it I got posted to NDA as Divisional Officer, 17 Div 'F' Sqn, around the same time i.e. from Jan 1979 to June 1981! It was during this period that the CNS came to the NDA twice [June 79 and Dec 80] to review the POP [Passing out Parade]! On both occasions, I was determined to meet my mentors come what may.

Interestingly, the first time the Admiral came to review the Passing out Parade in June 79, the Commandant, Maj Gen R K Jasbir Singh, had been posted out on promotion and had just taken over 15 Corps at Srinagar, and the Deputy was officiating. Ronnie refused to oblige without the Commandant being there. Well, the Army HQ's relented and Gen Jasbir Singh, was asked to come back as Officiating Commandant for the period of the POP flying the Corps Flag on his Staff car!

In the first instance, I made a request to the concerned staff to meet the Chief since I knew him, but for some reason it was turned down. But all Ex-NDA's are famous for finding a way out of a difficult situation. The CNS was to address all Naval Officers at the VIP guest house, Peacock Bay. I quietly made way to the venue and entered from a side door and parked myself in the adjoining room. **The address over, Mrs Pereira walked in and greeted me warmly and soon we were joined by the Admiral after he had changed into home clothes.** A simple T-shirt and plain trousers which showed faint signs of repairs here and there and finally, a pair of rubber Hawaii slippers on his feet completed this picture of utmost SIMPLISTIC ARROGANCE! **They both radiated a kind of warmth and affection which can only be felt and experienced. I didn't realise how long I basked in that blissful moment but I could have gone on and on!**

He was one of the few Chiefs to have passed out two courses and he next came in Dec 80 for 59th Course passing out. **This time around too I expressed an intense desire to meet my "Foster Parents", so to say but again came up against a dead end.**

But as they say if you have a strong will things happen. As is usually the programme we had the Riding and P T display a day prior to the POP at the Stadium and I too had participated. After the display had ended High Tea was laid out around the swimming pool for the passing out course and their parents. I, in my maroon Blazer, stood at a distance on one of the side exits of the Mess watching the proceedings. **I could see the Admiral and his wife on the Mess Portico chatting up with some of the parents when suddenly I heard a now familiar boom 'MORE'! When I gained consciousness I saw** both Ronnie and Phyllis walking towards me and subconsciously I too started walking. The three of us stood on the open space of the drive way while people all around us just stood and watched. **It felt like eternity, "how are you son?"**

We shook hands and how long that little chat took one doesn't know but I knew I was basking in the most sublime company almost ethereal! The pleasant aura that flowed was hitting me like a wave. There definitely was something heavenly about these two. Unfortunately, that was my last meeting with them.

Ronnie and Phyllis, no wonder God did not bless you with children of your own. because you were destined to be **Parents to so many like me**! Rest in peace both of you, you more than deserved it.

Dear Sambhaji,

We're sending these 2 little photographs of you to remind you of us & the N.D.A. We hope you'll have plenty of opportunity to keep up your doings at the I.M.A. & thereafter.

Our very good wishes for a successful year at the I.M.A. & we look forward to the day when you will be commissioned. Yrs sincerely

Phyllis Pereira

LYNYARD

LT GEN T S GILL

This story is enumerated by now retired Lt Gen TS Gill, AVSM, SM, VSM from the Parachute Regt, a tall broad shouldered and handsome Sardar from Punjab.

Quote "It was sometime in late May 1971 when I was in my first term of the 45th NDA course (**Alpha Squadron**) and only a week or so left for our much awaited summer break. I had the distinction of passing my Drill Square Test in my second attempt in the First Term earning my lanyard which allowed us to proceed on liberty to Poona on Sundays/Holidays, a big achievement for the first termers.

One morning I woke up with high fever and could hardly get out of my bed, so I walked up to the CSM (**Cadet Sergeant Major**), Nair who expectedly thought that I was shamming and did not allow me to report sick and was told to bugger off and proceed for end of term Passing Out Parade (**POP**) drill practice. The Deputy Commandant had come to witness the drill practice. As I was passing by the saluting dias in my squad, he observed that I was not doing the drill movements properly and found me a bit slow. There and then he pulled me out of my squad and removed my lanyard (**implying that I had to pass the Drill Square test again**), leaving me totally distraught and heart broken, but I was relieved that he did not bark 21 days and 4 Singarh hikes.

In the evening as I was still running high fever I was allowed by the CSM to proceed to the Military Hospital on special sick report. After a while as luck would have it, the Deputy Commandant walked in to the Military Hospital to check the sick report and catch anybody shamming. He of course noticed me and checked with duty Medical Officer and she confirmed that I was running high fever and had been given 48 hours Sick in Quarters. This interaction with the Medical Officer had happened without my knowledge. Later in evening the Deputy Commandant came to Alpha Squadron and asked for me. I ran down to the ground floor lobby where he was standing and stood in front of him with heart in my mouth and legs shivering thinking he has come to punish me more or relegate me. Before I realised, he asked me to sit in the car. Initially I thought I had heard him wrong, however he again said son get inside the car. I slowly slithered inside and sat motionless wondering what will happen next?? Without speaking a word he drove towards the swimming pool and then to his residence and all this while I could hardly breathe as he was a terror and I was wondering what next. We reached his residence and he took me inside to the Dining Table and offered me pastries, biscuits, cake and tea and more sweets and I kept eating thinking that I am – **BALLI KA BAKRA** being fattened before the kill. Anyhow I finished off whatever was on the table as cadets are always hungry and first termers more so. He then asked the driver Bahadur to drop me back to the squardon lines. Throughout this ordeal the Deputy Commandant did not utter a word which left me totally nervous, confused and baffled.

Two days later we had another rehearsal for POP and the Deputy Commandant appeared again on the prowl to catch some unfortunate victim. He entered the Drill Square and shouted for my name and I was sure that I was in BIG trouble again and may be relegated, all negative thoughts ran through my scared mind. I ran towards him and with proper drill movements halted and saluted and to my utter surprise he smiled and put the lanyard back on my shirt and said, **SORRY SON**, patted me on my shoulder and walked away leaving me in tears of joy as I marched back to my squad.

That was the greatness of Ronnie Pereira a man with no malice and intent, only **GOOD** for his beloved cadets whom he always wanted to make a man " **Unquote**

The above incident, though small left a big impact on me and taught me the value of **COMPASSION** alongwith **DISCIPLINE**. This small incident in my Army Career of 40 yrs was one of the factors which enabled me to acquit myself with honour when fighting the insurgents/terrorists as a Paratrooper in Sri Lanka (**OP PAWAN**), Nagaland (**OP ORCHID**) and J&K (**OP RAKSHAK**), earning me a gallantry award in **OP PAWAN**.

ANIL MAGO

Admiral always referred to the cadets as 'DEVILS' and he mentioned this in his letter dated 29th July 1985, quote *"I had the pleasure and privilege to mould the finest devils in the world that I could have ever wished for"*. The reason was; **on many occasions the cadets got the better of him.** I suppose one had no choice, as it was question of life and death! Therefore, you had to think fast and invent actions to out manoeuvre the dreaded Dep Com. God forbid if you are caught; you will end up with minimum 21 Restrictions and 4 Singarh Hikes!!

Cadet Anil Mago, 40th to 42nd course, Juliet squadron, was one of the few "Generals" from NDA, who did 8 terms instead of normal 6. During the period of Jan 71 to June 72, Anil Mago invariably found himself at the wrong place and at the wrong time with Dep Com hot at his heels. But Anil Mago had the sharpest brains and more often than not he escaped by the skin of his teeth and it is to his credit that he finally passed out in June 72! How??

I got Anil Mago's mobile number from one of my course mates Maj Gen Rajiv Kalra and called him up in Oct 2015, after a long gap of 43 years!! Yes, also it was first time in my life that I spoke to him. I said Sir, I am Mike Bhalla, 43rd Delta squadron and his reply was, yes I remember you and how are you? I informed him, Sir, I am writing a book on Admiral, he was so pleased to hear and said, **quote "Mike if I am alive today and talking to you, it's all because of Ronnie Pereira, I owe everything to him, he was God for me"**.

My next question was Sir, may I request you to go down the memory lane and narrate your **close encounters with Admiral?** He had a hearty laugh and few days later went on to narrate few incidents with the great man.

Quote "Ok Mike, one fine day I decided to spend a couple of prep periods in the comfort of my cabin instead of class room or library. The safest route to avoid the Drill Ustad was via Hut of Remembrance, the road behind Sudan Block going towards Military Hospital. I cycled down the slope as fast as I could, but as I approached the Military Hospital, what I dreaded happened – encountering a Drill Ustad, seeing me alone, he shouted '*halt, aur niche utro* (get down) and asked me where I was going alone on the cycle during classes time? I told him that I was not well. He then inquired what is wrong with you. I replied with straight face- Ustad am very ill and pregnant! The Ustad got confused and instead of exposing his ignorance he let me off and I rushed to the Squadron lines.

I think somehow Dep Com had noticed lone cycle movement near Military Hospital and as I reached my cabin on the third floor in the tea room flank, I heard a car screeching to a halt in the squadron parade ground. I looked down to check, and who do I see? None, else but Deputy, coming out of his car followed by his Labrador dog behind him. I panicked and I knew if am caught then I would cook my goose nice and proper and he will take me to the gallows. I had few minutes to think and my mind was working overtime. I saw one of the orderlies; Prabhu Dayal was sitting in the corridor polishing about 8 to 10 pairs of shoes placed around him. Suddenly I got a brainwave and asked Prabhu Dayal to take out his old vest and I quickly changed into his vest, put some polish on my face, tied his old towel over my head and threw some water on my face and vest and told Prabhu Dayal to vanish and hide himself in the toilet. I sat there polishing the shoes as vigorously as I could with my head almost touching the shoe. Sure enough after a while Deputy came to the third floor, first the dog approached me sniffing and making some noises, and I controlled myself and kept polishing. A while later Deputy arrived and as he approached I said 'Salam Sahib', he stood there and put his white shoes with some mud and dust in front of me and asked to clean them up and I did as a professional orderly and he then walked off to my great relief!! I did not move till I heard the car sound disappear. What a close escape?? " **Unquote**

Next Sunday, when I went home, Dep Com narrated this incident and told me son, I am 100% sure I noticed a lone cadet going into no 3 battalion and I looked around but couldn't locate him, he just disappeared into the thin air. I started to laugh, he looked at my face little perplexed and said son, why are you laughing. I told him, he did not disappear, he was sitting right under your nose, -is it so my son? – I said, he cleaned your shoes! He said, son, I can't believe it, he must be one hell of a smart devil. Aunty Phyll also had a good laugh and said, Ronnie you think you are smart!

However, Deputy NEVER asked me the name and said, son, good luck to him and am sure he will do well in war! But I will be more careful next time!

Major SK Sharma from 2nd Lancers was Squadron Commander Juliet Squadron. A handsome, broad shouldered, and a vintage Cavalry officer, who had represented Services in Squash and had a heart of gold. Maj Sharma was rather fond of Anil Mago and appointed him as DCC (Divisional Cadet Captain), hoping that he will concentrate on fulfilling his responsibilities and stay out of trouble, more importantly from Dep Com sights. But it was too much to expect from Anil Mago and soon he was in trouble again!!

Quote "One fine early morning at about 5.30am, Deputy decided to pay surprise visit to Juliet Squadron and he went to Tea Room to check the quality of the tea. There was no bulb in the tea room and surely whacked away by some cadet for exchange of a fuse bulb. So it was semi dark there. Deputy stood behind the tea bar and waited for the cadets. After a while a bleary eyed first termer walked in with 2 mugs. He filled the mugs and picked four biscuits and as he was about to leave the Tea Room, he heard –'stop son' and the poor chap just froze. Dep Com asked him about the second mug, he replied Sir, DCC Mago; the orders were clear that all cadets will collect their own tea and not detail first termers for the same. So he followed him, and knocked at the door of Mago's cabin. Mago shouted 'who is there?' Back came the reply from outside – your bloody Pop! I immediately realized that it is Dep Com and hurriedly got into my shorts and opened the door. Deputy said- Good Morning Sir, here is your tea! I stood motionless shivering in my legs, Deputy had great sense of humor and realized my plight and said Sir, can I have a biscuit? He looked at his watch, and said son it is 5.38 and you better be on time for morning Muster at 6am!! I never got ready so fast in my life, and flew down the stairs to reach before Dep Com!! Somehow he let me off?

As I mentioned I had no margin for any error and was very careful, but my luck ran out and lightening struck again. It was just 4 days before Passing out Parade and I was on my way to the Drill Square. Just little ahead of me, there was a squad of 8 cadets who were slouching by the roadside and suddenly out of nowhere Deputy's White Ambassador car appeared and screeched to a halt. Deputy came out of the car and barked 168 Restrictions and 32 Singarh Hikes - divide amongst yourselves, and then looked at me and said, you are DCC, then why didn't you check them. He asked the names of squadron from the cadets and then asked me to report to his office at 9.30 with the Squadron Commander. I felt my world crumbling around me and this was the proverbial last straw on the camel back. I was shattered with only 4 days to go for POP. I knew marching up means relegation and withdrawn from Academy and end of my career in the Army.

I went and informed my Squadron Commander, who held his head in both hands and said Anil Mago, what you have done and I don't think I can help you. **I pleaded please Sir, you have to save me or else it will be end of the road for me.** He said I don't think I can do anything now. Seeing my plight, he said let me try. At 9.30 I reported to the Dep Com office, Maj Sharma was already inside Deputy's office, apparently fighting my case and trying to convince Deputy. Sub Major Kashi Ram was ready to march me up. After a while Kashi Ram barked orders for march up and as I put one step inside the office, **I heard 'hold it there, son'- you have one foot inside my office on the banana peel and other outside also on banana peel, you can slip any where you want- 'next time'- EVEPORATE.** I couldn't believe what my ears heard and when it dawned on me, I turned back and ran for my life with tears rolling down my cheeks. Yes I owe it to my Squadron Commander Maj SK Sharma Sir.

After couple of days was Deputy's final rehearsal for POP and at the end of it as I was marching in slow order past the Quarter Deck and Deputy noticed me and hissed, **son, you are not passing out, you are "CRAWLING OUT".** I kept stoic expression on my face but laughed my guts out after the parade. He surely had great sense of humor!!" **Unquote**

In fact Anil Mago owes it to Major Sharma. Deputy was indeed very fond him and later told me son, I could not say no to SK, and let off the culprit. He also added, I am sure he will do very well in his career. Yes, Major SK Sharma rose to the rank of Lt General and retired as GOC-in-C, ARTRAC.

MY DATE WITH DESTINY

KIRAT VAZE

This is one of the **most** moving encounter which my course mate and dear friend Kirat Vaze, 43rd Echo Squadron experienced with the Admiral in our 6th term in 1972. In fact as I started with this noble venture to write a book on the **Greatman** on 25th August 2015, the first incident which came to my mind was Kirat's as I happened to be sitting next to him when Commodore Ronnie Pereiera, our Dep Com, came speeding down in his white Ambassador to our outdoor class behind D-3 Area and after getting down from his car, he shouted - is Cadet Vaze here??

I requested Kirat to please send me a write up of that fateful day and this is what he had to say ;

Quote "Whenever late Admiral RL Pereira's name is mentioned in any gathering in India, attributes such as **'One of the Chief Architect of the Indian Navy'** or **'A Soldier's Soldier'** or **'The Epitome of an officer and a Gentleman'** are often the norm. For those Armed Forces Officers who graduated from National Defence Academy in early seventies, he will always remain 'Our Dep Com', **arguably the best Deputy Commandant NDA ever had, before or since he held this appointment in the Prestigious Institution.** As a cadet under him, depending on the reason, place, situation and time you faced him, he could evoke emotions ranging from awe, fear, loyalty, love, hate, astonishment, or **absolute terror**. His was the defining presence and point of reference of every cadet who had the privilege and opportunity of having spent even a single term during his tenure. Most of these cadets have a story with 'One Day the Dep Com was on his usual unscheduled visits when I'...... **This** is my story which starts around 11 am on a fine wintery day at the NDA in 1972 when I was in my 6th term.

Day dreaming, albeit for short durations, is the prerogative of only Cadets in their SIXTH (final) Term at the NDA because of the simple reason that the First to Fifth Term Cadets are kept suitably occupied most of the day and night for them to have any time left for leisurely activity. During one such day dreaming session between two periods in my Sixth Term at the NDA, in the designated rest area of the grounds of the Army Training Team, my dream of seeing myself along with my course mates slow marching out of the portals of the NDA to the tune of 'Auld Lang Syne' was rudely shattered by my course mate's stage whisper "Vaze, he is asking for you". Hearing my name mentioned I sat up to hear another course mate - Mike Bhalla asking me in an urgent manner 'What have you done ?' while looking in a particular direction. On looking in the same direction, my daydream turned into a nightmare seeing the Dep Com purposefully approaching our group from a distance of 50 yards. Like I said, it was cool and fine winter day in Pune but only up till then. Now, for me the weather seemed colder than it would to a person about to face firing squad at the North Pole seeing the Dep Com was hunting for me to vent his wrath on me for violation of some rule or regulation. Desperately I tried to remember where and when I had committed an 'act prejudicial to good order and military discipline' over the past one week and to my dismay recollected at least three. However, my Divisional Officer (Divo) had let me off with four 'Singarh Hikes' as punishment. So I wondered what else I had done. By now the Devil in the form of the Dep Com was 25 yards away. My memory was now working at the speed of lightening and recalled that I had taken a short cut to the NDA Mess from the squadron Lines just that morning and concluded that somehow, somebody, (including the Almighty), must have ratted on me. I resigned myself to my fate and steeled myself for the worst scenario of spending another term at the NDA as I had already done 35 Restrictions in my Sixth Term and award (that's what it was called in our times) of even Seven Restrictions or more by Dep Com would mean Relegation to the junior course. And if that wasn't enough, as a matter of principle, this Dep Com always awarded more than 14 Restrictions. By this time my Destiny in the form of Dep Com was 5 yards from me. I sprung rigidly to attention and managed to squeak "Cadet Vaze here Sir" and waited for the axe to fall.

Flash back to about two months before this incident, we were playing a cricket match with the local team at the stadium and our (NDA) team wasn't doing particularly well. The Dep Com had come on one of his regular unannounced visits to see how the team was faring. I had been in the team since my fourth term after a lot of effort on my part primarily because of the fact that the matches were held only on Sundays and as a NDA Cricket Team Player, one was excused the 'Singarh Hike' you have been punished for some offence committed by you. To swap a 14 kms 'hike' with full Combat Gear for a fun day of cricket with fantastic lunch thrown in, was a great motivator to be in NDA Cricket Team!

That particular day at about 4 pm when Dep Com came to watch the match I went in to bat at No 6. The only instruction given to me was that the Match has to be saved by batting through the remaining one and a half hours. This was so since the opposing team had set us a herculean target to win and five of the best batsmen in our team were back in the Pavilion. I was essentially a bowler for my side and could bat a bit in emergencies. With bit of luck, fully aware that Dep Com hawk eyes were on us and following the Coach's periodic yells of 'play with the straight bat', me and my partner at the other end managed to salvage a draw. After the match, the Dep Com said while congratulating me, 'Cricket and Restrictions seems to run in your family, does it ? Here he was referring to the fact that the brother elder to me, Kumar, who was from 40th Course had been the Captain of NDA Cricket Team and had been awarded the highest recognition of a 'Blazer' in the game by the Dep Com himself. He however, had been relegated from 40 to 41st course for exceeding his quota of restrictions in one term and Dep Com was aware of the same. He later was commissioned into Indian Air Force. (I couldn't tell him that day but Cricket and Restrictions did run in the family. My eldest brother, Kiran, too was an NDA alumni who besides being a NDA Cricketer, had the honour, in NDA parlance of being a 'General'. Having been relegated from 27th to 29th NDA courses. He was commissioned into 2 Lancers of the Armoured Corps in 1967). That day at the Cricket Ground after his gruff congratulations and one liner, the Dep Com turned around to my Divo and said "Make sure that I am informed before this boy gets any more restrictions. I will be the one to award them" or words to that effect. Not knowing whether I had been rewarded or censured that day, I decided to follow the straight and narrow path as best as I could for the remainder of the Sixth Term.

Back in the present at the Army Training Team Ground, I relived the memories of only the bit about the Dep Com saying he was the person going to award me Restrictions in future. While saluting him I honestly felt like a prisoner on Death Row when he hears the Guards come to fetch him for the electric chair. I disbelievingly heard the Dep Com say "Boy, get into my car, I want a word with you". I ran and got into the front seat of his Staff Car while he slid into the rear seat and asked the driver to proceed to E Squadron which was my Squadron. My imagination ran wild and I saw myself being directly withdrawn from NDA when a soft voice from behind me said, "Son, I have seen you like to play cricket with straight bat and I will follow your lead by doing some straight talking. Remember, this Academy makes boys into men and you will become a man today". In still softer voice he went on, "your father was seriously injured in an incident when he tried to stop some burglars from entering your house in Belgaum at 4 am in the morning. He was taken to Military Hospital there and operated upon at 8 am today. The hospital authorities have asked us to inform you that your mother required your presence by her side. I am going to make sure that you reach Belgaum in shortest possible time. When we reach your Squadron, I am going to brief your Squadron Commander about the events. You will go in my car to the Railway Station at Pune and catch the first train or bus to Belgaum. Here is some money (**He took out Three Hundred Rupees from his wallet and gave it to me**). If you require anymore I will instruct your Squadron Commander to give you the same when you finish packing and come to the Squadron Office for your Leave Certificate. I am giving you 7 days emergency leave extendable to 10 days. Do not worry .Have faith in God. Remember Crises or Events like these separate men from boys. Do you understand what I have said, Son? I answered in affirmative. "Good", he continued, have faith and be the rock your mother can depend on. Good Luck. Within 15 minutes of reaching the Squadron I was off in Dep Com's car for Pune and by I pm on my way to Belgaum. (This was the era without mobiles when the call to NDA from Military Hospital. Belgaum was received around 10 am. I reached Belgaum Military Hospital around 7pm to find my father in the ICU in a critical condition with multiple injuries in the stomach and abdomen sustained while resisting the burglars. My mother though supported by friends and relatives was visibly relieved to see me. For my elder brothers it was not possible to reach Belgaum till the next day from where they were stationed. On the fourth day after the incident, after the doctors had placed him out of danger and my brothers had reached, one of the first words my father spoke to me was "I am OK now, Go back to the Academy tomorrow. (once a Maratha Light Officer, retired or otherwise gives you an order, try to say no). On the fifth day from the day 'Dep Com' had lent me his car to go to Pune Station, I reported back to the NDA. After he had spoken to him about my return on the telephone, my Squadron Commander told me to report to Dep Com's office. In his office, on asking me what my father had said, I told him what my Dad had said about rejoining the duty forthwith. He laughed and said "From now till your passing out keep playing with a straight bat or you will be in this office for very different reasons". Knowing that the Dep Com was a man who meant what he said. I kept my nose out of trouble from then on, and passed out with my original course mates, a record of sort in Vaze's Family History !.

In retrospect, had there been any cadet other than me among the 1500 or so cadets facing a similar situation in the NDA that day. I for one have no doubt that the Dep Com actions would have been the same. **The day when incident occurred, I learnt more about what a great leader of men is all about than what I have known all my life. The lessons learnt by me are too** numerous to state, but suffice to say that for me that day Admiral Ronald Lynsdale Pereira, PVSM, AVSM aka The Dep Com attained the status of a DEMI GOD !"Unquote

As I write this incident, I have no hesitation in confessing that by the end of it I had tears rolling down my cheeks!

Indeed Admiral was a Great 'HUMAN BEING'.

EVEPORATE

GEORGE JOSEPH / 43rd ECHO

When George got to know from Joy Nath that I was writing a book on our beloved Dep Com, he immediately sent me a mail:-

"My dear Mike - Hope I am not late in sending you this episode of my 'close encounter' with Ronnie Pereira. Of course I had few more but not as eventful as this one. **You also had a part to play in this.** I had written this during Dec 2010 for the 42nd course, when few of us were discussing about our NDA days I am reproducing the same with minor changes. **Its bit long and I am not sorry for it.**"

Quote "This incident happened in Mar 72, during my 5th term (first 6th term). I was doing extra drill (ED) at the Drill Square, one Saturday evening. As many of you may recall, it involved running in a squad around the Drill Square for about an hour, after the roll call was done. We were about 12 guys in the squad and had a nasty drill Ustad as our squad i/c. Four of us were the 6th termers in this squad. As 6th termers we were jogging as usual (not running), which infuriated the drill Ustad a great deal. Matters would have ended happily for all concerned, but for the arrival of the Duty Officer (DO) at the Drill Square, towards the end of running time. There were also other squads on ED, but our Ustad probably to attract the DO's attention, started hollering away at our squad. DO promptly came to us and told all 6th termers to fall out and start front rolling. We did roll but again as the 6th termers normally do. This wasn't taken very sportingly by the DO. As ill luck would have it, I was front rolling closest to him and he kicked me on my butt, asking to roll faster. Well, this wasn't taken very sportingly by me either. I got up and stood still. DO howled at me asking me to get down and continue rolling. I refused and told him in 'not so friendly' tone, that I don't intend to front roll any more. By now we had caught the attention of other squads and the drill staff. It must have been quite a sight. DO howling at me and I stoically refusing and asking him as to why has he kicked me. This went on for some time and reached a stalemate. (I could also get whiff of liquor in DO's breath). To break the impasse the DO asked me to report to the Swimming Pool immediately, where Inter Squadron Swimming competition was in progress.

Ronnie P was the officiating Commandant, that day. DO had preceded me to the pool, as I reached there on my cycle. I saw Ronnie, Adjt HK Trivedi, and my Sqn Cdr Dolly Kapoor. The DO and Himmat Sidhu (our SCC and Captain of the Squadron swimming team), all waiting for me. Well one was clearly overwhelmed by the occasion, but didn't show. Ronnie had already been briefed by the DO about my 'grave offence'. Ronnie didn't ask me much, but I did chip in that I was kicked in the butt. This apparently heckled Ronnie a bit but never the less, he relegated me on the spot and asked Adjutant to march me up to him on Monday. I returned to the squadron and waited. Soon Dolly and all the Div officers landed up and called me to the office. I was debriefed on the Drill Square incident and was told to report to the office again on Monday. I asked Dolly if I should attend parade/class with my course or the junior course. He said he will tell me on Monday. I **returned to my cabin feeling desolate and abandoned ... if you remember the movie 'The Longest Day' (Normandy Landings), that Sunday was the longest day in my life.** I now realized what 'Ike Eisenhover' must have gone through on 6th June 1944... Monday morning, Himmat Singh, our SSC and a dear friend, **had E sqn on their knees and pray for me during the morning muster. I think, Ronnie who was passing by, probably saw this.**

On Monday, I had the second round of briefing by our squady, Dolly Kapoor. He asked me repeatedly as to why I did not get down and roll when asked to do so. I told him that as I felt that he might kick me again, I had decided not to do so. I also informed him that I could get the smell of liquor in DO's breath. I was severely reprimand by Dolly and my Div Offr Lt (IN) Pandit, while leaving he told me not to attend classes that day and be available in the Squadron. Mean while, unknown to me then, some 'backroom' activities were in progress. Dolly and Adjutant HKT (they were course mates) felt that kicking a cadet openly was not a 'done thing' especially by an officer. **I, on my part had met a dear friend, Mike Bhalla the previous day and told him my side of the story. Both Ronnie and Madame Phyllis were fond of Mike. Mike promised that he will apprise Mrs. P about this.**

On Tuesday, the bugle sounded again for the second time in my life in NDA. I was marched up to Ronnie for formal relegation. **I have never stopped admiring Ronnie for very many qualities. One of the foremost was** his great ability to decide when injustice was done and correct the same irrespective of who had done it. Of course, I was guilty for open defiance of authority. It definitely deserved retribution. But a greater offence was committed by an officer, who manhandled a cadet in public, thus setting a bad example. **Of course I was certain that kind lady Mrs. Phyllis Beatrice Pereira also interceded on my behalf, having learnt my travails from Mike.** Many of these details were made known to me few years later by Adjt HKT (retired as Brig), when our paltans were in the same Brigade. He was then 2IC of 8 Grenadiers (approved to take over soon) and I was Adjt of my battalion – 6 MADRAS.

To cut the story short. I knew mine was the 'lost case' if I didn't speak up that day. **Oh boy …standing in front of Ronnie, I spoke for my life that day.** Ronnie let me speak but kept interrupting me at places. He was a patient listener that day. Of course I didn't forget to tell him that I smelt liquor in DO's breath and but for the kick up my posterior, I would have continued rolling. I also confessed that I was extremely sorry for what I had done and such a thing will never happen again. **Our tit-a-tat must have gone on for about 40 minutes or so! HKT, Dolly and No2 Bn Cdr were all at 'savdhan' all this while.** After I finished speaking there was a silence for a while. **And then Ronnie spoke…He was tough.** He didn't condone my act of disobedience and told me how completely he disapproved of my action. Thereafter, pointing his finger at my face, he said he will be keeping me in his 'sights' from then on. Any misdemeanor on my part, however minor will result in my relegation. And then looking sternly at HKT, Ronnie ordered him to march me out. My longest day was over".

Looking back on this incident, I now regret at times that such a thing happened. And I have never felt good about my conduct that day at the Drill Square. **But it taught me a very major lesson - that before deciding to initiate action against someone, always listen to his/her side of the story. And ultimately justice must prevail irrespective of persons/affiliations. And all lessons I learnt that day - of impartiality, compassion and being just are all kind courtesy …Ronnie P?**

Though belated I will be failing in my duty, if I do not express my sincere gratitude to late Ronnie and his gracious wife, late Mrs. Pereira (I attended her funeral in Nov 2013 at Bangalore), HKT, Dolly Kapoor, Himmat Sidhu, Mike Bhalla and the entire Echo squadron which remembered my intentions during the morning prayer, I am truly privileged to belong to an institution which produces such magnificent Comrades at Arms…**And for the beloved and much loved Pereira couple all I can humbly say is..**

"Death leaves a heartache no one can heal,

Love leaves a memory no one can steal". Unquote

What a moving description, yes, George spoke to me and I went home and narrated the story to Mrs. Pereira who heard me patiently and I told her that I am going to repeat the same to Boss. As I started, **Ronnie P said – son, don't teach me how to run my outfit and stay out of it.** I said please Unc, just hear me out and am not asking you to take cognizance of what I am going to tell you but **please** give me 10 minutes and I looked towards Mrs. P for support and she said Ronnie let the child speak and he reluctantly agreed but said **son, I am not going to change my decision,** I said doesn't matter and he quietly heard the other side of the story and I told him the **truth**. He didn't say anything. I came back and told George I have tried but chances are grim, let's pray for the best!

I really don't know what happened after that, may be Mrs. Pereira sage words or the scene of Echo squadron on their knees during morning muster and praying for George might have tilted the balance in George's favour. Admiral was a devout Christian and I think his dear late mother's words must have evoked his soft side!! I really don't know, it is my conjecture! But George was plain lucky and God was with him to walk out of Deputy's office **unscathed!**

All Admiral said later about his decision, son, I heard him and he had a point and gave him benefit of doubt. I kept quiet!

TRIBUTE TO A LEGEND

SJS GREWAL / 43rd KILO

It was on 2nd October 2015 that for the first time I sent a mail to all my course mates through kind courtesy Joy Nath, 43rd Delta, requesting for their contribution in the book I propose to write on Admiral RL Pereira. Sharan Jeet Grewal was one of the first to come forward and sent me a mail.

Quote "Hi Mike – regards: good to know that you are penning down and compiling all our stories and anecdotes that are related to our respected Dep Com. I will share something very important but not known to many of our course mates **that changed my career and life style because of his compassion and logical decision making acumen.** I will send the write up once I finish writing it. With best wishes – Garry" .**Unquote.**

Sharan Jeet kept his word and sent me his story as follows:-

Tribute

Quote "It was, I think 16th Dec 72 when I passed out from NDA as an Air Force cadet, marching with cane in hand, being Divisional Cadet Captain. But I was not happy as my future seemed very uncertain. Just prior to POP, final medical tests were held in **which I was temporarily declared medically unfit to join Air Force because of my chronic sinus problem.** The option was that either I go for immediate medical treatment and take a chance hoping that my sinus would cure and I will be able to continue with my flying training at Air Force Academy or if it hampers flying, I should accept to get grounded and remain a ground duty officer throughout my service. Later option was just not acceptable to me because flying aircrafts was my passion. Another option was to change over to Army and loose a term in NDA, to go through one term of Army training with my junior course i.e.;

44th course. In my heart of hearts I knew that this medical issue will not go away easily as I have been living with it since my school days and it had given me slight problems even while flying glider over the Lone Hill, Garware Hill, Pt 2475, and Pashan Gate near AFTT.

My Divisional Officer (Divo), Flt Lt Shirazee, and some of our flying instructors advised me to change over to Army, seeing my aversion towards ground duties specially when my course mates will be flying the machines and I will be doing some routine duties on the ground. But I was also not prepared to get relegated. So you can imagine the amount of tension and uncertainty that I was going through 7-10 days prior to POP. Firstly, knowing that I may not get to fly at all and secondly of getting relegated and spending 6 months with the cadets who were junior to me till now. I requested my Divo to defer any decision till I can discuss with my parents who were due to arrive for POP. He somehow managed to convince my squady and I got a breather.

The background as to why I had this sinus problem at such a young age, is that at the time of admission to Sainik School, Kapurthala in Jan 1963, my father was advised to get my tonsils removed, for the reasons best known to the school doctor. I was taken to a local civil hospital and got my tonsils removed without much medical expertise or proper procedure. I joined the school after the operation but suffered throughout my school days from after effects of this operation which over the time became chronic sinus.

I developed such a strong passion for flying after seeing low flying aircrafts and dog fights over our school premises during 1965 war that I started writing my name, of course informally – as Squadron Leader SJS Grewal !! Because of this passion I did not join NDA with 42nd course as Army cadet but waited for my next chance to try my luck for Air Force SSB. I was therefore, selected at AF SSB Varanasi for 43rd NDA as air force cadet and passed out also with them but to join Army, **thanks** to my Dep Com, Commodore RL Pereira. The following is a short narration of how the events unfolded after Passing out Parade.

After we marched past the Quarter Deck, we joined our parents for customary high tea and that is where I walked up to my Dep Com. "Admiral Ronald Lynsdale Pereira, PVSM, AVSM", then Commodore, with confidence in my gait and **hope** in my heart. I knew nothing worse can happen than what he had already decided i.e. relegation in case I choose to give up joining Air Force. After a smart salute, I took courage and told my story, which I suppose he knew already, **and in one breath told him that I want to opt out of joining**

Air Force and also I should not be relegated. Knowing him to be a terror that he was for us cadets, I mustered enough courage to look into his eyes and without waiting for him to say anything, I blurted out as to why I should not be relegated. I am losing out on my passion of flying and relegation for no fault and weakness of mine will further add to my disappointments; that I am an appointment holder and one of the very few who **survived his mass de tapping** of appointment holders of our course by him and that he may not be happy to see me as a plain cadet after relegation; **and how will he feel if he was in my shoes and words to that effect!!!!** I thought he smiled but maybe I was wrong. Before I could say anything more, he, being a tall man, looked down upon me and asked if I had any other option in mind. I had come prepared for this question, just in case my Dep Com would be in good mood and without blinking an eyelid I requested him to let me stay back during the term break and put me through the Army training, in condensed form, that my Army course mates have gone through and if I pass at the end of it, I may be sent to IMA directly from NDA. He looked around and asked me to take him to my parents who were standing some distance away. I thought the worst is going to happen now and he is going to tell them that their son stands withdrawn from the academy for indiscipline. How dare he has the guts to speak like this? Period!

He walked up to my father, a retired educationist, and after exchanging pleasantries told him something I couldn't believe. **He told him that I will not be able to go back with them for the term break and instead I will stay back to go through the Army subjects and after 20 days if I score 85 % or more in the test I will be spared from relegation and would be sent straight to Indian Military Academy, Dehradun.** Orders were passed to the Academy Adjutant on the spot and with a pat on my back he dismissed me. Did I expect this from him? No, not at that time with my maturity level at that age and the **circumstances. But, yes today I can say with conviction that he was a tough task master but gentle at heart.** His hard exterior was as good for us as his compassion and humane interior. **What a leader he was!?** Always immaculately turned out with perfect military bearing, ramrod straight, soldierly expressions. Seen everywhere and his aura felt in absence too, fair in doling out punishments and rewards, a man of few but precious words, physically fit and a wonderful leader in all aspects. Later on my wife and self had the privilege to meet him at DSSC Wellington and he remembered me from NDA days. Yet another trait of good leader and human being. **Was he a terror too? Of course but a well meaning one!**

Continuing with my story of joining Army---well, I scored more than 85% at the end of my so called 'training cycle' not because of my capabilities but because of compassionate team of ATT (Army Training Team) instructors who were assigned to me. God bless them and God bless my Dep Com's **pious soul!!!" unquote**

What a moving story and I must say Sharan Jeet had carried it in his heart all these 45 years and am grateful to him for sharing with us. Thanks buddy !

SALUTE TO MY MENTOR

JS KATARIA / 43 F

Walking down the memory lane Kats as he was popularly known recalls entering the hallowed portals of National Defence Academy as an Army cadet in 43rd course in Jan 1970 from a totally non Sainik/military school unlike most of his batch mates, he was totally raw and his young mind was in search of a mentor to shape him into a soldier and leader of men.

Come Jan 1971. Then Commodore Ronnie Pereira was posted as Dep Com to NDA and who, subsequently left an indelible print on his impressionable mind. Kat did very well for himself and won the coveted "Bayonet" in his 6th term, which he incidentally received from none other than the Dep Com himself. In Dec 73, he was commissioned into 13TH Rajputana Rifles.

On a fateful night of Oct 89, during the heightened militancy in Punjab, Kats while travelling in a civil bus with his wife and two small daughters was ambushed by Sikh militants on Moga – Firozepur road, causing serious injury to his wife and daughter. Kats single handedly overpowered three young militants and rescued all the civilians. **Could it be said that this was the acme of values imbibed under Ronnie Pereira?**

His tribute to the great man .

Quote "Dear Mike – my story is certainly not as touching as that of George and others. Nevertheless I must share with you.

The Pongos of 43rd were in Camp Torna, the closing phase of our 6th term. Captain DH Parab our Divisional Officer (divo) had nominated me as the leader of the final day escape run. My name was announced well in advance. But as luck would have it I developed fever a day prior to the run. As the Foxtrot Squadron Team was heading for the start line, Capt Parab came to give his words of encouragement. It is at this point of time, he came to know that I was running high fever. He looked at me and asked: "Will you be able to lead the squadron?" I stood in attention and replied in firm voice, "Yes Sir".

At the start line when the releasing officer shook hands with me to wish us good luck, he said, you can't participate - you are running high fever. He looked back at our very own Ronnie who was standing at a distance. Deputy Commandant showed no interest and appeared oblivious of our conversation. I stood my ground and said at this late stage I can't let down my squadron and belie the faith of my divo and course mates. I will lead the squadron come what may. The releasing officer said –OK, if your divo Capt Parab knows about your health and if you are keen, you can proceed.

I finished the run and after completing my firing I collapsed at the firing range. When I woke up I found myself in the hospital with a drip bottle on a stand hanging by my bed side.

In the meanwhile everyone went back to the squadron. The next day the 6th termers cadet of no 2 Battalion decided to skip the mandatory morning muster parade. Our dear Deputy Commandant Ronnie was on the prowl. Swinging in his Ambassador car in the wee hours of the day break, he caught them with their pants down. A special dose of Ronnie's style was inevitable!

There was mass de-tapping of the appointments and overnight those who never expected became appointment holders. This was not all, Ronnie's fertile mind came up with unique routine that would make the errant cadets remember the whole episode for rest of their lives and reinforce their mental and physical strength. The day for them would begin with 10 miles run in FSMO (Field Service Marching Order) starting at 4.30 am to the famous Poona crossing and back. After the run all cadets on punishment had to change into 'Drill Order' and assemble in their respective squadron's muster grounds by 6.50 am and go for drill at the Drill Square from 7am to 9am. After shower and breakfast they were required to fall in the famous 'Bajri Order' at 11.30 am for half an hour warming up exercises and then be ready for lunch by 1.30 pm. They were expected to get back at 4 pm for the evening run to Poona crossing in the FSMO, attend anti-room parade between 7 to 7.30 pm in the Mess Dress and then proceed for dinner. The finale of the day was the 10 pm assembling in front of the squadron in the 'Riding Rig' with Big Pack and break off at 11 pm. The routine was to continue till further order without a break. Ronnie was present most of the time, particularly for the morning and evening ten miles run.

I learnt the bunking incident while I was in the hospital. Capt Parab had come to look me up and was very appreciative of my performance. He assured me that I will be surely excused since I was not there at the time of the incident. After 5/6 days of hospitalization I requested the doctor for my discharge who was reluctant as he felt that I hadn't recovered fully. Most unusual of NDA doctors who were known for M & D (medicine and duty) which often landed us in trouble!

Finally the doctor let me go with medicine and excused outdoors. The next morning I joined my fellow termers for the 4.30 am run, quite confident that I would be let off. When Ronnie came, and he asked the reason for my standing separately. Capt Parab informed the Dep Com that when the incident took place I was in the hospital and hence I be exempted from the punishment. I was called forward in front of the Deputy Commandant, in the presence of my squadron commander and battalion commander. **Ronnie looked straight into my eyes and said, son, I vividly remember your conversation with the releasing officer who didn't want you to run and you insisted that you couldn't let down your squadron and your course mates, I had really liked that. My spirits soared sky high!**

Ronnie next question took the wind out of my sails' "Son, what would you have done if you were not hospitalized? Would you have been on parade or missed it like others? His sharp eyes were focused on my face. My soaring spirits came crashing down and sensing the reality on the ground. I replied Sir I would have been with my course mates. With a twinkle in his eyes Ronnie said "in that case you should be joining them, son" I had no choice but to join the gang.

As the passing out day was approaching nearer, we learnt that permission was taken from the Ministry of Defence to retain the passing out cadets on punishment for another fortnight. It was like 440 volts shock since number of the cadets in question had their parents arrive soon to witness the passing out parade. It was great humiliation for them. One fine morning to our pleasant surprise, the Dep Com announced that all those who finish ten miles run in one hour and twenty minutes will be exempted from punishment and proceed home after passing out. The run started and I being the first enclosure cross-country runner and best in no 2 battalion, ran at my usual speed and completed the run in just over an hour. **Observing me Ronnie cut down the timings to one hour and ten minutes.** With the change only few of us got exempted from the punishment.

On reaching the squadron all course mates pounced on me and accused me of letting them down. How I wished I had run slower or had the prowess to read Ronnie's mind. **But Ronnie being Ronnie always held the trump card in his hand.**

After the POP I came back to my cabin to pack my bags and say good bye to NDA and our Alma-mater, where we had spent three most memorable years of our youth. I suddenly heard the sounds of rejoicing in the squadron. I was over joyed to learn that during 'Tea with Parents' **our Dep Com Ronnie Pereira had magnanimously agreed to let the cadets go with their parents.**

Today, having retired after almost four decades with Infantry and Special Forces, I look up to the sky and thank our revered Ronnie Pereira who made soldiers out of ordinary mortals like me and prepared me to face the challenges of life squarely and smilingly!

May his 'MEMOIRS' continue to inspire generations in time to come! Unquote.

Kat rose to the rank of Major General and commanded a RAPID Division on the western border.

RECALLING ADMIRAL RL PEREIRA

MURALIDHARAN /43rd H

I like many of my contemporaries, my first recollection of Admiral RL Pereira or Ronnie P, as he was fondly known, is that of then Commodore Pereira as Deputy Commandant of the National Defence Academy, Khadakwasla, when we were cadets there in early 70's. Personally, I owe so much to that man, in that I may not have been in the Navy or in the Armed Forces for that matter, but for him. But I am jumping the gun and will come to that story little later.

When Ronnie P took over as Deputy Commandant of the NDA in Jan 71, I was not present, as I had been hospitalized due to a horse riding accident and possibly due to mishandling of the fracture of my hand. I had to spend a long spell in the hospital. When I rejoined, I immediately heard stories from my course mates of the new Dep Com, who was in total contrast to the earlier one – Col HKK Shukla. The new Dep Com had already gathered a reputation of being present at all spots where cadets could be found, whatever time of the day or night it was! The hushed buzz in squadrons and sports fields that Deputy is coming was often preceded by a booming voice, 'I am here'.

If I recollect, my first personal interaction with him was when he came to the practice session of the Battalion teams, preparing for Inter Battalion Bhavani Shankar Memorial Debate. All participants were coached by Professor Raina who was in charge of the event to ensure that we put up a good show. The Dep Com joined us and soon in his indomitable style was giving us tips on how to debate. While I do not recollect the subject that was being debated that day, Ronnie P threw in the name of Brigette Bardot. At that time many of us including yours truly did not get the name right nor did we realize who she was, till we ventured into the library a couple of days later to learn about the French heart throb. Dear readers, those were early 70's well before the days of Internet and mobile phone.

Once he got to know my existence, he always made a point to enquire about my progress whenever he saw me. Even though I was temporary low category, due to fracture of my hand, I had decided to take part in all physical activities irrespective of the fact that I was exempted being a low medical category. Soon, Ronnie P became aware of it and while he did not tell me directly, I learnt that he appreciated the spirit of my participation. One day he saw some of us in the swimming pool. Basically it was a way of skipping some other hectic activity, under the pretext that we were weak in Breast Stroke swimming and needed practice to clear swimming test. The moment he saw me, he inquired why I was there, when I told him that I was practicing breast stroke, he ordered me to swim half a length in that stroke. Even as I was mid way through, he called me out of the pool and he said that he found nothing wrong with my stroke and added "I always knew that no Malayalee can be weak in swimming". Pronto I was chased out of the pool and asked to rejoin in Squadron activities.

I could go on with many such anecdotes of Ronnie P, including the often story of turning the proverbial Nelson's eye when Naval cadets did not form proper squads on their way to Peacock Bay, but was promptly there to haul up the Army or for that matter Air Force cadets if they did not form a proper squads!

Let me come to the main incident for which I always remember him. As mentioned earlier. I had a fracture of my left hand in a riding accident and when time came for my re-categorization, the Surgical Specialist observed that I had not been able to obtain full movement of the hand in super nation/proration. He told me that until that movement became normal, I would not be upgraded medically. As a cadet, it implied that unless you were in fully fit medically category. You could not pass out from NDA, which actually meant closure of my military career? The Specialist actually made me Permanent Low Medical Category, but as luck would have it, the Medical Officer at Military Hospital at Khadakwasla knowing the implication took pity, on an unknown cadet and sent the medical papers back to the Specialist requesting him to make me a temporary category for another three months hoping that I would recover by then. I was not aware of all these details as the Medical Officer spoke only to my Squadron Commander. The Squady advised me that in normal official bureaucratic process, it would not be possible for me to get upgraded, nor he would be able to push my case. While I did not understand what he was saying at that stage, after many years in service I was able to grasp its importance. He then advised that I should go directly to the Dep Com and explain my case and he would find a way to help me. In normal case, one is only marched up to Dep Com's office, since I have been directed by my Squadron Commander; I went right into Dep Com's office. Of course his staff was not perplexed because they were used to cadets breaking protocol and coming to meet Ronnie P, and even directly summoned by him. I met Commodore Pereira and explained my predicament. I do not think he took even a minute to grasp the issue and told me, "Son, you go back to the squadron. I will let your Squadron Commander know when I need you. We will sort this issue out". He also encouraged me by saying that his own arm had been injured while in the Navy and he did not find any specific problems in managing and therefore, did not think I would have any issues in the Navy.

Later I learnt that Ronnie P who was soon going away on promotion as Rear Admiral to command the Eastern Fleet of the Navy had told Squadron Commander that once he hands over the job, he would resolve my issue prior to leaving for Vishakhapatnam. A couple of days later, I was called to the Squadron Commander office one morning and found Ronnie P with the jeep of No 1 Battalion Commander, as his own vehicle had been taken over by the next Dep Com. He then took me along to the Orthopedic Specialist at Military Hospital, Kirkee, who looked at my hand and told me "Son, don't worry I will upgrade you when you are due for re-categorization". Admiral Pereira then told me to wait outside the room and I could sense some kind of debate going on inside. Ten minutes later, Admiral Pereira emerged smiling with my medical papers and said "Son, you have been upgraded, and you can continue your normal training. See you on a naval ship soon". The Orthopedic Specialist was standing behind him smiling.

Ronnie P dropped me back in my squadron via the famous Manney's bookshop in Poona. The Squadron Commander later told me that the OC of the Military Hospital was upset that the cadet had gone and got himself upgraded without his knowledge and that too earlier than due. The Squadron Commander told him that it was under the orders of Admiral Pereira and if he had any issue he better sort out with the Admiral. There were no further calls from MH! Admiral Pereira had told me on our way back that he feared that once he had left the scene and incase the Specialist he had spoken to was away, some other doctor may have lower my category permanently which would have prevented me from passing out of the Academy. That would have been the end of my naval dreams and career.

Years later, when I discussed the issue with Admiral Pereira, he merely smiled and said something that is still ringing in my years; **"Son, if you can help any person and so long as you are not breaking any rules, and it is not for any personal gain, you should always do it."** Even now when I think back at that action of Admiral Pereira to help a young cadet, **I can do no better than to salute the noble soul.** It was not something that many of his contemporaries would have done or for that matter, I wonder how many of us would have done so?

Later when we were cadets on board training ship, Delhi. Admiral's Pereira flagship was berthed next to ours and we cadets were scrubbing the deck. Suddenly there was a booming voice from the other ship yelling "Murali how is your hand? "I quickly saluted and said its fine, Sir. On lighter vein, the flip side was that our Sub of the Gun (Training Officer), who was extra strict with the cadets, noticing my familiarity with the Fleet Commander, therefore gave me a lot of leeway! Later I met Admiral as FOC, Southern Naval Areas as it was then known and subsequently as Commander- in- Chief of the Western Naval Command. On all occasions we old cadets, always surrounded him and despite being the strict disciplinarian that he was as C-in-C, he always had soft corner for his old cadets, much to the surprise of other senior officers. I still recall meeting him in Bombay at a Command Reception. My hair was slightly longer than it should have been and it was windy evening when I walked up to him. Soon he started brushing my hair with his hands and said "firstly I am glad that you have not modified your uniform trousers into a bell bottom, secondly if your hair is long, brush it down when you come to see the C-in-C." I could see the stunned look in the eyes of Commodore and Captains who were around, when they observed that C-in-C to be so soft to a Lieutenant!

I ran into him on many occasions when he was the Chief of the Naval Staff as by then I had been appointed as Flag Lieutenant to one of the Commander-in-Chief , Vice Admiral Barboza, who was a contemporary of Admiral Pereira. It gave me many opportunities to interact with Admiral and Mrs. Pereira. Both of them treated all of us old cadets like their own children.

The impact he had on the entire generations of officers and men cannot really be explained in words. Even after his retirement, he was possibly one of the few officers who people were always keen to meet. Virtually every officer or jawan irrespective of his service, would stop to greet him .This was so evident in Wellington. I was at Kochi undergoing some training, when one evening I was booking a call through the naval telephone exchange to speak to my family at Wellington. As I got connected to the exchange, I heard the sobbing voice of telephone operator and on enquiry the lady told me that **they had just learnt that Admiral Pereira was no more and he was such a wonderful person.** I was equally numbed but was not at all amazed at the impact of Ronnie P had on people who were lucky to interact or merely hear about him.

As I moved up the ladder in the Navy, I never forgot the words of Admiral Pereira or kindness he showed to a cadet all those years ago. I always endeavoured to live up to his ideals and more so giving a helping hand to someone so long no rules were being broken even if it meant stretching them a bit.

Shano Varuna.

REMEMBERING RONNIE PEREIRA

MANOJ ASTHANA / 42 F

It was a normal day in the beginning of the term at the NDA. At least so it seemed.

The excitement of the 4th term writ large as we finally seemed to get little senior and couldn't be tossed around, or so we thought. Foxtrot squadron as always the most Royal Squadron was also a scene of activity to begin the term with cabin cupboard and putty parades. Capt DHC Parab's moral lectures kept us busy with our heads deep down in our James Hadley Chase novels cleverly concealed under the Physics précis, during the Squadron Period. Only a few like Sqn Cdr Lt Cdr Varghese knew of the plot but chose to take it easy as long as he could borrow some novels, once in a while.

We were the Champions, thanks to Arun Khetrapal, Jaat Singh, Jaiswal, Kaul, Manoj Pal Singh, CM Jaywant, Ravi Rajan, Ram Pal Suhag with his boxing gloves on. These stars of Foxtrot were all great at outdoors and always helped others as well. The venerable 38th course had got the Fox Squadron to be the Champions and the cockiness of the lanyard on the right, was overbearing.

Deputy Commandant Col HKK Shukla was moving out and the Academy was abuzz with the gleeful news that a non Ex NDA was coming in as the new incumbent, it was even more exciting to know that he was from the Navy.

White dress, picture of sobriety dignified and well, a little at Sea with the NDA! So we thought. We were in for cool times with a sober Deputy Commandant, who would not know the existence of room no 99 and room no 100. Nor would he know how to lock the cabins from outside and sleep inside. Certainly he would have no business to know, that we do report sick on double outdoor days, the only one to catch us was the Medical Officer who used to sit in the MH with his name tab, Maj Narayan Swamy written on it. In my service I never came across an officer who wrote his rank on the name tab. But he was effective as in place of medical books his office was laced with training programme of all courses. He would first confirm the course, checked the outdoor schedule and then very lovingly wrote M&D on the sick report book. I was the chosen few to get the M&D in red ink, which of course had its special privileges. While we basked in the comfort zone of non NDA Deputy, we were told to assemble in the Auditorium. As Bobby Shah gave the report to Adjutant and we waited for Deputy Commandant Commodore RL Pereira to arrive. Our monotony was broken by the arrival of a very lean, trim and tall Naval Officer as he climbed the steps to the stage. He thundered in his baritone voice that he is here not to molly coddle any one of you but to make you all into the finest leaders of men and I will not hesitate to kick your bloody backsides if warranted. I shall observe you for a while and then act. I will chase you all and chase very hard, which he soon started with a proverbial "bang".

He struck like lightening one early morning. SCC Manoj Pal Singh was taking the muster parade for the Foxtrot Squadron, when we heard a screeching sound of a car. The Deputy had struck!

A Black Dodge Kingsway opened its door and a lanky figure in whites emerged. Like a whirlwind he went around the cabins, ticking off 6th termers who normally never attend such fall-ins. There was a minor Tornado on in the squadron with appointment's tabs and stripes flying across the cabins windows. Then he arrived at the fall in area in front of the squadron. Two words I learnt that day which were new. Dirty brass work and poor leather work, as he continued on his liberal distribution of restrictions.

After dolling out handsome dosage, he sat inside his car and drove off like a receding avalanche. When we reached our classes , we were happy to note that we were not the only one with our jaws touching our groins, almost all squadrons seems to have been visited by the Black Dodge Kingsway ghost car! The terror multiplied when Deputy found new means of awarding punishments.

He would stop the cycle squads which were out of formation and award a number of restrictions to be equally divided by the cadets. Self help is the best help, he believed!

He introduced Singarh hikes as punishment to be done in FSMO full kit, in stipulated time. When I went for inaugural session for the first Singarh hike I was astonished to see a happy and smiling Deputy in white sports dress.

When you guys take "punga", you should be ready to face it too, said he in a thundering tone.

We were happy about the fact that the Deputy decided to walk with us to Singarh along with the PTO, Major Darshan Singh lovingly called Dhaka Singh. Enroute he cracked jokes with the cadets who were perpetual panga takers of the Academy. On top of Singarh, loads and loads of Nimbu pani and fruit cakes and biscuits awaited us. Ronnie Pereira did not believe in treating cadets shabbily, the message went down the Academy that day. His presence was being felt.

In one of the Singarh hikes when I went for the morning fall in, Subedar RP Singh, Rajput Regiment, who was from Fox, informed me that my name was not in the list for Singarh that day. Happily I turned back to return and sleep, CM Jayawant who was doing probably the maiden punishment in NDA asked me to come along, just for a company. When we returned from Singarh, I was shaken out of my lethargy seeing the ghost car, Black Dodge Kingsway parked right in the PT fields.

FSMO contents check up started, I was cursing my shit luck when I decided to undertake the hike even though my name was not on the list. Out of 14 contents of FSMO, seven were missing in my case. Deputy had a novel way of displaying his originality. Seven extra Singharh hikes were awarded to me, one for each missing item of the FSMO.

I decided to walk up to the Deputy in the PT field that day and told him my story of not being on the Singarh hike and said that I just went along to give company to CM Jaywant. In display of instant justice, Deputy increased the hikes to 14, seven for missing contents and other seven for going to Singarh when my name was not on the list. That day I learnt two important lessons, Deputy had taught me. One, that there is no graduate punishment, once you do something wrong then you should be ready for any punishment. Second, being most important lesson of my life, when you decide to partner a course mate, don't crib. Just go along come what may. Seven Singarh hikes have never killed anyone, but ditching buddies have!

Was Commodore Ronnie Pereira really a non Ex NDA??

He seems to be making magical impact on the cadet's psyche, despite dolling out punishments as if he was distributing Christmas gifts. Perhaps it was his sense of pride in uniform and love for the cadets. He would never demean anyone. If he lost his shirt during the day, he will make up for it during the Squadron social when he will surround himself with the indiscipline type and guffaw away with them. He had a special liking for panga takers and would often say, it's really between you and I, you manage to skip you are fine, if I get you, and then be graceful enough to show yourself on the drill square. Soon we knew him to be an Officer of extreme compassion, grace, élan and just behavior. His Officers like Qualities were infectious. His love for cadets was becoming increasingly evident, But Ronnie will never take any nonsense, was also a universal fact.

The term had just got over and we were back in NDA. Sub Maj Kanshi Ram informed us that all of us who had traveled by NDA special train 1, have been awarded 14 days restrictions for misbehaving at Ratlam railway station. By now I had gathered enough restrictions to push me to the next course, so I walked up to Sub Maj Kashi Ram and informed him that I never travelled by NDA special train No 1, as I had collected the ticket from my train JCO and clandestinely travelled by the Punjab Mail. I was happy that Kanshi Ram took my plea to the Deputy, who called me to his office and to my utter horror gave me strikingly familiar punishment. 14 days restriction for misbehaving while travelling on NDA special no 1 and another 14 days for not travelling by NDA special No 1! The lesson was driven home effectively that there was hardly a point in trying to act smart with him. He somehow could sense my utter discomfort; probably he knew that mere restrictions would not shake me. So I confided in him that my 28 restrictions will take my tally beyond 40, which is good enough to get one relegated.

Deputy did not take more than a moment to tell Kanshi Ram that no restrictions given by him shall be counted towards relegation. That's not the aim, he said!

His popularity had taken him deep in the heart of the cadets, who by now had clean forgotten that he was not an Ex NDA. Ronnie Pereira knew more about our pranks but that never deterred us from cooking up new stories.

The rules of game were simple and non negotiable, if you manage to skip, lucky you, but if you get caught, don't crib, face it with a smile. In one of the ante room socials I mentioned to him that the restrictions schedule is really very boring. He smilingly asked me what I had in mind. So I did tell him a time bound run in FSMO to Pashan gate would be interesting enough. He agreed.

Next day he drove on a scooter along with us to Pashan gate while we ran and he benchmarked the timing. As I was ready to leave, he casually asked what the catch is. So I did confide in him that the shooting of Bobby was going on near Pashan and every day we get to view the stars. Fine by me as long as you don't get late, he said.

More than Ronnie it was grace and kindness of Mrs. Pereira which had endeared them to the cadets. A grand lady that she was, she would treat the cadets with utmost love and care and in her presence Ronnie Pereira dare not raise his voice on a cadet.

A great couple, Pereira's had become the most loved couple for the cadets, this for their fine sense of justice, fairness, and concern for the cadets.

As I was passing out of NDA, he met me at the squadron social and confided that he loved those who took chances. Even Mrs. Pereira mentioned that Ronnie loves the panga takers but if caught, he'd come down hard, the trick was not to get caught. However, cases of moral turpitude and stealing were absolutely unpardonable and no mercy could be expected from him.

The NDA had special place for Ronnie Pereira, that's known as INS TRAINING SHIP PEREIRA at the Peacock Bay, a rare honor indeed.

I passed out from NDA in June 1972 and 9 years later when I was flying helicopters at Air Force Station, Bagdogra, we got a signal from HQs 33 Corps regarding the visit programme of Admiral RL Pereira, Chief of Naval Staff, for a visit Corps Zone from 6th to 8th May 81.

The prime reason for Admiral and Mrs. Pereira's visit was to meet their foster son Captain Mike Bhalla and his new wife, a local girl from Gangtok!!

Admiral and Mrs. Pereira landed at Bagdogra by the Air Force aircraft on the 6th May and were flown by Capt Arun Opal and self to Darjeeling, to visit their schools, i.e. North Point and Mount Hermon, where they studied in 30's. After that we flew them to Kalimpong for the night stay.

Next morning on 7th May, Arun and self flew them to Gangtok - barely 20 minutes flying time. I vividly remember the scene, when they saw Mike Bhalla at the Libing helipad and how both of them warmly embraced him, a touching sight, indeed. Mike Bhalla was the son to them that they never had.

On 8th May81, we flew them down to Bagdogra and it was the last time I ever met the "Great Man".

Finally, I can safely say that the National Defence Academy at Khadakwasla would always be proud of Ronnie Pereira, the profound Ex NDA.

ENCOUNTER WITH DEP COM

RN BHATTACHERJI / 43 A

"Bhatta", as he was popularly known in Academy days was one of the very interesting characters in our course and I was aware of his close encounters with the Deputy. I requested him to go down the memory lane and recreate those unforgettable moments, which are given as follows;

Quote "I joined NDA, Khadakwasla in Jan 1970 with 43rd course. Our Commandant was Rear Admiral RN Batra and Deputy was Col HKK Shukla. When we came back after our winter break in Jan 1971, we got to know that a new Deputy Commandant, Commodore RL Pereira from Indian Navy had been posted to the Academy. Like the good old saying 'A man's reputation precedes him wherever he goes', there were hushed whispers amongst our seniors that the new Deputy is a firebrand, very strict disciplinarian and 'No Non-sense' man. So be on the look out!

Soon, from the first day itself we all got to know; Who Ronnie P was? He was omnipresent all over the Academy from morning tea to dinner in the Cadets Mess. His very presence sent shivers down spine among the indiscipline cadets. At times it turned out to be 'hide and seek' game between the Deputy and the erring cadets and more often than not, Deputy got the better of them and surprised the unsuspecting defaulters. I did have few close encounters with the Great man, which are enumerated in the succeeding paras;

I recall an interesting incident of my 6th term. Alpha squadron tables were located next to the main entrance of the Cadets Mess. Once a week we had 'Dinner Night'; a formal dinner with Div Officer from each squadron in attendance and we finished the dinner by offering toast to the 'President'. Other evenings we had 'Supper Night' where the cadets could eat to their heart's content, if permitted by the seniors or else they would ask you to close the plate and disappear! On one such occasion, milk which was served after dinner fell short. We all kept waiting but no milk arrived. Meanwhile, one of our course mates DSC Verma (popularly known as Disco Verma, as he was a very good dancer) from Lima Squadron rang up the Deputy and most of us were not aware of it. At about 9.30 pm, suddenly we saw Ronnie P walking in through the main entrance, going past our table and asking some cadets if they had milk or not? In unison everybody said 'No Sir'. Seeing him, one of the Sergeants from Air Force, a member of the catering staff was walking up to Ronnie to greet him and explain the matter. The Deputy just said where is the milk? The Sergeant gave some wishy-washy answer, which I could not hear, but what I saw was the Deputy caught him by the scruff of his neck and pushed him towards the wall. The Sergeant barely 5 feet and few inches went skidding and skating at least 10 feet and hit the wall and fell down. It had to be so when a Six footer plus man and that too angry on the matters of welfare of cadets pushes a defaulter. Within 5 minutes, trolleys filled with mugs and milk arrived.

That was the stature of Ronnie and cadets loved him for it.

Another incident took place in my 5th term. We used to have 'self study' period from 6.30 pm to 8 pm, when every cadet used to sit in his cabin with the door wide open, so that the duty officer and squadron appointments taking the round could see if everyone was on his table and studying and not whiling away his time in idle gossip or absent from the cabin.

Ronnie in spite of his busy schedule, loaded with entire responsibilities to run a world class premier Training Institute as NDA, always found time to make surprise visit to the squadron lines every now and then.

On one such occasion, I was gossiping with one of my subordinates in his cabin when suddenly I saw three cadets running past the cabin shouting in hushed voices "Deputy, Deputy". I immediately realized that he will come up on the top floor also as climbing any numbers of steps were never insurmountable for him when out on the prowl. I tried to rush back to my cabin which was on one of the flanks of the top floor.

Just to give an idea of squadron layout, each squadron had three floors with a long corridor in the centre with cabins on both sides and a flank at each end of the corridor with cabins also on either side. Three stair cases are leading up each flank and one to the centre lobby in the corridor. As I turned into my flank, I looked and saw that Deputy had climbed up the stairs to the other flank and was looking down the corridor and we just had a glimpse at each other. I quickly hurried to my cabin, settled in my study chair and pretended to be engrossed in my studies, hoping like hell that he had not seen me, and even if he had, he may not recognize me. My heart beat went up and intermittently between looking at my books; I looked through the corner of my eyes, if he walked into the flank. After sometime I heard his voice in the corridor and thereafter an eerie silence prevailed. I thanked God, the worst was over I thought but alas! Was it to be so? Suddenly, I heard steps moving down our flank and saw him going past my cabin. A step or two he had gone, he turned back, came and stood at the door spreading his hands across it. We were face to face and 'one on one'. He asked me my name and term I was in? He asked "what were you doing in the corridor?" I said "Sir"; I was solving a mathematical problem for one of my friends. He said, "Now look whether you have brains or 'bhoosa' in your head, you stick to your bloody chair during the study period. Is that clear?" I said "Yes Sir". While going back he said, "See me tomorrow in my office at 2 pm". I said "Sir". That's all. Oh! The storm had gone past, what a relief it was. Next day, when I landed up outside his office at the appointed time, Subedar Major Padam Bahadur from GRENADIERS Regt was there waiting for all of us. I saw lot of my friends of Drill Square present there and we moved into his office one by one. On seeing me, he said "you are the 'brainy' type solving Maths for your friend; you thought I had not seen you! 14 x2. March him out". Sub Maj ordered me to march out of the office. The punishment was 14 days restrictions and 2 Singarh Hikes. Singarh meant walking 14 kms up to the fort one way in FSMO (Field Service Marching Order) on a Sunday.

It was during one such morning on Sunday while going to the Drill Square; I saw all officers i.e. Squadron Commanders and Div Officers of all three services going on two wheelers towards Pashan Gate. Curiosity was at its peak, as I was going on punishment drive to Singarh on Sunday morning at 6 am. I was keen to know the elite and privileged lot of the NDA, how come they were going to Pashan Gate and couldn't be to the Equitation Lines, which was located next to Pashan Gate. There has to be something more than that meets the eye. Once again rumours had that on one of the official functions in the Officers Mess, the officers were late and also there were few absentees. Our beloved Deputy, a 'No Non-sense' man took charge in his inimitable way, a 'fall in' for all defaulters. So, for Ronnie discipline was above all and made no exception, no matter who he was!

On another occasion, as a not too bad, yet not too disciplined a cadet, I was going to the Drill Square for the 'love' of it as much as I sincerely loved, admired and respected Ronnie as I grew up in NDA.

I saw Ronnie coming down the Sudan Block in his car, at 3.30pm, while I was on my bicycle going to my 'Mecca' (gift from Ronnie in those days), the Drill Square. When I paid my complements to him, he responded with a salute and a smile, as though he had recognized me and **I felt proud of the fact that he had recognized me. An officer of normal make and caliber of his rank would have possibly ignored with disdain.**

That was "RONNIE".

Last but not in ever the least I would say, while in NDA most of us were angry, felt bad and said few bad words or so about him, but today when I lay in my couch and reminiscence the days spent in NDA (four terms/2years) with Ronnie, I think what he did can be rightly summed up in these words; **"He received a cadet, turned him into Gentleman cadet for IMA, ingrained in him all the virtues and qualities of an officer of the Indian Armed Forces. 'Yes', I am proud to have been trained by him."**

I do remember the speech he gave at Hut of Remembrance was so motivating, invigorating, injected life for the budding officers, that all present of 43rd NDA were in tears surprised; **is this the Deputy we saw for 2 years.**

That was Ronnie; a man dedicated to his job and spared no efforts to attain his mission in NDA of training the potential officers of Indian Armed Forces, who would be second to none. Officers trained by him have always made an effort to keep his name HIGH'

Long Live Ronnie Pereira

PS; While attending Staff College, DSSC 43 in Wellington in 1987, one day I came across Admiral in the Coonoor Club. I walked up to meet him, he couldn't possibly recognize me, but when I recollected my association with him, he felt happy, offered me a drink and wished me well.

May God Bless His Soul—Ronnie was Ronnie

TRUE MOTIVATOR

BK SINHA / 42 H

Ronnie P was a veritable terror for the cadets in NDA. He could be seen at most unsuspecting places at odd hour's day in and day out. He had made life very tough for the cadets. Invariably he was present for the morning muster in some squadron and anybody late even by a minute, he was taken to task. De-tabbed if you were an appointment or else 21 days restrictions for ordinary cadets! We thought that he was a terror with no soft corner whatsoever, but I had the fortune to experience his other side.

Encounter on Golf Course

One Sunday morning in the spring term of 1972, I had gone to the golf course to play a round of golf. I had kept my blazer on the hanger outside the Golf Hut. After a while Deputy arrived and he noticed my blazer and was surprised to see four Blues written on the pocket i.e. **Football, PT, Squash and Mountaineering**, all won in previous term! He inquired from somebody; whose blazer is that and he was told that it belongs to DCC BK Sinha of Hunter Squadron and presently he is on no 16th hole. Deputy immediately called up Maj Midha, my squadron commander and asked him why DCC Sinha case not put up for **Best Sportsman Blazer?**

Next morning the first order in the Academy Routine Order was award of Best Sportsman Blazer to Division Cadet Captain BK Sinha, Hunter Squadron.

After couple of weeks one morning Deputy came to Hunter Squadron looking for me. He couldn't find me in my cabin as I was in the washroom. He spotted me and asked; son, have you got your blazer? I replied in negative. He then said; Ok son, I will take on the 'bania' and collect it after 4 days, which I did.

That was Ronnie P, as the years have passed on and all cadets under him already shed uniform except few i.e. Chief of Army Staff, Chief of Air Staff and may be few three stars Generals, if any? **We now realize the man's worth in GOLD.**

Punishment Ronnie Pereira Style

This incident took place about 20 days before the passing out of our course, 42nd. During the PT parade Deputy noticed that few of our course mates were late for the parade and to make matters worse they showed no urgency to join their squadrons. It was enough to get Deputy heckles up and he ordered the entire course to go back to the squadrons and fall in within 30 minutes in FSMO (Field Service Marching order) at the PT ground. We were asked to run to the Peacock Bay about 3kms one way and report to the Cadet's Mess. It was really hot day in the month of May and we all were really sweating and when we reached Cadet's Mess, to our great surprise we saw Deputy himself distributing orange juice and saying; **son, have some more!! That one action actually neutralized our fatigue.**

The more I think of Deputy, the more I get convinced that indeed he was the "**True Motivator**' we ever came across. Imagine after retiring as Chief of Naval Staff, he was riding on a Vespa scooter in the streets of Bangalore and in fact met with near fatal accident sometime in 80's.

MEETING WITH THE FLEET COMMANDER

PILOT OFFICER RAVI KRISHAN

After passing out from Academy in Dec 72, we went for the IAF flying in the 112 pilot's course. During our final stage in the fighter training wing at Hakimpet, we were given a mid-term break in May 1974 to visit our homes before commissioning ceremony. I decided to visit my elder brother, a Naval Officer in Vizag. My course mate Beniwal also came along with me to visit Naval base hoping to meet Rear Admiral Ronnie Pereira, The Fleet Commander Eastern Fleet. Beniwal was one of his blue eyed boys in NDA. We purchased a large 25 kg box of "Banginapalli" mangoes as gift for Admiral and Maam. As soon as we settled down in my brother's house in Naval Park officer colony, we asked him directions to Admiral's house. He showed us the Flag Staff House which was about 5 minutes down the road. My elder brother suggested that we should meet the Admiral's Flag Lt for an appointment. We were Flt Cadets and in this rank to approach even the Flag Lt was not easy. However, with some influence of my elder brother we managed to reach the Flag Lt. As we requested him for an early meeting with the Admiral, he informed us that Admiral was very busy and had no time for us that day. Therefore, he advised us to come next day in the morning to his office. Our pleading for slotting a meeting even late in the evening had no effect on the senior Flag Lt. Back to my brother's house, we the potential pilots of the IAF were not happy with the situation. We were not comfortable with the Flag Lt's attitude, Navy's red tape and our anxiety to meet the Admiral at the earliest. While sitting in the lawn, I requested my brother to at least tell us if the Admiral was at home or not. My brother showed the Fleet Commander flag majestically fluttering on top of the Admiral's house. "That is the indication for Admiral to be at home", my brother assured us. This information gave us some hope. We applied our minds and asked "what if we flout the naval protocol and land up in Flag Staff House without prior permission". We deliberated the issue and took the decision to at least go to the Flag Staff House. Time was around 1800 hours. Two Flt Cadets in smart shirts matching trousers and ties marched towards Admiral Pereira's Flag Staff House. Jointly they were carrying a big card box filled with 25kgs of delicious Banginapalli mangoes. Surprisingly no one checked us when we walked through the main gate and rows of colorful flowers with neatly trimmed soft grass of front lawn. We pressed the main door call bell. We stood and waited for some house staff to open the door. However, surprise was in store for us. Mrs. Pereira was even more surprised to see us. "Benny my son" she exclaimed in delight. She hugged us both and welcomed in their simple but elegantly decorated drawing room. As soon as we were comfortable in the drawing room, she rushed shouting Ronnie, Ronnie, look who has come. Ronnie Sir was so thrilled to see us that I can't describe it. They treated us as their children had arrived from a long journey. As we were sipping the tea, we saw his Flag Lt walking in. He gave us an angry look as though we have intruded in his private domain. However, he soon sobered down as Admiral told him our background and told him to treat us as his special guests. A proper itinerary was made for Admiral's guests for our visit to the naval base. Next day a special vehicle and escort was detailed to take us to visit important ships, submarine and Naval Dockyard. It was great memorable educational tour culminating in a sumptuous dinner in the Flag Staff House.

Admiral Ronnie Pereira was a true warrior, a capable Military leader with heart of gold. We were lucky to have known the great man so intimately.

PATTON

ANIL GARG / 43 F

By the time we were in our 5th term, Admiral (Dep Com) had already spent one year in the Academy. There was always hide and seek game that used to go on. We thought that we have become fairly smart after two years of training behind us. But at times the Deputy Commandant had his way and used to spring surprises and those unfortunate ones got caught, used to spend their afternoons doing restrictions in the Drill Square or hiking to Singarh Fort on early Sunday mornings, when others used to have a longish sleep, a real luxury for the cadets after the exhausting week.

Deputy Commandant had planned that the whole Academy should see a wonderful war movie **"PATTON"**.

Well, in the NDA auditorium we used to get an opportunity to see some of the best movies both English and Hindi, so what was so different in this case? It was different in a way that the whole lot of us in the academy were required to cycle down to Poona city to see the movie there in a civil theatre. The distance to be travelled was about 40 to 45 kms to and fro journey. The whole theatre was booked for us to watch this movie. We were asked to move in cycle squads as usual and there were strict instructions not to break the squad.

I vividly recall the opening dialogue of the movie by General Patton, **"No bastard ever won the war by dying for his country, he won it by making the other damn bastard die for his country."**

It was good fun as long as the movie lasted. The scorching heat of the Sun in the late afternoon and peddling up the slope while coming back to NDA was bit tiring. We were the tail-enders and spotted a shop selling sugar cane juice. Our squad thought that why not have a quick halt and enjoy the juice. So, all 12 of us halted, sat in the shade and waited for the juice to be served.

It was real good drink, more so when you are thirsty and tired. We all collectively decided as to why not have another round.

It may be appreciated that when the vendor has to squeeze sugarcane to make juice for 12 more glasses, it would be little time consuming and that is where we went wrong in our appreciation. Those were the days when there were no electrically driven devices as seen these days to squeeze sugarcanes. It was all manual.

Finally after waiting for 10 to 15 minutes our glasses were ready. As soon as we had the first sip, whoosh came a car and came to screeching halt right in front of the shop. Before even we could get up, Deputy jumped out of the car and shouted "why the hell you have broken the squad and not obeyed my orders". Even before we could muster courage to give a reply to him, he shouted, **"14 Singarh Hikes"** and asked me to hand over the names of all of us to him. This was not the end of it as other surprise waited for us .He said, "Once you reach Pashan Gate, lift cycles up on your shoulders and reach your squadrons"

That was the costliest sugarcane I ever had in my life.

REMEMBERING ADMIRAL

APS SAMRA / 44TH ECHO

Adarsh Pal Samra, 44th course, Echo, was one of the finest Horseman and Polo player produced by NDA, a tall well built Sardar with broad shoulders and strong wrists who could hit the ball a long distance and went on to become plus 2 handicap player. He was one of the pioneers along with Cdr John Sigar and Admiral Sushil Kumar, later Chief of Naval Staff who popularized Polo in Navy. Of course they had full support of Admiral Ronnie Pereira from early 70's.

APS Samra had close relations with both Admiral and Mrs. Pereira from his days in NDA and sent me a mail in their memory;

Quote "**What can one say about Admiral RL Pereira, in my entire life till date I have not found one who could come close to him**. When I joined NDA in 1971, he was the Deputy Commandant and ever since then he became an **idol** who one could look up to. He was so fond of cadets and treated them like children, but with a firm hand, and was extremely fond of sportsmen. I remember how he encouraged me when he saw me ride and told me "Son, I want you to join the Navy and play for the Navy team" At that time the only players who played Polo in the Navy were Admiral Sushil Kumar, Cdr John Sigar and Cdr JS Dhillon. He ensured that we all came back to NDA as instructors so that we continue to play as the Navy did not have any horses.

I remember when I went for my Sub Lieutenant course to Cochin in 1975, Admiral was FOC Southern Naval Areas and he told me to start Cycle Polo in Cochin. Cycles, sticks and balls were procured in no time. He himself could outride any of us youngsters in Cycle Polo. As a sportsman one had only to ask and he would ensure that it was made available. I remember asking to be posted to NDA, he called me and said "Son you are listed to go to Russia, which would be good for your career, but choice is yours". When I requested for NDA posting, I got my appointment letter the day I became Lieutenant. The stories are endless; one could just call and walk into his house and was warmly welcomed.

If I can remember correctly it was in mid 70's when the Navy played in Mumbai as a team and never looked back. Courtesy Ronnie P and Admiral Sushil Kumar that the Navy has horses in each Command and string of polo ponies both at Mumbai and New Delhi. The Navy since late 90's has been playing as a team and today has a number of young Polo players.

"A man who till date stands in memories as a great leader and Human being"

UNFORGETTABLE RONNIE PEREIRA

RAINA

Mike Bhalla had originally intended for my father (Late) Professor Trilokinath Raina to write a few words about his memories of Admiral Pereira. Unfortunately, my father breathed his last barely a couple of months before Mike conveyed the request and therefore the mantle fell on my shoulders to write on my father's behalf (as well as my own) and share some of my memories about the late Admiral.

Admiral Pereira is the stuff that legends are made of. I have yet to meet the person on whom he did not leave a profound impact. Yes, there were those who hated his guts because he did not allow them to stray from the straight and narrow, but even such people knew within their hearts that they were dealing with an incorruptible character and respected him even more for that.

By the time the Admiral, then Commodore, was posted as the Deputy Commandant at the NDA, I had already passed out and was a young officer serving in an artillery unit. But since my father was posted at the NDA, it was inevitable that our paths would cross. I first met him at the railway station in Pune. In July 1972 I was on my way back from Belgaum after having attended the Commandos Course. I had taken a couple of days off and broke journey at Pune. On expiry of my leave, my brother had come to see me off at the station. Coincidentally, Ronnie (as he was universally called) was travelling by the same train enroute to Ludhiana to attend a conference. Those days there was no direct train from Pune to Delhi. One had to travel to Bombay and change trains there. My brother introduced us and we got talking while waiting for the train to arrive. Neither of us had reservation so the first priority was to get a seat. Those were the days an officer had to travel with a lot of baggage when going on a course of instruction. One had to carry one's own bedding in a hold all. Uniforms, dresses for various occasions, boots etc would be accommodated in a trunk. To complicate matters, I was also carrying my service rifle. When the train arrived, I told my brother to look after my luggage and, rifle in hand, rushed to find a seat for Ronnie and myself. I found us two seats and rushed back to guide him there. I did what any junior officer would do; I picked up his suitcase and asked him to follow me. I told my brother that I would be back for the rest of the luggage. I happened to look back to see if he was behind me and I was flabbergasted to see him carrying my hold all. He then helped me with the trunk. I requested him to please sit and that I would get the rest of the luggage in two trips. But true to his nature he just brushed aside my reservations and said that it was more important to get the luggage on the train.

Once we were seated in the train, Ronnie dominated the entire conversation. He asked me about my course and about my stay at the NDA and my experiences as a cadet because it was obvious that I passed out from NDA barely a couple of years earlier and he was keen to pick my brains on what kind of behavior and qualities a cadet expects of his officers. On the other hand, I was less keen on speaking about myself and my time at the NDA and more on listening to his experiences about life in the Navy. So I asked him a couple of questions about the recent acquisitions in the Indian Navy because these acquisitions had coincided with similar acquisitions by the Indian Army. I was particularly intrigued by the fact that each good armament that we had acquired from the erstwhile USSR was invariably accompanied by another armament which was not as good. It was almost as the government had signed up for a 'buy one get one free' arrangement with the Soviets. He was happy with my question and when into a long diatribe against the Soviet system and the manner in which we had been hoodwinked, practically arm-twisted, into including substandard or antiquated equipment into our purchase list, just because they accepted payment in Indian rupees. It so happened that he had been involved in the acquisition of some warships and therefore had strong opinions about how the negotiations had been conducted to India's disadvantage. After about five minutes I came to the conclusion that he was definitely anti-communist and therefore, by default, a supporter of the west. I then shifted the topic towards the United States. Two minutes later he was criticizing them in the strongest of words. Not an acolyte of the west either; maybe I had gone too far west. So I went back across the Atlantic and talked of Britain and France. Well, he had enough to talk of these two countries also, and again not in very flattering terms. Finally, it dawned on me that this was a man who was very clear in his understanding of national interest and a very proud Indian. He made a statement which has stayed with me all these years, "**Pramathesh, remember there is no lasting** friendship between countries. Every country looks to its self interest first. We have to do the same and cannot afford to rely on any one country to come to our rescue in times of trouble. We have to be self reliant especially when it comes to the defence of the country". It was not just I who was held spellbound, but the entire group of people sitting next to us. When Ronnie took a washroom break, one of the co-passengers inquired of me in an awed tone as to who he was.

Over the next couple of years I had occasion to meet Ronnie a number of times. During this period he was fast acquiring a reputation which, I daresay, none of his predecessors had managed. That is not meant to detract from the ability of his predecessors. It is just the personality of Ronnie was such that he wove a magic spell over everybody he came into contact with. **He was the embodiment of integrity and totally immersed himself into the job at hand. There was not a single crooked bone in his body and he never allowed ego to interfere in the performance of his duty.** He could be totally harsh in inflicting a punishment (entirely legal, of course) on an errant cadet and at the same time surprisingly compassionate and tender in his dealings. I was witness to one such incident where three of the aforementioned traits were on display. It was evening time and the location was the swimming pool. There was an incident in which, due to the fault of one cadet, another was injured. I happened to be present at the spot and so were Ronnie and my father. Ronnie immediately took charge, meted out punishment to the defaulter, called for his staff car and sent the injured cadet to the hospital, thereafter, since he was getting late for another appointment, jumped on the back seat of my father's scooter and requested for a lift home. My father protested to the effect that it would not be nice for the deputy commandant of the NDA to be seen riding pillion on a scooter. Ronnie just dismissed his protestations with an impatient wave of the hand.

Years went by and the legend of Ronnie kept growing as he ascended the professional ladder. Much to everyone's astonishment, he was appointed the Chief of Naval Staff. **Not that anyone doubted his ability, but that such an outspoken, blunt and incorruptible individual could be acceptable to the political masters was unexpected. That again speaks volumes of his magnetic personality, and also of the sagacity of those behind the decision.**

My father kept in touch with him throughout. My own interaction with him however was limited and thereby hangs a tale. I was married in 1980 when he was the CNS. He attended the reception in Delhi and apologized for having come without a present. He asked me what I would like as a wedding gift. Naturally, my response was something to the effect that his very presence at the occasion was present enough for us. Someone present at the gathering jokingly remarked, **"Sir, why don't you get him posted to the NDA"**. He liked the suggestion and said that he would do so. I smiled and said that there was no way the MS branch was going to oblige because I had just completed the long gunnery course, had been retained as instructor and had to do my mandatory two year tenure at Devlali. I did get posted to the NDA but that was a good three years after this conversation and had nothing to do with the Admiral's commitment, or so I thought. Another three years went by and I was now serving in a rocket regiment. Our unit was shifting to Rajasthan on completion of its tenure in J&K. I was entrusted with the task of familiarising the commanding officer of the incoming unit with the operational area. At the end of a hectic day we retired to the officers' mess and he asked me whether I was the same Raina who had served in the NDA some years earlier. I confirmed I was the same person. His next question took me by surprise, "How do you know Admiral Pereira?" I told him that he was known to my father. That simple explanation did not entirely convince him. I asked him the reason why he connected me to the Admiral. To be honest, I had entirely forgotten about the conversation regarding the wedding present which had taken place six years earlier. He then narrated the story behind my posting to the NDA, which again reveals a lot about Ronnie's character. It turned out that the next day after attending my wedding reception, Ronnie summoned his staff officer and asked him to go across to the concerned department carrying his request for me to be posted to the NDA. (Incidentally, in the Indian Navy a posting to the NDA is quite a routine affair as compared to the Indian Army where it is considered a prize posting). The staff officer was directed to meet him as he was then posted in the relevant MS section dealing with postings to the NDA. My case was studied and it was conveyed to the staff officer that though I met the criteria for posting, it would not be possible in the normal course as I had yet to complete my present tenure. Thus he was unable to meet the Admiral's request without bending rules, for which he would have to take the approval of his superior officer. This was conveyed to Ronnie who immediately agreed that I should complete my tenure in the present assignment. But at the same time, he kept track of the case by tasking his staff officer to monitor the progress on a regular basis. The commanding officer told me that he used to get any number of requests from senior officers for out of turn postings with insistence on immediate compliance and scant regard for propriety. **Mine was the first and probably only case where a request had come from the level of a service Chief with absolutely no time pressure exerted on him, and yet it was ensured that the Chief's request was implemented absolutely in accordance with the rules and procedures.** I smiled and told him, "Sir, how typical of Ronnie. He ensured that he kept his word and yet was not party to any machinations".

I could go on with a number of similar anecdotes, but that is Mike Bhalla's prerogative. **I end with a tribute to the most complete man and ideal service officer I have had the privilege of knowing. He shaped my own character in a huge way.** Whenever I am faced with a morally challenging dilemma, I often ask myself how Ronnie would respond and more often than not I find myself acting accordingly without a care for the results, **knowing that I have followed the footsteps of one the greatest men to have ever donned the uniform.**

YASHWANT RAJAN

Cadet Yashwant Singh Rajan, 42nd Bravo squadron was a colourful character and die hard follower of Nazi regime. So much so he officially changed his name to "Yash Ryan". He had pasted 'Swastika' all over the walls of his cabin, and would religiously celebrate Hitler's Birthday with proper Cake cutting ceremony and this practice he carried on for the entire career in the Army and frequently got into serious trouble with the authorities and his superiors. He had to change three regiments, but that too had no affect on his honey moon with Hitler. He used to fly a small Swastika flag on his bike and always saluted with 'Hail Hitler' gesture and got away with it. He finally retired sometime in 2007.

This episode in NDA deals with a case of manhandling.

Rajan was an outstanding Cross-Country runner at Academy level and invariably finished in top three or four positions behind couple of Ethiopian Cadets. Major Nasib Singh Katoch, from Gorkha Regiment was Squadron Commander 'Bravo'. A great motivator and passionate about sports, particularly X-Country and obviously Rajan was one of his favorite cadets. In his 6th term Rajan was appointed CSM (Cadet Sergeant Major) and he proved to be a fire brand Nazi Sergeant and kept everyone on the run, particularly fifth termers viz 43rd.

Just couple of weeks prior to Passing Out Parade of 42nd course in May 72, one fine day Rajan caught hold of Dham, a Naval cadet from 43rd course and ordered him to front roll, Dham stood his ground and refused as Rajan was no more holding the appointment of Cadet Sergeant Major (few days earlier, he had been de-tabbed by the Dep Com !) Rajan lost his cool at the defiance displayed by Dham and hit him with the cane at his posteriors 4/5 times and also on the face with the knob of the cane. The matter was reported to the Squadron Commander, who expectedly let off Rajan with a warning.

However, the cadets of 43rd were not satisfied and coaxed Dham that he should urge Rajan for public apology. Rajan refused to bow down to the pressure and in his mould of arrogant Nazi said "**No way, even if you have me** thrown out of the Academy, I will NOT apologise" He was warned that the matter will be brought to the notice of Dep Com. Rajan couldn't care less, as he was sure that the Squadron Commander will stand by him.

So in next few days some cadets of 43rd got together viz Lalli Sandhu, Paul and SP Singh, and forced Dham to directly report the matter to the Deputy Commandant. So Dham was taken to Sudan Block and left outside the Adjutant, Major HK Trivedi's office. But before he could meet the Adjutant, the Academy Cadet Adjutant, MS Sikhon, who came out of Adjutant office, noticed Dham and asked him what was he doing there. Dham informed the ACA that he had come to see Adjutant to report Rajan's manhandling incident. ACA asked him to go back to the squadron and he will speak to his Squadron Commander, Dham meekly returned to the squadron much to annoyance of his course mates.

Once again the cadets of 43rd asked Rajan for public apology, who simply refused and told them to bugger off. Now this attitude incensed them and this time they took Dham quietly on the cycle behind the Sudan Block on Hut of Remembrance road and literally pushed him inside the Adjutant office. Dham narrated the whole incident to Major HK Trivedi, who immediately marched up Dham to Dep Com. After listening to Dham side of story, Dep Com called up Nasib Singh Katoch and asked him about the incident. Katoch informed Dep Com that Rajan was marched up to him, as only few days were left for POP, so I let him off with a warning. Dep Com will have nothing of it, as manhandling is a grave offence and Rajan must be taught a lesson or else later in his career he may misbehave again with his subordinate and end up with a 'Court Marshal'. Dep Com directed Major Katoch to inform his parents not to come for POP and Rajan will pass out with the next course. Next day Rajan was marched up to Dep Com for relegation. Before he relegated Rajan, Dep Com asked him few questions;

Dep Com; Son, would you like to change your squadron ?

Rajan; No, Sir.

Dep Com; You may have to face hostile environment from the cadets of the next course.

Rajan; Its OK, Sir.

Dep Com; Are you sorry for what you did ?

Rajan; No Sir!

Dep Com; You are relegated to 43rd course, march him out.

The aim was to teach him the correct conduct expected of an officer. Anyhow, Rajan was invited to Deputy's residence for a cup of coffee, before the end of the term and Dep Com explained to him why he had to take such a serious action against him.

Meanwhile Major Katoch was very upset about the whole episode and warned that all those cadets (Paul, Sidhu and SP Singh) instrumental in convincing Dham to bring the matter to Dep Com's notice will be on his hit list in the final term!! They all survived and Paul was appointed as Squadron Cadet Captain !! As per Lali Sidhu, Major Katoch had a heart of Gold and loved everyone in Bravo squadron.

Notwithstanding his relegation Rajan always had high regards for Admiral and being from Cavalry, we served in the same stations .He would always tell me not to forget to send his regards whenever I write to Admiral !

In 1983 when Admiral met with the scooter accident, being in the same station –Amritsar, I informed Rajan about it and he promptly sent a get-well card to Admiral. In his letter of 12th May 1983 Admiral wrote, **quote** *"Just today, I had a card from Rajan Hitler – who had heard from you about my accident. It was thoughtful and kind of him and I will write to him as soon as I am little better"* **unquote**

The point I want to HIGHLIGHT is that in spite of being relegated just few days before passing out parade, Rajan still held Admiral in great esteem and respect.

This episode speak volumes of Admiral's Code of Conduct and human values and that's why he is eulogized and worshipped by all cadets who came anywhere close to him .

RONNIE P WE LOVED

CP SHARMA

It was in my 6th term, I remember, I was going alone on a cycle to the Naval Training Team and Admiral appeared from nowhere and asked me to go running to the Khandwa Gate and back as punishment, which was more than 2kms one way. He being his good self stopped his car and asked me, son, in case there was an examination that I had to go? I told him there was none. So he said - well son, might as well keep running!

PS; The point I would like to highlight is- one could only see **how humane** he was that he stopped to confirm about the examination!

Just few days prior to POP, being the member of riding display team, one morning I was walking in my riding rig towards Equitation Lines which were about 3 kms away. Suddenly Dep Com car came to a screeching halt next to me and he called me. I thought I had it now, as I was alone and not in a squad, I stood at attention, he asked me why I was walking alone. I told him Sir, I am going to the Equitation Lines for display rehearsal and my cycle has been returned to MT Lines. He asked me to hop in the car and said do you mind if I pick up my dress from Sudan Block! **Before I knew he left me in his car all the way to Equitation Lines!!**

Having left the Navy a bit too early and venturing out on my own. Once Mrs Pereira called up our office to book some flight tickets, whilst she was in Delhi. My wife had no clue which Mrs Pereira it could be. She told her if she was Admiral Pereira's wife, it definitely she was. So much was the influence of Admiral Pereira on us. They both had a long chat!!

Though small incidents but it speak volumes of Admiral impact on all the cadets of NDA, who still worship him.

FIELD CRAFT AT ITS BEST

One fine morning during third period Mrs. Pereira decided to drive Deputy Commandant to office herself. As the car approached Sudan Block Deputy noticed three cadets ambling along without cycle - a crime at the Academy at the best of times, as the cadets were required to double up within the campus of the Academy, in an endeavour to encourage to keep their cycles 'on road'.

Not desiring to embarrass the cadets in the presence of Mrs. P, he jumped out of the car and ran up the steps of Sudan Block while the car drove off, and surveyed the scene, quite confident that he will deal with the defaulters expeditiously.

Not a soul appeared in view, but certain of his ability to handle the situation; he had two enthusiastic drill instructors quickly search the area behind the library and the cinema hall - the only two blocks adjoining the Sudan. The instructors quickly returned, but were disappointed to report that the cadets have not been found. Baffled as to their whereabouts, but accepting defeat, he retired to his office and thought no more on the matter till he went for lunch.

Greeted by a beaming wife, he was shot the question "Did you catch them?" catch who? He asked. "The cadets" said an even more delighted spouse. **"They fooled you completely by taking post behind the three cypress trees at the bottom of the garden.** I saw them as I drove past and was quite sure that they had you beaten."

When I went home the next weekend, the first thing Mrs. Pereira gleefully narrated this incident and for a change, how, Ronnie was hoodwinked by the smart cadets.

I then told them that there is a bit of twist to the story. They not only hide behind the trees but kept moving around the trees to stay out of drill ustad sights!! It was one of many spontaneous innovations by the erring cadets as they were aware that if caught then they had it and nothing short of 21 Restrictions and four Singarh Hikes!!!

We all had good laugh, and Admiral laughed the loudest, but never tried to find out their names. That was his greatness and all he said, son, I will catch them next time!!

That is why Admiral used to refer to all cadets as "devils".

SURVIVAL OF THE FITTEST

The event was a paper chase and the 165 horses at the equitation lines had been oversubscribed, twice over. However, the event was not without its falls, but fortunately no damage was done, except for one unfortunate cadet who could not hold a 16- hand hunter at a stretch gallop as it approached the crossing of a well macadamed road, watched over by Deputy Commandant for just such an eventuality.

The inevitable occurred with the animal slipping and the young cadet hitting the road with a sickening thud and visible evidence that his head and hands had taken most of the impact. Totally unconscious, he was hurried to the hospital by the Deputy, who was more than certain that he had fractured cranium and more broken bones in his body than it was good to think of. A report was immediately made to the Commandant in person, who hurried to the hospital to hear the worst from the doctor. Proceeding to the bed of the cadet, the horrified doctor found it empty and a search ensued for the cadet in obvious delirium, wandering around the campus in a daze. As the search intensified and the cadet was not found in the campus, doctor was threatened with dire consequences. Enquiries in his squadron, in his battalion and the Equitation Lines met with a negative reply, until in desperation and bankruptcy of further thought, a visit was even made by the Deputy Commandant to the dining hall. It was difficult to say at this juncture whether his wrath or relief was the over-riding consideration at the sight of the same cadet, sitting ceremoniously at his table with his right hand as raw as good leg of mutton and his head with a bump as large as a goose egg, shoveling breakfast down his throat as fast as he could eat it. **"What in hell's name are you doing here, when you are supposed to be dying in the hospital?"** said the Deputy Commandant to the startled cadet. With look of evident distress on his face and indeed surprise that the Deputy had not quite understood the problem, he replied, "Sir, if I don't have my breakfast now, I shall miss it at the hospital and they won't even put me on a "C" diet!

Deputy was speechless for once !!

ADMIRAL WITH HEART OF GOLD

BRIG VICKY MEHTA

Vicky Mehta 42nd/ India Sqn a second generation officer from Scinde Horse (14 Horse) sent me a write up on Admiral;

"Strict he was but Ronnie Pereira had heart of gold."

Quote "I was the DCC of 1st and 4th termers, with my cabin on the ground floor centre lobby in India Squadron. Since we have just bought a new stereo system for the ante room, I decided to keep the old one in my room and play soft music every morning when the first termers were having pre-muster and dress inspection.

One morning, someone banged open my door. I almost abused the SOB who had such guts but saw the Dep Com. He sternly asked me for my T, took them away and told me to meet him in the breakfast break. I went for Drill that day as OC, without my tabs. When I went to his office in the breakfast break, he asked me, why I had music system in my cabin. On hearing the facts as above, he picked up my Tabs from his table, flung them to me. Told me to put them on, gave me a cane which was lying in his office (how thoughtful) and told me to carry on. On seeing the look of indecision on my face, he clarified that I should continue to play the music in my room for the cadets for pre-muster.

That was Ronnie Pereira. **A hard exterior but understanding and soft interior.** He took no nonsense and was not hesitant in granting a person his due", **unquote**

GONE CASE

RAVI MALHOTRA / 42 I

QUOTE "I was in my 4th term in NDA. In this term we had external exams for our Intermediate Certificate and were known as tough in Education Term.

I had fever and reported sick, the doc told me that he is giving me Attend Cabin for 1 day, next time he will give extra duties. Fortunately we had extended weekend due to Monday being holiday. I had fever but did not report sick. I kept myself to my cabin. On Monday evening my course mates found me in a state of very high fever and called for an ambulance. I was taken to MH in semi conscious state.

I was diagnosed with Encephalitis, and was placed in DI list. Doc had given up on me as a **"Gone Case"** and accordingly my father was informed that I have very bleak chances of survival!

When I regained my conscious after two days, I found myself in Duty Doc's room and Dep Com sitting on a chair. I think it was evening time. Dep Com spoke to the doctor and told me, **"Son, all is fine, just get well"**. Every day Dep Com used to visit me, bring Reader's Digest Books for me to read. **I remained in hospital for 4 weeks and he visited me each day of 4 weeks!**

On discharge I was told to go on 6 weeks sick leave. I refused to go on sick leave, as 10 weeks absence would automatically relegate me to the next course.

The great man "Ronnie Sir" came and told me to go for sick leave. **He said, son, if you fail in your final exam up to 4 subjects, I will not relegate you!**

I proceeded on sick leave and on my return passed all my subjects and continued with my course.

He was the only person who visited me every day in my 4 weeks of hospitalization; he was the person who gave me assurances of not being relegated. It only speaks of magnanimity, kind heartedness, and great humane qualities of **Ronnie SIR**. How many Dep Com will ever do this to a cadet?- **NONE.**

People don't visit their kith and kin every day to hospital, but Ronnie Sir was from different world!

God bless his soul.

HIMMAT SINGH

Colonel Himmat Singh (63 Cavalry) was one of the most colourful cadets who passed out as Squadron Cadet Captain ,Echo sqn. Mrs Pereira was very fond of him along with his close friend and course mate GS Mahli and she used to address them as Jalebi and Barfi respectively due to their sweet tooth for them! .

I was aware that Himmat had lots of stories to tell about his close encounters with the Admiral and Mrs P, so on my request he sent me very interesting ones and here I go ;

Quote "I can never forget many instances of Ronnie Pereira and meeting him under circumstances which would at best have de-tapped me, at worst relegated me, however, his great **humane attitude** and complete backing for what is just and correct made all of us look up to him in awe and admiration. I was on a scooter with my wife in Delhi, at a street light and he in his Staff Car headed for Naval HQs. I pointed him out in admiration to my wife, he was reading a Newspaper, my action caught his eye as the lights changed to green. He crossed the light and stopped and met us. That's the man he was. Mrs Pereira I shall remember for the many 'Teas' one had for sports or as SCC at their 'Home'. She would always seek Mahli, Sekhon (late) and me out to stand next to her. She found the ladies and others short. She called me 'Jalebi' for the endless number one could eat them and she called Mahli – Barfi. Moments I cherish and are close to me till date."

"Towards the end of the 6th term one fine morning Muster was going on which I had happily skipped and was coming out of my cabin in the flank when I saw Ronnie Pereira was standing in front, I gave him a smart salute and wished him Good Morning to which he replied. I thought the matter was over and walked past him. Lo behold "SCC you should be at Muster and not in your cabin". I had no valid answer and was De-tabbed on the spot. He was a great man." **Unquote**

HUMILITY

PRABHJIT BEDI

Prabhjit 43rd Delta was a very close friend of mine and Admiral and Mrs Pereira were very fond him as they were of Anoop Singh and Arun Chand. Prabhjit was an excellent horseman and Polo player and he had lots of interactions with Admiral in NDA as he was very fond of Horse Riding and Polo. After passing out Prabhjit had few meetings with Admiral which he not only remember fondly but it taught him certain values in life.

Quote "Mike I was on short leave in Dec 77 to Delhi, where I had come to meet my fiancée, Pimmy. By then Admiral had moved to Naval HQs as Vice Chief and I was of course very keen to meet them after 5 years and also introduce Pimmy to Mrs. Pereira. Pimmy being from civil background was very hesitant to meet such a senior officer, but I told her not to worry, you will really love them once you meet them. I called up the Vice Chief's office and got an appointment for calling on. Admiral was residing in 5 Moti Lal Nehru Marg, and on the appointed day I borrowed my father-in- law's car and drove to Moti Lal Marg to be there before 7pm. We were received at the main door by Admiral and Mrs. Pereira. Pimmy of course was very nervous and shy but soon Mrs. P made her feel at ease. They asked me where I was posted and I told them at Leh, and indeed it is a place worth visiting once in a life time. We kept talking about the good old days in NDA and by the time we realized, instead of formal calling of 45 minutes, we had spent 2 hours with them, and then we begged to leave. I got into the car, but unfortunately it won't start!! And before I could come out, Admiral without any expression, said, **son, stay inside the car, and started to push with little help from Mrs. Pereira**, the engine coughed and started. We came out to say bye, they both hugged us and wished all the best for our marriage and Mrs. P promised that one day she will visit Leh.

I drove out of the gate, shaking my head in total disbelief, what **HUMILITY**, unbelievable. But that one act taught me a lesson for rest of my life. There is no better human quality than **Humility** .Indeed Admiral was a great man, Mike!

Visit to Leh

Admiral took over as Chief of Naval Staff on 1st March 1979. Soon he was invited to NDA as Reviewing Officer for Passing out Parade of 56th Course in June. However, there was minor hitch as the Commandant Maj Gen RK Jasbir Singh had moved out on promotion as GOC HQs 15 Corps, Srinagar, and the new Commandant had not taken over. The Army HQs directed Gen Jasbir to come back to NDA for couple of days to receive and welcome CNS. That's why in the photograph one can notice the 15 Corps formation sign!

A month after that Admiral and Mrs. Pereira paid an official visit to Srinagar as guest of the GOC. The visit also included a day in Leh. Expectedly the GOC 3 Inf Div Maj Gen Sommana personally detailed Prabhjit and Pimmy as Liaison officers to Admiral and Mrs Pereira respectively.

Quote "Mike the moment they landed at the airport, they were thrilled to see Pimmy and self and met us so warmly that it was really bit embarrassing in front of everyone present. In fact Mrs Pereira hugged both of us and held Pimmy's hand throughout and kept her next to her. **Not only that Mrs. Pereira insisted that Pimmy sat along with her on same table for the formal lunch**, they in fact treated us like VIPs. Instead of us looking after them, it was they who were looking after us to the amazement of all officers and ladies. May be they never experienced such humble behavior by such a senior officer and that too CHIEF." **Unquote**

KICKING ASSES

TA KUMAR / 43 D

Quote "I read Joe's moving 'kicking butts' story. That was one of the most fascinating and touching sides of our dear Ronnie P!

That was what triggered the memorable incident about Ronnie's "kicking asses" talk delivered to us one early morning, within the confines of NTT classroom!

Even now after 40 odd years, I cannot help chuckling to myself when I recall that memorable day! Ronnie P was on 'his prowl' and on the day in question, brought the ubiquitous white Ambassador to a screeching halt on one end of the lane in front of the NTT. Out sprang an extremely agitated Dep Com Ronnie P! The obvious reason for his ire was that he had spied from afar, a few of the naval cadets sauntering down the lane, on foot, casually! All of us who were in the vicinity froze to attention. They included those of us who had come on their cycles as required by the NDA "code of practice"(??), as well as those who come on foot. He ordered the defaulters to step aside but not one cadet did-including 'young' Shirgavi who was standing a little behind all of us. He ordered Shirgavi to fetch his cycle from the cycle rack and continued to rave and rant at us cadets. Thankfully Shirgavi had the presence of mind to go and pick up someone else's locked cycle, and rolling it on its front tyre, brought it a little towards us. Shirgavi was extremely fortunate to have escaped being deducted by the Dep Com. I dare not imagine what might have happened to him had he been noticed by the eagle eyed Ronnie P ! Perhaps he would have been instantly strung up from the yardarm of the NTT flag mast! (sometimes I wonder if Ronnie had turned a Nelson's eye on to Shirgavi !)

Anyway, what followed was the OIC of the NTT being ordered to assemble all of us in the class room. The fuming Ronnie P walked in and delivered a sermon befitting his status and reputation as a old sea dog! It is just one sentence that sticks out in my mind- after all these years. His opening statement went something like this- "you S---of ---B" I have kicked asses in the Navy for past 30 years and **"YOUR IS BUT SMALL ONE"**. He went on for a while more before a whirlwind exit and leaving all of us stunned and extremely relieved that we have been spared further and long retribution in form of Restritions and Singarh hikes?" **unquote**

PS; Mike, I wonder if this episode is worthy of inclusion in your book. But anyway-I just wanted to share my memories of that momentous (at least for me) day-TAK.

I wrote back to my friend TA Kumar (from my squadron), that every moment spent in great man's presence (good or bad) was worth its weight in gold, we were all blessed to have been under his wings in our formative years.

LIBRARY

In Jan 1955 when the Academy was formally opened at Khadakwasla, the library made its modest beginning in the Geography laboratory. It was named after Mr. TN Vyas, who was the 4th Principal from 1953-68. He was a renowned scholar, teacher, golfer and administrator. Later library moved to its present location situated on the left flank of the Sudan Block, in conjunction with Naval Training Team (NTT) building, it resembles an anchor from the aerial view.

In 1972 it was well stocked with magazines, journals, dozen Newspapers and over 20,000 books/ reference books. Thus library periods were always welcome for those who were keen readers as well as for those who were looking forward to deep and undisturbed snooze of 40 minutes or so. The sliding chairs provided ideal conditions to sleep in totally quiet environments.

When I went home on a Sunday Admiral narrated a story to me about his visit to the library, in fact he enacted the whole scene himself and kept Aunty and self in splits of laughter.

One day, during the last period Deputy decided to make a surprise visit to the library. As soon as he entered all cadets immediately pulled themselves up and pretended to read whatever was in front of them. There was pin drop silence and suddenly Deputy heard small noises of snoring and he tip toed to the corner to see who was indulging in mid-day siesta! As he approached, he made a gesture with his finger on the lips to the other cadets to be silent and not to try to shake the victim from his slumber! He went and stood in front of the unsuspecting cadet, after a while, touched his shoulder- no reaction, second time, tapped him harder and the cadet swatted Deputy hand and continued to enjoy his well earned snooze! Third time, Deputy decided to shake him hard, the poor chap half opened his eyes and saw a tall figure in whites standing in front of him and when he focused his eyes and realized who it was, out of sheer fear, he simply jumped from his chair and stood shivering in front of Deputy with his eyes wide open and nose almost touching Deputy's face, expecting him to bark 21 days and 4 Singarh Hikes?

However, for some reason Deputy soft side emerged and he just turned back and walked off! The poor cadet dropped into his chair out of sheer relief and happiness!

Deputy said, son, I think he must have had double outdoor that day and I just let him off!

After that no cadet ever slept in the library!!

ADMIRAL AS I KNEW HIM

PARDEEP SINHA – 43/A

It was in my third term in NDA, Khadakwasla, when I learnt that our Dep Com Col HKK Shukla from the Army had been posted out and he was being replaced by Commodore R L Pereira from the Indian Navy.

Our new Dep Com straight away went about understanding his job, which was very complex. He was the head of Administration and Training. He was a Martinet, a strict disciplinarian and had one aim in his mind to mould cadets into strong and disciplined leader of men. From a Martinet, the Admiral became a terror. He was omnipresent and we were surprised to see him in PT rig at PT time and next moment he was in speck less white Navy uniform present at the Drill Square. It was not surprising to see him attending Muster Fall-in of some Squadron (Sqn) or scanning the Sqn lines during study periods. He could be seen standing and watching the cycle discipline of the cadets while moving from one Trg area to another and God save those cadets who would not be in perfect lines of twos. A familiar sight used to be, the cycle squads being asked to get down for breaking their discipline and awarded restrictions or Singarh hikes as per his whims and fancies. **Overall we cadets were always under his scanner and he never hesitated to award stringent punishments to ensure that the cadets behaved in an Officer like manner and follow the rules & regulations in letter & spirit.** He never hesitated to tick the Officers and *Ustaads* on their follies. Such was the aura he created around himself, which the cadets dreaded and were always paranoid about **when he'll appear from nowhere and award punishments for smallest of mistakes.** There was no respite for those who were habitual offenders and he was very strict in enforcing discipline in the right perspective.

It would be pertinent to mention an episode which shook the Academy. It was our Sixth term and a much awaited first period in Sudan Block, Room No. 100, as prep period for non-tech stream. First period prep in Room No.

100 in Sudan Block meant trouble, as most of the cadets would skip being present and catch up with their sleep in their cabins. I was SCC, 'A' Sqn and too OG, always careful not to enter into any misdemeanor, especially with the Dep Com around. To my horror, I realized that only about 30 cadets were present and rest decided to skip. My heart started beating wildly, as my apprehensions of the Dep Com landing up became very strong. And lo! He was there. The worst was that, I was the senior most cadets present in the room. He yelled at me and wanted to know that being the senior most cadet, why I did not report the absence of cadets to him. Unlike IMA, in NDA the sixth termers believe in camaraderie and bonhomie to the core. The course spirit is such that sixth termers do not report against each other. I was quiet and knew the repercussions that were to follow. **The Dep Com came charging at me, ripped my SCC tabs off my shoulders and threw them from the window unceremoniously into the cycle stands below. "You are fired"**, were his words, which meant serious trouble. Next moment announcements were made that all non-tech stream cadets of sixth term to be present in the Assembly Hall in the next five minutes. We scrambled into the Assembly Hall and a few Squadies and Div Os were present, who were ushering all the appointments onto the stage.

A brief admonishment from the Dep Com and it was announced that all the non-tech appointments were to be de-tabbed after lunch in their Sqn in a promulgation parade. My Squady and Div O removed my tabs in front of the cadets who stood in silence and disbelief to see the plight of their favourite and popular SCC.

Now come the true side of the Admiral. The Dep Com was full of remorse, but he had to set an example for others. **In the evening, he visited me in my cabin and was literally feeling bad for me at the same time maintaining his stiff exterior. He was full of milk of human kindness and instructed the Squady not to change my cabin and for the rest of the term, I was to be treated as SCC.** During our Passing out Dinner in the Cadets Mess, **he especially came to my Parents and praised me like hell**, at the same time he expressed justification of the mass de-tabbing to prove his point of view. He **even called me once to his residence over a cup of tea** and confessed that although I was present in Room No. 100 but had to be de-tabbed to teach the other cadets a lesson.

I have no regrets about whatever happened on that fateful day, **but all the same, I have very high regards for this wonderful Officer, who had a stiff exterior but heart to heart, a very humble person. Mrs. Pereira was an epitome of grace and dignity. She would make-up for all the toughness** of the Admiral by consoling us who suffered, but in the true tradition of discipline required of NDA cadets.

The Admiral went on to become the Chief of the Naval Staff and is fondly remembered as "Ronnie" to many. He is no more amongst us but we pray for his soul to rest in peace. **A great human being who was largely misunderstood for being a Martinet.**

THE MASS DE-TABBING INCIDENT

NS KHERA – 43/C

National Defence Academy Khadakwasla is an institution that has shaped most of the illustrious officers of the Indian Armed Forces ever since its inception. If you have been fortunate enough to Pass Out through its hallowed portals, you can neither ignore nor forget its contributions towards making you a man, a gentleman and an Officer. Its memories of course would go with you to your grave.

While you go through the drills and the daily grind that are changing you every day and every moment, there are events and people that leave an indelible mark on your mental canvas.

For me, that person was the unforgettable Ronnie Pereira; the Late Admiral R L Pereira ex-Chief of Naval Staff who was then the Commodore R L Pereira, Deputy Commandant, National Defence Academy. He was every Cadet's and every young Officer's idol. A very principled and upright Officer and a thorough professional who commanded the respect of one and all. Simply the best of the best.

The De-tabbing Fiasco:

One of the events that I frequently reflect upon and which effected many of my illustrious (read appointment holders) course-mates at that time but left me unscathed even though I was the trigger point, of the infamous de-tabbing episode.

It was a fateful day, though to me it looked like a normal day that any final Term (6th) cadet would be going through.

We had a free period which we were expected to gainfully utilise in a disciplined and responsible manner to enhance our knowledge of military craftsmanship. Actually 'free' is a misnomer because its real importance may not be understood by those who have not gone through one of the greatest military training institutes of the world. Now being in the senior most Term (semester) one thinks one has done enough and learnt enough and is smart enough to deviate a bit here and there. That's what I did. Instead of devoting myself to improving my military knowledge in the Library, I decided I would steal a wink in one the empty class rooms of Sudan Block.

Near the end of the period I picked up my bicycle and started walking from Sudan Block towards the Science Block where our next period was. I was alone. Now NDA discipline demanded that when alone you can't ride a cycle but one is supposed to jog with cycle (not walk) to wherever one wants to go.

That is when the fate played its part. I saw Deputy Commandant's car with fluttering starred flag approaching the roundel from the other side. Now anyone saner would have started running with his cycle (as the discipline demanded). I did not. A lone cadet walking around the Ashoka Pillar roundel at that hour had to have a proper reason. I had none. I thought the Dy Comdt would take the first left turn towards Sudan Block and head for office. He did not. It seemed he had recognised me and his car took a full circle and stopped next to me. I heard his booming voice "Son, where are you going".

Ronnie Pereira, even though very senior by any cadet's standards, interacted directly with cadets and knew quite a few of them closely and by name. That was his style. I was one of those lucky cadets. Those who knew him well held him in great awe and respect but never feared him. He liked cadets to be honest and fearless.

Now back to event, I truthfully told him why/how I was there at that given moment. I had passed the test of being honest by telling him truthfully how I came to be around the Ashoka Pillar and I passed the test of being fearless by not starting to run on seeing his car and giving lame excuses for my action. Commodore Pereira listened attentively to what I said and he was very pensive. It was beyond me to fathom his thoughts though I could make out something troubled him. Finally he said "Okay son carry on".

Was I relieved. Oh boy!!! In hindsight I realised if any lesser mortal would have stopped me, he would have surely asked me to lift the cycle and run to the Science Block in addition to giving me some Restrictions or Extra-Drills as a punishment and the matter would have ended there.

As I jogged with my cycle towards the Science Block I heard screech of tyres and saw him drive off quickly towards Sudan Block.

I reached the Science Block and waited for other classmates to arrive for our next class. Unknown to me, I had started it all but thankfully missed out on drama that unfolded at the Sudan block and ended with de-tabbing of most of the senior appointment holders of non-technical stream of the 43rd NDA course in their final Term. It is a minor consolation that I was not the only one who mis-utilised the 'free' period. There were quite a few others, though I triggered an avalanche that effected quite a few of my dear friends (exalted appointment holders). Consequence was The Mass de-Tabbing (loss of appointment Tabs worn on the shoulders).

Commodore Pereira's logic was simple. It was the responsibility of the appointment holders to ensure cadet's discipline in the Academy. They were entrusted with that responsibility yet some of them were themselves found mis-utilising the 'free' period. So all those who got de-tabbed on that fateful day please don't hold it against me only.

On my part I did feel responsible for it and didn't have the heart to share this with anyone for over 5 decades. I also do sincerely believe that if I had known what the final outcome would/could be, I would not have been so upfront to Ronnie Pereira and tried to deflect the issue. After all we were also taught to protect our coursemates even to the extent inviting extra blame on ourselves. Finally, with this I hope to exorcise the ghost that I have lived with for a long long time." **unquote**

A total of 28 appointments including 6 Squadron Cadet Captains were detabbed. As a Cadet Quarter Master Sergeant, I too was detabbed!!

Encounters With Naval Officers

ADMIRAL MR SCHUNKER

Admiral Dick Schunker was barely a year junior to Ronnie P. Both from Executive Branch were very close friends since 1948.

First time I met them when Captain and Mrs Schunker along with their beautiful daughter Donna came to NDA in Autumn of 1972. I vividly remember him wearing a white bushirt and of course looking very handsome. I also remember Keith Soares, who was doing long course at IAT Girinagar near NDA had come home to meet his future wife Donna !!. On my request Vice Admiral Schunker (92 years)sent me a short story on his close friend whom he referred to as RP.

Quote "Lt Pereira who had completed his Long Gunnery Course in UK was deputed to meet a batch of us at Tilbury docks, London in March 1948. We were slated for the next Long G Course. There were 8 of us-Gandhi, Bindhra, Mathur, Cooper, Sandhu and self plus 2 Pakis .

I next met RP in Bombay in 1949 when he was the G of the frigate Jumna and I was 2nd G of the Cruiser "Delhi" the Flagship. Analysis of gunnery firing of the fleet ships had to be sent to the Flagship and my job was to analyse the firings. This gave me the opportunity of friendly banter over the phone about firings RP being one of them.

We served together in the make shift G school in Cochin in 1951/52, this was the beginning of our friendship. Engagement plans were in the air and the selection of an engagement ring was the order of the day. When my advice was sought I picked up an expensive one which was obviously unaffordable for a Lieutenant. His Fiancée visited Cochin in 1952 and RP being RP went to meet her on a cycle even without a carrier to bring her for dinner at our house. By the time they got to the station Phyllis was numb and decided to walk, she was tottering on her high heels by the time they got to our house.

Sometime in 1952 RP must have been selected for his Staff College. I cannot recollect when they got married but in 1952 when the naval students at the Staff course visited Cochin RP and his wife stayed with us. I then lost track of RP due to my appointments. As the Commander on the Cruiser Delhi he used to lead the Ship's Company on their morning run. This is where he was hit by TB and was sent to Aundh. This could have been end of his career but not RP. In due course he was promoted to Captain and took Command of Delhi and the rivalry started between the two Cruisers; Mysore the Flagship and Delhi and due to RP's leadership that Delhi came out on top and won the coveted prize the 'Cock of the Fleet'.

His other notable appointments were NOIC Bombay where we met up again and he proposed the toast to my daughter on her 21st Birthday on my ship Amba in 1969. As Flag Officer Commanding Eastern Fleet participated in a tactical exercise East versus West, he and his Fleet ended up in Bombay. As Chief of Staff, Western Naval Command I did the debriefing- Honours were even. When Vice Admiral Cursetji moved to Delhi, RP was FOC Southern Naval Areas and was moved by signal to take over a preventive move. I was then FOCWEF and displaying his usual trust in Humans I was left to get on with my job without any interference rather his full support. During my tenure with the Fleet he moved to Delhi as VCNS as the photos reveal.

This trait of trust I experienced when I was VCNS. When the sale of Swedish Fighter Aircraft were denied to India by the Americans as it was fitted with American Engines, RP would not touch anything American much to the displeasure of the Babus. Another contentious issue was the denial to acquire the Sea Harriers due to the Air Force objections as they believed that anything that flies must be with them. This resulted in lots of bitterness between the two Chiefs. We did get the Harriers in the end but at a greater cost as RP predicted at the meeting.

When he called on Mrs Gandhi she was amazed when he told her that from now on his transport would be a scooter" **unquote**

Tribute......

FOOTPRINTS ON THE SANDS OF TIME – REMEMBERING RONNIE

By Adolph Britto

"Lives of great men all remind us
We can make our lives sublime
And departing, leave behind us
Footprints on the sands of time"

These personal reminiscences are a tribute to a much loved Naval Chief, Admiral Ronald Lynsdale Pereira who 'passed on' in 1993 at the age of seventy. Ronnie, as I shall refer to my Admiral in this piece, was a truly inspirational role model who has left an indelible imprint on the minds and hearts of many, particularly on those like me who were privileged to associate and be commanded by him.

In 1962, on completion of degree course at the Naval College of Engineering, our batch of three Sub-Lieutenants was appointed for Engine Room Watch keeping Certificates to INS Kuthar, a new Blackwood Class Frigate acquired from the UK with Commander Ronnie Pereira in command. On introduction, the impressive Ship's Captain put us at ease, indicating that we all had much to assimilate in the newly acquired ship. On a personal note, he went on to add that since Kuthar had a small Officer's Wardroom Mess we may use his cabin, when free, for entertaining our guest. The ship was temporarily non-ops, awaiting materials for restoration of ship's boiler furnace. The Captain, restless in putting to sea, decided to understand technicalities for himself. Being of similar height, he borrowed my spare engineering overalls, and we crawled into the boiler furnace for a first hand appreciation. His drive magically unearthed 'non-available' imported materials

Ship's boilers restored, Kuthar met her sailing commitments. An exacting Captain, Ronnie ran a taut ship at sea, proving equally relentless ashore in honing the ship's smartness and team rowing skills for the Fleet Regatta. Hard days at sea were recompensed in harbour by the Captain declaring many a 'Make-and-Mend' (half-day in naval parlance), joining the Wardroom Mess for many a boisterous session over chilled beer. On Sunday's in Cochin harbour, he found time for God, and would invite Lt. Cdr. Claude Almeida, ship's XO, and me to partner him to Church. His exquisite stride had us breathless.

I next came across Ronnie as Captain in Naval Headquarters, Delhi, when he was Director of Combat Policy & Tactics (DCPT). Residing in the Officers Mess at Kota House, he spent long hours on files in office. He often joined in lively discussions or banter at the dining table; his impromptu bursts of booming laughter invariably had our waiter Munna Lal frozen in his tracks, if not dropping a plate. Ronnie went about life without much ado on his scooter, and borrowed mine at times, when his packed up.

Our next encounter was when Ronnie, as Rear Admiral, was Fleet Commander (Flag Officer Commanding Eastern Fleet), and I the Commander (E) of INS Brahmaputra, sent from Western Naval Command to Visakhapatnam, as Flagship for the Eastern Fleet. Our paths crossed one morning when Ronnie stopped me, and recalling our days on Kuthar, remarked "Britt, you seem to have shed your engineering overalls for sparkling whites ". I cheerfully replied that I had now migrated from steam ship environs to a diesel driven ship. Having immense regard for the tough life of engineers on steam ships, he remarked "God Bless the stoker mechanics, they have sinews of steel and hearts of gold."

In 1976, I was posted in Delhi. **Our three year old son Dhiresh had taken seriously ill with Acute Lymhoblastic Leukaemia, with low prognosis of survival**. After two months in Army Hospital, Delhi, we had taken him to Mumbai for a review by Tata Memorial Hospital (TMH). In the process, I had exhausted all leave, and TMH had advised that we either shift as family to Mumbai or continue Dhiresh's treatment at Delhi. Sharing my concerns with the Command Chief Staff Officer (Personnel), he in turn, brought this to the notice of Ronnie who was then the Flag Officer Commanding in Chief, Western Naval Command. **Hearing of our predicament and preferred option for treatment in Mumbai, Ronnie directed that my transfer orders be obtained from Naval Headquarters by signal and that I be allotted regular family accommodation. Both were done in 48 hours. Dhiresh lives today, a healthy 41 year old. Thanks to God and His marvelous instruments** like Ronnie, who was unstinted in upholding subordinates. In the 1980's, heading the Navy's Acceptance Authority as a Commander, I had rejected acceptance of a Leander Class frigate, INS Taragiri after conducting Full Power Trials, due to a vibrating engine. MDL, the Ship builders and the manufacturer BHEL resented my decision, contesting defects as marginal and as remedial work involved major dismantling in a ship due commissioning. The matter moved right up to CNS. Notwithstanding delay, Ronnie stood by our decision.

After Ronnie had retired, on a leave break in Bangalore, we called on him at his home 'At Last' in Whitefield. I had barely reached his gate, when he dropped his garden hose and ran up to open the gate, waving my car in. During conversation, we learnt of his financial propriety in building 'At Last'. Honest to the core, 'black money' was no way of life. On INS Kuthar, I happened to observe the ship's Captain briskly walking to ship from Lion Gate instead of driving in his stately Studebaker(?) sedan. On a casual query, he indicated that all had been well with the car, **but he had sold it for a pittance due to urgently needed medicines for his mother-in-law.** On another occasion, as Fleet Commander in Vizag, he was seen driving back to ship to unload an empty brass gun Cartridge case – he indicated his discomfort at having taken it in the first place to embellish his drawing room.

In 1991, while on a short duty from Hyderabad, I met Ronnie in Mumbai at the WNC Officers Mess Under treatment for his illness, he indicated his determination to fight it. On another visit months later, **during my morning walk for Mass to St. Joseph's RC Church, I came across him on the way, missal in hand, head bowed resting on his walking stick – he was trying to regain his breath. He who had led me in step since 1962 replied when I volunteered to help "Son, run along, you'll never keep this pace".** The indomitable spirit that had marked his earlier days stayed with him during the last two years of failing health – his resolution superbly **manifest in tune with God and neighbour.**

Admiral Ronnie Pereira, an exemplar in leadership and impeccable in character has been a great blessing to the Navy and indeed the tri-services. Unflinching in the line of duty, he set exacting standards of professional and personal conduct. He eschewed the trappings of post-retirement office and political patronage. **His enduring memory is well cherished by rank and file - those lives he touched and moulded -including an entire generation of cadets in the early seventies at the National Defence Academy.** In the words of Scripture, we may truly say of Ronnie :

"I have fought the good fight,

I have finished the race, I have kept the faith.

Henceforth, there is laid up for me the crown of righteousness."

– (2 Timothy 4)

– Adieu Admiral. Rest in Peace

PS: *Vice Admiral Adolph Britto, PVSM AVSM VSM of 16th NDA Course retired in 1997 as Chief of Materiel of the Indian Navy, and resides in Bangalore. His contact particularsare: adolphbritto@gmail.com*

COMMODORE KS RAI

Generally people from North East India join the Army; however, there are few who joined Air Force and couple of them rose to higher echelon viz Air Marshal PK Barbora retired as C-in-C Western Air Command and Air Vice Marshal Gagoi. But never heard anybody joining the Navy?

It was in March 2008, consequent to Gorkhaland agitation in Darjeeling, North Bengal. As Sub Area Commander located in Bengdubi, North Bengal, I was directed by higher Hqs to convene a meeting of all retired service officers in and around Darjeeling, Kalimpong and Siliguri and update them on the latest developing situation.

The senior most officers in that gathering was Colonel Rattan Bahadur Rai, PUNJAB Regiment from 1st NDA course, who was also accompanied by his younger brother, Commodore (retired) Kamal Shamsher Rai. After the meeting I invited Commodore Rai to my office for a cup of tea. As he entered the office, he noticed the photograph of Admiral and spontaneously came to attention and gave a crisp salute and said, Brigadier, he was the finest Chief Navy ever had. Next question was – what is this photograph doing on your table and he observed that it was duly signed by Admiral!! How did you get it? I had to tell him the whole story and he was indeed fascinated by it. Later he told me, Mike, do you know he was responsible for my posting as Naval Defense Attaché to Pakistan in 1981! And there is interesting story behind it.

When I started this project I met him and informed that I am in the process of writing a book on the great man and I would request you to please share your story about the posting to Islamabad, which he readily did in Feb 2016.

Quote "I joined NDA 24th course, A Sqn and passed out in June 1964 as a Naval Cadet. In fact initially after the 4th Term I did not qualify to become a naval cadet due to low grade in Mathematics. Fortunately for me, our Battalion Commander was a brilliant Naval Officer, who even in those days everybody thought that one day he will become Chief of Navy- Commander Kirpal Singh. I was called for interview of the Battalion Commander;

Cdr Kirpal Singh; Cadet Rai why do you want to join Navy?

Rai; Sir, my grandfather was in the Army, my father was in the Army and my two elder brothers are also in the Army. Sir…

Cdr Kirpal; Stop, that's enough, ok then you can join the Navy!

And that is how I joined the Navy and did pretty well for myself.

In the autumn of 1980, I was commanding INS Vagli submarine, from 9th Submarine Squadron based in Bombay. We were out on sea for an exercise with Western Fleet, when I received a message, that I should terminate the exercise immediately and move back to the harbour. I was wondering why I have been asked like this? There could be some emergency, I thought. On arrival on the shore, I was asked to wear proper uniform and a photographer was waiting to take my photo, which I was told that it is required forthwith by the Chief of Personnel branch, Naval Hqs Delhi. I was still not aware why my photograph was required by COP branch?

It was only after two months when I received a signal from COP branch, that I am required at Naval Hqs for an interview with 'Chief'. It was then I got to know that my name has been selected for the appointment of Naval Attaché to Pakistan. Till then I had not been interviewed by anybody!

When I arrived at the Chief's office, I was informed by NA Captain Kohli, that a panel of few officers was drawn by COP branch and forwarded to Chief's office. **When Admiral saw your photograph, he asked me –who is he? He looks like 'Chinese' officer, I think he is the guy; let's confuse the bloody Pakis and fix them! And that's** it.

Anyway I walked in and was interviewed by the Admiral and he told me –son, you are going on a very sensitive appointment, so be careful and do your job well, all the best. And I was on a flight to Islamabad in January 1981 in the rank of Acting Captain!

Brigadier MM Dhody was the Military Attaché. Few months later all Military Attaches were taken on a tour of Pakistan. When we landed at Karachi we were invited for high tea at Rear Admiral (later Pakistan Chief of Naval Staff) Khan's residence. After a while he inquired from Brig Dhody, **I don't see your Naval Attaché? Brig Dhody with tongue in cheeks replied –Sir, he is standing next to you!! All this while the Rear Admiral thought that I was from Chinese Navy!! So Admiral Pereira's idea of confusing the bloody Pakis was not far from its intended aim!**

Commodore Rai had the longest tenure ever in Pakistan by any Indian Attache-Jan 1981 to Jan 1985.

INS DELHI

COMMANDER AJB SINGH

In his entire career of 39 years, Admiral's best tenure without any doubts whatsoever was indeed the Command of INS DELHI; 1966-68. It was one of the two capital ships and most prestigious command for any naval officer. Admiral, though a strict disciplinarian with no-nonsense approach was still loved and admired by his men. He would repeatedly write and impress upon me to look after your men and you will have the finest troops to lead in battle on this earth. I was very curious and keen to interact with officers who had served with him on INS Delhi.

The first officer I contacted was Commander AJB Singh, who recounted his experiences with Admiral. **Quote** "I was commissioned in 1965 and still wet behind the ears, with 'half a dog watch' in the Navy, joined INS Delhi as Secretary to the Commanding Officer, Capt. RL Pereira. Our ship was based at Bombay and was part of the Indian Fleet. I sat in the Ship's Office which was rather small and invariably lots of officers would come to make calls etc making it difficult to get work done. I therefore decided to discourage entry into the office by putting a board outside saying "Keep off the Grass". We have a large number of Officers on a capital ship and on the Delhi most were senior to me. Unhappily the notice did not prevent a great many from coming in to that tiny Ship's office. On the other hand, after seeing my notice Ronnie, the CO never entered my office - and would speak to me from outside. **It was a small incident but it revealed his character - even though I was junior to most of the officers on the ship, he did not want to infringe on my authority.**

He had a rare affection for the Navy, its ethos and what was the right thing to do. He didn't compromise on work, never took out Duty free goods ashore and always played fair – which is why we all loved him so. I can think of two different examples.

Both Ronnie and his charming and endearing wife Mrs. Phyllis Pereira were very fond of me and every now and again, had me over for a meal to their house in Colaba. On one such occasion I asked him if I could have a shot at getting a 'Watch Keeping Ticket', since rules then allowed a 'Supply Officer' like me to try and qualify. I was permitted to give it a shot and so 'kept watch' both in harbour and at sea. But on our way back from Mauritius shortly before I was going on transfer, I thought I had him in a weak moment and asked him about getting my 'Watch Keeping Ticket'. "Sorry son" he said brutally yet almost affectionately, "you need to a lot more time". That was that.

But there was another soft side to him too in the way he dealt with matters official. Those days, in order to get leave a sailor would often produce a telegram saying 'Mother serious' or 'Father serious' and rarely if ever, did he refuse leave in such a case. He felt it would be terrible if leave was refused and the sailor lost a dear one. "I know" he said "it happened once".

He had a long, booming, hearty guffaw of a laughter that almost brought tears to his eyes. In fact he could see a joke in unsuspected places – such as a Division Officer's Record Book. Ships have 'Departments' and 'Divisions' the latter being handled by nominated officers to look after the men – their problems and the rest of it. Every Divisional Officer (DO) writes his observations about each sailor - how he's doing, his problems etc. These are sent periodically to the CO who goes through them, often only to find routine, platitudinous remarks about how each sailor in his Division is doing –swimmingly, more often than not. The remarks are usually dull, repetitive and boring stuff but one day I found Ronnie laughing uncontrollably as he flipped through one such Record book. It transpired that the noting on each sailor in that Division ended with the incisive and astute observation that the sailor "…is making good progress on his instrument!" It was the Ship's band that the DO was writing about, but really……

He had a puckish sense of humour too. So when we received the usual routine signal from the NOIC requesting information about the marital status of Lt. AJB Singh who was to report to Port Blair shortly, Ronnie couldn't help himself. Pat went the reply "…… despite best efforts Lt. Singh unable to find pretty bride with adequate dowry. Officer therefore comes un-accompanied with view to vetting suitable Jarawa or Onge"

It was Ronnie all the way.

REAR ADMIRAL RAVI VOHRA

Rear Admiral Ravi Vohra, who served as a young Lt in INS Delhi, very kindly narrated couple of incidents as follows;

Quote "It's been a long time Mike, when with barely 5 years of service I was posted as a young Lieutenant in INS Delhi in 1966. Our Commanding Officer was a firebrand with heart of gold. Ronnie P.

I remember when our ship was anchored in Cochin channel in 1966. I was on the Watch Duty on the bridge and our Captain had gone ashore to have dinner with his friends. The normal drill was, that on his return CO would shout "Boat" from the shore and the Captain barge would be sent to bring him on board. It must be close to 11pm, I was on the bridge when I was informed that some smoke has been noticed in the engine room and I rushed down to check what had happened? At that very moment Ronnie P reached the shore and shouted "Boat", obviously there was no response and when I came back and heard 'Boat' I immediately sent it ashore. By then Ronnie P had to wait 15-20 minutes and as soon as he reached Quarter Deck, he was very annoyed that I was not on the bridge and ordered me to continue the "Middle Watch" (midnight to 4am) till further orders ,that means the whole night. Being very junior I could not open my mouth and justify my absence as it could have landed me in further trouble. Next morning CO was informed about the engine room incident and he straightaway came to the bridge and asked me if I had my breakfast, to which I replied in negative. He said go and have breakfast and meet me ashore at 7pm in the evening.

I was wondering the worst but at 7pm was surprised when he asked me; where would you like to go for dinner?

That was his way to apologize for giving me extra duty!! What a wonderful gesture but that was Ronnie P, the best officer I ever had the pleasure to serve under, unbelievable leader of men. We all loved him.

The second incident took place when INS Delhi was on its way to East Coast. We had gone around Sri Lanka and were heading to the Bay of Bengal,

I was on the 'Watch Duty' on the bridge and there was movement of some fishing boats which must have drifted from the coast and I noticed one of them had capsized, with few fishermen hanging for life. After 20 minutes Ronnie P came on the bridge to check if all was well and I mentioned about the drowning fishing boat, he said why you didn't inform me that time, I told him that I thought we may be delayed to reach our destination. He said nothing is more important than human life and ordered me to turn back the ship. We managed to rescue one old man and two young boys and sailed them to Madras harbour, however, we could not save the old man who died enroute. That was the level of his concern for human life." **Unquote**

MY TWO INNINGS WITH RONNIE PEREIRA INS DELHI AND NHQ DELHI

VICE ADMIRAL BIMAL GUHA

INS DELHI

I had finished about a year in 1966, on board INS DELHI, as the Gunnery Officer after my Long G course, in December 1965, in the rank of Lieutenant – feeling rather, what do you say, a spring in my step, when then Captain Ronnie Pereira took command of the Cruiser INS Delhi .I had seen his name in the "Long G Board" in my alma mater Gunnery School, at INS Venduruthy. But this was the first face-to-face with my new Captain – **a six-foot man with a twinkle in the eye and a captivating smile.** From Day one, I was the "GUNS" – the "call" I am proud of.

INS DELHI, had served the Indian Navy for over decade and half, by then and with her three TWIN 6-inch turrets, was the second cruiser after INS MYSORE, with her triple 6-inch turrets. During practice shoot/ exercises and in other activities, like –sport, regatta, the competition was intense. Machinery and equipment of DELHI were aged but with Ronnie P, it was always" man behind the gun" and the motto**" Give the best – there is no runners-up in war**". Most importantly, Ronnie P believed in these and encouraged and guided others to achieve that BIT extra, setting the bar higher.

It is difficult to believe that the 6-inch gun control unit – Admirality Fire Control Clock (AFCC Mk) 4 had 13 motors to compute and all were run on "air from the compressor" – a special unit, the "heart" of the system. Believe you me when I say that I had 8 musicians (!) manning the various positions to "follow the pointer" – a practice followed from the Royal Navy as the musicians could sit in a stool for hours, as they usually did when performing in a concert. They were also my key-men, during "ACTION". Ronnie P came to know them by name and often when ship's Band was practicing in the Junior Sailors' Dining Room, would drop in to listen and could identify them with their special musical instruments. Coming to AFCC MK 4, the compressor gave the ship and Dockyard umpteen problems, consistently, and I remember that once, he having got a car (from the car pool) made me accompany him to the backyards of OLD docks like Mazagon/Sassoon and Junk Yards to locate part for that "special motor" – regrettably we did not succeed, much to his dismay.

INS Delhi also had twin turrets of 4-inch, two on each side and 10-odd L 40/60 guns (remember INS Delhi was of WW II vintage). He appreciated the efforts of the crew and their commitment. In addition to being GUNS, I was also the Quarterdeck Officer (wooden decks of yester years) - he used to come out of his cabin(aft) and talk to me before the COLOURS at 0800 hrs, when he was onboard (I was a bachelor, living on board).

REGATTA

Then the famous REGATTA of 1967 at Cochin. He enthused every crew – I was the Regatta Officer, as well as the Coxswain of the Officers' Boat (being a light weight). We won the **COCK**, but not without some anxious moments. The races were serially organized, department-wise, with crew changes rotationally, pulling in different boats (whalers), so that boat-advantage, if any was not appropriated by ONE ship. Regrettably, during the race for Supply and Secretariat Branch, the Engineering department crew, were towed to the starting line and they pulled and won. The result: DELHI got ZERO points and the tired crew of the Engineering Branch had to pull again in their correct race after 20 minutes Ronnie P was on deck with them, whilst able-bodied men were treading on the arms of the tired crew, and convinced them that the crew could win again for the SHIP and for the Captain to Lift the COCK (the silver Trophy). When the crew were being towed again to the starting line, he was going in his boat alongside their boat, shouting and gesticulating encouragement – it was a unique sight. Possibly, at that point in time, no one present believed that DELHI would win that race also. It was a day to remember – his face remained lit up for days. It was an example of "hands-on" determined leadership. Yes, CNS Admiral AK Chatterji, who was present, remarked INS Delhi won because of amazing leadership of Ronnie. **Unquote**.

In fact Montee Chatterjee told me **quote** "Mike the sailors loved Ronnie and they rowed like devils to win the race for their Captain." **unquote**

Another incident stands out in 1967 – the Chief Naval Staff exercises (CNX). Whole fleet used to put out to sea and do exercises (inclusive of Night Encounter) for the CNS. I had a perennial problem with my left gun of B turret - each barrel/gun had to be independently operated by the gun layer. Captain was aware of it as he himself had occasion to speak to the DGM (Weapons) of the dockyard – remember I was a Lieutenant! On the day of the shoot – CNS was onboard INS VIKRANT, stationed abreast of INS DELHI – left gun was again over ranging by 200 yards!! No correction could rectify it. As was known then CNS, Vice Admiral AK Chatterji (he became Admiral in 1968), was extremely fond of DELHI having commanded it as Young Captain in late 50s and wanted to come onboard. He was winched by a Helicopter and received by Captain and he strode to the Bridge. I was summoned – he made 3 points : the rate of fire was slow (as per Confidential Navy Order it had to be 6 rounds per minute), shoot was erratic (which it was by left gun of B turret) and he doubted whether I was competent to be the Gunnery Officer of the Cruiser (remember I was only a Lieutenant – possibly ONLY one of that Rank ever to be the Gunnery Officer of a Cruiser). Captain looked at me and nodded. My reply was: we were using reduced charges, which required gun to be elevated at a higher angle to achieve the same range (as for full/action charge), hence on extrapolation my rate of fire was 6.9 rounds per minute: The left gun of B turret was erratic, our efforts have yielded little progress but we would "Lick" it: I am proud of my men and the gunnery team. CNS looked at Captain, asked for the chopper and left ship. I did my full tenure on board the ship for 2 years!! **Ronnie P had given me the confidence to speak up and argue professionally.**

I got married in 1967 and during the reception given by the ships' officers – he simply lifted my wife and put her on a Wooden Grating so that my wife of 150 cm did not have to crane her neck!! He made his own family. I left in Jan 1968 to join the Gunnery School as Instructor – his parting advice was "Make them proud of the Navy and the profession". **How true of a man who never flinched from a challenge.**

NHQ – DELHI

In early 1979, I took over as Director of Naval Training (DNT), in the rank of Captain, at Naval HQ. Ronnie was CNS . My Principal Staff Officer was Chief of Personnel, Vice Admiral Manohar Awati, who had been my Fleet Commander. My office was in the Sena Bhavan and CNS sat in the South Block. As DNT, in addition to training, sports, rifle shooting (competition), yachting came under my part of ship. I was also a member of Joint Training

Committee (JTC), which was headed by Director General of Military Training, a three star General. I met Ronnie, in the meeting of Chiefs of Staff Committee, after about two months in my tenure as DNT. As CNS was also the President of Yachting Association of India, I had to prepare brief and send the same to NA to CNS.

As CNS, he was keen for the Navy to do well in sports and excel in Yachting and shooting .I regularly sent him Inter-Services Sports Fixtures being held at Delhi and on two occasions, I saw him present during such events to cheer the Navy team. In my interactions with officers from other two services on many occasions we discussed **RONNIE, for his commitment and for his contribution, when he was Deputy Commandant at NDA in the early 70s.**

I remember receiving a call from him in late 1979, when he enquired whether JTC was meeting that day in the afternoon to discuss "Change of Service", of some 4th term cadets, in NDA. On getting an affirmative, he requested me to speak in JTC for change of service to Navy from the Army, for cadet Farouk Tarapore – an accomplished yachtsman, who had been a Sea Cadet and Navy had always stood by him – though he could not get into the merit list for Navy, during induction in NDA. Believe you me, when I mentioned this request from CNS, Lt General SS BRAR, then DGMT and Director of Air Training, both agreed without any discussion – such was the respect that he had in all three services .On my own, I offered and they agreed that in the next induction, Navy will surrender vacancy of One Naval cadet to the Army. On return, I rang him up – he was delighted and asked me to convey his personal thanks to the other two service members of JTC.

In Sep 1980, when I had been DNT for over 20 months, COP called me to his office and told me that I was to go to USSR, to command the Second Kashin Class Destroyer (61 ME) in Jan 1981. From then, till end-Dec 1980(3 months), I was to attend office in the forenoon as DNT and go to JNU from 1430 -1700 hrs to learn preliminary Russian Language. As I was leaving his office, he called me back and said that CNS had personally preferred for me to go for Command now than doing RCDS (Royal College of Defence Studies, UK). **I am ever Grateful to RONNIE P, my Captain and CNS.**

POST SCRIPT: I last met RONNIE in Mar 1993, at Wellington MH. I presented to him the Coffee Table Book on Golden Jubilee of Submarine Arm. He thanked me and his face lit up.

IN MEMORY OF ADMIRAL PEREIRA

COMMODORE P FRANKLIN

The Anglo-Indian community of post-independent India was a jolly lot. They were not exceptionally intelligent, but were practical people who were good with their hands. The bulk of them served in the railways as that was the opening available to them in colonial times that was not easily available to the 'natives'. They were honest, fun-loving, and a very sociable lot as a community. They were not hard-working. In post-independent India, the 'fairer' of the lot migrated to the UK, Canada, and Australia. A few remained in India.

Admiral Pereira was one of a bunch of few who joined the Indian Navy as commissioned officers. He joined at a time when there was a huge vacuum ahead of officers of his seniority, the senior ones being Royal Navy Officers who left India after Independence. Officers were yet to be commissioned through the National Defence Academy. Some of these early officers joined through the Dufferin, some from the Customs, others from the Royal Indian Navy, and still others from the Reserve List (RINVR). Promotions therefore came easily to them, and there was no 'rat race' like in present times.

With this background, if you looked at Admiral Pereira, one saw a bold man with very high integrity, average knowledge of naval affairs, and a good sense of humor. He was no outstanding officer. He just about managed to handle the ships he commanded without the usual aplomb and finish of a good ship-handler. He made many mistakes in his profession, but was man enough to stand before a huge crowd in uniform and admit them. He learned from his mistakes. He was well-loved for his personality. People saw in him a caring and kind human being and took all the yelling and shouting he gave without feeling offended because it was from him – Pereira. This love and affection that he earned made him a great leader of men. The Navy has not seen a better leader of men at the helm of its affairs.

Had the Congress Govt. remained in power, he would NOT have made it to Chief. That post was going to Vice Admiral Rusi Gandhi. He was Indira Gandhi's man. However, the Congress lost the elections and the Janata Party won. They dumped Vice Admiral Rusi Gandhi in favour of Vice Admiral Pereira. However, that was a short-lived period for the Janata Government, and the Congress came back in power to find Admiral Pereira heading the Navy. His tenure as Chief was therefore fraught with resistance at every stage, over every matter, from no less a person than Indira Gandhi. This uncomfortable relationship percolated down to the Ministry of Defence and his job became an uphill one till the end. Whenever he threatened to resign (when he found the Services getting a raw deal), Indira Gandhi was quick in asking him from which date he wanted to go. He withdrew his threats. But he was the man who opposed the 'babus', and managed to get the Services 'free rations' in preference to cash in lieu.

He was ably supported by Phyllis who was no less a personality. They made an excellent team. She was also well-liked in the Navy. She vividly remembered the names of every sailor who she came in contact with, right till a few years before she lost her memory. If one were to find any fault with them, it was the fact that they both smoked heavily!

The Navy loved them when they were in Service, after they retired to reside in Bangalore and Coonoor, and still loves them long after they have moved on.

The above article is written by Commodore P Franklin, who served with Admiral on INS DELHI in 66/67.

Encounters With Staff

RONNIE PEREIRA REMEMBERED

VICE ADM PREMVIR DAS

I was commanding the Missile ship INS VIJAYDURG based in Mumbai and had just completed a year out of the normal tenure of the 18 months when, towards end May 1979, I received a call from Personnel in NHQ that I was to move to Delhi as NA to CNS within a week. This came as a bolt from the blue. RLP had taken over as CNS just a few months earlier and subsequent enquiries revealed that his incumbent NA had some domestic issues to resolve. Anyhow, that is how I became NA to CNS! I had first met the CNS in 1963 when he, as Commander, was commanding a frigate and I was the Flag Officer to the Fleet Commander. Twelve years later, in 1975, I as a Commander, was a member –secretary of a naval delegation under his leadership (he was FOC Southern Naval Areas, Cochin) which visited Tanzania; his childlike reactions when we toured the game sanctuaries was seen to be believed and from him I learnt to pronounce the name of an animal called Wild Beeste - there were thousands of them around! I had never met Mrs. P.

I was to serve as his NA for 14 months, for the first 8 as a Commander and last 6 as a Captain. At our first meeting in the office, he told me that I was not to inconvenience my family and I was told not to reach the desk before 8.30 am and leave latest by 5.30 pm .These were just not words and he walked the talk. Mrs. P got to know that my wife was a working lady and ensured that nothing came in the way of her working life saying that she, herself, had been in those shoes for many years. Over a period of time, we got to know them as human being, of how the CNS would attend personally to his father-in-law's needs at night and how they cared deeply for the people who served on the staff. He had a straight forward black- white approach to any issue and no time for the 'greys' which many tried to persuade him was more useful thing to do.

He was the CNS when we negotiated the contract for purchase of four submarines from Germany – buy two build two. His recommendation was to buy from the Swedes and this was the way in which the case was processed right up the ladder except at the Cabinet meeting. It was decided that the boats would be German. Why this change took place was conjectural but the deal later led to the HDW scandal and its fall out. He took an appointment with the PM Indira Gandhi which was granted. She listened to him quietly but did not speak and to HDW we went!

Towards late 1981 he faced a major dilemma under his Chairmanship. Navy's promotion board had rejected the selection of Captain to Rear Admiral. Inevitably the aggrieved officer put up representations and surprisingly reached the office of Prime Minister. Normally as a NA I was not in the loop for personnel oriented files coming into his office, these being processed by his civilian PS. One day CNS called me to his room and, himself, bolted the door from inside. Then he gave me a file and asked me to read a noting by a JS in the PMO. It was a very harshly worded indictment of the Navy's promotion system referring, in particular, to the case of this officer. It ended with the sentence "PM has seen and approved". RLP was furious and said that he would resign that very moment. Later, the Defence Secretary came to meet him and gave the assurance that he would not let CNS's position to be compromised and, to his credit, this he stood by. The PMO was told that CNS resigning would be far more damaging to the Government's image than any benefits that the offended officer's promotion could bring. RLP retired three months later and as long as he remained in the office the gentleman promotion was not given effect. **It is different matter that within weeks of the new CNS taking over, the situation was reversed, the new incumbent accepted reversal of the earlier decision and officer was promoted with ante date seniority!!**

The CNS did not make any foreign trips during the time I was with him but undoubtedly his inclination to interact with his British counterparts, Admiral Sir Terence Lewin and Admiral Sir Henry Leach was more noticeable as was his mistrust with the Russians. If this was a slight failing, he admitted it openly. Possibly the Russians also felt it and no meaningful overtures came from them during my association with RLP. On the other hand he made several trips to Army and Air Force institutions in the country and was well received wherever he went. Some more in the mind than the others were visit to Leh where he received a Lhasa pup in the basket and the other to Jodhpur where he played baseball with officers of host regiment – 16th Light Cavalry, where he went to see **Mike Bhalla**! He had no hang ups about interacting with young officers with whom he was very popular.

Ronnie was hugely popular with rank and file and not just in the Navy. He was tough and played by the rules and did not bend them even for people for whom he had great personal liking. He played Golf with his Staff officer three times a week but made no effort to ensure his promotion when he was overlooked for his next higher rank by the relevant promotion board. There were occasions when I pleaded with him on behalf of some to whom I felt injustice was being done and he responded that being 'namby pamby' was not a quality he had inherited from his father. Both he and Mrs. Pereira were Masons and deeply religious without believing in rituals.

In June 1980 he called me in and told me that he had approved my selection to undergo a course at Naval War College in the USA. He asked me to suggest some names as my relief and is happy that one of the two I gave to him came to occupy the chair I vacated. When the time came for me to leave, I was worried what to do with my old Fiat fearing that if I sold it I would not be able to buy a new one on coming back. He noticed my troubled state and said that the car would be left at the Navy House and that the CNS will look after the car. Later, many people told me that the blue 1968 Fiat would almost always be seen at private social functions to which the CNS was invited with RLP at the wheel. When, on coming back from USA in 1981, I went to Navy House to collect the car, he gave me the keys saying that the Fiat was in better state than what it was I gave it to him!

An incident which speaks volumes for the person he has bears recounting. In the Navy we had a system where by a pilot who had flown 1000hrs was awarded the Nao Sena Medal. A proposal advocating the same award for the Commanding Officers of Submarines who completed 1000 dived hours underwater was put up for the submariners. This was opposed by the PSO (DCNS) concerned who sent up the file which passed through me as NA enroute to CNS. I clipped a note to it saying that leading a crew of 100 odd in the strenuous environment of a submarine was as deserving recognition if not more than that accorded to pilots who were essentially individual performers. I attached to this note the Ching Chow cartoon that had been published in the TOI that very morning. In it, Ching Chow was seen advising his King that "Reward and Punishment are both hallmark of good administration". The file came back to me with the CNS merely having initiated it but on the file itself, below the DCNS's note was recorded CNS's decision **"I see merit in the proposal. Approved"** The submariner who had initiated the case became the first of many, who were, in later years, awarded the Neo Sena

Medal. I kept my note, as I did all others, and few years later, presented it as a memento to the submariner who had retired by then and resettled in USA; he has kept it with him till today!

After his retirement I met the Pereiras once in Coonoor where they had settled down and again at their home ATLAST in Whitefield near Bangalore. They received us warmly and with great affection as, always.

ADMIRAL KK KOHLI

In June 1980, Captain Premvir Das, the first NA to CNS was selected to attend Naval War College, Norwich, USA. Prior to his departure Admiral consulted Capt Das for his reliever and told him to find out a suitable replacement. Premvir Das is the one who proposed Captain KK Kohli's name, who at that juncture was posted as Instructor, Staff College, Wellington.

Admiral KK Kohli had visited Gangtok with Admiral and Mrs. Pereira in May 1981 and I spoke to him just prior to his departure for USA in mid 82. Thereafter, met him briefly in Feb 87, when group of Army students from Staff College visited INS Ganga during Bharat Darshan. At that juncture he was commanding INS Ganga in Bombay. I, therefore, had no hesitation speaking to him after a gap of nearly 30 years. He instantly recognized me and I informed him that I am writing a book on Admiral Pereira and he was very happy to know and said, Mike,how can I help you . My first request was to know how he was selected as NA to CNS. I called him back after few days and this is what he had to share:-

Quote "Mike, yes, let me narrate the whole incident. It was sometime in June 80, when I was at Staff College, Wellington and one day I received a letter from the Chief's Secretariat, and when I opened the envelope I was surprised to notice that it was a letter from the Chief himself and initially wondered what it could be and the contents were as follows:-

"My dear Kailash, as you are aware that my incumbent NA Capt Premvir Das is proceeding for a course at Naval Warfare College, Norwich, USA. Though I do not know you personally but from your record of service which indeed is outstanding and brilliant, I do not have any doubts that you will make a very fine NA. **I must inform you that I am very difficult person to get along. However, if you wish to serve with me and accept the** appointment, then let me know so that I can instruct COP to issue the posting order. Regards Admiral RL Pereira"

Needless to say I was indeed happy and replied:-

"Dear Admiral, Sir, thank you very much for your letter and I am indeed happy and honored to serve as NA to you. I would humbly like to submit that I am not an easy subordinate to have as matter of course, and I will disagree with your opinions and opinions of other senior officers on matters military in case I feel so in the interest of our Navy. **In other words in brief I am not a 'yes man'.** If I am permitted to free and frank opinion it will be my honor to serve you, Sir."

Apparently Admiral was impressed with my forthright reply and I was transferred to Naval HQs with immediate effect. I had a wonderful innings of nearly two years and later in 82 proceeded to attend long course Naval Warfare College, Norwich, USA. **Unquote.**

Admiral Kohli added - Mike you know, Admiral Pereira was very **Honest, Humble and HUMANE.** Every one around him was instantaneously attracted to his personality. I still cherish his handwritten letter received about 30 years ago.

Quote "*dated 5th June 87- My dear Kailash, We had a letter last week from C-in-C telling me that your new assignment was CI (Navy) at the DSSC, but he made no mention that you are getting your Flag Rank with the appointment. I immediately thumbed thru an old copy of the Navy list, but I could not work out the junior lot in the list of RAs. However, from your last letter, you had indicated that you would have to wait a bit, before being due.*

Be that as it may, the assignment would more than indicate that you are through, and it is mere formality if the board has not been held.

None the less Kailash, Mrs P and myself are really delighted, and offer you our warmest good wishes and congratulations, though none of us had any doubts whatsoever. Mrs P's first comment was, that Kumad would make an excellent Flag Officer wife at the DSSC. I couldn't agree more and I am equally sure that you will not only enjoy the assignment but will make an excellent CI.

I don't really remember Wadhwani whom I have been told has gone to Cochin Shipyard. However, the feed back from my old cadet was, he was not too impressive, could not quite put his view over. I must say i was saddened at this view point of a CI (Navy).

Our love and good wishes to Kumad and please drop in a line to let us know what exactly is happening. I certainly find it rather puzzling. your sincerely Ronnie Pereira" **Unquote.**

Captain Kohli did very well for himself and missed the appointment of Chief by a whisker and retired as Vice Chief in 1997. He shared his experiences with Admiral which are covered in chapter on 'Matters Military'.

CAPTAIN MONTEE CHATTERJEE

Undoubtedly Montee Chatterjee was the closest naval officer to Admiral. He was indeed Admiral's soul mate which is very evident from his correspondence with Montee C, who very kindly sent me the copies of letters received from the Admiral.

In early spring of 1980, the incumbent Secretary to CNS, Captain Krishnan was posted as Naval Attaché to Moscow. Admiral had no hesitation in selecting his reliever and wrote to Montee C who was away to USA to attend Advance Defense Management Course in Naval Academy Post Graduation School, Monterrey, California.

In his letter of 25th Feb 1980 Admiral wrote, **quote** "*My dear Monty; Thank you very much for your letter which I received this morning. I am glad to hear that it's going well.*

I can see that you will be burning up the Delhi Golf Course when you get back. What with new Citation and the added benefits of watching the best in American Golf! It is for this reason that I have taken the added precaution of keeping somewhat a close tag on you- on your return, and have had you appointed as my Secretary. You will not therefore, will able to take the imprudent step of beating the hell out of your boss!!! I have unfortunately been off golf for the last month, what with my own tours and a bit of extra work thrown in. Khushru has also been out of station and as the 4 ball has been disrupted. However, I hope to get together with him from March and get back to the old programme of golf, 3 times a week.

Our good wishes to you and all the best. Looking forward to seeing you soon after mid April- sincerely Ronnie Pereira." **Unquote**

Montee C had a memorable tenure of 17 months as Secretary to CNS. He accompanied Admiral for tour of Australia (photo), however, he missed out the visit to Sikkim which he said he was very keen to come but Kailash Kohli beat him to it as Admiral was informed that there may be some operational discussions and NA presence was necessary. Montee C shared a number of "**amazing incidents**" while he served with Admiral and they have been covered in detail on the chapters of "Matters Military and Golf".

Quote "Mike, you know I shared a very special relation with the Admiral and he was my Godfather and let me share a very touching and wonderful incident. When I made it to Captain's rank in my 3rd look, after the selection board meeting, Ronnie P left a small chit in my hand 'Montee, you are in'! What a nice gesture." **unquote**

However, Montee put in his papers for pre mature retirement and bid adieu to services in Oct 81. Few moments after his last meeting with CNS, Admiral sat down to write a very touching letter of thanks to Montee.

Admiral wrote in his letter dated 3rd Oct 81 **quote** "*My dear Montee, You have just left my office for the last time as my Secretary, and as I am not too good in the oral expression of my feelings. I felt I should do so, on this little piece of paper.*

Secretaries like navigators, have to establish an affinity with their "boss" and unless this works out, the team does not survive. I have often tried to analyze our own relationship in and out of the office- and I can only say that it has been much closer to brotherly relationship than officer to officer, if, you know what I mean.

You had always had my implicit trust and this must have stemmed from the intense loyalty and devotion you have always given me. I can only say that I have appreciated this more than anything else. We have shared not only my inner most thoughts of office, but many of my personal problems and I must always thank you for being a patient listener, for it is not always possible to unburden to all and sundry. Thank you too for all your good advices-often and erroneously not taken, but always remembered. As one gets older, one values good friends, young and old, and I will always value our association.

Finally Montee, thank you for pulling me out of office so regularly and so often, to put the care of the world behind me, as I endeavoured to hit a little white ball better than you, and seldom succeeded!!!

My love and good wishes to Leela and Poppet- sincerely Ronnie P" **unquote**.

After Admiral retired in Feb 82, Montee was in touch with the Admiral and there was correspondence between them. Admiral wrote in his letter dated 1st March 1983 from Bangalore.

Quote "*My dear Montee; I was delighted to receive your letter, and I must admit that the earlier letter with a line from Poppet that you say was addressed* to Goa never got to me. Nonetheless this is not unlike Goa, where letters and telegrams are often not delivered to the addressee!!

To begin with I was sorry to hear that, you are leaving Delhi Golf Club but Ronnie Durant has a bad habit of pushing people around and his reputation is well known for this. Ronnie certainly works hard but he is totally autocratic and can never see anyone else's point of view. I can well appreciate; therefore, that he is a difficult man to get on with. Your departure will be equally disastrous for the club, as finding golfers as Secretaries can be almost impossible task and they have a wealth of experience on this. Your departure, therefore, will have them in deep trouble, but I can well appreciate that the committee must understand that a paid Secretary is not someone they can have at their beck and call and unless they change their tune, they will never be able to find someone of your caliber.

Thank you for all you have done in settling up my accounts, Montee. I am indeed grateful. I shall continue my absentee membership for some time, but I doubt that I will ever be in a position to use the club for any length of time, as I cannot see myself settling down for any length of time in Delhi and as we settle down in AT LAST, the question of move become more and more remote, as the time goes by.

It would surprise you; indeed it may not, seeing that you have your own flat, to learn how long it really takes to settle into one's house. We are always finding things to do, whether it is painting the garage door or building some furniture for a specific intention or redesigning the windows, or planning a sit out. It just goes on indefinitely, but one seems to revel in it as being for one's very own house and the added expensive are somehow acceptable to one's mind because it's for own house.

AT LAST is now really begun to look up. Phyll has got working on the garden though in B'lore, one can only plant perennials, as there is not only water shortage, but the soil is dreadfully poor and manure is not readily available, even in our village.

Summers have set in early this year and we are already in 33*'s and 34*'s C. When in fact, we should be in high 20's. However, B'lore has had no winter rain whatsoever, with a lousy monsoon last year, we have water problem on our hands, that will certainly be severe, to say the least.

Our love and good wishes to Leela, Poppet and the boys. Bombi must be doing house surgeons, if he has not completed that already and he should be deciding his avenue of specialization. How is Robin?I hope the accident is behind him and he is back to normal.

Well Montee I will close. I cannot really thank you enough for everything you did for me in and out of service. Yoy will always be as close as a brother. God bless you —afftly Ronnie P" **Unquote**

LT DINABANDHU JENA

Lt Jena was the first Flag Lt that I ever met . When Admiral moved to Cochin in Dec 74 to take over as FOC Southern Naval Areas , Lt Cdr Keith Jonathan (36 NDA) had moved along as Flag Lt from Vizag, however, he did not stay very long and proceeded to Australia on pre mature retirement in April 75.

Admiral was very particular in selection of his personal staff. Having a reputation of fire brand and hard task master, many were mortally scared to serve with him. But once they were under his wings, then over a period of time the whole perception would drastically change and by end of their tenure, more often than not, they ended up idolizing him for his great human qualities of head and heart.

It was not at all easy to get Commodore Jena contact no after a long gap 40 years. Last I met him was in INS Shivaji, Lonavala in April 76 where I spent a day with Admiral and Mrs. Pereira and I had no idea when and in what rank he retired? Captain Biswajit Bhattacharya, Director, Naval Veteran Officer Cell, who has been a great help, finally got Jena's contact number from the Flag Lt at HQs Southern Naval Command, during his visit to Cochin.

I called up Commodore(retired) Dinabandhu Jena, initially he could not place me, naturally as I was speaking to him after 40 years, then I said, Sir, 2/Lt Mike Bhalla-Ronnie Pereira-Cochin-Aug 1975. Then all the memories came flooding back and he was happy to hear from me and usual question about Army and my family. I informed him that I am writing a book on Admiral. Needless to say he was excited and said, Mike anything I can do to help you please let me know.

I humbly asked, that I want to know from him as to how Admiral selected him as Flag Lt? He said: Oh! most certainly but give me some time to gather my thoughts as I have to travel back more than 40 years! I told him Sir, please take your time and I will call you after few days. I must admit that Jena Sir certainly had an excellent memory and narrated the story as follows:-

The Admiral I Knew – A True Story of Admiral Ronald Lynsdale Pereira

Quote "Ok, Mike, it must be in early 75 when Admiral on his visit to Naval HQs met Vice Admiral Rusi Gandhi, COP (Chief of Personnel), equivalent to Military Secretary in the Army, who deals with posting and promotion of officers. Admiral Pereira requested Rusi Gandhi to help him to find a good Flag Lt. Five dossiers were put up to him and after due perusal Admiral somehow selected my name. It was revealed much later why he selected my name without even meeting me personally or taking interview and of course – **not even asking my consent**!

I was subsequently informed by the Admiral that it was my report initiated by Commander Dalip Kumar Ghosh, CO, INS KILTAN, popularly known in the Navy circles **as No1 Ghosh, his number at NDA was 001** and it was known fact in the Navy that what Commander Ghosh wrote was like writing on the stone and am sure Admiral was aware of this fact. I barely had 2 years of service when Commander Ghosh initiated my Annual Confidential Report as his Signal Communication Officer and he gave me an outstanding report and also mentioned in the pen picture '**that the officer is strongly recommended for the appointment of Flag Lt**' and probably that one sentence did the trick and turned the tide in my favour. Admiral made up his mind and requested COP to send a signal for my move to Cochin forthwith!?

At that time I was serving as Missile Officer on INS VINASH at Bombay, which had participated in Indo-Pak war of 1971. It was Sunday morning when the signal arrived about my posting to move with immediate effect and I was totally taken aback as it was like bolt from the blue, this was the last thing I wanted in my life!! I immediately requested the Duty Officer in the Communication Centre to please confirm from the Naval HQs the validity of the signal, and I gave my personal no 01226K and full name as per the Navy list - Dinabandhu Jena. After a while the Cipher Officer after confirming from Naval HQs informed me that it was me only and I have to report to Cochin the next day!

My first reaction was, how to get out of this situation as I knew Ronnie P will sack me within a month if I am not able to cope with the pressure of the work!! So I decided to hit the bar- the last day of my freedom- and proceeded to Cochin the next day.

I said my prayers and reported to the Admiral and came out of his office rather confused as I could not comprehend his anglicized English. However, I got moral support from unexpected quarters- Kittu- Admiral's driver, Mr Chanerasen, PA to Admiral and above all Lt Cdr KKR Nair, Secretary to

FOC Southern Naval Areas!! Kittu assured me that Bara Sahib is very 'strict' but very nice and Madam is very, very nice, rest I will handle. I survived till May 76 and then proceeded for long course". **Unquote**

India Blazer

In September 75, Admiral was nominated by Naval Hqs to proceed to Tanzania for one month for establishment of a Naval Academy. There couldn't have been better news for Jena.

Quote "When I got to know that Admiral will be out for a month, I felt very happy as it will give me a break from hectic schedule and give me an opportunity to meet my friends and go out for dinner and generally have good time!! I had lots of ideas in my mind, how I am going to spend next one month, however, all my dreams came crashing down when Admiral called me to his office and told me that he has been informed by Commander Nagpal, OC Anti Submarine School that you are very good yachtman, to which I replied in affirmative. Next question was – Do you want to go to Colombo? I asked –what for, Sir? Admiral replied to participate in the 1st South Asian Yachting Regatta which was being held at Colombo in Oct/Nov 75.

The team was being led by Lt Cdr Mongia, who was posted at Staff College, Wellington. The Naval HQs instructed that another yachtman be detailed from Southern Naval Areas to accompany Lt Commander Mongia for the Championship at Colombo. Out of the blue I got this opportunity.

There were more than ten teams from different countries of South Asia and we were put up in five star hotels and Championship was conducted over a period of one month. Along with Lt Cdr Mongia, who was a National Champion, we won the Lewis Brown Cup and I earned not only India Blazer but also Navy Blazer in one stroke all at the age of 26 years.

I was very concerned about Admiral smoking habit, and he used to smoke Gold Flake about 40 to 60 cigarettes a day. One day Mrs. Pereira informed me in confidence about Admiral losing part of his left lung post attack of Tuberculosis in 1956 and requested me to somehow cut down on his smoking. Then I managed to get a silver case for cigarette and carry it myself and every time Admiral wanted to smoke he used to look for me and I used to give him a slip and gradually brought down to 20/30 cigarette a day!" **Unquote**

Married Accomodation

Quote "Mike, I must share with you about the family accommodation situation in Cochin. In 1975 like most of the naval stations there was acute shortage of married accommodation in Cochin and the waiting period, particularly for Lt Cdr and below was from 2 to 3 years and by then one's tenure be over. One day Admiral came across a builder, who had constructed "Furnson" apartments but somehow he had some issues with Income Tax Authorities. Admiral got a brain wave and offered to help him if he gave all 48 apartments on hire to the Navy. Admiral was gracious enough to approach concerned authorities in Bombay and got the penalty reduced to minimum resulting in resolving the problem for the builder as well as the families of Navy. No Admiral before him did anything like this, but Ronnie P always had the welfare of his officers and sailors upper most in his mind. Subsequently these flats were sold to the Navy, apparently the son of the builder became drug addict and there was no one to run the business! What an irony?" **Unquote**

However, the most exciting incident in Cochin was the impromptu move of Admiral to Bombay to take over as FOC-in-C Western Naval Command in end Feb 76 which has been covered in the Chapter on "Admiral in the Making".

Jena served with Admiral till May 76 and thereafter he went on two months annual leave and then to Cochin to attend Long Gunnery Course in July 76.

PK VIJAYAN

This is the story of Lt Vijayan who was first Flag Lt to Admiral when he took over as Fleet Commander, Eastern Fleet at Vishakapatnam in February 1973.

Quote "I was serving on board INS Amba when Admiral took over as FOC Eastern Fleet. On his taking over, the Admiral did not have a permanently appointed Flag Lieutenant. He was still in the process of selecting one.

INS Amba was the Flag Ship of the Eastern Fleet, commanded by Captain HS Punia , who called on the Fleet Commander. At the time the Admiral returned the call on board, I was the Guard Commander for the presentation of the Guard. The Guard Drill was excellent and Admiral, being a Gunnery Officer, was very impressed and commended me and the squad.

The vessel subsequently sailed for exercises. A day before the vessel was to enter harbour, after about a week, the Commanding Officer, Capt Punia, received a signal that the Admiral would like to see and interview Lt PK Vijayan on the following day on berthing. When the vessel berthed, FNO, Cdr PP Sivamani, was at the jetty to take me to the Fleet Office. Cdr Sivamani mentioned that another officer, Lt Nirmal Verma was also summoned for interview for Flag Officer to the Admiral. I was first to enter Admiral's office and he had already obtained our dossiers from NHQ .There was mention of Summary Court Marshal (SCM) in my dossier sometime in May 71. The Admiral enquired about it and I explained to him that it was a minor service jeep accident while I was driving. I had lost a month's seniority due to SCM. At that time, I was also selected as ADC to the Governor of Kerela. The Admiral asked me if I would like to serve with him as his 'Flag Lt' and I replied 'Yes Sir'. After me Lt Nirmal Verma was interviewed. Subsequently, both of us were called inside together. Nirmal Verma was not selected as he was my junior and the Admiral felt that he needed to spend more time at sea. Later Nirmal Verma went on to become Chief of Naval Staff.

That is how I came to serve him as the first Flag Lieutenant.

After serving Admiral Ronnie Pereira, my entire impression of the Navy and its senior officers changed completely. In my eyes no one was comparable to him. He was way above anybody else in all respects- **totally honest, straight forward, caring and down to earth**. He respected one and all, whether he was a sailor, an officer or an officer's/sailor's wife. As the axiom goes, there was no other officer in the Navy who could hold a candle to the Admiral. In my view, he was by far **the best leader and human being** the Navy ever produced.

Once on our way back after fleet exercise on the West Coast, the Eastern Fleet was sailing back to Vizag via Cochin. The Southern Naval Areas had hosted a reception for the Fleet. Admiral and self were staying in the mess during the two days we were in Cochin. After the reception, the Admiral said "let's go out for dinner, Flag" I told him I have a Dentist friend, Dr Mathews Verghese, in Cochin and I would request him to arrange dinner for us. We changed into civvies and went to the Lotus Club, where Dr Verghese was the President. After dinner when Admiral expressed his desire to have coffee, Dr Verghese insisted that we go to his house to which Admiral agreed. Since Doctor's wife was out of station, Dr Methews went to the kitchen to make the coffee. Admiral followed him in the kitchen, rolled up his sleeves and insisted on making the coffee himself. **That's how down to earth he was.**

We were on visit to Bombay and were staying in the Command Mess. I wasn't keeping well and after returning late from a party, I just threw myself on the bed in my cabin and fell asleep in my red sea rig. When I opened my eyes in the morning, I found that my shoes had been removed and I was covered with the sheet. The next morning he said "Flag, you must have been very tired last night". That's when I realized that it was **Admiral who had removed my shoes and covered me** as my cabin was adjacent to the Admiral's. What can I say for man like him??

I spent 17 months with the Admiral before proceeding for my specialist Long Course to Cochin .Before my departure, I went to Delhi to pick up my car and drove alone back to Vizag . A farewell party was arranged for me at the Navy House by Admiral and Mrs. Pereira. However, when I reached Vijaynagram I had a breakdown and I realized that I won't be able to make it to Vizag that evening for the party. I called up Mrs. Pereira from a PCO and informed her. She mentioned to me that she had invited all the Fleet Commanding officers with their wives and other officers and ladies for my farewell but it wouldn't matter and she would postpone it to the following day. She said, son don't rush back and come safely. That was her primary concern. The Admiral did not allow me to drive further down to Cochin, as I had planned. Instead, he told me to go by train and he would ensure that the car was delivered to me in Cochin. The car was delivered as promised by a Landing Craft, which called at Cochin on her way to Bombay from Vizag.

Later when Admiral was CNS, I had wanted to quit the Navy as I was offered a good job in Dubai. I had requested the Admiral to help me to quit the service. He refused and said "over my dead body. You will be an Admiral , so stay on". I was later sent to Russia in the Training Team for the 'Rajput' class frigates.

Eventually, I left the Navy in 1991 on premature retirement after 22 years of service as I had suffered a heart attack in 1985." **Unquote**

That is the story of Cdr PK Vijayan, whom I have never met personally, but when I spoke to him for the first time in early 2015, he was really excited to hear that I am writing a book on the Admiral and true to his word he has been very kind and forthcoming- all because of his **deep LOVE and RESPECT for the Admiral.**

Cdr Vijayan has kindly sent me lots of photographs of Admiral including the one with Col Morris Ravinderan , my first Commandant in Jan 1974. In addition he has always extended whatever information I have asked for past 8 months. Being an Aide myself I do understand the relationship between Boss and Aide!

BHASKAR RANJAN SEN

Admiral moved to Bombay to take over as C-in-C Western Naval Command in end Feb 1976 and Flag Lt Jena moved along with him. However, in May Jena was detailed for Long Course and Admiral was once again on the lookout for another Flag Lt.

Bhaskar Sen had the pleasure of serving under Admiral on two occasions and indeed Admiral and Mrs. P were very fond of him. I first met Bhaskar when I visited Bombay in Aug 1976. He also visited 16 Cavalry along with Admiral in Mar 1980 and we were good friends. Therefore, the moment I started on this project I contacted him after a gap of more than 30 years and requested to please narrate; how he was picked up as Flag Lt to the Admiral?

Quote "Mike, in end May 1976 I was in Cochin, serving in INS Delhi under the command of Captain Podgy Nadkarni (later CNS). Ronnie P was very fond of him and probably being an ex CO himself, asked him to look for a smart officer from INS Delhi for the appointment Flag Lt. Podgy Nadkarni selected me and I was directed to report within 24 hours for formal interview.

Next morning I boarded a Dakota from INS Garuda for Bombay, however enroute it developed a snag and had to make emergency landing in Goa. I then took a civil flight and reached Santa Cruz airport at about 7.30 pm. A staff car was waiting for me which took me straight to Western Naval Command HQs. By the time I got there it was past 9pm. And Admiral was still in the office, without any other staff member. I was ushered in his office by the lone sailor for the interview;

Self;   Good Evening , Sir.

Admiral;   Son, Do you drink?

Self ;   Yes Sir.

Admiral;   Do you smoke?

Self ;   Yes Sir.

Admiral;   Which Brand?

Self ;   Four Square.

Admiral;   Good, that's my brand too and I am sure we will get along well!

That was the end of my interview.

Admiral was schedule to go to NDA for POP at the invitation of Rear Admiral Awati, Commandant. The POP was scheduled for 5th June76, and Admiral was very keen that I should accompany him. However, I had to go back to Cochin to fetch my luggage. I could not afford to and fro air ticket and travelled by train and missed the trip to NDA!!

The next 10 months were most memorable tenure in my career. Unfortunately in April 1977 Admiral was suddenly moved to Naval HQs as Vice Chief. My tenure was prematurely truncated as VCNS is not entitled to have Flag Lt and moved out.

Come November 1978, the Government of the day nominated Admiral as "Chief Designate". Couple of weeks later I received a letter from Admiral asking me to join on his staff as Flag Lt once again. I went on to serve with him till June 1980.

I must admit, that I was very fortunate to serve with a man like Admiral from such close quarters. He was a man of fierce integrity and strong principles and never wavered in most difficult and hostile environments. Hats off to him! **Unquote**

Bhaskar Ranjan Sen had very eventful tenure with Admiral for 15 months and then proceeded for long course in June 1980. I am reproducing a letter which he received had from Admiral dated 04th Aug 91, **quote** *"My dear Ranjan-Thank you for your letter of 24th July and both Ma and I were delighted with the news that you are in command at sea. I don't think anything could give you as much satisfaction and pleasure, for command is really the epitome of Naval officer's career.*

I am sure, Ranjan, you will enjoy every minute of it, and moulding of young cadets as you would wish them to be , would give you added satisfaction.

A s I look back on my service and time at sea, I realize more and more, that it is your team of officers that makes or break a ship. Men are always excellent; it is a matter of leading them and that leadership stems from the wardroom. Officers today have, and I hope I am wrong- lost touch with men. However, the relations which are so important in today's context of business be it cooperate or service, is not given the importance that it must always have. Young mind and ambitious thoughts are carried away with the mistaken belief that "HI-TECH" is answer to every problem and human relations are relegated to peripheral importance wholly sad and disastrous. You will find that you will have to drive your wardroom. Do not hesitate to do so. They will not like it, but it is vital for the success of the service and necessitates this treatment to get it back on line. Both Ma and I wish you every success and good future, and you will always be in our prayers.

We were deeply distressed with the sad news of your dear father's demise. I well know what you have gone through, for it hits me hard, many years ago- in 1957- I lost both father and mother in a matter of 15 days. Their loss always leaves a hole in one's heart, which only time can heal and words and comfort from others in times like this, means little. It always comforting to remember, son, that what you are, they have made you and therefore your hard work and sweat is like paying them back in some measure for all their endeavors.

Our love and good wishes Debjones and Kasturi. I shall let you know when I shall be visiting Cochin again, Look after yourself, sincerely Ronnie P". **Unquote**

LT NALIN DEWAN

As narrated by Nalin, **quote** "In June 1980 Lt Bhaskar Ranjen Sen, Flag Lt to CNS was to proceed for his Long Course. At that time, I was 24 and posted on board the Missile Boat INS Chapal at Bombay. I was on leave at Delhi - to get engaged (for marriage!!!). My father was posted at NHQ [now Integrated HQ of MOD (Navy)]. One morning I got a call at home and was informed that I was being considered for a 'special' assignment at Delhi and was required to report to Capt Ravi Sikka, DOP (Director of Personnel) by 1200h. I was surprised, as there were no known assignments for a young Lt except ADC to the President and Flag Lt to the CNS. I blurted this out to the DOP, as also the fact that I had just got engaged to get married, and to my mind this assignment would require a bachelor. DOP replied saying that we would see about that! In any case I was not yet 25 and could not get married - he had probably knowingly overlooked the clause that as per Naval rules one had to be 25 or a Lt to get married. I also told him that by rights I should always have my uniform with me, but I did not. "Come in shirt and tie he blared." Considering the fact that I was going to South block for the very first time, I put on a pair of trousers in addition.

The maze of South Block to a young Lt was mind boggling. I however made it to CNS' office (after a brief tete a tete with DOP and the NA to the CNS, Capt KK Kohli). I entered the CNS' office (huge to the eyes of a young Lt) and was offered a chair. The following conversation ensued:-

I had no option but to go. As I entered Chief's office the Admiral looked at me and said-

Admiral: Son, do you know me?

I: Yes Sir. You are the CNS and were the Deputy Commandant when I was a cadet at the NDA. In fact when I reported to NDA to join the 49th course (Foxtrot) on 10 January 1973 you were the first person I met and you remarked - "Hurry up son, time doesn't wait for you and neither do I." I also remember you climbing through my cabin window from the battalion area at midnight to catch unsuspecting smokers.

Admiral (with a twinkle in his eyes): Ex NDA eh. Oh! So, you know me. Good. You are selected. Such was his confidence in training at the NDA. He then went on to outline what was expected of me.

I (rather sheepishly): Thank you very much for the confidence that you have placed in me. I would however like to tell you that I have yesterday been engaged to get married in October. It would be unfair on my part at this stage to tell my fiance to wait for a couple of years.

Admiral (picking up the intercom): Montee (Capt Chatterjee, SO to the CNS), please see that the new Flag Lt gets out of turn married accommodation.

That, in a nutshell is the story of my selection as 'Flag Lt' the single ADC that the Chief of the Naval Staff has.

I learnt a lot from him, the most important being that one should do their job to the best of their ability and be a good human being at the same time. There are many stories and incidents that can be recounted. Each day was an adventure in Professionalism, Management and being Humane without compromising on work. I was with the Admiral till he retired on 28 Feb 1982."

CONCLUSION

MOIST EYES: It has taken me better part of two years to compile my "Karmic" journey with Admiral. As I trudged along the memory lane of 46 years, I recalled all the moments from the day; 15th Jan 1971, when Commodore RL Pereira joined National Defence Academy, Khadakwasla as "Deputy Commandant" and soon he had all 1500 cadets running helter-skelter to avoid getting caught by him.

I got back to my course mates and ex-NDA cadets from 40th to 49th course to share their experiences with the Great man. Many I spoke after 20/30 years and some after 40 years. The very mention of Admiral's name evoked instant emotional reactions: awe, admiration, respect and pride. All conversations with them were long and laced with laughter recounting those days in early 70's and how we tried to get the better of Dep Com!? Though most of the times we failed and ended up with 21 Restrictions and 4 Singarh Hikes!

All memories came flooding back of that fateful day – Wednesday, 4th August 71, when Dep Com eyes froze on my terrified face and within span of one week, a non-descript Cadet Sant Pratap Singh Bhalla was graduated to "Mike Bhalla". For me Dep Com was upgraded from Sir to Uncle and subsequently to Unc and Mrs. Pereira – Aunty Phyllis to Aunty Phyll, (Aunty Phyll and self often used to refer Dep Com as "Boss").

There onwards I was literally transported to altogether a different world-a world full of love, affection and concern.

In Admiral Shekhawat words, quote "Mike, Admiral had very hard exterior but soft interior. The problem was how to penetrate his exterior? Once you did that and touched his soft side, then you were exposed to altogether a different personality; kind and benevolent. You fortunately succeeded". Unquote.

I reckon that like any normal human being Admiral had his flaws, however, personally I did not experience any in my association of 22 years, except his "quick temper". He was simply driven by righteousness and good human conduct without any malice in his heart. Aptly engraved on his Tomb Stone:

I have fought the good fight,

I have finished the race,

I have kept the faith.

2- Timothy 4.7

RIP

Finally, for me, he had acquired the status of a "MESSIAH". Not a day passed in last two years without shedding a tear in his memory.

GOD BLESS HIS SOUL.

About the Author

Brigadier SPS Bhalla alias Mike Bhalla did his entire schooling (1963-69) from Sainik School, Kunjpura, Karnal and joined 43rd course, National Defence Academy on 7th Jan 1970. He was commissioned into 16th Light Cavalry in Dec 1973 and went on to command 6 Armoured Regiment in the sensitive Chicken Neck area in Akhnoor in 1995-1997. Later he commanded an Armoured Brigade in Rajasthan, Infantry Brigade in Punjab and Sub Area in Siliguri corridor in North Bengal.

He has also held various staff appointments in the fomations deployed in the counter insurgency areas in the Northeast.

After retirement in July 2009, he settled down in a small town of Bagdogra (District - Darjeeling) in North Bengal.

Email ID: mikebhalla@rediffmail.com

Mobile: 919800000070

www.ingramcontent.com/pod-product-compliance
Lightning Source LLC
Chambersburg PA
CBHW021413300426
44114CB00010B/476